# The Resounding Soul

# VERITAS
## Series Introduction

"... the truth will set you free" (John 8:32)

In much contemporary discourse, Pilate's question has been taken to mark the absolute boundary of human thought. Beyond this boundary, it is often suggested, is an intellectual hinterland into which we must not venture. This terrain is an agnosticism of thought: because truth cannot be possessed, it must not be spoken. Thus, it is argued that the defenders of "truth" in our day are often traffickers in ideology, merchants of counterfeits, or anti-liberal. They are, because it is somewhat taken for granted that Nietzsche's word is final: truth is the domain of tyranny.

Is this indeed the case, or might another vision of truth offer itself? The ancient Greeks named the love of wisdom as *philia*, or friendship. The one who would become wise, they argued, would be a "friend of truth." For both philosophy and theology might be conceived as schools in the friendship of truth, as a kind of relation. For like friendship, truth is as much discovered as it is made. If truth is then so elusive, if its domain is *terra incognita*, perhaps this is because it arrives to us—unannounced—as a gift, as a person, and not some thing.

The aim of the Veritas book series is to publish incisive and original current scholarly work that inhabits "the between" and "the beyond" of theology and philosophy. These volumes will all share a common aspiration to transcend the institutional divorce in which these two disciplines often find themselves, and to engage questions of pressing concern to both philosophers and theologians in such a way as to reinvigorate both disciplines with a kind of interdisciplinary desire, often so absent in contemporary academe. In a word, these volumes represent collective efforts in the befriending of truth, doing so beyond the simulacra of pretend tolerance, the violent, yet insipid reasoning of liberalism that asks with Pilate, "What is truth?"—expecting a consensus of non-commitment; one that encourages the commodification of the mind, now sedated by the civil service of career, ministered by the frightened patrons of position.

The series will therefore consist of two "wings": (1) original monographs; and (2) essay collections on a range of topics in theology and philosophy. The latter will principally be the products of the semi-annual conferences of the Centre of Theology and Philosophy (www.theologyphilosophycentre.co.uk).

Conor Cunningham and Eric Austin Lee, *Series editors*

# The Resounding Soul

## Reflections on the Metaphysics and Vivacity of the Human Person

*Edited by*
ERIC AUSTIN LEE &
SAMUEL KIMBRIEL

CASCADE *Books* • Eugene, Oregon

THE RESOUNDING SOUL
Reflections on the Metaphysics and Vivacity of the Human Person

Veritas 16

Copyright © 2015 Wipf and Stock Publishers. All rights reserved. Except for brief quotations in critical publications or reviews, no part of this book may be reproduced in any manner without prior written permission from the publisher. Write: Permissions, Wipf and Stock Publishers, 199 W. 8th Ave., Suite 3, Eugene, OR 97401.

Cascade Books
An Imprint of Wipf and Stock Publishers
199 W. 8th Ave., Suite 3
Eugene, OR 97401
www.wipfandstock.com

ISBN 13: 978-1-4982-3207-4

*Cataloging-in-Publication data:*

    The resounding soul : reflections on the metaphysics and vivacity of the human person / edited by Eric Austin Lee and Samuel Kimbriel.

    Veritas 16

    xviii + 406 p.; 23 cm—Includes bibliographical references and index.

    ISBN 13: 978-1-4982-3207-4

    1. Soul. 2. Theological anthropology—Christianity. 3. Philosophical anthropology. 4. Human beings. I. Lee, Eric Austin. II. Kimbriel, Samuel. III. Series. IV. Title.

BT701.3 L222 2015

Manufactured in the USA.

*In memoriam*
Revd. Dr. John Mark David Hughes
(December 13, 1978–June 29, 2014)

# Contents

*Preface* xi

*Acknowledgments* xiii

*List of Contributors* xv

Introduction 1
— *Samuel Kimbriel and Eric Austin Lee*

**Section I: The Soul and the Saeculum**

1. The Experience of Death: The Immortality of the Soul and the Unity of the Person in Landsberg, Scheler, and Augustine 25
— *Anna Piazza*

2. Bernard Stiegler's Politics of the Soul and His New *Otium* of the People 40
— *Johann Rossouw*

3. Eucharistic Anthropology: Alexander Schmemann's Conception of Beings in Time 60
— *Andrew T. J. Kaethler*

4. The Psychology of Cosmopolitics 78
— *John Milbank*

**Section II: Fracture and Unity**

5. "Know Thyself": The Soul of Anatomical Dissection 93
— *Kimbell Kornu*

6 Persons and Narratives: A Physicalist Account of the Soul  114
— K. Nicholas Forti

7 Transcending the Body/Soul Distinction through the Perspective of Maximus the Confessor's Anthropology  135
— Sotiris Mitralexis

8 Nous (*Energeia*) and Kardia (*Dynamis*) in the Holistic Anthropology of St. Gregory Palamas  149
— Nichifor Tănase

9 Souls, Minds, Bodies, and Planets  175
— Mary Midgley

**Section III: Moving to Wholeness**

10 The Soul in the Novel: From Daniel Defoe to David Foster Wallace  199
— Edmund Waldstein, O.Cist.

11 Difficult Conversion: Shakespeare and the Soul of Religion  211
— Anthony D. Baker

12 Both, Between, and Beyond: The Third Term and the Relation Constituting Being  231
— L. C. Wilson

**Section IV: The Soul's Regard**

13 Strategies of the Gift: Body and Soul in John Paul II and Levinas  249
— Nigel Zimmermann

14 Redeeming Duality: Anthropological Split-ness and Embodied Soteriology  266
— Lexi Eikelboom

15 Music and Liminal Ethics: Facilitating a "Soulful Reality"  285
— Férdia J. Stone-Davis

**Section V: Vivacity**

16 The Soul and "All Things": Contribution to a
   Postmodern Account of the Soul  307
   — *W. Chris Hackett*

17 The Soul at Work: A Reading in Catholic Romanticism  330
   — *Simone Kotva*

18 Soul Music and Soul-less Selving  352
   — *William Desmond*

*Name and Subject Index*  391

# Preface

SINCE 2005, THE CENTRE of Theology and Philosophy at the University of Nottingham has held semi-annual conferences on a number of topics, providing space for theologians, philosophers, Scripture scholars, scientists, politicians, political analysts, and literary scholars to come together and engage in lively dialogue. Under a "wide umbrella" of themes, the Centre primarily aims to bring faith and reason into conversation with one another to see what kind of fruit emerges from such soil. In 2011 in Krakow, Poland, at the Centre's "What is Life?" conference, a number of threads converged amidst especially scientific, philosophical, and theological papers that left us continuing to consider dimensions of the human person. The simple—and intentionally general—topic of "The Soul" readily presented itself as the theme for our next conference almost immediately. From June 28th to July 1st in 2013, a delegation of over 130 persons convened at St. Anne's College at the University of Oxford to present various papers relating to this theme. The following essays selected from this conference include Keynote addresses by John Milbank, Mary Midgley, and William Desmond along with a number of other papers selected through blind peer review.

# Acknowledgments

THIS VOLUME COULD NOT have been possible without the help of a number of generous souls. First and foremost, the conference on The Soul was made possible with the guidance of Centre of Theology and Philosophy staff John Milbank, Alison Milbank, Conor Cunningham, and especially Simon Oliver, who helped keep the conference running smoothly at every step along the way. A big debt of gratitude is also owed to our colleagues David Mosley, Michael DiFuccia, Kimbell Kornu, Jarrod Longbons, and Justin Devore for providing daily on-the-ground support. Neil Turnbull, Brent Driggers, Christopher Ben Simpson, Peter M. Candler, Jr. were also a great help, if none other than for their encouragement of us through their presence and constant support of the work of the Centre.

The vibrancy of our conference arose not least from the presence of our keynote speakers: Conor Cunningham, William Desmond (the Dusty Springfield rendition was a hit!), John de Gruchy, David Bentley Hart, Ian McGilchrist, Mary Midgley, John Milbank, Marilynne Robinson, and Graham Ward. Including our keynote sessions, we had a total of over 50 panels which were generously chaired by friends and colleagues—thank you. We were thrilled to see Owen Barfield, Jr., in attendance, and are thankful that he took the time to be with us as well as the special effort he took to promote his grandfather's body of work at the book stalls. And a special thanks is due to Graham Ward, not only for making us feel at home in Oxford, but also for the beautiful way in which he facilitated conversation with Mary Midgley, who served as our final keynote speaker of the conference.

Regarding the conference volume you are holding in your hands, its existence is possible in the first instance due to the generosity of John Milbank, Conor Cunningham, and Simon Oliver who entrusted us to take over this editorial project. We are grateful to our good friends at Cascade Books, Christian Amondson, Jim Tedrick, and especially Robin Parry, who continually take very good care of us. We would also like to offer our thanks to Blake Allen for reading drafts of our introduction and providing insightful suggestions. Many thanks to those who submitted papers, as well as to all of our anonymous referees for giving their time and insight in order to help us make our editorial selections. For very good reasons, it is not typical to reveal those who serve in this anonymous capacity, but in this case, given the untimely death of Revd. Dr. John Hughes, we would like to extend a special thanks to him for being one of our referees. We have dedicated this collection to him.

# List of Contributors

**Anthony D. Baker** is Associate Professor of Systematic Theology at Seminary of the Southwest in Austin, Texas. He is the author of *Diagonal Advance: Perfection in Christian Theology*, and is currently working on a book on Shakespeare and theology.

**William Desmond** is Professor of Philosophy at the Institute of Philosophy, Katholiecke Universiteit Leuven, Belgium. He is the author, amongst many works, most notably of the "Between" trilogy: *Being and the Between*, *Ethics and the Between*, *God and the Between*, as well as *Desire, Dialectic, and Otherness* (2nd ed.); *Beyond Hegel and Dialectic: Speculation, Cult, and Comedy*; *Is There a Sabbath for Thought?*; *Hegel's God: A Counterfeit Double?*; and most recently, *The Intimate Strangeness of Being: Metaphysics after Dialectic*.

**Lexi Eikelboom** is a DPhil candidate in Theology (Modern Doctrine) at the University of Oxford. She is currently working on a thesis on rhythm as a theological category, and has published in the *Heythrop Journal* and *Studies in Christian Ethics*.

**K. Nicholas Forti** is an Episcopal priest in the Diocese of Virginia. He recently completed a Master of Sacred Theology at the School of Theology at Sewanee: The University of the South.

**W. Chris Hackett** is Research Fellow/Lecturer, School of Philosophy, Australian Catholic University. He is the translator of Jean-Yves Lacoste, *From Theology to Theological Thinking* and Emmanuel Falque, *God, the Flesh and the Other*, and co-author of *Quiet Powers of the Possible: Interviews in Contemporary French Phenomenology*.

**Andrew T. J. Kaethler** recently completed his PhD in systematic theology at the University of St Andrews. He has published in *Modern Theology*, *Logos:*

*A Journal of Catholic Thought and Culture*, and *New Blackfriars*. In addition, he has one monograph based on his MA thesis titled *The Synthesis of Athens and Jerusalem: George Grant's Defense Against Modernity*.

**Kimbell Kornu** is an Instructor in Palliative Medicine and Health Care Ethics at Saint Louis University in St. Louis, Missouri. He is currently working on a genealogy of medical knowledge following the paradigm of anatomical dissection.

**Simone Kotva** recently completed her PhD at the University of Cambridge, Emmanuel College. Her research explores the relationship between vitalism and Stoic revivalism in nineteenth- and twentieth-century French philosophy. Her work has appeared in *Radical Orthodoxy*; *Theory, Culture & Society*; and *Noesis*. She also publishes in Swedish.

**Mary Midgley** is a retired Senior Lecturer in Philosophy at the University of Newcastle. She is author of over fifteen books, including *Beast and Man*, *Animals and Why They Matter*, *Evolution as a Religion*, *Science as Salvation*, *Science and Poetry*, *The Myths we Live By*, *The Solitary Self: Darwin and the Selfish Gene*, and most recently, *Are you an Illusion?* She is regarded as one of the UK's most eminent and influential philosophers of recent decades.

**John Milbank** is Professor in Religion, Politics, and Ethics at the University of Nottingham, and is Director of the Centre of Theology and Philosophy. He is author, most notably, of *Theology and Social Theory: Beyond Secular Reason* as well as being the co-editor of the *Radical Orthodoxy* series (along with Catherine Pickstock and Graham Ward). Additionally, he is author of *The Word Made Strange: Theology, Language, Culture*, *Truth in Aquinas* (with Catherine Pickstock), *Being Reconciled: Ontology and Pardon*, *The Suspended Middle: Henri de Lubac and the Debate Concerning the Supernatural*, *The Future of Love: Essays in Political Theology*, and *The Monstrosity of Christ: Paradox or Dialectic?* (with Slavoj Žižek). Most recently, he has written *Beyond Secular Order: The Representation of Philosophy and the Representation of the People*, the first part of a two-part sequel to *Theology and Social Theory*.

**Sotiris Mitralexis**, Dr.phil. in Philosophy at the Freie Universität Berlin and Visiting Scholar at Boğaziçi University, Istanbul. He has recently earned his PhD with a thesis entitled *Ever-Moving Repose: The Notion of Time in*

*Maximus the Confessor's Philosophy through the Perspective of a Relational Ontology.*

**Nichifor Tănase** is Lecturer of Orthodox Spirituality and History of Christian Literature at Eftimie Murgu University, Resita (Romania). He holds a PhD in theology with a thesis on the hesychast dispute of the fourteenth century and its influence on twentieth-century neo-patristic theology: "The Receptarea spiritualității Sfântului Grigorie Palama în Teologia Ortodoxă a secolului XX: Dumitru Stăniloae, John Meyendorff și John Romanides" [Reception of the Spirituality of St. Gregory Palamas in the Orthodox Theology of the Twentieth Century: Dumitru Staniloae, John Meyendorff and John Romanides"]. He is a member of The Society for the Promotion of Byzantine Studies (SPBS), of the Association des Amis de Sources Chrétiennes (AASC), of the International Association of Patristic Studies (IAPS), and of The Nordic Society for Philosophy of Religion (NSPR); he is also the coordinator of Didactic Theology degree program. His publications include: *Ontology of the Incarnation: Being-Essence-Phenomenon Triptych* and *Christ and Time: The Living Present of the Life-Energetic Perichoresis between Time and Eternity*, and *Orthodox Spirituality: Neopatristic-palamite Synthesis*. He is currently working on a book entitled *Logic and Spirituality: Deification Rhetoric in Saint Gregory Palamas* (forthcoming).

**Anna Piazza** is currently working as a PhD student at Max Weber Kolleg Erfurt with a dissertation on Max Scheler's philosophy of religion. She has published in various philosophical journals including *Phenomenology and Mind*. She is currently translating two works of Scheler's, to be published with FrancoAngeli.

**Johann Rossouw** is Senior Lecturer in Philosophy at the University of the Free State, South Africa. He completed his doctoral thesis on the theological in Bernard Stiegler's philosophy and politics at Monash University, Melbourne in 2013.

**Férdia J. Stone-Davis** received a BA, MPhil, and PhD from the University of Cambridge before proceeding to Trinity College of Music, London, where she gained a MMus, specializing in early music performance. Since graduating, she has combined research, performance, and teaching. She is an interdisciplinary academic working in the fields of music, philosophy, and theology. Publications include a monograph *Musical Beauty: Negotiating the Boundary between Subject and Object*, a co-edited collection *The*

*Soundtrack of Conflict: The Role of Music in Radio Broadcasting in Wartime and in Conflict Situations*, and an edited collection *Music and Transcendence*. She is currently a research assistant in the Department of Musicology, Georg-August-Universität Göttingen, Germany.

**Edmund Waldstein**, O.Cist. doctoral candidate in theology at the University of Vienna, Austria, and monk of the Abbey of Heiligenkreuz. His dissertation is on the work of David Foster Wallace.

**L. C. Wilson** is a PhD candidate at the University of Nottingham. Her research focuses on the theology of melancholy.

**Nigel Zimmermann** is Lecturer in Theology at the University of Notre Dame Australia (Sydney). He is author of *Levinas and Theology* and *Facing the Other: John Paul II, Levinas, and the Body*. He has also published in *The Heythrop Journal* and *The Tablet*. He completed his doctorate at the University of Edinburgh and was granted funding for a postdoctoral project by the Wingate Foundation.

# Introduction

## Samuel Kimbriel and Eric Austin Lee

> But (*thou*) which didst man's soul of nothing make,
> And when to nothing it was fallen again,
> To make it new, the form of man didst take;
> "And God with God, becam'st a man with men."
>
> Thou that hast fashion'd twice this Soul of ours,
> So that she is by double title thine,
> Thou only know'st her nature and her pow'rs;
> Her subtil form thou only canst define.[1]

There is something curious about the frequency with which the term "soul" is now used in English in reference not to human beings but to inanimate objects. There is soul food and soulless fast food,[2] soul music and soulful music, and apparently, according to a friend, even my old Raleigh 3-speed bike has "got soul."

Such language is one of many indications hidden within modern life that, whatever one may think in the clamorous halls of the academy *about* human nature, there are certain practices of humanity with which we are

---

1. Sir John Davies, "*Nosce teipsum*: Of the Soul of Man and the Immortality thereof," stanzas 16, 17 (p. 4).

2. As William Gibson's *Pattern Recognition* puts it "My God, don't they know? This stuff is simulacra of simulacra of simulacra. A diluted tincture of Ralph Lauren, who had himself diluted the glory days of Brooks Brothers, who themselves had stepped on the product of Jermyn Street and Savile Row. . . . But Tommy surely is the null point, the black hole. There must be some Tommy Hilfiger event horizon, beyond which it is impossible to be more derivative, more removed from the source, more devoid of soul." Gibson, *Pattern Recognition*, 17–18.

intertwined in daily existence. When faced with one another, we serve and we cherish, we enjoy and we mourn, we forgive and make promises. All of this is enacted because, so to speak, "that is the kind of animal that I am," and, likewise, in so enacting, I acknowledge the weight, not of the other's brain (roughly 1.25 kgs), but of their person, their substance. The act of making a promise to another person, for example, is a granting of a claim that is not expected of non-human things.[3] In such actions we are revealing in lived conviction that human persons differ from other things for they are "animate."[4]

This enacted conviction is nowhere more evident than in our treatment of disability. We do not treat human beings with severe mental affliction, life-threatening ailments, and debilitating diseases as "lost causes" or "on their way out," because we know that as persons they are still our friends,[5] and this relationship is not severed even after their body may deteriorate or depart. To take a recent example, the *New York* magazine film critic David Edelstein makes an illuminating observation about a scene from the film *Still Alice*,[6] which is about a fictional professor named Alice Howland who discovers that she has Alzheimer's. In an appendix to the film, a speech from Tony Kushner's "Angels in America" is delivered in light of the news that the movie's co-director Richard Glatzer had been diagnosed with the disease ALS (amyotrophic laterals sclerosis). Edelstein remarks, "It's a speech in which Tony Kushner, writing at the peak of a violent, hopeless AIDS epidemic, finds words to convey what remains when our earthly bodies seem lost. The scene takes you somewhere a neuroscientist can't—to the soul."[7] Why would Edelstein be so bold about "what remains when our earthly bodies seem lost," about this "more" which animates us even amidst such bodily degradation? On the level of everyday encounter with one another, it should not be surprising that we intuit this basic aspect of human interaction. We rightly balk at crude reductions of persons to some observable trait, which is why we find racism, eugenics, and even most stereotypes to be heinous misrepresentations of the full breadth of one's humanity.

To this point, all parties—those who embrace the old language of soul and those who reject it—must agree. Even the vociferous commentator who

---

3. For more on this, see Spaemann and Zaborowski, "An Animal that can Promise and Forgive."

4. "Between the psyche of an animal and the spirituality of a man there is an enormous distance, an uncrossable gulf." Wojtyła, *Love and Responsibility*, 121.

5. See especially Hans Reinders meditations on disability in his *Receiving the Gift of Friendship*.

6. Adapted from a novel of the same title by Lisa Genova.

7. Edelstein, "Still Alice."

is dedicated to convincing us that "you're nothing but a pack of neurons,"[8] does not intend, when he is attempting to argue for the radical nature of his hypothesis,[9] to introduce an ethic by which promising and forgiving are rejected and eugenics is embraced. On the contrary, if the hypothesis is to stand, the aim is to take everything that we now call human and reveal just how it emerges from the material basis described. Such a person, who believes that the soul is imaginary,[10] is similarly likely to find the continued ubiquity of the language of soul[11] at most puzzling, not unnerving. This confidence is based upon an implicit sense of the separability of these different usages. There is, so it is asserted, on the one hand, a primary and literal notion of "the soul" as a hypothesis by which the pre-modern world accounted for human mental functioning in roughly the same way that we now do with the brain. But though this primary sense is rejected, that does not prevent the term being used in looser and more figurative ways elsewhere.[12]

Perhaps the sentiment behind this breezy dismissal is coherent or even sufficient, but there remains something perplexing about the lingering need to express certain aspects of lived experience with reference to a "dead hypothesis." Why is the word "soul" still so damn useful?

To answer this question, it is worth reflecting further on the notion of "soulfulness." It is surely little accident that most of the references with which we started are to *made* things, objects of human artifice. To say that a bike has soul (which is different than saying that it has *a* soul) is surely to say something about the bike—about its vigor, perhaps, or its weathered wisdom—but it is also to say something about human beings. We might, in part, be alluding to the way that the human skill of the artisan is particularly manifest in the made object, or, perhaps to the way that the object is able powerfully to elicit a certain quality "of soul" from those who encounter it, or perhaps both. Nonetheless, to say that fast food is soulless would not, even for someone who believed in souls, mean "fast food is not a human product." Instead, it seems that we are saying that "this human product fails

---

8. Crick, *Astonishing Hypothesis*, 3.

9. See Crick, *Astonishing Hypothesis*, 258.

10. "I myself, like many scientists, believe that the soul is imaginary and that what we call our minds is simply a way of talking about the functions of our brains." Crick, *Of Molecules and Men*, 87.

11. Though one cannot make too much of this, it is interesting to note that according to Google's Ngram database, whilst the word experienced a steady decline in usage across the twentieth century, this trajectory surprisingly reversed in the mid-1980s to such an extent that as of the most recent data available, it was more common in English than the word "brain."

12. For an example of such a separation, see Musolino, *Soul Fallacy*, 23.

adequately to express humanity." Amongst other things, the term "soul" in these phrases is being used as an intensifier, to express the power of human vivacity as it relates to the given objects in various ways.[13] To put this another way, the term is indicating something about human potential. To say a dance has soul is to indicate that the seed of humanity has flourished and flowered in those actions more completely than elsewhere. In the best art, the human form seems to ring with life in a fashion that can summon tremors of vitality from forgotten depths within the human person.

Just as our lives enact reference to a certain weightiness both in ourselves and in those around us, so also our art implicitly refers to the possibility for growth, for enhanced weightiness to be achieved. It just so happens, furthermore, that the term "soul" is particularly apt in referring to both aspects. This, of course, is no accident. In historical terms the idea of humans as "ensouled" arose not as some bloodless hypothesis, but from within a powerful set of practices concerned with fostering human potentiality and vitality. To understand this point is also to understand why, despite protestations to the contrary from certain academic circles, the soul is still very near at hand.

## Know Thyself

There is no doubt that "anthropological enquiry" (in the broadest sense, which now takes place under titles such as philosophy of mind, psychology, cognitive science and neuroscience, theological anthropology, and evolutionary biology) has undergone significant transformation in recent centuries. As the story is generally told, from the sixteenth century onward Western thought forcefully turned away from the old dualist idea of human nature to such an extent that, as one commentator now puts it, "substantival minds are no longer a live option for most of us."[14] The hard work of science and philosophy regarding the human mind, and related matters such as agency, consciousness, and intentionality have, so it is said, rightly left the soul in the past with other defunct hypotheses. What tends to go

---

13. The quality of this term can be highlighted further by replacing the term "soul" with "brain" in the prior uses. Rather than highlighting vitality, the later term highlights more of an intellectual or nerdy quality. Thus, "brain food" means "food that feeds the brain" and "brainless fast food" means "stupidly prepared" and so on. A decided shift in the nature of the expressions has occurred.

14. Jaegwon Kim, *Phsyicalism*, 9. A recent translator of Aristotle's *De anima* similarly writes: "The predominant philosophic and scientific tradition of the last four hundred years has taken away our souls." Translator's introduction by Joe Sachs in Aristotle, *On the Soul*, 5.

unremarked in this way of telling the story is the fact that the most decisive departure from the older anthropological tradition in which the concept of "the soul" was developed has always been anterior to any of these debates.

Anthropological study is unlike any other, for it is the study of what we ourselves are. The self-reflexivity of the enterprise has some crucial consequences. For one thing, one cannot arrive at an understanding of human beings that does not allow for the possibility of self-knowledge without undermining the whole endeavor.[15] For another, the question of why human beings should seek self-knowledge—why am I, that is, engaging in the present activity?—takes on similarly critical importance. It is with regard to this latter issue particularly that the two traditions divide.

To treat the soul as a defunct hypothesis is, rather obviously, to treat it as a hypothesis (or rather a proto-hypothesis[16]) in the first place.[17] But this is to import a great mass of assumptions, including, most critically for our purpose here, assumptions regarding the motivations and aim of gaining knowledge about this particular entity (in this case, ourselves). Hypotheses, that is, have been developed as part of a procedure to gain a very specific kind of propositional knowledge, either for the purposes of technical mastery or out of a sense of the intrinsic value of "mapping the world." To treat the soul as a hypothesis is to assume either that it has always been part of this procedure and is fit to be directed toward such aims, or that it can be imported with minimal damage to the sense of the concept. Both possibilities must, however, on historical grounds, be denied.

To understand why, consider a notable moment from the *Phaedrus*. Before turning to offer some of his most sophisticated reflections on the nature of the soul and its relationship to materiality, immortality, and love, Plato recounts the following interaction between Socrates and his young interlocutor. Phaedrus asks Socrates' opinion regarding the veracity of the legend of Boreas carrying the princess Orithuia away from a nearby place. Socrates responds that Athenian intellectuals are fond of demystifying the story, saying that Boreas simply stands in for a gust of wind that swept Orithuia away over the cliff to her death. Far from endorsing such rigor (as we might expect a modern "lover of wisdom" to do) Socrates goes on to say that whilst these explanations

---

15. This feature undergirds arguments such as those presented in Lewis, *Miracles*, ch. 3, and Plantinga and Tooley, *Knowledge of God*, 33–49.

16. As the term hypothesis, in a strict sense, belongs to a procedure involving empirical evidence-based testing not yet developed in the ancient world.

17. For paradigmatic examples of handling the soul as a hypothesis/proto-hypothesis see Churchland, *Brain-Wise*, ch. 2; Churchland, *Engine of Reason*, 17; Musolino, *Soul Fallacy*, 24–25; Metzinger, *Being No One*, 504–5.

> are amusing enough . . . they are a job for a man I cannot envy at all. He'd have to be far too ingenious and work too hard. . . . I have no time for such things; and the reason, my friend, is this. I am still unable, as the Delphic inscription orders, to know myself; and it really seems to me ridiculous to look into other things before I have understood that. That is why I do not concern myself with them. I accept what is generally believed, and, as I was just saying, I look not into them but into my own self: Am I a beast more complicated and savage than Typhon, or am I a tamer, simpler animal with a share in a divine and gentle nature? (229d3–230a6)[18]

At the heart of the Socratic temperament is the conviction that focus must fall, before all else, to the cultivation one's own being into its just shape. This theme is articulated to great effect in the *Alcibiades*. There, through highly pointed and personal questions, Socrates gradually enables his young interlocutor to see that the cultivation of any ambition—be it economic or political success or even happiness itself—will end up being both futile and destructive until he learns how to cultivate himself. As he shows him, it is only in this self-cultivation that one can come to see the truth and worth both of oneself and of everything else in the world (see, for example, the progress that Alcibiades makes in 116–24). As they finally come to agree in one of the dialogue's culminating passages: "it is not possible, unless one is moderate and good, to be happy. . . . So it's not one who's gotten rich who will avoid being wretched, but the one who has become moderate. . . . If you are going to manage the affairs of the city correctly and admirably, you must give excellence to the citizens. . . . So you must first get possession of excellence yourself" (134a13–c7).[19] Socrates argues, further, that the only way to cultivate the self is through apprenticing oneself to the Delphic command. As he says, "oh Alcibiades, whether it is easy or not, the situation still holds us like this: if we know ourselves, then we might know how to care for ourselves, but we could never do this when ignorant" (129a7–9, translation ours; cf. 128e10–11).

This Socratic conviction that human life is only worth living in the context of having prioritized the Delphic imperative above all else came to be crystallized in the philosophical schools as they developed over subsequent centuries. As Proclus would write over 750 years later in his commentary on

---

18. Quotations from Plato, *Phaedrus*, translated by Nehamas and Woodruff. We have consulted the Greek text in Plato, *Phaedrus*, edited by Yunis.

19. Unless otherwise noted, quotations from Plato (disputed), *Socrates & Alcibiades*, translated by Johnson. We have consulted the Greek text in Plato, *Alcibiades*, edited by Denyer.

*Alcibiades*, "we consider the strongest and steadiest foundation for . . . the whole of philosophical contemplation, so to speak, to be the discernment of one's own being. For when this has been rightly set, we will also be able, in every way, to perceive accurately the good that belongs to us and the evil that fights it."[20]

It is in the context of this practice that the notion of "the soul" would be developed.[21] This is apparent in both the *Alcibiades* and the *Phaedrus*.[22] In the *Alcibiades*, the soul is introduced as the answer to the question of what the "it" is that one seeks to know in self-knowledge, which is itself the primary task in cultivating oneself.[23] But this "knowledge of the soul" is equated not with gaining a model of the human person, but rather with a kind of contemplative union with the most elevated aspect of the soul and the reality that underpins it:

> S: So, my friend Alcibiades, if a soul is to know itself, it must look into a soul, and particularly into that region of it in which the excellence of the soul, wisdom, resides and to anything else that this is similar to?
> A: It seems so to me . . . .
> S: So it is to God that this aspect of soul is similar, and one looking to this and knowing all that is divine, both God and thought, would in this way also most know himself. (133b7–c6)[24]

Although the second Socratic speech in the *Phaedrus* is famous for its description of the tripartite soul, the purpose of this vivid depiction is too

---

20. Our translation; Greek text: Proclus, *Alcibiadem*, 20, lines 1–7. With regard to the question of authorship: in one sense, our case would in fact be strengthened if *First Alcibiades* was written not by Plato, but by a philosopher from a subsequent generation as it would thereby evince just how powerful these faithfully Platonic ideas would come to be, even in the early academy. In any case, it is either genuine or an artful emulation, as can be seen, for example in the linguistic parallel between the argument in 133a–b and *Phaedrus* 255d. For a thorough summary of current debate on authorship see: Jirsa, "Authenticity"; cf. Denyer (ed.), "Introduction," *Alcibiades*.

21. To grasp just how subservient the concepts developed in the ancient schools were to these aims of self-cultivation and ascent, see: Hadot, *Philosophy as a Way of Life*, esp. chs. 3, 5, 7; Hadot, *What is Ancient Philosophy*, parts 1, 2.; O'Daly, *Plotinus' Philosophy of the Self*, part 1; Gerson, *Plotinus*, ch. 7.

22. The description of the nature of the soul in the *Phaedo* is obviously directed to much the same aim, but so too in the *Timaeus*; see the exhortation in 90a–e.

23. "So he who commands that one know oneself bids us to know our souls" (130e7–8).

24. These lines come just before a fascinating exhortation of disputed origin (Denyer, *Alcibiades*, 236–37, for example, argues that it is a later insertion) regarding the need to gaze into the greater clarity and purity of God in order to know oneself.

rarely considered. The idea that Socrates advances of the soul is a direct response to his questions in the passage on self-knowledge quoted above, with the dark horse representing the bestial aspect of the soul "more complicated and savage than Typhon" and the charioteer (and to a lesser extent, the virtuous horse) manifesting the dignified soul, which shares "in a divine and gentle nature" (230a5–6; see 246a–251c). Here again, however, the purpose in providing these descriptions is not simply to get a model of the soul, but to learn how to inhabit the divine aspect of the soul and to rule over the bestial so that the human can achieve its fullest state. The entire discussion of the character of the soul—of the charioteer and the horses, of the soul's wings, of its capacity for self-motion, of its immortality, its relation to matter and its immortality—is offered with the single goal of enabling Socrates to reveal the path by which such a soul can seek its highest end. Socrates commends this path and the underlying self-knowledge required as the way to "divine gifts" (256e3), not only "bliss" and "shared understanding" in this life (256b1), but also the enslavement of the bestial aspect below the divine such that the wings of the soul regrow to their full expanse, enabling the soul to move upward in its ascent to the highest things (256b1–7).[25]

Once one sees that the movement from the language of soul to the language of brain is not a shift between two different hypotheses, but between two different traditions with wildly divergent goals a number of things become clear. The first is why "the soul" has fared so badly in modernity. Just like we would be incomplete and likely even mistaken in attempting to describe a hammer without reference to the use for which it was developed ("ungainly hunk of metal"), so too, the sense inherent in the idea of the soul can only be spotted with regard to the aim of philosophical contemplation. Now of course, one can still use a tool in some sense without knowing what it was for—repurposing a hammer, for example, as a desk leg—but one ought not be surprised when its performance is less than ideal. What is shocking about those who maintain that the soul is imaginary, however, is that rather than pausing to understand whether they have misunderstood the soul's use, they are content to go on berating it for its poor performance in propping up the escritoire.

---

25. A. E. Taylor, in commenting upon Plato's *Phaedrus*, says regarding the soul: "The goal of the whole pilgrimage is reached by an ascent to a region outside the whole heaven, 'the plain of reality', where the procession pauses and enjoys a Sabbath rest in the contemplation of 'bodiless reality, without figure, colour, or tangible quality' (in other words the forms); this is the true home of souls, and the source of their spiritual food." Taylor, *Plato*, 307. For an illuminating reading of Plato on the soul and the "World Soul," see Oliver, *Philosophy, God and Motion*, 21–22.

In considering whether the soul as a concept can safely be transported out of its own tradition and into the scientific one, it is perhaps sufficient to note that many of the features that make it perform so poorly in the lab were its greatest strengths in its own environ. Take, for example, Patricia Churchland's consideration of the question "as a hypothesis about the nature of mind, how does substance dualism stack up against physicalism?" She responds:

> The short answer is that substance dualism chronically suffers from the lack of any *positive* description of the nature of the mental substance and any *positive* description of the interaction between the physical and the nonphysical. The content of the hypothesis is specified mainly by saying what the soul is *not*: that is, it is *not* physical, *not* electromagnetic, *not* causal, and so forth. . . . Because the soul-brain hypothesis lacks a substantive, positive characterization, it . . . is hard to take seriously, especially at this stage of science.[26]

Churchland is frustrated by the lack of precision in the construct that could be operationalized into a viable empirical test. What she does not pause to ask, however, is whether the features that she faults for lack of precision might have been developed with some other end in mind, as indeed they were. Socrates' descriptions of the soul, for example, lack Churchland's desired "positive content," not because he is sloppy or intentionally attempting to sidestep more rigorous scrutiny, but because of the conviction that the specific character of the soul's vitality is such that it cannot be defined in advance, but can only be understood by being inhabited in the fullest sense. What Churchland perceives as insufficiency or evasiveness (but which could be termed more charitably an "apophatic pause") is in fact an invitation to the hearer to give up trying prematurely to define the soul and learn rather to cultivate it.

To put this another way, the apparent victory won by those antagonistic to the soul has come about only because they have been jousting with a straw-man of their own devising. To strip a term of its original structure and usefulness only to find it wanting is not to refute an idea, but to ignore it.[27]

---

26. Churchland, *Brain-wise*, 47, emphasis in original.

27. Another indication that this argument is being conducted against a strawman can be found in the structure that the case tends to take. Much of the text in works like Crick's, *Astonishing Hypothesis*, Churchland's *Brain-Wise*, or Musolino's *Soul Fallacy* is concerned, in the simpler form of the argument, with reviewing evidence that shows that there is strong correlation between certain material neurological events and particular traits of human thought or consciousness, or, in a slightly more complex form, showing that when particular material conditions are altered or impaired, the

An understanding of this Socratic tradition does more, however, than simply to challenge in conceptual terms the ease with which the soul has been imported as a hypothesis; it critiques the very impulse that motivates the attempt. As noted above, any anthropological enquiry faces serious self-reflexive questions regarding why we should go about studying the human being in the first place. The contemporary scientifically-minded tradition might, when faced with the question, resort to arguing that it is a modern successor to this old Delphic approach (for example, are not questions of how consciousness can be grounded in material processes or how the mind's habits have been shaped by evolutionary forces about as basic as it gets in considering the nature of the human being, in coming "to know ourselves"?). Sufficient introduction to that older tradition has already been given to see what is flawed with that claim. This issue, and its paradoxical consequences, have attentively been noted by the phenomenological school. As Maurice Merleau-Ponty aptly puts it, "Scientific points of view, according to which my existence is a moment of the world's, are always both naïve and at the same time dishonest, because they take for granted, without explicitly mentioning it, the other point of view, namely that of consciousness . . . ."[28] The problem, in other words, is that science looks outward before looking inward. As Merleau-Ponty explains,

> I cannot conceive myself as nothing but a bit of the world, a mere object of biological, psychological or sociological investigation. I cannot shut myself up within the realm of science. All my

corresponding "mental traits" are also impaired. Without any further steps, these authors tend to reach the conclusion that it must be very embarrassing for those who believe in the soul to be confronted with the intertwining of thought and matter. What tends to escape notice, however, is that a great many of those who developed the old idea of the soul were highly aware of this interwoven relationship (as is nearly anyone who observes that death happens through violence to the *body*), and, far from finding it embarrassing, were, in fact, transfixed by what they perceived as the great beauty and dignity of the arrangement. Aquinas writes this way in *Summa Theologiae* I, q. 76 a. 5, for example, but it is more eloquently stated by John Donne, who thanks the body for being that from which the soul emerges: "On man heaven's influence works not so,/ But that it first imprints the air;/ For soul into the soul may flow,/ Though it to body first repair.// As our blood labours to beget/ Spirits, as like souls as it can;/ Because such fingers need to knit/ That subtle knot, which makes us man." "The Ecstasy," lines 57–64. Sir John Davies' beautiful poem "On the Immortality of the Soul" culminates its initial reflection on soul and body with the lines: "Doubtless, this could not be, but that she turns/ Bodies to Spirits, by sublimation strange;/ As fire converts to fire the things it burns;/ As we our meats into our nature change.// From their gross matter she abstracts the forms,/ And draws a kind of quintessence from things; / Which to her proper nature she transforms,/ to bear them light on her celestial wings." Section IV, stanzas 12,13.

28. Quotation from Merleau-Ponty, *Phenomenology of Perception*, translated by Colin Smith, ix.

knowledge of the world, even my scientific knowledge, is gained from my own particular point of view, or from some experience of the world without which the symbols of science would be meaningless. The whole universe of science is built upon the world as directly experienced, and if we want to subject science itself to rigorous scrutiny and arrive at a precise assessment of its meaning and scope, we must begin by reawakening the basic experience of the world of which science is the second-order expression.[29]

What seems to be essential for Socrates as for Merleau-Ponty is a matter of prioritization, that the first order of business must be the task of coming to know, and accordingly to be at home in, one's own self. But what Merleau-Ponty is sensing in this passage is that the path that has been taken by more scientifically-minded studies of the human is much too circuitous for comfort. They have, that is, arrived at anthropological enquiry by way of precisely the distraction of which Socrates was so wary when speaking of the legend of Boreas. Rather than attending to self knowledge as the first order of business they have: 1. rushed about analyzing the external appearance of things and then 2. attempted to assimilate the self (upon which such observations are all the while dependent) back into the mold of what they spied outside. Socrates would rightly be concerned: what looks to be a human-centric mode of enquiry is in fact the opposite, for its governing impulse is to ignore, or (worse) to "assimilate away," the human itself in an effort to make all of reality conform to the distraction.

The aims toward which scientific enterprises are shaped are representational (building a map of reality) and technical (finding ways to manipulate nature for practical ends). As we have seen, for Socrates, in contrast, all such projects are prone to catastrophic error until we understand what is actually *worth* doing, and the only way to find that out is through cultivation of the self in virtue through self-knowledge. Here the redefinition of the term "theory" in modernity is evident. Socrates is seeking *theoria*, contemplative union with the true nature of the soul and the highest things (as he says in *Phaedrus* 247c8, "that being that really is" οὐσία ὄντως οὖσα). The modern anthropologist seeks *theory*, a neutral model that represents an external reality in propositional form. To see the contrast, consider how an aspiring cognitive scientist who refused to conduct experiments until she could understand precisely how this activity is a *just* thing for her type

---

29. Ibid. For the original, see *Phénoménologie de la perception*, 8–9. For precursors to this critique, see Husserl, "Philosophy as Rigorous Science"; Heidegger, *Being and Time*, 45–50.

of being to undertake would be shown the door before ever making it to graduate school.

From a Socratic perspective, there are a variety of problems here. The first is that these enquiries have succeeded in mis-marketing themselves and we must come to see that the energy fueling so much frantic activity in these disciplines is not the desire of true self-knowledge, but rather a fear of that very task and a resulting desire to force the conformity of the one lingering aberration (ourselves) into the model of the distraction. The second is that no enquiry, no matter how methodical, can proceed aright without first attending to this basic thing. For Socrates and the phenomenologists alike, the point is practical. We are quick to wipe clear our lenses and telescopes, but what if the grime is in my very self? If I am muddy and confused then all else will be the same *for me* (even if I don't recognize this fact).

Both of these points derive from a deeper and more encompassing point. Whatever we may think *about* human beings we also *are* human—a fact that we enact in many ways, including those noted at the start of this introduction. But, from a Socratic perspective, to be human as we are in this life is also to be in need of fostering, to be as a seedling, not yet a tree. The trick played by modern anthropological enquiries is, in other words, not merely disingenuous, but tragic. In substituting this game of hypothesis swapping in place of the true Delphic task, we have lost what we most desperately need, a pathway toward vitality, toward the full life.

## Gaining the Soul

The following essays arise from this spirit of restless searching for ourselves in the company of others. We approach this task not as experts seeking to give a comprehensive definition of the soul (or of its relation to matter, immortality, etc.)—as we have indicated above, such a task would be a fool's errand. Instead, these essays, which represent papers given at the Centre of Theology and Philosophy conference at Oxford on "The Soul," are undertaken in the Socratic spirit of the novice. We seek, however fumblingly, to find our way again into the full life of the soul.

Just as we cannot pre-define the soul without inhabiting it, so too we cannot pre-determine the path by which its nature might be realized. That path can only be discovered by searching, and that, to put it mildly, is a difficult endeavor, not least for those born into a culture infused with powerful evasions and obstacles to such discovery. It is also, however, as we have been arguing all along, a task that is incumbent upon our nature. We are on this path whether we own up to this fact or not. We either seek, in a Socratic manner, to find this full human life, or we suffer in the poverty of not having found what we should be.

The authors in this volume attempt this search in different manners (drawing on philosophical, theological, historical, literary, and musical modes of analysis) and arrive, at times, at different conclusions (see for example the contrasts between Wilson, Mitralexis, and Eikelboom on the question of unity). Together, the volume presents a variety of possible itineraries, all within that Socratic country between poverty and abundance.[30] The volume is arranged thematically in five sections: "The Soul and the Saeculum," "Fracture and Unity," "Moving to Wholeness," "The Soul's Regard," and "Vivacity." Our description of the content of the volume follows these categories to a degree, but we have also attempted to narrate the work in a way that reveals crucial interconnections and contrasts that arise apart from these thematic headings.

In seeking this Socratic path, the first need is to confront the reality of our current situation. As Socrates says to Alcibiades, the condition most capable of causing great harm is to be one who does not know what is just, but to think that one does.[31] The contrast here is stark. To confront one's true condition and seek to become just is to open oneself to the possibility of attaining ever greater heights of goodness, beauty, and perfection.[32] The obverse example is that of the tragic life in which one remains intent on evading one's true face—attaching oneself to wealth, fame, or even, as in the case of the Athenian demythologizers, "knowledge"—so as to insulate oneself from the vulnerability of the Delphic task. As Socrates argues, these will ultimately find themselves condemned to wander the earth for nine millennia, devoid of understanding.[33] This relates to the argument in the previous section that much of what passes in the contemporary world for Delphic investigation (what we have called "anthropological enquiry") is in fact the opposite, as the evasion has circled back on itself.

Three approaches to these issues can be found in the first half of the volume. On the one hand, there is a diagnostic voice, attempting both to

30. *Symposium* 203b–d.

31. 117c–118b.

32. It should be noted here that the person cannot, of course—nor should she want to—escape creaturely approaches to discerning soulful things. It is a matter of "where one ends up". While perception arises through the senses first in knowledge, it is being (ontology) that is in fact primary—similar to how we do not know God's essence directly, but first through God's effects. We are here following Aquinas. See, e.g., *Summa contra Gentiles*, I, c. 11, n. 4; II, c. 15; *Summa Theologiae* I, q. 1, a. 7 ad 1; q. 2, a. 1; q. 2, a. 2; q. 12, a. 8; *De Veritate*, q. 2, a. 14.

33. *Phaedrus* 256e–257a.

reveal the poverty of the current situation and to consider how we got here.[34] Kimbell Kornu, for example, shows how both Galen and Melanchthon influence Western thought such that anatomical dissection becomes the primary paradigm for locating and achieving knowledge about the soul. Where for Aristotle "the soul is in a certain way all beings [ψυχὴ τὰ ὄντα πώς ἐστι πάντα],"[35] now the soul, as Kornu shows, begins to be seen only as real within a spatialized, knowable nature. Likewise, K. Nicholas Forti turns to recent reductive accounts of the soul from Nancey Murphy to Daniel Dennett, highlighting significant difficulties hidden within the narratives of this new physicalism. As he argues, in addition to being unable to call certain human beings "persons" within their limited criteria, on the one hand, such accounts fail to be truly "physical" in the end, and on the other, they are so concerned with reacting against realistic accounts of soulful encounter that "truth" becomes an arbitrary concern. Forti paves a way forward with an account of souls that are narrated by a different, promising word. Mary Midgley extends these analyses by charting the trajectory by which the idea of "the soul" came to be abstracted, in modernity, into "mind" and then further reduced to mere "body." She unpacks Descartes' dualism of body and soul as a theistic dualism that later descends into a materialistic monism as the soul, now extrinsic to the body, is eschewed. A significant strand of Midgley's argument leads into the second approach as she exhorts us to attend to the *whole* of our experience such that we can abide in our outer and inner realities.[36]

This diagnostic approach complements the strategy deployed by Anna Piazza and Andrew Kaethler, who reflect on the soul's continued accessibility through experience. Piazza considers the experience of mortality, arguing that such experience in fact verifies rather than refutes the idea of the underlying vitality and immortality of the soul. She provides a comparison between Max Scheler, Paul Ludwig Landsberg, and Augustine, showing how Landsberg and especially Augustine give our souls hope in ways that can truthfully guide our affections along the journey. Andrew T. J. Kaethler meditates similarly on the experience of time through a study of Alexander Schmemann's understanding of a "Eucharistic anthropology" of persons

---

34. Interestingly, as can be seen by their placement in the second section, all three of these diagnostic papers are also heavily concerned with issues of unity and fragmentation.

35. Aristotle, *De Anima*, Book III, ch. 8; 431b 21. Thomas Aquinas approvingly quotes this passage from the philosopher in *De Veritate*, q. 1, a. 1c. See the paper by Hackett for further discussion of this understanding of the soul.

36. This diagnostic strategy is also prominent in the essays by Milbank, Hackett, and Desmond.

ensconced in and bounded by the finite limitations of time. These finite limitations, he argues, can be either enslaving or freeing, depending upon our descent away from, or ascent into the offering of ourselves to God. The nature of thanksgiving transports us into a further participation of this reality where time is redeemed.

A third approach can be seen in the essays by Johann Rossouw and John Milbank, both of whom reflect on the political conditions that result from our ability or inability to inhabit the soul rightly. In contrast to many essays in this volume, Rossouw, drawing on the work of Bernard Stiegler, takes for granted, to a certain degree, the severing of the old connection between the soul and God. He suggests that we must now find an alternative societal mechanism by which the needs previously met by the divine can be serviced in another way. John Milbank disagrees. Over against Stiegler's "mix and match" approach, Milbank argues that we must recognize the stark contrast between a cosmos of soul and that without it. Against those theologians who seek now simply to defend a minimalist view of mind and human dignity, Milbank argues that we must rather see that the true confrontation is between comprehensive visions of reality and their attendant political embodiments. Thus, to use the language we used above, "the soul" is not simply a hypothesis (as "mind" tends to be) but a whole way of inhabiting reality in integral ethical community stretching from plants to humans to God himself. In contrast, our post-soul world, with all of its incoherencies, is built upon a much more unilateral notion of the human being who works as the uninvolved technocrat who oversees and manipulates, but never loves.

The work of confronting one's present condition—however difficult—is undertaken out of the desire to find a way behind it, and Milbank's point regarding the integrated nature of the soulful cosmos is useful here. When one takes the Socratic path, with all of the sacrifice that it entails, one is also opening oneself to a kind of bounty in a number of different areas, including, amongst others: 1. the integrating of oneself, 2. the communication or communion with other beings, 3. the ascent to God and the highest things. It is the concern of the remaining essays in the volume to explore one or more aspect of this abundance and the difficulty of the path to it in various ways.

Amidst such diagnoses regarding the fractured state of the soul, a perpetual concern regards the soul's quest to be integrated or unified. Sotiris Mitralexsis and Nichifor Tănase have each contributed similar-yet-differing papers to this collection that attend to issues of a unified—and fully ensouled—human person. Mitralexsis and Tănase both aim to provide a wholistic anthropology through specific studies of Maximus the Confessor and Gregory Palamas, respectively. While their papers differ widely in their specifics, both point toward a unified account of the human hypostasis such that the person becomes more unified by their own response to reflecting the unity of God through the unity of Christ. This technical philosophical and theological method approaches, from another (and often very useful) angle, a reality that is at the same time deeply personal.

When we examine the nature of our own experience along these paths, we frequently discover that the journey itself, like Kierkegaard so often mentions, is inherently fraught. A phenomenology of Abraham's ascent up Mount Moriah with his son Isaac, despite its shockingly paradoxical nature,[37] provides an analogy for our own foray into a truthful life, one which Kierkegaard says in fact *should* be difficult.[38] The truth of this realism is not ultimately expressed in writing, but is one that has to be lived, or performed.[39] Saint Augustine echoes the struggle embodied in these sentiments when he states, "If you are in love with the earth, your journey is taking you far from God. If you are with God, you are climbing toward him."[40] Mere bodies cannot find rest in and of themselves, for we are always more than that, guided by the heart's desire: "The body travels from place to place; the soul travels by its affections."[41] The soul, therefore, must undertake the toil of conversion and pilgrimage if there is to be ascent.

Within the fraught nature of this experience we are continually impeded, furthermore, by a hidden shadow-like darkness, a sinful proclivity. L. C. Wilson writes on Evagrius of Pontus and Søren Kierkegaard against such a melancholic backdrop. Acedia, despair, and the demonic attempt to destroy the unity of the person into a dispersion of multiplicities resulting in dejection of heart, escapism, and a lack of earnestness about the eternal. Wilson shows how Evagrius and Kierkegaard, in their own ways, offer a path toward a harmonious, balanced, integrated soulful person. Lexi Eikelboom also considers the challenge of the unified person, but from a different perspective, questioning the parameters of unity itself. She suggests that perhaps the philosophical disunity of the body and soul may not be primarily due to the affects of sin (so her focus is very different from Wilson's), and thus, by looking to the work of Giorgio Agamben with some necessary

---

37. Kierkegaard, *Fear and Trembling*.

38. See, e.g., "But the ideality with regard to being a Christian is a continual inward deepening. The more ideal the conception of being a Christian, the more inward it becomes—and indeed the more difficult." Kierkegaard, *The Point of View*, 137.

39. This is why, for Kierkegaard, Socrates is the existential person *par excellence*.

40. Saint Augustine, *Psalms*, 507 [Commenting upon Psalm 119:5–6 in Augustine's Latin text; Psalm 120:5–6 in current translation].

41. Ibid.

modifications, Eikelboom offers not a disunity for its own sake, but rather a "redeemed duality" with an emphasis on relationality (and so in this sense presents a concern very much *like* Wilson's).

The papers by Edmund Waldstein and Anthony D. Baker complement Wilson's reflections on such *difficulty* by bringing these practical and pastoral concerns into conversation with literary resources. Waldstein considers the history of the modern novel, arguing that its primary features, which aimed at giving the reader a "peep-hole" into another's consciousness emerged out of dualisms which saw the inner and outer as radically divorced from one another. Waldstein argues, however, that as this tidy eighteenth-century anthropology has broken down, so too has the idea of the novel itself, particularly in post-modernity as our fractured experience of being human also undermines the books that we pen. Considering finally the work of David Foster Wallace, Waldstein argues, however, that this erosion is in fact providing an opportunity, as the novel comes again to be a "performance," and, in particular, a performance of fracture and of difficulty capable of providing healing. Baker, using the works of Shakespeare, similarly reflects upon these issues of masks and performances in order to consider the nature of conversion. As Baker argues, "all true conversions in Shakespeare are difficult" such that the least masked characters (and he considers Falstaff especially) are also those that have the most trouble with conversion, for, what do they have to give but their very selves? By reflecting in this literary fashion on the soul's obstinacy, these papers force one again to consider just how much is required if one is to be successful in the truly Socratic task of conversion (this is surely part of the reason that many opt for the much easier work of hypothesizing).

Relationality is a significant concern of a number of the authors under the conviction that it is impossible to understand the soul in isolation, for its essence is bound up with its capacity for community. As W. Norris Clarke puts it, "the full dimensions of what it means 'to be' can be found only in *personal being*, in its *interpersonal manifestation*."[42] More primary than the "I am," as Clarke says, is the "we are" of interpersonal dialogue. The papers by Nigel Zimmermann and Férdia J. Stone-Davis establish this foundational connection between souls and their inherent regard for one another (as does the essay by Eikelboom). Zimmermann engages in a comparison between Saint John Paul II and Emmanuel Levinas, highlighting different strategies of gift reception, looking particularly at how each of these thinkers gives attention to "the other." While both John Paul II and Levinas are known for providing strong accounts of alterity/otherness, Zimmermann points

---

42. Clarke, "The 'We are' of Interpersonal Dialogue," 42, emphasis Clarke's.

out significant divergences that make a real difference when it comes to the flourishing of a *communio personarum* without eliding the irreducibility of the singular person. Stone-Davis considers the effects of music on the body in establishing what she calls a "liminal ethics" focusing particularly on the challenging interstices between proximity and distance. By examining a cacophonous "Music Immersion Program," she brings to the forefront various assumptions about how music can "world-make" and therefore create a reality, however positive or (as it seems here in her example) negative. This analogy enables her to reflect upon music's role in establishing soulful worlds as the music's "thresholds" resounds in the person's own porous relationality.[43]

This idea of the soul as the window by which relationality is opened to the creature extends, for many of our authors, far beyond *human* community. The soul becomes intertwined in intimacy with creation itself, both ringing with the divine song and, in its turn, singing as well. In this vein, soulful eyes become the "eyes to see" creation as iconic, and other faces as icons of the friendship and love of Christ. A beautifully recreated fictional diary of the poet Francis Thompson speaks movingly to this theme as the poet ruminates on the interplay between isolation and community, darkness and light:

> My own darkened life has here at Storrington been irradiated by the light of the lives of these holy monks. Their faces are icons of Christ, radiant with His love and compassion. How fortunate I am to abide among them.
>
> When I gaze upon Father Sebastian's face, I am gazing upon Christ. "Our faces are forged within the soul," he once said to me on one of our afternoon walks. How else explain the sublimity and dignity and repose of such a face as his?
>
> Faces and therefore eyes. I shall never forget the day I looked into Sebastian's eyes and felt that Christ was gazing at me. Under his gaze I became myself.[44]

The final three essays in this volume reflect in different ways upon the vitality of soul as it participates in the community of God and of creation. Simone Kotva's essay brings out that facet of the novice's journey related to work as a liturgical activity. The spirit of the Socratic novice, contrary to much of our modern inclination toward specialist expertise, is to look afresh on all reality, again and again, in a child-like way, striving for what

---

43. In this sense there are some striking parallels with William Desmond's paper in this volume.

44. Waldon, *The Lost Diary*, 48.

Chesterton calls an "eternal appetite of infancy."[45] Kotva's paper analyzes Friedrich Schlegel and the concept of work, for Schlegel Kotva finds that the knowledge involved in this enterprise reverses our notion of work such that we allow ourselves to be grasped by love.[46] It is in divine worship where we "let things be" in such a way that life is a liturgical celebration, Being is resplendent with love, and work becomes, in turn, truly leisure.[47]

Through examination of medieval, modern, and post-modern understandings of the human person, W. Chris Hackett charts a series of tensions regarding the possibility of ascent back to the highest things. As he emphasizes, the goal of the ascent, finally, is to share in God's own self-knowing. This is only possible as that highest comes low to bring us high in various ways, not least in the gift of being ensouled in the first place. We *are* our ascent and all human knowledge and action can only be understood as an interpretation of this ascending itself. What is the soul but the analogical presence of this passage to God? This ascent is enabled, furthermore, communally in the gift of the community of the church that stretches all the way to the end of the ascent through the *beati* who stand now before the divine essence. As Hackett argues, modern thought has been centrally concerned with alienating us from these realities and his final challenge is to reflect upon how the soul as a living concept can be recovered, and, indeed, reinhabited.

The final and culminating essay in the volume by William Desmond is itself, when read aright, a Socratic journey. In his spiraling reflection one comes into confrontation at various moments with Aristotle and Descartes, with science and Kant, with singularity and intimacy, with music and death, with self and soul. In all of this, Desmond gradually opens a space in which one's present music-less stasis might crack apart as a deeper resonant soul music emerges all around.

It is finally for the sake of this resonance, for Desmond and for us, that the soul must turn to itself, must endeavor to find its face. One does not walk the Socratic path so as to be left simply with more "ego"; Alcibiades had quite enough of this to begin with. That self was always a counterfeit, a substitute for a true name that Alcibiades had never bothered to find. For in order to come to say "I" truly, one must awaken to that truer self that has always already been ringing with melodies not its own. This soul is, as

---

45. See the full wonderful passage in Chesterton, *Orthodoxy*, 58.
46. Cf. 1 Cor 8:2–3.
47. Pieper, *Leisure*, 65.

Jean-Louis Chrétien says, "the place where the world transforms its light into song."[48]

## Bibliography

Aristotle. *De Anima*. Greek Text. Edited by W. D. Ross. Oxford Classical Text. Oxford: Oxford University Press, 1956.

———. *On the Soul* and *On Memory and Recollection*. Translated by Joe Sachs. Santa Fe, NM: Green Lion, 2001.

Saint Augustine. *Expositions of the Psalms* 99–120. Translated by Maria Boulding, O.S.B. Edited by Boniface Ramsey. New York: New City, 2003.

Chesterton, G. K. *Orthodoxy*. New York: Image, 2001.

Chrétien, Jean-Louis. *The Unforgettable and the Unhoped For*. Translated by Jeffrey Bloechl. New York: Fordham University Press, 2002.

Churchland, Patricia. *Brain-wise: Studies in Neurophilosophy*. Cambridge: MIT Press, 2002.

Churchland, Paul. *The Engine of Reason, the Seat of the Soul: A Philosophical Journey into the Brain*. Cambridge: MIT Press, 1995.

Clarke, W. Norris. "The 'We Are' of Interpersonal Dialogue as the Starting Point of Metaphysics." In *Explorations in Metaphysics: Being—God—Person*, 31–44. Notre Dame, IN: University of Notre Dame Press, 1994.

Crick, Francis. *The Astonishing Hypothesis: The Scientific Search for the Soul*. New York: Touchstone, 1994.

———. *Of Molecules and Men*. Amherst, NY: Prometheus, 2004.

Davies, Sir John. "The Immortality of the Soul." In *The Poetical Works of Sir John Davies*, 100–103. London: Davies, 1773.

Denyer, Nicholas, ed. "Introduction." *Alcibiades*. Cambridge: Cambridge University Press, 2001.

Donne, John. "The Ecstasy." *Poems of John Donne*. Vol. 1. Edited by E. K. Chambers. London: Lawrence & Bullen, 1896.

Edelstein, David. "'Still Alice' Is a Triumph for Julianne Moore, But the Rest of Film Is Thin." Fresh Air, National Public Radio. January 16, 2015. Online: http://www.npr.org/2015/01/16/377716242/still-alice-is-a-triumph-for-julianne-moore-but-the-rest-of-film-is-thin.

Gerson, Lloyd P. *Plotinus*. New York: Routledge, 1994.

Hadot, Pierre. *Philosophy as a Way of Life*. Edited by Arnold Davidson. Translated by Michael Chase. Oxford: Blackwell, 1995.

———. *What is Ancient Philosophy?* Translated by Michael Chase. Cambridge, MA: Belknap, 2002.

Heidegger, Martin. *Being and Time*. Translated by Joan Stambaugh. Revised by Dennis J. Schmidt. Albany, NY: State University of New York Press, 2010.

---

48. The full quotation reads: "the human body does not respond solely by itself and for itself, that its task and dignity are to speak for all that does not speak, to be the place where the world transforms its light into song. Human dialogue lives only in also being a response to things and to the world. Such are the command and compassion of the song." Chrétien, *The Unforgettable and the Unhoped For*, 128.

Husserl, Edmund. *Philosophie als strenge Wissenschaft*. Hamburg: Meiner, 2009.
———. "Philosophy as Rigorous Science." Translated by Marcus Brainard. *The New Yearbook for Phenomenology and Phenomenological Philosophy* 2 (2002) 249–95.
Genova, Lisa. *Still Alice*. Lincoln, NE: iUniverse, 2007.
Gibson, William. *Pattern Recognition*. London: Penguin, 2004.
Jirsa, Jakub. "Authenticity of the *Alcibiades* I: Some Reflections." *Listy filologické* 132.3/4 (2009) 225–44.
Kierkegaard, Søren. *Fear and Trembling*, Edited and translated by Howard V. Hong and Edna H. Hong. Princeton, NJ: Princeton University Press, 1983.
———. *The Point of View*. Edited and translated by Howard V. Hong and Edna H. Hong. Princeton, NJ: Princeton University Press, 1998.
Kim, Jaegwon. *Physicalism or Something Near Enough*. Princeton, NJ: Princeton University Press, 2005.
Lewis, C. S. *Miracles: A Preliminary Study*. Rev. ed. Glasgow: Collins, 1960.
Metzinger, Thomas. *Being No One: The Self-Model Theory of Subjectivity*. Cambridge: MIT Press, 2004.
Merleau-Ponty, Maurice. *Phénoménologie de la perception*. Paris: Gallimard, 1945.
———. *Phenomenology of Perception*. Translated by Colin Smith. New York: Routledge, 2002.
Musolino, Julien. *The Soul Fallacy*. Amherst, NY: Prometheus, 2015.
O'Daly, Gerard. *Plotinus' Philosophy of the Self*. Shannon, Ireland: Irish University Press, 1973.
Oliver, Simon. *Philosophy, God and Motion*. London: Routledge, 2005.
Pieper, Joseph. *Leisure: The Basis of Culture*. San Francisco: Ignatius, 2009.
Plantinga, Alvin, and Michael Tooley. *Knowledge of God*. Oxford: Blackwell, 2008.
Plato. "Phaedrus." In *Plato: Complete Works*, edited by John Cooper; translated by A. Nehamas, and P. Woodruff, 506–56. Indianapolis, IN: Hackett, 1997.
———. *Phaedrus*. (Greek Text). Edited by Harvey Yunis. Cambridge: Cambridge University Press, 2011.
Plato (disputed). *Socrates and Alcibiades*. Translated by David Johnson. Newburyport, MA: Focus, 2003.
———. *Alci1'biades*. (Greek Text). Edited by Nicholas Denyer. Cambridge: Cambridge University Press, 2001.
Proclus. *Procli diadochi in Platonis primum Alcibiadem* in *Procli philosophi Platonici opera inedita*. (Greek Text). Edited by V. Cousin. 2nd ed. Paris: Durand, 1864.
Reinders, Hans S. *Receiving the Gift of Friendship: Profound Disability, Theological Anthropology, and Ethics*. Grand Rapids, MI: Eerdmans, 2008.
Sachs, Joe, ed. "Introduction." In *Aristotle's On the Soul and On Memory and Recollection*, 1–42. Santa Fe, NM: Green Lion, 2001.
Spaemann, Robert, and Holger Zaborowski. "An Animal that Can Promise and Forgive." *Communio* 34.4 (2007) 511–21.
Taylor, A. E. *Plato: The Man and His Work*. New York: Meridian, 1957.
Waldon, Robert. *The Hound of Heaven at my Heels: The Lost Diary of Francis Thompson*. Milwaukee, WI: Wiseblood, 2014.
Wojtyła, Karol. *Love and Responsibility*. Translated by H. T. Willetts. San Francisco: Ignatius, 1981.

# SECTION I
# The Soul and the Saeculum

# 1

## The Experience of Death
### The Immortality of the Soul and the Unity of the Person in Landsberg, Scheler, and Augustine

ANNA PIAZZA

ONE OF THE MOST fecund themes of Paul Ludwig Landsberg's anthropology, which stands out for a presentation of man's potential "self-comprehension" on the basis of a lived "inner-experience," is his reflection concerning death and the confrontation with the human conscience of death, which threatens the sense of life and the search for an overcoming of transitoriness. It was in *Esprit* where Landsberg published, in 1935, the two essays related to this topic, *Die Erfahrung des Todes* and *Das moralische Problem des Selbstmorder*. In particular, we would like to analyze the former, and compare it with the positions of two other important thinkers, both "fathers" of Landsberg: Max Scheler and Augustine of Hippo.

With Landsberg, we will first confront the question of death in all its radicalism, and then undertake through Scheler a retrospective path until turning back even further to Augustine's theory. If Landsberg and Scheler grasp the matter of death adequately, relating it to the consciousness of modern man and, phenomenologically, to an intentional temporal synthesis, we will see that Augustine will offer an even more integral answer to the problematic.

At the beginning of *Die Erfahrung des Todes*, Landsberg writes that human beings, unlike all other living creatures, are the only ones to be characterized by the knowledge of their own inevitable death.[1] This self-awareness does not just derive from empirical observation or biological laws, but is an innate perception of the human being's own finitude. "The being (*das Dasein*) does not just exist as mere fact, but in a certain way has to experience himself—as Heidegger recognized—as a 'being for death' (*Dasein zum Tode*),"[2] and has to find in this fact a decisive and qualifying feature.

This fact brings man face to face with a choice that demands he take a position: it can be alternatively explained, for example by reducing it, as evolutionary theories do, to the purely biological need for species survival; or it can be valued as a privileged moment in which man comes face to face with his personal existence as a whole. In fact, the experience of death cannot be relegated to a merely biological need as it questions the very essence of the human being. As Landsberg puts it:

> The question about meaning is the unique, common, original root of other philosophical fundamental problems: who am I, where am I going, where do I come from? But also: what do I have to do? Both questions refer to the threat of death (*Todesbedrohlichkeit*), [and are activated by this]. The question about the meaning of life arises for man in relation to the precise degree of his individualization, from a particular kind of knowledge about his being destined to die. . . . Man's self-conception (*Selbstauffassung des Menschen*) is inseparably tied to a conception of survival beyond death.[3]

## A New Method Faithful to Experience: Max Scheler and the Phenomenology of Death

In the whole course of history, philosophers have attempted to make sense of the human being's desire to survive death's inevitability. Plato initially reacted against the finitude of our corporal body by stressing the superiority of the spiritual over the physical. In his *Phaedo* he demonstrates how the soul, since it can know eternal things as *condicio sine qua non,* has to have a kindred nature to that which is immortal. Along the whole course of history, from Neoplatonism to medieval philosophy with Augustine, then in modernity from Descartes to every subsequent spiritualistic or rationalistic philosophy, attempts have been made to prove that the soul is an

---

1. Cf. Landsberg, *Einführung in die philosophische Anthropologie*, 51.
2. Ibid., 52.
3. Ibid., 64–66.

irreducible disembodied kernel where the essence and dignity of the person are preserved.

However, belief in a substantial soul, separated from the body, was discredited by natural psychology and evolutionary biology in the nineteenth century. The second half of that century saw the development of a "psychology without a soul,"[4] which tried to observe the empirical laws of psychological life while avoiding metaphysical assumptions, such as the possible existence of a "soul." From there, philosophers like Wundt[5] or Brentano[6] claimed the impossibility of supposing and theorizing about anything beyond purely observable phenomena.

In opposition to these new theories, the German phenomenologist Max Scheler offers a dissenting approach. While embracing a naturalistic framework,[7] Scheler does not eliminate the question of the soul and does not reduce his notion to a psychophysical product. Admittedly, he strongly rejects the concept of substance, i.e., the old Platonic and medieval theory of the body as "the prison of the soul" (*Kerkertheorie*), together with the rigid Cartesian alternative according to which everything has to be either physical or spiritual.[8] At the same time, however, by using a phenomenological method that observes the givenness of experience whilst remaining faithful to it, he proposes an irreducible transcendence of the person.

To shed light on this phenomenological method proper to Scheler's school of thought (which Landsberg himself also follows), a quotation from an article that Landsberg published in *Esprit* in 1939 will be instructive: "Phenomenology requires that the phenomena are accepted for what they are.... The philosophers get to peek at the logos *immanent* to the phenomenon.... Husserl [rightly] calls for reason to penetrate the whole variety of experience. It is not about offering an explanation but rather faithfully describing what is given (the phenomenon). It also concerns determining the way the phenomenon originally manifests itself in our experience."[9]

4. *Psychologie ohne Seele*.

5. Wilhelm Wundt is widely regarded as the "father of experimental psychology." His "structuralistic" approach to consciousness consisted in breaking it down into elemental sensations and feelings.

6. In his work "Psychology from an Empirical Standpoint" Franz Brentano affirms that his psychology will utilize the model of mental life of a "psychology without a soul" as proposed by Lange.

7. Scheler does not reject the naturalistic view, while admitting the subordination of the body to empirical-biological laws. He even gave some classes in the years 1908–9 about biology. Moreover, it is well known that Henri Bergson and Hans Driesch exercised considerable influence on Scheler.

8. Cf. ANA 375, B III 12.

9. Cf. Landsberg, "Notes pour une philosophie du marriage," in *Esprit* (avr. 1939),

In the phenomenological experience as an authentic lived-experience, the "universal-concrete" gives itself. Here, Landsberg remarks how in the category of *Jedermann* ("anyone"),[10] the singular experience mirrors universal experience,[11] because in every particular experience, essential phenomenological structures come to light. In this sense, the category of *Jedermann* represents a contrast to Heidegger's public and impersonal *Das Man* ("the one"/"the they"), because it is tied instead to a philosophical personalism. Indeed, even Scheler's phenomenological reflection on death is not to be seen as unbound from his phenomenological and personalistic studies, in particular the ones concerning the person defined as a "concrete and essential unity of being of acts of different essences."[12]

For Scheler the human being reveals his irreducible nature through *acts* that belong to a transcendent personal dimension beyond the reach of death. In his essay concerning the idea of man, *Zur Idee des Menschen* (1914), he describes man as the being "who, thanks to the activity of the spirit (which is laughable for what concerns his biological goals of conservation), he can transcend every form of 'mere life' and, in the sphere of life, even his own life. 'Man' in this new sense is the intention and the gesture of transcendence itself." His nature possesses "a spirit and a love in which every movement and act have a direction towards Something."[13] From this viewpoint Scheler understands that the body, though in itself subject to biological laws, is not a prison for the immaterial soul, but is rather the *condition* for the development of personal acts and spiritual potencies that remain independent of organic existence.

Furthermore, Scheler states in his essay "Death and survival" that from a cognitive point of view, the awareness of death becomes an evident fact for the human conscience, thanks to the correlation of senses which build up among different temporal acts. Using the Augustinian notion of temporality, Scheler states that man, who awaits the spatial enlargement of his own past with the concomitant contraction of the dimension of the future, grasps intuitively that his own life is being progressively consumed. Readopting the Augustinian theory of *memoria*, *contuitus*, and expectation, he observes that

---

it. Trans. *Note per una filosofia del matrimonio*, in Landsberg, *Scritti filosofici*, vol. I, 573–81. Translation mine. Unless otherwise stated, all translations are my own.

10. Cf. Landsberg, "Bemerkungen zur Erkenntnistheorie der Innerwelt."

11. Cf. Zucal, "Il silenzio infedele: la morte come 'esperienza di prossimità' in Paul Ludwig Landsberg," 294.

12. Scheler, "Person ist die konkrete, selbst wesenhafte Seinseinheit von Akten verschiedenartigen Wesens," in *Der Formalismus in der Ethik und die material Wertethik*, GWII, 382.

13. Cf. Scheler, GWIII.

the experience of aging is not just a mere biological decadence, but is also a temporal experience pregnant with a particular teleology. In other words, he affirms that to experience himself is to be subjected to a "directional tendency," which is an intentional "death-directedness" (*Todesrichtung*). In the same text, Scheler affirms that "the first condition to believe in a life beyond death is to eliminate the forces that push modern man ... to remove the idea of death."[14] Scheler, like his disciple Landsberg, is deeply critical of modern society, for it reduces every phenomenon to mechanistic movement, generating a stance of removal from the world, thus giving rise to an immoderate will to manipulate and dominate nature. In his eyes, the idea of death promulgated within modernity represents the pathological result of a vision of life, and consequently of death, that is typical of the modern bourgeois—characterized by their own subversion of values—where the constitutive finite limit of every living being is denied.[15]

Scheler pleaded therefore on the one hand for a reintegration of the religious conscience of man, which would open upon the possibility for a renewed awareness of the limits of the human condition, one's "being-for-death." On the other hand, Scheler proposes a phenomenological observation that demonstrates the existence of a personal sphere transcending the merely vital dimension of existence.

However, Scheler emphasizes that the object of his research is not the existence of the soul or the immortality of the spirit as such; rather, his focus is upon the presence of *acts* that remain *independent* of the psychophysical structure of man. He thus ascertains this excess to be the "spirit's surplus of life," something he also describes as an experience of "leaping" (*aufschwung*). However, despite all these remarks gesturing toward a transcendent personhood, Scheler affirms that "he does not know anything."[16] Therefore, in taking care not to hold to a rigid metaphysical hypothesis about the person that is removed from phenomenological experience, Scheler avoids formulating a definitive conclusion concerning man's status.

## Landsberg: Experience of Death in Individualization and the Death of the Other

In his desire not to go beyond the sort of analysis proper to the phenomenological method, Scheler tries to ground the spiritual within the organism. However, he thereby overlooks some other essential facts that are given by

14. Scheler, *Morte e sopravvivenza*, 34.
15. Cf. Simonotti, *Introduzione*, in *Morte e sopravvivenza*, 6.
16. Cf. Scheler, *Morte e sopravvivenza*, 98.

experience, and demands a higher unity of the human being. Scheler indeed limits himself to the claim that there is a non-physical "surplus" revealed within the boundaries of the body, but his verification of this claim remains mired in a dualism between spirit and biological body. Here, his student Paul Landsberg takes a step further by focusing on the very structure of the experience of death.

In his book *Die Erfahrung des Todes*,[17] he begins with Scheler's analysis and criticizes it. Once again, Landsberg convincingly defends the value of the phenomenological method, which shows how experience is something qualitatively richer than what empiricism pretends to offer. Experience, he argues, is never a sum of isolated data, but rather a connection between necessary structures and essential relationships. But, he argues, the way Scheler focuses on the knowledge of death as given in a temporal process at the utmost limit of individual biological evolution does not give a reasonable account of the abundance of given data and of the radicality of the question that arises in the face of this fact. Landsberg argues that there are rather two ways in which man can experience death: in the first case, we know death as an immanent future for one's own life; in the second case, we know it as the death of what is most familiar to us. In respect to the first case Landsberg claims:

> I do not just have the evidence that I will have to die one day, when the limit of natural death will be reached; rather, I have the evidence that I am directly confronted with the real possibility of death, every instant of my life, today and every day. . . . Human uncertainty about the sudden arrival of death is not simply a gap in biological science, but signals an ignorance of one's own destiny, and this ignorance is itself an act that constitutes a presence as well as an absence of death. *Mors certa, hora incerta.* Death has its own intimate dialectic. It is for us *present in its absence.*[18]

In the section entitled "Experience of death and individualization" (which treats Lévy-Bruhl's *La mythologie primitive*[19]), Landsberg theorizes that the consciousness of death is in step with human individualization, viz., there is an emergence of unique individualities that originate from a personal center. In primitive societies, the person is minimally differentiated from the group in order to recognize himself as something besides his posi-

---

17. This section will primarily treat Landsberg's book, *Die Erfahrung des Todes* ("The Experience of Death"), which is not available in English translation.

18. Landsberg, *L'esperienza della morte*, 23.

19. Lévy-Bruhl, *La mythologie primitive*.

tion and function in the group itself. In these societies death is merely the overtaking of a psychical force in another individual, the obverse of birth. While gaining a clearer consciousness of his own singularity, man actualizes a content proper only to himself, which goes beyond the confines of the group: he realizes he will die one day, and he begins to feel existentially threatened.

According to Landsberg, the proof of this kind of evolution is that the "richest epochs of individuality" present a stronger anxiety toward thought of the death: for example, in late antiquity, with the dissolution of the city-state, a new individuality of the *élite* takes form and gives birth to a renewed anguish for death. This results in the rise of religious cults, philosophical sects, and prepares the way for Christianity.[20] Something similar happens with the Renaissance and Reformation, epochs where the predominant theology was guided by the question of one's possible personal salvation upon death.

Concluding his analysis about individualization, Landsberg argues that just the Christian concept of survival, in its relationship with an ontological category of eternity, contains a definitive subtraction of earthly time and becoming that itself ends in death. Christ in fact promises a rebirth, where death relinquishes its sting. The victory of grace over sin and the corruption of earthly things is synonymous with to victory over death.

Interrupting his excursus on Christianity (only to resume it later), Landsberg proceeds to the second case of death's possible experience. He observes that in so far as man individualizes, he must also perceive the uniqueness of the others. In this regard, Landsberg describes the experience of a friend's death, arguing that death is the only way that allows us to get close to the person as such and to the relationship that he or she has with death. In this kind of experience we meet, according to Landsberg, an intimate unity of necessity and universality; the *universal necessity* he's remarking upon does not belong to a logical order, but to a *symbolic* order. He states,

> Insofar as we individualize ourselves, we also feel the personal uniqueness of others. In personal love, we touch this uniqueness .... The death of a neighbor is infinitely more than the life of the other in general. There, where the personal self is given to us in love, just there, with intrinsic necessity however, we touch the ontological problem of his relationship with death.[21]

---

20. While Landsberg does not give us a full account here of a historical "preparation," we suggest that his intention concerns an anxiety for justification along with a requisite eschatology.

21. Landsberg, *L'esperienza della morte*, 32.

Thus, if in every instant of our lives death is present in its absence, our beloved who is now deceased remains *absent in his presence*. And from there we comprehend the intimate problem of the coincidence of this biological limit with the sudden disappearance of the spiritual dimension. The death of a friend seems to break the communion between us, but what I realize is that, to a certain extent, this communion implicates myself, and to this same extent death penetrates the intimacy of my existence and becomes immediately perceptible. Just this experience of the death of the other teaches us what *qualitative absence* and *qualitative distance* really are: we discover how our existence mysteriously overcomes its earthly form, even if we do not yet possess a real knowledge of the direction of such an overcoming. As Landsberg underlines, the intensity of such experience varies depending each instance: it is namely founded on the possibility of personal love, in which we escape isolation.[22] Landsberg speaks further about the *tragic infidelity* of the person we love: the deceased person physically departs from us, thus leaving us alone. That provokes the emergence of a restlessness that is equivalent to an open question. Through the beloved's *ontological infidelity* we understand that the nothingness of death opposes the deepest tendency of our being. We recognize our desire for eternity, which is the "ontological hope" that the beloved has not departed for good and that he/she will last forever. In the words of Gabriel Marcel, "To love someone is to say that you, at least, will never die."[23] Personal love is also, according to Landsberg, one of the reasons why Catholics cannot renounce belief in purgatory, the place where the existence of the deceased person is not yet completely inaccessible to the loving action of the living.

All these matters raise a question that remained undecided for Scheler: is it possible to speak about a superior unity of the person, which would not be corrupted by bodily decomposition in death? Landsberg undertakes a precise qualitative analysis of human phenomena, but he recognizes that the problem of death raises a fundamental issue: the difference between a "living being" and a "person," and thus the person's ontological status.

## Landsberg's Ontological Foundation

Landsberg cares first of all about giving a definition of what it means to be a person: "With 'person' we mean an existence which constitutes itself in acts, a building-of-oneself as actualization of a 'being-in-becoming' that gives

---

22. In this regard Landsberg criticizes Heidegger's position: according to him, Heidegger's category of *Mit-sein* remains completely formal because Heidegger's philosophy does not in any respect consider other human categories like faith, hope, and love.

23. Marcel, *Il mistero dell'essere*, 131–32.

sense and unity to the whole of individual human existence."[24] Furthermore, he affirms that there is a specific relationship between this transformation of the person and a vital process that, if one isolates it, could be easily compared with the vital processes found in plants and animals. With Scheler, Landsberg notices that the organic process presents an ambiguous meaning for the actualization of the person: on the one hand, through its resistance, it obliges the person to struggle for the achievement of his realization; on the other hand, it offers him the place for such realization. However, Landsberg observes that such facts could offer easy support for a spiritualistic anthropology, which would serve as the obverse to a materialistic monism. That is exactly the risk of Scheler's position, which, though not furthering the apparent contradiction of such a stance—i.e., the presence in the human experience of different directions, such as organic processes on the one hand, and personalization and desire of fulfillment on the other hand—hangs in a dangerous dualism between *spirit* and *drive* (in fact, this contradiction becomes established in the metaphysics of his last period).

Landsberg clarifies the way in which the matter of human death denies such "spiritualism":

> In the self of man we continuously happen upon a multiplicity in which there is a predominant tendency towards unity. Therefore, human life is never absorbed in personalization. The fulfillment of human life does not coincide with the instant of the death.... This missed coincidence shows that death cannot be considered originally as the possibility of personal existence, of the Being proper to man. Coming from the sphere of corporal life that is originally foreign to itself, it is in our existence that death seems to turn up suddenly from outside. Surely the spiritual appropriation of having-to-die is a decisive task for every person. But, this effort of appropriation indeed assumes this character of the extraneousness of the death that has to be defeated.[25]

This means that man's existence, as it remains before its being-for-death, is oriented to *his own realization* and to *eternity*. The person "tends to his own perfection, also overcoming the old, hard, sorrowful boulder of physical death, whose ontological extraneousness can be transformed only if the person makes death a vehicle for his own fulfillment."[26]

---

24. Landsberg, *L'esperienza della morte*, 45.
25. Ibid., 47.
26. Ibid.

The person must decide for the possibility that situates itself between the original extraneousness of death and the hope of the spirit, which overcomes death itself. Clashing with Heidegger's position, Landsberg explains how the anxiety of death manifests death's own nothingness, which is opposed to the deepest and unavoidable tendency of our being. He does not speak about a mere Will-to-Live, as in Schopenhauer, which could be equalized with the animal need for self-preservation, but about a personal act towards eternalization: an affirmation of himself that shows how faith in personal survival is an expression and *actualization* of one of our fundamental *ontological structures*.

Additionally, Landsberg founds his argument for the unequivocal presence of hope in the human condition. Accordingly, hope tends towards being, enduring in the progressive actualization of the human person. "It is not about hope in this or that other thing, but in the creation and natural foundation of hope about which it is written that hope will not let us die."[27]

In support of his argument, Landsberg turns to St. Augustine, although it should be said that he probably does not completely grasp Augustine's position, or at least he does not consider the depth of the passages from Augustine where he deals with the problem of death and temporality. Rather, Landsberg is interested in the more existential aspects of Augustine's reflections. Quoting a passage from *The Confessions*,[28] Landsberg describes how, faced with the death of his mother Monica, and even despite the certainty of Christian hope, Augustine cannot avoid the painful heartbreak of natural man. Surely, his hope in God will be stronger than the sadness of life, but according to Landsberg, it seems as if Augustine's experience remains in a sort of "in between," where human feelings are not totally defeated and do not give us a satisfactory answer in the face of death. This is probably why Landsberg finally decides to turn to the mystical experiences of Teresa of Avila, claiming that within these final moments, the idea of death can be truly illuminated, showing a particularly superior grade of the Christian life. In fact, he argues, Augustine's experience occurs "in the middle of humanly Christian life, but generally just at the threshold of specifically mystical life."[29] Thus, Landsberg maintains that it is precisely in the "authen-

---

27. Ibid., 53; Landsberg refers here in particular to Romans 5:5 "and hope does not disappoint, because the love of God has been poured out within our hearts through the Holy Spirit who was given to us."

28. Landsberg refers to book IX of the *Confessions*, noting especially two passages: "Illa nec misere moriebatur, nec omnino moriebatur" [IX, 12, 29], "Quoniam itaque deserebar tam magno eius solacio, sauciabatur anima et quasi dilaniabatur vita, quae una facta erat ex mea et ilius"[IX, 12, 30].

29. Ibid., 97.

tically mystical souls" that the idea of death shines in a "clearer light," since here a strong "love for death" proceeds from lived experiences of an event analogous to death: this experience is the *anticipation of death in raptures*, which is exactly the *"arrobamientos"* of St. Teresa of Avila. In Teresa, the sentiment of the existing God replaces the very sentiment of earthly reality as the saint lives in a sort of dream in life, in *"una manera de sueño en la vida."* This sentiment, according to Landsberg, reveals an act in which "being joins itself and affirms itself"; that is, the fulfillment of the ontological hope is enacted by something that does not come from itself, but nevertheless completes it.[30] Here, "death and becoming" becomes a lived rule of life. Landsberg concludes his reflection with a quotation from Meister Eckhart, where the mystic says, "Whoever is not radically dead does not know anything about the sanctity that God always reveals to his beloved friends."[31] Normal men and philosophers, he adds, cannot have a similar experience of their own destiny. This is to say that the mystical experience remains something restricted to a few chosen people. Also, without underestimating the mystical experience of such great figures and Landsberg's rightful claim to them, we want to explore another possible philosophical foundation of the problem of death: a foundation that perhaps does not result in mysticism, but takes a step in a theological direction. I would therefore like to examine some passages from *De civitate Dei* and *Confessiones* that deal with Augustine's position on the problem of death in a manner that does justice to the complexity of Augustine's account.

## Temporality in Augustine of Hippo

Both Scheler[32] and Landsberg recognize the correlation, identified in Augustine, between death and temporality as the transcendental dimension of the human soul. "Uniform time does not exist concretely," affirms Landsberg, "but it spreads out continuously in three forms of time, and they belong inseparably to the soul, *'sunt in anima tria quaedam'.* They correspond to three faculties of soul: *'Memoria, contuitus, expectatio',* memory, intuition, and waiting."[33]

---

30. Ibid., 101.
31. Quotation from Dempf, *Maister Eckhart*, 225.
32. Cf. Scheler, *Morte e sopravvivenza*, 40. Scheler speaks about three variables of temporality: the immediate present, the immediate past, and the immediate future.
33. Landsberg, *L'esperienze della morte*, 87.

In Landsberg's reflection about the dialectic of temporality/eternity,[34] there are, in principle, several similarities with Augustine's phenomenological analysis; however, as we have just observed, Landsberg's investigation remains at a more descriptive level and also some of his observations are less ontologically founded, whereas they are sufficiently founded in Augustine. Naturally, we ought not to overlook how Augustine's reflections are woven together with his activity as a theologian: his analyses are surely valid as phenomenological, but they always and inevitably proceed according to a theological plan, since in the epoch in which Augustine writes there was not yet a clear distinction between the philosophical and the theological disciplines.

To better understand how the dialectic of time/eternity turns out to be an essential correlation for Augustine, it is fundamental to examine his account of original sin, which he carries out in Books XIII and XIV of *De civitate Dei*. For Augustine it is necessary to begin by considering human existence from its origins, in order to understand how historically and ontologically this rift becomes established. Indeed, Augustine indicates that "the Fall" broke the original unity between creatures and God, and Adam and Eve fell from a state of eternity to an earthly temporality, which brought confusion and instability and permitted, for the first time, the subjection of the body to earthly needs and lacks, like hunger, thirst, and sensual desire; the body began feeling pain, getting sick, and deteriorating with age.[35]

In *De Peccatorum Meritis et Remissione*, Augustine says that once man lost the privilege of remaining stable in the age in which he was created, it was through the mutation of aging that he set out on a path toward death.[36] From this moment, mortality will characterize man: death comes into history, it lends time a new essence, it transforms human knowledge of reality, and demolishes the intimate coincidence between soul and body. Therefore, the full spectrum of the problem of temporality emerges as the original relationship between God and creature is now broken, and temporality becomes therefore a symptom of dissolution.

Augustine calls this descent from the Edenic state to a submission to temporality and death *alienation*. Henceforth, the existence of man will

34. Cf. ibid., 28.

35. Cf. Nightingale, *Once out of Nature: Augustine on Time and the Body*, 39.

36. "tunc etiam morbo quodam ex repentina et pestifera corruptione concepto factum in illis est, ut illa in qua creati sunt stabilitate aetatis amissa per mutabilitates aetatum irent in mortem. Quamvis ergo annos multos postea vixerint, illo tamen die mori coeperunt, quo mortis legem, qua in senium veterascerent, acceperunt. Non enim stat vel temporis puncto, sed sine intermissione labitur, quidquid continua mutatione sensim currit in finem non perficientem, sed consumentem," (Augustine, *De Peccatorum Meritis et Remissione*, 1, 16, 21).

be defined as *ex-istentia*, i.e., being thrown from his foundation, from the status of being in unity with God to a status of *being-in-the-World*. From here, temporality will be characterized no longer as progression but as corruption. "*Ego in tempora dissilui, quorum ordinem nescio, et tumultuosis varietatibus dilaniantur cogitationes meae, intima viscera animae meae*,"[37] where *dissului*, dissolution, takes the place of *in fieri* to describe this new situation of the creature.

The issue of temporality is analyzed by Augustine in its entirety in Book XI of *Confessiones*, while it is more properly observed in its connection with death, as we said, in Book XIII of *De civitate Dei*. Without going into the whole argument as laid out in *De civitate Dei*, we can note here that Augustine analyzes this concept from a more existential point of view, which is, again, not to separate it from its theological frame.

As we just touched upon in our comparison of Augustine's notion of temporality with Scheler's and Landsberg's, temporality is defined by the church father as being in relationship with the time of the soul, i.e., as *distensio animi*,[38] and such a concept implicates on Augustine's part the oneness of eternity. The *distentio animi* indicates namely the laceration of the soul which is deprived of relationship with eternity: the dialectic of *intentio/distentio* that belongs to time turns into an existential dialectic since the moment of *distentio* refers to a dispersion of multiplicity, while *intentio* refers to the inner man, who recomposes himself by following the One. Likewise, time is experienced as *distentio* because the subject is no more a *coniuctum* of body and soul: therefore, the creature is determined by a sort of dualism such that the soul strives for the One, but the person is at the same time subject to disintegration through time. Augustine thus associates the dynamic of time with the oneness of death: it lets things pass through being and non being, letting things disappear and be consumed. The whole temporal existence of man is death, a continuous disappearance, a "becoming dead." Time and death thus reveal the ontological *mobilitas* proper to the creature, who, originally alienated from a relationship of unity with the Eternal, cannot help but now descend into his own "consuming": that is, his status of *ex-sistentia*, where the being of man is a being in time—that is a living while dying—is now a being in his own not-being.

---

37. Augustine, *Confessiones*, 11, 29, 39.

38. "In te, anime meus, tempora metior. Noli mihi obstrepere, quod est: noli tibi obstrepere turbis affectionum tuarum. In te, inquam, tempora metior. Affectionem, quam res praetereuntes in te faciunt et, cum illae praeterierint, manet, ipsam metior praesentem, non ea quae praeterierunt, ut fieret; ipsam metior, cum tempora metior. Ergo aut ipsa sunt tempora, aut non tempora metior" (*Confessiones*, 11, 27, 36).

So a phenomenology of time leads to a phenomenology of death, which, with the words of Lettieri, can be seen as the highest point of the *confessio*: the recognition of this unimpeachable "negative" dialectic between time and eternity is namely at the same time an invocation and an acceptance of the Other.[39] In the end this acceptance is possible thanks to the Incarnation of the Eternal Word and His assumption of the negative, which is the experience of time even unto death.[40]

The *animus* that measures time, ordering it in the past and the present, can find its destination in a stable future, which realizes itself already in the present, orientated to the Eternal. The orientation of time presumes a realization, and that is why time constitutes itself as a waiting, as a projection of the awareness to the future. But this waiting, what Landsberg calls this "ontological hope," becomes an "eschatological hope" because the future is no longer condemned to sinking into non-being, but transcends time itself. That happens when the soul lives in *intentio*, i.e., when, still living in time, it can accept its full course, because it is supported by the Eternal. This awareness is no longer shuttered in by time, but is recomposed, adhering in its hope to the *Unus*. Furthermore, the intention is no longer a dynamic belonging merely to temporal experience, but becomes the guiding principle of history, in the form of hope. Likewise, the memory (*memoria*) in conjunction with this meaning of waiting, becomes memory of the Origin and at the same time the memory of sin, i.e., what initially disconnected man from his Origin, for whom he always longs. The life of man happens within this continuous dialectic, in the relationship between these two poles, which are time and the Eternal, between creatures and the Creator.

To conclude, we can see how first of all Scheler adequately grasps the matter of death, adopting the phenomenological method of Augustine that allows him to connect it to an intentional temporal dimension: in this vision, temporality is no longer the objective time of science; rather, it is an ontological dimension of the soul, which in its *extentio* grabs in a certain way the extreme limit of biological life. Temporality coincides thus with "mortality" as the constitutive finitude of the human being. Scheler's gain consists moreover in recognizing the transcendental origin of the soul's acts, which remain independent from the sphere of vitality. Yet, he still understands the "independency" as radical separation between the spiritual and the biological life of the body, so (firstly) he remains stuck in a sort of

---

39. Cf. Lettieri, *Il senso della storia in Agostino d'Ippona*.

40. "Sed quoniam melior est misericordia tua super vitas, ecce distentio est vita mea, et me suscepit dextera tua in Domino meo, mediatore Filio hominis inter te unum et nos multos . . . ut per eum apprehendam, in quo et apprehensus sum, et a veteribus diebus colligar sequens Unum." Ibid. 11, 29, 39.

dualism, and (secondly) he does not see in experience adequate reasons to express a metaphysical hypothesis.

Landsberg goes deeper, recognizing in the temporality of human beings a possibility both of his own realization and of the actualization of his real structure. Indeed, he sees in the *expectatio* the human desire for eternity—his structure of "waiting"—which constitutes an ontological structure of the person. However, even if he rightly points out how hope constitutes a fundamental element of man, in the end he turns to mystical experience to redeem the possibility of complete knowledge and rest in this life in the face of death. Only Augustine presents a possible complete answer to this problem, demonstrating that with the assumption of the One and Eternal self of the mortal condition by His resurrection, the human situation can be completely redeemed: "ontological hope" becomes finally "eschatological," the whole unity of the mortal person can immediately find meaning, and the question can be resolved.

## Bibliography

St. Augustine. *Confessiones*. Edited by Carlo Carena. Rome: Città Nuova, 1988.
Dempf, Alois. *Maister Eckhart*. Leipzig: Hegner, 1934.
Landsberg, Paul Ludwig. "Bemerkungen zur Erkenntnistheorie der Innerwelt." *Tijdschrift voor Philosophie* I (February 1939) 363–76.
———. *Einführung in die philosophische Anthropologie*. Frankfurt am Main: Vittorio Klostermann, 1960.
———. *L'esperienza della morte*. Trento: Il Margine, 2011.
———. "Notes pour une philosophie du marriage." *Esprit* (April 1939) 48–57; translated by Marco Bucarelli in *Note per una filosofia del matrimonio*, in Paul Ludwig Landsberg, *Scritti filosofici*, vol. I, 573–82. Milan: San Paolo Edizioni, 2005.
Lettieri, Gaetano. *Il senso della storia in Agostino d'Ippona*. Roma: Edizioni Borla s.r.l., 1988.
Lévy-Bruhl, Lucien. *La mythologie primitive*. Paris: Alcan, 1935.
Marcel, Gabriel. *Il mistero dell'essere*, vol. 2. Torino: Borla Editore, 1971.
Nightingale, Andrea. *Once Out of Nature: Augustine on Time and the Body*. Chicago: University of Chicago Press, 2011.
Scheler, Max. *Der Formalismus in der Ethik und die material Wertethik*, GWII. Bonn: Bouvier-Verlag, 1986.
———. *Morte e sopravvivenza*. Brescia: Morcelliana 2010.
———. *Zur Idee des Menschen*. GW III. Bonn: Bouvier-Verlag, 1986.
Simonotti, Edoardo. *Max Scheler, Morte e sopravvivenza*. Brescia: Morcelliana, 2010.
Zucal, Silvano. "Il silenzio infedele: la morte come 'esperienza di prossimità' in Paul Ludwig Landsberg." In *Da che parte dobbiamo stare: il personalismo di Paul Ludwig Landsberg*, edited by Michele Nicoletti, Silvano Zucal, and Fabio Olivetti, 289–327. Soveria Mannelli, CZ: Rubettino, 2007.

# 2

# Bernard Stiegler's Politics of the Soul and His New *Otium* of the People

JOHANN ROSSOUW

I side with what Bataille called an *atheology*, that is, atheist thought which nevertheless *does not forget* all that it *owes* to its theo-logical past.[1]

The confrontation of the spirit with itself of which I speak here is thus simultaneously aesthetic, economic, political, juridical,

---

1. Stiegler, *Constituer l'Europe* 1, 122. All emphases in Stiegler citations are by him unless otherwise indicated. All citations from his texts are my translations from the original French, and references those texts, except for Stiegler, *La Technique et le Temps* 1 (*TT*1), of which the English translation *Technics and Time 1: The Fault of Epimetheus* (*TT*1*E*) is so outstanding that all citations from *TT*1 are from the English translation and hence references its pagination. Otherwise where translations of Stiegler's texts are available in English, I did check my translations against those translations in order to ensure the best possible translation. This applies mostly to the volumes 2 and 3 of Stiegler's *Technics and Time* as well as to the first volume of his *Disbelief and Discredit*. Translating Stiegler's French with its play on words, neologisms, and particular style is not always easy. Hence, the published translations were often an invaluable help, but sometimes proved to be not entirely satisfactory, in which case I did my best to improve on the published translation to do justice to Stiegler's very precise phrasing. Where I cited from French texts by other authors the translations are also my own except where indicated otherwise. Any possible errors of translation in this chapter are therefore on my account.

institutional, scientific, technological and industrial—not to speak of the theological stock from which it stems implacably.[2]

## Introduction

THIS CHAPTER WILL CONSIDER Bernard Stiegler's political ideal, the new *otium* of the people, which, as will be shown, reveals his philosophical project ultimately to be not the consideration of "the pursuit of life through means other than life" (technics),[3] but the pursuit of Christianity through means other than Christian. As will also be shown, of these means, art and the aesthetical are crucial for Stiegler, as is his "atheological" reading of Aristotle's three levels of the soul.

For Stiegler, the central crisis of Western modernity is of a theological nature, namely, its loss of faith in its social order and in its future. He takes the restoration of Western modernity's faith in its social order and its future to be the main political challenge of today. Stiegler wants to meet this challenge with his proposal of the creation of the new *otium* of the people[4]—a proposal that draws heavily on medieval Latin Christendom and the broader Christian tradition, and that ultimately hinges on Stiegler's attempts to execute two questionable moves.

The first of these moves is his attempt to hold up the twentieth century's "cult" (his term) of art as a substitute for Christianity that can do socially, politically, and spiritually for the contemporary Western social order what Christianity did for the Western social order before the so-called death of God. As will be seen, this move rests on a questionable attempt to interpret the creation and experience of art with reference to Christian liturgy. The aim of this move is to legitimate art as the successor of Christianity, which can stamp its authority on the contemporary social order and thus equal

---

2. Stiegler, *De la misère symbolique* 2, 17.
3. Stiegler, *Technics and Time* 1, 17.
4. Stiegler takes as his model the *otium* of medieval Latin Christendom where work (*negotium*) and prayer (*otium*) each had their place, a social order in which the *negotium* was the material support of the *otium*, and the *otium* the spiritual support of the *negotium*. That state of affairs he contrasts with the present one in explaining why it has come to pass that the *negotium* is now supported by the *otium*—why leisure has been turned into an industry. The new *otium* of the people must first and foremost be brought into being by the contemporary equivalent of the medieval clergy, that is, creators and intellectuals of all sorts. It is a promise that is carried by the new mnemotechnologies— one that must place at its heart participatory democracy as a cult where everybody cares for and takes responsibility for everybody—so that a new European way of life that can illuminate and re-enchant the world can be achieved.

the authoritative example of Christianity in previous Western social orders: Christianity is used to authorize art.

The second of these moves is Stiegler's attempt to extend his techno-anthropology[5] to an aesthetic anthropology whereby the aesthetical is not only construed to be pivotal to the constitution of individuals and groups (what he calls psychic and collective individuation), but also to religion and politics. Religion, especially Christianity, is first and foremost interpreted as an aesthetic phenomenon, while the aesthetical is interpreted as the ground of politics. Here, the authority of Christianity is made to rest on its claimed aesthetic contribution to individuation and politics in previous Western social orders: art is used to authorize Christianity.

In order to assess Stiegler's ideal of the new *otium* of the people this chapter will begin in section 1 with a critical overview of a number of crucial conceptual refinements of his diagnosis of the ills of Western modernity, including his restatement of the theological crisis of Western faith as the result of the *negotium* (historically, activities related to business and subsistence) encroaching on the *otium* (historically, leisure of the kind that favors activities related to education, artistic creation, intellectual work, and spiritual contemplation). Then, in section 2, a closer look will be taken at Stiegler's new *otium* of the people with regards to his preliminary suggestions on what this must look like, what promise contemporary mnemotechnologies hold for the new *otium*, and what examples of the tentative realization of this promise he identifies. Finally, in section 3, we shall turn to what I call Stiegler's aestheology, that is, his attempt to make a case for the cult of art as the successor of Christianity and, hence, as the spearhead of the new *otium* of the people and its politics.

## 1. Refining Stiegler's Diagnosis of the Ills of Western Modernity

### Subsistence, Existence, Consistence

However, before the latter proposal can be understood, one first needs to understand the development of the concept of individuation that Stiegler undertakes with his distinction between the interdependent triad of subsistence, existence, and consistence. These are the three levels on which groups and individuals may find themselves at any given moment, with subsistence the lowest level, existence the intermediary level, and consistence the highest level. Once the lower needs of subsistence have been met—the provision

---

5. As he develops it in *Technics and Time* 1.

of food, clothing, and shelter—collective and individual existence may strive towards something more, better or higher, which Stiegler calls the consistent. But whereas the subsistent is tangible and concrete, and the existent is the level on which the consistent is realized through action, the consistent never is tangible and concrete. Stiegler calls this "the consistent that does not exist." The consistent that does not exist is made up of motifs or ideals that motivate groups and individuals to act in particular ways—setting up institutions, executing actions, cultivating practices in the name of these motifs or ideals. These concrete expressions on the level of collective and individual existence are nothing else than individuation, and the lack of such motifs and ideals to inspire such expressions leads to a loss of participation and the disindividuation of groups and individuals. In Stiegler's words: "Existence lies between subsistence and consistence, and only a consistence, as idea, can animate a process of individuation . . ."[6]—which takes place on the level of existence. In section 3 it will be shown that, for Stiegler, subsistence, existence, and consistence corresponds to the three levels of the soul that Aristotle distinguishes, namely, the vegetative, the sensitive, and the noetic.

The various and ongoing expressions of the consistent that does not exist—the realization of motifs and ideals—always occur on the level of existence when groups and individuals are sufficiently motivated to participate in the expression of these motifs and ideals, while such expressions, in turn, also depend on sufficiently inspiring motifs and ideals, as well as the right institutions and practices to embody them. Stiegler writes: "[T]hat which *consists* is not that which *exists*: it is that which gives meaning (its direction and its movement, or its *driving force*) to what exists, without reducing itself to this existing. Existing is a *fact*. But existing only consists as that which *surpasses* its factuality."[7] As a concept which refers to that which inspires and sets groups and individuals in motion to surpass themselves towards something more, better or higher, the notion of the consistent that does not exist is to Stiegler's atheist thought or "atheology"[8] what God is to Christianity—the cornerstone of his atheological edifice. Stiegler says in an interview:

> God was the incalculable, but theology said: God exists. But God is dead, which signifies that God does not exist. This means the incalculable does not exist. Effectively, everything is calculable. And yet, existence does not reduce itself to subsistence. Existence distinguishes itself from subsistence, which is itself

6. Stiegler, *Mécréance et discrédit* 1, 47, footnote 1 continued from 46.
7. Ibid., 70.
8. Stiegler, *Constituer l'Europe* 1, 122.

entirely calculable. . . . The death of God thus opens the question of what I call consistence, which gives to belief its necessity.[9]

God is Stiegler's prime example of the consistent that does not exist, but the concept also includes motifs or ideas that are invoked to inspire people collectively or individually to something more, better, or higher: "In other words, *there is not just God who, although not existing, consists*. There is also art, justice, ideas in general."[10]

While the pre-modern religious and philosophical traditions would explain the consistence of the motifs or ideas that inspire people to something more, better, or higher as emanating from some sort of transcendent source, Stiegler is oddly quiet about *why* the consistent that does not exist, consists—especially in a so-called post-traditional, post-theological social order.

In section 3, when discussing Stiegler's atheological reading of Aristotle's three levels of the soul, subsistence, existence, and consistence will be considered further, but now we come to Stiegler's analysis of how the *negotium* in Western modernity encroaches on the *otium*.

## *Negotium* and *Otium*

As an example of how Stiegler's thought is situated in the tension between a medieval Christian social order and its secular variant, Stiegler affirmatively cites Max Weber's argument in *The Protestant Work Ethic and the Spirit of Capitalism* that capitalism is a "mutation" (Stiegler's word) of Christianity, and that it leads to the transition from *belief* inscribed in a tradition to *trust* in innovation that constitutes a rupture with tradition.[11] He also follows Weber's analysis of Benjamin Franklin as exemplary of the Protestant embrace of capitalism, interpreting Franklin's statement that "Time is money" as the blurring of the boundary between *negotium* and *otium*, which means that service to God becomes "calculable and rational," what with the heritage of Calvinism consisting "in the doctrine that believes in the fulfillment of one's duty through temporal affairs (in the *negotium*)."[12] "Temporal affairs" in this citation refers to the medieval division between the spiritual and the temporal, the heavenly and the earthly represented on Earth by the church and the polity. This, then, transforms belief into trust as embodied in credit:

9. Ibid., 124.
10. Ibid., 125.
11. Stiegler, *Mécréance et discrédit* 1, 96–97.
12. Ibid., 97.

"Belief is transformed into *credit* obtained through trust insofar as it is itself calculable and *measures occupied time (negotium)*."[13]

The transition from belief to trust also brings about a new system of value, based on calculation in the general equivalent of money.[14] According to Stiegler, leisure—as the modern form of the *otium*—is, from the beginning of the twentieth century in the USA, brought into this regime of value with the program and cultural industries and the invention of the consumer.[15] Stiegler interprets the transition from belief to trust as one of the adoption of new forms of behavior brought about by incessant technological advances.[16] For Stiegler, the precise nature of the trust that in capitalism comes to replace belief is one of "absolute trust in the innovations of capitalism, in *capitalism as the spirit of innovation*."[17] The irrational motivation of putting money as motif above all else can function so long as the belief in the expansion of the economy as social progress is maintained.[18]

In Stiegler's view, the effacement of the difference between the medieval Latin Christian *negotium* and *otium* that started with Luther and the printing press is completed by hyper-industrial capitalism's effacement of the distinction between subsistence and existence, so that the *otium*—through the industrialization of leisure—is now an extension and support of the *negotium*. The *negotium* "finally absorbs the world of clerics into its functions and its forces of production just as it controls all sensible life, by replacing the sensible experience of singularity with the aesthetic conditioning of consumer behavior."[19]

And so, to sum up: in this section it was shown that Stiegler refines his diagnosis of the ills of Western modernity through the conceptual development of the interdependent triad of subsistence, existence, and consistence, with the atheological notion of the consistent that does not exist being to Stiegler what God is to Christianity. This process Stiegler recasts with reference to the *negotium* and the *otium* to argue that the tendency of the *negotium* through the industrialization of leisure now dominates its

---

13. Ibid., 98. It should be noted that the concept of credit, which is central to Stiegler's analysis, is the English translation of the French *crédit*, which, when it refers to belief, is better translated into English as credence. Nevertheless, maintaining the English translation of *crédit* is important, since Stiegler's argument depends on interweaving the financial and theological senses of "credit."

14. Ibid., 98.
15. Ibid., 99.
16. Ibid., 100–101.
17. Ibid., 102.
18. Ibid., 104.
19. Ibid., 119–20.

counter-tendency, the *otium*. In spite of the apparent lack of hope for an alternative, it will now be shown in section 2 that Stiegler believes that, via the restoration of the composition of the *negotium* and the *otium*, individuation can be reinstated, thus restoring Western modernity's belief in itself and its future. Thus Stiegler appeals to the medieval Latin Christian motif of belief as opposed to its modern substitute, trust. Let us now turn to Stiegler's proposed cure, the new *otium* of the people, through which it will become clear why *attention and its liturgical cultivation* is, for him, at the core of contemporary politics.

## 2. The New *Otium* of the People

In this section it will be argued that with his "atheology" Stiegler is engaged in a full-blown theoretical attempt at repeating what Christianity did for the medieval social order, namely, to bring about a stable society that believes in itself and its future, while pursuing cultural and spiritual elevation.

Stiegler gives an interpretation of the resurrection of Christ that puts the cultivation of attention via liturgy at its heart:

> But here, I believe, the resurrection first designates the *return* of a spirit, that is, its resurrection across *generations that remember because they retentionalize and protentionalize precisely to the extent that they attentionalize*, if I may put it like this; that is, to the extent to which they are *attentive*, and attentive precisely through the *repetition of a cult* through which they cultivate the *memory of a sacrifice*. Through such a cult Christ . . . returns, and, effectively, opens the spirituality of the community of the faithful as their common spirit, and as message of hope. But *this hope, much more than life after death, is love*.[20]

This is an absolutely key passage that makes clear to what extent Stiegler sources his notions of the incalculable and the infinite from his interpretation of Christian love. Here he also takes liturgical Christianity as a model of remembering and projection on the basis of the liturgical cultivation of attention.

We can now turn to his proposal for the new *otium* of the people, in which it will become clear to what extent this proposal is a secular version of the medieval Latin Christian *otium*—which will, in section 3, lead me to raise the question of the viability of the new *otium* of the people as a purely secular proposal.

20. Stiegler, *Mécréance et discrédit* 2, 158, my emphasis.

The first point about the new *otium* of the people is that the responsibility to bring it into existence lies with creators and intellectuals in a broad sense—"the thinkers, scientists, artists, philosophers, and *other clerics*."[21] The latter emphasis is mine to emphasize that in his new *otium* of the people, Stiegler sees creators and intellectuals in a broad sense as the equivalent of the medieval clergy (*clercs*), which is in line with the twentieth-century French tradition of extending the notion of the *clercs* to include the secular intelligentsia. This is nevertheless very much an Enlightenment proposal, whereby art and knowledge—instead of religion *inclusive of art and knowledge*—are central.

The second point about the new *otium* of the people is that, in his techno-theology, Stiegler's great hope for the new *otium* of the people does not stem first and foremost from a belief in some or other religion or philosophy, but from his belief in *technics itself*, and more specifically, the possibilities that he sees offered by contemporary mnemotechnologies or, as he also often calls them, technologies of the spirit. He argues that because these technologies are cognitive and cultural, they must constitute a "new spirit"[22] that will be central to the new *otium*.

That democracy must in the new *otium* stand as the equivalent to Christian faith aiming at the *telos* of the heavenly city during the Middle Ages is made even clearer when Stiegler links democracy to spiritual elevation and the new technologies of the spirit:

> [D]emocratic participation is precisely the participation in an *effort of the raising of the group* above itself, and through the force of the instruments of the democratic cult, which are none other than the instruments of thought as *hupomnémata* (memory aids), noetic techniques and cognitive and cultural technologies, and as *social instruments* of delegation and representation, that permit the development of collective intelligence.[23]

Stiegler's definition of democratic politics is also strikingly reminiscent of how the early Christian church saw itself as a family where everyone takes care of the other:[24] "Politics as democracy consists in ensuring that

21. Stiegler, *Mécréance et discrédit* 1, 192, my emphasis.
22. Ibid., 192.
23. Stiegler in Marc Crépon and Bernard Stiegler, *De la démocratie participative*, 72.
24. "Now God, our master, teaches two chief precepts, love of God and love of neighbor; and in them man finds three objects for his love: God, himself, and his neighbor; and a man who loves God is not wrong in loving himself. It follows, therefore, that he will be concerned also that his neighbor should love God, since he is told to love his neighbor as himself; and the same is true of his concern for his wife, his children, for the members of his household, and for all other men, so far as is possible. And, for the

everybody has the right and the duty to *take care of everybody*, to be *responsible for everybody*, and to be able *to speak about everything, to say everything they want to.*"[25]

Thirdly, Stiegler also has a soteriological hope for the "democratic cult" insofar as democratic participation must bring about "a truly new form of economic and social organization in all aspects of human existence," a new "European way of life."[26] And: "A new European way of life must again put existences and their conditions, and consistencies . . . at the heart of a new industrial project that must be invented and that aims to *intensify the singular as incalculable[;]* . . . it must effectively re-enchant the world."[27] Here Stiegler is arguing that to the contrary of the hyper-industrial *negotium* where the industrialization of leisure reduces existence to subsistence, the new *otium* must elevate existence to consistence as that which is infinite and incalculable—exactly what God was for the medieval Latin Christian *otium*. This is a proposal for the construction of a social order that can re-associate people in a European *We* as opposed to the hyper-industrial disassociation of producers and consumers—a secular version of the Christian *We*.

Summing up, then: the new *otium* of the people must first and foremost be brought into being by the contemporary equivalent of the medieval clergy, that is, creators and intellectuals of all sorts. It is a promise that is carried by the new mnemotechnologies, one that must place at its heart participatory democracy as a cult where everybody cares for and takes responsibility for everybody, so that a new European way of life that can illuminate and re-enchant the world can be achieved.

Considering how powerfully affective the medieval Latin Christian *otium* was, with its Augustinian link between the contemplation of God and the love of one's neighbor, the success of its association between its elites (nobility and clergy), and the ordinary people in the inclusion of all in the *res publica Christiana* and the church, it can be argued that Stiegler needs to produce a vehicle for the new *otium* that can carry the burden of the (religious) affect, as well as the inclusion and association of everybody with everybody. As will now be shown in section 3 this is precisely what he tries to do with art, and where his pursuit of Christianity by means other than Christian takes on its most extreme forms.

---

same end, he will wish his neighbor to be concerned for him" (St. Augustine, *City of God* 19.14).

25. Stiegler, *De la démocratie participative*, 115.

26. Ibid., 74.

27. Stiegler in Bernard Stiegler and Ars Industrialis, *Réenchanter le monde*, 95–96.

## 3. Stiegler's Aestheology

Stiegler contends that the political battle that must be fought today to establish the new *otium* of the people is above all aesthetic,[28] "not to speak of the theological stock from which it stems implacably."[29] In the introduction above I called this Stiegler's aestheology, that is, his attempt to make a case for the cult of art as the successor of Christianity and, hence, as the spearhead of the new *otium* of the people and its politics. To state it differently, art is for Stiegler what religion is for believers—a position that he seeks to maintain by reworking a number of classic Christian theological motifs such as belief, love, hope, the promise, liturgy, participation, and community in order to legitimate the quasi-soteriological value that he gives to art. As was also stated in the introduction above, Stiegler tries to execute two questionable moves, that is, to authorize art through Christianity, and to authorize Christianity through art. The latter move involves Stiegler drawing on Freud's notion of sublimation to argue that sublimation in collective and psychic individuation is the creation of a motif from its desire, which is, for example, what happens when the imagination "creates" a god or God. Following Nietzsche, Stiegler argues that sublimation is best executed by art:

> [It is] art that trans-forms and trans-values the immotivated (*l'immotivé*) into motifs—into motifs to live and to love, into motifs of desire. The immotivated of language is for example that from which poetry makes its sublime motif: sublimation is always such a sort of transformation of lead into gold.[30]

### Re-reading Aristotle's Three Levels of the Soul

Central to Stiegler's attempt to construe art as the main vehicle of the new *otium* of the people is his re-reading of Aristotle's notion of the three levels of the soul, which Stiegler links to the interdependent triad of subsistence, existence, and consistence. In Stiegler's view, the vegetative soul, which is concerned with people's basic needs, relates to subsistence; the sensitive soul to existence; and the noetic soul to consistence. The noetic soul, which is the highest level on which the soul functions when it is creating, thinking, or praying, is only experienced intermittently—according to Aristotle only God can constantly be noetic. Stiegler calls the intermittent movement from the sensitive to the noetic soul a "becoming-symbolic," and most

---

28. Stiegler, *De la misère symbolique* 2, 16.
29. Ibid., 17.
30. Stiegler, *Mécréance et discrédit* 2, 171.

importantly expresses itself in reaction to its intense experience of the sensible, which Stiegler calls "exclamatory":

> This becoming-symbolic as *logos*, which only is in the course of its being-expressed, is what I call an *ex-clamation*: the *noetic* experience of the soul is *exclamatory*. It exclaims itself before the sensible insofar as it is *sensational*. . . . The exclamatory soul, that is, sensational and not only sensitive, *enlarges* its sense by exclaiming it symbolically.[31]

As will soon become clear, this capacity of the noetic soul to express its experience "by exclaiming it symbolically" is vital to Stiegler's hope for greater participation in the social order via the experience and creation of art, and via the conception of the social order as an artwork in which everybody participates.

Stiegler follows Hegel in arguing that the sensitive and the noetic soul are not in opposition, but in composition: "The sensitive soul, according to Hegel, is the *dunamis* of the noetic soul that is only ever in action (*energeia, entelecheia*) intermittently."[32] According to Stiegler—and here he introduces the theological motif of belief—as an act of *aisthesis*, the nous itself is "aisthesic"[33] and belief: "as act of *aisthesis*, *nous* itself is aisthesic, but in an elevated sense, in some way lifted up by *nous*—by *nous* as the *power and action of exclamation*. That is to say, as belief. As, for example, when one says: *what beauty*!, One *believes* then that it is beautiful . . . ."[34] In Stiegler's view, for Aristotle, the knowledge that is noetically produced is the same as the movement that God produces in the soul—God, for Aristotle, being the mover of the sensitive soul to the level of the noetic soul.[35]

Stiegler stresses that the potential of the noetic action could also be its "impotential": whether it passes into noetic action or not depends on what sensations it experiences, and this is precisely where the culture and program industries get a hold, and where they today make the sensitive soul descend to the level of the vegetative soul.

Stiegler argues that there is an intimate link between the noetic soul and fiction, which is decisive for the politics that he advocates:

---

31. Stiegler, *Mécréance et discrédit* 1, 179.
32. Stiegler, *Mécréance et discrédit* 2, 180.
33. While *aisthesis* is a Greek word that Stiegler uses, "aisthesic" is his neologism, meaning "pertaining to or characterized by sense perception."
34. Stiegler, *Mécréance et discrédit* 1, 181.
35. Stiegler, *Mécréance et discrédit* 2, 181–82.

> [T]he *noetic* life is *intrinsically* fictive, fictional and thus *to decide*, to decide *in the political economy* of that *spiritual and libidinal* economy that a city constitutes, is to decide to *realize a fiction*. It is to want to believe in a fiction: the law as a difference we must *make*. This also means: to have *imagination*—or, yet again, *to invent*.[36]

In other words, since Stiegler by his own admission[37] decides to read the noetic soul atheistically and aesthetically, he has to install fiction and the will to believe in the place that metaphysics occupies for Aristotle.

## Art as Main Vehicle of the New *Otium* of the People

It was noted above that Stiegler has to work out in greater detail what the main vehicle of the new *otium* of the people can be, and that he chooses art for this task. One of the steps that he takes towards this goal is to propose an equivalent to the believer in the medieval Latin Christian *otium* in the form of the contemporary art amateur. According to Stiegler, there must be a passage from

> the age of the consumer (who consumes him- or herself in believing that it is possible to consume works [*œuvres*]—let us call this their self-consumption . . .) to the age of the amateur, who *loves* because, in his or her way, through their practices . . . they *work and open up* and, thus, they are open: their eyes, their ears, their senses are wide open to sense.[38]

As will soon be shown, the amateur as the model of recultivated attention is crucial for the popular establishment of the new *otium* of the people—the equivalent of the ordinary believer in the medieval *otium*. In Stiegler's view, the amateur tendency of sampling and musical creation from pieces of music sourced electronically is an example of what André Leroi-Gourhan called "participating in order to feel,"[39] whereas the appearance of recorded music allowed for the appearance of a musical amateur who "if he or she often does not know how to read notes, on the other hand is furnished with a new form of historical consciousness of the repertory."[40] Importantly, Stiegler bases this ability to participate on his re-reading of the

36. Ibid., 194.
37. Ibid., 183.
38. Stiegler, *De la misère symbolique* 2, 32.
39. Ibid., 34.
40. Ibid., 35.

three Aristotelian souls: "This participation relates, in Aristotle's terms, to what he precisely calls *participation in the divine*."[41]

It was seen above that, for Stiegler, the noetic soul responds to the sensible experience with an exclamatory expression. That is, whatever one feels needs to be expressed, which is something one gives to the greater social order—for example, when people speak about a film, or about an important public event. When the noetic soul expresses what it received sensibly, it participates in the social and in its own individuation, states Stiegler. And here Stiegler identifies the value of art as substitute for the Aristotelian God in moving the soul noetically: "Artworks, insofar as they tend to provoke a noetic experience, are the tensors of noetic individuation that is only social in this: they help noetic souls to pass into action."[42]

This argument can be understood if one thinks of engaged citizens who would explain their engagement by saying that such and such a film, novel, or other artwork "changed their life" and inspired them to "make a difference," which is really the essence of why Stiegler rates art so highly. This is why he argues that the social order is purely and simply the accumulated result of this process of aesthetically and affectively mediated receiving and giving.[43] In other words, his thesis is that the exclamatory expression that constitutes collective and psychic individuation is first and foremost brought about by the aesthetic experience, the possibility of which is today threatened by the instrumentalization of the aesthetical for social control.

In invoking the amateur and the passage into noetically-inspired action as part of the individuation process, Stiegler finds a great ally in Joseph Beuys with his two concepts of social sculpture and the artist, the latter being that all people are artists in principle. Stiegler concurs with Beuys' claim that "every human existence is intrinsically artistic, and thereby every human being is an artist."[44] He also affirmatively cites Beuys' view that the task of art as social sculpture is "to create a new social organism" that implies the forging of concepts "which will give form to feeling and willing" that must produce imprints on the social order.[45] For Stiegler, Beuys shows that art, when it marries technics and concepts as Beuys did with his own very material and political artworks, can contribute to social transformation. Since not everyone is, of course, a practicing artist in the conventional sense in which art is understood, Stiegler argues that Beuys' two concepts necessitate

---

41. Ibid., 40.
42. Ibid., 67.
43. Ibid., 67–68.
44. Beuys cited in ibid., 108.
45. Ibid., 122.

an enlarged conception of art. As will now be seen, Stiegler undertakes such an expanded notion of art where he holds that the amateur (or the artist that people all are in principle) is crucial. This is also where he makes his move to authorize art through Christianity.

## Art as Liturgy

The essence of this move is to *give a liturgical reading of the experience of art*. Stiegler begins this argument by first providing a broad reading of what happens in liturgy, and why it is important to the stability of an epoch. In his view one of "the conditions of an effective communitization . . . is the time of the *frequenting* of the works of the spirit." In keeping with his customary mediation between spirit and matter he stresses that with the works of the spirit he refers to "all forms of artifacts." In liturgical vein he then concludes that the "organization of this time is a complex always inscribed in a calendar structure."[46]

In other words, the elevating regular exposure to and engagement with works of the spirit (including technical artifacts) is essential to a social order, and this regularity must be institutionalized and made part of a calendar. Stiegler takes his cue for this argument from medieval Catholicism. He argues that for faithful Catholics over the centuries, Catholicism thus was "the time of the contemplation of images and repeated songs (chants), and, through these images and songs, [it was also] the time of contemplation through the interiorization and exteriorization of the divine *in the monotheist version of the consistent*."[47]

After this secular reading of Catholic liturgy as "the monotheist version of the consistent" and Stiegler's emphasis on the aesthetic aspect of liturgy, he then goes on to argue that liturgy is the basis of faith in discussing Proust's descriptions of his church visits:

> What is true of the young Marcel [Proust] who frequents the cult is true of all faithful, and herein lies their faithfulness. Every Sunday the faithful see and see again, in their churches and cathedrals, in their places of cult, those paintings, those stained-glass windows, those tapestries, those sculptures, those arabesques, those perspectives, those interlacings and those corbellings, and they look at them while singing psalms and while listening to the sermon that guides their eyes and their bodies, where those eyes are aware of their hands, the coldness

46. Ibid., 137.
47. Ibid.

of the stone and the warmth of the heart. Listening in this way, responding by singing, they look and look again at what they see. In this gaze there is an inadvertence that the cult invites them to meditate upon, and this meditation is a culture, the culture of this *looking* as it becomes a *contemplating*.[48]

This is a key passage because it allows Stiegler to not only correctly identify liturgy as the support of faith but, more dubiously, to foreground the *aesthetic* aspect of liturgy, from which it is only a small step to argue that art is actually the source of belief, and Christianity a proof of that. This is exactly what Stiegler does when he sets out to make liturgy the model for art:

> But this [Catholic] cult is only possible because in *every* gaze (*regard*) there is an "again" (*re*), that is, a repetition and a maintaining, a tenacity and a "keeping" (*garde*): the experience of a painting is an experience of a repetition that keeps something.
> 
> This is what the faithful know, *like* true art amateurs know that, to be able to see, one must see again, and that seeing again is to look/keep again (*re-garder*), that the gaze is a seeing again (*revoir*) and that a painting always, in a way, says to you "See you again" (*au revoir*), *and that you must therefore believe in it.*
> 
> And it is only thus that it says something. It says: "You will have to come and see me again, otherwise you won't see me . . . ."[49]

What Stiegler is doing here would be regarded as quite disingenuous by a Catholic—making belief and the revelation of meaning dependent on the tenacity of the believer, whereas a Catholic would make those things conditional not on the effort of the believer, but on the work of the Holy Spirit. A Catholic would say that the tenacity with which the believer returns again and again to the liturgy is a response to the gift of faith and revelation, and not that faith and revelation eventually follows from one coming back again and again. The irony of Stiegler's take on this is that he bases his argument partly on the art historian Daniel Arasse recounting how certain paintings time and again "revealed" their meaning to him after he spent hours looking at them or returned to see them again, and the paintings that Stiegler quotes Arrasse mentioning are all from Catholic medieval art![50] Thus, Stiegler

---

48. Ibid., 139.

49. Ibid., 139–40.

50. Ibid., 140–42. The paintings to which Arrasse refers in the passage cited by Stiegler cites Piero della Francesca's frescoes in the San Francesco church, Arezzo and Raphael's Sistine Madonna, Dresden.

repeats the same Derridean move that he makes with writing:[51] meaning derives from the interaction between the reader and what is read—here meaning derives from the interaction between the looker and what is looked at. It is the same reading strategy that some Protestant strands propose, and the same explanation of the production of meaning that Freud proposes with his notion of sublimation: ultimately, meaning resides in the individual receiver of the text or the artwork. Never for a moment does Stiegler allow for the fact that, as the pre-modern religious and philosophical traditions have it, meaning is also inherent in the message itself, and in the community in which it is received, and that the liturgy is not the production of meaning *but a response to and an embodiment of it*. Similarly, Stiegler would have it that the meaning of music is "revealed" by re-listening to it.[52]

## Art as Successor of Christianity

This then allows Stiegler to make his boldest move in holding up art as the vehicle of the new *otium* of the people, namely, to anoint the "cult of art" as the successor of Christianity after the so-called death of God. Proust's repetition of works of the spirit "forms a cult, but it is no longer a religious cult."[53] According to the spirit of Stiegler's "atheology," he might as well have described this as an "areligion," since he goes on to qualify it as nothing less than a secular cult of *fin-de-siècle* art lovers: "This cult, which is a mode of existence, constitutes a coherent ensemble of practices, typical of the amateur of art and the man or woman of the spirit of the beginning of the twentieth century *insofar as they repeat*."[54]

In a grand statement about art, belief, and the amateur whereby Stiegler links them—as is to be expected—to technics, he reaches the crescendo of his aestheology when he writes the following, which is nothing less than his credo:

> *The aesthetic experience is a belief where a consistence is produced on condition of a tenacity and an insistence*—of the gaze, the hearing, the senses, the flesh, which are constituted in

---

51. "[From] the stripping away of the context of the statement results a paradoxical opacity of the stated in the effects of the (re)contextualization of which reading consists: it is as if although the indecision with regard to any reading's meaning is reduced, the variability of its meaning is proportionally increased, freeing up the possibility of always new interpretations" (Stiegler, *La technique et le temps* 2, 70–71).

52. Stiegler, *De la misère symbolique* 2, 143.

53. Ibid., 144.

54. Ibid.

practices which call for knowledges, that is, *tekhnaï*, whether work-knowledge or life-knowledge, that is, collective and individual modes of existence as *otium*, for example, as rituals and cults in the everyday sense. Like all belief . . . aesthetic credence requires practices through which it is *voluntarily* maintained (there are no spontaneous beliefs). And it is only thus that the figure of the *amateur* can be constituted, that is, of he or she who *loves an object*, and who *sublimates*, and who hence believes in it, and who can sometimes lose the "faith," that is, no longer believe in his or her object: this love of the object can be, as passing into noetic action, just as intermittent as the participation in the divine. It is even, according to Pascal, the *imperative* condition of belief, of faithfulness or of faith. And it is this in which we must therefore *trust in the prostheses of faith that repetitions are* in which what we rightly call practices, whether religious or artistic, consists . . . .[55]

Thus, by claiming that the aesthetic (and the religious) experience depends on the tenacity of the art lover, Stiegler not only repeats the modern gesture of making meaning the product of its receiver, but also the modern approach of making experience the heart of belief, and belief the precondition of the experience; whereas the experience is the *result* of the liturgical participation in a tradition and its institutions. For Stiegler, the religious believer's place is taken by the amateur, who—via his or her love—constitutes the object of belief, instead of the object of belief being constituted by a tradition and its liturgy. Last, but not least, the prosthesis is substituted for liturgy. All that is left to complete Stiegler's aestheological imitation of Christianity is the equivalent of the church, which he takes to be the goal of a new politics, that is, "the reconstitution of an organological community opening the possibility of a new 'sharing of the sensible.'"[56]

And although culture and its cultivation is central to the new *otium* of the people, Stiegler leaves no doubt that he sees such cultivation in quasi-religious terms. He states that it "will be . . . practically (*quasiment*) cults, and not just cultures, through which," he hopes, "the degrading figure of the consumer of images and sounds will be substituted with the more desirable and distinguished figure of the true amateur." That the amateur is to the new *otium* of the people what the believer is to Christianity is underscored by Stiegler's quasi-religious description of the amateur as "the one who loves

---

55. Ibid., 153.
56. Ibid., 154.

and believes in what he or she loves, and who knows that their love and their belief must be cultivated."[57]

Stiegler completes his modeling of the new *otium* on Christianity (Christianity authorizing art) by reading Christianity as aesthetic, sublimatory phenomenon (art authorizing Christianity): "Christianity, which is the *cradle of the images that became what we today call the history of Western art*, would itself have been, in its time, as religion of declared love, and *in this*, as *new organisation of sublimation and participation*, a libidinal economy."[58]

In sum: it has been shown that Stiegler sets out to make art the main vehicle of the new *otium* of the people. This leads him to creating an "aestheology," that is, a theology of art constituted by classic Christian theological motifs—belief, love, hope, the promise, liturgy, participation, and community. In the process, on the basis of his utilization of the medieval Latin Christian *otium* as a model, Christianity is used to authorize art as the vehicle of the new *otium* of the people, something that Stiegler can only execute if he can argue the case that art can repeat everything done by Christianity. In order to do the latter, he not only develops his theological account of art, but, in turn, he is bound to re-figure the *aesthetic, affective experience* as the heart of Christian belief, whereas St. Augustine states that the Christian conception of *truth* is at the heart of Christian belief and "thanks to the liturgy the human mind reaches the truth and proclaims its faith in the Lord."[59] For liturgical Christianity—Catholic, Orthodox, or Anglican—the affect is the result of the liturgical participation in the truth, which is a knowable person that, in Stiegler's language, through the incarnation of Christ was the consistent that came into existence instead of remaining gnostically unknowable as some consistent that does not exist, but yet mysteriously consists.

And yet, notwithstanding Stiegler's questionable atheological imitation and attempted repetition of medieval Latin Christianity, there can be little doubt that liturgical Christians or adherents to other pre-modern religious and philosophical traditions from the West and the East who are exposed (like the vast majority of humanity today) to hyper-industrialism and its constant solicitation of attention can find common cause with this atheologian—if only because his analyses clearly owe so much to these traditions. Thus, although those of us who live, write, and think from within these traditions may find much to protest about in Stiegler's thought, we may also find much with we can be in accord in his thought. After all, in a

57. Ibid., 158.
58. Ibid., 159.
59. St Augustine. "St Augustine of Hippo on the Liturgy" as broadcast on Ancient Faith Radio (http://www.ancientfaith.com). No date. Transcription made from sound file of citation as received from the station manager via e-mail on 2 August 2011.

very moving passage that straddles the divide between traditionalists and modernists, between secular atheist humanists and believers, Stiegler describes something that is undoubtedly an example of John Rawls' overlapping consensus that Charles Taylor also often cites affirmatively:[60]

> The true question of the meaning of the future, that is, of the spirit, is the question of *knowing what the world will become after my death*—and this is the question of the future that worries Catholics, and all of us today, whether we believe in heaven or not. That this question passes and *is figured* in the course of history and still today through the representation of the soul after death, particularly in Catholicism, is neither contestable nor negligible, and even less contemptible. But this only has sense, this only *gives sense to existence* . . . insofar as such belief constitutes a *guide for life* here below, and in particular, to live *beyond the self*, in the *attention to others* and in the *succession of generations*.[61]

I am in accord with Stiegler that the question of the future and the health of the spirit is of common concern to secular moderns as well as contemporary adherents of pre-modern religious and philosophical traditions. Where the former and the latter are likely to disagree, is on how the future and health of the spirit is to be cultivated. Contemporary adherents of pre-modern religious and philosophical traditions will probably agree with Catherine Pickstock's often cited statement that "traditional communities governed by liturgical patterns are likely to be the only source of resistance to capitalist and bureaucratic norms today."[62]

Does Stiegler's new *otium* of the people as parody of liturgical tradition not ironically validate Pickstock's statement?

---

60. For example in Taylor, *A Secular Age*, 532, 693, 701.
61. Stiegler, *Mécréance et discrédit* 2, 157–58.
62. Pickstock, "Liturgy and Modernity," 24.

## Bibliography

Crépon, Marc, and Bernard Stiegler. *De la démocratie participative. Fondements et limites*. Paris: Mille et une nuits, 2007.

Augustine. *City of God*. Translated by Henry Bettenson. London: Penguin, 1984.

———. "St Augustine of Hippo on the Liturgy" as broadcast on Ancient Faith Radio (http://www.ancientfaith.com). No date. Transcription made from sound file of citation as received from the station manager via e-mail on 2 August 2011.

Pickstock, Catherine. "Liturgy and Modernity." *Telos* 113 (1998) 19–41.

Stiegler, Bernard. *Constituer l'Europe 1. Dans un monde sans vergogne*. Paris: Galilée, 2005.

———. *De la misère symbolique 2. La Catastrophè du sensible*. Paris: Galilée, 2005.

———. *Mécréance et discrédit. 1. La décadence des démocraties industrielles*, Paris: Galilée, 2004.

———. *Mécréance et discrédit. 2. Les sociétés incontrôlables d'individus désaffectés*. Paris: Galilée, 2006.

———. *La technique et le temps, 2. La désorientation*. Paris: Galilée, 1996.

———. *Technics and Time 1, The Fault of Epimetheus*. Translated by Richard Beardsworth and George Collins. Stanford: Stanford University Press, 1998.

Stiegler, Bernard, and Ars Industrialis. *The Decadence of Industrial Democracies. Disbelief and Discredit, Volume 1*. Translated by Daniel Ross and Suzanne Arnold. Cambridge: Polity, 2011.

———. *Réenchanter le monde. La valeur esprit contre le populisme industriel*. Paris: Flammarion, 2006.

———. *Technics and Time, 2. Disorientation*. Translated by Stephen Barker. Stanford, CA: Stanford University Press, 2009.

Taylor, Charles. *A Secular Age*. Cambridge: The Belknap Press of Harvard University Press, 2007.

# 3

# Eucharistic Anthropology

## Alexander Schmemann's Conception of Beings in Time

ANDREW T. J. KAETHLER

IN A BROADCAST TO the Soviet Union, Alexander Schmemann boldly announced, "Christianity began with a new experience of time, in which time ceases to be bound-up with death. 'O death, where is thy sting? O hell, where is thy victory?' (1 Cor 15:55). This new experience is the very heart of Christianity and its fire . . . ."[1] Yet, throughout Schmemann's extensive writing on time and the kingdom of God and his heavy emphasis on these themes, he does not explicitly, nor systematically lay out how this new experience of time shapes his theological anthropology. That is not to say that it is not there, but it is to say that it must be pieced together in light of Schmemann's overarching theological orientation.

This paper explicates five important elements of Schmemann's theological anthropology: 1) the nature of time outside of Christ, 2) redeemed time, 3) the "relationality" of Eucharistic personhood, 4) the role of the body in personhood, and 5) the function of the soul. The first element illuminates the human predicament and the historicity of the human person. Redeemed time, the second element, is the result of God's response to our predicament in which Christ is the new end of time. With Christ as the new *telos*, time, the landscape of human existence, has become relational. The

---

1. Schmemann, *The Church Year*, 26.

third and fourth elements look at this "relationality" in terms of Christology and embodiment. While the first four elements concern the human person's relational historicity (her becoming), the fifth element, the soul, is the static element that preserves personal identity in the midst of the relational flux. It is here that Schmemann runs into some problems. His conception of the soul is in tension with the rest of his relational Eucharistic anthropology. Nevertheless, the problem is easily overcome and such a corrective is offered in the final section, a remedy that is consistent with Schmemann's relational approach.

## Time as Death

The human person is a historical being; as Heidegger has articulated so powerfully in *Sein und Zeit*, she is embedded in time.[2] Therefore, it is impossible to conceive of what it means to be human without taking time into account. Schmemann posits that our experience of time is two-fold. First, "man experiences time as cyclical: day follows night, spring follows winter, in an eternal rotation, an eternal cycle of beginning and ending enclosed within time."[3] This cycle, an unending circle, symbolizes the completeness of time, in which beginning and end are connected. Schmemann titles this the cosmic aspect of time, and he sees it as positive because of its completeness. With the completeness there is joy, and this can be seen in our seasonal festivities.

The second aspect of time is that we are beings toward death—Heidegger's "thrownness" toward the ultimate possibility, namely, the end of all possibilities. All life is projected towards its end, death; "wherever time exists, death is always present."[4] The final word of time, even in its positive cosmic dimension, is death. Thus, man lives in the tension between the pregnant joy of life's completeness, and the vacancy and meaninglessness of death. Dramatically, Schmemann emphasizes that from the minute of our birth we are progressing towards death, adding "whether I die tomorrow or in thirty years, all I am trying to do, all that I am trying to be, is void of meaning because I will disappear. So, the time of human existence is meaningless unless there is something somewhere that can overcome this meaninglessness."[5] For Schmemann the meaninglessness of human existence is the conclusion of the philosophers and the great men of the ages; his

2. Heidegger, *Being and Time*.
3. Schmemann, *The Church Year*, 24.
4. Ibid.
5. Schmemann, *Liturgy and Life*, 75.

conclusion is potently and poetically expressed by the writer of Ecclesiastes: "For of the wise as of the fool there is no enduring remembrance, seeing that in the days to come all will have been forgotten. How the wise dies just like the fool! So I hated life, because what is done under the sun was grievous to me, for all is vanity and a striving after wind" (Eccl 2:16–17).

The human person lives in the strange tension between cycle and end, completeness and meaninglessness. And we are left with the fundamental question, how can the joy of completeness be reconciled with the nihilism of death? This question inescapably faces us, and yet we seek to avoid it. Technological society assists us in this denial; specialization and naïve hopes of progress turn our gaze away from our slavery to time and death. Yet, it is this hopeless duality that frames the human situation and sheds light on the radical sanctification of time that takes place in Christ's resurrection. Without Christ, argues Schmemann, time culminates in death, in meaninglessness.

## Redeemed Time

Time is redeemed because Christ entered into death, and in so doing conquered it. When Christ died normal life and meaningless time came to its end and are no longer possible.[6] With death overcome, "normal" time lost its end and thus time became something new; time became intertwined with joy rather than death, for death was transformed into a passage that leads to Joy Himself, He who is life. The resurrection stands at the center of time. The past as salvation history is clarified as the resurrection works its way backwards through time impregnating time with meaning, making time history; the future, touched by resurrected time is gathered back to the event that always is. The resurrection pulls all time into the kingdom as if it were a whirlpool pulling everything into itself. Christ, therefore, is the new *telos*. To unpack this further we will turn to Schmemann's explication of Lazarus Saturday (the liturgical day before Palm Sunday).

Typically Saturday services within the Orthodox tradition are services that commemorate the dead. Lazarus Saturday is unique in that it does not follow the pattern. In fact, paradoxically Lazarus Saturday is a "Sunday celebration" celebrated on a Saturday. This means that the typical day that remembers the dead is turned into a day that celebrates the power of resurrection over death—Sunday is the day of resurrection. Hence Lazarus

---

6. "The Pascha of Jesus signified its end to 'this world' and it has been at its end since then. This end can last for hundreds of centuries, this does not alter the nature of time in which we live as the 'last time.' 'The form of this world is passing away . . .' (I Corinthians 7:31)." Schmemann, "A Liturgical Explanation of Holy Week," para. 10.

Saturday is a service permeated by joy as the participants celebrate Christ's "forthcoming" victory over death. According to Schmemann, the resurrection of Lazarus provides the interpretive key to the mystery of Pascha.

It is important to understand that Lazarus personifies the whole of humanity, and his home, Bethany, is a symbol of the whole world as humanity's home. Jesus' friend Lazarus is destroyed by a power that God did not create, death. Here, facing Lazarus' death, Jesus comes face to face with the power that destroys His creation. He experiences the meaningless power of death and destruction, and He weeps. He weeps for his friend who is caught up in this meaningless power, and in so doing Christ weeps for humanity and the world. Christ knows that he will resurrect Lazarus, and yet he weeps because he has encountered the sorrow of this world, the triumphing of the powers that destroy all that which He created and loves.

The Saturday of Lazarus reveals that the enemy is death, preparing the way for Christ's own battle with death. Death, and thus meaningless time, arose from humanity's choice to be alienated from God, "having no life in himself and by himself, he dies."[7] Christ enters into our humanity so that we can be reconciled with God, made one—"at-one-ment"—and through His humanity and in His love Christ enters into death to bring life to death. Death parted humanity from all her relationships, divine and human, or perhaps more accurately death is the name given for absolute separation. Yet, in Jesus Christ, the God-Man, death runs into a problem. While the human person has no life in herself (i.e., she is totally contingent), and thus can be separated from life, death cannot rob Christ of His life and of His goodness, for He is good and He is life. If life and goodness are excluded then so is Christ. Therefore, paradoxically, death enveloped life (Himself), but could not overcome it.[8] As a result, death itself has become a passage on to life "and because His dying is love, compassion and co-suffering, in His death the very nature of death is changed. From punishment it becomes the radiant act of love and forgiveness, the end of alienation and solitude. Condemnation is transformed into forgiveness . . . ."[9]

Death has been transformed, but we must still pass through it. Our death and resurrection waits to be appropriated by us, but "it is already His Resurrection, but not yet ours. We will have to die, to accept the dying, the separation, the destruction. Our reality in this world, in this 'aeon,' is

---

7. Ibid., para. 38.

8. "The One who dies on the Cross has Life in Himself, i.e., He has life not as a gift from outside, a gift which therefore can be taken away from Him, but as His own essence. For He is the Life and the Source of all life. 'In Him was Life and Life was the light of man'" (Ibid., para. 49).

9. Ibid., para. 38.

the reality of the Great Saturday."[10] The center of time is still gathering the future to itself and we live in the Saturday, in midnight waiting for the dawn of day. In celebrating Pascha we celebrate the past which is also our future; "Pascha is always the end and always the beginning. We are always living *after* Pascha, and we are always going *toward* Pascha."[11] Pascha is the beginning of the new time, but for now we live in the middle of Christ's two comings: what was and what will be. And yet in this Saturday He is with us as he promised: "behold, I am with you always, to the end of the age" (Matt 28:20). Although we live between two comings, Christ is still present. Therefore, the new time involves past, present, and future. These three tenses are essential to the Christian life and to time in its totality:

1. "Christ has come": we ascertain the meaning of our lives.

2. "Christ is present": this makes our meaning possible.

3. "Christ is coming": time is given meaning (leading to the fulfillment of the kingdom).[12]

The meaninglessness of time as death has been replaced by the joy of Christ. And as resurrection time reaches back and at the same time gathers the future into itself, the events of this life are impregnated with life and meaning. Life now sits at the end and the center of time. Schmemann writes, "It is a time radically different from that of a person whose only concern in life is to mow his lawn, to have money in the bank, and then to trade in his Chevy for a Cadillac and the Cadillac for something else, and finally to die saying, 'Well, I had all this and nothing has a meaning.' It is sad, it is tragically sad, not to know that the past, the present, and the future have been given by Christ a new and joyful meaning."[13]

But how do we participate in the three tenses of time? Simply put: in Christ. This occurs in two ways: eschatologically and cosmically. First, through the divine liturgy climaxing with the Eucharist, the Christian person enters into Christ and his kingdom. In other words, in Christ we participate in the new aeon (the kingdom), and it is this aeon, the time of Christ, that brings all time together as meaningful time. To sweep away the cobwebs of confusion, for Schmemann the new aeon as the kingdom is a personal/relational concept. The kingdom is love, the kingdom is paradise, paradise is thanksgiving, Christ as Eucharist is thanksgiving and Christ is love; therefore, Christ, so to speak, is the kingdom. The kingdom, in the

10. Ibid., para. 63.
11. Schmemann, *Liturgy and Life*, 76.
12. Ibid., 87–88.
13. Ibid., 80.

eschatological sense, is the Christian experience of the future in the present. However, it also transports one into the past, specifically the Last Supper. Since Schmemann sees the Last Supper as the inauguration and manifestation of the kingdom he can say that the historical event, Jesus breaking bread with the twelve disciples, does not remain an event in the past:

> And when, approaching for communion, we pray, "Of Thy Mystical Supper, O Son of God, accept me *today* as a communicant," this identification of what is accomplished *today* with what was accomplished *then* is *real*, and precisely in the full meaning of the word, for *today* we are gathered in the same kingdom, at the same table, where *then*, on that festal night, Christ was present among those whom "he loved to the end."[14]

The Last Supper is the quintessential event in which the old aeon becomes a place for the new, or as Schmemann calls it in his journal, the chalice of eternity.[15] The Last Supper is an event in history that is eternal.

Second, the cosmic way has to do with what Schmemann calls meaningful events.[16] Like the eschatological way, the Eucharist remains central because it brings us to the center of time. Clearly, the cosmic cannot be separated from the eschatological. What the cosmic way does is make past events present as a meaningful event. Schmemann is referring specifically to historical events that the liturgy celebrates—perhaps we could call them "kingdom events." The celebrant in the liturgy—and this is important for Schmemann—does not re-enact the event, but re-enters.[17] She re-enters via participation in the liturgy into the meaning of the event, and it is through participation that she experiences the meaning in the present event, the liturgy.[18] In other words, it is an event of today because it manifests the efficacy of the historical event.[19] To be clear, a meaningful event is not simply one of recollection. For example, one recalls that Jesus raised Lazarus from the dead, and thinks about this as a foretaste of the universal resurrection of the dead. It is not an abstraction. Rather, in Christ, in whom all meaning is found, the reality of the resurrection event is made present in and through

---

14. Schmemann, *The Eucharist*, 200.
15. Schmemann, *The Journals*, 78.
16. Schmemann, *Great Lent*, 82.
17. Schmemann, *Introduction to Liturgical Theology*, 106–9.
18. "A feast thus is an entrance into, and communion with the eternal meaning of an event of the past, through which we taste of the Kingdom of God." Schmemann, *Liturgy and Life*, 19.
19. Schmemann, *The Journals*, 219.

the participant re-entering the meaningful depths of Lazarus Saturday by the Spirit.

In light of what Lazarus Saturday reveals about Pascha, Christ's entering into death and becoming the *telos* of time, what exactly can we say about redeemed time? First, time is relational. It is in relation to the kingdom, and the kingdom is Christ. Second, as a consequence of the previous point, time is known in reference to life rather than death. Therefore, joy can truly be experienced in this world. Third, time as meaning signifies that time does not enslave all people to the present in this world's past, present, and future dichotomies, nor to the old aeon. Fourth, time is history, or put differently, time is meaningful. Fifth, in light of the previous two points, time does not equate to progress, at least not in a linear fashion. Christ is the end of history, and thus the future has already happened in the past event of the Last Supper. Sixth, time is a movement towards God. Christ sits at the end, or we could say the center of time, and therefore the time of this world is the time of salvation, or what Schmemann calls the time of the church. It is the time in which the church lifts the world, including time, to God impregnating it with eternity, with meaning.

## Eucharistic Anthropology

The previous section concluded by asking how humans can participate in past, present, and future, and this question leads nicely into Schmemann's theological anthropology. I have broken down Schmemann's anthropology into three interrelated claims about the human person: 1) we are beings in relationship, 2) we are Eucharistic beings, and 3) being must be understood as becoming. All three claims bring together time and being.

Pure and simple, Christ is the center of Schmemann's anthropology. Schmemann writes, "Eucharist (thanksgiving) is the state of perfect man. Eucharist is the life of paradise. Eucharist is the only full and real response of man to God's creation, redemption and gift of heaven. But this perfect man who stands before God is *Christ*."[20] In participating in Christ, scripturally speaking to be hid with Christ in God, one becomes more truly a person. Not human, but person, for "human nature does not exist outside of *persons* . . . ."[21] Abstract human nature has no reality—what is real are persons, persons in time. I have used the phrase "persons in time" keeping in mind that time is relational, is in relation to Christ. We are persons via relationship, and being in relationship with Christ means we become truly

---

20. Schmemann, *For the Life of the World*, 37–38.
21. Schmemann, *Of Water and the Spirit*, 139.

relational, or even extra-relational by being brought into relationship not only with all of creation, but with God Himself the Ultimate Relation.

In Christ we become Eucharistic beings. This is twofold. First, we participate in Christ's thanksgiving. Here in the fullest degree we fulfill our essence as worshipping beings, *homo adorans*, giving thanks to God. "For thanksgiving is truly the first and the essential act of man, the act by which he fulfills himself as man."[22] We can give thanks fully because we do it in Christ, and thus it is an unblemished whole act of gratitude. On another level, we are able to be thankful in and for this life because death has been transformed by Christ. Once again we can feast, we can celebrate for death no longer enslaves us. The joy of cyclical time is no longer overshadowed by death, and it is restored and made revelatory as the chalice of eternity.

Schmemann argues that "it is in time . . . that we find the first and the most important condition of our life."[23] We are persons in time and this means that a person is to be understood dynamically rather than statically. Schmemann uses language that involves movement: preparation, pilgrimage,[24] following Christ, and climbing up Mount Tabor.[25] He writes, "God revealed and offers us eternal Life and not eternal rest. And God revealed this eternal Life in the midst of time—and of its *rush*—as its secret meaning and goal. And thus he made time, and work in it, into the *sacrament of the world to come*, the liturgy of fulfillment and ascension."[26] Personhood grows as one ascends Mount Tabor towards transfiguration. The pattern of living and growing here in "this world" carries on into the hereafter.[27] With Christ as the archetype of the human person we are and always will be in a state of becoming rather than being:[28] creaturely eternity moving into the everlastingness of God.[29]

## Relational Body Static Soul

Time and being coalesce in Christ. Time has become relational and likewise our ontology is relationally rooted. Since time involves extension (space and

---

22. Ibid., 46.
23. Schmemann, *Liturgy and Life*, 75.
24. Schmemann, *Great Lent*, 69.
25. Schmemann, *Liturgy and Life*, 83.
26. Schmemann, *For the Life of the World*, 65.
27. For more see Brandon Gallaher, "Chalice of Eternity," 5–35.
28. Schmemann does not use the language of being as becoming, but it fits with his dynamic and relational understanding of personhood.
29. Ibid.

movement) it is only natural to look at extension and ontology, or to put it in a less obfuscated manner, embodiment and personhood. In *For the Life of the World*, Schmemann sets out to unpack the meaning of life. He asks, "What *life* is both motivation, and the beginning and the goal of Christian *mission?*"[30] Schmemann suggests that there are two general approaches given in response. The "spiritualists" approach, known historically as the gnostic, in which one stoically faces the trials of this life while focusing on the spiritual life; eating, playing, creating, and so forth are all but irrelevant. In contradistinction, the "activists" approach aims to recover the world lost in the previous approach and in so doing the social, political, and economic trump the liturgical and contemplative. With both approaches, "this life" and the world are left without meaning; "one eats and drinks, one fights for freedom and justice in order to be *alive*, to have the *fullness of life*. But what is it? What is the life of life itself? . . . Whether we "spiritualize" our life or "secularize" our religion . . . the real life of the world, for which we are told God gave his only-begotten Son, remains hopelessly beyond our religious grasp."[31] According to Schmemann, the problem with both approaches is that they place the spiritual and material in fundamental opposition. The same pattern of opposition is seen in the way that the body is all too often misunderstood. It is either construed in a strict dualistic sense of body and soul from which stems the idea of the immortality of the soul,[32] or in a strict physicalist sense in which there is nothing beyond the physical body (e.g., Nancey Murphy).[33] Schmemann does not connect the two approaches to life with the body and soul "problem," but it does mirror his method. The likes of Murphy are not on his radar; however, her non-reductive physicalism[34] fittingly represents one extreme, matching, in some ways, the "activists" approach to life. Like Murphy, the pressing concern for Schmemann is the notion of the immortality of the soul. Nonetheless, it is easily deduced from his rejection of the opposition of spirit and matter that physicalism is incongruent with Schmemann's anthropological vision. He does leave room for the soul, but in a problematic way, which we will return to in the section that follows. In this section we are asking and seeking to answer the follow-

30. Schmemann, *For the Life of the World*, 12.

31. Ibid., 13.

32. Schmemann, "The Christian Concept of Death."

33. "My central thesis is, first, that we are our bodies—there is no additional metaphysical element such as a mind or soul or spirit." Murphy, *Bodies and Souls, or Spirited Bodies?*, ix.

34. The "non-reductive" clause, according to Murphy, means that the attributes traditionally attributed to the soul (reason, free will, morality, and spirituality) are all capacities of the body. Ibid., 72.

ing questions: What role does the body play in regards to being a person? How does the body participate in man's identity as *homo adorans*? What is the soul, and what part does it play in our personal identity?

Schmemann's reflections on the subject of the body are most explicit in his writings on death and in contrast with the notion of the immortality of the soul.[35] All of this sits in the background of the Paschal hope: Christ is risen; He is risen indeed. The affirmation "I believe in the resurrection of the body" of the Apostles Creed is the corollary for what follows. Schmemann fears that Christians have inadvertently moved away from the Paschal hope and returned to Plato's notion of two opposing worlds—the idea that the immortal soul, in death, leaves the imperfect changing and shifting world and enters the perfect, unchanging other world. Schmemann adamantly asserts, "Christ never spoke about the immortality of souls—he spoke about the resurrection of the dead! . . . [S]urely, if the question is strictly about the immortality of souls, then we need not concern ourselves with death as such, and what need have we of all these words about victory over death, about its destruction, and about resurrection?"[36] For Schmemann, resurrection of the body and immortality of the soul are incongruent. The immortality of the soul sanctions death as liberation; it "is the justification of death and one of the chief arguments in favor of reconcilement with it."[37] Whereas, resurrection is the overcoming of death and its aim is to obliterate it. Christ is life itself and death strives to be life's antithesis. This brings us back to Lazarus Saturday and Christ weeping at Lazarus' tomb. Death is the great enemy. It is not created by God and is therefore unnatural.[38] Schmemann goes so far as to say that "death is the denial of God, and if death is natural, . . . if it is the highest and immutable law about all creation, then there is no God . . . ."[39] In the story of Adam and Eve death is literally the denial of God. Man and woman chose other than God and the result was death. There is no life apart from God. The great tragedy is that man desired life apart from God, and by moving away from God man moved into death.

"This life" and this world were given to us to be communion with God, and here is the crux of the argument: "The horror of death is, therefore, not in its being the 'end' and not in physical destruction. By being separation

35. Schmemann, "The Christian Concept of Death"; Schmemann, *O Death, Where is Thy Sting?*; Chapter 6 in Schmemann, *For the Life of the World*; Chapter 2 in Schmemann, *Of Water and the Spirit*, 60–66.

36. Schmemann, *O Death*, 26–27.

37. Schmemann, "The Mystery of Easter," 18.

38. See Schmemann, *For the Life of the World*, 99–100; Schmemann, "The Christian Concept of Death"; Schmemann, *O Death*, 29–36.

39. Schmemann, *O Death*, 32.

from the world and life, it is *separation from God*. The dead cannot glorify God."[40] Our human life, embodied/bodied existence, finds its *telos* and its life in worship, in relationship—the opposite of separation—with God. In other words, without a body there is no interaction with this world[41] and thus no communion with God. Yet, Schmemann is not a physicalist, for resurrection includes both soul and body.[42] The body is what enables relationship to the world and to others. The body is for communion: "without exception, everything in the body, in the human organism, is created for this relationship, for this communion, for this coming out of oneself. . . . [T]he body is that which sees, hears, feels, and thereby leads me out of the isolation of my *I*."[43] The body is the soul's freedom, "for the body is the soul as love, the soul as communion, the soul as life, the soul as movement. And this is why," writes Schmemann, "when the soul loses the body . . . it loses life; it dies, even if this dying of the soul is not complete annihilation, but a dormition, or sleep."[44]

In the last three quotations in the previous paragraph an obvious lacuna can be seen: Schmemann asserts much about the body but little about the soul. Nonetheless, we can deduce something about the soul from his comments on the transitory nature of the body and from his comments on death as sleep. Biologically speaking, the cells that form our bodies are replaced every seven years, and Schmemann is quick to adumbrate that "physiologically, every seven years we have a new body."[45] Therefore, if all I am is my body then my identity is short-lived. This is why Schmemann describes our bodies as our "individual incarnation in the world . . . ."[46] What we glean from this is that it is the soul that maintains one's "static identity," the identity of oneself that perdures through time. It is the soul that "sleeps" in biological death waiting for the resurrection of the body, and like "biological sleep" the soul is suspended waiting for the body to awake. Without the body the soul is imprisoned in sleep. This separation is not liberation, "for Death is the severance of the soul from the body and it is this severance which is evil, because God has united them that they live, and in this union

---

40. Schmemann, *For the Life of the World*, 100.

41. "Each of our bodies is nothing other than our individual incarnation in the world, as the form of my dependence on the world, on the one hand, and of my life and of my activity in the world, on the other." Schmemann, *O Death*, 42.

42. Schmemann, "The Christian Concept of Death."

43. Schmemann, *O Death*, 42.

44. Ibid., 42–43.

45. Ibid., 41.

46. Ibid., 42.

implement the life of man."[47] He repeats this idea but with greater detail in *The Christian Concept of Death*: "it is precisely this union of spirit, soul and body that is called *man* in the Bible and in the Gospel. Man, as created by God, is an animate body and an incarnate spirit . . . ."[48] Without a body the soul does not live, meaning the soul cannot commune, be in relationship. In that sense death is not destruction, one's annihilation, "for creation may not destroy that which God has called from nothingness into being. But man is plunged into death, into the darkness of lifelessness and debility."[49] The life of man is one in relationship, and this is why if man is to live (be in relationship) after death there must be a resurrection of the body. In other words, body equals relationship. But what sort of body is to be had in the eschaton? And what does the resurrected body reveal about our current bodies?

It is only in Schmemann's radio address published in *O Death, Where is Thy Sting?* that he reflects on the resurrected body:

> When Christianity speaks about the vivification of bones and muscles, for bones and muscles and the whole material world, its whole fabric, is nothing more than certain basic elements, in the end—atoms. And in them there is nothing specifically personal, nothing eternally mine.
>
> Christianity speaks about the restoration of life as communion, it speaks about the spiritual body that over the course of our whole life we have developed through love, through our pursuits, through our relationships, through our coming out of ourselves. It speaks not about the eternity of matter, but about its final spiritualization; about the world that finally becomes truly a body—the life and love of mankind; about the world that has become fully communion with Life.[50]

There are six interesting points concerning the new body that Schmemann makes in the quotation. First, the resurrected body will in some way be deeply personal, deeply unique, so much so that atoms are too limited to express the personal reality that will be eternally one's "own." Second, and this is key, life will be restored as communion, and something about our new bodies will take one beyond the current communal limitations of the present body. Third, our new bodies are called spiritual bodies. I think what Schmemann seeks to express is that there will be no disjunction between the "body and soul"—a perfect mirroring, perfect oneness. One caveat: the

---

47. Schmemann, "The Mystery of Easter," 18.
48. Schmemann, "The Christian Concept of Death," para. 12.
49. Ibid.
50. Schmemann, *O Death*, 43–44.

new body is not the amalgamation of body and soul (old and new) but the complete spiritualization of matter (the old becomes new). This fits with Schmemann's emphasis upon God making the world anew. Reflecting on Revelation 21:5 ("Behold I make all things new"), Schmemann points out "that Christ does not say 'I create new things,' but 'all things new.'"[51] Fourth, our spiritual bodies are formed in this present life. In other words, what we do in this life forms us for the hereafter, and there is continuity that is carried on in the new. Fifth, the spiritual body, although deeply unique, is somehow permeable to the other, open in such a way that there is no need to come out of the self. Sixth, the spiritual body continues to commune with God, as always intended, through the world; the world, with the final destruction of death, reaches a final climax of spiritualization and fully becomes communion. God "will transfigure it [the world] into 'a new heaven and a new earth,' into man's spiritual body, into the temple of God's presence and God's glory in creation."[52] This highlights the second point. The new heaven and new earth conceived as "man's spiritual body" and "the temple of God" refer to the world as man's means of communing with God.

What do the aforementioned six points reveal about our current bodies? First, respectively, our current bodies are limited in expressing personhood. Although physical bodies distinguish one human person from the next—both literally in that I cannot "leave my own skin" and in the sense of our defining characteristics (brown curly hair, average height, long nose etc.)—they are limited. Second, similar to the previous point, even though our bodies enable communion, they are limited: I am stuck within "my own skin." Third, Schmemann may reject traditional body-soul dualisms, but there is a disjunction in that there is not complete "spiritualization" of the body in our current state. Further evidence for this disjunction is revealed in the way that Schmemann describes sleep: "for in sleep it is precisely the body that sleeps and is inactive."[53] Fourth, this life is the beginning of life eternal and we are "growing into" our spiritual bodies. Time and space are where God forms us in relationship.[54] Everything we do here matters, and is part of our future. Or, as C. S. Lewis perspicuously put it, explaining the virtue of courage, "Now it is quite true that there will probably be no occasion for just or courageous acts in the next world, but there will be every

---

51. Schmemann, "Liturgy and Eschatology," 97.

52. Schmemann, "The Christian Concept of Death," para. 13.

53. Schmemann, *O Death*, 43.

54. Kallistos Ware acutely expresses this: "Time is part of the 'distancing' or 'contraction' on God's side which makes it possible for us humans freely to love. It is, as it were, the interspace which enables us to move towards God unconstrained and by our voluntary choice." Ware, "Time," 188.

occasion for being the sort of people that we can become only as the result of doing such acts here."[55] Fifth, faith and communion involve an exodus of the self,[56] a dying to the self and this is possible on this side of the eschaton. Hence, the import of baptism as "the restoration of *true life*, the life that man has lost in sin."[57] Man dies to the world and the self (self-sufficiency) in Christ (who reveals in His relationship with the Father absolute dependence), and through this death man rises in Christ. Therefore, in this life, in this body, we can enter into Christ and exit the self, yet this is a bodily act: baptism. It is also an act that we repeat. Liturgy, like the sacraments, is a passage. In every Eucharistic service we ascend to the kingdom of God enabling us to live the liturgical life climbing mount Tabor.[58] Although in "this life" and with this body we are hid with Christ in God (Col 3:3) we have yet to reach the fulfillment of personhood. Sin and the brokenness of "this world" weighs us down. Sixth, we are incarnated creatures, priests in and for the world and not purely separate from it. The world is God's gift to us, given to be transformed into life and to be offered back as our gift to God.[59] Therefore, "we should concentrate upon this world lovingly because it is full of God, because by way of the Eucharist we find Him everywhere . . . ."[60] Simply put, our bodies enable us to participate in God's created order and through this we participate and give thanks to God.

In conclusion, our bodies, both in this age and the age to come, are for communion, for relationship. The soul separated from the body is a tragedy, for it has lost its means of communing. Schmemann adamantly argues that the immortality of the soul is not a Christian doctrine; contrary to Christianity, it imbibes the pre-Christian idea of death as liberation from the body. In regards to constructive notions of the soul, Schmemann writes little and we are simply left with the idea that the soul is one's "static identity." Perhaps, with so little attention paid to the soul it is not surprising that we run into some inconsistencies in Schmemann's thinking.

---

55. Lewis, *Mere Christianity*, 81.

56. Schmemann, *The Eucharist*, 144.

57. Schmemann, *Of Water and the Spirit*, 20. Also see Schmemann, "The Mystery of Easter," 21–22.

58. Schmemann, *Liturgy and Life*, 82–83.

59. Schmemann, "The World as Sacrament," 223.

60. Ibid., 226–27.

## Identity without Relationship?

Schmemann offers a beautiful vision of the physical body: the body enables communion, communion between man and the world, man and humanity, and man and God. Yet, every seven years the cells that comprise our bodies are replaced. Constancy of identity, consequently, does not depend upon our body, otherwise we would each be a new person every seven years. "Static identity," according to Schmemann, rests in the soul. Even though personal identity may rest statically in the soul, it only exists in relation to God, in the I-Thou relationship—God "recognizes" one's name. To put it clearly, the relationship between God and the human person is what gives the person identity, not to mention his or her personhood. Following Schmemann's logic, in death the soul, one's "static identity," can only be sustained via relationship with God. Unless one is willing to assert that death ends one's identity, which Schmemann is not, it must be possible to have communion with God without the body. Ironically, Schmemann's inconsistency arises as a result of too strong a dualism, a dualism of functionality. When Schmemann writes that man was meant to be an embodied creature and he states that it is through the body that we commune, both in heaven as it is on earth, he leaves out the soul. In other words, he separates body and soul according to functionality. The body communicates, relates, and thus leads one out of the imprisonment of individuality. The soul simply retains one's identity, which again, is problematic since identity is based on relationship.

As a possible solution, with a weaker dualism Schmemann could speak of the horror of death and at the same time retain his strong relational understanding of existence and personhood. Contrary to what one would expect, what Schmemann needs for a weaker dualism is a stronger and more developed notion of the soul.[61] If the soul shares the functional characteristics of the body and the body is the expression of the soul then the two could be seen as working together—unified.[62] Similar to Schmemann's dualism, the soul in this case is also incomplete without the body. A bodiless soul is severely limited within a weaker dualism; after all, man is an embodied creature (e.g., a cyclist needs a bike to cycle). Death is a tragedy, for it separates a person from his body leaving him hardly a human person, like a cyclist without a bike, a lion without a mane, or a bird without its wings.[63] However, what rests "beyond" the grave, the soul, can and must

---

61. For example, see Ratzinger, *Eschatology*, 104–61.

62. I am thinking along the lines of Aquinas in which "the soul is the 'form' of the body." See Aquinas, *Summa Contra Gentiles*, II, 56.

63. The liturgical theologian David Fagerberg puts his finger on the issue. Describing Plato's misunderstood and overlooked insight concerning the tension between

commune (albeit limitedly) with God in order to be sustained as person and to maintain identity.

It is arguable that Schmemann's error arises as a result of misreading Plato, an error common to his time.[64] By reacting to Plato, Schmemann all too eagerly sought to minimize the role of the soul, a proper reaction to his misconceived reading, and in so doing he unintentionally created a dualism that is incompatible with his relational ontology. The incoherency and contradiction within Schmemann's body-soul construal is problematic but not devastating. The error can be amended without damaging Schmemann's overall approach simply by insisting that the soul, like the body, albeit in a limited way, is functionally relational.

## Human Person as Priest

In conclusion, according to Schmemann, time is an inescapable feature of human existence. However, time can be either enslaving or freeing. Outside of Christ one experiences time as enslavement to the present, which, like life, continually slips out of one's grasp as it passes into nonexistence. For those hid in Christ time becomes the space, the chalice, for eternity to fill, impregnating time with meaning and joy.

The human person is one in relationship who lives out of gratitude as a Eucharistic being. In this regard, life is passage; in Christ, one continually moves deeper into the life of God. The six points I made concerning redeemed time are bound up with these three notions of personhood. The first three points of time—time is relational, crowned by life, and not locked to the present—correspond to person as one in relationship and as Eucharistic-being. The last three points about time—time is history, movement, and yet is not a linear progress—corresponds to Schmemann's idea that being is becoming.

---

body and soul, Fagerberg writes: "Plato was wrong when he said the body is a prison for the soul, but he did notice a truth even in being wrong. His detractors have not even noticed this much. One party says there is no tension between soul and body because there is no soul; another party says there is no tension because the soul should make itself hedonistically at home in the body and not seek anything loftier. Both of these parties err by overlooking the tension that Plato noticed. Christianity says neither the body nor the spirit fell: rather, anthropos fell, putting body and spirit in tension." Fagerberg, *Theologia Prima*, 230.

64. For a perfect example of this see Oscar Cullmann, *Immortality of the Soul or Resurrection of the Dead?*, 15–27. Cullmann's work had a large influence on Schmemann as evidenced in *Introduction to Liturgical Theology*. Ratzinger provides a brief and insightful overview of the development of this anti-Platonic approach in *Eschatology*, 72–75.

Schmemann offers us a beautiful image of personhood and time, but he struggles to consistently maintain identity. By arguing that the body and soul have drastically different functions he creates a disjunction between identity and relationship. According to Schmemann's own schema this is deeply problematic: there cannot be a divide between identity and relationship because identity is found in relationship. Ironically, it is the relational element between body and soul that needs to be increased or tightened in order to consistently maintain Schmemann's relational ontology. The soul without the body must remain capable of communion with Christ, albeit in a limited way, in order to preserve its "static identity" in death.

Perhaps it is possible to collapse all the distinctions about what it means to be a being in time with one simple phrase from Schmemann's book *For the Life of the World*: "the basic definition of man is that he is *the priest*."[65] Time is the space within which we lovingly and freely offer all back to God.[66] This means that, in Christ, we offer not only ourselves, but the world and time back to him. What has been given as gift we give back in thanksgiving as gift. Here we fulfill the relational element and our existence as Eucharist. Here time is offered up and opened up to eternity, to Love. And out of this Love, time takes on meaning. Thus, for Schmemann, our priestly identity means that we bless God by offering all to Him, and in so doing we give time meaning. Yet, we must not forget that as priests we also participate in this meaning. Through participation we move into deeper communion with God always climbing further up and further in to everlasting love. And it is because this journey begins here in "this world" that Schmemann suggests we can wholeheartedly echo St. Peter: "'Lord, it is good for us to be here.'"[67]

## Bibliography

Aquinas, Thomas. *Summa Contra Gentiles*. Online: http://www3.nd.edu/Departments/Maritain/etext/gc2_56.htm.

Cullmann, Oscar. *Immortality of the Soul or Resurrection of the Dead? The Witness of the New Testament*. London: Epworth, 1958.

Fagerberg, David W. *Theologia Prima: What is Liturgical Theology?* 2nd ed. Chicago: Hillenbrand, 2004.

---

65. Schmemann, *For the Life of the World*, 15.

66. In a more lucid manner than Schmemann, Kallistos Ware argues that "time is the interval between God's appeal and our answer. We humans need this interval of time so as freely to love God and one another; without the interval we cannot engage in the dialogue of love." Ware, "Time," 188–89.

67. Schmemann, *Liturgy and Life*, 88.

Gallaher, Brandon. "Chalice of Eternity: An Orthodox Theology of Time." *St. Vladimir's Theological Quarterly* 57.1 (2013) 5–35.

Heidegger, Martin. *Being and Time*. Translated by Stambaugh Joan. New York: State University of New York Press, 1996.

Lewis, C. S. *Mere Christianity*. New York: Harper Collins, 2001.

Murphy, Nancey. *Bodies and Souls, or Spirited Bodies?* Current Issues in Theology 1.3. Cambridge: Cambridge University Press, 2006.

Ratzinger, Joseph. *Eschatology: Death and Eternal Life*. Translated by Michael Waldstein. 2nd ed. Edited by Aidan Nichols. Washington, DC: Catholic University of America Press, 2007.

Schmemann, Alexander. "The Christian Concept of Death." No pages. Online: http://www.schmemann.org/byhim/thechristianconceptofdeath.html.

———. *The Church Year*. Translated by John A. Jillions. Vol. 2 of Celebration of Faith. Crestwood, NY: St. Vladimir's Seminary Press, 1994.

———. *The Eucharist: Sacrament of the Kingdom*. Translated by Paul Kachur. Crestwood, NY: St. Vladimir's Seminary Press, 1987.

———. *Introduction to Liturgical Theology*. Translated by Asheleigh E. Moorehouse. Crestwood, NY: St. Vladimir's Seminary Press, 1966.

———. *For the Life of the World: Sacraments and Orthodoxy*. 2nd ed. Crestwood, NY: St. Vladimir's Seminary Press, 1973.

———. *Great Lent: Journey to Pascha*. Crestwood, NY: St. Vladimir's Seminary Press, 1969.

———. *The Journals of Father Alexander Schmemann, 1973–1983*. Translated by Juliana Schmemann. Crestwood, NY: St. Vladimir's Seminary Press, 2002.

———. "A Liturgical Explanation of Holy Week." No pages. Online: http://orthodoxinfo.com/general/a-liturgical-explanation-of-holy-week.pdf.

———. "Liturgy and Eschatology." In *Liturgy and Tradition: Theological Reflections of Alexander Schmemann*, edited by Thomas Fisch, 89–100. Crestwood, NY: St. Vladimir's Seminary Press, 2003.

———. *Liturgy and Life: Christian Development Through Liturgical Experience*. New York: Department of Religious Education: Orthodox Church in America, 1993.

———. "The Mystery of Easter." *St. Vladimir's Seminary Quarterly* 2.3 (1954) 16–22.

———. *O Death, Where is Thy Sting?* Translated by Alexis Vinogradov. Crestwood, NY: St. Vladimir's Seminary Press, 2003.

———. *Of Water and the Spirit: A Liturgical Study of Baptism*. Crestwood, NY: St. Vladimir's Seminary Press, 1974.

———. "The World as Sacrament." In *Church, World, Mission: Reflections on Orthodoxy in the West*, 217–27. Crestwood, NY: St. Vladimir's Seminar Press, 1979.

Ware, Kallistos. "Time: Prison or Path to Freedom?" In *The Inner Kingdom: The Collected Works*, Vol. 1, 181–91. Crestwood, NY: St. Vladimir's Seminar Press, 2000.

# 4

# The Psychology of Cosmopolitics

## John Milbank

IN THE CONTEMPORARY WORLD, defending the mind against reduction to the brain might seem task enough, without trying to defend that antique ghost, the soul. Theologians may presumptively seek to safeguard mind and the dignity of human status as a necessary first step, before mounting in some fashion an argument for the soul and its immortality.

But I would argue that this is a mistaken strategy. Outside a theological or a metaphysical purview, mind is actually indefensible and the human properly evaporates. Instead, the theologian needs to go for broke at the outset: soul is far more arguable than mind, and without the psychic the mental becomes incredible, even though the incredible now makes no less sense than the credible, since sense itself has become a dissolving phantom.

The difference between mind without soul and soul as including mind can be simply expressed. Mind without soul belongs to a gradually emergent modern, dualistic picture, for which there is no inherent connection between thought and nature on the one hand, and thought and God on the other. Nature is a realm without meaning, sensation, thought, or even spontaneous vitality. It can be presumed to be there by accident, even though it is all that is really there at all. Mind, on the other hand, which is conscious and willing, is a detached capacity to observe nature, and a power to erect artificial realities above and beyond it. Trying to explain how these two realities, nature and mind, belong together in one finite existence, has preoccupied much of the efforts of modern philosophy. How can awareness arise from non-aware matter; how can intentional decision arise from blindly propelled processes?

In the face of this double problem, three broad options have been pursued. The first is "physiological"—an attempt to explain mental processes in purely natural terms. The second is "ideological" (in the original sense of the term)—a Lockean insistence on the integrity of the mental sphere as following its own laws of association and connection of observed empirical realities.[1] If ideology becomes discontented with this dualism, it can develop into idealism, which seeks to explain even physical reality in terms of the immanent self-development of thought. The third option, from Kant onwards, suggests that in the case of human awareness the natural and the mental have been always already blended. This mixture is simply an obscure given into which we can have no real insight. Moreover, despite epistemological interfusion the given still really splits into two: there remain given nature and given mind and just why they should "correlate" remains unexplained.[2] One could perhaps live with such transcendental agnosticism, but the problem is that philosophy so construed seems to contradict the naturalism of the physical sciences for which not only is matter the only reality, but mind has emerged as part of a natural evolutionary process.

In the second two cases of ideology and transcendentalist duality, one can still hope to climb apologetically from mind to God. But the God so invoked tends to be an idolized God brought in to mend the unexplained gap between mind and nature. Or else, and in addition, he tends to be a fideistic God who has inexplicably dumped us in a dualistic world, in which matter serves our temporary bodily conveniences, but does not sacramentally relate to the true concerns of salvation. The ensuing theology may readily collude with the more brutal physiologies in permitting the ravaging of the planet and species other than the human. In the case of ideology become idealism, the resulting pantheistic voluntarisms can look little different in the end from materialisms acknowledging only force and power as final realities.

The problem then with defending mind is that it appears to be an anomaly, fit to be explained away or else defensible only as a surd intrusion by a voluntarist deity. This will ensure that mind itself is reduced to a power of choice and arbitrary domination.

The case with soul is quite otherwise. Soul is not an anomaly, because it is conceived as an integral and central part of a cosmic reality in most

---

1. See Janicaud, *Ravaisson et La Métaphysique: Une Généalogie Du Spriritualisme Français*, 1–35; Heller-Roazen, *The Inner Touch: Archaeology of a Sensation*, 219–36.

2. See Meillassoux, *Après la Finitude: Essai sur la nécessité de la contingence*.

anciently derived philosophies and religions, both East and West. It is therefore at once more natural and more elevated than mind.

How is it more natural? First, as for Aristotle, it is the form of animal bodies. Every material reality has a shape or a pattern that is both visible and elusive in its determinable properties. This form, because it can migrate from particular material instantiation, and be abstracted, is more than matter—leaving the concreteness of matter, which must always be informed, a paradoxically negative mystery. Something more than matter therefore begins in matter itself, and there is evidence that this something more can often "apprehend" as well as cause or be caused, as both Francis Bacon (in *De argumentis scientarum*) and later Alfred North Whitehead claimed.[3] Soul is at one level merely a more complex form, integrating many sub-shapes and patterns, even though these are not integral forms in themselves.

The soul is not therefore an alien guest in nature. But it involves two unprecedented natural realities: self-motion and reflexive apprehension. These two realities are deeply connected, since they emerge from the way in which animal surfaces touch other realities through offering to them an obscure resistance. To try to explain this resistance in terms of an initial passivity of sensation is to remain within a Lockean, representationalist paradigm, which is too "ideological" and insufficiently naturalistic. For why should an animal, or maybe even a plant "sense anything" as coming from without were it not already offering a certain opposition which distinguishes itself as itself. And it is just this resistance that also gives rise to a reflexivity which is already present in every sensation as the very condition of its possibility. In this way, by rooting sensation in bodily *action,* we avoid any Lockean problems as to why animals should become aware of passively received sensations and why they should be either pleasant or unpleasant—the latter being accountable as a matter of the relative assimilability or non-assimilability of what the animal encounters.[4]

Thus, because animals move they sense, and because they move they are self-aware. Is this movement a pure internally-generated spontaneity? No, because that notion would be the reverse face of the idea of a given passivity; it would belong to the model of double givenness and inexplicable correlation. Instead, one has to realize that animal resistance begins from the outset as a contact—as a partial embrace of an external reality which also holds it at a distance. For this reason, the nineteenth-century French philosopher Félix Ravaisson, moving beyond the early work of Maine de Biran at this point (Ravaisson was unfamiliar with the later work), spoke of

---

3. See Heller-Roazen, *The Inner Touch,* 176–77.
4. See Janicaud, *Ravaisson,* 1–35.

a fundamental animal "desire" both for relation and for self-sustaining in a certain dynamic shape.[5]

This suggests that in the case of embodied animal life, we cannot even think of the material aspect of this life without at the outset invoking the psychic. Inversely, we cannot think of the psychic except as incarnated. One can demonstrate this reality further by considering the phenomena of both touch and habit, which are consequent upon the process of reception and resistance.

All sensation requires a medium, such as light for seeing, which sustains encounter as the drawing near of the distant, essential for alterity. For this reason we see "over there" and we hear "over there." Touch, including tasting and smelling, retains this pattern, since, however intimate, touch must be "of something." But in the case of touch it is the surface of our body, as Aristotle taught, which is itself the medium, and we cannot experience touch unless we experience our own bodies as touching themselves in touching something: this is one reason why our having two hands capable of touching each other is so significant. In such a fashion, it is the most directly material of sensations which most of all "proves the soul," since our difference to what is close and our reflection upon what is close is only possible because of a psychic distancing, even though without this distancing the close impact of touch would not be present at all.[6]

Yet this psychic character of all perception has no taint of Cartesian solipsism or possible doubt as to exteriority. For we cannot touch ourselves or sense ourselves through corporeal reflexivity unless we encounter something external. The foetus in the womb may already be self-sensing because of this, but Ibn Sina's flying man aware of nothing outside himself could never have attained to any *cogito*.[7] Certainly one can agree with Michel Henry that there is something in consciousness irreducible to the reflexive, a sense of self that is not self-relation, but one cannot really think any such auto-affection that is not *also* reflexive and externally orientated. It is for this reason that Merleau-Ponty is the better reader of Maine de Biran and the tradition of "spiritual realism" that stems from him: sensing is intentional because it is resistance. And since, as Henry rightly says, one cannot fully reduce this intentional resisting of a radical ontological exteriority to phenomenological givenness, there is no complete phenomenology of intention. Nor can one have such a phenomenology of the act of intending itself without an infinite regress, since the intentionality of intending can only be

---

5. Ibid., 23; Ravaisson, *Of Habit*.
6. See Milbank, "The Soul of Reciprocity Part Two: Reciprocity Granted."
7. See Heller-Roazen, *The Inner Touch*, 219–36.

preserved if something in the experience of intending escapes experiential awareness.[8]

But this does not, against Henry, show that pure phenomenology should reduce to a mentally archaic level before intentionality. It rather shows that one cannot possibly do so and still be aware of what one is doing—and therefore that, given the impossibility of an entire phenomenological reduction of intentionality, pure phenomenology is impossible. It is rather from the outset crossed by a speculative ontology, as Merleau-Ponty eventually considered.[9] The animal, to apprehend, to touch at all, must resist and must resist by conjecture, by an uncertain reading of the signs that naturally appear. Such activity is integral to the psychic, but not to the Cartesian mental—to which citadel Henry seeks to retreat. For the psychic, unlike the mental, is inherently embodied, which means that to think is to incorporate within oneself external encounter. Indeed, only through these patterned encounters does the self have any characterized personal identity, whereas Henry's autoaffecting ego is absolutely identical in each and every one of us.

It is with respect to these constitutive encounters that, as Xavier Bichat first realized in the romantic era, the mark of animal as opposed to merely plant life is stereoscopy: two arms, legs, eyes, ears, lungs, kidneys, and brain hemispheres superimposed upon a still plant-like monodic growth ruled by a single fragile heart—sometimes resulting in the death of the former before the death of the latter.[10] And since nothing is received without reflection, it becomes impossible to say, as Aristotle already realized, that animal sensation is merely for the sake of function. Here all goes round in a circle: the animal's pleasures and fears both help to sustain it, but equally they sustain it so that it may maximize its pleasures and minimize its fears.[11]

Through the ever-renewed process of its primitive "conjecturing" the animal starts to evolve *habits* of interaction with the outside world. All its encounters follow certain patterns that are entirely irreducible to any preceding laws: indeed, a less anthropomorphic science might validly conclude with Ravaisson that this is true of nature as a whole.[12] But if habit goes all the way down, we are left with two problems. First, what gives rise to habit in the first place, if we abandon the myths of the double given and of correla-

---

8. Henry, *Phénoménologie matérielle*, 13–59.

9. Merleau-Ponty, *The Visible and the Invisible*; Merleau-Ponty, *L'Œil et l'Esprit*; Milbank, "The Soul of Reciprocity Part Two."

10. Bichat, *Recherches Physiologiques sur La Vie et La Mort (première partie)*.

11. Aristotle, *De Anima*, 424a 28; 431a 9–13.

12. Ravaisson, *On Habit*.

tion? Ravaisson, as already mentioned, thought that habit can only be lured forward by an obscure desire, which must be instigated by something like prevenient grace. Thus his solution to a mystery arising from a more radical and consistent naturalism was not merely metaphysical, but theological in the sense of raiding the terminology of revealed theology. He was very explicit about this maneuver, especially in his unpublished notes.[13]

The second problem was already considered by Maine de Biran and many others. How is it that normally a repeated action tends to diminish, such that many habits are "bad habits," inherently linked to degeneration, and yet any animal excellence or skill requires the formation of a good habit and cannot arise spontaneously and sporadically without memory, practice, or acquired skill.[14] For however much a fine tennis player or dancer or painter may "think with" her body during performance or execution, and only fall back upon a pure unconsciousness in a crisis, it remains the case that most of the thinking remains acquired and unconscious and can sometimes produce the flash of genius as much as supply the automatic emergency resort.[15] So just how is it that "merely" material processes as unthought tend to result in enfeeblement and decline, and yet the same material processes are required to ensure the greatest mental achievements, including a fluidity of speech and writing?

De Biran here suggested that one has to suppose a secret occult action at work between mind and matter: something that appears less strange if one admits the reality of Aristotelian *eidos*. His later work, like that of Ravaisson, is able to see that the very *acme* of intelligent action can be embodied and unconscious habit, just because, from the outset, action is not pure self-derived spontaneity, but the achievement of a certain sinuously variable relationship with the outside world.[16]

Following David Hume here even more closely than he thought, De Biran extended such considerations into a four-step process of argumentation which overcame modern mentalism and representationalism, including the

13. Ravaisson, "Fragments de Ravaisson" in Janicaud, *Ravaisson*, 236–68.

14. Maine de Biran, *Influence de l'habitude sur la faculté de penser*; Janicaud, *Ravaisson*, 1–35.

15. For arguments concerning this issue see Hubert L. Dreyfus "The Myth of the Pervasiveness of the Mental" and Barbara Montero, "A Dancer Reflects" in *Mind, Reason and Being-in-the-World*. In the passage above I split the difference between Dreyfus who argues for the unconscious intelligence of the body (though he insufficiently allows that this is "intelligence" at all, with no real fidelity to Merleau-Ponty) and Montero who (perhaps surprisingly) argues for the perpetually accompanying conscious guidance of the dancer's steps.

16. Maine de Biran, *Nouvelles Considérations sur les Rapports du Physique et du Moral de l'Homme*; Janicaud, *Ravaisson*, 1–35.

supposedly critical perspectives of Kant. These four steps were: 1. a physiological attempt to explain mental ideological processes as physical motion; 2. the discovery—after Hume—that physical causal connections are themselves inexplicable; 3. the suggestion—again after Hume—that the best clue we have to causality, since we ourselves know nature from within, is our own inward experience of habitual sensation, movement, and thought; 4. the speculative projection of animal touch and habit onto all of physical nature to engender a new tradition of physical vitalism, which will continue through Ravaisson, Bergson, Merleau-Ponty, Deleuze, and beyond.[17]

The only real counter-argument to these perspectives would be to deny the objective validity of valuation. Perhaps good habits are delusions: merely the consistent outweighing of weaker material forces by stronger ones. Perhaps the entirety of apprehensive and qualitatively judging sensation is mere epiphenomenon and physiology reigns after all. Or perhaps, as for Henry, a non-reflexive interior and materialized *cogito* remains "equally close" to all our physical activities and sensations, without hierarchy and with a reserve of judgment concerning a realm that is inherently alienated and without any real value (this is Henry's dubious ontologization of Marx).

Though *value* is here the wrong word, since it really belongs to the modern picture for which valuation is arbitrary and subjective, in contradistinction to the antique *good,* which was convertible with being itself.[18] Therefore, to reinstate valuation as inherent to apprehension, in the manner of the French spiritual realists from the Romantic era onwards, is in effect to reinstate the good and to deny any cosmic amorality.

In this respect we can locate another, and yet more crucial, contrast between mind and soul. The notion of mind is above all "apolitical," or else political in a perverse sense. "Mind" is fundamentally the mind of a detached representing spectator, who doubles up as an intervening technocrat. The only possible political paradigm for this was suggested by Descartes: the way to think is to follow the model of an absolute monarch possessed of an undivided sovereignty and consulting no traditions or mediating influences.[19] But this is not politics in the ancient sense that is invoked, but rather the technological and biopolitical control of populations. This is of one piece with Descartes' entirely novel pursuit of a truth so amoral and so apolitical that it would remain true (in a wholly new sense of "true," entirely

---

17. See Milbank, "What Lacks is Feeling: Hume versus Kant and Habermas" in *Habermas and Religion,* 322–46.

18. On this point see Brague, *Les Ancres Dans Le Ciel: L'Infrastructure Métaphysique,* 30–54.

19. Descartes, *Discourse on the Method,* Part Two, 12.

divorced from its ancient links to being and goodness), even if the apparent order of the cosmos was the trickery of a demon.[20]

But the attitude of ancient philosophy, East and West, and of most medieval thought was different. The philosopher had both to see aright and to live well, and he could not do one without the other. It was because philosophy involved ethos as well as vision that it was to some degree esoteric and incommunicable: you had to join in and join with a whole culture if you were really to "get it."[21] This meant that politics was viewed ontologically and the cosmos politically. If one rejected that interchange, then, like Thucydides or the sophists, one espoused a duality of *physis* and *nomos*, a duality of meaningless nature versus imposed culture.[22] By contrast, as Giorgio Agamben has argued, the fusion of metaphysical with political discourse was intensified by biblical influence in Philo, the New Testament, and the church fathers. Being was now personal and law-giving—"natural law" was no longer an oxymoron as it often was for the pagan Greeks.[23] Inversely, the *politeia* had to be a microcosm of cosmic order, like the temple at Jerusalem.

For this outlook, which I would argue is in keeping with ordinary human thought, to think at all is to think God. So once more it is not that we should first defend the reality of mind and of human uniqueness and then try to erect a ladder from this to the absolute. It is instead to realize that every spontaneous thought transgressively goes from fact to value, and receives the landscape before it either as gift or as abnormal hostility. And this means that all thought is either the experience of the arrival of the divine or of the disruption of the demonic. To get rid of this "magical" dimension of thought and language as receiving the real as good or evil is simply to leave oneself with no way to defend the irreducibility of the mental against the physiological.

Hence to think at all is automatically to receive being as the good or else as but deficiently itself. In this way all ontology is spontaneously politicized in the manner of all ancient human societies and of Shakespeare's plays: today, the cosmic order is operating well or not and influencing the human sphere for good or ill. Inversely, politics is naturally ontologized. Not only must politics take account of human and other natures, but also, in imagining a future improved good it sustains a kind of performative

---

20. Descartes, *Meditations on First Philosophy*, First Meditation, 22.

21. See Hadot, *What is Ancient Philosophy?*; Milne, *The Mystical Cosmos*.

22. See Sahlins, *The Western Illusion of Human Nature*.

23. Agamben, *The Kingdom and the Glory: For a Theological Genealogy of Economy and Government*, 68–108.

ontological argument: the best imaginable society has to include its own existence, therefore it can exist—or even has and will exist, if we live in a divinely governed reality.

Traditionally, the consideration of the soul lay at the exact juncture of these two realities: a politicized cosmos and an ontologized politics. For the soul is at once "in a manner all things" as knower, and governs itself and other creatures as mover. To know correctly it must value things correctly—which can only spring from a true self-cultivation. To act correctly it must imagine well, according to both the nature of things and their teleological betterment—for which once more the "better" must include actual instantiation.

To separate these ontological and political aspects of the soul is to erect the modern duality of nature over-against mind. It is to suggest that mind knows a world without value on the one hand and posits for itself values with no grounding in reality on the other. It is to abolish metaphysics in favor of the manipulation of nature unconstrained by values that constitute essences, and it is to abolish politics in favor of technocracy and pop culture. For the only objective aspect of the political process will now be the manipulation also of humans (of course, by other, privileged human beings) as part of nature, while all else will be handed over to whim, giving license to a kind of demonic sustaining of degenerate habits, not just beyond their natural shelf-life, but seemingly in all perpetuity. One-dimensional science to the sound-track of bad music is then one's cultural lot.

By contrast, the ancient and medieval understanding of soul saw it not as a site of spectating or of controlling, but rather as a microcosmic pivot that mediated pure mind all the way down to pure matter and back up again. Equally, it mediated between the fixed and the mutable, which included a relating of ontology to politics. Thus if, in the *Republic*, Plato's arguments for the right political order are psychological ones, then, equally, his arguments for the right psychic order are political ones. Were there no transcendent realm of forms, then the power exercised by *nous* over *thumos* and *epithumia*, the power of reason over force and desire, would have no legitimacy: the sophists would be right and it would be but a more wheedling and dissembling higher power in disguise. This follows because the measure of mind is its power to keep all the other faculties in the right place, yet *nous* itself only has a right place and a distinct job to do if it can contemplate the forms and on the basis of this vision know not just the right spatial positionings of psychic faculties and civic roles, but also the right new configurations of these things and the right action for the performers of these roles at the right moment in the shifting course of time.[24] If there is no eternal pattern of truth, however hard to discern, then thought reduces to more subtle force and more refined but meaningless self-delectation.

At this point one can illustrate again the way in which nature and divinity are natural allies against the modern alienation of the mental. Tradition spoke little of consciousness and much more of *synaesthesia* or self-sensing: what Daniel Heller-Roazen calls "the inner touch."[25] For this reason it was much more open than the post-Cartesian era to seeing quasi-human and proto-rational functions at work in animals. What Catherine Pickstock nicely dubs "the naturalism of the ancients" was far less frenetically preoccupied with showing the absolute difference of humans from animals than are modern apologists.[26] This was just because they thought that reason suffused the cosmos—or was the very work of reason, once one had the doctrine of creation *ex nihilo*. Equivalently to the relative elevation of animals, they built human reason and consciousness on a base of sensory reflexivity. Thought was an intensification of this: it was a more complete "return to self." But as such it remained an ecstatic reach out to things and a literal bringing of the forms of things within the human mental space.

Augustine is sometimes read as proto-Cartesian. Yet in the *De Libero Arbitrio*, he sees human reason as an additionally reflective awareness, not just that we sense, but that we have the awareness that we can sense our sensing and thus an ability to direct and control it. As with Plato, this would be an entirely naturalistic account *unless* one invokes the dimension of cosmic, or in this case divine, government. For this doubled reflection might be just an intensified animality and greater power to fulfill our animal instincts. How can we know that in fact it exercises a higher power of *judgment*? Augustine's answer is entirely cosmopolitical: our reason is proved, he says, by our power *to tame and govern animals*.[27] But even this could be mere higher animal tyranny were we not divinely illumined, did we not participate in the mind of God, which is non-animal and non-animated (above the psychic), both as purely spiritual and as eternal, unmoving and independent of anything outside itself.

Mind, according to both Aristotle and Aquinas, is but one power of the soul: it is not its essence, as for Descartes. It is, as it were, a spin-off from the psychic reality of forming the body and providing the spring of motion.

24. See Pickstock, *After Writing: On the Liturgical Consummation of Philosophy*, 3–46, and Planinc, *Plato's Political Philosophy; Prudence in the Republic and The Laws*.

25. Heller-Roazen, *The Inner Touch*, passim.

26. Pickstock, "What is Given? Truth, Mind, World and Arrival" (unpublished).

27. Augustine, *De Libero Arbitrio*, Book One, 7. And see the whole of books One and Two.

Already in Aristotle mind is a kind of superaddition, almost a kind of grace, since it concerns a teleological lure of the soul beyond the merely psychic, indeed a participation in eternal divine self-thinking, according to the *De Anima*.[28] Yet this "proper accidentality" of mind, as underscored by Aquinas, still pervades the entire operation of the psychic, raising its animality to a new level. The seemingly extra is actually the most fundamental, since teleology implies an eschatology—a drawing of natures finally beyond themselves within a cosmic order, yet in a way that most defines their essences.

Such teleology would seem to be unavoidable if we are to explain how mind is in continuity with nature and yet exceeds the rest of the natural altogether. Its higher value must somehow be naturally intended, else souls dissolve into mere mind and mind itself evaporates. Consciousness, animal self-sensing, animal and human valuation, plus the idea that language and science give the "truth of things" in a way that is not just another mutation of things, all require, as the atheist philosopher Thomas Nagel argues, the invocation of teleology, else these realities must be deemed but illusory epiphenomena.[29]

Therefore, one can conclude, that if one is to defend the irreducibility of mind one must from the outset defend the reality of soul, which means to defend the microcosm and pivot of a divinely ordered cosmos. The soul reaches down into the darkest natural depth of things and yet up to the most ethereal heights. And outside this suspension we cannot understand ourselves as "thinking" at all.

For this reason it is impossible to achieve a non-dualism and to overcome both the double myth of the given and also correlationalism merely in ways that are post-metaphysical, phenomenological, analytical, and non-teleological. For thereby one is always left with two inexplicable and separate sources of life and understanding, however this may be nuanced. Kant, at least before the biological and once more metaphysically teleological (and therefore post-critical) turn of the *Opus Postumum*, posits independent sources of reception and spontaneity. In Hegel and idealism these become inexplicably original dialectical poles; in Heidegger the obscure gaze of *Dasein* on its own alienated animality and the unexplained correlation of an arbitrarily chosen mood with Being as such. In Wittgenstein, on pain of skepticism, transcendental patterns of grammar disclose and guide a region

---

28. Aristotle, *De Anima*, 415a 30–415b: "For this is the most natural of functions among living creatures . . . to reproduce one's kind . . . in order that they may have a share in the immortal and divine in the only way that they can (*in tou aei kai tou theoin metexosin e dunantai*)."

29. Nagel, *Mind and Cosmos: Why the Materialist Neo-Darwinian Conception of Nature is Almost Certainly False*.

of nature. More recently, in Hubert Dreyfus's misreading of Merleau-Ponty, unconscious habits become pure unthought vitalities, while his opponent John McDowell makes the opposite mistake of reading the always-presupposed involvements of thought in sensation and action as the intervention of unexplained categorial constraints (however newly fluid) imposed upon material processes that are still in the end just received by us by a process of sheer efficient causality.[30]

So in slight disagreement with Charles Taylor I do not think that we can overcome representationalism and correlationism in a non-reductive rather than materialist fashion merely by invoking the refinements of Kantianism as phenomenology and linguistic analysis.[31] As Christian theologians and philosophers we must admit there exists no such apologetic crutch to lean on. No way of securing the human along with other humanists in the hope that we will eventually lure them to God. Instead, we have to take posthumanism more seriously than this—as the enemy that is also our dialectical friend. For it is demonstrable, as I have explained, that we need God and notions of divine government from the outset if we are to defend the soul and then mind in its train. Hence our modern allies are not Kant and all that follows in his wake, but rather Hume read otherwise and romantically (with very diverse if complementary emphases) by Jacobi in Germany and de Biran in France.[32] This twin legacy allows us to rethink the perennial soul and cosmology in yet more dynamic, more corporeal, and more faith-imbued terms than was attained by the ancients and the medievals.

In this way we can resume the pre-critical psychic and the pre-critically metaphysical. Not by a spurious spiritualization, but exactly by showing that modernity and its proud suspicions have failed to inhabit the body, to respect matter or to regard nature.

## Bibliography

Agamben, Giorgio. *The Kingdom and the Glory: For a Theological Genealogy of Economy and Government*. Translated by Lorenzo Chiesa. Stanford, CA: Stanford University Press, 2011.

Aristotle. *De Anima*. Translated with an introduction and notes by Mark Shiffman. Indianapolis, IN: Focus, 2011.

Augustine, Saint. *De Libero Arbitrio* [On Free Choice and the Will]. Translated by Thomas Williams. Indianapolis, IN: Hackett, 1993.

---

30. Dreyfus, "The Myth of the Pervasiveness of the Mental"; McDowell, "The Myth of the Mind as Detached" in Schear, ed., *Mind, Reason and Being-in-the-World*, 41–58.

31. Taylor, "Retrieving Realism" in *Mind, Reason and Being in the World*, 61–90.

32. See Milbank, "What Lacks is Feeling."

Bichat, Xavier. *Recherches Physiologiques sur La Vie et La Mort (première partie)*. Paris: Flammarion, 1994.

Brague, Rémi. *Les Ancres Dans Le Ciel: L'Infrastructure Métaphysique*. Paris: Seuil, 2011.

Descartes, René. *Discourse on Method and Meditations on First Philosophy*, 4th ed. Translated by Donald A. Cress. Indianapolis, IN: Hackett, 1998.

Dreyfus, Hubert L. "The Myth of the Pervasiveness of the Mental." In *Mind, Reason, and Being-in-the-World*, edited by Joseph K. Schear, 15–40. London: Routledge, 2013.

Hadot, Pierre. *What is Ancient Philosophy?* Translated by Michael Chase. Cambridge: Harvard University Press, 2002.

Heller-Roazen, Daniel. *The Inner Touch: Archaeology of a Sensation*. New York: Zone, 2007.

Henry, Michel. *Phénoménologie matérielle*. Paris: PUF, 1990.

Janicaud, Dominique. *Ravaisson et La Métaphysique: Une Généalogie Du Spriritualisme Français*. Paris: Vrin, 1997.

Maine de Biran, François-Pierre-Gonthier. *Influence de l'habitude sur la faculté de penser*. Paris: L'Harmattan, 2006.

———. *Nouvelles Considérations sur les Rapports du Physique et du Moral de l'Homme*. Edited by Victor Cousin. Brussels: Hauman, 1841.

McDowell, John. "The Myth of the Mind as Detached." In *Mind, Reason, and Being-in-the-World*, edited by Joseph K. Schear, 61-90. London: Routledge, 2013.

Meillassoux, Quentin. *Après la Finitude: Essai sur la nécessité de la contingence*. Paris: Seuil, 2006.

Merleau-Ponty, Maurice. *L'Œil et l'Esprit*. Paris: Gallimard, 1964.

———. *The Visible and the Invisible*. Translated by Alphonso Lingis. Evanston, IL: Northwestern University Press, 1968.

Milbank, John. "The Soul of Reciprocity Part Two: Reciprocity Granted." *Modern Theology* 17.4 (2001) 485–509.

———. "What Lacks Is Feeling: Hume versus Kant and Habermas." In *Habermas and Religion*, edited by Craig Calhoun, Eduardo Mendieta, and Jonathan VanAntwerpen, 322-46. Harvard: Harvard University Press, 2013.

Milne, Joseph. *The Mystical Cosmos*. London: Temenos Academy, 2013.

Montero, Barbara. "A Dancer Reflects." In *Mind, Reason, and Being-in-the-World*, edited by Joseph K. Schear, 303–19. London: Routledge, 2013.

Nagel, Thomas. *Mind and Cosmos: Why the Materialist Neo-Darwinian Conception of Nature is Almost Certainly False*. Oxford: Oxford University Press, 2012.

Pickstock, Catherine. *After Writing: On the Liturgical Consummation of Philosophy*. Oxford: Blackwell, 1998.

———. "What is Given? Truth, Mind, World and Arrival." Unpublished article.

Planinc, Zdravko. *Plato's Political Philosophy; Prudence in the Republic and The Laws*. London: Duckworth, 1991.

Ravaisson, Félix. "Fragments de Ravaisson." In Dominique Janicaud, *Ravaisson et La Métaphysique: Une Généalogie Du Spriritualisme Français*, 236-68. Paris: Vrin, 1997.

———. *Of Habit*. Translated by Clare Carlisle and Mark Sinclair. London: Continuum, 2008.

Sahlins, Marshall. *The Western Illusion of Human Nature*. Chicago: Chicago University Press, 2008.

# SECTION II
# Fracture and Unity

# 5

# "Know Thyself"

## The Soul of Anatomical Dissection

### Kimbell Kornu

### Introduction

In *The Sciences of the Soul*, Fernando Vidal masterfully tells the story of the development of psychology as a discipline. He notes that the eighteenth century was the century of psychology, the empirical science that enables "knowing oneself."[1] He argues that the "science of the soul" grows out of the Aristotelian-Galenic tradition of the Renaissance, evidenced by the introduction of the term *psychologia* by Protestant Scholastics in the later sixteenth century. On the one hand, the Aristotelian tradition maintains that body and soul are a unity, whereas the Galenic emphasizes the importance of anatomy for understanding physiology, on the other. Philip Melanchthon synthesizes these insights to ground the importance of anatomy for understanding the workings of the soul as the seat for human action and morality. Thus, the science of anatomy plays a key role in the knowledge of the soul.[2] In other words, anatomy allows one to "know thyself."

1. Vidal, *Sciences of the Soul*, 1–20.
2. Ibid., 21–47.

Contrast this Renaissance development with the ancient notion of the Delphic maxim, as seen in the Platonic dialogues. In *Charmides*, Critias equates "know thyself" with the virtue of temperance. In Socrates' interpretation, temperance is a science of oneself.[3] In *Alcibiades*, Socrates regards "know thyself" as knowledge of one's soul.[4] In *Phaedrus*, Socrates understands "know thyself" to be knowledge of one's own human nature, which is either a complicated beast or a simple animal with a share of the divine.[5] Clearly absent in the Socratic notion is knowledge of anatomy, as contrasted by the sixteenth-century anatomical illustrations that are accompanied by *Nosce teipsum*.

How does the "know thyself" maxim undergo such a radical transformation from antiquity to the early modern period? Since Vidal begins in the early modern period, his account does not address this important shift. I argue that a developing "anatomical rationality"[6] contributes to this mutation, already starting in antiquity. The etymology of anatomy comes from Greek *anatomē*, meaning "to dissect or cut up." Cutting up as a methodology begins with anatomical investigations of the human body to further knowledge of natural philosophy and medicine, evidenced by Aristotle and Galen respectively.[7] I then argue that it takes on a broadened semantic range applied to knowledge in general. In this way, anatomical rationality means an attitude toward reality whereby knowledge is acquired through the cutting up of the object of inquiry into its parts. I show that this anatomical rationality as applied to the study of man, both body and soul, results in a transformation of self-knowledge. To this end, I will briefly trace the transformation of the paradigm of anatomical rationality from antiquity to the early modern period by looking at the changing relationship between anatomical dissection and self-knowledge through historical sketches of Galen, Avicenna, and Philip Melanchthon.

---

3. Plato, *Charmides*, 164d-e, 165d.
4. Plato, *Alcibiades*, 132c.
5. Plato, *Phaedrus*, 229e-230a.
6. I borrow this term from French, *Dissection and Vivisection*, although I use the term more broadly.
7. For useful introductions see Cosans, "Aristotle's Anatomical Philosophy," 311–39; Carlino, *Books of the Body*, 121–28.

## Birth of the Anatomical Rationality[8]

Galen, the great second-century philosopher-physician, highly valued anatomical knowledge, both for physicians and philosophers. In *On Anatomical Procedures*, a practical anatomy manual, Galen gives several applications for anatomical knowledge: (1) love of knowledge for its own sake; (2) demonstration of the teleology of Nature; (3) investigation of mental and physical functions; and (4) surgical practice.[9] The first two applications serve theoretical purposes for philosophers, while the latter two are practical for physicians. For Galen, the best physicians are also philosophers with anatomical knowledge.[10] He advises prospective patients seeking the best physician first to "find out how wide his knowledge is and how penetrative is his training in anatomy."[11] Following Hippocrates, he regards accurate knowledge of the body as the starting-point for the whole of medicine.[12] All medical practice is grounded upon anatomical knowledge, which is obtained through anatomical dissection.[13] In other words, without anatomical knowledge, one cannot be an effective physician.[14]

Yet, while anatomical knowledge is necessary, it is not sufficient to be a good physician. In Galen's *The Best Doctor is Also a Philosopher*, the true physician knows all the parts of philosophy: logic, physics, and ethics. Following the Hippocratic ideal, Galen places a high value on ethics, not just for

---

8. The best pre-Galenic example of the anatomical rationality that relates knowledge of the soul and anatomical dissection is the pseudepigraphical story of Hippocrates and Democritus. The council of Abdera summons Hippocrates, the divine physician, to heal Democritus from what is thought to be madness. Hippocrates finds Democritus with poor hygiene, emaciated, and surrounded by papyrus scrolls and dissected animals. Yet, when Democritus speaks, he is pleasant and highly rational. Ironically, he declares that he is writing a treatise on madness. He cuts up animals to look for the nature and location of gall, the build up of which was believed to be the cause of dementia in humans. He later admits that he should look to men themselves for the cause of madness by opening up men's homes to see what is happening inside, acting as a surrogate for opening up men's souls. Hippocrates, *Pseudepigraphic Writings*, 73–93.

9. Galen, *On Anatomical Procedures*, 33–34.

10. Galen, "The Best Doctor," 30–34.

11. Galen, *On Examinations*, quoted in Rocca, "Anatomy," 242.

12. Galen, "The Best Doctor," 30.

13. Tieleman, "Methodology," 53.

14. Galen loosely identifies with the Dogmatist school of medicine, which affirmed the importance of anatomy to guide medical reasoning and therapeutics, in contrast to the Empiricist and Methodist schools, which had no need for anatomy. For ancient accounts of the various schools of medicine, see Galen, *Three Treatises*; Celsus, *De Medicina*, Prooemium 1–75. For a modern account, see Edelstein, *Ancient Medicine*, 173–203.

medical practice, but also for the physician himself. The manner in which Galen discusses ethics is akin to Pierre Hadot's notion that philosophy is a spiritual exercise and a way of life.[15] For Galen, because the goal of the art of medicine is the common good, the physician must possess the cardinal virtues of justice, temperance, courage, and wisdom. In a treatise on the affections and errors of the soul, Galen meditates on the Delphic maxim to "know thyself."[16] "Know thyself" during Galen's era meant knowledge of one's own soul and measure, including one's limitations, mortality, and faults, as an embodied person.[17] As a youth he thought the injunction to be excessive, but in his maturity he found this to be justified. Only the wisest of men know themselves fully. Truly knowing oneself is one of the hardest things to do, for it is a lifelong discipline of hard work that must be pursued in the context of friends who can point out when one's soul is in error.[18] But this growth in wisdom holds out the greatest reward: "the wise man is like a god."[19] One could say that, for Galen, "know thyself" is a concise injunction for divinization. The pursuit of wisdom is required to be a good physician and to be a good human being.

So far we have seen that Galen places utmost importance upon anatomical knowledge and self-knowledge as necessary for medicine and philosophy. Galen employs an anatomical rationality by utilizing anatomical dissection to investigate the nature, function, and location of the soul. Nowhere does Galen attempt to prove the existence of the soul, but rather he simply assumes its existence. He holds that the soul shares an interdependent relationship with the body. On the one hand, the soul is the form of the body, making the body dependent on the soul.[20] On the other hand, there is a dependence of the soul and its faculties on the mixtures[21] of the bodies in which they reside.[22] Thus, the soul's capacities correspond to the mixtures of the bodily organs and those same capacities use the bodily organs

---

15. Hadot, *Philosophy as a Way of Life*; Hadot, *What Is Ancient Philosophy?*
16. Galen, "The Affections and Errors," 101.
17. Wilkins, *Delphic Maxims*, 52–69. According to Wilkins, there is only one instance where "know thyself" refers to knowledge of the body which leads to knowledge of the soul (Julian, *Or.* vi. 183b–c, 190b), ibid., 62.
18. Galen, "The Affections and Errors," 116, 106.
19. Ibid., 104. Galen is likely drawing from the Hippocratic and Platonic traditions: "For a physician who is a lover of wisdom is the equal of a god." Hippocrates, "Decorum"; and Plato, *Phaedrus* 249c–d.
20. Galen, *On the Usefulness*, 67.
21. In ancient medicine, the mixtures are hot, cold, wet, and dry. For Galen's most extensive treatment of mixture theory, see Galen, "Mixtures," 202–89.
22. Galen, "The Soul's Dependence, 157.

to perform the functions of the living thing.[23] However, Galen maintains his agnosticism about the nature and essence of the soul, chiefly on the question of the immortality of the rational part of the soul, because he does not think that this can be demonstrated based on his rational, scientific method, that is, his anatomical rationality.

Despite agnosticism about the nature and essence of the soul, he thinks that the function and location of the soul can be scientifically demonstrated through anatomical dissection, mapping the Platonic tripartition of the rational, spirited, and appetitive parts of the soul onto the physiological organs of the brain, heart, and liver, respectively. In *On the Doctrines of Hippocrates and Plato*,[24] he attempts to refute the Stoic view that the heart is the seat of the ruling part of the soul as the source of sensation and voluntary movement in favor of his own using both rational argumentation and empirical observation. He begins with the premise that the organ that contains the ruling part of the soul must initiate every voluntary movement in all parts of the animal and be responsible for sensation. He asks rhetorically, "Where will the proof of all of this come from? Where else other than from dissections?"[25] Anatomical dissection and experimentation make evident by ocular demonstration what would otherwise be hidden to the senses and the mind, providing absolute clarity that the vessels originating from the heart have nothing to do with sensation and voluntary movement, which instead are attributed to the nerves arising from the brain.[26] Based on his anatomical findings, he develops two premises: (1) "where the source of the nerves is, there too is the ruling part of the soul"; and (2) "the origin of the nerves is in the brain."[27] Therefore, he concludes, the ruling part of the soul resides in the brain. Galen's anatomical rationality and scientific reasoning already anticipates modern neuroscience, which correlates functions of the body with locations in the brain, with the premise that the soul is localizable and that there is nothing beyond the material.

Having established that the ruling part of the soul resides in the brain, he then argues for the interrelationship between the soul, ethics, and virtue

23. Donini, "Psychology," 185.

24. Galen, *On the Doctrines*. Hereafter, *PHP*, followed by book number.

25. *PHP*, II, quoted in Donini, "Psychology," 190.

26. As an experimental example, Galen famously performed public anatomies for the Romans to demonstrate this anatomical rationality by severing the recurrent laryngeal nerve in a living, squealing pig thereby silencing it. See Galen, *On Anatomical Procedures*, 208–9. For a more detailed narrative, see Mattern, *Prince of Medicine*, 147–48. For more on the performative dimensions of Galen's anatomical demonstrations, see Gleason, "Shock and Awe, 85–114.

27. *PHP*, VIII, quoted in Donini, "Psychology," 191.

in the appropriately titled work, *That the Faculties of the Soul Depend on the Mixtures of the Body*. While Galen pleaded agnosticism on the nature and essence of the rational soul, it appears that he tended toward a physicalist direction. Recruiting Plato, Aristotle, and particularly Hippocrates for his purposes, he argues that the mixtures of the body directly influence the faculties of the soul, such as character, virtue, intellect, and understanding. Mixtures are affected by both nature and nurture (to use anachronistic terminology). Galen thinks that mixture accounts for natural differences in children's temperaments and abilities as well as for environmental effects such as nutrition, medications, seasonal changes, and certain kinds of training and education. The foundational therapeutic regimen in ancient medicine is the manipulation of nutrition and environment to ensure proper balance of the humors, which constitutes health. Since physicians are the experts in therapeutics, and souls are directly influenced by the humors of the body, physicians have a role to play in cultivating virtue by improving souls. Galen is so bold as to proclaim that philosophers have something to learn from physicians in cultivating virtue, which is typically the domain of the philosopher:

> So it would be wise of my opponents—those men who are unhappy at the idea that nourishment has this power to make men more or less temperate, more or less continent, brave or cowardly, soft and gentle or violent and quarrelsome—to come to me even now and receive instruction on their diet. They would derive enormous benefit from this in their command of ethics; and the improvement in their intellectual faculties, too, would have an effect on their virtue, as they acquired greater powers of understanding and memory. Apart from food and drink, I would teach them about winds and mixtures in the ambient air, and places, instructing them which to select and which to avoid.[28]

However, Galen is so convinced of the soul's dependence on bodily mixtures, which are, in turn, influenced by environmental factors and unalterable natural constitution at birth, that he seems to paint a deterministic picture of human character, where the will plays a minimal role in the cultivation of virtue while medical therapeutics plays a large one. Consequently, he advocates for a proto-biopolitics that exalts medical intervention to improve virtue and social usefulness for the sake of the common good and supports the killing of the "irredeemably wicked" from the body politic because their souls are beyond repair:

28. Galen, "The Soul's Dependence," 169.

We even kill the irredeemably wicked, and for three good reasons: so that they may not harm us while they live; as a deterrent to others like them, who will fear punishment for their crimes; and, thirdly, because it is actually better from their point of view to die, when their souls have been so severely damaged that they can no longer benefit from training at the hands of the Muses, nor be improved by Socrates, or even by Pythagoras.[29]

Indeed, for Galen, if wicked souls are beyond the help of medicine, then they are beyond hope for the common good.

## Maturing the Anatomical Rationality

Galen bequeaths to the subsequent medical tradition an unintended *aporia*. On the one hand, his philosophical sensibility valued the singular importance of lifelong growth in wisdom encapsulated in the maxim "know thyself," highlighting the vital role of the will in the process of perfecting oneself. On the other hand, his medical sensibility developed such a sharp anatomical rationality that he tended toward a quasi-deterministic, physicalist physiology only amenable to medical intervention. Avicenna, the great eleventh-century physician-philosopher,[30] addresses this *aporia* in attempting to synthesize the Aristotelian philosophical tradition with the Galenic medical tradition, leading to profound consequences. Avicenna exerted considerable influence on Islamic and Western medicine and philosophy with *The Canon of Medicine*[31] and *The Book of the Healing*. Yet, it is through his philosophical work that Avicenna transforms anatomical rationality and self-knowledge. I will briefly address each in turn.

First, I will sketch how Avicenna develops a different anatomical rationality that does not deal with the anatomy of the body as such, but rather the anatomy of being.[32] Avicenna receives Aristotle's *Metaphysics* through

---

29. Ibid., 173.

30. In his autobiography, Avicenna does not shy away from proclaiming his own precocious brilliance as a physician: "Medicine is not one of the difficult sciences, and therefore I excelled in it in a very short time, to the point that distinguished physicians began to read the science of medicine under me. I cared for the sick and there opened to me some of the doors of medical treatment that are indescribable and can be learned only from practice. In addition I devoted myself to jurisprudence and used to engage in legal disputations, at that time being sixteen years old." In Avicenna and Juzjani, *The Life of Ibn Sina*, 25–27.

31. The *Canon* continued to be used as a medical textbook in European medical curricula as late as 1650. See Siraisi, *Avicenna in Renaissance Italy*.

32. Cf. Nasr, "Anatomy of Being." Nasr uses the phrase "anatomy of being," but not

two distinct interpretive positions, each representing a particular side of an *aporia* that appears to arise from Aristotle's text.[33] On the one hand, Al-Kindi understood metaphysics chiefly as a "divine science" with God being its primary subject matter, whereas Al-Farabi defined metaphysics rather as the science of being *qua* being, on the other.[34] Avicenna's solution to this *aporia* employs Aristotle's *Categories* and the methodology of Aristotle's *Posterior Analytics* and ontologizes them for his own *Metaphysics*.[35] Avicenna's goal is to obtain clear and certain knowledge of the underlying causes of reality. To this end, he discards dialectic and instead relies upon demonstration via Aristotelian logic applied to being as such as the surest way to knowledge. This is clearly at odds with the notion of ancient philosophy as pursuit of wisdom that we have seen with Galen.

As Amos Bertolacci has shown, Avicenna's ontology becomes logicized. Close overlap between his logic and metaphysics results in an "'ontologization' of logic" that is "compatible with a conception of logic as universal tool for knowledge, coextensive with philosophy understood as general ontology, and therefore partially overlapping with metaphysics understood as the science of being qua being."[36] Avicenna's logicized ontology consequently broadens the notion of "anatomical rationality," but remains true to the original semantic range. Recall that the Greek etymology of anatomy is "to cut up." In what I call Avicenna's "*anatomia entis*," anatomical dissection includes abstract concepts, not just concrete objects.[37] Logical

---

in the same sense that I employ it here.

33. For more on the *aporia* of being in Aristotle, see Booth, *Aristotelian Aporetic Ontology*; Dumont, "Scotus's Doctrine of Univocity, 193–212.

34. Bertolacci, *Reception of Aristotle's Metaphysics*, 113.

35. Ibid., 115.

36. Bertolacci, "'Ontologization' of Logic," 51.

37. Owen Barfield similarly claims that analytical method of thought directly leads to physical anatomical dissection, exemplified by the Alexandrians: "On the whole, the Alexandrians probably collected, arranged, and renewed the meanings of more words than they actually created. This is even truer in the case of medicine. The analytical method of thought led naturally in Alexandria to the actual dissection of bodies, living and dead. Aristotle himself is still regarded as the founder of comparative anatomy (cutting up) and it was he who first used this word in its medical sense." Barfield, *History in English Words*, 108. Cf. Ernest Gellner who explicitly charges analytic philosophy with dissecting abstract concepts like dissecting an organism, although he does not make the semantic connection with anatomy. Gellner, "Analysis and Ontology," 408–15; Gellner, *Words and Things*. For explicit use of "anatomy" and "dissection" applied to logical analysis, see Wittgenstein, *Tractatus Logico-Philosophicus*, 16. Cf. Tertullian who assumes the broad semantic range of "dissection" applied to the abstract functional divisions of the soul in *De Anima* 14, entitled "The Soul Variously Divided by the Philosophers; This Division is Not a Material Dissection": "Thus variously is the soul dissected by the

categories are applied to ontology resulting in the logical dissection of being into its constituent parts, with God subsumed under this logicized ontology. The existent is the most universal reality that encompasses even God, whom Avicenna qualifies as a particular type of existent, the Necessary Existent: "There are specific properties that belong individually each to the Necessary Existent and the possible existent. . . . That which in itself is a necessary existent has no cause, while that which in itself is a possible existent has a cause."[38] In this way, all being is neatly categorized and known through the operations of the mind via mental dissection. As Bertolacci shows, such mental dissection can even prove God's existence: "The remainder of I, 6 and chapter I, 7 [of *The Metaphysics of The Healing*] are mainly devoted to provide an investigation of the Necessary Existent based on the sole analysis of concepts. In this way Avicenna shows that metaphysics is able to prove the existence of the Necessary Existent, or First Principle, without taking into account sensible data."[39] As Avicenna's use of metaphysical necessity and possibility testifies, Taneli Kukkonen regards *The Metaphysics* "as initiating a new phase in the history of Western ontology: it constitutes the first real stab at a modal metaphysics in the Western tradition . . . ."[40] Avicenna's logical dissection of the anatomy of being becomes the paradigm for all knowledge of reality, and thereby also provides the grammar for the practice of anatomical dissection.

Now I will turn to how Avicenna's psychological theory develops a different notion of "know thyself" (although he does not use the term) by rejecting Aristotle's theory of knowledge and by modifying Aristotle's doctrine of the soul, adumbrating a proto-Cartesian substance dualism and a proto-mental representation theory of cognition. Robert Hall has argued that Avicenna's "psychological theory is really the spine of the [philosophical] system,"[41] influenced by his medical learning. The Islamic medical tradition that Avicenna received drew heavily from Greek medicine in a largely Galenic form. However, Galen's physiological psychology by Avicenna's time had become materialist. Avicenna responded indirectly, arguing for the immateriality of the soul in order to safeguard his theory of knowledge and

---

different schools. Such divisions, however, ought not to be regarded so much as parts of the soul, as powers, or faculties, or operations thereof, even as Aristotle himself has regarded some of them as being." Tertullian, "Treatise on the Soul," 193.

38. Avicenna, *The Metaphysics*, I.6.

39. Bertolacci, *Reception of Aristotle's Metaphysics*, 171.

40. Kukkonen, "Dividing Being," 37. In this sense, one could say that Avicenna is the long forerunner to the sensibility of analytic philosophy, which places the philosopher at a distance from the object of inquiry.

41. Hall, "Intellect, Soul and Body," 63.

the immortality of the soul. He defines the soul as the principle of action following volition.[42] However, he does not call the soul the form of the body, but rather its perfection, because he wants to protect the soul's immortality. Avicenna's most famous argument for the soul's immateriality and the non-identity of the self with the body is his "Flying Man" thought experiment.[43] It goes like this: imagine a man, newly created in an instant, who appears in a void such that no parts of his body are touching each other and he cannot feel the air, completely deprived of all sensation. While he cannot feel his own body, nevertheless, he has certain awareness of the existence of his own self without asserting its own extensionality. Thus, concludes Avicenna, the bodily members are like clothes to the self. He calls the "I" that which aims to know about himself as self. For Avicenna, then, "know thyself" goes in a rationalist, disembodied direction that anticipates Descartes' *cogito* by 600 years.[44] In contrast to Aristotle, who espouses an interdependence of soul as the form of the body, in Avicenna's conception, the body is only an instrument for the soul to grow in knowledge and ascent. In the state of blessedness there is no need for the body, for the latter distracts the soul from its perfection in pure contemplation.[45] Avicenna opens the door to conceiving the nature of the human person as the conjunction of an animated corpse inhabited by the actual person, the essence of which is the soul, the "I."

Avicenna further develops Aristotle's faculty psychology by incorporating Galen's more physiological approach, yet departs from Aristotle's notion that knowledge entails the identity of the soul and the object known,[46] arguing that such a theory is impossible on the grounds of numerical identity.[47] Instead, he opts for increasing levels of abstraction of the form from the object that the faculties of the soul retain as an image. While the idea of "abstraction of form" is clearly Aristotelian, Avicenna makes two novel contributions to the tradition: (1) the notion of internal senses (i.e., sense perception that does not require the use of the external five senses) and (2) the corresponding notions of intention and representation. It has been shown that the scholastic philosophical terms for intention[48] and represen-

---

42. Avicenna, *Avicenna's De anima*, I.1. See the useful translation by McGinnis and Reisman, *Classical Arabic Philosophy*, 175–209.

43. See Marmura, "Avicenna's 'Flying Man,'" 383–95, which summarizes and reviews all three versions of the "Flying Man" in the Avicennian corpus.

44. Wisnovsky, *Avicenna's Metaphysics*, 155–56. See also Hasse, *Avicenna's De Anima*, 81–92; Druart, "Soul and Body Problem," 27–49.

45. Avicenna, *Avicenna's De anima*, V.5.

46. Cf. Aristotle, *De anima* III.5, 430a.19–20; and III.7, 431a.1.

47. Avicenna, *Avicenna's De anima*, V.6.

48. Of course, intention as a philosophical concept is reintroduced into modern

tation were introduced in the twelfth century through the Latin translation of Avicenna's works.[49] Avicenna's notion of intention is illustrated by his classic example of the sheep that senses the intention of the wolf, by which the sheep knows the wolf is dangerous. The intention then becomes a representation in the estimative faculty. However, it should be noted that, for Avicenna, it is the internal senses that represent an image, not the intellect that represents a mental concept. But the notion of a subject, an "I," that apprehends the internal representation as a perceived object becomes part of the grammar of medieval discourse on psychology. Representation undergoes transformation through the medieval scholastics culminating in Ockham, who makes intention a mental concept that represents an external thing, with the result that the form of the thing has objective existence only in the mind, not extra-mentally.[50] As the initiator of this representational theory of cognition, Avicenna begins paving the road to knowledge as representation.[51]

## Representing the Anatomical Rationality

Now I will turn to the rise of anatomical dissection as a routine practice and how it further transformed the anatomical rationality. Recent scholars have tried to answer the puzzling question why human anatomical dissection arose in medieval Europe after a long silence since antiquity but did not arise in other cultures. I will not attempt to answer that question here.[52] The first anatomy manual appeared in 1316 by Mondino de Luizzi,[53] which inaugurated anatomy instruction in academic medicine and remained influential into the Renaissance.[54] As part of the growing humanism that began to influence medical education, Galen's works were translated from Greek

---

philosophy by Franz Brentano.

49. Gyekye, "Terms 'Prima Intentio' and 'Secunda Intentio,'" 32–38; Spiegelberg, "'Intention' and 'Intentionality,'" 108–27; Lagerlund, "Terminological and Conceptual Roots," 11–32; Tweedale, "Representation," 63–79.

50. Kneale and Kneale, *Development of Logic*, 229, 266.

51. For more on the medieval transformation of knowledge as representation, see Boulnois, *Etre et représentation*.

52. For the various attempts to answer this question, see Sawday, *Body Emblazoned*; Cunningham, *Anatomical Renaissance*; French, *Dissection and Vivisection*; Carlino, *Books of the Body*; Park, *Secrets of Women*.

53. Ketham and dei Luzzi, *Fasciculo Di Medicina*.

54. For example, see the later anatomists, Berengario da Carpi and Alessandro Benedetti. For a sample of their work in English translation, see da Carpi, *Short Introduction to Anatomy*; Lind, *Pre-Vesalian Anatomy*.

into Latin by the early 1500s. Against this intellectual backdrop, Andreas Vesalius published *De humani corporis fabrica libri septem* in 1543,[55] which overturned aspects of Galenic anatomy, marking a watershed moment in anatomical knowledge. Before Vesalius, classic anatomical texts dictated the interpretation of the body, whereas after Vesalius, the visually seen and manually manipulated human body dictated the interpretation of classical texts.[56] In other words, the text of the body took primacy over the text of the book.

In the Preface to *Fabrica* Vesalius calls anatomy the chief branch of natural philosophy and the foundation for medicine.[57] Medical knowledge requires accurate knowledge of anatomy, which is only gained through visualization. Vesalius encouraged all aspiring physicians to learn anatomy through first-hand dissection of the body. As an aid to this learning, the *Fabrica* provided illustrated representations of human anatomy. The *Fabrica* depicted the structure of the human body, while downplaying its function. In contrast, Galen's anatomy was both structural and functional because of its overarching teleology. Whether or not Vesalius intended to do so, the *Fabrica* effectively represented the human body in frozen, static terms, rather than in its functional activity. In a sense, knowledge of the human body is captured on the space of the page, frozen in time.

---

55. Hereafter, *Fabrica*.

56. Carlino, *Books of the Body*.

57. Farrington, "Preface," 1360. Richardson and Carman translate the same phrase "important part of natural philosophy." Vesalius, *On the Fabric of the Human Body*, l. Garrison and Hast translate the phrase "particular branch of natural philosophy" as part of a new translation of Vesalius' *Fabrica*. Daniel Garrison and Malcolm Hast, "De Humani Corporis Fabrica," Northwestern University, accessed December 11, 2013, http://vesalius.northwestern.edu/flash.html; Vesalius, *The Fabric of the Human Body*.

Despite the translation variations which regard anatomy as either the "chief branch of natural philosophy" or simply one branch of many, there are reasons internal to the Preface itself that support the translation "chief branch." At the end of the Preface, Vesalius remarks that the study of anatomy is the most pleasing of all natural philosophy since it enables one to "know thyself," verging on theology, with a direct appeal to the microcosm analogy: "Yet I surmise that out of the entire Apolline discipline of medicine, and indeed all natural philosophy, nothing could be produced more pleasing or welcome to your Majesty [Charles V] than research in which we recognize the body and the spirit, as well as a certain divinity that issues from a harmony of the two, and finally our own selves (which is the true study of mankind). . . . So as it is inescapable that you are uniquely interested in the science of the universe, so you would sometimes be delighted to ponder the construction of the most perfect of all creatures, and take pleasure in considering the lodging place and instrument of the immortal soul—a domicile which, because it admirably resembles the universe in many of its names, was fitly called a microcosm by the ancients" (trans. Garrison and Hast).

With the growth of anatomical knowledge, philosophical psychology also changed during this same period.[58] Park and Kessler note that in the Renaissance, "psychology was seen both as the apex of natural philosophy and as a transition to the higher study of medicine,"[59] with Aristotle's *De anima* as central to the university curriculum. Yet, within both philosophy and medicine, anatomy and physiology began to replace demonstrative Aristotelian natural philosophy as explanatory for the organic soul (that is, the vegetative and animal souls functioning below the level of the rational soul). Rather than disputing the number, location, and functions of the various faculties of the soul, Renaissance philosophers utilized the anatomical knowledge of the day and attributed the faculties of the organic soul to different organs in the body.[60] Not surprisingly, a growing number of philosophers in this period were describing the organic soul as material, extended in space, and divisible.[61] In other words, the organic soul was becoming spatialized. Philosophical psychology had employed an anatomical rationality to answer metaphysical questions.[62]

During the early 1500s, "know thyself" took on an increasingly anatomical application. The anatomical use of the Delphic maxim explodes over the course of the sixteenth century, precisely during the time of Vesalius and Philip Melanchthon. As William Schupbach remarks, "know thyself" became the catch-phrase of anatomy, evidenced by its use with anatomical illustrations.[63] Moreover, at public anatomies anatomists placed a great deal of importance on "know thyself." Before opening up the corpse for dissection, the anatomist would speak of the dignity of man as the microcosm, the peak of creation. Created in God's image, the body of man is raised above the other animals with certain unique anatomical properties as evidence of divine craftsmanship. But in order to gain knowledge of these divine ele-

---

58. The ideas for this paragraph are deeply indebted to Park and Kessler, "Concept of Psychology," 455–63; Park, "Organic Soul," 464–84; Nutton, "Anatomy of the Soul," 136–57.

59. Park and Kessler, "Concept of Psychology," 457.

60. Park, "Organic Soul," 478–79.

61. Ibid., 483.

62. Note the explicit language of Philip Melanchthon: "there has been a great and foolish battle in the schools about the distinction of the faculties. Concerning the organic powers, it is clear that they are distinguished by their organs; for the soul produces different operations in different organs, just as different sounds are produced in different pipes. Thus if anyone wants to enquire into the faculties and actions of the soul, he must know the organs and parts of the body." Melanchthon, *Liber de anima*, quoted in ibid., 479.

63. Schupbach, *Paradox of Rembrandt's*, 31–32. Jonathan Sawday calls the Renaissance a "culture of dissection." Sawday, *Body Emblazoned*, 3.

ments within oneself, it was necessary for man to "know himself," and this required anatomical dissection.[64] In other words, anatomy provided a dual knowledge of God and of oneself. Here we see anatomical rationality and "know thyself" take on a new theological key.[65] After anatomical dissection and an anatomical understanding of "know thyself" are dressed in terms of natural theology, anatomical rationality becomes knowledge of God.

Philip Melanchthon plays a vital role in this genealogy, because he moves the coupling of anatomical rationality and the "know thyself" maxim out of the anatomy theater and into the theology curriculum. Because he holds a high view of the intimate interaction between soul and body, anatomy as knowledge of the body is instrumental for gaining knowledge of the workings of the soul. Furthermore, he thinks that knowledge of anatomy is one of the clearest ways in discerning the divine wisdom with God as architect. Thus, all students in philosophy, theology, and medicine at the University of Wittenberg learned anatomy. In an oration on the life of Galen, Melanchthon recalls, "Galen said that the knowledge of anatomy is the beginning of theology, and the path to the knowledge of God."[66] In his 1540 commentary on Aristotle's *De anima* Melanchthon states:

> At this point truly you think yourself introduced into a temple and a kind of shrine; on this account you ought not to simply look at the material with particular reverence, but to take into consideration the plan and diligence of the Maker. For the scheme of the work bears witness that men do not exist by chance, but take their rise from some infinite Mind which has arranged its individual parts with astonishing care and destined them to certain goals and which has impressed knowledge and mind on it, which is the clearest mark of divinity.[67]

In no uncertain terms, Melanchthon declares the theological importance of anatomy: through anatomical knowledge, the body is a temple

---

64. Some anatomical theaters, particularly those in Holland, were housed in chapels, sometimes taking place on former altars. See Heckscher, *Rembrandt's Anatomy*, 29–34.

65. Cf. Jean Riolan the Younger, French rival to William Harvey, who viewed dissection as "anatomical liturgy." See French, *Dissection and Vivisection*, 237.

66. Melanchthon, *On the Life of Galen*, in Melanchthon, *Orations*, 218. Melanchthon is likely citing this quote from Galen: "Then a work on the usefulness of the parts, which at first seemed to him a thing of scant importance, will be reckoned truly to be the source of a perfect theology, which is a thing far greater and far nobler than all of medicine." Galen, *On the Usefulness*, 731.

67. To the best of my knowledge, there is no modern edition of the *Commentarius*. Melanchthon, *Commentarius de anima*, f. 44v–45r. Translation from Cunningham, *The Anatomical Renaissance*, 231.

where one can visually see the knowledge of God imprinted in its innermost, anatomical parts. In other words, the "clearest mark of divinity" is spatialized onto the anatomical body.

In the 1553 revised edition of his commentary on *De anima* Melanchthon assimilates Vesalius' *Fabrica*, including anatomical sheets to accompany the text. His language regarding the theological importance of anatomical knowledge becomes even stronger:

> looking at this wonderful variety of work and these designs of God from without and through a thick darkness, we are struck dumb and grieve that we cannot look nature and discern causes. But then at last when we discern the "idea" of nature in the divine mind we shall look into that whole machine as if from the inside, and we shall understand the designs of the Maker and the causes of all the divine works. Now, through this incomplete consideration, we know that God is the Architect, and we should be inflamed with desire for that perfected wisdom.[68]

I would like to highlight two things in this quote. First, he describes the human body as a "machine." This manifests the philosophical shift during the Renaissance that attributes various faculties of the soul to different organs of the body. Melanchthon was not alone in calling the human body a machine, but he was the most theologically influential. Secondly, he echoes St. Paul's phrase about seeing in a mirror dimly, meaning that through anatomy we see imperfectly into God's mind as revealed through His divine works, epitomized in the human body. Anatomical knowledge enables direct knowledge of God as architect and the path toward divine "perfected wisdom." Elsewhere in the oration *On Anatomy*, he declares that true wisdom is "recognition of God and the contemplation of nature."[69] In this context Melanchthon appeals explicitly to "know thyself," which he interprets as an admonishment to examine both the wonder that we have in ourselves as the pinnacle of nature and the sources of actions of life. Recall that for Melanchthon, studying anatomy leads to knowledge of how the soul

---

68. Melanchthon, *Corpus Reformatorum*. Translation from Cunningham, *Anatomical Renaissance*, 232. In several places throughout his writings on the soul and anatomy, Melanchthon describes the human body as a machine (*machina*). See Preface to the *Commentary on the Soul* (1540); Preface to the *Book on the Soul* (1553); *On Anatomy* (1550), in Melanchthon, *Orations*, 145–46; 155–56; 160–61, respectively.

69. Melanchthon, *On Anatomy*, in Melanchthon, *Orations*, 164–65.

functions.⁷⁰ Since the soul is also a moral agent, anatomical knowledge is the starting point for moral philosophy.⁷¹

The dual knowledge of God and self through anatomy took on new form with the printing press and the subsequent explosion of anatomical fugitive sheets in the later 1500s by which knowledge becomes spatialized. Vesalius' *Fabrica* was copied and plagiarized into anatomical fugitive sheets for popular consumption.⁷² Anatomical illustrations broadened its popularity because of its corresponding moralistic tone to "know thyself."⁷³ Knowledge of the person that was previously gained through dialogue either with oneself or with another person now can be captured on the space of paper, frozen in time. This cultural development, widely disseminated through the printing press, influences the paradigm for knowledge of the self, which can now be exactly represented in images. By seeing the inner parts of the anatomized body, one can contemplate the divine power. Through anatomical illustrations, one can know oneself and know God.⁷⁴ This provides the conditions for knowledge as exact representation that is fully inaugurated by Descartes with the modern subjective turn.⁷⁵

---

70. The influence of Melanchthon's emphasis on anatomy for knowledge of the soul cannot be overstated. Unlike other contemporary treatises on *De anima*, his commentary included anatomy as central to understanding the soul, comprising up to half of the content. It became one of the most frequently printed commentaries on *De anima* in the sixteenth century. See Kusukawa, *Transformation of Natural Philosophy*, 86. The teaching of anatomy as part of the philosophy and theology course, which he started at Wittenberg, became common at other Protestant universities, such as Glasgow in the 1570s and Edinburgh in the 1580s, persisting into the seventeenth century. See Cunningham, *Anatomical Renaissance*, 233–34.

71. For discussion on how anatomical knowledge becomes the starting point for moral philosophy, see Kusukawa, *Transformation of Natural Philosophy*, 75–123; Nutton, "Wittenberg Anatomy," 11–32.

72. Carlino, *Paper Bodies*, 46–73. Carlino defines anatomical fugitive sheet as "a printed, iconographical and textual genre of their own. Their main characteristic, common to them all throughout the centuries, is to show the human anatomy by means of a printed figure made out of flaps of paper one can lift up, and surrounded with a brief explanatory text." Ibid., 74.

73. The moralistic text with "Nosce teipsum" (know thyself) was found in the preface of nearly all sixteenth-century treatises on human anatomy, inscribed in frontispieces and illustrations, evidenced by varying anatomical fugitive sheets. For an example of a representative *Nosce teipsum* inscription, see the appendix in Carlino, *Paper Bodies*, 333.

74. Ibid., 104–13.

75. For more on spatialization and knowledge as representation as the metaphysics of modernity, especially as it relates to Descartes, see Pickstock, *After Writing*, 47–100.

## Conclusion

Through this brief genealogy of anatomical dissection and "know thyself," I have suggested that "anatomical rationality" plays a major role in the transformation of knowledge. It is birthed with Galen's use of anatomical dissection to search for the location of the soul, matures with Avicenna's logical dissection of being and dissection of soul from body thereby providing the grammar for the practice of anatomical dissection, and becomes fully spatialized in the Renaissance with Vesalius' anatomical illustrations and Melanchthon's anatomical theology. Through this spatialized knowledge of God and self, anatomical rationality paves the way for a distinctly modern approach to know nature in general. The "culture of dissection" provides the intellectual conditions for the anatomical rationality of Francis Bacon's *Novum Organum*, wherein to know nature is to dissect it:

> The human intellect's very nature carries it towards things abstract and to fancying that things fleeting are fixed. But to abstract from nature is not as effective as to dissect it . . . .[76]

> For we are laying the foundations in the human understanding of a true model of the world. . . . But this can be done only by performing a most careful dissection and anatomy of the world.[77]

Indeed, Wordsworth succinctly captures, and laments, the anatomical rationality towards nature in "The Tables Turned":

> Sweet is the lore which Nature brings;
> Our meddling intellect
> Mis-shapes the beauteous forms of things;
> —We murder to dissect.[78]

## Bibliography

Avicenna. *Avicenna's De anima: Being the Psychological Part of Kitab al-Shifa'*. Edited by Fazlur Rahman. London: Oxford University Press, 1959.

———. *The Metaphysics of The Healing: A Parallel English-Arabic Text*. Translated by Michael E. Marmura. Islamic Translation Series. Provo, UT: Brigham Young University Press, 2005.

76. Bacon, *Novum Organum*, 89.
77. Ibid., 96.
78. Wordsworth, *William Wordsworth*, 131.

Avicenna, and ʿAbd al-Wahid Juzjani. *The Life of Ibn Sina: A Critical Edition and Annotated Translation*. Translated by William E. Gohlman. Studies in Islamic Philosophy and Science. Albany, NY: State University of New York Press, 1974.

Bacon, Francis. *The Instauratio Magna Part II: Novum Organum and Associated Texts*. Translated by Graham Rees and Maria Wakely. The Oxford Francis Bacon XI. New York: Oxford University Press, 2004.

Barfield, Owen. *History in English Words*. New ed. London: Faber, 1954.

Berengario da Carpi, Jacopo. *A Short Introduction to Anatomy (Isagogae Breves)*. Translated by L. R. Lind. Chicago: University of Chicago Press, 1959.

Bertolacci, Amos. "The 'Ontologization' of Logic: Metaphysical Themes in Avicenna's Reworking of the Organon." In *Methods and Methodologies: Aristotelian Logic East and West, 500–1500*, edited by Margaret Cameron and John Marenbon, 27–51. Investigating Medieval Philosophy 2. Leiden: Brill, 2011.

———. *The Reception of Aristotle's Metaphysics in Avicenna's Kitab al-Sifa: A Milestone of Western Metaphysical Thought*. Islamic Philosophy, Theology, and Science 63. Leiden; Boston: Brill, 2006.

Booth, Edward. *Aristotelian Aporetic Ontology in Islamic and Christian Thinkers*. New York: Cambridge University Press, 1983.

Boulnois, Olivier. *Etre et représentation: Une généalogie de la métaphysique moderne à l'époque de Duns Scot, XIIIe-XIVe siècle*. 1st ed. Paris: Presses universitaires de France, 1999.

Carlino, Andrea. *Books of the Body: Anatomical Ritual and Renaissance Learning*. Translated by John Tedeschi and Anne C. Tedeschi. Chicago: University of Chicago Press, 1999.

———. *Paper Bodies: A Catalogue of Anatomical Fugitive Sheets, 1538–1687*. Translated by Noga Arikha. Medical History, Supplement No. 19. London: Wellcome Institute for the History of Medicine, 1999.

Celsus. *De Medicina*. Translated by William George Spencer. Vol. 1. 3 vols. Loeb Classical Library. Cambridge: Harvard University Press, 1935.

Cosans, Christopher E. "Aristotle's Anatomical Philosophy of Nature." *Biology and Philosophy* 13.3 (1998) 311–39.

Cunningham, Andrew. *The Anatomical Renaissance: The Resurrection of the Anatomical Projects of the Ancients*. Aldershot, UK: Scolar, 1997.

Donini, Pierluigi. "Psychology." In *The Cambridge Companion to Galen*, edited by R. J. Hankinson, 184–209. Cambridge: Cambridge University Press, 2008.

Druart, Therese-Anne. "The Soul and Body Problem: Avicenna and Descartes." In *Arabic Philosophy and the West: Continuity and Interaction*, 27–49. Washington, DC: Center for Contemporary Arab Studies, Georgetown University, 1988.

Dumont, Stephen D. "Scotus's Doctrine of Univocity and the Medieval Tradition of Metaphysics." In *Was Ist Philosophie im Mittelalter?*, edited by Jan Aertsen and Andreas Speer, 193–212. Miscellanea Mediaevalia 26. New York: de Gruyter, 1998.

Edelstein, Ludwig. *Ancient Medicine: Selected Papers of Ludwig Edelstein*. Edited by Owsei Temkin and C. Lilian Temkin. Translated by C. Lilian Edelstein. Baltimore, MD: Johns Hopkins University Press, 1967.

Farrington, Benjamin. "The Preface of Andreas Vesalius to De Fabrica Corporis Humani 1543." *Proceedings of the Royal Society of Medicine* 25.9 (1932) 1357–1366.

French, Roger K. *Dissection and Vivisection in the European Renaissance*. Brookfield, VT: Ashgate, 1999.

Galen. "The Affections and Errors of the Soul." In *Selected Works*, translated by P. N. Singer, 100–149. Oxford: Oxford University Press, 1997.

———. "The Best Doctor Is Also a Philosopher." In *Selected Works*, translated by P. N. Singer, 30–34. Oxford: Oxford University Press, 1997.

———. "Mixtures." In *Selected Works*, translated by P. N. Singer, 202–89. Oxford: Oxford University Press, 1997.

———. *On Anatomical Procedures: Translation of the Surviving Books with Introduction and Notes*. Translated by Charles Joseph Singer. Publications of the Wellcome Historical Medical Museum 7. London: Oxford University Press, 1956.

———. *On Examinations By Which the Best Physicians Are Recognized*. Translated by A. Z. Iskandar. Corpus medicorum Graecorum, Supplementum orientale 4. Berlin: Akademie-Verlag, 1988.

———. *On the Doctrines of Hippocrates and Plato*. Translated by Phillip De Lacy. 3 vols. Corpus medicorum Graecorum 4. Berlin: Akademie-Verlag, 1978.

———. *On the Usefulness of the Parts of the Body*. Translated by Margaret Tallmadge May. 2 vols. Cornell Publications in the History of Science. Ithaca, NY: Cornell University Press, 1968.

———. "The Soul's Dependence on the Body." In *Selected Works*, translated by P. N. Singer, 150–76. Oxford: Oxford University Press, 1997.

———. *Three Treatises on the Nature of Science*. Translated by Richard Walzer and Michael Frede. Indianapolis, IN: Hackett, 1985.

Gellner, Ernest. "Analysis and Ontology." *The Philosophical Quarterly* 1.5 (1951) 408–15.

———. *Words and Things: An Examination of, and an Attack on, Linguistic Philosophy*. Rev. ed. London: Routledge & Kegan Paul, 1979.

Gleason, Maud. "Shock and Awe: The Performance Dimension of Galen's Anatomy Demonstrations." In *Galen and the World of Knowledge*, edited by Christopher Gill, Tim Whitmarsh, and John Wilkins, 85–114. Greek Culture in the Roman World. New York: Cambridge University Press, 2009.

Gyekye, Kwame. "The Terms 'Prima Intentio' and 'Secunda Intentio' in Arabic Logic." *Speculum* 46.1 (1971) 32–38.

Hadot, Pierre. *Philosophy as a Way of Life: Spiritual Exercises from Socrates to Foucault*. Translated by Arnold I. Davidson. Malden, MA: Blackwell, 1995.

———. *What Is Ancient Philosophy?* Translated by Michael Chase. Cambridge: Belknap Press of Harvard University Press, 2002.

Hall, Robert E. "Intellect, Soul and Body in Ibn Sina: Systematic Synthesis and Development of the Aristotelian, Neoplatonic and Galenic Theories." In *Interpreting Avicenna: Science and Philosophy in Medieval Islam: Proceedings of the Second Conference of the Avicenna Study Group*, edited by Jon McGinnis and David C. Reisman, 62–86. Islamic Philosophy, Theology, and Science: Texts and Studies 56. Leiden: Brill, 2004.

Hasse, Dag Nikolaus. *Avicenna's De Anima in the Latin West: The Formation of a Peripatetic Philosophy of the Soul, 1160–1300*. Warburg Institute Studies and Texts 1. London: Warburg Institute, 2000.

Heckscher, William S. *Rembrandt's Anatomy of Dr. Nicolaas Tulp: An Iconological Study*. New York: New York University Press, 1958.

Hippocrates. *Hippocrates: Volume II*. Translated by W. H. S. Jones. Loeb Classical Library. Cambridge: Harvard University Press, 1923.

———. *Pseudepigraphic Writings: Letters—Embassy—Speech from the Altar—Decree*. Translated by Wesley D. Smith. Leiden: Brill, 1990.

Ketham, Johannes de, and Mondino dei Luzzi. *The Fasciculo Di Medicina: Venice, 1493*. Translated by Sebastiano Manilio and Charles Joseph Singer. 2 vols. Monumenta Medica 2. Florence: Lier, 1925.

Kneale, W. C., and Martha Kneale. *The Development of Logic*. Oxford: Oxford University Press, 1962.

Kukkonen, Taneli. "Dividing Being: Before and After Avicenna." In *Categories of Being: Essays on Metaphysics and Logic*, edited by Leila Haaparanta and Heikki J. Koskinen, 36–61. New York: Oxford University Press, 2012.

Kusukawa, Sachiko. *The Transformation of Natural Philosophy: The Case of Philip Melanchthon*. New York: Cambridge University Press, 1995.

Lagerlund, Henrik. "The Terminological and Conceptual Roots of Representation in the Soul in Late Ancient and Medieval Philosophy." In *Representation and Objects of Thought in Medieval Philosophy*, 11–32. Ashgate Studies in Medieval Philosophy. Aldershot, UK: Ashgate, 2007.

Lind, L. R. *Studies in Pre-Vesalian Anatomy: Biography, Translations, Documents*. Memoirs of the American Philosophical Society v. 10. Philadelphia: American Philosophical Society, 1975.

Marmura, Michael E. "Avicenna's 'Flying Man' in Context." *Monist* 69 (1986) 383–95.

Mattern, Susan P. *The Prince of Medicine: Galen in the Roman Empire*. New York: Oxford University Press, 2013.

McGinnis, Jon, and David C. Reisman, eds. *Classical Arabic Philosophy: An Anthology of Sources*. Indianapolis, IN: Hackett, 2007.

Melanchthon, Philip. *Orations on Philosophy and Education*. Edited by Sachiko Kusukawa. Translated by Christine F. Salazar. Cambridge Texts in the History of Philosophy. Cambridge: Cambridge University Press, 1999.

Melanchthon, Philipp. *Commentarius de anima*. Vitebergæ: Ex officina Petri Seitz, 1540.

———. *Corpus Reformatorum: Philippi Melanthonis opera quae supersunt omnia*. Edited by Carolus Gottlieb Bretschneider. Vol. 13. Halle: Halis Saxonum, 1846.

Nasr, Seyyed Hossein. *An Introduction to Islamic Cosmological Doctrines: Conceptions of Nature and Methods Used for Its Study by the Ikhwān al-Safā, al-Bīrūnī, and Ibn Sīnā*. London: Thames and Hudson, 1978.

Nutton, Vivian. "The Anatomy of the Soul in Early Renaissance Medicine." In *The Human Embryo: Aristotle and the Arabic and European Traditions*, edited by G. R. Dunstan, 136–57. Exeter, UK: University of Exeter Press, 1990.

———. "Wittenberg Anatomy." In *Medicine and the Reformation*, edited by Ole Peter Grell and Andrew Cunningham, 11–32. London: Routledge, 1993.

Park, Katharine. *Secrets of Women: Gender, Generation, and the Origins of Human Dissection*. New York: Zone, 2006.

———. "The Organic Soul." In *The Cambridge History of Renaissance Philosophy*, edited by C. B. Schmitt et al., 464–84. Cambridge: Cambridge University Press, 1988.

Park, Katharine, and Eckhard Kessler. "The Concept of Psychology." In *The Cambridge History of Renaissance Philosophy*, edited by C. B. Schmitt et al., 455–63. Cambridge: Cambridge University Press, 1988.

Pickstock, Catherine. *After Writing: On the Liturgical Consummation of Philosophy*. Oxford: Blackwell, 1998.

Rocca, Julius. "Anatomy." In *The Cambridge Companion to Galen*, edited by R. J. Hankinson, 242–62. Cambridge: Cambridge University Press, 2008.
Sawday, Jonathan. *The Body Emblazoned: Dissection and the Human Body in Renaissance Culture*. London: Routledge, 1995.
Schupbach, William. *The Paradox of Rembrandt's "Anatomy of Dr. Tulp."* Medical History, Supplement No. 2. London: Wellcome Institute for the History of Medicine, 1982.
Siraisi, Nancy G. *Avicenna in Renaissance Italy: The Canon and Medical Teaching in Italian Universities after 1500*. Princeton, NJ: Princeton University Press, 1987.
Spiegelberg, Herbert. "'Intention' and 'Intentionality' in the Scholastics, Brentano and Husserl." In *The Philosophy of Brentano*, translated by Linda L. McAlister, 108–27. London: Duckworth, 1976.
Tertullian. "A Treatise on the Soul." In *Ante-Nicene Fathers*, edited by Alexander Roberts, James Donaldson, and A. Cleveland Coxe, translated by Peter Holmes, 3:181–235. 1885. Reprint. Grand Rapids: Eerdmans, 1953.
Tieleman, Teun. "Methodology." In *The Cambridge Companion to Galen*, edited by R. J. Hankinson, 49–65. Cambridge: Cambridge University Press, 2008.
Tweedale, Martin. "Representation in Scholastic Epistemology." In *Representation and Objects of Thought in Medieval Philosophy*, edited by Henrik Lagerlund, 63–79. Ashgate Studies in Medieval Philosophy. Burlington, VT: Ashgate, 2007.
Vesalius, Andreas. *On the Fabric of the Human Body: Book I, Bones and Cartilages*. Translated by William Frank Richardson and John Burd Carman. San Francisco: Norman, 1998.
———. *The Fabric of the Human Body: An Annotated Translation of the 1543 and 1555 Editions of "De Humani Corporis Fabrica Libri Septem"*. Translated by D. H. Garrison and M. H. Hast. Basel: Karger, 2014.
Vidal, Fernando. *The Sciences of the Soul: The Early Modern Origins of Psychology*. Translated by Saskia Brown. Chicago: University of Chicago Press, 2011.
Wilkins, Eliza Gregory. *The Delphic Maxims in Literature*. Chicago: University of Chicago Press, 1929.
Wisnovsky, Robert. *Avicenna's Metaphysics in Context*. Ithaca, NY: Cornell University Press, 2003.
Wittgenstein, Ludwig. *Tractatus Logico-Philosophicus*. Translated by David Francis Pears and Brian McGuinness. Rev. ed. Routledge Classics. London: Routledge, 2001.
Wordsworth, William. *William Wordsworth: The Major Works*. Edited by Stephen Gill. Oxford World's Classics. New York: Oxford University Press, 2008.

# 6

## Persons and Narratives

### A Physicalist Account of the Soul

K. NICHOLAS FORTI

IN THE END, IT did not take the promise of gaining the whole world to convince us to forfeit our souls; it just took a transformation of our minds by a reorientation of our hearts to a new story. Of course, some of the defenders and tellers of the new tale at times bemoan the vestiges of the old that still possess our language and thoughts, trapping the unenlightened in a demon-haunted world of make-believe. Among the concepts, tropes, phrases, and words that many of the heralds of the new age wish to sweep away like late day cobwebs obstinately clinging to the corners of modernity is the "soul." Indeed, the question of the soul in modern debates about anthropology betrays this determinative narrative of the age and its correlative metaphysics.[1] The metaphysical commitments of much of modern science and philosophy have not only provided the foundation for the debates between physicalism and dualism, but they have set the discussion within the bounds of that debate. Theology, for its part, has largely

---

1. Hart, *The Experience of God*, 64: "Today the sciences are not bound to the mechanical philosophy as far as theoretical and practical methods are concerned; they never were, really, at least not beyond a certain point. Even so, the mechanical philosophy's great metaphysical master narrative—its governing picture of nature as an aggregate of mechanistic functions and systems, accidentally arranged out of inherently lifeless and purposeless elements—remains the frame within which we now organize our expectations of science and, consequently, our reality."

allowed the resulting narrative to shape its own reflections on anthropology, but with the addition of "God" as a character or "the spiritual" as a kind of plot device that the secular versions of the story have overlooked. For this reason, talk about the soul has become problematic even for some Christian philosophers and theologians who think they recognize *the-writing-on-the-wall* as dualism seems to lose more and more ground to physicalism by way of advances in neuroscience. However, their alternatives tend to remain trapped in the metaphysical commitments of modernity.

After briefly sketching the provenance of these modern anthropologies, I will look at three contemporary examples. Two of those contemporary examples—those of Nancey Murphy and Lynne Rudder Baker—represent attempts to construct non-dualistic anthropologies amenable to the Christian witness. However, the third example, drawn from the work of Daniel Dennett, is an account that is, at best, unconcerned with the Christian witness and, perhaps, implicitly against it. Ultimately, all three accounts will be shown to rest on the hollow foundation of the ontologically given of the ethically accountable will (Murphy), the embodied first-personal perspective (Baker), or the cultural units and narratives constitutive of consciousness (Dennett). Moreover, by building their accounts from the physically dependent though ontologically ethereal, but lacking any account of the transcendent or the donation of being, these anthropologies betray a retreat from a truly robust physicalism. I will then argue that such a truly physicalist anthropology demands metaphysical commitments that are only intelligible in the kind of narrative found within the witness of Christian Scripture and Tradition. For it is only Scripture and Tradition, as embodied witness to the incarnation, that narrates the creation in such a way as to provide for the reality of bodies, persons, words, and stories—all of which are necessary for any meaningful discussion of the relationship between consciousness and physicality, as well as the formative narrative of that physicality, its soul.

## The Soul of the (Synaptic) Gaps

Despite attempts, from both within and outside of the tradition, to narrate the history of Christian thought as being persistently committed to a dualistic anthropology until the most recent generation of theologians and philosophers, one need only look to the work of the most important medieval theologian, Thomas Aquinas, for an example of a nondualistic Christian anthropology. Aquinas' concern for the unity of the human person was an attempt to provide a corrective to the Augustinian anthropologies of his day.² For inchoate in the Neoplatonic perspective of Augustine and the later anthropologies based on his theology was the danger of privileging the rational soul over the body by dividing the person into a hierarchy of parts with the rational soul at the top and the rest of the parts—particularly the body—in service to it. Drawing on an Aristotelian anthropology and account of causation, Thomas argued that each human has only one soul, a rational soul incorporating the powers of the vegetative and sensitive souls of other creatures, which provides the substantial form of the body.³ So, for example, Augustine spent the length of his theological career struggling with the question of how an incorporeal soul comes to be joined to a particular body—vacillating between creationist and traducian accounts—while for Thomas such a question misunderstands the relationship between soul and body, since the soul operates as formal cause on the material substance constitutive of the body. In other words, there is no particular body with which a soul must be joined since a body cannot exist without its particular soul to make it a body. As such, according to Thomas, a person is not their rational soul trapped within and moving or making use of their body; rather, a person is an embodied rational soul or, put differently, the body formed by a rational soul.

Still, the desire to privilege the rational soul as the seat of the self persisted after Thomas and found expression in the subtle work of Duns Scotus, who argued that the soul is the intellective and first-personal part of a human and is distinct from the form of the body.⁴ In this way, Scotus was able to preserve the Neoplatonic and Augustinian identification of the person with the reasoning part of the soul or rational mind, but at the expense of dividing the person perhaps even more substantially than those anthropologies that preceded Thomas' work. For Duns Scotus, the rational or animating soul must be joined to the body and its form through an act of God's will. Similarly, that rational soul then relates to its body through the function of the will, and not as the form of the body, as Thomas would have it.

In this way, Scotus' division of the human person anticipated Cartesian dualism. For Descartes, as for Scotus, the rational soul (or *res cogitans*) and the body (or *res extensa*) are substantially distinct and the causal influence of the one upon the other has been flattened to *efficient* causation via the voluntaristic power of the rational soul alone.⁵ Of course, Scotus' view is not

---

2. Turner, *Thomas Aquinas*.
3. *Summa Theologiæ*, I q. 76, aa. 1–3.
4. Cross, "Philosophy of Mind," 263–84.
5. For Duns Scotus, the causation is efficient and material. The rational soul is, in

identical with Cartesian dualism, since the form of the body cannot sustain the life of the body on its own without the animating rational soul, but as a consequence of Scotus' division between the soul and the form of the body, one is left with the sense that the body is a machine waiting to be put to use by the rational soul.[6] It is this view, shared by Duns Scotus and Descartes, of the soul's will acting as efficient cause upon the distinctly separate body (to which it is joined only by divine will) that would become the foundation for the anthropologies of early modernity—the precursor of what Charles Taylor calls "the punctual self," first articulated by John Locke.[7]

From the beginning, this perspective has been burdened with at least one important and stubbornly persistent problem: namely, the question of how the will of an incorporeal soul could be the efficient cause of the body's actions. This problem loomed larger and larger as Aristotelian ideas departed from scholastic readings and were developed solely along an immanent trajectory in the natural philosophy of the Enlightenment, wherein all causation was flattened into efficient causation and matter was no longer thought to require forms.[8] In light of these changing ideas, the Unitarian clergyman and natural philosopher Joseph Priestley and his friend Thomas Jefferson sought to reintroduce Tertullian's concept of the corporeal soul. Empirical evidence, however, never lent weight to this hypothesis and it mainly persisted into the late nineteenth-century among those convinced by the romantic, yet pseudo-scientific Spiritualism of the age, which held that souls were composed of ectoplasm, making them corporeal enough to be photographed and move things other than the bodies they once inhabited. But by that time, the more scientifically rigorous, influenced by the Lockean punctual notion of the self, had exchanged talk of the soul for

---

a sense, a substantial form for Scotus, but it does not seem to operate as a form of the body. See Cross, "Philosophy of Mind," in *The Cambridge Companion to Duns Scotus*, 273: "This sort of view, according to which there is a *plurality of forms* in an animate composite, makes it harder to give an account of the unity of a composite. In fact, we might find it hard to see what sense can be made of calling the animating soul a 'form' at all, given the basic claim that forms of material objects ought to have some role in the structuring of a body. Scotus is well aware of both of these two difficulties and spends some time trying to work out a philosophical solution to them—though it must be admitted that his solution to the second is ultimately aporetic."

6. Based on his division of the rational soul from the form of the body, a corpse is still the same species as a living body according to Duns Scotus. However, for Thomas, a corpse, because its physicality is no longer formed by a rational soul, is no longer a body and can only be spoken of as such by analogy.

7. Taylor, *Sources of the Self*, 143–76.

8. This notion that matter does not necessarily require forms was, again, anticipated in the work of Duns Scotus.

speaking of consciousness, which they assumed was in some kind of causal relationship with the brain.

In his seminal work first published in 1890, *Principles of Psychology*, William James dismissed talk of the soul as a superfluous relic from pre-scientific philosophy that could do no real work in a modern anthropology. Like many of his colleagues, James preferred to speak of consciousness rather than the soul. Still, he eventually became dubious of popular level uses of this term as well. "Consciousness" may be a better word than "soul," but as long as it is used in such a way as to suggest there is some other substance to the universe than the material of its physicality, then the word is as technically improper as soul. James' arguments anticipated, if not inaugurated, a good deal of the philosophy of mind that developed during the twentieth century and has continued into this century. According to this account, consciousness—which has superseded the soul—is best understood as the functions of the physical brain; albeit, with innumerable debates over interpretation and explanation of the details of this type of physicalism.

Yet it has not only been philosophers, psychologists, and neuroscientists who have accepted this narrative. For a number of current theologians, a physicalist anthropology has become more persuasive than the dualistic anthropology that has been taken as the default Christian position in modernity. Nevertheless, many of these theologians have not owned up to the implications of adopting physicalism. Nancey Murphy is a theologian who has taken these implications seriously, hence her suggestion that the soul should be seen as a failed ancient-medieval *scientific* hypothesis, clung to by modern Christians who mistakenly think it theologically essential.[9] Still, Murphy recognizes that the reductive materialism that underwrites physicalism should raise concerns for a Christian anthropology. In particular, Murphy fears the strict determinism correlative of such reductive materialism—a determinism that robs the human person of any agency necessary for moral responsibility. Therefore, Murphy has argued for the role of "downward causation" or "whole-part constraint"—the ability of a complex system to place constraints on the bottom-up causation of its parts —in maintaining the agency of the complex systems we call *persons*. This personal agency, which is the key to a nonreductive physicalism for Murphy, is significantly enhanced by the uniquely human ability for language.[10]

However, it is difficult to see why the kind of personal agency described by Murphy should put the "non" in nonreductive physicalism, since

---

9. Murphy, *Bodies and Souls, or Spirited Bodies?*

10. Ibid., 121: "Nonreductive physicalism grants . . . that we are biological organisms, but emphasizes that our neurobiological complexity and the history of cultural development have together resulted in the capacity for genuine moral reasoning."

her account of agency is similar enough to that of Daniel Dennett's narrative that both accounts could hypothetically be argued from the same set of metaphysical commitments.[11] And it is precisely on these grounds that proponents of the "Constitution View" of human persons, like Lynne Rudder Baker, object to the kind of solution Murphy has proposed in response to the problem of materialistic reductionism.[12] In the words of Baker, "*person is an ontological kind.*"[13] Hence, persons can never be reduced to the complex, organic systems that constitute them. "Persons are one kind of thing; human bodies are another."[14] Though a person and his or her body may share the same space, the same name, even the same constitutive cells, molecules, and atomic particles, that person is not identical to the constitutive body of the human animal with which he or she is identifiable. For Baker, a person is a kind of thing that "has a capacity for first-person perspective."[15] In a later work, Baker qualifies that definition with the distinction between a rudimentary and robust first-person perspective, thereby allowing for a rudimentary first-person perspective in an animal that is not constitutive of a person, but nevertheless displays consciousness and intentionality.[16] Human infants are, for Baker, an example of an animal with a rudimentary first-person perspective; however, by a further qualification Baker is able to retain the ontological designation of person for human animals in the state of infancy. A human person may be constituted by a human infant despite the fact that the infant only has a rudimentary first-person perspective because the infant also has a "remote capacity" to develop a robust first-person perspective as it matures. That is to say, a human animal in the state of infancy has the real potential, even if it is never actualized, of developing the kind of first-person perspective that distinguishes human persons from other kinds of things in the world, but for Baker a first-trimester human fetus is not a person because it lacks the physiological prerequisites for a remote capacity to develop a robust first-person perspective. Human infants have this potentiality because their physiology allows them to acquire language, which is necessary for the kind of first-person perspective that Baker identifies as robust.

11. See Dennett, *Freedom Evolves*. To be clear, I am not critiquing Murphy's account of personal agency (or Dennett's), *per se*. Rather, I am suggesting that there is nothing inherently nonreductive about her account; hence, the comparison with Dennett, who *is* an advocate of reductive physicalism. More on Dennett below.

12. Baker, *Persons and Bodies*; and Corcoran, *Rethinking Human Nature*.

13. Baker, *Persons and Bodies*, 11.

14. Ibid., 25.

15. Ibid., 20.

16. Baker, *Naturalism and the First-person Perspective*.

Language, then, is crucial for both Baker's Constitution View of human persons and Murphy's defense of personal agency as a uniquely human characteristic. Furthermore, without explicitly adopting the Constitution View or reflecting on their ontological status, Murphy begins to make similar claims for persons as Baker in the last chapter of *Bodies and Souls, or Spirited Bodies?*[17] By rejecting the dichotomies of body-soul and brain-mind, while reformulating the question in terms of a person's relation to their body, and then answering that question by proposing that persons are constituted by their bodies, these anthropologies have attempted to avoid the supposed difficulties associated with a concept such as the "soul." Baker's persons are not immaterial "things" that subsist without a constitutive body with the capacity for first-person perspective, as souls are according to Thomas Aquinas.[18] And, since Baker, like Locke before her, makes the persistence condition of a person the continuation of the dispositional property of the person's first-person perspective, she further avoids any confusion of persons with the Cartesian *res cogitans*. Nevertheless, there remains a kind of ghostly quality to this view of persons. For example, Baker is willing to argue that persons can persist beyond the destruction of the embodied animal that initially constituted them. This persistence of the person extends beyond the replacement of essential parts of the constitutive animal's natural body with prosthesis. In Baker's view, God could miraculously provide a person's robust first-person perspective with a new constitutive body, having no continuity with that person's original constitutive body, and that person would persist as the same person. But such a view strains against the central Christian narrative of the incarnation and specifically the narratives of Christ's own resurrection wherein the risen Christ retains the historically inflicted wounds of crucifixion.[19]

Finally, there is another corollary of Baker's Constitution View that might be problematic for a theological anthropology situated within the Christian tradition. According to the Constitution View, a human being that is born with only a brain stem would not properly be a person, since that human being will never possess the cognitive apparatus necessary for a remote capacity for a robust first-person perspective. Such a being would be a human animal, but not a human person. This account of human persons is not necessarily problematic as long as it remains an academic point;

---

17. Murphy, *Bodies and Souls, or Spirited Bodies?*, 132–42.

18. *Summa Theologiæ* I, q. 75, aa. 2, 6.

19. See, 1 Cor 15:42–44. Although Paul suggests that the resurrection body (*sōma pneumatikon*) is as different from the pre-mortem body (*sōma psychikon*) as a plant is from the seed, the metaphor still suggests continuity. His description employs the language of change, not replacement.

however, if the distinction between human persons and human animals becomes normative for ethics, then Christians may find the implications unacceptable.[20] But this just is the corollary that makes Baker's account of human persons problematic, for if it cannot be applied to the ethical practices of the Christian community, then—at least for that community—that account is insufficient. And, to the extent that this anthropology is incompatible with the embodied practices of the Christian community over time, the person is abstracted from all connection to its constitutive physicality.

## A Word about Memes

Lynne Rudder Baker's argument for the ontological irreducibility of persons rests on her unflagging commitment to resist the reductive narratives determinative in modern philosophy of mind. However, it may yet be helpful to follow Nancey Murphy's lead in inching closer to the precipice to see what can be learned. Similar to Murphy, the (teleo)functionalist Daniel Dennett[21] claims that "language, when it is installed in the brain, brings with it the construction of a new cognitive architecture that *creates* a new kind of consciousness—and morality."[22] Indeed, Dennett would surely agree with Herbert McCabe's Wittgensteinian-Thomistic description of the human as "a linguistic animal,"[23] since Dennett claims that language actually shapes the plasticity of the brain and provides the building blocks for the brain's creation of *self*. "Our human environment contains not just food and shelter, enemies to fight or flee, and conspecifics with whom to mate, but words, words, words. These words are potent elements of our environment that we readily incorporate, ingesting and extruding them, weaving them like spiderwebs into self-protective strings of *narrative*." And, he continues, "when we let in these words . . . they tend to take over, creating us out of the raw materials they find in our brains."[24] Dennett's characterization of words as outside of us, as "elements of our environment" suggests they have

---

20. See Hauerwas, "Must a Patient Be a Person to Be a Patient?," 596–602.

21. Dennett, *Consciousness Explained*, 460: "Am I then a functionalist? Yes and no. I am not a Turing machine functionalist, but then I doubt anyone ever was. . . . I am a sort of 'teleofunctionalist,' of course, perhaps the original teleofunctionalist (in *Content and Consciousness*), but as I have all along made clear, and emphasize here in the discussion of evolution, and of qualia, I don't make the mistake of trying to define all salient mental differences in terms of biological *functions*."

22. Dennett, *Freedom Evolves*, 260 (emphasis original).

23. McCabe, *Law, Love, and Language*, 68.

24. Dennett, *Consciousness Explained*, 417.

obduracy. Or as McCabe writes, "I can't just mean what I like by words,"[25] because the meaning of a word is not dependent on personal subjectivity or will.

So it seems that words have a kind of ontological "weight" for Dennett (at least in some of his work), which can be seen in his description of the way language makes consciousness possible. Words, according to Dennett, are *memes* that can be spoken, and memes are the "stuff" of consciousness. "Human consciousness is *itself* a huge complex of memes (or more exactly meme-effects in brains) that can best be understood as the operation of a *'von Neumannesque'* virtual machine *implemented* in the *parallel architecture* of a brain that was not designed for any such activities."[26] In this description of consciousness, "a meme is an information-packet with attitude—a recipe or instruction manual for doing something cultural."[27] According to Dennett, they are invisible, require some form of physical media to migrate, are subject to natural selection and evolution, and are parasitic—requiring human brains to reproduce.[28] Such a description lends a kind of creaturely gravitas to memes. And, if this "weight" or obduracy is true for words as spoken memes, it is also true for narratives—both the narratives we tell and the narratives that tell us. So, Dennett says, "Our fundamental tactic of self-protection, self-control, and self-definition is . . . telling stories, and more particularly concocting and controlling the story we tell others—and ourselves—about who we are."[29] Dennett calls the story-telling *self* of each individual *linguistic animal* its "center of narrative gravity."[30] And he reminds us that, in fact, the narrative precedes and produces that *center of narrative gravity*. "Our tales are spun, but for the most part, we don't spin

25. McCabe, *Law, Love, and Language*, 88.
26. Dennett, *Consciousness Explained*, 210 (emphasis original).
27. Dennett, *Freedom Evolves*, 176.
28. Following the predilection of the *episteme* of science, Dennett suggests breaking culture down into atomistic units of information replication that are modeled on genes. These units of replicating information include words, symbols, beliefs, ritual actions, tropes, and any other discrete cultural elements that can and do get replicated, for which Dennett adopts Richard Dawkins' term, memes. In this way, Dennett is intentionally and explicitly building the analogy between biology and culture. More specifically, he is arguing that these units of culture are selected for or against in a way similar to genes, and complexes of memes can be studied in the same way as complexes of genes, or organisms—the continuation and adaptation of which are dependent on the fitness selectors of the evolutionary process. While this analogy has come under attack from some anthropologists and theologians, I am not here concerned with the philosophical viability of the concept of memes. Rather, I am interested in the conditions for their existence and the metaphysical implications of their use by Dennett.
29. Dennett, *Consciousness Explained*, 418.
30. Ibid.

them; they spin us. Our human consciousness, and our narrative selfhood, is their product, not their source."[31] Just as the "narratives" encoded in our DNA form the matter of our physicality into our bodies, so also our embodied narratives form our*selves* and give rise to consciousness.[32] But Dennett is quick to insist that there is no magic in play here. The life of these invisible, incorporeal creatures called memes is completely reducible to physical processes, and a *center of narrative gravity* is as much a "theorist's fiction" as the physical center of gravity.

So, finally, the metaphysical commitments of Dennett's narrative of reductive physicalism trump his commitment to the obdurate reality of narratives, words, or memes—revealing that the two commitments are ultimately irreconcilable. Nevertheless, unlike the eliminative materialist Patricia Churchland, Dennett is not prepared to dismiss the evidence that language plays a crucial role in the formation and functioning of human consciousness.[33] To engage in such a dismissal cannot help but philosophically call into question the whole project of science itself (as well as any other human, cultural project). But Dennett is aware that the admission of the power of words or memes to change the way we think, recollect, reflect, and thus react in future situations provides a layer of causality that strains against purely physical, atomistic (efficient) causality.[34] He therefore struggles to establish some elbow room in the efficient causality and reductive physicalism of the *episteme* of science for the causal power of such immaterial things as words and memes. By resisting the temptation to treat a person's consciousness as something apart from their physicality, he is able to avoid the dualism of the mind's will and the body's action; however, he never seems to arrive at giving an account of how the words and narratives that spin that consciousness into existence and change the patterns of its web exercise causality.[35]

Moreover, as Baker has pointed out, Dennett has been unable so far to explain away the first-person perspective from a third-personal stance, despite the fact that to do so is the intended goal of his "neutral method" for studying the data provided by conscious subjects, *heterophenomenology*.

31. Ibid.

32. Recent work in epigenetics suggests that these two types of narratives may be connected by more than just analogy.

33. Churchland, *Touching a Nerve*.

34. Dennett, *Freedom Evolves*.

35. Dennett suggests that language works in a way similar to the way software runs on the hardware of a computer; although, he is willing to admit that the plasticity of the brain allows for that linguistic or memetic software to actually alter the hardware of the brain. But the differences that this analogy inevitably highlight only serve to beg the question.

Furthermore, Baker notes that Dennett's narrative-based concept of the "self is much richer than the idea of a first-person perspective."[36] Her point is that a first-person perspective is necessary for Dennett's narrative-self, but the narrative-self is not necessary for a first-person perspective. However, it is exactly on this point that I think Dennett's work is most helpful. His recognition that the self is given through narratives that are not necessarily of that self's own making underscores the contingency of who we are. Even the emergence of the robust first-person perspective might only be made possible through the narrative-selves that are spun for us while we are yet in a state of rudimentary first-person perspective. I did not choose my own name nor did I narrate my own personhood as an infant; rather, I was given a name and my life was narrated by others who treated me like a person before I ever developed the robust first-person perspective necessary for me to have an active, conscious share in that narrative.[37]

Yet the contingency of the self and its first-person perspective on the narratives that form and inform who we are just pushes the question of being back further rather than answering it. Even the attempt to put those narratives under the microscope in the hopes of discerning their fundamental elements—their memes, according to Dennett—does not yield an explanation of what they are contingent upon, ontologically. But this question remains key. For if the contingency of all narratives or memes is unhooked from truth (and thus being), then all attempts at meaning-making—even science—are simply an imposition of the will. Though, in the case of Dennett's understanding of memes and meme-complexes, which exist and persist for the sake of their own existence, the determinative will is not that of the human host, but of the memes themselves. According to this account, science, no less than any other body of knowledge and practice, is a complex of memes whose continual cultural replication does not rely on its truth, validity, or even usefulness for human flourishing, but on its survival fitness. The whole *episteme* upon which Dennett's philosophy and anthropology are built has no more claim to truthfulness than any other narrative or meme-complex.[38]

36. Baker, *Persons and Bodies*, 87.

37. Hauerwas, *A Community of Character*, 148: "The necessary existence of the other for my own self is but a reminder that the self is not something we create, but is a gift. Thus we become who we are through the embodiment of the story in the communities in which we are born."

38. Dennett is aware of this danger and attempts to counter it throughout his book on religion, *Breaking the Spell*. He takes this challenge on in small sections throughout the book, whenever it begins to loom over his argument from within, and then in a more sustained way in an appendix in the back. In summary, Dennett's answer to the challenge is that science is an endeavor for truth for which methods and disciplines

## In the Beginning Was the Word

When Gregory of Nyssa asked his saintly sister about the soul, what it is and whether it stands up against the attacks of the skeptics, Macrina began her answer by directing Gregory to the way in which all of creation acts as a book of signs, a narrative that tells of its Creator and Sustainer.[39] Macrina's conviction was that knowledge of the things of creation must begin with the recognition that they are created and sustained by One that is uncreated and transcendent. The being of any creature is not its own, but a gift from the One whose essence is existence, a gift received by participation in the gift.[40] To the extent that this metaphysical presupposition has been ignored or rejected in modern accounts of reality, much of the language of the Christian narrative—that is, Scripture and Tradition—has become problematic.

To be sure, there have always been accounts of creation that have approached reality as something to be known in itself, apart from the transcendent. But following the argument above, it was René Descartes who made the definitive move in this direction in the history of ideas when he sought a foundation for epistemology in a mathematical rationality. According to Étienne Gilson, Descartes' "systematic application of the mathematical method to reality could only have as its immediate result the substitution of a limited number of clear ideas, conceived as true reality, for the concrete complexity of things."[41] Catherine Pickstock reads the Cartesian epistemological project through his ontology, symbolized as a planned and mapped-out city. She characterizes this project as *immanent spatialization*[42]—according to which, the arrival of contingent being in time as gift is replaced with the flattened-out map of self-subsistent being beneath

---

have been established to reduce the personal, subjective biases of the individual scientists, thereby increasing the probability of objective results. Dennett is surely correct that the disciplines and method of science have this outcome; however, he is missing his very own point. Memes are *for* memes—they are for their own replication. His own argument is that religions may provide benefits for their human hosts, and some of those beneficial aspects of religion may have been selected for fitness because of their benefit to their hosts, but a religion, as complex of memes, exists and replicates for the sake of existing and replicating itself. *Mutatis mutandis*—science may provide benefits for humanity, but science, as a complex of memes, exists and replicates for the sake of existing and replicating itself. If truth and objectivity are memes, the replication and persistence of which is based on their selective advantage, then there is no way to determine whether or not the goal and methods of truthfulness and objectivity correspond to anything in reality or are simply successful memetic adaptations.

39. *On the Soul and the Resurrection.*
40. *Summa Theologiæ*, I, q. 44, a. 1.
41. Gilson, *Methodical Realism*, 62.
42. Pickstock, *After Writing*, 47–100.

the omniscient Cartesian gaze.[43] When the spatialized city is applied analogously to the human person, "there will follow absolute divisions between mind and body newly conceived as 'areas,' and the mind itself conceived as the spatial traverse of an inevitable order of intuited deductions."[44] It is this Cartesian gaze and dualism that Dennett and Murphy are both keen to reject. From their perspective, the only counter to such dualism is to dismiss the "area" of the person that is resistant to empirical observation and might well be reducible to the physical "area." However, such an option is already based on the same metaphysics of the Cartesian project as opposed to the earlier metaphysical first principles of the narrative developed from the patristics through Thomas Aquinas.

This narrative, the narrative of Christian Scripture and Tradition, is centered on Jesus Christ, who is the Transcendent entering the categories of creation in the unique way of actually being indivisibly joined to an immanent, creaturely nature. Moreover, this narrative says that "in him all things . . . were created."[45] The hypostatic union makes Macrina's claim about the creation intelligible—for the Trinity's work of creation and incarnation are inextricable. Apart from the Second Person of the Trinity, there is no Jesus Christ, and apart from the gift of being that Creator and Sustainer provide *through* Jesus Christ, there is no creation. Yet also, apart from the contingent being of the creation, there is no Jesus Christ. It is by the incarnation, it is in Jesus Christ, that the being of the world is suspended, for "in him all things hold together."[46] As the incarnate Word, Jesus is the Truth revealed[47]—that is, communicated—in the fullness of his person and life, but this is first and foremost ontological, not epistemological.[48] For when the Word of God goes forth, it accomplishes what He purposes—calling into being the conditions for revelation and communicating the narrative of creation.[49]

So, a Christian anthropology must begin with this one in whom all things hold together, the one about whom it can most truthfully be said that he was fully human; it must begin with the Word becoming flesh and dwelling among us. That the Word not only took on flesh but also dwelt among

---

43. Ibid., 69: "The interiorized 'flattening-out' of this new intellection thus offers an immanentized version of the angelic vision for which diverse perspectives are unified into a single omniscient gaze. But the Cartesian gaze is inward and reflexive, gazing only at its own projection of order and sign, as if in its own mirrored reflection."

44. Ibid., 61.

45. Col 1:16 (NRSV).

46. Col 1:17 (NRSV).

47. John 14:6; 17:17.

48. Sonderegger, "The Humility of the Son of God," 60–73.

49. Isa 55:10–11.

us clarifies that this is not just a matter of matter, but of embodiment. And human bodies, like the persons they constitute, are inextricably bound to language *in general* and narratives *in particular*, since the body is the site of the self.[50] Herbert McCabe's description of this begs for extended quotation:

> All animal life, then, is a matter of communication, of creating a significant world out of an environment. In the case of man this communication reaches the point of being linguistic, that is to say man is able to some extent to create the media through which he makes his world significant. These media have their roots in the sensuous life of man and their creation is the history of a community leading into biographies, which are themselves the histories of minor communities.
>
> It is because I have this sort of body, a human body living with a human life, that my communication can be linguistic. The human body is a source of communication; we must be careful not to think of it as an instrument used in communication like a pen or a telephone; such instruments can only be used because there is a body to use them. If the human body itself were an instrument we would have to postulate another body using it—and this, indeed, is what the dualistic theory really amounts to; the mind or soul is thought of, in practice, as a sort of invisible body living inside the visible one. Instead of this we should recognize that the human body is intrinsically communicative. Human flesh, the stuff we are made of, the intricate structure of the human organism, is quite different from wood or stone or even animal flesh, because it is self-creative. It does not simply produce other bodies which are its children in its own image, it produces *itself* at least to the extent of creating the media, the language and communication systems which are an extension of itself.[51]

This is to say, in Thomistic fashion, that being formed by a rational soul means that everything that the human body does—even those things that are not done with conscious deliberation or followed by linguistic-symbolic reflection—are done rationally, or linguistically. Hence, both the behaviors and even, to an extent, the physicality of human bodies are formed by habits that may go unacknowledged, but still bear a rationality or narrative.[52] And this habituated knowledge that is the formation of the body toward the world in a particular way comes through that human body's participation in

50. Damasio, *Self Comes to Mind*.
51. McCabe, *Law, Love and Language*, 90–91.
52. Smith, *Imagining the Kingdom*.

communities or social bodies with their own unique structures of linguistic signification. As James K. A. Smith writes, "to acquire a *habitus* is to have been incorporated into a social body and its vision of a way of life."[53]

It is the body that provides the self with its boundaries and situates the self in society. From the narratives encoded in a body's genes to the narratives encoded in the brain's memes, the physicality constitutive of a body is formed into the body of a particular person in a society of persons. Hence, Jesus' historic life also embodied the socially particular narratives of being a child of Israel, the son of Mary, the friend of tax collectors and sinners, the awaited Messiah, and the criminal to be crucified. Jesus Christ was not only the eternal Word through whom creation was spoken into existence and in whom all things hold together, but he was also a particular person with the persistent dispositional property of his own first-person perspective, and with a narrative-self that provided the integrity of his conscious self-understanding within the larger narratives of his relationships, his family, and his culture. He was also the recipient of genetic and memetic narratives that formed his living, human body capable of bearing his narrative self-consciousness and first-person perspective. Yet, as the unique fulcrum of history and human signification, Jesus Christ draws together the narrative of all creation. His story begins with the first moment of creation and points to the fulfillment of all time.

## The Word Became Flesh

The narrative of Jesus Christ could not have been completely apprehended by a glance at the body of the babe lying in the manger because narrative—like being—must unfold over time, arriving as a seemingly inexhaustible gift. When we speak of Jesus Christ as incarnation, we are certainly making metaphysical and theological claims that we should not try to obscure, but primarily we are talking about the unfolding gift of a particular life.[54] The narrative that is embodied in the life of Jesus of Nazareth is the Word through whom the Father spoke creation.[55] But as the life of the person of Christ, he is also a particular narrative embodied within the story of creation. In one sense, the story of creation is told for the sake of the narrative that is embodied in his life.[56] So, given the significance of Christ's life, one might expect that the seeming inexhaustibility of his narrative and being

53. Ibid., 125.
54. Hauerwas, *The Peaceable Kingdom*, 75.
55. John 1:1–4, 10.
56. Col 1:16.

should be perfectly manifest in that life. But, of course, the gift of embodied narratives—the stories that are refracted by the *center of narrative gravity* that is the self and participated in through first-person perspective—are exhausted when the bodies that carry them, that they formed, die or are killed. This was no less true for Jesus than it is for each of us.

Indeed, this is what can be seen with Jesus' life as it unfolds towards his own passion and death on the cross in the textual narratives of the Gospels. For the most part, the Gospel texts are not overly-burdened by plot. Rather they are each a pastiche of oral sources—aphorisms, parables, pronouncement sayings, miracle stories—given narrative sequence by geographic and temporal change. However, this changes when Jesus turns his face towards Jerusalem.[57] In fact, the passion of Christ in the Gospel according to Mark is so coherent in plot and marked by such narrative verisimilitude that it is strikingly different from the rest of the Gospel. Starting with the proleptic anointing of Jesus for burial by the unnamed woman in Bethany, the narrative overtakes Jesus and constricts around his body. As Jesus is led towards torture and death, the process of self-expansion through language "is reversed. The immediacy of pain, its monopoly of attention and its incommunicability, reduces the world of the sufferer down again to the limits of the body itself . . . . In torture this phenomenon takes an extreme form. The immediacy of the pain shrinks the world down to the contours of the body itself; the enormity of the agony is the sufferer's only reality."[58] Christ, whose own words had earlier driven the narrative, whether in the telling of parables, the proclamation of the kingdom, or the pronouncement of healing, becomes mute.[59] While those who are against him force false narratives onto him through lies and physical abuse,[60] and even those whose language had been elevated through discipleship to speak truthfully about him[61] descend into lies and self-deception.[62]

Approaching the crucifixion, the narrative embodied in the life of Christ becomes hijacked by the narrative of the powers and principalities. Crucifixion was a public statement—an advertisement—of Roman imperial power embodied in the humiliated wretch dying on the cross and being left there to waste away without proper burial; for the point of the crucifixion, from the Roman perspective, was the silencing of the narrative through

57. Crossan, *The Historical Jesus*, 367.
58. Cavanaugh, *Torture and Eucharist*, 37.
59. Mark 14:61; 15:5.
60. Mark 14:55–59; 15:2–3.
61. Mark 8:27–29.
62. Mark 14:66–72.

the obliteration of the body. It was not simply the death of the person that was the goal of crucifixion; it was the complete eradication of the body.[63] A corpse can still carry the ghost of its narrative, haunting its decaying boundaries as the dénouement of the dead—allowing for the possibility of traces of the narrative to continue upon the boundaries of other bodies whose own narratives had once included the deceased. It is the empty cross that ultimately advertises the narrative of Roman power, since the act of crucifixion co-opts the body of the crucified for its own narrative until that body has been completely silenced, its communicative power completely exhausted, and by its absence no other narrative remains but the power of death told by those who claim to wield that power. However, ultimately this just reveals the vacuity of such fallen narratives, for the empty cross calls into question the significance of any narrative and suggests that human rationality and meaning-making are acts of *libido dominandi* in the face of the nothingness that provides it with its supposed power.

## (The First and) The Last Word

At the heart of history and the nexus of all narratives, the story that was ended on the cross of Calvary, though truly exhausted and erased, burst back in upon the deafness of the world that had silenced it. In the bodily resurrection of Christ, narrative itself was redeemed, and meaning restored. Had there been no resurrection, irrationality would have triumphed, the silenced story refusing to ultimately provide meaning and form to the substrate of matter.[64] Bodies would cease to have been bodies. Matter would have ceased to be any thing. By conquering the irrationality of death, Christ—the Word and Truth—restored the rationality of the universe, making possible truthful narratives of it from the smallest subatomic particle to the fullness of the cosmos itself. More than that, Christ's resurrection opened the way for the embodied narratives of each and every person to subsist in his own body. For Christ's resurrected body, as the first-fruits, is an eschatological body—a body that tells the fullness of creation's narrative. This is to say that, by his resurrection, "Jesus Christ is himself the medium in which men will in the future communicate, he is the body in which we shall

---

63. Crossan, *Who Killed Jesus?* 161.

64. McCabe, *Law, Love and Language*, 132: "After the crucifixion, to interpret the defect of the world as sin, to interpret it, that is, as involving the rejection of the Father's self-giving, is the same as to say that given the sin of the world, the crucifixion was bound to happen. It is to say that this is the kind of world we have, a crucifying world, a world doomed to reject its own meaning."

all be interrelated members, '*la cellule première du cosmos nouveau*,' he is the language in which we shall express ourselves to each other in accordance with the promise and summons of the Father."[65] And, McCabe continues, "this language, this medium of expression, this body which belongs to the future is made really present for us in the church."[66]

The church is the embodied narrative of the crucified and resurrected one—the Word made flesh. The church is his embodied narrative in that it participates in that great cloud of witnesses who remember and reflect the narrative of the Word, thus having their own narrative formed by the embodied narrative of the Word. This witness is Scripture, mediated through the Scriptures. And that which is mediated through the Scriptures is the narrative of the church unfolding over time in liturgies and embodied practices of the people drawn into the narrative.

From the beginning, the witness to the Word was embodied and enacted rather than simply reported and recorded. In part, the church was formed by its reflection on and participation in the scriptural tradition of Israel fulfilled in Jesus Christ. Its further formation came in its enactment of that witness to Jesus Christ—doing that which he commanded in remembrance of him and proclaiming his life and death by imitation and repetition, habit and ritual, word and deed.[67] In this living out of the developing tradition, the witness came to be written down, the word became text, though never divorced from that cloud of witnesses in whom it was embodied. That is to say, the narrative of the witness continues to unfold over time, moving toward the inexhaustible *telos* of Truth embodied in the resurrected Christ, but not fully realized in the narratives of the individual lives that have been grafted into that narrative through the worship and disciplines of the tradition. Each individual life, each embodied narrative, bears the witness in part even as it is continually drawn further into the story of Christ, being formed in his image and likeness. But our sanctification, indeed the very realization of who we are, the knowledge of our souls, comes through the grace of faith lived out in the embodiment of the church's worship, in the learning of the new language of God in Christ, and in those disciplines and "those practices that 'carry' the true story of the whole world as articulated in the Scriptures, centered on Christ."[68] To be human is to be an embodied life formed by a narrative that is as much a gift as one's own existence—a narrative whose

---

65. McCabe, *Law, Love and Language*, 140-41.

66. Ibid., 141.

67. See, for example, Crossan, *The Birth of Christianity*, 403-6; Horsely and Draper, *Whoever Hears You Hears Me*; and Theissen, *Sociology of Early Palestinian Christianity*.

68. Smith, *Imagining the Kingdom*, 163.

ultimate provenance is in the grace of God's work of creation. To be *born anew to a living hope through the resurrection of Jesus Christ from the dead*[69] is to have one's embodied life grafted into the eschatological body of the one by whom and for whom the narrative of creation is told.

## Conclusion

To the extent that the modern mind has been captivated by the narrative of reductive materialism, physicalist anthropologies have emerged as particularly persuasive. And inasmuch as this physicalism has broken the hold of Cartesian dualism on the Christian imagination, it has proven useful. So, this essay has looked to how three different modern, nondualistic anthropologies have responded to the narrative of reductive physicalism that dominates certain sections of philosophy and science today. Lynne Rudder Baker's proposal that persons are an ontological kind that emerge from their constitutive bodies is a clear rejection of that reductive physicalism. Daniel Dennett's conception of the self as the *center of narrative gravity* is formulated to exist comfortably within reductive physicalism (though, it is not at all clear that it does so). And Nancy Murphey's attempt to construct a nonreductive physicalist anthropology is meant to chart a *via media* in the debate. However, each account begins with ontological givenness. So, for example, Baker's view that persons emerge from their constitutive animality as new things in an ontologically plural reality does not require an account of the donation of being from a Creator any more than Dennett's view. And because Baker emphasizes the first-person perspective of consciousness and Murphey emphasizes personal agency, both of their anthropologies seem to be haunted by the modern "punctual self," just as Dennett's account is also beholden to such a view.[70] However, Dennett's acknowledgment of the narrative character of the self and its contingency and reception from sources outside itself strains against this Cartesian and Lockean view to the extent that Baker's account of persons and Dennett's view of the self seem mutually exclusive. This need not be the case, though, as long as the being of persons, their constitutive bodies, and their formative stories are understood as contingent and sustained by the donation of being.

To begin the story in this way, however, reveals that the problem with anthropologies that presume the metaphysical commitments of modernity's narrative is that they are not physicalist enough. The scandal of the cross is that bodies can be drowned in the silence of nothingness as completely

69. 1 Pet 1:3.
70. My thanks to Eric Austin Lee for pointing this out to me.

as the narratives they signify. But the story embodied in the life of Jesus of Nazareth could not have stayed silent, for this embodied narrative signifies the eternal Word, whose being truly is inexhaustible and necessary. The resurrection of Christ was not simply the raising of an individual and his narrative from death and silence and the reestablishment of Jesus' robust first-person perspective in a spiritual body; though, it was at least this. But more than that, Christ's resurrection was the renewal of all creation. Therefore, it included both the resurrection of his body and the gathering of a cloud of witnesses into that body, whose membership therein proclaims the gospel, the story of God in Christ. Moreover, it is through this particular embodied narrative—Jesus Christ, who was dead and has been raised to new life—that the contingent being of the whole creation (subatomic particles, persons, genes, memes, words, and stories) is suspended. Finally, if the eternal Word lends such weight to words as revealed in the Christian narrative, then it seems that we should not, after all, abandon the tradition's word for the narratives that "spin us" and which we embody—namely, the soul.

## Bibliography

Baker, Lynne Rudder. *Naturalism and the First-person Perspective*. New York: Oxford University Press, 2013.

———. *Persons and Bodies: A Constitution View*. New York: Cambridge University Press, 2000.

Cavanaugh, William T. *Torture and Eucharist: Theology, Politics, and the Body of Christ*. Malden, MA: Blackwell, 2008.

Churchland, Patricia S. *Touching a Nerve: The Self as Brain*. New York: Norton, 2013.

Corcoran, Kevin. *Rethinking Human Nature: A Christian Materialist Alternative to the Soul*. Grand Rapids: Baker Academic, 2006.

Cross, Richard. "Philosophy of Mind." In *The Cambridge Companion to Duns Scotus*, edited by Thomas Williams, 263–84. Cambridge: Cambridge University Press, 2003.

Crossan, John Dominic. *The Birth of Christianity: Discovering What Happened in the Years Immediately after the Execution of Jesus*. San Francisco: HaperCollins, 1998.

———. *The Historical Jesus: The Life of a Mediterranean Jewish Peasant*. San Francisco: HarperCollins, 1991.

———. *Who Killed Jesus?: Exposing the Roots of Anti-Semitism in the Gospel Story of the Death of Jesus*. San Francisco: HarperCollins, 1996.

Damasio, Antonio. *Self Comes to Mind: Constructing the Conscious Brain*. New York: Vintage, 2012.

Dennett, Daniel C., *Breaking the Spell: Religion as a Natural Phenomenon*. New York: Penguin Viking, 2006.

———. *Consciousness Explained*. Boston: Little, Brown and Company, 1991.

———. *Freedom Evolves*. New York: Penguin, 2003.

Gilson, Étienne. *Methodical Realism: A Handbook for Beginning Realists.* Translated by Philip Trower. 1990. San Francisco: Ignatius Press, 2011.

Hart, David Bentley. *The Experience of God: Being, Consciousness, Bliss.* New Haven, CT: Yale University Press, 2013.

Hauerwas, Stanley. *A Community of Character: Toward a Constructive Christian Social Ethic.* Notre Dame, IN: University of Notre Dame Press, 1981.

———. "Must a Patient Be a Person to Be a Patient? Or, My Uncle Charlie Is Not Much of a Person, But He Is Still My Uncle Charlie." In *The Hauerwas Reader*, edited by John Berkman and Michael Cartwright, 596–602. Durham, NC: Duke University Press, 2005.

———. *The Peaceable Kingdom: A Primer in Christian Ethics.* Notre Dame, IN: University of Notre Dame Press, 1983.

Horsely, Richard A., and Jonathan A. Draper. *Whoever Hears You Hears Me: Prophets, Performance, and Tradition in Q.* Harrisburg, PA: Trinity, 1999.

McCabe, Herbert. *Law, Love, and Language.* London: Continuum, 2003.

Murphy, Nancey. *Bodies and Souls, or Spirited Bodies?*. New York: Cambridge University Press, 2006.

Pickstock, Catherine. *After Writing: On the Liturgical Consummation of Philosophy.* Oxford: Blackwell, 1997.

Smith, James K. A. *Imagining the Kingdom: How Worship Works.* Cultural Liturgies Volume 2. Grand Rapids: Baker Academic, 2013.

Sonderegger, Katherine. "The Humility of the Son of God." In *Christology, Ancient and Modern: Explorations in Constructive Dogmatics*, edited by Oliver D. Crisp and Fred Sanders, 60–73. Grand Rapids: Zondervan, 2013.

Taylor, Charles. *Sources of the Self: The Making of the Modern Identity.* Cambridge: Harvard University Press, 1989.

Theissen, Gerd. *Sociology of Early Palestinian Christianity.* Philadelphia: Fortress, 1978.

Turner, Denys. *Thomas Aquinas: A Portrait.* New Haven, CT: Yale University Press, 2013.

# 7

# Transcending the Body/Soul Distinction through the Perspective of Maximus the Confessor's Anthropology

## Sotiris Mitralexis

Does the question of the soul *always* and *necessarily* entail the dualistic dichotomy so characteristic of the body/soul discourse? And, if we do accept the existence of immortal souls and the prevalence of free will, how can these two coincide? How can the soul of a human person possessing a truly free will be *compulsorily* eternal? In this article I will address these two different but interconnected questions through examination of selected passages from Maximus the Confessor's writings, in an attempt to trace possible answers.

A unique system of philosophical anthropology is to be discerned in St. Maximus the Confessor's (580–662 AD) works. Due to his extended involvement in the Monothelite controversy, Maximus developed an elaborate anthropology largely in connection with the task of working out his significant Christological insights. The careful examination of faculties pertaining to the human person, for example, such as the natural and gnomic will, the activities/operations (ἐνέργειαι) etc., was undertaken within the context of his battle against the Christological heresy of his time.

Whilst the distinction between body and soul holds a prominent position in the Confessor's anthropology, Maximus sees this distinction in a unique and truly illuminating way. The importance of these insights, however, can only be grasped on the basis of a firm understanding of his ontological terminology. The soul was not always considered as "something" that "exists somewhere" or "does not exist," i.e., in the sense that it is widely understood today as an entity that is to be rejected or confirmed. As is common knowledge, the Greek words for soul and spirit (ψυχή and πνεῦμα, both etymologically related to breath) were used to denote and signify the difference between a living, breathing human person and his dead body, bereft of life. This difference was deductively located in the presence or absence of the breath, i.e., the soul or spirit. Philosophical theories entailing a strict duality or even a dichotomy between body and soul as seen, for example, in Cartesian philosophy are not a necessary corollary of speaking about the presence of a soul. But what is Maximus the Confessor's stance on this subject?

The first thing to note is that Maximus uses the philosophical language of his time, what we call today "Neoplatonism." However, this does not *make* him a Neoplatonist: the question is not which philosophical language he uses, but which philosophical and theological testimony he is trying to articulate and to whom it is directed. As Torstein Tollefsen puts it, Maximus "received a Christian intellectual heritage that could freely express itself in this kind of vocabulary, and, strictly speaking, these are not 'Neoplatonic terms', rather they are Greek words, used by the Fathers."[1] For example, one of his primary concerns is not to contemplate about the soul[2] in general, but to counter the Origenist theory of the pre-existence of the soul,[3] using the same language used by the Origenists. This makes it very easy for someone to conclude from the study of some of Maximus' works that he proposes a strict dichotomy of body and soul: for example, he speaks of the soul as a "bodiless, intelligible and simple substance, residing in the body, being the cause of life and not being subject to corruption, dissolution or death": οὐσία ἀσώματος, νοερά, ἐν σώματι πολιτευομένη, ζωῆς παραίτια,[4] ἀσύνθετος, ἀδιάλυτος, ἄφθαρτος, ἀθάνατος.[5]

---

1. Tollefsen, *Christocentric Cosmology*, 11.

2. On a side note: Maximus writes *both* about a distinction of body and soul *and* about a distinction of mind, body and soul (νοῦς, σῶμα, ψυχή). In this short article we will focus on the contrast of body and soul, not attempting to analyze the latter distinction, which is treated in Thunberg, *Microcosm and Mediator*, 107–13.

3. See for example Maximus, Περὶ διαφόρων ἀποριῶν, PG 91, 1325d: οὔτε προΰπαρξιν οὔτε μεθύπαρξιν ψυχῆς ἢ σώματος, συνύπαρξιν δὲ μᾶλλόν φαμεν / "We are not speaking of an existence of the soul either before or after the existence of the body, but of their co-existence [their concurrent emergence]."

4. Maximus, Περὶ ψυχῆς, PG 91, 361a. The reader should note that the authorship of this treatise is disputed, and this further supports the general claim of this article.

5. Maximus, Περὶ ψυχῆς, PG 91, 357c.

However, Maximus' concern is also to guard the oneness and wholeness of the human person, of the human hypostasis. In understanding this, one must keep in mind that in the common patristic terminology there is no οὐσία ἀνυπόστατος,[6] no unactualized substance, that we cannot speak of any substance insofar as it has not been hypostasized and is not to be encountered as a hypostasis, a specific realization and manifestation. Maximus follows the common patristic terminology of his time, in which οὐσία (substance) is synonymous with φύσις (nature) and the specific realization of the substance (ὑπόστασις) is in the case of the human person and God synonymous with πρόσωπον (the person).[7] Even this distinction between substance and hypostasis is not a distinction between two "things"—and Maximus' dual understanding of the body/soul relationship vividly illustrates this.

Substance, οὐσία, is the homogeneity of the particulars, the "what" of something, the reason that it is what it is. "Substance" denotes the way in which something participates in existence. "Cat," "human," and "horse" are substances; however, these cannot be encountered isolated, as pure substances/natures, but only in particular existences, in hypostases. Hypostasis, ὑπόστασις, is the particular existence, the "how" of something, the specific way in which it is what it is. This particular human being, this particular horse, and this particular table are hypostases actualizing the substances "human," "horse," "table"—they *hypostasize the substance*.[8]

I must stress here again that both terms (substance and hypostasis) are not to be thought of as *things*, but circumscribe the mode of the beings' existence; they are *modes, modes of existence* (τρόποι ὑπάρξεως). The substance is not a "thing," it is the mode of the homogeneity's existence, the mode of its participation in being. It is not merely a question of what a thing's substance is, but it is instead a question of a thing or object's *whatness* (i.e., its mode, or how it exists). Even the word hypostasis, the particular, signifies a *mode of existence* when used in conjunction with the word "substance"; the mode of the particular's existence. The patristic terminology does not introduce a disjunction and dualism through the use of these terms: they describe the different *modes of existence* of beings, the mode of homogeneity and general participation in being (substance) and the mode of the particular realization and actualization with all of its accidents (hypostasis). That is

6. Maximus expresses that in Πρὸς Μαρῖνον, PG 91, 149b.
7. See for example, Maximus, Ἐπιστολαί, PG 91, 485d–545a–545ab–549b–552a.
8. Yannaras, *Elements of Faith*, 26–28. A note on the Confessor's terminology: Maximus applies the term *hypostasis* to everything that exists, to all particulars (Ἐπιστολαί, PG 91, 549bc), which is not the case with the term πρόσωπον, a term exclusively reserved for persons (human and divine).

why it is a common patristic *topos* that there is no οὐσία ἀνυπόστατος, i.e., no substance or nature that is not actualized in one or more hypostases, no "naked" nature: Maximus the Confessor is very clear on that.[9]

Maximus is in line with the common patristic terminology: "Substance, and nature, is the common, the universal, the general. The hypostasis, and the person, is the particular and the partial."[10] In his view, of all created beings only the human being is endowed with the tendency of becoming a person, of existing in-relation-to (man *is* a person, as his otherness is manifested and actualized in relations and communion, but simultaneously *can become* a person in the fullest sense of the world: this simultaneous co-existence without division and without confusion—the "Chalcedonian logic"—of a future state wished for and of the present state that is already a reality is also a *topos* of patristic thought, due to the atemporal character of the uncreated). A more concise formulation would be that, compared to other creatures, the human person is a person *par excellence* due to his creation "in the image and likeness" of the triune prototype. It is under this light that we must understand Maximus' explicit assertion that "*person* and *hypostasis* are one and the same."[11] Nature is nature, and the tendency of the created (the cause of which is outside of itself) towards individual onticity (non-relation; corruption; death) is *non-prosopic*, it does not describe personhood. However, there is also the tendency towards relation, the tendency and motion towards the return to the uncreated source of createdness and towards the full communion with it, the hope for the *redemption* of creation. In this we see that the *possibility* of personhood, of existing relationally and in communion, is to be found in all created beings; all created beings are characterized by the tendency to personhood "according to the [uncreated]

---

9. Maximus, Πρὸς Μαρῖνον, PG 91, 149b. A thorough examination of the use of these terms by Maximus is to be found in Zizioulas, "Person And Nature," 85–113.

10. Maximus, Ἐπιστολαί, PG 91, 545a. Cf. 549b. For a comprehensive analysis of Maximus' notion of a human hypostasis, see Tollefsen: "St Maximus' Concept of a Human Hypostasis," 115–27. Tollefsen implies that his analysis of these terms differs from that of Zizioulas, but these substantial disagreements could not be traced. Tollefsen seems to imply that to stress the inexistence of an οὐσία ἀνυπόστατος, to stress that there is no "naked" substance or nature (which has implications for the ontological importance of hypostases and persons) would necessary entail, more or less, the inexistence of substances. But this is not Zizioulas' position. On p. 118, n. 15, Tollefsen voices his doubts on the correctness of Maximus' assertion that, should all the hypostases of a universal perish, the universal is abolished as well. However, Maximus' statement is practically a rephrasing of the fact that there is no οὐσία ἀνυπόστατος: should the hypostases perish, their substance is not hypostasized (i.e., actualized) any more and ceases to exist (in the sense of ὑφίσταται<ὑπόστασις).

11. Maximus,Ἔργα θεολογικὰ καὶ πολεμικά, PG 91, 152a: ὑπόστασις καὶ πρόσωπον, ταυτόν.

λόγος of their nature" (κατὰ τὸν λόγον τῆς φύσεως), and all the λόγοι[12] are recapitulated in the one person of the Λόγος. However, this *personalization* of nature (i.e., the redemption of creation) cannot be achieved by nature alone, it is the task of the human being, the priest and mediator of creation; it is the task of *mediation*.[13] In that sense, and without losing the relative and apophatic character of formulations in language, I could say with Maximus that each hypostasis is also a person(-in-waiting).

Returning to the body/soul question, I will examine how Maximus uses the substance/hypostasis distinction with utmost versatility in order to shed light upon this problem. In this, it will become apparent that Maximus thinks of the "substance" and the "hypostasis" as *modes*, not as *things*; otherwise, we would have to consider him as gravely inconsistent, which is not the case.

The Confessor makes *two seemingly contradictory statements* when he speaks about the soul and the body and when he constructs his anthropology parallel to his Christology. He states (1) that the human person, in contrast to Christ, has a "composite nature"[14] (φύσις σύνθετος, whereas in Christ we can only speak of a composite hypostasis), and in another text (2) that the human person constitutes a hypostatic union of two different substances,[15] the body (as substance) and the soul (as substance), in an analogy to Christ's hypostatic union of the divine and human nature.[16] In

12. The polysemy of the word λόγος in Greek, and especially in its philosophical use, is vertiginously staggering (cf. LSJ or Lampe's *Patristic Lexicon*): attempts at translating it in English (as "word", "principle," etc.) are seldom satisfactory, and consequently the term will remain here untranslated. A comprehensive overview of the philosophical use of the term λόγος (plural: λόγοι) would be outside the scope of this article. From a philosophical perspective, the word λόγος signifies every referential activity that manifests an otherness: as such, a primary meaning of λόγος is *disclosure*. Λόγος is also an inherently relational concept: the λόγος of an object *speaks* to us ("I speak": λέγω), i.e., informs us of its identity, of its *what*-it-is, of its substance or nature. The λόγος of something is its *mode* of communicating its existence and nature to us, the *mode* of its disclosure. Existence manifests itself as "logical" when its identity becomes a personal disclosure to a subject bearing the consciousness and personhood needed to actualize the relationality of this disclosure. In Maximus the Confessor's use, the λόγοι are the uncreated *intentions*, *wills*, and *utterances* of God concerning each created being and particularly each created being's substance/nature—*intentions, wills,* and *utterances* that are (pre)existent in God.

13. Masterfully expounded by Thunberg in his *Microcosm and Mediator*.

14. E.g., Maximus, Ἐπιστολαί, PG 91, 488d.

15. Maximus, Ἐπιστολαί, PG 91, 552d.

16. On the analogy between the unity of body and soul in the human person and the unity of divine and human nature in Christ, on the "hypostatic union" of soul and body in man, see e.g., Thunberg, *Microcosm and Mediator*, 101–4, as well as Karl-Heinz Uthemann's mention of Maximus' understanding of the unity of soul and body as both

(1), the body and the soul are two natures/substances which merge into one composite nature/substance, the "human" nature/substance. Whereas in (2) the substance "body" and the substance "soul" co-exist in one single hypostasis, in one actual realization, retaining their distinct nature in a way similar to Christ's hypostatic union. "Composite nature" and "union of two natures in one hypostasis" are two diametrically opposed formulations (and the essence of the Chalcedonian controversies); to use them both as acceptable in a context other than Neochalcedonianism could be seen as philosophically problematic. If we accept that Maximus *consciously* employs both to denote the body/soul relationship, then we need to abandon the dualistic understanding of the notions "body," "soul," "substance," and "hypostasis" in order to understand him and see his seemingly contradictory references as different languages in order to signify the totality and wholeness of the human person.

Polycarp Sherwood regards this as an inconsistency on Maximus' part, as Thunberg remarks,[17] but I maintain that it is perfectly consistent, not only with Maximus' logic, but also with the *inner logic* of the terminology he uses. His (1) first exposition, that the substance of the human person is one "composite nature," a φύσις σύνθετος, is a natural corollary of the philosophical language that Maximus uses: each human person, each human hypostasis, partakes in the common nature of being human, the common substance of all human beings, that, which makes a human being human. This human nature, each specific manifestation of which is every human being, has most certainly a dual character in the Confessor's eyes: "each one of us is of a dual nature, both from a soul and from a body."[18] It is characterized by materiality, which is a nature in itself, a distinct way of partaking in existence (it is the *mode* of materiality, the λόγος of its being), but at the same time possesses qualities that are to be ascribed to an intelligible nature, beyond pure materiality, a way of partaking in existence different than that of pure materiality: a soul, a distinct λόγος of being, a distinct mode (τρόπος) of existence: "the logos and mode of the soul is different from that of the body."[19] These two natures, these two substances,[20] coexist in human nature, in the common substance of all human beings.

---

a hypostatic union and a natural synthesis (Uthemann, "Das anthropologische Modell," 230). Note that this analogy is not Maximus' invention, but quite a *topos* in his time.

17. Thunberg, *Microcosm and Mediator*, 101, fn. 49.

18. Maximus, Περὶ διαφόρων ἀποριῶν, PG 91, 1373c: ἕκαστος ἡμῶν διπλοῦς ἐστι τὴν φύσιν, ἐκ ψυχῆς καὶ σώματος συνεστώς.

19. Maximus, Περὶ διαφόρων ἀποριῶν, PG 91, 1321c: ἄλλος ὁ λόγος καὶ ὁ τρόπος τῆς ψυχῆς, ἄλλος τῷ σώματι.

20. Maximus, Ἐπιστολαί, PG 91, 488a.

However, (2) Maximus also approaches the subject from a seemingly radically different perspective (even incompatibly so), understanding the human person not as one composite nature and hypostasis, but as one hypostasis in two distinct natures, as a "hypostatic union" of some sort. He makes it clear: "Man is not of one nature which is constituted of body and soul,"[21] rejecting the definition on which I just elaborated above. Maximus compares Christ's union of two natures in one hypostasis with man's union of body and soul in one hypostasis, but not in one (composite) nature: as he writes, "the one and single Christ is known by the natures from which and in which he is constituted, just as each one and single human being is known by the natures [i.e., body and soul] from which he has been constituted and in which he exists."[22] In speaking about a *hypostatic union* of soul and body in man, Maximus changes perspective and chooses to focus on the two natures and substances that constitute every specific human being and not on the qualities of man's general nature, which in the former exposition make it a composite nature. However, this is not to suggest a dichotomy, but quite the contrary: Maximus proposes it to underline the oneness and wholeness of the human person, a oneness and wholeness similar but not identical to the co-existence of Christ's two natures in his person *without confusion, without change, without division, and without separation*.[23]

And here I come to my point: *in both of Maximus' definitions on the relationship of soul and body, the hypostasis—the specific manifestation of the general substance "soul"—is the particular human person as a whole*:

1. In Maximus' view of the composite human nature and substance, composed of the substance "body" and the substance "soul," its specific manifestation and actual existence, the realization of this composite nature, is the human person as a whole.

2. In the Confessor's view of a hypostatic union of these two natures and substances in man, there is again one and specific actual existence, one hypostasis: this specific human person—we could say, following Chalcedon, "*without confusion of the two natures, without change in them, without division and without separation.*"

Maximus does speak of a soul, of the soul as an immortal, bodiless, intelligible, and simple substance:[24] however, in the field of *actual existences*,

---

21. Maximus, Ἐπιστολαί, PG 91, 488b: Ἀλλ' οὐδὲ τὸν ἄνθρωπον μίαν φύσιν τὴν ἐκ ψυχῆς καὶ σώματος.

22. Maximus, Ἐπιστολαί, PG 91, 488a.

23. ἀσυγχύτως, ἀτρέπτως, ἀδιαιρέτως, ἀχωρίστως, as the Symbol of Chalcedon, the decree of the Chalcedonian Council would put it.

24. Maximus, Περὶ ψυχῆς, PG 91, 357c–361a.

the whole human person is that which actually exists: *the soul in itself would be an οὐσία ἀνυπόστατος.* There is no hypostasis of the substance "soul," apart from the human hypostasis as an undivided whole, the whole of the human person.²⁵

I mentioned a union "without division" and "without separation." But isn't the soul separated from the body after death? An examination of Maximus' writings would suggest that his answer would be "yes *and no*." For him, the dead body and the intelligible soul are only the parts of a whole: it is the body of *this* human person; the soul of *this* human person. Neither body nor soul is to be thought of in itself—even in death—as separated from the one human person that together they constitute, i.e., the person that they constitut*ed* and, in Maximus' view, do still constitute and will constitute again. Maximus writes:

> The soul is not simply called "soul" after death, but this specific person's soul. And the body is not simply called "body" after death, but this specific person's body, even if that body is subject to decay. Thus, one cannot speak of body or soul separately, as if they were irrelevant to one another.²⁶

Later in the *Ambigua*, Maximus remarks again that "one cannot conceive of a soul without body or of a body without soul."²⁷ Even after death, the hypostasis, the specific manifestation and realization, continues to be the whole human person. This shifts the ontological and soteriological focus from a notion of the soul as a bodiless human to that of the whole human person, of the human person as we know it.

Furthermore, as Maximus speaks of the *immortal* nature of the human soul, I come to my second question, which is integrally connected to the first one: if the human person truly possesses a free will as an ontological fact, could his soul or his hypostasis be *necessarily* eternal? The answer to God's

---

25. See also: Maximus, Περὶ διαφόρων ἀποριῶν, PG 91, 1336a: Ἡνώθη δὲ τῷ Θεῷ Λόγῳ μετὰ τῆς ψυχῆς καὶ τὸ σῶμα. Ἄρα μετὰ τῆς ψυχῆς καὶ τὸ σῶμα σωθήσεται. ("The body as well as the soul have joined the God Logos. That is, the body will also be saved along with the soul.") *Ibid.*: σαρκοῦται ὁ τοῦ Θεοῦ Λόγος ἵνα καὶ τὴν εἰκόνα σώσῃ καὶ τὴν σάρκα ἀθανατίσῃ. ("The Logos of God has been incarnated both in order to save the image/icon and to immortalize the flesh.")

26. Maximus, Περὶ διαφόρων ἀποριῶν, PG 91, 1101b-c: Οὐχ ἁπλῶς γὰρ λέγεται ψυχὴ μετὰ τὸν τοῦ σώματος ἡ ψυχή, ἀλλὰ ἀνθρώπου ψυχή, καὶ τοῦ τινος ἀνθρώπου ψυχή. . . . Οὐ γὰρ ἁπλῶς λέγεται σῶμα μετὰ τὸν χωρισμὸν τῆς ψυχῆς τὸ σῶμα, ἀλλ' ἀνθρώπου σῶμα, καὶ τοῦ τινος ἀνθρώπου σῶμα, κἂν εἰ φθείρεται καὶ εἰς τὰ ἐξ ὧν ἐστιν ἀναλύεσθαι στοιχεῖα πέφυκεν. . . . Οὐχ ἔστιν οὖν ὅλως σῶμα δυνατὸν ἢ ψυχὴν εὑρεῖν ἢ λέγειν ἄσχετον.

27. Maximus, Περὶ διαφόρων ἀποριῶν, PG 91, 1324b: Καὶ τούτῳ τῷ λόγῳ οὔτε σώματος χωρὶς ἡ ψυχή, οὔτε ψυχῆς σῶμά ποτε νοηθήσεται.

creative call that creates us "from non-being into being" or into eternal being cannot but be *necessarily* affirmative? And if so, is the freedom of the person true freedom, or does God force the person to accept an existence that this person could otherwise deny?

Speaking about the answer to God's creative call, I am not referring to an event *before our birth* or *after our death*, but to a continuous event, or to be more precise an event *outside of time* as we know and experience it. If freedom and free will allow us to prepare during our life a receptiveness to the possibility of being given existence beyond the constraints of natural life, beyond the grave, then freedom would also allow us to deny such a possibility. However, the price of such a choice would not be an eternal punishment imposed by a God who is only defined as love, but, simply, inexistence; the denial to participate in His love, which calls us "from non-being into being." The inability to revisit such a choice, as "there is no repentance after death," would be, truly, hell. It must be duly noted that when we are speaking about "freedom" in the context of ontology and fundamental anthropology, there can be no *grades* of freedom: a being can either have the capability to transcend all limitations, to *become what it is not* (for example, in the context of Maximian "deification," θέωσις, according to which "we are becoming fully and utterly Gods except of an identity in substance"[28]) or not. In the second case, there could definitely be internal grades of freedom within the operation of a being that cannot attain full ontological freedom and thus is defined by necessity. However, these instances of relative freedom would not change the ontological status of said being: it would be still defined by *necessity*, not by *freedom*. As such, the question whether the human person can reject God's creative call from non-being into being, even after the conclusion of his life, is essentially identical to the question whether the human person is constituted as a free person, possessing an undiluted free will, or not, or as a being defined by necessity.

Christos Yannaras, commenting on Maximus the Confessor's fragments on "our hopes hereafter,"[29] has analyzed the possibility that "what we term in our language as 'hell' could refer to man's free choice not to exist. If the foundation of existing is the relationship with God, and the 'logical'-per-

---

28. Cf. Maximus, Ἐπιστολαί, PG 91 376ab: ὅλοι δι' ὅλου γινόμεθα θεοὶ χωρὶς τῆς κατ' οὐσίαν ταυτότητος. And Πρὸς Θαλάσσιον, PG 90, 320A: πάντως καὶ τῆς ἐπὶ τῷ θεωθῆναι τὸν ἄνθρωπον μυστικῆς ἐνεργείας λήψεται πέρας, κατὰ πάντα τρόπον, χωρὶς μόνης δηλονότι τῆς πρὸς αὐτὸν κατ' οὐσίαν ταυτότητος, ὁμοιώσας ἑαυτῷ τὸν ἄνθρωπον. "Then God will also completely fulfill the goal of his mystical work of deifying humanity in every respect, of course, short of an identity of substance with God; and he will assimilate humanity to himself."

29. Yannaras, "Ontological Realism," 379–86.

sonal relationship (which, to be logical-personal, must be free) constitutes the logical-personal existence, then this relationship-existence can be either accepted or even rejected, leading to nonexistence."[30] Yannaras considers this view well founded in the texts of church fathers like the Confessor:

> Hell, says Maximus, is the negation to participate in being, in well being and in ever being: the free self-exclusion from existence, from relation-participation in being, the negation of the relationship and as such the negation of existing, of existence. And this voluntary nonexistence as a deprivation and loss of the gift of deification can perhaps only be signified symbolically in language with the image of endless torture, of the suffering and weeping. Thereby is the unbearable scandal dispelled, that a God who is love preserves His deniers eternally in existence only to see them suffer hopelessly.[31]

Maximus' relevant passage is revealing: according to him, the participation or the refusal to participate in being, well being, and ever being is a punishment for those who cannot participate and a bliss and delight for those who can participate.[32] Maximus does not explicitly write that hell is inexistence, that the negative answer to God's call would result in inexistence—this would be contrary to his ascertainment that the soul i.e., the human person is "immortal." However, Maximus denotes the totality of existence with his three categories of being (εἶναι), well-being (εὖ εἶναι), and ever-being (ἀεὶ εἶναι): the refusal or inability to participate in *any of them* cannot but mean the refusal or inability to participate *in existence, in reality*, if we follow Maximus' language concisely. And he is right in writing that we cannot but perceive this conscious choice of inexistence as "punishment." It is interesting to note that Maximus speaks in another context of the "irrational and absolute and substanceless *inexistence*" that results from a life in sin, i.e., a life "contrary to our [real] nature" (παρὰ φύσιν).[33] Judging from the Confessor's generally concise use of philosophical and theological signifiers, I think that his reference to the "irrational and absolute and substanceless *inexistence*" that results from a life that embodies a conscious denial to God's creative and relational call is not merely a literary or rhetorical

---

30. Yannaras, "Ontological Realism," 385.

31. Ibid.

32. Maximus, Περὶ διαφόρων ἀποριῶν, PG 91, 1329b.

33. Maximus, Σχόλια εἰς τὸ Περὶ θείων ὀνομάτων, PG 4, 305b: Τῆς κατὰ φύσιν κινήσεως ἤτοι τάξεως ἀποτυγχάνοντες φερόμεθα εἰς τὴν παρὰ φύσιν ἄλογον καὶ παντελῆ καὶ ἀνούσιον ἀνυπαρξίαν.

*topos*.³⁴ In such a case, hell would be a signifier (and not merely a "symbol") of *inexistence*, the result of a life consistently "contrary to nature." However, the question arises: is it possible at all for the human being's answer to God's creative call to be *wholly negative and rejective* (or wholly affirmative, for that matter)? Can man's life be constituted as a continuous and absolute choice of non-relation, death, non-communion and inexistence (or of communion, relation, and life)? Or are these absolute choices extremities that cannot be truly attained in their wholeness, thereby annulling the possibility of a human person's life truly resulting in "absolute and substanceless inexistence"? In such a case, "irrational and absolute and substanceless inexistence" would remain a potentiality/possibility (a signifier of the will's true freedom) that cannot be truly actualized in its wholeness. The possibility that a person's life has been a chosen rejection God's creative call, relation, communion, and life, but has not "achieved" the completeness of rejection that would result in inexistence (thereby being granted a participation in existence that cannot but be incomplete due to the person's overwhelming rejection of it) illustrates an existential drama; an eternal hell.

Certain passages of the Confessor's could lead to this conclusion. In Πρὸς Θαλάσσιον, Maximus mentions the delight (ἡδονὴ) of those that will be united with God by his nature and grace³⁵ and the pain and anguish (ὀδύνη) of those that "will be united with God by his nature but contrary to grace."³⁶ The criterion is "each human person's own quality of disposition" (κατὰ γὰρ τὴν ὑποκειμένην ἑκάστῳ ποιότητα τῆς διαθέσεως),³⁷ each human person's preparedness for this union, i.e., the full and absolute union of God with each and every one at the "end of the ages."³⁸ According to the Confessor, this union with the uncreated, a union effecting the continuation of existence through life-giving relation and communion, will take place in any case due to God's own nature. The ones whose answer to God's continuous creative call from nonbeing into being is a negative one are bound to experience this union as pain and anguish, for it is a union contrary to their

---

34. I believe that Yannaras' position on the subject is an interesting one that could provide the basis for a truly productive philosophical and theological debate. Essentially, this is not a question of philological and exegetical conciseness, but of ontological consistency, much in the vein of Maximus the Confessor's own primary concern as a church father. The affirmation of both a truly free will and immortality of the soul in the context of the ecclesial testimony remains, in our opinion, an unresolved philosophical *problem* in need of bold attempts at consistently addressing it; I hope that this debate will indeed take place in the near future.

35. Πρὸς Θαλάσσιον, PG 90, 609c.

36. Ibid.

37. Ibid.

38. Ibid.

preparedness for receptiveness and communion, contrary to their quality of disposition. This reading of Maximus', contrary to his passage concerning the "irrational and absolute and substanceless inexistence,"[39] accounts for a *tendency* of the disposition towards inexistence that, regrettably, cannot be truly actualized; an existential hell.[40]

In this paper I have attempted to examine the question of the soul, of whether it is "something" that "exists" or "does not exist," in the light of Maximus the Confessor's writings and in the light of a distinction between substance and hypostasis, rather than between body and soul. In this context, Maximus' analogy between the unity of body and soul in the human person and the hypostatic union of the divine and human nature in Christ's person has been shown to be of particular importance, as he speaks about the body and soul as "substances," the common "hypostasis" of which is the whole human person—while an οὐσία ἀνυπόστατος, i.e., an unactualized substance, would be inconceivable. This analogy overshadows certain formulations of the church father which would seem to suggest a dichotomy characteristic of the Neoplatonic philosophical language that Maximus uses, but not of the Confessor's testimony itself. Furthermore, in the context of the soul's alleged immortality, the following question has been addressed: if the human person truly possesses a free will as an ontological fact of philosophical anthropology, could his soul or his hypostasis be *compulsorily eternal*? Doesn't man's "quality of disposition" (ποιότητα τῆς διαθέσεως) give him the choice of inexistence? And wouldn't the inability to revisit such a choice be, truly, hell?

It is customary to think of Christian anthropology as reflecting a dualistic conception of humanity and the human person, to say the least. It is also customary to think of the Christian's hopes hereafter as being defined by either "punishment" or "reward"—categories pertaining to a juridical mindset so often encountered in the context of religion and categories pertaining to morality and moral justice, not to ontology and the anthropology that would derive from it. I am proposing that there can be interpretations of church fathers of Maximus the Confessor's stature that could indicate otherwise. According to this interpretation of Maximus' unified anthropology, constitutive *modes* (τρόποι) of the whole and actually existing human person can be discerned, i.e., constitutive *hows* instead of constitutive *whats*, leading to an anthropology beyond said dualisms and polarizations. In this interpretation, Maximus' unified, whole human person is then defined as a

39. Maximus, Σχόλια εἰς τὸ Περὶ θείων ὀνομάτων, PG 4, 305b.

40. The reader is here reminded of Maximus the Confessor's aforementioned explicit reference to "the *risk* of dissolving into nonbeing" in Μυσταγωγία, Cantarella 1.70–72.

πρόσωπον and, consequently, as freedom: as someone whose existence is a free answer to God's creative call, which is at the same time a call to relate with the Creator, to enter a personal relationship with Him. An integral part of this freedom would be the capability to *reject* this call-to-relate, to *reject* God's call, thereby "risking inexistence," as Maximus says. However, is the human person able to be wholly actualized as a negation, or would this possibility of accepting inexistence remain an unactualized option, leaving the human person in the desire of a rejection-constituting-inexistence that he cannot fully commit himself to accomplish? These questions may contribute an ontological aspect to the problem of the semantic content of "hell." However, these questions cannot but remain unanswered—and, at the same time, in need of further and deeper philosophical inquiry. When our sources (scriptural, patristic, or otherwise) do not provide us with definitive answers concerning possible internal inconsistencies of ontological and anthropological propositions, an ontological/anthropological inquiry applying the criterion of philosophical consistency is of utmost importance.

In referring (a) to the substance and the hypostasis as *modes of existence*, (b) to the soul and body not as a dichotomy and duality between two realities, but as the very affirmation of the human person's totality and wholeness, and (c) to the problem of the simultaneous affirmation of the soul's *immortality* and the person's *freedom*, I have only provided hints on subjects that by far exceed the limitations of a short article. I have done so in the hope that these subjects and questions will receive the attention they deserve in the future, with the aid of the Maximian *corpus*' vast potential for illuminating them. The articulation and formulation of the ecclesial testimony's ontology, as well as of its hope for humanity and the world, is not to be seen as a philological exercise at annotating fixed givens, but rather as a perpetual and demanding inquiry.

## Bibliography

Maximus the Confessor. Ἐπιστολαί. In *Patrologiae Cursus Completus—Series Graeca*, edited by Jean-Paul Migne, Vol. 91, 364–649. Paris: Migne, 1857–66.

———. Μυσταγωγία. In *S. Massimo Confessore. La mistagogia ed altri scritti*, edited by Raffaele Cantarella. Florence: Testi Cristiani, 1931.

———. Περὶ διαφόρων ἀποριῶν τῶν ἁγίων Διονυσίου καὶ Γρηγορίου. In *Patrologiae Cursus Completus—Series Graeca*, edited by Jean-Paul Migne, Vol. 91, 1032–1424. Paris: Migne, 1857–66.

———. Περὶ ψυχῆς. In *Patrologiae Cursus Completus—Series Graeca*, edited by Jean-Paul Migne, Vol. 91, 353–61. Paris: Migne, 1857–66.

---. Πρὸς Θαλάσσιον, περὶ διαφόρων ἀπόρων τῆς θείας Γραφῆς: In *Patrologiae Cursus Completus—Series Graeca*, edited by Jean-Paul Migne, Vol. 90, 244–785. Paris: Migne, 1857-66.

---. Σχόλια εἰς τὸ Περὶ θείων ὀνομάτων. In *Patrologiae Cursus Completus—Series Graeca*, edited by Jean-Paul Migne, Vol. 4, 185–416. Paris: Mignr, 1857-66.

Thunberg, Lars. *Microcosm and Mediator: The Theological Anthropology of Maximus the Confessor*. Chicago: Open Court, 1995.

Tollefsen, Torstein. *The Christocentric Cosmology of St. Maximus the Confessor*. Oxford: Oxford University Press, 2008.

---. "St Maximus' Concept of a Human Hypostasis." In *Knowing the Purpose of Creation through the Resurrection—Proceedings of the Symposium on St. Maximus the Confessor, October 18-21 2012*, edited by Maxim Vasiljević, 115–27. California: Sebastian Press, 2013.

Uthemann, Karl-Heinz. "Das anthropologische Modell der hypostatischen Union: ein Beitrag zu den philosophischen Voraussetzungen und zur innerchalkedonischen Transformation eines Paradigmas." In *Maximus Confessor: Actes du Symposium sur Maxime le Confesseur, Fribourg, 2–5 septembre, 1980*, edited by Felix Heinzer and Christoph von Schönborn, 223–233. Fribourg: Éditions universitaires, 1982.

Yannaras, Christos. *Elements of Faith*. Edinburgh: T. & T. Clark, 1991.

---. "The Ontological Realism of our Hopes Hereafter: Conclusions from St. Maximus the Confessor's Brief References." In *Knowing the Purpose of Creation through the Resurrection, Proceedings of the Symposium on St. Maximus the Confessor, October 18–21, 2012*, edited by Maxim Vasiljević, 379–386. Alhambra, CA: Sebastian, 2013.

Zizioulas, Metropolitan John of Pergamon. "Person and Nature in the Theology of St. Maximus the Confessor." In *Knowing the Purpose of Creation through the Resurrection—Proceedings of the Symposium on St. Maximus the Confessor, October 18–21, 2012*, edited by Maxim Vasiljević, 85–113. Alhambra, CA: Sebastian, 2013.

# 8

## *Nous* (*Energeia*) and *Kardia* (*Dynamis*) in the Holistic Anthropology of St. Gregory Palamas

NICHIFOR TĂNASE

### Introduction

ATHONITE SPIRITUALITY OF THE fourteenth century is situated at the confluence of a theology of divine names already present in the Old Testament and of the ancient practice of monastic traditions, and is also illustrated by the writings of Evagrius and Ps.-Macarius. Hesychasm provides a deep, spiritual theological meaning by grafting the uncreated energies and a single word of prayer onto a theological conception of divine glory. Hesychastic spirituality is "able to assimilate and integrate creatively, as in the case of Evagrius, for whom the mystical tendencies are colored by Neoplatonism and Stoicism."[1]

The three stages of development of the Hesychastic movement are: the Sinai, Symeon the New Theologian (Sec. XI), and Athonite hesychasm (XIV–XV). The name "hesychasm" usually signifies that current of spiritual life among Eastern Orthodox monks which is wholly directed to pure contemplation and prayerful union with God. The "re-establishment of

---

1. Behr-Sigel, *Lieu du coeur*, 61–62, 75.

hesychasm," such as a return to the contemplative life or as spiritual renewal of interior life of the contemplative spirit, was brought about by Gregory the Sinaite.[2]

The Holy Mountain becomes the center from which the hesychastic practice of the prayer of the heart spread. Gregory the Sinaite uses the name of Jesus eucharistically, while Maxime the Huts Burner (*Kausokalybe*) unites "the remembrance/memory of Jesus" with that of Mary, Mother of God. Theoleptos of Philadelphia offers one role in prayer to each of the spiritual powers: discursive (*dianoia*), intellectual (*nous*), and spiritual (*pneuma*). In this context, St. Gregory Palamas protected the integrity of the Christian mystery and the authenticity of spiritual experience for the mystical monks, with full affirmation of the reality of deification in which man participates in his psychosomatic totality. A famous distinction of the unknown being of God and his participating energies is intended to preserve the experience of the contemplative—meaning the uncreated nature of the Tabor light.

Gregory teaches that man possesses the divine likeness in a greater measure than an angel: the body as well as the soul reflects the image of God; precisely because he has a body, he is more truly sealed with divine image than the pure spirits, the angels. The intellectual (νοερός) and rational (λογικός) nature of the soul created with an earthly body has received a life-giving spirit from God. The nature of soul is endowed both with intellect (νοῦς), reason (λόγος), and life-giving spirit being, to a higher degree than the angels, in God's image.[3] Impassivity (ἀπάθεια) itself is no mere mortification of the physical passions of the body, but is its new and better energy and, in general, the body shares in the spirit's life of grace, not only in the world to come, but even now.[4]

Understanding the spirituality of St. Gregory Palamas will involve a downward movement (*katabasis*) from triadology to anthropology and then reverse, traversing upward (*anabasis*) from anthropology back to triadology, whose finality is the deification of man through uncreated divine energies. But analysis of this palamite triadological anthropology will send us, as we will see, toward the differentiated reception of Augustinian categories by the authors of the so-called "hesychastic dispute."

Therefore, it is necessary to recognize the *important role played by theological anthropology* in the doctrine of St. Gregory Palamas.

Thus, only man was truly made in the image of the trihypostatic God. Palamas was intermingling two analogies for the Trinity and associated

---

2. Krivosheine, *Ascetic and Theological*, 51–52, n. 2.
3. Palamas, *One Hundred and Fifty* (chapters 34–40), 116–27.
4. *Haghioriticus Tomus*, 418–25.

both with God's image in man. The first was mind, word, and spirit, but the second analogy was the relation of the mind to its immanent knowledge (*logos*), a relation described as love (*eros*). The application of the analogy of love to the Spirit is almost unprecedented in the East, while at the same time it is a hallmark of Augustine's theology of the Trinity. The analogy of mind, word, and spirit had a venerable patristic heritage, although it was rarely associated with the divine image in man. These triads, whether the Trinitarian nature of the soul (intellect, *logos*, mind), or the triune nature of knowledge (spiritual, rational, sensible), or triple character of the intellect when it returns to itself and ascends to God (intellect, knowledge, love).

*The distinction between hypostasis of the Holy Spirit and His grace or energy is likewise the central node of Palamism.*

In this regard, Augustine confuses or makes no distinction between the economic and the immanent Trinity, because in *De Trinitate* Augustine concludes that *within the Trinity* the Father and the Son constitute together one principle in relation to the Holy Spirit, a concept Palamas did of course not share. Thereby, there is clearly a conceptual antagonism between Augustinianism and Palamism. Indeed, in the context of Palamas' rejection of the argument by his opponents that energy is just an accident, he makes use of Trinitarian analogies of the human mind. But, to Augustine's transfiguration grace—presently experienced now in hope, but in reality fully present only in the eschaton—Palamas categorically opposes the real possibility of enlightenment as a deifying experience, anticipated and visible here among the saints. Already in the *Triads*, Gregory Palamas laid emphasis on deification as an experiential reality.

In the present study we propose to analyze the noetic implications of deification or *theosis* in four dimensions: 1. *nous-logos-pneuma*; 2. *nous* (intuitive intellect) and *dianoia* (discursive intellect); 3. *nous* and *kardia*, and 4. being and energies of mind in the psycho-somatic method of hesychast prayer.

Even though Palamas did not accept the entirety of Augustine's thought on the Trinity, he made use of Augustine in various writings, letting himself be inspired by some of Augustine's arguments for a different purpose, in order to *clarify the analogy of the Spirit as love*. Thereby, firstly we will try to point out that the *triad logos-nous-psyche is not so much Augustinian* and secondly that *Palamas was not an "Augustinian" theologian* since, in some cases, he used Augustine's words in order to support a concept that was the *opposite* of what Augustine originally intended. Therefore, it will be necessary to study the relationship between *Nous* and other concepts of hesychastic spirituality such as: *logos, pneuma, dianoia, kardia*, and *energeia*.

God's image in man reflects both the immanent life and the economic processions of the Godhead. Because of man's corporeality, the image has a Christological and incarnational dimension as well as a pneumatological character. The *Christological corrective* is operative in Gregory's doctrine of the divine image. Man's *taxis* in the hierarchies is placed immediately after God and above the angels. In the case of man, his corporeality adds an incarnational dimension to the triadic character of the image.

Then we analyze the distinction between the noetic ("nous," *intuitive intellect*) and the intellectual ("dianoia," *discursive intellect*) made by hesychasts within the faculties of the soul. *Nous* is more an organ of mystical union and *noesis* is a form of a deeper, simpler, contemplative thinking. Our mind is also made by the image of the Father, the supreme Mind. The νοῦς is a purely philosophical term that has no biblical foundation. Byzantine authors fully inherited the meaning and connotations that ancient philosophy gave to the concept. Νοῦς is the ability of men to surpass themselves and participate in God. The task of the hesychast is to direct not the nature of the mind, but its activity inwards. Misunderstandings arise from the confusion between the nature of the mind and its activity. There is a very interesting similarity between Palamas and Theoleptos' conception of *dianoia* and *nous* during prayer.

In connection with his doctrine of man, we must note the role that Saint Gregory assigns the heart (*kardia*) in the spiritual and intellectual life. He looks on it as the principal center of man's spiritual life, the organ of thought (the *seat of the mind* and of discernment). Palamas explains how the noetic faculty isn't the essence of the soul, but an energy. He advocates for a holistic anthropology of prayer and of grace through a complementarity between the heart and intellect. Nous is understood both as *energeia* (activity) of the mind, and as *dynamis* ("power" called "*kardia*") that activates *noera energeia* ("the human spirit in the heart"). The heart, therefore, is the first fleshly organ of the mind. St. Gregory Palamas provides a theological and anthropological foundation of the prayer of Jesus, which is simultaneously a prayer both of the heart and the mind. In the prayer the mind becomes unified and triadic. "Heart" in this context is to be understood in the Semitic and biblical rather than the modern Western sense, as signifying the totality of the human person, our innermost being.

Related to the common energies of the soul and the body and their role in mental prayer, we have two theological assertions: the mind must return to the heart. Following such fathers as St. Basil the Great, Palamas explains that the noetic faculty is not the essence of the soul, but an energy. Irénée Hausherr make a mistake when he identifies the essence of mental prayer with its auxiliary methods. Gregory Palamas does not give any detailed account of its methods as do his predecessors (Symeon the New Theologian, Nicephorus the Monk, and Gregory the Sinaite), but we find in him a most brilliant ascetico-philosophical defense of some of these methods. There is no mechanical technique, whether physical or mental, that can compel God to manifest his presence. For St. Gregory Palamas, the essential thing is not the external control of the breathing, but the final objective described by the patristic term *theosis*, "deification" or "divinization." The Jesus Prayer, by uniting us to Christ, helps us to share in the mutual indwelling or perichoresis of the three Persons of the Holy Trinity. The noetic prayer stops in ecstatic union. In the "silence of mind," the *nous* unites itself with the Divine Mind beyond its own nature. The intellect of man has a "straight" movement and a circular movement. In the latter man comes to the work without beginning and is the contemplation of himself. This ineffable divine dynamism must also be the work of the true man, by which "the unity of the intellect becomes triple, remaining one."[5] This latter is clearly the Augustinian psychological triad. However, even if there is a relationship between Augustine and Palamas, there are nevertheless considerable differences in their uses of the same image, resulting from the different theological presuppositions of each. This is mainly due to the fact that St. Augustine does not know the distinction between essence and energy. For St. Gregory, only the Trinitarian energy is accessible to man, being the "work" and the eternal "movement" of the Triune God and His manifestation *ad extra*. For him, the soul's many powers reflects in "an obscure way" the Triune God, and while using the psychological method, he does not adhere to the psychological analogy of triads.

Thus, starting from comparison between Augustine and Palamas on their different approaches to the Trinity, especially with regard to the Holy Spirit and energies, in our exposition of the ascetico-gnoseological teaching of Gregory Palamas we wish to note the following peculiarities. Firstly, the importance he attributes to the sharing of the whole, integral man in the work of bringing him to the knowledge of union with God. This *conception of man as an integral being* is vividly expressed in Gregory's teaching that man possesses the divine image to a higher degree than the angels, a possession that is stamped on the whole of his psycho-physical composition. In the domain of asceticism this idea is expressed in the teaching on the *co-operation of the body in the spiritual life*, its capacity to be illuminated by and united with the Divinity in one contemplative operation that embraces the whole man. Gnoseologically Gregory opposes one-sided intellectual

---

5. Palamas, *One Hundred and Fifty* (chapters 40 and 63), 126–27, 156–57; Palamas, *Triads* (I.ii.5, I.ii. 8), 44, 46; Palamas, *Homilies* (60, 4), 495–96.

cognition, inadequate in the matter of the knowledge of God, to a supra-rational knowledge proper to the man whose being has been enlightened and who attained union with God. Another peculiar feature is his antinomism, namely combining the idea of an inaccessible and unapproachable Divinity with his assertion that it is possible to attain the union with God through grace and direct vision of Him.

## *Nous, Logos, Pneuma*

There is clearly a conceptual antagonism between Augustinianism and Palamism. Indeed, in the context of Palamas' rejection of the argument by his opponents that energy is just an accident, he makes use of Trinitarian analogies of the human mind (chapter 37 and the *Trinity* IX, 12, 18). But, Palamas very clearly did not conclude, like Augustine, that the Holy Spirit is the relation of love between the Father and the Son. Palamas had access to the famous treatise *De Trinitate* of Saint Augustine through the Greek translation made in 1281 by the Byzantine humanist scholar monk Maxim Planudis, who was educated at court and developed a special interest in Latin.[6] From the fact that Palamas comes into contact with the translation of the Augustinian work *De Trinitate,* various hypotheses about the Augustinian influence on Palamite theology were proposed. Martin Jugie and John Meyendorff (1926–92) are the first who clearly pointed to the Augustinianism that emerges from the fourteenth century hesychast theologian's work.

Jugie first notes (in 1932) the parallelism of Trinitarian Palamite "theopsychology" to that expounded by Augustine in *De Trinitate*: *mens, verbum, spiritus* (*nous, logos, pneuma*) or *mens, notitia, amor* (*nous, gnosis, eros*).[7] Meyendorff also calls Palamas "one of the most Augustinian authors of the Christian East"[8] and admits a "close similarity"[9] between the two theologians. To be sure, Meyendorff had also seen Barlaam as a "nominalist," though a Byzantine one,[10] and therefore had excluded any direct Latin influence on him during the time of the controversy.[11] However, there are also more recent theologians who deny that Palamite theology related to

6. Constantinides, *Higher Education*, 66–89.

7. Jugie, "Palamas," 1766.

8. Meyendorff, *Introduction*, 175. This has been rejected by Romanides, "Notes on the Palamite I," 196, 205.

9. Meyendorff, *Introduction*, 316; Bobrinskoy, *Mystère de la Trinité*, 30–34.

10. Meyendorff, *Introduction*, 65, 74, 281.

11. Meyendorff, "Les débuts de la controverse," 90–96.

a specific Augustinian influence and refer instead to fourteenth-century Byzantine Platonism as the source. Endre von Ivanka tried to convince us of "Palamas' unconscious Platonism," which resulted in the "metaphysics of uncreated energies" in "a pluralist spirit outside the Unity."[12]

In the context of modern debates on the dependent relationship between Palamas and Augustine, there is a second group who denies any influence of Augustine, placing St. Gregory Palamas exclusively in the context of Eastern patristic theology. Thus, Edmund Hussey had already considered Didymus' *De Spiritu Sancto* as a possible *alternative* to Augustine,[13] while Constantine Tsirpanlis pointed out that "Palamas totally avoided the 'Augustinian temptation' and its Trinitarian analogies," but instead "clarified the orthodox analogy of the Spirit as love."[14] John Romanides, the most bitter critic of Meyendorff and perhaps the most anti-Augustinian Orthodox theologian of the twentieth century, argues that Gregory must have positively rejected the polemics of *De Trinitate* I–IV. Romanides argues that this section of *De Trinitate* was not only used by Barlaam to refer to the question of the biblical theophanies, but it was also where Augustine broke with prior tradition in order to deny the *Visio Dei* to the saints.[15] Romanides labelled Barlaam a Christian Platonist who was theologically schooled in the works of Duns Scotus, Thomas Aquinas, and Augustine.

Reinhard Flogaus and Robert E. Sinkewicz represent two theologically divergent approaches to the reception of Augustinian theology in the fourth century, concerning themselves with correctly interpreting Palamas' reliance on those who came before him. In his 1988 edition of the *Capita*, the Basilian father Sinkewicz strongly rejected this kind of dependence and deliberately omitted this connection, supporting a direct dependence of his contemporaries, Gregory of Sinai and Theoleptos of Philadelphia. Thus, Sinkewicz develops a discussion of this triadic theopsychological analogy from the holy fathers (Theophilus, Origen, Gregory of Nazianzus, Gregory of Nyssa, John of Damascus).[16] Gregory spoke of the relation of the mind to the knowledge immanent in it as one of love, but he did not describe this as the mind's intending its own self-love (*amor sui* and *voluntas sui*).[17]

---

12. Ivanka, "Hésychasme et palamisme," 389–402.
13. Hussey, "The Palamite Trinitarian," 83–89.
14. Tsirpanlis, "Epistemology, Theognosis," 9.
15. Romanides, "Notes on the Palamite I," 194–98, and "Notes on the Palamite II," 247–49, 257–62.
16. Sinkewicz, "St. Gregory Palamas and the Doctrine of God's Image," 857–81.
17. Sinkewicz, *Doctrine of the knowledge of God*, 18.

Flogaus, a Lutheran theologian, noted that Palamas' *Discourse-Treatise on Christ's Economy* was based on the reading notes from the books IV, XIII, and XIV of Augustine's *De Trinitate*. Contrary to Sinkewicz, Flogaus discusses Augustine's reception in the *One Hundred and Fifty Chapters*, especially when he discusses "energies as accident" (125–35) and the "Trinitarian image of man" (35–38). Inspiration, exploitation, and distortion: these three keywords were also appropriated by Flogaus to describe the contemporary scholarly discussion about Augustine in the hesychast controversy.[18] Furthermore, Flogaus says that "Palamas obviously did read Augustine as a father belonging to the tradition of the Church."[19]

In contrast to Fr. Meyendorff, Flogaus never claimed that Palamas was an "Augustinian" theologian. Flogaus' line of interpretations was recently continued by theologians like Jacques Lison and Josef Lössl, or exactly replicated by Demetrakopoulos. In this vein, Lison argues that Palamas was not influenced by Augustinian thought.[20] He refuses, following in this way Sinckewicz, to see any Augustinian influence in the well-known passage of Gregory Palamas about the Holy Spirit.[21] However, there is a lack of any references in the analysis of Lison to the two *Apodictic Treaties* and, secondly, to *Against Bekos*. Demetrakopoulos analyzes the reception of Aristotelian categories both in Palamas and Augustine's thought and, at same time, the reception of Augustine's psychotheological triadology by Palamas.[22] He practically reproduced all the parallel passages from the *Capita* that were listed in Flogaus' publications, but did not mention the publications of the latter.

Lössl, totally indebted to Flogaus, wanted to see in Augustine rather a Palamite in the making, or render Palamas a crypto-Augustinian thinker.[23] Also he looked for further evidence of Augustinian influence in the work of Prochoros Kydones who tried to place Augustine in the Hesychast tradition. Having been one of Palamas's most ardent followers during his lifetime, Prochoros ended up being condemned a heretic, not in line with Palamas's teaching, and has ever since been known as an "anti-Palamite."[24] Quoting from *De Trinitate* I. 3. 30, Prochoros's use of Augustine worked

18. Flogaus, "Inspiration-Exploitation-Distortion," 75; Flogaus, "Palamas and Barlaam Revisited," 1–31.

19. Flogaus, "Inspiration-Exploitation-Distortion," 73, 80.

20. Lison, "L'Ésprit comme amour," 325–32.

21. Lison, *L'Esprit répandu*, 88–89.

22. Dēmētrakopoulos, *Augoustinos kai Grēgorios Palamas*. See also Dēmētrakopoulos, *Is Gregory Palamas an Existentialist?*

23. Lössl, "Augustine in Byzantium," 281.

24. Flogaus, *Prochoros Kydones*, 7–8.

against him by "Combining the Augustinian concept of grace with Chalcedonian Christology."[25] In the case of Prochoros we may see a kind of "palamite soteriology in Augustinian dress": "Prochoros, said Lössl, applied the scholastic method (i.e., dialectics and syllogistics) as well as the patristic argument (i.e., from authority and tradition). He perceived no conflict between [them]. . . . For him both went hand in hand."[26]

We have a positive perception of Flogaus' discoveries in Alexander Golitzin. Starting from the Augustinian interpretation of the Old Testament theophanies, he developed his own theological analysis of the hesychastic dispute and the influence of Augustinian theology on this fourteenth-century Byzantine dispute. Thus, in *De Trinitate* II, 19-20 and III, 27 Augustine's solution to the problem of theophanies is the most drastic in the literature or simple symbolophanies.[27] Therefore, from Books I-IV Barlaam could have drawn the criticism against the Old Testament that the theophanies are reduced to the level of simbolo/angelophany, and Palamas took over the idea of the soul as *Trinitatis imago* of the last books. The triad *logos-nous-psyche* is borrowed from St. Symeon the New Theologian. Golitzin notes that Palamas did not then accept the whole of Augustine on the Trinity, but only that which he appears to have felt could be "*enfolded without rupture or strain into the already existent theological* Gestalt *of the Greek East.*"[28]

At this point, it is also necessary to make a comparison between Augustinian mystical theology and the hesychastic version of Byzantine spirituality. While the differences between Augustine and Palamas are obvious in triadology, we ask ourselves, can the ground of union between this two opposite theologies be found within spirituality or mystical experience? However, while the rule of *lex orandi, lex credendi* contradicts us from the start, in order to elucidate this aspect, we must make a brief analysis.

David Bradshaw calls Barlaam "the unwitting representative of the West" in this "confrontation between Augustinian metaphysics of the divine essence and the apophatic theology of the East."[29] The stamp of Neoplatonism is reflected in Augustine's conception of divine intelligibility. God is intrinsically accommodated intellect. While the Eastern fathers speak of the Old Testament theophanies as appearances of the *Logos*, in conjunc-

---

25. Lössl, "Augustine in Byzantium," 293.

26. Lössl, "Palamite Soteriology," 36-37.

27. Golitzin, *Mystagogy—God Experience*, 209-12. Regarding Augustine's revolutionary theology of the theophanies, see also Barnes, "Arians of Book V and the Genesis of *De Trinitate*," 385-95; Barnes, "Visible Christ and the Invisible Trinity," 329-55; Bucur, "Theophanies and Vision of God," 67-93.

28. Golitzin, "Dionysius the Areopagite," 182-83.

29. Bradshaw, *Aristotle East and West*, 222, 229.

tion with the concept of "glory of God" as a manifestation of the uncreated divine presence, Augustine understands the nature of revelation as *sight of God in the truth of the intellect* (the third type of theophany, the intellectual one, alongside physical and spiritual theophanies).[30]

Augustine's idiosyncratic commitment to Divine intelligibility is the "key strain" of theological difference between East and West and "makes his brand of Platonism unique in the orthodox Christian traditions."[31] In remarking upon the intelligibility of God, Phillip Cary notes: "Where Augustine differs from the rest of orthodox Nicene Christianity is in attaching the Platonist predicate 'intelligible' to the divine side of the Creator/creature distinction."[32]

Augustine describes his deepest and most "mystical" experiences in terms of Reason's vision of God as Truth. Beatific vision, in short, is simply the fullness of intellectual vision. Augustine's inward turn (Latin: *conversio*; Greek: *epistrophē*) is a project of awakening oneself to that vision; it is an epistemology, a pedagogy, and an ethics for the mind that desires to see God. Augustine is also doing something new by locating Christ as eternal Wisdom and Truth within the soul. Christ is the Inner Teacher, and He dwells in the inner man as "the eternal Wisdom of God."[33] For the purpose of our study we shall note that Augustine's use of the scriptural term "heart" is wide-ranging, often co-extensive with the term "soul," but sometimes referring specifically to the soul's higher part, the mind, or intellect. That is to say, sometimes Augustine says "heart" and means "mind."[34] It is evident that Augustine's account of intellectual knowledge is indeed ontological. For Augustine "all intelligible things (i.e., all things that are properly understood by the intellect) are contained in God, as uncreated Forms in the mind of God."[35] According to Ronald Nash, "no other important aspect of Augustine's philosophy is as difficult to understand and to explain as this notion that God in some way illumines the mind of man."[36]

Against Augustine's transfiguring grace, which appears in the present as hope, but in reality is only present in the eschaton, Palamas categorically opposes the real possibility of enlightenment as a deifying experience,

---

30. Ibid., 234–37; Jensen, *Face to Face*, chapter 3 "The Invisible God and the Visible Image. Justin Martyr: Refutation of Idols and Divine Theophanies," 69–74.

31. Cary, *Augustine's Invention of the Inner Self*, 55.

32. Ibid.

33. Cary, *Outward Signs*, 101.

34. Ibid., 96.

35. Ibid., 69; Cary, *Inner Grace*, 33–68.

36. Nash, *The Light of the Mind*, 92; Schumacher, *Divine Illumination*, 4; Schumacher "Theo-logic of St. Augustine's theory," 375–99.

anticipated and visible here and now among the saints. Far from being contraries, Christology and the uncreated energies, salvation and deification—these do not cancel each other out in the theology of St. Gregory Palamas, but as the Romanian theologian Father Ică jr. concludes, are mutually reinforced and require each other.[37]

In conclusion, we could ask Flogaus, if he was so convinced of the "Augustinian Patristic Authority,"[38] then why doesn't Palamas quote Augustine, and also, why did he "distort" his concepts? Considering how subtle Palamas was during his controversy with Barlaam, it was almost impossible not to discover Augustine's theological limitations. Because Augustine was becoming increasingly known and quoted in Byzantium, Palamas offers an example of exegetical inculturation. The answer to our question to Flogaus above could lie in the subtle references in the theological-philosophical discussions of the humanistic Byzantine environment that make use of these Augustinian quotes, which were well-known to Palamas' contemporaries and also selectively identified in the work of St. Gregory Palamas. Thus, he reinterprets them in an effort to keep an irenic silence, avoiding direct appeal to Augustine (being cautious about future controversies), instead referring to a process of elucidating Augustine's theological deviation from the patristic line. As Lössl shows us, it is as if Palamas is responding over and over to searches for Augustine himself, standing in as the exact Greek theologian for whom Augustine was seeking to make contact. Palamas did not need Augustine to express his patristic doctrine or teaching because the tradition of fathers was sufficiently wide-ranging. Quite confident and sure of his faith, however, Palamas himself enters into the Augustinian mind, ultimately in the interest of the Latin theologian, and with no dismissive intent. In my opinion, the issue here is not about "reception," for Palamas was concerned with concrete "answers" to some of the theological and philosophical opinions of Augustinian origin that were circulating in Byzantium at his time.

---

37. Ică jr., "St. Gregory Palamas," in Palamas, *Virgin Mary and Peter the Athonite*, 77.

38. Flogaus, "Inspiration-Exploitation-Distortion," 80–83; Flogaus, "Palamas and Barlaam Revisited," 1–31.

### *Nous* (intuitive intellect) and *Dianoia* (discursive intellect): The Distinction between the Noetic and the Intellectual Made by Hesychasts within the Faculties of the Soul

The distance that the Platonists put between intellect and feeling is considerably reduced by the fathers. A distinction is made between *nous* and *dianoia*. Abba Evagrius protests against those who will not grant to the intellect what everyone recognizes in the senses: intuition, immediate perception of its object. Intellect (*nous*) is a "sense," the spiritual sense. Nuanced meaning of the term "mind" intellect (*nous*) and its evolution to the term "heart" (*kardia*) removes the danger of intellectualism. In this context we can say that *the organ of contemplation is "spiritual feeling" or "heart" with her intuition.*[39]

The Greek word "*nous*" is usually translated with "mind" or "intellect." The problem is that none of these words is as rich in derived forms as the Greek *nous*. We say "I think, therefore I am," which means that thinking is an *activity* which I activate and so there must be an "I/me" to activate it; the Greeks would say, "I think, therefore there is what I think—*to noeta*." What I think is something that goes through my head; what the Greeks think, *to noeta*, are objects of thought, which exist in a higher, more real world. This means that *nous* and its derivatives have a different meaning to our words of *mind, mental, intellect, reason*, etc. Our words suggest our reasoning, our thinking, *nous, noesis*, etc., are an almost intuitive understanding of reality.[40] *Nous* is more an organ of mystical union and *noesis* is a form of a deeper, simpler, contemplative thinking. As already mentioned, νοῦς is a purely philosophical term that has no biblical foundation. Byzantine authors wholly inherited the meaning and connotations of the concept bequeathed by ancient philosophy. They continue to call νοῦς the active and directing organizing principle. Ontologically speaking, it is the highest level of being. Analyzing νοῦς in the Byzantine tradition, Sofia Avramova, said: "Byzantine authors put more emphasis on three aspects, introduced and developed by Christianity: first, νοῦς possesses a personal and free character; secondly, its ultimate goal is found in God; and finally, it is νοῦς's nobility to be, by nature, created in the divine image." Νοῦς is the ability of men to surpass themselves and participate in God, for the object par excellence of

---

39. Špidlík, *Spirituality of the Christian East*, 383, 133. Nous, divine faculty is God's place.

40. Louth, *Origins of the Christian Mystical*, xiv.

νοῦς is God."⁴¹ Νοῦς is the ability of men to surpass themselves and participate in God. The object par excellence of the νοῦς is God. Historically, under the influence of Origen, the Cappadocian fathers replace the spirit of the Pauline trichotomy "spirit (πνεῦμα), soul, and body" with νοῦς. God himself is also Νοῦς. However, to emphasize the divine transcendence and inaccessibility of its essence, the Byzantine authors prefer to call God Νοῦς ἀνόητος and Νοῦς ὑπὲρ νόησιν.⁴²

Saint Gregory, like Dionysius the Areopagite, speaks of a threefold operation of the mind whereby it ascends to God: directed towards exterior objects (first operation), returns into itself (second operation), and then ascends to God through prayer (third operation). These two last operations are also called "rolling up" as a scroll, and "stretching upwards," with the explanation that the turning of the mind to itself is its guard, while its ascent to God is achieved through prayer.⁴³ At the same time Gregory Palamas insists that it is always necessary to keep the mind within the limits of the body (τὸ ἀσώματον ἐν σώματι, a well-known ascetic rule of St. John Climacus;⁴⁴ he said: "Strange as it may seem, the hesychast is a man who fights to keep his incorporeal self shut up in the house of the body"⁴⁵). Remaining in this activity, a certain "intellectual sense" (αἴσθησις νοερά) occurs. The task of the hesychast is to direct not the nature of the mind, but its activity inwards. Misunderstandings arise from the confusion between the nature of the mind and its activity.⁴⁶

John Meyendorff develops the peculiar theory that both Barlaam and Palamas belong to hesychast traditions,⁴⁷ with the difference that the Calabrian is a member of an Origenistic, Evagrian, Nyssan, Pseudo-Dionysian, Platonic dualistic anthropological tradition, while St. Gregory Palamas is heir mainly to a Macarian, Stoic, biblical monistic anthropological tradition,⁴⁸ although he makes full use of the terminology of the other group.⁴⁹ Therefore, according to Meyendorff, both accepted the hesychast practice of uninterrupted prayer: for the Calabrian it is a *passive disincarnation of the intellect* (νους), whereas for Palamas it is an *active state in which*

41. Avramova, *Le rapport de l'Un*, 150.
42. Ibid., 160, 162–63.
43. Krivosheine, *Ascetic and Theological*, 7.
44. Climacus, *Ladder of Divine Ascent*, 260–63.
45. Step 27: On Stillness, cf. Climacus, *Ladder*, 262.
46. Krivosheine, *Ascetic*, 7–8.
47. Meyendorff, *Introduction*, 174.
48. Ibid., 195.
49. Ibid., 219–20.

*the total man, body and soul, fully participates.* After Romanides, Barlaam defines St. Paul's unceasing prayer in terms of Augustinian irresistible grace as a *habitus*, a sort of passive state, and the Calabrian formally accepts the hesychast term "noetic prayer," but tries to force it into the categories of the wordless prayer of non-discursive intuitive ecstasy, which in certain Western mystical circles is considered to be the highest form of prayer.[50] Palamas reminds Barlaam that no one in this life can attain to uninterrupted or ceaseless ecstasy. The hesychasts make a clear distinction between the noetic and intellectual.[51]

There is a very interesting similarity between Palamas and Theoleptos of Philadelphia's conception of *dianoia* and *nous* during prayer. In Theoleptos' mystical thinking,[52] the ascetic dyad virtue-humility (*arete-tapeinosis*) corresponds to the contemplative dyad vigilance-prayer (*nepsis-proseuche*). The remembrance of God is joined to thinking or reasoning (*dianoia*) through prayer (*proseuche*). Prayer of reason/thinking united with attention of mind makes the knowledge of God arise, and love attaches the contemplation of mind to the knowing of God. Interceding through an apophatic unknowing of the mind's union with God, love makes the soul replace the sweet dialogue of prayer with deep silence (*Word* 6).[53] Mystical prayer is a total act of man whose entire liturgical ministering to God is a dialogue of thought (*dialogos dianoias*) invoking the name of the Lord that is constantly overseen by the attention of the mind (*prosoche nous*) and warmed by the spirit's compunction and love (*katanyxis kai agape pneumatos*). This prayer unifies the three powers of the soul (*nous/logos/pneuma* or *nous/dianoia/psyche*) and unites the tripartite soul with the One God in three Persons: Father, Son, and Holy Spirit. Therefore, Theoleptos makes a distinction on the one hand between prayer (*proseuche*) to God made in the inner speech of thinking (*dianoia*—discursive intellect) and, on the other hand, with the word of language and remembrance of God (*mneme*), which is a silent act of sight and of light of the mind's eye (*nous*—intuitive intellect). The mind becomes the temple of God and in entering into its depths (*en adytois tou nou*), it mysteriously sees the Unseen:

> Prayer is a dialogue of the discursive intellect (διαλογή διανοίας) with the Lord, in which the discursive intellect runs through

---

50. Romanides, "Notes on the Palamite II," 226.

51. Ibid., 230.

52. Theoleptos, *Monastic Discourses*, chapter 5 "Catechesis on the Feast of the Transfiguration of our Lord, God and Saviour, Jesus Christ," 187–91; Hero, *Life and Letters of Theoleptos* (Letter 3, 66), 74–75.

53. Theoleptos, *Monastic Discourses*, chapter 6, "Hesychia and Prayer," 192–99.

the words of supplication with the mind's gaze fixed entirely on God. For when the discursive intellect is repeating the Name of the Lord without ceasing and the mind has its attention clearly fixed on the Invocation of the Divine Name, the Light of the knowledge of God overshadows the soul completely like a luminous cloud.... For Scripture says, "You shall love the Lord your God with all your strength, with all your heart (καρδίας σου) and with all your mind (διανοίας σου)."[54]

Thus, the mind (*nous*) has two powers (*dynameis*), rational (*logike*) and loving (*erotike*): through reason it actively seeks and finds God, distinguishing things, and through love it unites itself with a contemplative and passive God. The ascetical-mystical teachings of Theoleptos is a synthesis between the Simeonian and Evagrian mysticism developed as a subtle mystical psychology.

Within this ascetical-mystical teaching we also find an integrated hesychasm in Palamas. As Palamas shows, "if our mind could not overcome itself, it would have no view and understanding beyond the works of the mind."[55] The mind has the power to overcome itself, but only by God can it pass from potency to act. Our mind is also made by the image of the Father (i.e., Christ), the supreme Mind. The mind initiates the word and love for Him. The understanding and rational nature is: mind, word of mind, and love of mind towards the word. The word, which is born from the Father as the supreme Mind, is like the "word" planted in our minds along with our creation as a knowledge without which the mind cannot meditate; as a virtual knowledge that is continuously updated. Along with the Word that comes from the Mind, love comes from the word that is "this pre-eternal joy of the Father and the Son [which] is the Holy Spirit in that he is common to them by mutual intimacy. Therefore, he is sent to those who are worthy by both, but in his coming to be he belongs to the Father alone and thus he also proceeds from Him alone in his manner of coming to be."[56] Our mind is the image of the Father-Mind, because, along with the word that comes out of it, its love for this word also comes out from it. "The threefold character of our knowledge shows us to be more in the image of God than the angels, not only because it is threefold but also because it encompasses every form of knowledge. For we alone of all creatures possess also a faculty of sense perception in addition to those of intellection and reason."[57]

54. Theoleptos, *Monastic Discourses* (chapter 6, 17–18), 96–97.
55. Palamas, "In Defense of Those," 331.
56. Palamas, *One Hundred and Fifty*, 123.
57. Ibid. (chapter 63), 157–58.

### *Nous* and *Kardia*: Juxtaposition of Two Different Spiritualities or Expressions of the Same Spiritual Reality?

In connection with his doctrine of man, we must note the role which Gregory assigns the heart in the spiritual and intellectual life. He looks on it as the principal centre of man's spiritual life, the organ of thought (the *seat of the mind* and of the discernment), as the sources and guardian of man's intellectual activity and the most inward part of the body.

Palamas explains how the noetic faculty isn't the essence of the soul, but an energy. He advocates for a holistic anthropology of prayer and of grace through complementarity between heart and intellect. *Nous* is understood both as *energeia* (activity) of the mind and as *dynamis* ("power" called "*kardia*"), which activates *noera energeia* ("the human spirit in the heart"). The heart, therefore, is the first fleshly organ of the mind. Palamas summarizes the patristic tradition: "something is the being of mind and something else her work. . . . [M]ind has not only a moving straight line, but turns around and acts on it, when viewed itself, action called circular movement. This latter work of mind is higher and more proper for itself; thus, sometimes, mind rising above it, is united with God" (*Triad* I.2.3).[58]

Palamas provides a theological and anthropological foundation for the prayer of Jesus, which is at the same time a prayer of the heart and mind. In the prayer, the mind becomes unified and triadic (*One Hundred and Fifty chapters*, § 40[59])—*nous*-mind, *logos*-word, and *pneuma*-spirit—as the Holy Trinity. "*Nous*" means both the activity (*energeia*) of mind through thoughts and meanings, and power (*dynamis*) which activates what Scripture calls the "heart" (*kardia*). Mind's energy (work) is purified by praying in a concentrated single thought (*monologistos*). But *dynamis/kardia* (power or the root of it) is cleaned only by purification of all faculties of the soul.

"Heart" in this context is to be understood in the Semitic and biblical rather than the modern Western sense, as signifying the totality of the human person, our innermost being. The physical heart is an outward symbol of the boundless spiritual potentialities.[60] To accomplish the journey inwards and to attain true prayer, it is required of us to enter into this "absolute centre," that is, to descend from the intellect into the heart. Prayer of the heart is a return to paradise, as it is also an eschatological reality. For the heart has a double significance in the spiritual life: it is both the center of the

---

58. Stăniloae, *Viața*, 168.
59. Palamas, *One Hundred and Fifty*, 127–30.
60. Ware, *Power of the Name*, 142–43.

human being, the point of meeting between the human being and God, and the place of self-transcendence, where we understand our nature as a temple of the Holy Trinity, where the image comes face to face with the Archetype. In the "inner sanctuary" of our own heart we cross the mysterious frontier between the created and the Uncreated.[61]

Meyendorff attempts to describe the present controversy in terms of an opposition between a Neoplatonic "intellectual mysticism" and a biblico-Stoic "mysticism of the heart."[62] He is following Hausherr, who made it conventional to juxtapose, the "*spiritualité intellectualiste*" of Evagrius of Pontus and the "*école du sentiment ou de surnaturel conscient*" of Makarios/Symeon.[63] One of the very few people to seriously detract from this dichotomist viewpoint has been Golitzin: "The contradistinction of 'mind' and 'heart' reflects the medieval Western opposition between 'intellective' and 'affective' mysticisms a little too much for my comfort. Evagrius is not an Eckhardt, nor is Macarius a Bernard of Clairvaux . . . . I do not, in short, believe that Evagrius' *nous* and Macarius' *kardia* are all that different from each other."[64]

The heart is certainly less integrated into the Evagrian teaching than is the intellect in the Macarian. In fact, Evagrius' *nous* is contained within Macarius' *kardia*.[65] Evagrius has simply substituted the word "heart" where he would normally use "intellect." He speaks of the light of prayer most often as the light of the human intellect: "during prayer it will see its own nature like sapphire or the colour of the sky. In Scripture this is called the realm of God that was seen by the elders on Mount Sinai" (*Thoughts* 39).[66] When the *intellect* reaches such a state it truly becomes the dwelling-place of God. The place of God therefore is the rational soul, and his "*dwelling place*" the luminous intellect (*Skemmata* 25). The luminous intellect is the inner Sinai, the place of God's self-revelation. His descriptions of the light of the intellect deliberately evoke the divine *shekinah*.[67] Therefore, Marcus Plested claims that "the anthropology is the key one."[68] Evagrius is familiar

---

61. Ware, *Power of the Name*, 143–44.
62. Meyendorff, *Study of Gregory Palamas*, 137–38.
63. Hausherr, "Les grands courant," 114–38; Plested, *Macarian Legacy*, 59.
64. Golitzin, "Hierarchy Versus Anarchy?" 153; Ware, "Prayer", 14–30; Plested, *Macarian Legacy*, 61.
65. Brock, "Prayer of the Heart," 131–42; Plested, *Macarian Legacy*, 62.
66. On this theme see also: Guillaumont, "La vision de l'intellect," 255–62; Harmless and Fitzgerald, "The Sapphire Light of the Mind," 513–14; Corrigan, *Evagrius and Gregory*, 37–51; Hammerling, *A History of Prayer*, 137–66; Bitton-Ashkelony, "The Limit of the Mind," 291–321.
67. Plested, *Macarian Legacy*, 67–68.
68. Plested, *Macarian Legacy*, 70.

with the world of the heart from the Bible and the traditions of the Egyptian desert, while Macarius has picked up on the concept of the intellect from the Hellenic tradition. Although Macarius integrated the intellect with the heart within his teaching more convincingly than Evagrius, both express the same spiritual reality in their divergent approaches.[69]

## The Being and the Energies of Mind in the Psycho-Somatic Method of Hesychast Prayer

Through prayer we are assumed into the perichoresis, the mutual love of the Trinity. God as Trinity is the source and end-point of all our prayer.[70] Related to the common energies of the soul and the body and their role in mental prayer, we have two theological assertions: the mind must return to the heart (*Triad* I, 2.4) and the divided soul in essence and energies (*Triad* I, 2.5). The body is not bad in itself, as the body will also be deified, the whole being itself deifies. The Orthodox spiritual tradition makes little use of systems of "discursive meditation," such as were elaborated in the Counter-Reformation West by Ignatius of Loyola or François de Sales, as with the *lectio divina* of Benedictine and Cistercian monasticism.[71]

Following such Fathers as St. Basil the Great, Palamas explains that the noetic faculty is not the essence of the soul, but an energy.[72] Barlaam is, therefore, misrepresenting the hesychasts. It is the noetic faculty as an energy of the soul that must be circumscribed within the body. Palamas retorts that "to cause the noetic faculty to wander outside the body in order to seek intelligible visions is the source and root of Greek errors and all heresies, an invention of demons."[73]

Irénée Hausherr makes a mistake when he identifies the essence of mental prayer with its auxiliary methods.[74] He fails to see the skilled-art of prayer as an organic part of the general ascetical teaching of the church. Gregory Palamas does not give any detailed account of its methods as do his predecessors (Symeon the New Theologian, Nicephorus the Monk, and

---

69. Ibid., 70–71.

70. Ware, *Praying*, vii, xii.

71. Ware, *Orthodox Way*, 111.

72. *Triad* II, 2, 25–26, in Palamas, *Défense des Saints Hésychastes*, 373.

73. Romanides, "Notes on palamite II," 231–32.

74. Hausherr, *La méthode d'oraison hésychaste*, 111; Hausherr, "Note sur l'inventator," 66; Hausherr, *Solitude et vie contemplative*, 176; Jugie, "Les origines de la méthode," 179–85; Brock, "The Prayer of the Heart," 131–42; McGuckin, "The Prayer of the Heart," 69–108; Krausmüller, "The Rise of Hesychasm," 101–26.

Gregory the Sinaite), but we find in him a most brilliant ascetico-philosophical defense of some of these methods. The defense is based on the idea that since the body is not in its essence an evil principle, but a creature of God and the temple of the Spirit who dwells in us, its use to aid us in our prayer is natural, and he insists on this: to confine his mind without distraction within himself in the region of the heart, like a scroll neatly rolled up into one cylinder. The fundamental idea is that of the connection between the psychical and the physical phenomena, confirmed by psychology. Without any ascetical purifications, the methods have no infallible efficacy, showing thereby a secondary and not a primary importance.[75] There is no mechanical technique, whether physical or mental, which can compel God to manifest his presence.[76] Kallistos Ware speaks about the completeness of the Jesus Prayer. In one brief sentence it embodies the two chief mysteries of the Christian faith, the incarnation and the Trinity.[77] In the Old Testament, as in other ancient cultures, there is a close connection between someone's soul and his name. His personality, with its peculiarities and its energy, is in some sense present in his name. In the Hebrew tradition, to do a thing in the name of another, or to invoke and call upon his name, are acts of weight and potency. To invoke a person's name is to make that person effectively present. The power and glory of God are present and active in His Name. The Name of God is *numen preasens*, God with us, Emmanuel. Attentively and deliberately to invoke God's Names is to place oneself in His presence, to open oneself to His energy.

A human being, in the biblical view, is a psychosomatic totality—not a soul imprisoned (*soma/sema*) in a body and seeking to escape, but an integral unity of the two. The body has a positive part to play in the spiritual life and it is endowed with energies. Every psychic activity, they realized, has repercussions on the physical and bodily level.

For Palamas, the essential thing is not the external control of the breathing, but the final objective described by the patristic term as *theosis*, "deification" or "divinization." The Jesus Prayer, by uniting us to Christ, helps us to share in the mutual indwelling or *perichoresis* of the three Persons of the Holy Trinity.

The noetic prayer stops in ecstatic union. In the "silence of mind," the nous unites itself with the Divine Mind beyond its own nature.[78] For Isaac

---

75. Palamas, *Défense* (I, II, 7), 97; Krivosheine, *Ascetic*, 14; Ware, "Praying with the Body," 6–35.

76. Behr-Sigel, *Lieu du cœur*, 127.

77. Ibid., 132–35.

78. Palamas, *Défense* (Tr. I, 3, 21), 155.

the Syrian the discoveries or revelations *(ghelyâne)* made by the revelations of the Holy Spirit take place in one way: "in the feeling of heart." It is just a "work of the Spirit," the man being in "astonishment," in non-prayer.[79] With their revelations, angels clean the man in order to make him a temple of the Holy Spirit, Who, in His turn, sanctifies man with the revelation of Him. Revelations are therefore aimed at cleansing and sanctifying man, in order that, remembering God unceasingly, one may become the temple of the Trinity. In the framework of this topic, I think we can find that Palamas is very close to Isaac the Syrian. This teaching on holy silence as the state of the soul, and as the means of attaining to the knowledge of God and deification, was most vividly expressed by Gregory in his splendid *Sermon on the Presentation in the Temple of the Most Holy Mother of God*.[80] In the Holy of Holies, in constant prayer and meditation, separated from mankind and from the world, one attains the highest and most perfect realization of silent and mental prayer. The Mother of God unites her mind with God by turning it back on itself, by attentive and unceasing divine prayer in intellectual silence (νοητὴν σιγήν).

In the *Triads* Gregory had already laid emphasis on deification as an experiential reality (*Triad* 1.3.5).[81] The monks see the hypostatic light as a reality, and not in a symbolic fashion. Accordingly, Palamas maintains that the deifying light is essential, not symbolic, but is not itself the essence of God (*Triad* 3. 1. 29).[82]

# Conclusion

For Augustine God is intrinsically accommodated to the intellect and Divine Being is inherently compatible to the human intellect. In *De Trinitate* Augustine concludes that *within the Trinity* the Father and the Son constitute together one principle in relation to the Holy Spirit, a concept Palamas did not share. He confuses, or makes no distinction between, the economic and the immanent Trinity, or, to put it in another and rather anachronistic way, he regards the immanent Trinity as directly revealed in the New Testament. In the Trinity the Father and the Son jointly send the Spirit and therefore in the immanent Trinity He must proceed from them both (this

---

79. Chialà, *Isaac the Syrian*, 177–78.

80. *Homily* 53, in Ică jr., "St. Gregory Palamas", 173–216.

81. Russell, "Theosis and Gregory Palamas," 377.

82. Russel, *Doctrine of Deification*, 304–8; Williams, *Ground of Union*, 128–56; Collins, *Partaking in Divine Nature*, 99–102; Flogaus, *Theosis bei Palamas und Luther*, 83–93; and Mantzaridis, *Deification of Man*, 15–39.

is close to the *filioque*). This would justify the conclusion that the Spirit, insofar as He is one, must be the communion that exists between them. However, his imprecise thinking on the distinction between the immanent and the economic Trinity does not permit us to clarify this point further.

It is necessary to recognize the important role played by theological anthropology in the doctrine of St. Gregory Palamas. Thus, only man was truly made in the image of the trihypostatic God. Palamas was intermingling two analogies for the Trinity and associated both with God's image in man. The first was mind, word, and spirit, but it was the second analogy that occasioned Jugie's comment. Here the relation of the mind to its immanent knowledge (*logos*) was described as love (*eros*). The application of the analogy of love to the Spirit is almost unprecedented in the East, while at the same time it is a hallmark of Augustine's theology of the Trinity. The analogy of mind, word, and spirit had a venerable patristic heritage, although it was rarely associated with the divine image in man. However, the mind's relation of love (*eros*) to its own immanent knowledge (*logos*) represents a transformation of the common patristic analogy, not in the direction of a doctrinal innovation, but rather as an organic development within the mainstream of orthodoxy.

Unlike the angels, man's knowledge is threefold in character. Man alone possesses three faculties of knowledge: the intellectual or spiritual faculty (*noeros*), the rational or discursive faculty (*logikon*), and the faculty of sense perception (*aisthetikon*). The last faculty is unique to man among sentient creatures. To summarize, then, the angelic image reflects only the immanent life of the Trinity, whereas God's image in man reflects both the immanent life and the economic processions of the Godhead. Because of man's corporeality, the image has a Christological and incarnational dimension as well as a pneumatological character. The Christological corrective is operative in Gregory's doctrine of the divine image. Man's *taxis* in the hierarchies is placed immediately after God and above the angels. In the case of man his corporeality adds to the triadic character of the image an incarnational dimension. Man's place above the angels in the hierarchical order is based on the special pneumatological character of the Trinitarian image in the soul. Because man possesses a body for its own sake, his spirit manifests a life-giving energy. This aspect of the triadic image mirrors the Father's gift of the life-giving Holy Spirit (his energy, not the hypostasis) to the worthy. The soul of man, therefore, is a microcosm reflecting both the immanent life and the economic processions of the Trinity.

By Gregory's analogy of a human being's inner triad of *logos-nous-psyche* with the three Divine Persons, within the *imago* the soul reflects the movement of love within the Holy Trinity. The Athonite saint *par excellence* has a dynamic anthropology in both directions of God's image in man, Trinitarian and Christological. Man is the only being in the image of the tri-hypostatic nature, because it possesses mind, reason, and life-giving spirit. For Palamas man is truly rooted in the Trinity, ontologically and gnoseologically.

These triads, whether the Trinitarian nature of the soul (intellect, *logos*, mind), or the triune nature of knowledge (spiritual, rational, sensible), or the triple character of the intellect when it returns to itself and ascends to God (intellect, knowledge, love), or the ability of the soul to have multiple powers by distinction from its essence—all these manifest and represent the same thing: the Triune God. Thus man does not only represent God's existence, but also by his "work," by his "circular" dynamic Trinitarian movement, and his unitary character. By his moving, man represents the eternal movement of God, which exists in the Triune God as a movement of love (*eros*) and charity (*agape*).

# Bibliography

Augustin. *De Trinitate*, in *Oeuvres de Saint Augustin* 15, 2ième serie: *La Trinité*. Edited by M. Millet and T. Camelot. Paris: Éditions Desclée de Brouwer, 1955.

Avramova, Sofia. *Le rapport de l'Un et de l'intellect dans la centurie de Calliste Cataphygiotès*. Quebec: Université de Montréal, 2010.

Barnes, Michel René "The Arians of Book V and the Genesis of *De Trinitate*." *Journal of Theological Studies* 44.1 (1993) 385–95.

———. "The Visible Christ and the Invisible Trinity: MT. 5:8 in Augustine's Trinitarian Theology of 400." *Modern Theology* 19 (2003) 329–55.

Behr-Sigel, Élisabeth. *Le lieu du coeur. Initiation à la spiritualité de l'Église Orthodoxe. Avec une contribution de l' évêque Kallistos Ware «La puissance du Nom»*. Paris: Cerf, 1989.

Bitton-Ashkelony, Brouria. "The Limit of the Mind (νοῦς): Pure Prayer according to Evagrius Ponticus and Isaac of Nineveh." *Zeitschrift für Antikes Christentum / Journal of Ancient Christianity* 15.2 (2011) 291–321.

Bobrinskoy, Boris. *Le Mystère de la Trinité. Cours de théologie orthodoxe*. Paris: Cerf, 1986.

Bradshaw, David. *Aristotle East and West: Metaphysics and the Division of Christendom*. Cambridge: University Press, 2004; Romanian translation by Dragoş Dâscă and Vasile Bârzu. Sibiu: Ecclesiast, 2010.

Brock, Sebastian P. "The Prayer of the Heart in the Syriac Tradition." *Sobornost/ECR* 4.2 (1982) 131–42.

Bucur, Bogdan G. "Theophanies and Vision of God in Augustine's *De Trinitate*: An Eastern Orthodox Perspective." *St. Vladimir's Theological Quarterly* 52.1 (2008) 67–93.

Cary, Phillip. *Augustine's Invention of the Inner Self: The Legacy of a Christian Platonist*. Oxford: Oxford University Press, 2003.

———. *Inner Grace: Augustine in the Traditions of Plato and Paul*. Oxford: Oxford University Press, 2008.

———. *Outward Signs: The Powerlessness of External Things in Augustine's Thought*. Oxford: Oxford University Press, 2008.

Chialà, Sabino. *Isaac the Syrian: Asceticism Lonely and Endless Mercy*. Translation by Cornelia Maria and Deacon John I. Ică jr. Sibiu, Romania: Deisis, 2012.

Climacus, John. *The Ladder of Divine Ascent*. Translation by Colm Luibheid and Norman Russell, notes on translation by Norman Russell, introduction by Kallistos Ware, preface by Colm Luibheid. London: SPCK, 1984.

Collins, Paul M. *Partaking in Divine Nature: Deification and Communion*. London: T. & T. Clark, 2010.

Constantinides, Costas N. *Higher Education in Byzantium in the Thirteenth and Fourteenth Centuries (1204–c.1310)*. Texts and Studies of the History of Cyprus XI. Nicosia, Cyprus: Cyprus Research Centre, 1982.

Corrigan, Kevin. *Evagrius and Gregory: Mind, Soul and Body in 4th Century*. Farnham, UK: Ashgate, 2009.

Dēmētrakopoulos, Giannēs. *Augoustinos kai Grēgorios Palamas: ta provlēmata tōn Aristotelikōn katēgoriōn kai tēs triadikēs psychotheologias*. Athēna: Parousia, 1997.

———. *Is Gregory Palamas an Existentialist?* Athēna: Parousia, 1996.

Flogaus, Reinhard. "Inspiration-Exploitation-Distortion: The Use of Augustine in the Hesychast Controversy." In *Orthodox Readings of Augustine*, edited by Aristotle Papanikolau and George Demacopoulos, 63–80. Crestwood, NY: St. Vladimir's Seminary Press, 2008.

———. "Palamas and Barlaam Revisited: A Reassessment of East and West in the Hesychast Controversy of 14th Century Byzantium." *St. Vladimir's Theological Quarterly* 42.1 (1998) 1–31.

———. *Prochoros Kydones: Übersetzung von acht Briefen des Hl. Augustinus*. Vienna: Hunger, 1984.

———. *Theosis bei Palamas und Luther: Ein Beitrag zum okumenischen Gesprach*. Berlin: Vandenhoeck & Ruprecht, 1996.

Golitzin, Alexander. "Dionysius the Areopagite in the Works of Gregory Palama: On the Question of a 'Christological Corrective' and Related Matters." *St. Vladimir's Theological Quaterly* 46.2–3 (2002) 163–90.

———. "Hierarchy versus Anarchy? Dionysius Areopagita, Symeon the New Theologian, Nicetas Stethatos, and Their Common Roots in Ascetical Tradition." *St. Vladimir's Theological Quarterly* 38.2 (1994) 131–79.

———. *Mystagogy—God Experience in Orthodoxy. Studies of Mystical Theology*. Translated by and with a presentation by Ioan I., Ică jr. Sibiu, Romania: Deisis, 1998.

Guillaumont, Antoine. "La vision de l'intellect par lui-même dans la mystique évagrienne." *Mélanges de l'Université Saint-Joseph* 50 (1984) 255–62.

Hammerling, Roy. *A History of Prayer: The First to the Fifteenth Century*. Leiden: Brill, 2008.

Harmless, William, S.J., and Raymond R. Fitzgerald, S.J. "The Sapphire Light of the Mind: The Skemmata of Evagrius Ponticus." *Theological Studies* 62 (2001) 498–529.

Hausherr, Irenée. "Les grands courants de la spiritualité orientale." *Orientalia Christiana Periodica* 1 (1935) 114–38.

---. *La méthode d'oraison hésychaste.* Orientalia Christiana, 9.2. Rome: Notarius Sander Bücherstube, 1927.

---. "Note sur l'inventator de la méthode d'oraison hésychaste." *Orientalia Christiana* 20.66 (1930) 179–82.

---. *Solitude et vie contemplative d'après l'Hésychasme*; Spiritualité orientale et vie monastique, no. 3. Bégrolles-en-Mauges, France: Abbaye de Bellefontaine, 1980.

Hero, Angela Constantinides. *The Life and Letters of Theoleptos of Philadelphia.* Brookline, MA: Hellenic College Press, 1994.

Hussey, Edmund. "The Palamite Trinitarian Models." *St. Vladimir's Theological Quarterly* 16 (1972) 83–89.

Ică jr., Ioan I. "St. Gregory Palamas: Hesychast Spiritual Writer and his Era." In Grigorie Palama, *Virgin Mary and Peter Athos: Hesychastic Life Prototypes and Other Spiritual Writings*, Writings II, 5–150. Sibiu, Romania: Deisis, 2005.

Ivanka, Endre von. "Hésychasme et palamisme." In *Plato Christianus. La réception critique du platonisme chez les Pères de l'Eglise*, French translation from German by Elisabeth Kessler, revised by Rémi Brague and Jean-Yves Lacoste, 389–402. Paris: Presses Universitaires de France, 1990.

Jensen, Robin Margaret. *Face to Face: Portraits of the Divine in Early Christianity.* Minneapolis: Fortress, 2005.

Jugie, Martin. "Les origines de la méthode d'oraison des hésychastes." *Échos d'Orient* 30.162 (1931) 179–85.

---. "Palamas Grégoire." *Dictionnaire de Théologie Catholique* XI (1932), tome 11, col. 1735–76.

Krausmüller, Dirk. "The Rise of Hesychasm." In *The Cambridge History of Christianity, Volume 5: Eastern Christianity*, edited by Michael Angold, 101–26. Cambridge: University Press, 2008.

Krivosheine, Basil. *The Ascetic and Theological Teaching of Gregory Palamas.* Reprint of *The Easter Chrches Quaterly*, 4 (1938). Edited by Dom Bede Winslow. London: Geo. E. J. Coldwell, 1954.

Lison, Jacques. "L'Ésprit comme amour selon Grégoire Palamas: une influence augustinienne?" *Studia Patristica* 32 (1997) 325–32.

Lison, Jacques. *L'Esprit répandu. La pneumatologie de Grégoire Palamas.* Paris: Cerf, 1993.

Lössl, Josef. "Augustine in Byzantium." *Journal of Ecclesiastical History* 51.2 (2000) 267–95.

---. "Palamite Soteriology in Augustinian Dress? Observations on Prochoros Kydones' Writings and Translations of Works of Augustine." *Journal for Late Antique Religion and Culture* 2 (2008) 33–43.

Louth, Andrew. *The Origins of the Christian Mystical Tradition: From Plato to Denys.* Oxford: Oxford University Press, 2012.

Mantzaridis, Georgios I. *The Deification of Man: St. Gregory Palamas and the Orthodox Tradition.* Crestwood, NY: St. Vladimir's Seminary Press, 1997.

McGuckin, John A. "The Prayer of the Heart in Patristic and Early Byzantine Tradition." In *Prayer & Spirituality in the Early Church*, vol. 2, edited by P. Allen, W. Mayer, and L. Cross, 69–108. Queensland: Australian Catholic University, Centre for Early Christian Studies, 1999.

Meyendorff, John. "Les débuts de la controverse hésychaste." *Byzantion* 23 (1953) 90–96.

———. *Introduction à l'étude de Grégoire Palamas*. Patristica Sorbonesia 3. Edited by H. I. Marrou. Paris: Seuil, 1959.

———. *A Study of Gregory Palamas*. Translated by George Lawrence. London: Faith, 1964.

Nash, Ronald. *The Light of the Mind: St. Augustine's Theory of Knowledge*. Lexington, KY: University Press of Kentucky, 2003.

Palamas, Gregory. *Défense des Saints Hésychastes*. Introduction, texte critiques, traduction et notes par Jean Meyendorff. Louvain: Spicilegium Sacrum Lovaniense, 1959.

———. "In Defense of Those Who Devoutly Practice a Life of Stillness." In *Philokalia, The Complete Text*, Vol. 4, edited by G. E. H. Palmer, Philip Sherrard, Kallistos Ware. London: Faber & Faber, 1998.

———. *Haghioriticus Tomus*, P.G. 150, 1233b. "The Declaration of the Holy Mountain in Defense of Those Who Devoutly Practice a Life of Stillness." In *The Philokalia: The Complete Text*, Vol. 4, translated by G. E. H. Palmer et al., 418-25. London: Faber, 1998.

———. *The Homilies*. Translated by Christopher Veniamin. Waymart PA: Mount Thabor, 2009.

———. *The One Hundred and Fifty Chapters: A Critical Edition, Translation and Study*. Edited by Robert E. Sinkewicz. Toronto: Pontifical Institute of Medieval Studies, 1988.

———. *The Triads*. Edited with an introduction by John Meyendorff, translation by Nicholas Gendle, preface by Jaroslav Pelikan. Toronto: Paulist, 1983.

———. *Virgin Mary and Peter the Athonite: Hesychastic Life Prototypes and Other Spiritual Writings*. Sibiu, Romania: Deisis, 2005.

Plested, Marcus. *The Macarian Legacy: The Place of Macarius-Symeon in the Eastern Christian Tradition*. Oxford: Oxford University Press, 2004.

Romanides, John S. "Notes on the Palamite Controversy and Related Topics (I)." *Greek Orthodox Theological Review* 6 (1959–60) 186–205.

———. "Notes on the Palamite Controversy and Related Topics (II)." *Greek Orthodox Theological Review* 9 (1963–64) 225–70.

Russell, Norman. *The Doctrine of Deification in the Greek Patristic Tradition*. Oxford: Oxford University Press, 2006.

———. "Theosis and Gregory Palamas: Continuity or Doctrinal Change?" *St. Vladimir's Theological Quarterly* 50.4 (2006) 357–79.

Schumacher, Lydia. *Divine Illumination: The History and Future of Augustine's Theory of Knowledge*. Oxford: Wiley-Blackwell, 2011.

———. "The Theo-logic of St. Augustine's Theory of Knowledge by Divine Illumination." *Augustinian Studies* 41.2 (2010) 375–99.

Sinkewicz, Robert E. *The Doctrine of the Knowledge of God in the Initial Discussions between Barlaam the Calabrian and Gregory Palamas*. Oxford: Oxford University Press, 1979.

———. "St. Gregory Palamas and the Doctrine of God's Image in Man according to the Capita 150." *Theologia* 57 (1986) 857–81.

Špidlík, Tomáš. *Spirituality of the Christian East: A Systematic Handbook*. Cistercian Studies. Collegeville, MN: Cistercian, 1986. Romanian translation by Ioan I. Ica jr., Sibiu, Romania: Deisis, 1997.

Stăniloae, Dumitru. *Viața și învățătura Sfântului Grigorie Palama*. București: Scripta, 1993.

Theoleptos of Philadelpheia. *The Monastic Discourses. A Critical Edition*. Translation and study by Robert E. Sinkewicz, C.S.B. Toronto: Pontifical Institute of Mediaeval Studies, 1992.

Tsirpanlis, Constantine. "Epistemology, Theognosis, the Trinity and Grace in St. Gregory Palamas." *Patristic and Byzantine Review* 13 (1994) 5–27.

Ware, Kallistos. *The Orthodox Way*. Crestwood, NY: St. Vladimir's Seminary Press, 1995.

———. *The Power of the Name: The Jesus Prayer in Orthodox Spirituality*. Oxford: Fairacres/SLG, 1986.

———. "Prayer in Evagrius and the Macarian Homilies." In *An Introduction to Christian Spirituality*, edited by Ralph Waller and Benedicta Ward, 14–30. London: SPCK, 1999.

———. "Praying with the Body: The Hesychast Method and Non-Christian Parallels." *Sobornost* 14 (1992) 6–35.

———. *Praying with the Orthodox Tradition*. Crestwood, NY: St. Vladimirs Seminary Press, 2002.

Williams, A. N. *The Ground of Union: Deification in Aquinas and Palamas*. Oxford: Oxford University Press, 1999.

# 9

# Souls, Minds, Bodies, and Planets[1]

## Mary Midgley

### Separate Substances?

WHAT DOES IT MEAN to say that we have got a mind-body problem? Do we need to think of our inner and outer lives as two separate items between which business must somehow be transacted, rather than as aspects of a whole person?

Dualist talk assumes that we already have before us two separate things which we don't see how to connect. This is a seventeenth-century way of seeing the problem. It is tied to views in physics and many other topics that we no longer hold.

"Mind" and "matter," conceived as separate in this way, are extreme abstractions. These are terms that were deliberately designed by thinkers like Descartes to be mutually exclusive and incompatible, which is why they are so hard to bring together now. In Descartes' time, their separation was intended as quarantine to separate the new, burgeoning science of physics from views on other matters with which it might clash. It was also part of a much older, more general attempt to separate reason from feeling and establish reason as the dominant partner, feeling being essentially just part of the body. That is why, during the Enlightenment, the word "soul" has

---

1. Another version of this article appears in *Science, Consciousness and Ultimate Reality*, edited by David Lorimer and published by Imprint Academic in July 2004.

been gradually replaced by "mind," and the word "mind" has been narrowed from its ordinary use ("I don't mind" . . . "I've a good mind to do it") to a strictly cognitive meaning.

That was the background against which philosophers designed the separation of soul and body. And they saw it as an answer to a vast metaphysical question of a kind which we would surely now consider ill-framed. This was still the question that the pre-Socratic thinkers had originally asked, "What basic stuff is the whole world made of?" The dualist reply was that there was not just one such stuff, but two—mind and body.

In the seventeenth century, hugely ambitious questions like this were much in favor. Perhaps because of the appalling political confusions of that age, seventeenth-century thinkers were peculiarly determined to impose order by finding simple, final answers to vast questions through pure logic, before examining the complexity of the facts. In philosophy, as in politics, they liked rulings to be absolute. The grand rationalist structures that they built—including this one—supplied essential elements of our tradition. But there are limits to their usefulness. We do not have to start our enquiries from this remote distance. When we find the rationalist approach unhelpful we can go away and try something else.

## How Consciousness Became a Problem

Officially, we English-speaking philosophers are supposed to have done this already over mind-body questions. Half-a-century back we agreed that we should stop talking in terms of a ghost in a machine. But our whole culture was much more deeply committed to that way of thinking than we realized. Existing habits made it seem that our next move would be quite simple. We could at last triumphantly answer that ancient, pre-Socratic question—which was still seen as a necessary one—by once more finding a single solution for it. We could rule that everything was really matter. We could keep the material machine and get rid of the mental ghost.

So behaviorist psychologists tried this. They tabooed all talk of the inner life, with the effect that, through much of the twentieth century, people who wanted to seem scientific were forbidden to mention consciousness or subjectivity at all. But this turned out not to work very well. A world of machines without users or designers—a world of objects without subjects—could not be made convincing. Gradually it became clear that the concept of the machine had been devised in the first place to fit its ghost and could not really function without it. Attempts to use it on its own turned out so artificial and unreal that the learned population eventually rebelled. Some thirty years back, scientists suddenly rediscovered consciousness and decided that it constitutes a crucial problem. But the concepts that we now have for dealing with it are still the ones that were devised to make it unspeakable in the first place.

Colin McGinn has stated this difficulty with admirable force in his book *The Mysterious Flame: Conscious Minds in a Material World*:

> The problem is how any collection of cells ... could generate a conscious being. The problem is in the raw materials. It looks as if, with consciousness, a new kind of reality has been injected into the universe.... How can mere matter generate consciousness? ... If the brain is spatial, being a hunk of matter in space, how on earth could the mind arise from the brain? ... This seems like a miracle, a rupture in the natural order.[2]

McGinn's drastic answer is that this state of affairs is indeed a real mystery—a puzzle that our minds simply cannot fathom because it lies outside the area that they are adapted to deal with. His suggestion is that there must be an unknown physical property, which he calls $C^*$, that makes consciousness possible. This property is present in the stuff of brains, but it may be something that it is altogether beyond us to understand.

It is surely good news to find a respected analytic philosopher recognizing mysteries—insisting that there are limits to our power of understanding. But I shall suggest that we don't need to fall back on his rather desperate solution. This particular difficulty arises from a more ordinary source. Our tradition is leading us to state the problem wrongly. We really do have to start again somewhere else.

I will suggest that a better starting-point might be to consider directly the relation between our inner and outer lives—between our subjective experience and the world that we know exists around us—in our experience as a whole, rather than trying to add consciousness as an afterthought to a physical world conceived on principles that don't leave room for it. The unit should not be an abstracted body or brain but the whole living person. In order to show why this is necessary it will be best to glance back first at the tradition to see just how and where things have gone wrong.

## Rationalist Wars

This takes us back to Descartes. But of course he is not personally to blame for our troubles. If he had never written, sooner or later someone else would

---

2. McGinn, *Mysterious Flame*, 13, 115.

certainly have made the dualist move. And it is most unlikely that they would have done it any better than he did.

As I have suggested, one factor calling for dualism was the general, lasting wish to establish reason as a supreme ruler, a separate force able to arbitrate the confusion caused by disputes between warring authorities in the world. But the special factor that made this need pressing at that time was the advent of a new form of reason, one that seemed likely to compete with old forms of knowledge—namely, modern physics.

Once that discipline was launched into an intellectual world that had been shaped entirely round theology—a world, too, where theological opinions were dangerously linked to international politics—some device for separating these spheres had to be invented. That device ought to have been one that led on to pluralism—meaning, of course, not a belief that there are many basic stuffs, but a recognition that there are many different legitimate ways of thinking. Different conceptual schemes can quite properly be used to trace the different patterns in the world without conflicting. But, instead, the train of thought stopped at the first station—dualism—leaving its passengers still stranded there today.

We see signs of this trouble whenever people raise this kind of question—for instance over the problem of personal identity. When we talk about relations between mind and body, we are asking what a person essentially is. Modern analytic philosophers have puzzled a great deal about this, usually setting out from John Locke's discussion of it and concentrating on just one point in that discussion—his famous example of the prince and the cobbler.[3]

Locke argued that, if we ask whether someone is "the same person" as he was in the past, the answer must depend on the continuity of his memory, not on continuity of substance, "For," says Locke, "should the soul of a prince, carrying with it the consciousness of the prince's past life, enter and inform the body of a cobbler ... everyone sees he would be the same person with the prince, accountable only for the prince's actions."[4] So the "person" must be the memory lodged in the soul, not the body.

Starting from this little example, philosophers have produced a striking monoculture of science-fiction stories. They have repeatedly asked whether various kinds of extraordinary beings would count as "the same person" after they had undergone equally extraordinary kinds of metamorphosis. Their answers tend not to be very helpful because, when we go beyond a certain distance from normal life, we really don't have a context that might

---

3. Locke, *Essay Concerning Human Understanding*, Bk. 2, ch. 27, Section 15.
4. Ibid.

make sense of the question. And—as students often complain—these speculations seem fairly remote from the kind of problems that actually make people worry about personal identity in real life, which are mostly problems that arise over internal conflicts and clashes of loyalty to different groups around us. We will come back to these conflicts presently.

The difficulty of talking sense about detachable souls afflicts real, professional science-fiction writers too, for their art is deeply committed to dualism. They often produce transmigrational stories in which characters in a wide range of situations keep jumping into other people's bodies, or having their own bodies taken over by an alien consciousness. It even happens in *Star Trek*, which shows how natural the thought still is today. But, in order to be convincing, the authors have to fill in a rich imaginative background that links this situation to normal life. And these stories are still strangely limited because they proceed on such an odd assumption.

They treat soul or consciousness as an alien package radically separate from the body. They go on as if one person's inner life could be lifted out at any time and slotted neatly into the outer life of someone else, much as a battery goes into a torch or a new cartridge into a printer. But our inner lives aren't actually standard articles designed to fit just any outer one in this way. The cobbler's mind needs the cobbler's body. It is not likely that two people with different nerves and different sense organs would perceive the world in the same way, let alone have the same feelings about them, or that their memories could be transferred wholesale to a different brain. Trying to exchange their bodies is not really at all like putting a new cartridge in the printer. It is more like trying to fit the inside of one teapot into the outside of another. And this is something that few of us would attempt.

## Ships and Pilots; Batteries and Torches

It is surely very interesting that so many writers of science fiction (sci-fi) have signed up for this strange metaphysic. Of course, there is nothing odd about their dealing in metaphysics in the first place. Sci-fi arises out of metaphysical problems quite as often as it does from those in the physical sciences, and good sci-fi stories can often be metaphysically helpful. But reliance on this particular metaphysic seems to be part of a rather unfortunate recent attempt to simplify the relation between our inner and outer lives by talking as if they were indeed completely separate items. This has the unlucky effect of making it even harder to connect them sensibly—even harder to see ourselves as a whole—than Descartes' separation of mind and body had already made it. Since his time, dualism has persisted. In fact, it has grown a good deal cruder.

It is interesting that Descartes himself did not actually show souls as totally irrelevant to their bodies. Though he ruled that they were substances of different kinds, he placed them both firmly within the wider system of God's providence. He thought God must have good reasons for connecting them, even though those reasons were obscure to us. In fact, Descartes surprises his reader by saying twice explicitly that the soul or self is *not* actually a loose extra added to the body. He writes: "*I am not only lodged in my body as a pilot in a vessel . . . I am besides so intimately conjoined, and as it were intermixed with it, that my mind and body compose a certain unity. For if this were not the case, I should not feel pain when my body is hurt.*"[5]

Descartes actually knew quite a lot about nerves. He saw that treating the soul as an alien, arbitrary item raised great difficulties about action and perception, so he assumed some underlying connection. And in this he was in tune with Christian thinking, which insisted on the resurrection of the body. Souls needed bodies, so God would restore the bodies at the resurrection.

But unfortunately Descartes' occasional statements of this link don't stop him arguing all the rest of the time that the separation is absolute. He identifies his self, his "I," entirely with the soul, the pure spark of consciousness. He speaks of the body as something outside it, something foreign which the soul discovers when it starts to look around it. (The pilot wakes up, so to speak, and finds himself mysteriously locked into his ship.) Descartes rules that, "the natures of these two substances are to be held, not only as diverse, but even in some measure as contraries."[6] They have no intelligible relation. Only God's mysterious plan can hold them together.

A soul conceived in this way is, of course, well-fitted to survive on its own after death, which is something that concerned Descartes. It could travel well. *But immortality is not the first thing we need to consider when we form our conception of ourselves.* Before we fit our minds out for the afterlife we need, first and foremost, to have a view of them that makes good sense for the life that we have to live now. By making them so thin and detachable as to be thus independent, Descartes put our inner lives in danger of looking unnecessary.

As the Enlightenment marched on and God gradually faded into the background, the enclosing framework of providence was lost, while the

---

5. Descartes, *Meditations on the First Philosophy*, Meditation 6, "Of the Existence of Material Things," 135.

6. Ibid., Synopsis of the Meditations, 76.

conviction of a gap between soul and body remained and hardened. Increasingly, the advance of physical science made matter seem intelligible on its own. Mind and body did indeed start to look more like ship and pilot. And then, starting from that picture, people began to wonder whether the pilot was actually needed at all. If perception and action were physical processes that could go on without him, had he any function?

These were the thoughts that led the behaviorist psychologists to drop him overboard, leaving a strictly material world of self-directing ships—uninhabited bodies. Descartes' theistic dualism turned into materialistic monism. Subjective experience was dismissed as an ineffective extra, a mere by-product, irrelevant froth on the surface of physical reality. That is why, for a time, people who wanted to seem scientific were not allowed to mention their own or anybody else's inner experience.

But it is very hard to discuss human life intelligibly if you have to ignore most of its more pressing characteristics. Even the most docile of academics don't obey these vetoes forever. So, as we have seen, eventually some bold people who had noticed that they had inner lives suggested that there was after all this "problem of consciousness." (Apparently, it was just one problem . . . .) And now everybody wants to talk about it. But it is notably hard to do so.

One thing that makes the difficulty worse is that scientifically-minded people tend to see this problem of consciousness as a problem of how to insert a single extra term—consciousness—into the existing pattern of the physical sciences and handle it with methods that are already recognized there as scientific. Thus, the famous Tucson conferences on the subject set themselves the goal of producing, not an understanding of consciousness, but "science of consciousness," which it is presumably hoped would be just one more scientific speciality, perhaps something comparable with the sciences of particular kinds of material?

This project is an attempt to revive Descartes' highly abstract soul—his pure spark of consciousness—and to fit it in somehow within the study of the physical world. Since the whole point of separating off this soul-concept in the first place was that it couldn't be handled by the methods used on the physical world, this can't work. Descartes was right about that and McGinn is right to follow him here. What we need now instead is to stand back and consider human beings quite differently—not as loose combinations of two incompatible parts, but as whole complex creatures with many aspects that have to be thought about in different ways. Mind and body are more like shape and size than they are like ice and fire, or oil and water. Being conscious is not, as Descartes thought, a queer extra kind of stuff in the world. It is just one of the things that we do. Verbs are needed here, not nouns.

To grasp this, we need to start by abandoning both the extreme abstractions that have reigned on the two sides of the divide so far.

## Inner Lives Are Neither Simple Nor Solitary

At the mental end, we need to get right away from Descartes' idea that the inner life is essentially a simple thing, a single, unchanging entity, an abstract point of consciousness. He put this point strongly. Unlike body, which is always divisible, mind, he says,

> cannot be conceived except as indivisible. For we are not able to conceive the half of a mind, as we can of any body, however small . . . . When I consider myself as a mind, that is, when I consider myself only in so far as I am a thinking thing, I can distinguish in myself no parts, but I very clearly discern that *I am somewhat absolutely one and entire*.
> . . . [A]lthough all the accidents of the mind be changed, —although, for example, it think certain things, will others and perceive others, *the mind itself does not vary with these changes*.[7]

This story abstracts entirely from the inner complexity, conflict, and change that are primary elements in all subjective experience. Locke's discussion shows well how misleading this abstraction is. Locke did not dismiss the idea of a separable self or soul, but he asked what it would have to be like if it did exist. He was intrigued by the idea of reincarnation because he had (it seems) a friend who claimed to have been Socrates in a former life. So he asked what we would say if we did come across a case like this where the familiar whole seemed to be divided.

Is the transmogrified prince still the same person? Yes he is, said Locke, provided that he keeps his memories. The word *person* is, he says, essentially "a forensic term," one centring on responsibility, and we are only responsible for what we can remember doing. With continuity of memory you can still be called "the same person." But if you now have a different body, you can't be called "the same man."

This suggestion notoriously led to further muddles. But Locke was surely right that any usable idea of a self or person does have to be the idea of something complex and therefore of something socially connected with the surrounding world. It must be an entity that incorporates the whole content of a life, the richness of a highly contingent individual experience. The cobbler would not be who he is without the connections established

---

7. Ibid., 76, 139, 77.

by his cobbling. Even within the restricted forensic context, Locke sees this need for complexity because of its bearing on justice. What (he asks) is to happen if an offender really has no continuity of memory? In that case, he says,

> the same man would at different times make different persons; which, we see, is the sense of mankind in the solemnest declaration of their opinion, human laws not punishing the mad man for the sober man's actions, nor the sober man for what the mad man did, thereby making them two persons; which is somewhat explained by our way of speaking in English, *when we say, such an one was "not himself" or is "beside himself."*[8]

If this defendant was not himself, then who was he?

It seems that after all people are not simple unities, they are highly complex items often riven by inner conflict. Even the law, which usually ignores these complications, cannot always do so and in ordinary life they are matters of the first importance. We often have to consider, not just "is this man in the dock the same person?" but "am I myself altogether the same person? Am I (for instance) really committed to my present project?" or again "which of us within here should take over now?" There are lawcourts inside us as well as out in the world. A friend of mine used to say that he unfortunately contained a committee. The trouble was not just that the members didn't always agree, but that, when they disagreed, all too often the wrong person got up and spoke all the same

The truth is that the unity of a human being is not something simple and given. We could easily go to pieces and that would be our final disaster. Harmonizing out inner life is a project central to our existence, a difficult, continuous ongoing enterprise, an aim that has to be continuously struggled for and is never fully attained. Carl Jung called it "the integration of the personality" and thought it was the central business of our lives.

## The Importance of Conflict

Plato, who was a very different kind of dualist from Descartes, thought so too and gave conflicts of this sort a central place in his theory. These conflicts take place (he said) within the soul itself and they are a torment to it. The soul is by no means a unity. It is divided into three parts: good desires, bad desires, and reason, which is the unlucky charioteer trying desperately

---

8. Locke, *Essay On Human Understanding*, 196. Emphasis mine.

to drive this mixed team of horses.[9] This is, of course, primarily a moral doctrine. But it is also an integral part of Plato's metaphysic and its psychological acuteness has been widely recognized.

Its difference from Descartes' scheme shows plainly that *there is not just one way of dividing up a human being*. There is no single perforated line marking off soul from body, no fixed point at which we should tear if we want to separate them. Many ways of thinking about this are possible. None of them is especially "scientific." Each is designed to bring out the importance of some particular aspect of our life. Plato's main concern was with emotional conflicts within the self, notably those that surround sex. Descartes, by contrast, was most disturbed about an intellectual conflict, one that arose between two different styles of thinking. It is not surprising that these different biases led them to different views about what a person essentially is. But something that they have in common, and which we may want to question, is that they both wanted to settle the matter by finding one ultimate arbitrator—by crowning one part of the personality as an absolute ruler and calling it reason.

Just as Hobbes, in trying to end political feuds, put all his trust in a single absolute sovereign, so these moralists, in discussing the feuds within us, want to appoint an inner monarch against whom there is no appeal. They aren't prepared to leave decisions in the hands of a committee. And plenty of people have tried to find that monarch. But their efforts have never been altogether satisfactory. Today, we may well think that, although the committee system gives us a lot of trouble, it is perhaps the least bad alternative that is available to us.

Once we notice this inner complexity we begin to see that it makes the solipsistic isolation of the simple "thinking thing" impossible too. Inner complexity echoes, and is linked to, a corresponding complexity in the world around us. The divided self is not an independent unit, quarantined from outside interference. Wider patterns outside affect its structure. As Locke saw, a person who has a memory must be an active social being, one capable of being involved in responsibility. Our personal identity is shaped by the surrounding world, depending radically on the attitudes of others.

Thus, when King Lear's daughters begin to treat him rudely, he first says to Goneril "Are you our daughter?" and then

> Doth any here know me? Why, this is not Lear;
> Doth Lear walk thus? speak thus? Where are his eyes?
> Either his notion weakens, his discernings

---

9. See Plato, *Phaedrus*, sections 246–57.

Are lethargied – Ha, waking? – 'tis not so.
Who is it that can tell me who I am?
To which the Fool replies, "Lear's shadow." [10]

At this point Lear is speaking somewhat sarcastically. But he soon has to confront these questions literally. The whole point of the play is that his identity has so far centred on being treated as a king. He can't see how to exist without it. And though his case is a specially dramatic one, this point about the crucial importance of social context holds for all of us. The role that we play in the social drama has huge force in shaping who we are. No human being exists in the artificial isolation of the Cartesian pure thinker. When Lear asks who he is, it would not help him to be told that he is a thinking thing.

## The Price and the Rewards of Dualism

Descartes supposed himself to be abstracting from all social influences. He thought he had withdrawn into a realm of pure intellect, designing *a priori* an impartial picture of human knowledge. But the most withdrawn thinkers still take the premises of their reasoning into their study with them. Descartes was in fact responding to certain quite particular pressures of his own time, trying to resolve the doubts and debates that fuelled the fierce religious wars of his day. He hoped to find a system of thought so universal, so compelling that it could accommodate conflicting theological views and also take in physical science, which might soon begin to rival them.

He devised his dualism as a way of fitting that new science into European culture without harming its Christian background. And, because he wanted above all to unify the system—to avoid doubts and divisions within it—he concentrated intensely on the problem of knowledge. He made the assumption, which has turned out not to be a workable one, that by reasoning we can get absolute, infallible certainty for our beliefs. That is why the soul that he pictured turns out to be essentially an intellect, a reasoning and knowing subject rather than an acting or a feeling one. For him, the centre of our beings is the scientist within.

For a time this ingenious division of intellectual life did succeed. It suited Newton well enough. For a great part of the eighteenth century, scientists managed to divide themselves internally to suit the two permitted viewpoints. In their work, they could function as pure thinking beings— that is, essentially as mathematicians. They could view the world around

---

10. Act 1. Scene iv, lines 215 and 223–28.

them as an abstract moving pattern, a mass of lifeless, inert particles driven ceaselessly here and there by a few simple natural forces. The rest of the time they could respond to it normally as a familiar rich, complex jumble full of living beings who supplied the meaning for each other's lives. A benign God still regulated the relation between the two spheres.

But as time went on and technology advanced, the more abstract, scientific way of thinking gained strength and pervaded people's lives. Inevitably, conflicts between these two approaches were noticed. As the gap between them widened and became more disturbing, it grew hard to treat them as having equal importance—hard not to ask "but which of these stories is actually the true one? Which tells us what the world is really like?" People felt that this question had to be answered—that one realm must be accepted as genuine and the other demoted to an illusion. They felt this because it seemed that, if both were equally real, there was no intelligible way of connecting them and reality was irremediably split. Hence McGinn's worry about "a new kind of reality." Hence the question that disturbs him and many other people: "If the brain is spatial being a hunk of matter in space, and the mind is non-spatial, how on earth can the mind arise from the brain? . . . This seems like a miracle, a rupture in the natural order."[11]

Or, as he puts it after citing a lively sci-fi illustration, "The point of this parable is to bring out how surprising it is that the squishy gray matter in our heads—our brain-meat—can be the basis and cause of a rich mental life."[12]

But this is an extraordinary abstraction from reality. Brains do not go about being conscious on their own. Meat is, by definition, dead and these brains belong to conscious, living creatures. Conscious pieces of matter are never just consignments of squishy grey matter, sitting on plates in a lab like porridge. They are living, moving, well-guided bodies of animals, going about their business in a biosphere to which they are naturally adapted. And the question about them is simply whether it makes sense to diagnose *consciousness* as an integral, necessary, appropriate, organic part of the behavior of such entities—including ourselves—or whether it is more reasonable to suppose that they might all just as well actually be unconscious.

## What Sort of Explanation?

It is important to notice exactly what we are trying to do here if we want to "explain consciousness" in a way that resolves McGinn's metaphysical

11. McGinn, *The Mysterious Flame*, 115.
12. Ibid., 8.

difficulty. The point is not, of course, just to find some physical condition that is always causally conjoined with it. We want to make that junction intelligible—to show that the one item is in some way suitable to the other.

When one is trying to find the connection between two things in this way—for instance the connection between roots and leaves or between eyes and feet—the best approach is not usually to consider these two on their own in isolation. It is to step back and look at the wider context that encloses them. In the case of consciousness that context is, in the first place, organic life and, in the second, the power of movement.

Any being that lives and moves independently, as animals do, clearly needs to guide its own movements. And the more complex the lives of such beings become, the more subtle and varied must be their power of responding to changes that are going on around them, so that they are able to respond flexibly. That increasing power of responding calls for an ever-increasing power to perceive, think, and feel. So it necessarily calls for consciousness, which is not an intrusive supernatural extra, but as natural and appropriate a response to the challenges that confront active life as the power of flying or swimming. Plants can get on without such a power, but animals could not because they are confronted with problems of choice. We ourselves do a lot of things unconsciously—that is, without attention. But when a difficulty crops up and a choice is needed, we rouse ourselves and become conscious of it.

There is no miracle here. The really startling factor in this scene is something that is usually ignored in these discussions, namely the introduction of life itself. Indeed, one might be tempted to say that consciousness is merely the superlative of life—just one more increase in the astonishing power of spontaneous development and adaptation which distinguishes living things from stones. Once life is present, the move from inactive creatures to highly-organized moving animals is simply one more stage in the long, dazzling creative process which is already a kind of miracle on its own, but one that is not usually treated as a scandalous anomaly.

## Discontinuities Within

Can it be true that there is not really an alarming gap here? If so, what is it that has made this particular transition seem so strange?

The answer is, I think, that the sense of strangeness arises simply from *the shift that we have to make in our own point of view when we consider it*. When we are confronted with a conscious being such as a human, all our social faculties at once leap into action. We cannot doubt that it has an inner life. Questions about its thoughts and feelings at once strike us. We bring to bear a whole framework of social concepts, a highly sophisticated apparatus that works on quite different principles from the one we would use if we were thinking about squishy grey matter in the lab.

This shift of methods can raise great difficulties, particularly on the many occasions when we need to use both these ways of thinking together. To use an image that I have suggested elsewhere, it is as if we are looking into a large aquarium through two opposite windows—trying to harmonize views of the same thing from quite different aspects. This trouble arises for instance over mental illness. We find it very hard to bring together our thoughts about the inner and the outer life of disturbed people—again, perhaps including ourselves. We often run into painful confusions. But *the clash in these cases is not a cosmic clash between different forms of reality. It is not a clash between ontological categories in the world, not a clash between natural and supernatural entities. It is a clash between two distinct mental faculties within ourselves, two distinct ways of thinking, along with the various emotional attitudes that underlie them. It constantly raises moral questions about how we should act in the world, questions about what is most important in it.*

This discontinuity does not, then, actually raise metaphysical questions about what is real. But of course that does not mean that it is trivial—quite the contrary. The difficulty of bringing together the different parts of our own nature so as to act harmoniously is a crucial one that pervades our lives. The reason why we are so highly conscious is that we are complex social beings and this means that our choices are never likely to become simple.

## Matter Is Not Simple Either

As I suggested earlier, the sense of bizarreness infesting the mind-body conjunction is made worse by the extreme abstraction to which both these terms have been subjected. Here I think the parallel with apartheid is actually quite illuminating. "Black" and "white" are extremes of the color-range. If they are colors at all they are colors that are never actually seen on any human skin. The use of this dramatic contrast to categorize the vast range of people found in South Africa or anywhere else imposes a quite irrelevant, artificial way of thinking, an approach that distorts all perceptions of these populations and makes it impossible to understand their diversity realistically. In the same sort of way, the sharp contrast between extreme conceptions of mind and body has obscured our thinking when we try to meditate on the complexities of our nature.

We have seen how, at the mental end of this mind-body axis, the idea of soul or mind became narrowed to a bare point of consciousness. But at the other end of it too the idea of matter has also been narrowed. Indeed, muddles about matter have probably been even more disastrous than muddles about mind.

Under a blindly reductive approach, the conscious animal that we ought to be asking about is reduced to a brain and even the brain loses its structure, becoming just a standard consignment of chemicals—inert porridge, squishy grey matter-as-such. It was indeed a central doctrine of seventeenth-century dualism that matter-as-such is inert and can do nothing, all activity being due to spirit. That is surely the conviction that still makes people like McGill feel that a miracle must be involved if something material takes the enterprising step of becoming conscious.

This thesis of the inertness of matter is not often stated explicitly today, but it is often implied. Peter Atkins expressed it strongly in his book *The Creation* when he made the startling remark, "Inanimate things are innately simple. That is one more step along the path to the view that *animate things, being innately inanimate, are innately simple too.*"[13]

Animate life, Atkins suggests, is not a serious factor in the world. It is just a misleading surface froth that obscures the grand, ultimate simplicity revealed by physics. Life has no bearing on consciousness, which (he explains) appears in the universe independently of it:

> Consciousness is a property of minute patches in the warm surfaces of mild planets.... Here now (and presumably cosmically elsewhere at other times) the patches are merging through the development of communication into a global film of consciousness which may in due course pervade the galaxy and beyond. ... Consciousness is simply complexity.... Space itself is self-conscious.... Consciousness is three-dimensional.[14]

This is scandalously muddled talk. Consciousness is not a property of such patches, but a property that (as far as we know) is found nowhere in the universe except in certain rather complex living beings—in fact, in animals. And that is the only context in which its presence makes sense.

This kind of attempt to make consciousness respectable as an isolated phenomenon, without mentioning biological considerations, by inserting it directly into physics and treating it mainly as a basis for cybernetics, the

13. Atkins, *The Creation*, 53.
14. Ibid., 71, 73, 83, 85.

IT revolution, and the colonization of space is rather prevalent at present. Similarly David Chalmers suggested that, in order to avoid reducing mind to body, we should take "experience itself as a fundamental feature of the world, *alongside mass, charge and space-time*."[15] This list shows his conviction that, in order to be fundamental, a feature must belong to physics. He does not name life as one of these fundamental features, and he goes on to remark with satisfaction that, if this view is right,

> then in some ways a theory of consciousness will have more in common with a theory in physics than a theory in biology. Biological theories involve no principles that are fundamental in this way, so *biological theory has a certain complexity and messiness about it*, but theories in physics, insofar as they deal with fundamental principles, aspire to simplicity and elegance.

In talk like this, the desire to keep one's theories clean of messy complications takes precedence over any wish to get a useful explanation. Such physics-envy is one more consequence of the unlucky fact that, in the seventeenth century, modern physics gained huge status because it was invented before the other sciences. This gave the Newtonian vision of the physical world an absolute standing as the final representation of reality, which is why that vision is still the background of much thinking today. It is surely the source of Atkins's amazing contention that all the things in the world are innately (whatever that may mean) simple.

That drastic assumption of simplicity was a central part of the seventeenth century's determination to get final, authoritative answers to all its questions. Physicists today have learnt better; they do not make this assumption. Like other scientists, they still look for simplicity, but they know they have no right to expect it. And they have, of course, altogether abandoned the simplistic doctrine of inert matter. Solid, billiard-ball like atoms have vanished entirely. As Heisenberg pointed out long ago,

> Since mass and energy are, according to the theory of relativity, essentially the same concepts, we may say that all elementary particles consist of energy. This could be interpreted as defining energy as the primary substance of the world. . . . With regard to this question *modern physics takes a definite stand against the materialism of Democritus* and for Plato and the Pythagoreans. The elementary particles are certainly not eternal and indestructible units of matter, they can actually be transformed into each other.[16]

---

15. Chalmers, "Facing Up to the Problem of Consciousness," 200–219.
16. Heisenberg, *Physics and Philosophy*, 58–59.

In fact, when physicists abandoned the notion of solid particles, the word "materialism" lost its old meaning. Though this word is still used as a war-cry it is by no means clear what significance it ought to have today. That change in the ontology of physics is one scientific reason why it is now clear that the notion of matter as essentially dead stuff—hopelessly alien to conscious life—is mistaken. But an even more obvious reason is, of course, the Darwinian view of evolution.

We now know that matter, the physical stuff that originally formed our planet, did in fact develop into the system of living things that now inhabit its surface, including us and many other conscious creatures. So, if we are still using a notion of physical matter that makes it seem incapable of giving rise to consciousness, we need to change it. That notion has proved unworkable. We have to see that the potentiality for the full richness of life must have been present right from the start—from the first outpouring of hydrogen atoms at the big bang. This was not simple stuff doomed forever to unchanging inertness. It was able to combine in myriads of subtle ways that shaped fully active living things. And if it could perform that startling feat, why should it be surprising if some of those living things then went on to the further activity of becoming conscious?

## Disowning the Earth

Many people have pointed out that Descartes' notion of the secluded soul played a part in the rise of individualism by cutting us off from our fellow-humans. But until lately less attention has been paid to the way in which it cuts us off from the living world around us. Descartes viewed all non-human animals, equally with plants, as literally unconscious automata. An animal, he said, does not *act*. It is driven. Human bodies too were automata; their only difference from the rest of the machinery was that they were driven by the alien soul set within them. All organisms, along with the planet they inhabited, were merely arrangements of inert matter. Life belonged only to spirit. And though views about consciousness have softened somewhat since his time, the more general idea that the rest of the biosphere is something foreign and decidedly beneath us has not shifted half as far as it should have done.

This idea still centres on the old notion of physical matter as inert and alien to us. It is worthwhile to notice here where this notion came from. Though Descartes used it for his purpose of isolating physics, it is not an objective conception demanded by science. It is part of an ideology that was long encouraged by Christian thinking, an ideology that centred on fear and contempt for the earth, which was seen primarily as the opposite of heaven. Human souls were conceived as having their real home in a remote spiritual paradise. Earth was at best a transit-camp, a place of trial through which they must pass. All sorts of nuances in our language still reflect this drama. Thus, the Oxford dictionary gives as the meaning of *earthy*: "Heavy, gross, material, dull, unrefined, . . . characteristic of earthly as opposed to heavenly existence."

Pre-Copernican cosmology set this heaven literally in the sky, beyond the concentric spheres that bore the sun, moon, stars, and planets. The earth was held to be merely the dead point in the middle of the system, the midden to which worthless matter that could not move upwards eventually drained. That central position was *not* seen as a sign of importance, as is often said, but as a mark of worthlessness, of distance from the celestial heights that held everything of real value. After all, what lay at the centre of earth itself was hell.

Accordingly, when Copernicus displaced our planet from its central position, Christian people did *not* feel the humiliation that is often said to have followed that move. Of course there was a sense of confusion and insecurity. But human souls still had their celestial citizenship. Their salvation was still essential cosmic business.

This sense of complacent independence from the earth did not die away, as might have been expected, when confidence in the Christian vision declined. Secular Westerners who stopped seeing themselves as Christian souls subject to judgment did stop expecting their previous welcome in the sky. But this did not lead them—as one would think it might have done—to conclude that they might be only rather gifted earthly animals. Instead, they still managed to see themselves in the terms that Descartes had suggested as pure intellects—detached observers, set above the rest of the physical world to observe and control it. When they stopped venerating God, they began instead to venerate themselves as in some sense the supreme beings in the universe—intellectual marvels whose production must have been the real purpose of evolution. This rather surprising position is expressed fully today in the Strong Anthropic Principle, and to some extent by other manifestoes of what is now called Human Exceptionalism.

Human intellect, in fact, now shone out as supreme in isolation from the whole animal background that might have helped to explain it, and from the rest of the biosphere on which it depended. "The mind" did indeed begin to look like a miracle, a self-supporting phenomenon without a context. As Roy Porter says, "In a single intrepid stroke, Descartes had disinherited almost the whole of Creation—all, that is, except the human mind—of the attributes of life, soul and purpose which had infused it since the speculation of Pythagoras and Plato, Aristotle and Galen."[17] The physical universe no longer seemed to be what Plato had called it, a mighty living creature. It was simply a more or less infinite pile of raw material provided for humans to exploit.

That exploitation accordingly went on without much check throughout the Industrial Revolution. The pile of resources did indeed seem infinite. Doubts about this are, of course, beginning to be felt now. But the sense of humans as essentially independent, powerful, super-terrestrial beings is still extraordinarily strong.

Some people—apparently quite a lot in the United States—still ground this confidence in the Christian heaven, expecting to be carried off there in chariots when disaster strikes. Others use the sky differently, advertising future desirable residences in outer space rather than in the traditional heaven. And even among people who don't go for either of these scenarios, many are still confident that scientific ingenuity will always resolve our difficulties somehow. The vision of ourselves as essentially invulnerable minds independent of earthly support, colonists whose intellects will get them out of trouble whatever may go wrong, is still amazingly strong.

## Life and Its Effects

This flattering illusion of human separateness and self-sufficiency is surely the really disastrous legacy still left over from Cartesian dualism. It is closely linked to the idea that physical matter is inert. That idea makes our planet appear as a mere jumble of blindly interacting particles senselessly forming themselves into handy products for us to consume. If we want to move to a more realistic notion of ourselves, we need to have a more realistic conception of what the earth itself is—namely a living, working system.[18]

That is why we now need James Lovelock's concept of Gaia. This idea is not just some idle Californian fancy, a futile substitute for traditional religion. It is the worldview that fills in the appropriate background to our new, more realistic idea of ourselves as working parts of the biosphere.

The point is that this biosphere does not consist of two separate parts any more than we ourselves do. It is not an inorganic machine that has accidentally got infested by some irrelevant life. Instead it is a working whole—an organic system, whose living components continuously affect the rest in a way that determines the fate of the whole. There is now plenty of evidence

---

17. Porter, *Flesh in the Age of Reason*, 65–66.
18. I cannot discuss this topic at length here, but I have done so in the end section of my book *Science and Poetry*.

that the reason why our planet has not become a dead one—one unable to support life, like Mars and Venus—is that the biota on it have continuously modified its soil and atmosphere in a way that has made possible their own survival and development. Without this work, they would not be here and neither would we. We are not the owners and engineers of this system. We are a tiny dependent part of it.

Today, this idea of the self-preservative function of life is no longer dismissed as bad science. It is widely accepted. There are now many Departments of Earth Science where the interdependence of living things with non-living is taken for granted. In these departments geologists and biologists work together, in a way that they never used to do, to investigate the details of this process.

But, of course, these scientists are not required to look at the wider implications of that interdependence. It is not their business to consider how this new view of the earth ought to affect our conception of ourselves. In fact, they usually manage not to notice how far-reaching those implications are, how many questions they raise about the notoriously puzzling concept of *life* itself. And they are helped in this inattention by avoiding the actual name Gaia. Indeed, in order to make it easier for them to accept his scientific message Lovelock himself at one time considered dropping the name Gaia and substituting "geophysiology."

But in the end he decided that the wider problems are too important to allow this kind of evasion. The change needed cannot be encapsulated in this way. It is not one internal to the physical sciences; it affects the whole shape of our thought.

## The Mystery Is Within

After the enquiry that we have been making, two questions may well occur to us. One is, "Why has the unworkable mind-body dualism that we have been examining lasted so long?" The other is, "Why did scientists studying the earth not notice earlier that organisms might have causally affected the planet, as well as vice versa? Why did they take it for granted that life was merely an inconsequential by-product of inorganic phenomena? Why, in fact, did biologists and geologists not talk to each other on these matters until the last few decades, when, to their own surprise, they have suddenly brought themselves together in departments of Earth Science?"

I think the answers to these two questions are related. The delay on both points springs from the difficulty that we have in bringing together two very different ways of thinking—two sides of our personality—two distinct approaches. When we are dealing with conscious subjects we think socially. When we deal with lifeless things we treat them as objects. These two approaches call out different faculties within us.

The relations between these faculties are not at all simple. It is often hard to see which of them to use. We see cases (such as trees) that seem intermediate. We also see others (such as mentally ill people) for which we are sure that both methods are needed. In fact, because our social life is so pervasive, it is probable that both play some part on most of our transactions with the world around us. The art of combining these two approaches—of making them work together in our lives—is as necessary as the art of using our two eyes together, or as using sight together with touch. The idea that it is always scientific to avoid the personal approach—that we should be always "objective" in the sense of treating everything as an inert object—is an unworkable fantasy. It can only produce a terrible mental squint.

McGinn is quite right to say that there are real mysteries in the world, matters that we are not at all well-equipped to understand. Foremost among these mysteries are those that concern the inner structure of our own minds, the relation between different parts of our lives. We are not totally helpless here. We can make some sense of this structure if we attend to it carefully. But if, instead of attending to it, we simply project its conflicts onto the outer world and try to deal with them there by metaphysical conjuring, we shall get nowhere.

## Bibliography

Atkins, Peter. *The Creation*. Oxford: Freeman, 1987.
Chalmers, David J. "Facing Up to the Problem of Consciousness." *Journal of Consciousness Studies* 2.3 (1995) 200–219.
Descartes, René. *Meditations on the First Philosophy*. Everyman's Library. Translated by John Veitch. London: Dent & Dutton, 1937.
Heisenberg, Werner. *Physics and Philosophy*. New York: Harper & Row, 1962.
Locke, John. *Essay Concerning Human Understanding*. London: Penguin, 1997.
McGinn, Colin. *The Mysterious Flame: Conscious Minds in a Material World*. New York: Basic, 1999.
Midgley, Mary. *Science and Poetry*. London: Routledge, 2001.
Porter, Roy. *Flesh in the Age of Reason*. London: Penguin, 2003.

# SECTION III
Moving to Wholeness

# 10

# The Soul in the Novel
## From Daniel Defoe to David Foster Wallace

Edmund Waldstein, O.Cist.

## Introduction

THE NOVEL DEVELOPED AS a literary form particularly suited to a certain typically modern view of the division between soul and body—a view that makes a very sharp distinction between the inner, psychic reality and the outer corporeal reality; between the *res cogitans* and the *res extensa*; between interiority and exteriority; between the subject and the object; between the world of "the first-person" and that of the "third person." The novel, I claim, was particularly suited to expressing the world as experienced through this dualism. I shall illustrate this by looking at Daniel Defoe's *Robinson Crusoe*. I shall then go on in the second part of this essay to consider what happens to the novel when this view is rejected, a task I shall undertake by examining the novels of David Foster Wallace.

Daniel Defoe is one of the first novelists in the modern sense. David Foster Wallace, on the other hand, is a (near) contemporary novelist who has been described as "post-postmodern." If postmodernity dissolved the Cartesian distinction between subject and object by radically questioning the very idea of the subject, and thus seemed to entail the end of the novel, then Wallace's project could be described as an attempt to revive the novel through finding a new mode of human subjectivity.

Wallace's friend and rival Jonathan Franzen compared Wallace to Defoe in an essay in which he (Franzen) describes how he went to Selkirk Island in the Pacific, where Alexander Selkirk (one of Defoe's inspirations for Robinson Crusoe) was stranded. Franzen camped out on the island for a while, read *Robinson Crusoe,* reflected on novel writing, and tried to come to terms with Wallace's death.[1] (Wallace had committed suicide two years earlier.)

Franzen recounts how he and Wallace had worked out an account of the purpose of the novel as overcoming existential loneliness by giving "access" to the consciousness of its characters. Franzen sees Defoe as one of the first novelists to try to do this, and he sees Wallace as working in the same tradition. The details of Franzen's comparison are highly questionable,[2] but what I want to draw attention to here is his view of what the novel is: a genre that begins with Defoe and Richardson in the eighteenth century, and which is concerned with giving the reader a peep-hole (as it were) into the consciousness of other subjects.

Steven Moore has recently attacked Franzen's view in the first volume of his new history of the novel. Moore argues that there have always been novels, not just since the eighteenth century, and that the best novels have a different purpose:

> [We] don't read such novels "to sustain a sense of connectedness, to resist existential loneliness." We read them for the same reason we might go to the opera or the ballet: to be dazzled by a performance.[3]

Moore's championship of "performance" over peep-hole-ism is, I think, the reason why he rejects the traditional view of the novel as a modern genre, and it is symptomatic of a collapse of the view of the relation between soul and body on which the "modern novel" was based. "Performance" is actually more typical of a certain pre-modern view of the relation between soul and body, of the exterior and the interior. A view that sees the external

1. Franzen, *Farther Away.*

2. Franzen sees himself as working in a slightly different version of the tradition of the novel from Wallace—one inaugurated by Samuel Richardson, the pioneer of the courtship-marriage plot in the novel. Franzen argues that while novelists such as Defoe and Wallace tried merely to portray the existential isolation of the modern subject, and thus overcome it, Richardson and Franzen try also to depict the overcoming of that loneliness through a certain kind of relationship. I claim that Franzen exaggerates the similarities between Wallace and Defoe.

3. Moore, *The Novel,* 9.

as immediately expressing the internal; that sees the soul as not foreign to the body, but as forming with it a microcosm that mirrors the macrocosm— a macrocosm that is itself no Cartesian *res-extensa*, but rather an ordered whole, full of intrinsic teleology and form. Think of Dante's *Commedia* in which the visible is the immediate expression of a deeper order. Performance in this view of things is the best way of expressing the truth, because the truth itself is primarily public.

But in modernity performance is problematic, because the relation between the inner and the outer is problematic. Truth is not public, but private, a matter (above all) of the interior monologue within the hidden depths of the *res cogitans*. The novel thus tries to avoid the impression of performance, of artificiality. Even if it is in fact a work of very careful art, it tries to give the impression of merely peering into another mind. The first great master of this technique was Daniel Defoe.

## I. Daniel Defoe

Defoe's great literary innovation was what Ian Watt in his classic study of the early novel calls "formal realism;" a style marked by a great many details, many of them unremarkable, and which therefore stresses the particularities of its characters, rather than their universal characteristics.[4] To call such a style "realism" is somewhat question begging—it assumes that the individual is more real than the universal.

But *Robinson Crusoe* is not only important because of its formal innovation, but also because of the peculiar character of its hero. Crusoe's character has two sharply distinguished parts: first, what we might call the economic or technological, and second, the spiritual.[5] The first part of his character is, I'm afraid, more interesting, and is the part that appeals to children; Robinson's tireless and inventive labor, by which he produces everything that he needs. (Note however, that this labor is only rendered so interesting by a Utopian feature: it is wholly un-alienated; there is neither division of labor nor separation of labor and capital.[6]) Robinson is the exemplary representative of the project of the domination of nature through the application of mathematics to the physical world, inaugurated by Francis Bacon, and carried forward by Descartes. As Robinson himself notes:

---

4. See Watt, *The Rise of the Novel*, especially 32–34.

5. For the following analysis I am much indebted to Brann, "The Unexpurgated Robinson Crusoe."

6. Marx points this out in his discussion of Crusoe: Marx, *Capital*, ch. 1.

> So I went to work; and here I must needs observe, that as Reason is the Substance and Original of the Mathematicks, so by stating and squaring every thing by Reason, and by making the most rational Judgment of things, every Man may be in time Master of every mechanick Art.[7]

The Baconian-Cartesian project of dominating nature is of course a key element in the "disenchantment" of the world in modernity. Descartes' method of universal doubt can be seen as a method of stripping the world of all features that are not relevant to the Baconian programme. The intrinsic teleology of things is of course irrelevant to such a project, since domination involves substituting one's own end for the natural end of the thing. And therefore the teleologically determined substantial forms of things (in the Aristotelian sense) are irrelevant. The only form that is left in the world is the most extrinsic and accidental sort of form: mathematically metrical figure.

In the capitalist economic system, which Baconian-Cartesian science helped to bring about, the mechanization of nature is extended to a mechanization of human relations. As Karl Marx famously put it in *The Communist Manifesto*:

> [It] has put an end to all feudal, patriarchal, idyllic relations. It has pitilessly torn asunder the motley feudal ties that bound man to his "natural superiors," and has left remaining no other nexus between man and man than naked self interest, than callous "cash payment."[8]

Now, this poses a problem for the human subject: she is not at home in the mechanized world she has brought about. The more the subject advances in reductive, mechanical knowledge of the world of objects, the more she becomes a riddle to herself. "Lost in the cosmos" as Walker Percy would say.

Robinson Crusoe's solitude on the island can be taken as an unconscious symbol of the isolation of the modern subject. Defoe gives this remarkably eerie expression in a scene in which Robinson Crusoe is awakened by the voice of his parrot:

> But judge you, if you can, that read my Story, what a Surprize I must be in, when I was wak'd out of my Sleep by a Voice calling me by my Name several times, *Robin, Robin, Robin*

---

7. Defoe, *Robinson Crusoe*, 78–79.
8. Marx and Engels, *Manifesto*.

> *Crusoe,* poor *Robin Crusoe,* where are you *Robin Crusoe?* Where are you? Where have you been?[9]

These are, of course, questions that the parrot has heard Crusoe pose to himself, and they bring us to the second part of Crusoe's character—the spiritual part.

*Robinson Crusoe* is largely concerned with Crusoe's religious journey, with his growing recognition of God in his life. The long spiritual introspections in *Crusoe* are often left out in children's versions of the novel as being too boring, but for our purposes they are of crucial importance. Crusoe's religion largely functions as a means of giving his life *meaning*. This is a very modern sort of religion. Pre-modern Christians tended to see the world about them as saturated with meaning and intentional agency, much of it dangerous; they did not pray to God for meaning, but for salvation.[10] But Crusoe's relation to God above all gives him the comfort of the sense that his life has meaning, despite the emptiness and solitude about him. Ian Watt has noted that Crusoe's religion has little effect on his actions; it remains in the subjective sphere, and does not influence his treatment of objects.[11]

It is, of course, true that Crusoe sees even the external events of his life as guided by divine providence. Crusoe is not a twentieth-century liberal Protestant—his religion is not *merely* subjective. And yet, one can see in Crusoe tendencies that already tend in the direction of reducing religion to the subjective. In a passage where Crusoe speaks of praying for deliverance from cannibals, he notes his dissatisfaction with his prayer, since prayer ought really to be a matter of finding internal comfort, rather than facing objective threats:

> I must observe with Grief too, that the Discomposure of my Mind had too great Impressions also upon the religious Part of my Thoughts, for the Dread and Terror of falling into the Hands of Savages and Canibals, lay so upon my Spirits, that I seldom found my self in a due Temper for Application to my Maker, at least not with the sedate Calmness and Resignation of Soul which I was wont to do. . . . For these Discomposures affect the Mind as the others do the Body; and the Discomposure of the Mind must necessarily be as great a Disability as that of the Body, and much greater, Praying to God being properly an Act of the Mind, not of the Body.[12]

9. Defoe, *Robinson Crusoe,* 168.
10. Cf. Taylor, *A Secular Age,* ch. 1.
11. Watt, *The Rise of the Novel,* 81.
12. Defoe, *Robinson Crusoe,* 193.

Given this subjective view of religion, it is not surprising that when Crusoe's solitude has been relieved, near the end of his stay, and his island has become a political society in miniature, he decides to tolerate various religions:

> It was remarkable too, we had but three Subjects, and they were of three different Religions. My Man *Friday* was a Protestant, his Father was a *Pagan* and a *Cannibal,* and the *Spaniard* was a Papist: However, I allow'd Liberty of Conscience throughout my Dominions.[13]

Politics for Crusoe belongs to the external, objective world—it is a matter of managing external affairs. Religion is primarily a matter of the subjective, interior, and thus essentially private. The ancient idea of politics as the art of governing souls has faded.

## II. Relationships, Hylozoism, Epic, and the End of the Novel

Defoe provided the model for the novel formally, but not thematically. Samuel Richardson was to provide the novel with its principle theme; namely the overcoming of the isolation of the individual through freely chosen personal relations. Capitalism having destroyed the interpersonal ties of more organic societies and replaced them with cold contractualism, freely chosen relationships took on a great importance: especially the relationship of husband and wife, which, disengaged from other areas of life, becomes a matter of personal choice.[14]

As the novel develops after Defoe and Richardson one sees a great many complications of the picture that I have been drawing. The Cartesian view of the subject is very soon questioned in philosophy—first by the so-called empiricists. This has an effect on the novel, but it does not change the fundamental separation of the inner and outer that I have been describing. Indeed I would argue that it aggravates it. Laurence Sterne writes in his highly philosophical novel *Tristram Shandy,* written in the 1760s: "our minds shine not through the body, but are wrapt up here in a dark covering of uncrystalized flesh and blood."[15]

---

13. Defoe, *Robinson Crusoe,* 287.

14. See: Watt, *The Rise of the Novel,* ch. 5; cf. Charles Taylor's discussion of "affirming ordinary life": Taylor, *Sources of the Self,* ch. 13.

15. Sterne, *Tristram Shandy,* 60.

In the nineteenth century the novel is further complicated by various reactions against Enlightenment rationalism. Goethe's hylozoism, for instance, is an expression of a yearning for a pre-modern, organic-holistic world, but it remains something toward which he strives, rather than the background picture of his work.[16] Later still come epic social novels, such as Tolstoy's *War and Peace*, in which Enlightenment individualism is tempered by a sense of the action of social "forces." But again, such novels are more similar to Defoe than they are to classical or medieval literature. Their very form continues to embody an Enlightenment picture of the subject. Thus Tolstoy is one of the great masters of the art of giving the reader the impression of a view into the subjective depths of his characters.[17]

The twentieth century sees a more radical change in the form of the novel—Joyce's stream of consciousness begins to unravel the idea of a coherent inner life that can be narrated. But it is the postmodern novels and "metafiction" of the late twentieth century that question this most radically. The work of writers such as John Barth, William Gaddis, and others question both the idea of narratable human life and the very idea of communication through signs.

At the level of literary form, metafiction draws attention to its own status as fiction; it does not invite the reader to "suspend disbelief" and enter into an illusion, but rather to keep the illusory character of the narrative in the foreground. Thematically, postmodern novels are concerned with portraying human subjects as mere epiphenomena of material and economic reality, or linguistic constructs that mask the irrational imposition of power. The centrality of the human subject was, however, the *raison d'être* of the novelistic form, and thus postmodern novels are deeply ironic—they are novels about the impossibility of novels. The pleasure of the most brilliant postmodernists is the pleasure of, as it were, *being in the know*, of "getting" the ironic nihilism that sees through all pretense to the meaningless chaos that pretense hides.

## III. David Foster Wallace

Wallace thought the postmodern project rather empty. He thought he knew "in his gut" that the great literature of the past was more than mere illusion, that it involved a real communication between human beings, and that it

---

16. See, for example, his novella *Die Wahlverwandschaften* (1809) with its attempt to portray an analogy between human and chemical interaction.

17. Tolstoy in fact uses the technique of directly reported thought, which was already falling out of fashion in his day (to be replaced by "free indirect speech"). See: Pascal, *The Dual Voice*, 123–24.

was able to show the possibility of really being human.[18] Thus he saw the task of literature today as being a double one: first, to face those aspects of late capitalist life and thought that make it difficult to "be human," and that lend so much plausibility to postmodern nihilism, and second, to try to find ways of reviving the *humanum,* even in these times. As he once put it in an interview:

> Look man, we'd probably most of us agree that these are dark times, and stupid ones, but do we need fiction that does nothing but dramatize how dark and stupid everything is? In dark times, the definition of good art would seem to be art that locates and applies CPR to those elements of what's human and magical that still live and glow despite the times' darkness.[19]

Wallace made use of many of the literary techniques of postmodern metafiction, but he uses them to very different ends. While metafiction drew attention to its own status as text in order to ironize and debunk itself, Wallace used its techniques to get the reader to enter into a communicative relationship with the author. Unlike the classical modern novel, which tries to be entirely transparent to the reader, so that the reader has the impression of an unmediated look into other subjects, Wallace wanted his readers to have to *work* on his works. What he once said of his story "Little Expressionless Animals" applies to all of his work:

> it's trying to prohibit the reader from forgetting that she's receiving heavily mediated data, that this process is a relationship between the writer's consciousness and her own, and that in order for it to be anything like a full human relationship, she's going to have to put in her share of the linguistic work.[20]

The novelist and critic Lee Konstantinou has argued that while postmodern metafiction tries to get readers to become conscious of the questionable activity in which they are themselves engaged, "revealing that what the reader reads ought to be disbelieved," the literary form that Wallace developed opens the reader rather to the activity of the writer and asks the reader to *believe* to enter a "full human relationship" with the writer, a relationship of trust.[21] Konstantinou borrows a term from Raoul Eshelman to describe this sort of literary technique as "performatist."[22]

18. Wallace, "Greatly Exaggerated," 144.
19. McCaffery, "Interview," 26.
20. Ibid., 34.
21. Konstantinou, "No Bull," 97.
22. Ibid., 96.

I argued above that "performance" is a literary style typical of a pre-modern view of the human being. And in this respect Wallace's work is closer to pre-modern literature than to the classical novel—since it is consciously artificial. But Wallace's performatism differs from pre-modern literary performance in the "unfinished" character that he gives it. Pre-modern literature could afford a very high degree of formal completion and resolution, because the anthropology that it expressed was unproblematic. For Wallace, in contrast, the status of the human is highly problematic. The modern isolation of the subject has lead inevitably to the postmodern disappearance of the subject. The "linguistic work" that the reader has to do in order to have "anything like a full human relationship" with the author is a path towards a recovery of humanity.

Wallace's 1996 novel *Infinite Jest* is his most ambitious attempt at getting his readers to do this kind of linguistic work. Most of the book is narrated in the third person with remarkable formal complexity; hundreds of characters appear in fragments of various lengths and styles. It seems initially that the world being described is an irrational swirl of bits and pieces, but as one reads further, patterns emerge. There are hints at a completion that is, however, never reached.

The novel begins, however, with a section narrated in the first person—the form of narrative used by pioneers of the novel such as Defoe—by Hal Incandenza an eighteen-year-old intellectual and athletic prodigy. This first section is a frighteningly exaggerated description of the isolated subject. "I am in here," Hal tells us, "I'm not a machine. I feel and believe." And yet we soon learn that he is totally unable to speak his interior life to others. When he tries to speak the other people in the room hear only inarticulate bestial noises "like a drowning goat. A goat, drowning in something viscous."[23] It later emerges that Hal's father has made a film in the hopes of drawing Hal out of his isolation, of finding a way of communicating with him:

> [Hal's father] spent the whole sober last ninety days of his animate life working tirelessly to contrive a medium via which he and the muted son could simply *converse*. . . . Make something so bloody compelling it would reverse thrust on a young self's fall into the womb of solipsism, anhedonia, death in life. A magically entertaining toy to dangle at the infant still somewhere alive in the boy, to make its eyes light and toothless mouth open unconsciously, to laugh. To bring him "out of himself," as they say.

---

23. Wallace, *Infinite Jest*, 3, 12, 14.

The film's title is significantly the same as the novel's, *Infinite Jest,* but (as I read it) the film ultimately fails in its objective. The film turns out to be not a means of communication, but rather a means of fleeing the lonely self through Pascalian diversion. The film becomes like a drug; a distraction so powerful that it drowns the internal monologue.

Diversion is, for Wallace, *the* great temptation of the hypermodern society that he describes. The attempt to *flee* the loneliness of modern subjectivity prevents the problem from being faced, and thus ensures that it will never be truly overcome. *Infinite Jest* deals mostly with two sets of characters—the students and staff of an elite tennis academy and a halfway house for recovering drug addicts. Drug abuse is portrayed as Pascalian diversion; as the attempt to flee the self by drowning it in pleasure. Of course, the drug addicts soon realize that what they are doing is self-destructive, but they cannot escape. Seeing through the problem with their minds only makes the problem worse. "It's the newcomers with some education that are the worst, according to [the director of the half-way house]. They identify their whole selves with their head, and the Disease makes its command headquarters in the head."[24] In this they resemble the postmodern fiction writers, who recognize the problem of modern of subjectivity, but offer no alternative.

The tennis academy tries to overcome interiority by a mechanistic monism. The students are submitted to a discipline that is meant to turn them into machines. The human soul, however, protests against this monism; as dramatized by Hal's opening monologue: "I'm not a machine."

A more promising path is indicated by one of the recovering addicts in the halfway house, Don Gately, arguably the true protagonist of the novel. Gately is forced to participate in the Alcoholics Anonymous. AA's approach seems hopelessly naïve and cliché ridden to Gately, but it turns out to work. One of the disciplines that AA imposes on him is "giving thanks" to "a higher power." Gately does not believe in God, but it turns out that the body ritual of kneeling down and giving thanks in prayer is a remarkably effective counter ritual to the giving away of the self that takes place in addiction. AA and the halfway house also help Gately to integrate himself into a community, turning him away from his own interiority toward the needs of the others. Finally, Gately learns the discipline of "abiding in the moment," which is an ascetic, almost a monastic discipline. "Everything unendurable was in the head, was the head not Abiding in the Present but hopping the wall and doing a recon and then returning with unendurable news."[25] Abiding in the present allows one, as Wallace once said in a speech,

24. Ibid., 272.
25. Ibid., 861.

to experience a crowded, hot, slow, consumer-hell type situation as not only meaningful, but sacred, on fire with the same force that lit the stars: love, fellowship, the mystical oneness of all things deep down.[26]

The "force that lit the stars" is, of course, a reference to Dante's *Commedia*. Wallace is no Dante, but the humanity that he makes faltering steps toward recovering resembles the soul-body unity described by Dante more than the stranded subject evoked by Daniel Defoe.

## Bibliography

Burn, Stephen J., ed. *Conversations with David Foster Wallace*. Jackson: University Press of Mississippi, 2012.

Brann, Eva. "The Unexpurgated Robinson Crusoe." *American Dialectic* 1.1 (2011) 90–111.

Defoe, Daniel. *The Life and Strange Surprizing Adventures of Robinson Crusoe of York, Mariner: Who lived Eight and Twenty Years, all alone in an un-inhabited Island on the Coast of America, near the Mouth of the Great River of Oroonoque; Having been cast on Shore by Shipwreck, wherein all the Men perished but himself. With an Account how he was at last as strangely deliver'd by Pyrates. Written by Himself.* London: Taylor, 1719. Online: http://www.pierre-marteau.com/editions/1719-robinson-crusoe.html.

Franzen, Jonathan. *Farther Away*. New York: Farrar, Straus and Giroux, 2012.

Goethe, Johann Wolfgang von. *Die Wahlverwandtschaften*. Stugart: Reclam, 1986.

Konstantinou, Lee. "No Bull: David Foster Wallace and Postironic Belief." In *The Legacy of David Foster Wallace*, edited by Samuel Cohen and Lee Konstantinou, 83–112. Iowa City: University of Iowa Press, 2012.

McCaffery, Larry. "An Expanded Interview with David Foster Wallace." In *Conversations with David Foster Wallace*, edited by Stephen J. Burn, 21–52. Jackson: University of Mississippi Press, 2012.

Marx, Karl. *Capital: A Critique of Political Economy*, Vol. I [1867]. Translated by Samuel Moore and Edward Aveling, edited by Frederick Engels (1887). Marx/Engels Internet Archive 1999. Online: http://www.marxists.org/archive/marx/works/1867-c1/ch01.htm

Marx, Karl, and Engels, Frederick. *Manifesto of the Communist Party* [1848]. Translated by Samuel Moore and Frederick Engels (1888). Marx/Engels Internet Archive [1987] 2000. Online: http://www.marxists.org/archive/marx/works/1848/communist-manifesto/ch01.htm

Moore, Steven. *The Novel: An Alternative History*, Vol. 1. New York: Continuum, 2010.

Pascal, Roy. *The Dual Voice: Free Indirect Speech and Its Functioning in the Nineteenth-Century European Novel*. Manchester: Manchester University Press, 1977.

Sterne, Laurence. *Tristam Shandy*, Vol. 1 [1760]. Edited by Ian Cambell Ross. Oxford: Oxford University Press, 1983.

Taylor, Charles. *A Secular Age*. Cambridge: Belknap-Harvard University Press, 2007.

---

26. Wallace, "Kenyon Commencement Speech," 362.

Wallace, David Foster. "Greatly Exaggerated." In *A Supposedly Fun Thing I'll Never Do Again: Essays and Arguments,* 138–45. Boston: Back Bay, 1998.

———. *Infinite Jest.* 1996. Reprint. New York: Little, Brown, 2006.

———. "Kenyon Commencement Speech." In *The Best American Nonrequired Reading,* edited by Dave Eggers, 355–64. Boston: Mariner, 2006.

———. *The Pale King.* Edited by Michael Pietsch. New York: Little, 2011.

Watt, Ian. *The Rise of the Novel.* London: Chatto and Windus, 1957.

# 11

# Difficult Conversion

## Shakespeare and the Soul of Religion

ANTHONY D. BAKER

### Soul-Steering

WHEN THE CHARACTER PROLOGUE comes to the stage in Ben Jonson's *Staple of News*, he delivers an injunction at the bidding, he claims, of the playwright, that the audience mark "a difference 'twixt Poetique elves, and Poets," as something like the difference between imitators and the real thing:

> All that dable in the inke,
> And defile quills, are not those few, can think,
> Conceive, expresse, and steere the soules of men,
> As with a rudder, round thus, with their pen.[1]

On one level, this is a simple brag that Jonson puts in the mouth of his narrator: I am a poet, not a "poetic elf" who dabbles in ink in order to amuse an audience. On a more sophisticated level, it is a deeply ironic opening to a

---

1. Quoting from the Yale Studies in English edition, 21–24. This essay has improved greatly during preparation for the present volume under the careful readings of Samuel Kimbriel and an anonymous reviewer. I am also most grateful for the incomparable research and editing assistance of Christine Havens.

play which puts on stage the beginnings of consumerism—the consumption of both goods and information—and demonstrates just how easily the dealers of shallow words and promises can "steere the soules of men." The poet will attempt to move us in a way that reveals the manipulations of the media and market to be a shallow ruddering that never touches the deep waters of a person. The true poet will make us laugh at what once steered us.

What is the soul that appears here as the target of the poetic craft? It is perhaps not altogether different from the hidden person that the French essayist Montaigne had conjured for the previous generation: "It is no part of a well-grounded judgment simply to judge ourselves by our exterior actions. A man must thoroughly sound himself and dive into his heart, and there see by what wards or springs the motions stir."[2] Jonson had no patience for the dilettantish ways of essayists who extol in one essay the very thing they discredit in another.[3] Perhaps though Jonson and his Prologue imagine the soul to be a thing too easily discovered? Montaigne's "heart" is less a ship in the harbor than an exotic and elusive creature who swims on the ocean floor, camouflaging itself among the rocks and seaweed. Montaigne, for his part, was skeptical of the way theatrical performances of Jonson's sort celebrated disingenuousness: "Everyone may play the juggler and represent an honest man upon the stage. But within, and in bosom, where all things are lawful, where all is concealed—to keep a due rule or formal decorum, that's the point."[4] Perhaps though Montaigne imagines his essays as less "theatrical" than they actually are? We are all wearing costumes, to paraphrase the great Frank Zappa, and the self-revealing essay may have more in common with the staged juggling act than we care to think. In any case, both essayist and playwright imagine here a non-obvious, perhaps rarely expressed truth of a person's existence, and it is to steer this one that they lift their pens.

With Jonson's concerns for authenticity and Montaigne's for the "bosom, where all things are . . . concealed," it may seem as if "soul" here is a synonym for interiority, a kind of kernel of selfhood available only to self-reflective subject. Yet it is the pen of the poet that acts as a rudder on the souls of the audience, for Jonson. As he puts it elsewhere, the true poet can "informe yong-men to all good disciplines, inflame growne-men to all great

---

2. Quoting from the new edition of Florio's 1603 translation: Stephen Greenblatt and Peter G. Blatt, eds., *Shakespeare's Montaigne: The Florio Translation of the Essays. A Selection*, 98. The essays were first published, posthumously, in 1595, and had begun appearing in manuscript translations in London by around 1600.

3. "What they have discredited, and impugned in one worke, they have before, or after, extolled the same in another. . . . Such are all *Essayists*, even their Master *Montaigne*." Quoted in Greenblatt's introduction to *Shakespeare's Montaigne*, xxv.

4. "Of Repenting," in *Shakespeare's Montaigne*, 200.

vertues, keepe old-men in their best and supreme state."[5] Thus, the truth of oneself is not simply an introspective discovery, but a "best" self that the artful poetry of another may summon. Similarly, Montaigne, ever suspicious of his own powers of self-deception, finds the soul to be a complex creature, always able to fool the self with more camouflage. Searching for a trustworthy guide to true and soul-disclosing repentance, he warns himself against mistaking for repentance a "general wish to be other than I am," or a vague loss of appetite for the sins of youth. "I acknowledge no repentance . . . [that] is superficial, mean, and ceremonious. It must touch me on all sides before I can term it repentance. It must pinch my entrails and afflict them as deeply and thoroughly, as God himself beholds me." To find the true soul that inhabits our many costumes, "God must touch our hearts."[6]

In this sense, soul may be a mode of encounter before it is a metaphysical entity. Or perhaps we can call it a metaphysical entity only in light of our experience of it as a mode of encounter. "Of course there is such a thing as a soul," we might exclaim in a Jonsonian-Montaignian mode: "have you never been moved by da Vinci's *Head of a Woman*?" As a mode of encounter, soul is conversion. When we leave the theater or museum or library "untouched," we leave unchanged by the encounter with an other; we leave having failed, in fact, to encounter any other at all. However, once we respond "from the soul," that is, with a deep and self-forgetting singularity, we have experienced a turn of both our attention and intention, a change in orientation. We have met with something that lies both deep within and far above the mundane order that normally guides us; something other has steered our souls. This may manifest bodily as goosebumps or a shiver: that my body is responding to the poet or musician on stage and not the positioning of the air conditioning ducts beneath it may be more than I can discern about myself with any immediate finality; still, the poet and prose writer stake their success on the hunch that an encounter with this ontological depth of a human beings is, if elusive, yet possible. It is the highest ideal of their craft. "Oh for a muse of fire," says the Prologue of a rival to the London stages of Jonson's day, "that would ascend/the brightest heaven of invention."[7]

In Montaigne's observation that the search for the human bosom is ultimately the search to meet with God, the moral injunction of the poet meets with that of the preacher. The sermons and devotional literature of the turn of the seventeenth century called for a similar stripping down to

---

5. From the dedication to his *Volpone*, ll.24–26, quoted and discussed in Richard S. Peterson, *Imitation and Praise in the Poems of Ben Jonson*, 55.

6. "Of Repentance," 206–10.

7. Shakespeare, *Henry V* Prol. 1–2. All Shakespeare references are from Stephen Greenblatt et al., eds., *The Norton Shakespeare. Based on the Oxford Edition*.

truth, an honesty before oneself that serves as a prelude and pathway to an honest reception of divine grace. "Descend into thyself, and looke into thy Life," exhorts a Jesuit devotional manual.[8] Conversion, says the great Anglican preacher Lancelot Andrewes, is a turning of the whole heart: "For which cause, as if some converted with the brimme, or upper part only, doth the Psalme call for it, *de profundis* [Ps. 130.1]; and the *Prophet* [Joel 2.12], *from the bottome of the heart.*"[9]

Religious conversion involves what Charles Taylor has called a "transformation beyond our usual scope."[10] Here too, however, and perhaps especially here, we ought to be wary of the layers of camouflage we wear. How much is involved in the turning to God from the *profundis*, and not merely from within the shallows? Conversion always involves an element of the theatrical, and this is especially true of the turn of the early Reformation era English church, when joining the Established church was key to political favor and financial success, and, alternatively, failing to attend the local parish for a specified number of Sundays was a minor act of treason, punishable by fine. In this context, can Anglican baptism be a disinterested conversion? On the other hand, a public disavowal of the official church is no more obviously "pure," since the refusal of one source of political sponsorship will always manifest as alignment with another. Indeed, the same Andrewes who preached conversion *de profundis* also had the privilege of preaching the Gunpowder sermon for many years running, thus stoking the fires of an anti-Catholic cult of the state of England. In religion especially, the soul is prone to juggling acts.

The question of religious conversion, and all the complexity of will, motivation, and expression it entails, is one that animates Shakespeare's plays. Jonson's senior by nearly a decade, the latter seems to have been periodically enamored of and annoyed by the emerging reputation of the former.[11] Though the two shared many tools common to the playwrights of the day, on the matter of soul-steering there is a pronounced difference. Whereas Jonson allows his Prologue to give a moral charge to the audience, Shakespeare never offers anything so resembling his own point of view as that. Rivals in love or war will moralize, but the plays tend to multiply

---

8 Quoted in Alison Shell, *Shakespeare and Religion*, 136.

9. Story, ed., *Sermons*, 129.

10. Taylor, *A Secular Age*, 729.

11. Alongside the famous praise in his edition to the First Folio, that Shakespeare wrote "not for an age, but for all time," we have Jonson's response to the players who marveled at Shakespeare's ability to write plays in a single draft, without blotting out a line: "My answer hath been, would he had blotted a thousand." Quoted in Stephen Greenblatt, *Will in the World*, 189.

rather than reduce the "moral" of the tale. Shakespeare, that is to say, is not preaching, or doing anything that might be taken as preaching, in his plays. In fact he seems to delight in displaying the proteanism of the human character (and not least of the character Proteus).[12] He makes us question the reliability of such religious bedrocks as the deathbed confession, and the "false seeming" of holy men and women.

How should we take this subversive element in Shakespeare? In refusing to preach, is he refusing the theological? The easy reading might be that he neatly exposes the hypocrisy of any religious purity, and gestures toward a secular soul beyond any politically religious intrigues: that, as Alison Shell puts it, he engages in "a ruthless subordination of religious matter to dramatic effect,"[13] making use of the former only in service of the latter. Harold Bloom puts the matter more emphatically, arguing that Shakespeare's greatness lies precisely in his discovery of a universal humanity beyond the strictures of Christianity.[14] While these two critics disagree about Shakespeare's motives as well as his ultimate place in the canon, they are in accord on the question of theology: he refuses it, and so renders a secularized conversion. His great character pivots work as they do precisely by being something other than religious.

In what follows, I will suggest that something else is going on in Shakespeare's plays. At their most ambiguous turns, Shakespeare's plays hint at the possibility of a soul-steering conversion that is also a turning toward God. They challenge any assumption of the priority of a non-religious soul by angling religious and especially theological conversion in such a way, to be sure, given the various Tudor and Stuart acts restraining religious references on stage, to avoid censure; secondly, though, they invoke the possibility that a public act that has become thoroughly politicized might again grasp men and women in the depths of their humanity—that religion might sink below the surface, and move us, steer us, at the level of soul. He toys with a hard and fast dichotomy between an aesthetic soul and a religious soul only to reject it, or rather to gesture toward the coinciding of the one with the other. In Shakespeare we get a hint, though it is the subtle and slanted hinting of an artist, not simply that a religious conversion toward God might

---

12. See Shell, *Shakespeare and Religion*, 21–29.

13. Ibid., 116. These subordinations are pivotal for Shell's narrative of a Shakespeare whose religious and moral non-directiveness "allows his audiences, if they choose, to practice a kind of hypocrisy" (174). She also cites, apparently approvingly, Graham Greene's judgment that Shakespeare represents "the blind eye exchanged for the coat of arms, the prudent tongue for the friendships at Court and the great house at Stratford" (118).

14. Bloom, *Shakespeare: The Invention of the Human*, 10.

be as profound a conversion as an aesthetic steerage by the poet, but more impressively, that all traceable conversions, all soul-steerings, may be refractions of the central great conversion of the soul toward God.

## Shakespeare's Converted Souls

Shakespeare's plays tend to open with a recognizable pattern: there is a tremendous release of energy into the world, and then a concerted effort by the key characters to work toward resolving the crises initiated by this release.[15] As such, the plays are, at the very structural layer of the plot, "about" conversion: the conversion of desire, ambition, or insult, into warfare, trickery, or manipulation, and then to marriage, death, peace, reconciliation between brothers, or victory over an enemy.

This kind of movement is not of course unique to Shakespeare. What is, or at least what emerges with a new intensity in his plays, is the playing out of this release in the minds and motivations of characters: the "psychological" dimension that so fascinated commentators like Coleridge.[16] All drama is about "conversion;" the essence of Shakespearian drama is to make conversion a matter of the soul. One fascinating example of this is the supplemental material that Shakespeare added—if, that is, we can assume the Coleridgean thesis, which is recently gathering support in handwriting and meter analysis, that it was in fact Shakespeare who made the revisions[17]—to Thomas Kyd's *The Spanish Tragedie*.

The play is about revenge: first the revenge of a courtier's ghost on the prince who killed him in battle, secondly and more in the foreground, the revenge of a father and a young woman for the murder of a youth. As it happens, both revenge plots converge on the Prince of Portugal, as it was he who both slew the courtier and brought about the murder. After the murder, the plot hinges on the character of Heironimo, the murdered youth's father, and in particular on the question of his action or inaction. The original text of 1592 presents an almost clownish Heironimo, running on and off stage, shouting "catch me if you can" (3.13.129),[18] at once seeming to desire vengeance and then re-affirming his allegiance to the Portuguese court. When two men ask him for directions he speaks to them in echoes and riddles,

---

15. See Gibson, *Shakespeare's Game*.
16. Holmes, *Coleridge: Darker Reflections*, 264–86.
17. See Vickers, "Shakespeare's Additions to Thomas Kyd's 'The Spanish Tragedy': A Fresh Look at the Evidence Regarding the 1602 Additions," 106–42.
18. All quotations taken from *The Spanish Tragedy*, edited by Clara Calvo (London: Arden Shakespeare, 2013).

dismissing them finally with "Farewell, good 'Ha-ha-ha'" (3.11.31). One of the men replies to the other with the more or less obvious "doubtless this man is passing lunatic" (3.11.32). However, as it is the dialogue alone that suggests his decent into madness, we are never quite sure whether it is real or a ruse. Even at the play's end, when he bites off of his own tongue, this comes across as either a moment of pure insanity, or else a rational act to remove the possibility of admitting that his son's beloved was his own co-conspirator in the revenge plot.

But with the lines added in 1602—and let us assume, again, that they are Shakespeare's—we are taken deep into the grief of a father for his son, and the struggle with a terrifyingly real madness that is precisely the struggle to move from inaction to action. Following his son's murder, he laughs at his wife and his servant for insisting that the dead man is his son, insisting, with a dizzying flash of partial self-awareness, that they "are more deluded than myself" (2.5.45.26). When he returns and looks again, his words become the trajectory of his journey through the remaining acts, and thus of the plot itself: "How strangely had I lost my way to grief!" When the two men ask him directions, he responds with a long meditation, asking "What is a son?" a speech which carries him from the notion that sons are more trouble than they are worth, that "a young bacon/ Or a fine little smooth horse-colt/ Should move a man as much as doth a son," to the consoling thought that violence may yet come to his son's murderers (3.11.1.4–47). The "tongue scene" is likewise transformed, as Heironimo now casts himself as an actor having completed his role, and also as the only audience who can applaud him for it. The final line of the 1602 addition is made to rhyme now with the next line from the original, giving in a new theme:

> Now to express the rupture of my part, [1602]
> First take my tongue and afterward my heart. [Both] (4.4.187.48–49)

He is an actor, and his role is complete; his tongue is no longer useful to him.

These extra lines take us into the soul of the grieving father, revealing the chaotic delusion at work there. They also, though, reveal the origin of the change in Heironimo's expressed action and speech, which in turn becomes the catalyst for the play's final scene. Heironimo flirts with forgiveness, and with the Pauline "vengeance is mine," only at last to give in to the summons of Revenge (3.13.1–45). His movement toward retribution gives his character the integrity that his madness has been at work eroding, since he can longer hesitate over whether his son is dead if he is firmly resolved to avenge his murder. Thus, under Shakespeare's hand, the "conversion" of energy in the play, an energy loosed by lust, murder, and madness, transfers from the level of plot to the level of character. For Kyd, the tension mounts and is resolved in a final act of blood vengeance in which Heironimo is the principal actor. After Shakespeare, this plotted conversion takes hold only because Heironimo himself has undergone a conversion—he has found the true role to which he will give himself utterly, unreservedly—and can thus drive the plot toward its final scene.[19]

In Shakespeare's own plays, the characters into whose souls we descend are sometimes those through whom the dramatic catharsis of the plot occurs, sometimes those on whom the catharsis breaks. In the latter vein, the enduring chill produced by Richard III and Macbeth comes at least in part from both tyrants' revelations to the audience, not only of their "plots," but also of their internal deliberations. "Therefore since I cannot prove a lover/ To entertain these fair well-spoken days," Richard tells us, "I am determined to prove a villain/ And hate the idle pleasures of these days./ Plots have I laid . . ." (1.1.28–32). "Stars, hide your fires," says Macbeth, "Let not light see my black and deep desires" (1.5.50–51). For both, their ultimate conversion is in essence the conversion of the plot in reverse: as the plot moves from spectacular tyranny to a world re-ordered, the title characters "convert" from supreme confidence in their own auto-deification to an introspective and pathetic self-pity. We know that the end of their reigns of terror is at hand not primarily due to the gathering of armies against them, but because we watch their souls self-destruct before us. Hamlet, a play that owes a great deal to Kyd's *Tragedie*, goes so much further into the psycho-dramatics of its hero. The "most foul, strange, and unnatural" (1.5.28) state into which murder and incest have led Denmark must be converted toward justice, and Hamlet's descent into suicidal madness is, as with Heironimo, a vacillation between inaction and action, between channeling a conversion toward justice in his own soul or watching an unjust world solidify around him.

These plays demand conversion, and Shakespeare is most interested in what the external conversions of war to peace, disorder to order, do to his characters' internal depths. We name those plays in which the conversion of plot and character align as comedies; tragedies are those plays in which the plot conversions break the characters in whose souls they are played out—whether those characters are working for the conversion, like Hamlet, or against it, like Macbeth.[20]

19. See Coleridge's argument from Table Talk I in *The Collected Works of Samuel Taylor Coleridge*, 355ff.

20. This is obviously contested territory, beginning from the post-mortem arrangement of the plays by genre. There is something undeniable in Dr. Johnson's assertion that the plays tend to mingle and even burst the types that they employ. See Maslen,

Heironimo is expressly aware of Christian accounts of justice, perseverance, and reconciliation, and implicit in the tragic label of Kyd's play is his rejection of all three. Most often Shakespeare's characters convert—or toy with conversion—in the other direction, toward the theological, even in cases like Richard, whose demonic prayer, "Let hell make crooked my mind" (3 *Hen. VI* 5.6.79), returns as the less spectacular admission of guilt: "all several sins, all used in each degree,/ Throng to the bar, crying all, 'Guilty, guilty!'" (*Rich. III* 5.5.152-53).

Still, only rarely do these theologically self-aware transformations come near territory we would commonly refer to as "religious conversion." More often, a religious conversion is a consolation for a character's desolate state: Richard II's "I'll give my jewels for a set of beads" (3.3.146) or Thaisa's lament for her lost husband, "But since King Pericles,/ My wedded lord, I ne'er shall see again,/ A vestal liv'ry will I take me to,/ And never more have joy" (*Per.* 14.7-10). The conversion of a soul toward a life of prayer would seem, on this evidence, to be a foil to the greater conversions of war to peace, injustice to justice, loss to recovery.

The play that makes the most explicit reference to a religious conversion, a change in this case from Judaism to Christianity, does so in a glaringly problematic fashion. Antonio's demand in *The Merchant of Venice* that Shylock "become a Christian" (4.1.382) is unsettling not only because of the theological unsuitability of conversion as judicially enforced punishment, but also because, aesthetically, the true conversion of the plot has already taken place. It is Portia's out-legalizing the legalist that resolves the building chaos between the merchant's misfortune and the moneylender's resolve. While the religious conversion leaves the "convert" unwell and leaves the audience feeling strangely cold, Portia's resolution reaches into the depths of the anxious souls on stage (and perhaps too in the audience). The plot converts without Shylock who, like the rich young ruler in the Gospel, goes away sad. The effect of the play is to cause us to value a deep conversion of humans toward a mercy-tinted justice, but at the same time to devalue "becoming a Christian," since here such a movement remains external to the "convert," coming nowhere near his soul. Religious conversion in this play is a parody of a true re-routing of the soul.

---

*Shakespeare and Comedy*, 3-4. Danson, *Shakespeare's Dramatic Genres*, 139-40, makes the observation, with appropriate qualifications, that comedies tend to name a theme (*Much Ado about Nothing*), while the tragedies name a figure (*Hamlet*). Combining this with my distinction, we might venture the following: a comedy offers a setting which will ultimately unify the many characters who have been working with and against one another through the play; a tragedy by contrast names a great character or characters (*Antony and Cleopatra*) who must be titularly named, since he or they will ultimately refuse the unity of any thematic at all.

Does this mean that Shakespeare's plays stand for a humanizing secularization? The cheapening of religious conversion is not in fact concomitant with a disavowal of theology. The soul-steering conversion in the *Merchant* takes on the great theological question of the co-incidence of justice and mercy, which was as perplexing a matter for the authors of the Talmud as for the preachers of the first Easter sermons. Portia's resolution, while something of a stretch (to put it mildly) from a legal and philosophical perspective, is an eschatological gesture to a convergence point where one need not choose whether to uphold promises or to forgive. Even in the tragedies, where the tortured (and/or torturing) hero lies dead on the stage, a Christian impulse gathers the threads toward hints of comedy. Hamlet exchanges forgiveness with Laertes before he dies, and Horatio promises to unveil the "carnal, bloody, and unnatural acts" (5.2.325) that the King's ghost first announced, thus bringing a rebellious world a measure of reconciling righteousness. All the major tragedies, in fact, bear a similar hint of evil's unveiling in service of a triumph of grace. "Pure" tragedy may not be possible within a Christian frame of reference, as Auden suggests.[21] If this is true, then Shakespeare never shows his Christianity more clearly than in his relentless pressure toward a "comic" horizon. There is no Christian tragedy, only difficult Christian comedy.

The critique of religious conversion, then, is not a critique of the theological possibilities of a full and profound change in the course of one's life; perhaps we could best read it now as a critique rather of the failures of religion to achieve those depths. Again: whether one's conversion implies affirming the episcopacy or a newly empowered Parliament, honoring the King's government or attempting to blow it up, there is no escaping the political ramifications.[22] We may be tempted to read Shakespeare, as Bloom and others have read him, as the great secularizing poet who gives us a depth of humanity that can replace all these failed attempts of Christianity to find the soul. I suggest, rather, that we read him as indicating the failure of Christianity to achieve the depths of human contact that are written into Christian theology.

## Testing the Convergence

The *Henry IV* and *V* plays present the single dramatic cycle that attempts to do what the *Merchant* fails to do, and bring the aesthetic conversion into alignment with a religious one. I do not mean the conversion narrative that

21. Auden, *The Dyer's Hand, and Other Essays*, 176.
22. A point that Shell gently underemphasizes throughout her book.

sits in the foreground of the plays, the infamously problematic "reformation" (*Hen. V* 1.1.34) of Hal that leaves its mark on all four plays. The young Prince Hal is a well-known sinner, daily frequenting London's taverns while in the presence, as his newly crowned father puts it, of "unrestrained loose companions" (*Rich. II* 5.3.7). Falstaff is the chief among these companions, the "white-bearded Satan" (1 *Hen.* 2 2.5.422) who holds a kind of anti-court at Mistress Quickly's tavern. At one obvious level, the tetralogy is an epic morality play, with Hal caught between his kingly father and the Lord of Misrule, and we expect the plot, as in the medieval *Everyman*, to move toward the renunciation of Satan and the life of virtue that follows.[23] This is precisely what occurs at the end of 2 *Henry IV*, at Hal's coronation, in what turns out to be Falstaff's final appearance in the plays.

> Falstaff: My king, my Jove, I speak to thee, my heart!
> King Hal: I know thee not, old man. (5.5.44–45)

Hal's turning from Falstaff is the key moment of the turning of the meta-plot of the four plays from Richard II to Henry V, and thus very much a conversion in the dramatic-aesthetic sense: it is the punctuation point at which the "nimble-footed madcap Prince of Wales" (1 *Hen. IV* 4.1.95) becomes the "mirror of all Christian kings" (*Hen. V* 2.0.6). But it is, in terms of his own soul, in terms that is of the depth of his character that Shakespeare knew how to reach and to steer, all an act. Hal announces his intentions to "convert" in his very first scene, in so many words letting the audience in on his plan, to put it in the Pauline idiom, to sin boldly so that grace might increase: "I'll so offend to make offence a skill,/ Redeeming time when me think least I will" (*Hen. IV* 1.2.194–95).

His rejection of the fat knight's ilk is a complex turn of the plot that gathers up the building tensions and failures of the king and installs the possibility of a monarch who knows how to "act" like a king; whatever else it is though, it is neither a religious conversion nor a staging of Jonsonian soul-steering. Hal is an actor; a self-aware actor, to be sure, yet at his most transparent moments we see that he is the same role-player on the battlefield on St. Crispin's Day as in that opening soliloquy in the tavern.[24]

---

23. This is central to the argument of Tillyard's classic, *Shakespeare's History Plays*, 161ff., but also plays a key role in Hugh Grady, "Falstaff: Subjectivity between the Carnival and the Aesthetic," 609–23, and in Moody Prior, "Comic Theory and the Rejection of Falstaff," 159–71.

24. See Neema Parvini, *Shakespeare's History Plays: Rethinking Historicism*, 40–42. Tillyard makes a hard distinction between the grand scope of Henry IV and the ideology of *Henry V*, and so misses this continuity in Hal's character (*Shakespeare's History Plays*, 307–9).

It is, however, in the fat knight himself that a new possibility of religious and aesthetic conversion emerges. If Falstaff begins his plotted life as a tempting devil, he is, as more than one critique has noted, far too successful a character to stay in that role.[25] It would hardly do in a stock morality play for the Lord of Misrule to forget himself and consider repenting of his sins; the fulsome, life-loving brilliance of Falstaff's personality may make us forget that he is, from his first appearance to his last, obsessed with the question of his own conversion.[26] "I must give over this life, and I will give it over," he says in his first scene. "By the Lord, an I do not, I am a villain," he adds, reaching into his inexhaustible supply of comic counterfactuals. Death truly worries him—that he might face the gallows or "die of sweat" (2 *Hen. IV*, Epil. 25–26) before he has the chance to perform this giving over. Later, concerned that he is dwindling physically due to too much worry and too little drink, he re-emphasizes the point: "Well, I'll repent, and that suddenly, while I am in some liking. I shall be out of heart shortly," he says, punning on heart as both "mood" and the actual organ that keeps him alive, "and then I shall have no strength to repent. An I have not forgotten what the inside of a church is made of, I am a peppercorn, a brewer's horse—the inside of a church! Company, villainous company, hath been the spoil of me" (3.3.4–9).

This "villainous company" includes Hal, but also a red-faced companion whose color makes him think of Christ's parable of Lazarus and Dives; later, a sorry band of soldiers puts him in the mind of the Prodigal at his worst, when in his famished state he was reduced to stealing husks from pigs. These two parables in fact recur throughout the two *Henry IV* plays in Falstaff's speeches, as he inadvertently returns to the question of judgment looming over his lengthening days. While cheating Mistress Quickly out of the bulk of his bar tab, he tells her not to worry over the poverty into which he is throwing her, as she can simply sell her tapestries and put up a cheap rug painting, for instance "the story of the Prodigal" (2 *Hen. IV* 2.1.132). But the image occasionally strikes him more explicitly as suited for his final days. When he is frightened into thinking that his judgment is at last upon him in the clownish *Merry Wives of Windsor*, he locks himself in his rooms, which he paints throughout with a giant mural of the parable.

As often as this sort of desire to give his life over recurs, we tend to miss it, or to refuse to take him at his word, because of the other, more obvious pull of his will, to be what and whom he has always been. He is a thief,

---

25. Shell, *Shakespeare and Religion*, 144.

26. Auden misses this constant nagging of past sins and future judgment, calling him instead a man for whom "the historical world does not exist" (*The Dyer's Hand, and Other Essays*, 186).

a coward, a drunk, a fornicator, a gambler, and a cheat; and he loves this life as much as his audience (both on stage and in the house) loves watching him love it. In his opening scene, even while promising to give his life over, he makes a case for the honor of his chosen habits: "Marry then, sweet wag," he says to Hal, "when thou art king let not us that are squires of the night's body be called thieves of the day's beauty." If what is thought wicked is simply looked at differently, it might emerge that there is no need at all for transformation. "Let us be 'Diana's Foresters, 'gentlemen of the shade,' 'minions of the moon', and let men say that we be men of good government, being governed, as the sea is, by our noble and chaste mistress the moon, under whose countenance" he concludes, being chronically unable to resist a pun, "we steal" (1 *Hen. IV* 1.2.20–26). Rather than ask him to stop thieving as a means to avoid the gallows, he suggests a simpler solution: "Do not thou when thou art king hang a thief" (1.2 54). Problem solved.

Immediately after lamenting that he has forgotten what the inside of a church looks like, he waffles again: his life has in fact not been a wicked one, so what need is there of repentance? The speech is as full of potential for comic double and triple entendres as any he delivers: "I was as virtuously given as a gentlemen need to be: virtuous enough; swore little; diced not [pause . . .]—above seven times [pause . . .] a week; went to a bawdy house not—[pause . . .] above once [pause] in a quarter—[pause] of an hour; paid money that I borrowed [pause . . .]—three or four times . . ." (3.3.12–15)— not, observe, three or four times what I borrowed, but simply "three or four times." "Watch tonight," he tells Mistress Quickly, "pray tomorrow" (2.5.254–55). Emerging from his muralled den in *Merry Wives*, he blames his fatness for his failure to return home to his father's house: "Well, if my wind were but long enough, I would repent" (4.5.83–84).

Falstaff may have started his life in Shakespeare's drafts as a Puritan caricature who doubled as a morality demon; by the time he blossoms on the stage, he is as grand a celebration of humanity as any the playwright crafted. When he plays dead in order to avoid being killed by the fearsome Earl of Douglas, he says,

> 'Sblood, 'twas time to counterfeit. . . . Counterfeit? I lie, I am no counterfeit. To die is to be a counterfeit, for he is but the counterfeit of a man who hath not the life of a man. But to counterfeit dying when a man thereby liveth is to be no counterfeit, but the true and perfect image of life indeed. The better part of valour is discretion, in the which better part I have saved my life. (1 *Hen. IV* 5.4.111–18)

A dead Falstaff on the battlefield would be a poor imitation of the great geyser of life that the live one is, he insists, and the audience cannot help but think he has a point. It is not, further, just any life Falstaff desires: he wants to go on being Falstaff. In a realm filled with disloyalties and political dissembling, Falstaff is the voice of authenticity. He refuses to counterfeit himself.

To be sure, he attempts at various times to wear a disguise: as a priest, as a deaf man, as Prince Hal, as King Henry. But all this is to no avail, since his size, his roar, his love of playing Falstaff give him away. "Play out the play!" he cries, as the sheriff comes in and interrupts his attempt to act Hal's part in their play extempore, "I have much to say in the behalf of that Falstaff" (1 *Hen. IV* 2.5.442–43). Here he presents a marked contrast with Hal, who sinks perfectly into a variety of roles. Falstaff is, like Nick Bottom and his rude mechanicals in *A Midsummer Night's Dream*, a stage character who is utterly unable to act. As such, he raises profound questions for an audience about identity and authenticity, but filtered ironically through the air of the theater. There is no obvious lesson for us here, as in the morality plays; or, if there is a lesson, it is put in the form of a question: can you avoid admiration for Falstaff's indefatigable love of himself? We share his hesitation about conversion, and it is not simply the glistering seduction of sin. In the great shadow he casts, we come to wonder if any change of character that fails to reach the fullness of person from which Falstaff's self-love originates really counts as a conversion of the soul. It may be easy enough, as Montaigne suggested, to entertain the giving over of life in one who is dissatisfied with herself, and looking for something better: conversion as a means to a greater happiness. This is not all that far from Hal's conversion as a means to political advance, or Shylock's conversion as judicially enforced punishment. If religious conversion is a step in a larger plan of any sort, the plan itself becomes an unchanging, unconverted arena.

Falstaff's dilemma, and the dilemma that he presents to readers and theatergoers, is the struggle between love of life and the surrender of that life to God. According to his most revealing pun—one missed by the appropriately named "Judge Shallow," who squeals gleefully at the more painfully obvious ones—he has "heard the chimes at midnight." His entire life is a late night revel, but one haunted by a looming death.

Though he is denied an appearance in the final play, the question of his conversion is staged one last time, recounted by Quickly. She insists, prone as ever to malapropisms, that he "made a finer end" as any "christom" child, and so is "in Arthur's bosom, ever man went to Arthur's bosom" (*Hen. V* 2.3.9–11). We sense through her errant narration that she and Falstaff, the two old enemies/companions, each had one last and perhaps inadvertent laugh at each other's expense, and thus are we left in doubt about this deathbed conversion.[27] So she replies to his cry of "God, God, God," with the comfort that he "should not think of God; I hoped there was no need to trouble himself with any such thoughts yet." Here Quickly echoes the advice he gave her earlier, "Watch tonight, pray tomorrow," and in so doing denies him the prayer that he began to make—if, in fact, he was beginning a prayer, and not crying out in pain, or perhaps recalling a particularly fine evening with Doll Tearsheet. Falstaff, for his own part, asks for covers for his feet, and in so doing manages to get her hands to run up his legs, and then "up'ard and up'ard," where all was "cold as any stone" (2.4.17–23). Thus, apparently, the great fat knight died as bawdily as ever he lived.

The brilliance of Falstaff's life and death is that he forces us to confront the question of whether conversion is, in itself, not always at some level an act. Hal, the master of costume changes, is without depth; Falstaff is a profound character who is ultimately too much himself to change.

Even the great deathbed or scaffold confessions from other characters come here under Falstaff's suspicious gaze. For we expect such a confession: it is the role that we demand of characters like Buckingham in *Richard III* and Cardinal Wolsey in *Henry VIII* play out, and to the extent that they do so, they remain emplotted. "Have I not hideous death within my view?" asks Melun in *King John*. "What in the world should make me now deceive,/ Since I must lose the use of all deceit?" (5.4.22, 26–7). But the point is that he is still deceiving, "playing false" like any actors plays false. He is acting for us, in *The Life and Death of King John*, saying precisely what we need him to say so that the play can continue. Wolsey is "ever double," says Katherine, even in death (*Hen. VIII* 4.2.38). They say what they always were going to say when life had no more to offer, just as Hal was always going to reject Falstaff when the tavern life had dried up. This, as Montaigne said, is a loss of appetite; it is not repentance.

Here again, Falstaff cannot act. When Anthony Quayle, who played him in the BBC's 1979 screening of the plays, turns to the camera to deliver his soliloquies, he makes the point with an unsettling brilliance: Falstaff cannot even pretend to be a character in a Shakespeare play. As the plot turns toward the ultimate conversion for which Hal's "I know thee not" is key, Falstaff has to drop out of the action altogether, and this in spite of the fact that the playwright promised to bring him back. For *Henry V* is, from the opening speech by the Chorus to the King's wooing of Catherine of Valois, all about acting, and Falstaff has too much soul to find a place in this

---

27. Shell's characterization of the scene bears repeating: it is a masterful display of "designed ambiguity" (*Shakespeare and Religion*, 143).

world. For the final play to work as a capstone to the tetralogy, for Henry V to emerge as the leader that neither his father nor the deposed Richard II were, he must make this final costume change, and leave the question of soul behind him at the tavern. Thus Falstaff becomes a morality demon in the end, after all: a strange demon, to be sure, tortured by his desire to go to church and confess his sins to God. But a demon nonetheless, a white-bearded Satan whose path must be rejected and whose character must be denied, so that England, the real character of the tetralogy, can be restored as God's "other Eden" (*Rich. II* 2.1.42).[28]

If conversion is easy, even at death, it has not yet touched a soul; Falstaff lives deeply, and for that reason makes of conversion an almost insurmountable difficulty. Falstaff cannot convert because there is nothing but Falstaff flowing under the surface of his ample body. To give over his life is, as Christ said, to hate it, and Falstaff could never pretend to hate his own life. Or perhaps he could pretend, but absolutely no one would believe him.

## Tragi-Comic Conversion

Falstaff is authenticity itself, manifesting the shallow game that is religious conversion; but does he manifest soul? Returning to Jonson's boast, soul is a thing steered—not simply the "self" deep within a person, but the capacity for change toward another that lies at the very heart of a person. In theological terms, soul is the desire for Godward movement that makes one both utterly unique and essentially related to every other. A theology of creation suggests the movement toward another creature is, at its fullest, an awakening of the soul toward this ultimate Godwardness.[29] Falstaff has the tormenting desire for this sort of change, but that desire is locked in a battle with a desire precisely not to change—to go on being who he is without any movement toward another at all.

Said differently, Falstaff is, throughout the plays, chronically in love with no one but himself. Hal, at the very least, loves the England which (whom) he must one day become. Falstaff enjoys the company of others—Hal, Bardolf, Quickly, Doll Tearsheet—but this is never a joy that provokes a change in his life or character. This is even the case when his presence evokes seemingly authentic passions in others, such as when Tearsheet's confesses

---

28. Tillyard, *Shakespeare's History Plays*, 266ff, sees England as the new Everyman of the tetralogy.

29. See David Kelsey's distinction between humanity's ultimate context, "God's relating to them as Creator," and the proximate context, creation as such, "the lived world of the quotidian" (*Eccentric Existence: A Theological Anthropology*, vol. 1, 162, 190).

that she loves him, and then with a kind of serious playfulness asks whether he is perhaps too near his end to keep living at his current pace:

> Thou whoreson little tidy Bartholomew boar-pig,
> When wilt thou leave fighting 'o days and foining
> o' nights, and begin to patch up thine old body for heaven?
> (*2 Hen. IV* 2.4.206–08)

"Do not bid me remember mine end" (2.4.210), he chides her gently, in a rare moment of punless rhetoric. He will not deny his Falstaffianism, even at her pleading. And where there is no change, no movement toward anything at all, only a stagnant return to oneself, there can be no soul.

It is this incapacity for others that haunts Falstaff like the chimes at midnight. A giving over of the life could only ever be a staged hatred of the only thing he truly loves. The call to conversion is not a call to love God more than he loves himself, but rather simply to hate himself. He is in the position of a Prodigal who is having the time of his life in the far country. And though he suspects that he should go home, he has no notion of where that home is or of anyone living there. There is no epiphanic "coming to himself" as in the parable (Luke 15:17), only the bothersome suspicion that he is expected to give up his prized possession, his life, and act a part for which he has no script or inclination.

This is the point at which Shakespeare's plays might lead us back into a more richly theological notion of conversion, one which reaches into the soul in a way that the Wolseyian, Shylockian conversions never could. For his plays are, to repeat, from start to finish about conversion, the conversion of hate, or injustice, or indifference. These conversions lead characters to places and decisions beyond any they had foreseen or planned. An easy conversion is no real conversion, because it does not have the weight-bearing capacity to support the turning of an entire life. When the Archbishop and the Bishop of Ely discuss Hal's remarkably rapid transformation, there is a hint of winking and nodding, since such an immediate change as his has the air of the miraculous, and "miracles are ceased" (*Hen. V* 1.1.8).[30] Surely the wildness was a self-imposed veil, a carpet of nettle under which his virtue was always growing "like summer grass" (1.1.66). Indeed, rather than see him under the figure of fallen Adam, turned back towards Eden, he is Eden itself, finally free from "offending Adam" (1.1.30). In other words, the immediacy of Hal's conversion is itself the evidence that no conversion ever took place.

---

30. Despite Tillyard's insistence that this dialogue be read with no sense of irony (*Shakespeare's History Plays*, 310).

All true conversions in Shakespeare are difficult. Claudio's behavior toward Hero and her father in *Much Ado* is reprehensible, and in light of the reprehension, the audience is poised for him to give his life over. Thus when his would-have-been father-in-law says that his own revenge will die only when Claudio marries his niece, and without every laying eyes on her, we consider this a just measure. Claudio does as well, and his dying-to-self response marks the beginning of his conversion: "I do embrace your offer; and depose/ For henceforth of poor Claudio" (5.1.279–80). Similarly, when Paulina refuses, for sixteen long years, to let King Leontes forget the suffering and destruction wrought by his unprovoked jealousy, we who have been privy to the mad release of energy in Act One feel sure that she is right. She is right, and not the lords who gather around Leontes insisting, "Sir, you have done enough" (*Winter's Tale* 5.1.1).

There is an aesthetic of justice at work here, but it is closely tied, as Claudio makes explicit (*Much Ado* 5.1.257–58), to a theology of penance. In fact, the two mutually inform one another. If *The Winter's Tale* suggests, in terms of balance and fittingness, that Leontes has earned every day of those sixteen years of sorrow, it is just this fittingness that suggests the possibility of some sort of ultimate, miraculous event of reconciliation. The resurrection of the lost love, so prominent an event in the late comedies and romances, presents the occasion for a reunion in which the aesthetics of justice can meet with a supernatural grace.[31] Leontes's suffering has prepared him to ask Hermione's forgiveness—Paulina has seen to that. At the moment when his contrition finally penetrates to his soul, a moment which Paulina and, through her eyes, the audience claims the right to determine, he finds himself standing before Hermione's statue. And it is already moving downstage to greet him.

This theological aesthetics turns on the ability of the plays to suggest to us that the hero is ready to convert. Penance, in its fullest sense, is about such preparation before it is a punitive, imposed measure. It is thus a kind of penance that Pericles endures when he enters a period of grief so deep that it becomes a living death, and he takes food and water "but to prorogue his grief" (*Per.* 21.20). The depths of his sorrow are, aesthetically, the tension on the bowstring that will soon send him soaring with rapture. Pericles suffers not for his own sins but for the sins of others; his conversion, therefore, will convert the play's entire world. Theologically, he has here entered the silence of Holy Saturday, which places him exactly where he must be in order to

---

31. See Beckwith, *Shakespeare and the Grammar of Forgiveness*, and Boitano, *The Gospel according to Shakespeare*, both of which revive and revise G. Wilson Knight's reading of the late romances as delivering the richest theology of all the plays in *Wheel of Fire: Interpretations of Shakespearian Tragedy, with Three New Essays*.

embrace his lost bride. "O come, be buried/ A second time within these arms" (22.65–66). Penitential suffering, the point of intersection, especially in the late tragicomedies, where aesthetics and theology meet, is about encountering the hero's soul. The conversion must be difficult, or we will suspect that Pericles and Leontes are pulling a Prince Hal on us.

Falstaff will never pull a Prince Hal on us. The conversion that he desires is the giving over of his life to God, reconciliation with his maker "inside of a church." By leaving his end in an ambiguous place, Shakespeare leaves the question of the quality of religious conversions suspended. Could a giving over of a sinful life to God ever strike us as aesthetically fitting as Claudio's giving of his life to Leonato and his "niece"? Could our interpersonal encounters of reconciliation and recovery prepare us, perhaps, for a meeting with God? Is it possible, aesthetically speaking, to imagine a fitting scenario in which God's presence transports (soul-steers) a whole person as unreservedly as Thaisa's presence transports Pericles? "O come, Christ, be buried a second time in these arms"?

The only definitive response Falstaff can give to these questions is "not without love." Without love of another's life, conversion is self-hatred. For the despairing soul, hatred of self may be easy enough, but it will not present a conversion. For the lover of life like plump Jack, on the other hand, such a claim would be a pretense. He still has far too much to say in behalf of this Falstaff. Without the capacity to love another, which is to say the ability to imagine the prospect of a conversion to more rather than less life, giving himself away as Claudio did will be, strictly speaking, beyond the pale.

If Shakespeare leaves open the question of whether a religious conversion could ever reach the real depths of a human person, he does at least make clear, through the marriage of aesthetics and theology, that preachers and poets are, in the end, talking about the same soul. He is not a secularist, constructing a non-religious space for a character to achieve a soul-conversion. For conversion is always for him a kind of mundane miracle: a long daily struggle to encounter the truth of oneself, for which each must ultimately await those presences that are beyond our capacity to resurrect: the lost, the dead, the past. Conversion is a difficult journey toward an end that is, ultimately, a supernatural gift.

## Bibliography

Auden, W. H. *The Dyer's Hand, and Other Essays*. London: Faber and Faber, 1962.
Beckwith, Sarah. *Shakespeare and the Grammar of Forgiveness*. Ithaca, NY: Cornell University Press, 2011.
Bloom, Harold. *Shakespeare: The Invention of the Human*. New York: Riverhead, 1998.

Boitano, Piero. *The Gospel according to Shakespeare*. Translated by Vittorio Montemaggi and Rachel Jacoff. Notre Dame, IN: University of Notre Dame Press, 2013.

Coleridge, Samuel Taylor. *Table Talk*. In *The Collected Works of Samuel Taylor Coleridge*, edited by Carl Woodring. Vol. 14. Princeton, NJ: Princeton University Press, 1990.

Danson, Lawrence. *Shakespeare's Dramatic Genres*. Oxford: Oxford University Press, 2000.

Gibson, William. *Shakespeare's Game*. New York: Atheneum, 1978.

Grady, Hugh. "Falstaff: Subjectivity between the Carnival and the Aesthetic." *The Modern Language Review* 96 (July 2001) 609-23.

Greenblatt, Stephen. *Will in the World: How Shakespeare Became Shakespeare*. New York: Norton, 2004.

Greenblatt, Stephen, ed. *Shakespeare's Montaigne: The Florio Translation of the Essays*. Trans. John Florio. New York: New York Review of Books, 2014.

Greenblatt, Stephen, et al., eds. *The Norton Shakespeare*. Based on the Oxford Edition. New York: W. W. Norton, 2008.

Holmes, Richard. *Coleridge: Darker Reflections*. London: HarperCollins, 1998.

Jonson, Ben. *The Staple of News*. Yale Studies in English edition. Edited by De Winter. New York: Henry Hold and Company, 1905.

Kelsey, David. *Eccentric Existence: A Theological Anthropology*, Vol. 1. Louisville, KY: Westminster John Knox, 2009.

Knight, G. Wilson. *Wheel of Fire: Interpretations of Shakespearian Tragedy, with Three New Essays*. London: Methuen, 1956.

Kyd, Thomas. *The Spanish Tragedy*. Edited by Clara Calvo. London: Arden Shakespeare, 2013.

Maslen, R. W. *Shakespeare and Comedy*. London: Arden Shakespeare, 2005.

Parvini, Neema. *Shakespeare's History Plays: Rethinking Historicism*. Edinburgh: Edinburgh University Press, 2012.

Peterson, Richard S. *Imitation and Praise in the Poems of Ben Jonson*. New Haven: Yale University Press, 1981.

Prior, Moody E. "Comic Theory and the Rejection of Falstaff." *Shakespeare Studies* 9 (1976) 159-71.

Shell, Allison. *Shakespeare and Religion*. London: Methuen, 2010.

Story, G. M., ed. *Lancelot Andrewes: Sermons*. Oxford: Clarendon Press, 1967.

Taylor, Charles. *A Secular Age*. Cambridge: Harvard University Press, 2007.

Tillyard, E. M. W. *Shakespeare's History Plays*. London: Chatto & Windus, 1948.

Vickers, Brian. "Shakespeare's Additions to Thomas Kyd's 'The Spanish Tragedy': A Fresh Look at the Evidence Regarding the 1602 Additions." *Shakespeare Quarterly* 62.1 (2011) 106-42.

# 12

# Both, Between, and Beyond

## The Third Term and the Relation Constituting Being

L. C. WILSON

SEPARATED BY CENTURIES, BUT united by their faith, and a certain kind of idiosyncratic genius, both Evagrius of Pontus and Søren Kierkegaard developed the traditional concept of "the soul" within anthropologies grounded in their dynamic metaphysics. Each posited a tripartite composition of the human being, consisting of body, mind/soul, and soul/spirit. Despite the variable terminology used by the thinkers (and their translators), both employed a "third term" to designate the relation between the person's corporeal and incorporeal aspects: a relation that is, itself, constitutive of the character of one's being and a litmus test for one's moral and spiritual health. Though the ascetic monk of the fourth century and the romantic and ironic nineteenth-century Danish philosopher may, at first glance, seem to have little in common, their understandings of intra-human relationality, established in the imagination and, as we shall see, tested by melancholy, proceed along similar paths, and meet at several important landmarks on the way to relationship with God. For both, the tripartite understanding of human nature grounds an integrated account of body and soul that mediates time and eternity, earth and heaven to the person they inseparably constitute. It is in the imagination that this mediation explores its own dynamism and in melancholia that it reveals its decisive importance.

Furthermore, this dynamic is both illustrated and challenged by contrast and encounter with beings whose dynamic is of a different, but not entirely alien, character from that of our own: demons.

Evagrius of Pontus lived and fought for his spiritual life in the city-like desert of fourth-century Egypt, after scandal had exiled him from a more bustling, and tempting, urban scene. His ascetic retirement was not into a life of ease, but became the elucidation and elaboration of a theory and practice of Christian monastic practice that drew on both the high Alexandrian theology of Origen, with its roots in Neoplatonic philosophy, and the evolving traditions of the coenobites and, particularly, the anchorites who had followed St. Anthony into the wilderness. For Evagrius, the fall of humanity as *nous* "thickened" the being of mankind from that of simple *logikoi* to that of creatures composed of bodies bound to their minds by souls. Indeed, he writes in the *Gnostic Chapters* that "The soul (*psyche*) *is* the *nous* which through negligence, has fallen from the Unity."[1] However, rather than simply characterizing a kind of inferior mind, the soul in Evagrius acts as the integrating hinge between the material and immaterial parts of the person. Indeed, it is through the passionate parts of the soul that the person is enabled to integrate the demands of body with that of the mind and that the mind is propelled to escape the tyrannical gravity of selfish drives. Human thoughts are not in themselves evil, but must be energetically (one might say, passionately) "shepherded" and guarded. "The Lord has confided to the human person the mental representations of this age, like sheep to a good shepherd."[2] It is to guard these precious impressions, as noted above, that God bestowed upon humanity its irascible aspect, while its counterpart the concupiscible was given that we might love and cherish the good and work for its protection and furtherance. The responsibility of the shepherd does not only extend to guarding the flock, but to its proper pasturage, too, for our "sheep" are fed on whatever virtues or vices the monk cultivates, and Evagrius warns his reader not to graze them alongside passions such as lust or pride, but rather, especially in times of weariness and discouragement, to "graze our sheep at the foot of Mount Sinai," in contemplation of "the rock of knowledge."[3] To succumb to "unnatural," that is, selfish, temptations would be not only to degrade and disregard the rationality and potential for *gnosis* of the mind, but also to commit an indignity against the proper nature of the body: in this life, the two are inseparable. Nevertheless, as the metaphor of a

1. Evagrius, *Kephalia*, 3.28.
2. Evagrius, *Logismoi*, 17.
3. Ibid.

potentially unruly flock suggests, their relation is variable. Both must work in tandem to maintain their proper harmony.

Søren Kierkegaard, on the other hand, takes this understanding of the intra-relationality of human ontology deeper. Humanity, for him, is suspended dialectically between the opposing poles of the finite and the infinite: the eternal and the temporal, the particular and the abstract. This synthesizing relation between the poles of human ontology is called by Kierkegaard, "spirit." The third term alongside the aforementioned dialectical aspects of body and soul, time and eternity, and necessity and freedom, is, properly, the self itself. "The self is not the relation, but the relation's relating to itself."[4] This is the anthropology by which Kierkegaard fundamentally understands the pure dynamism of the humanity's nature.

However, it is impossible for this relationship to be balanced without being grounded in and scaled against the divine that established it. The human self is a "derived" self, "a relation which relates to itself and in relating to itself relates to something else."[5] Therefore, "the self cannot by itself arrive at or remain in equilibrium or rest, but only, in relating to itself, relating to that which established the whole relation."[6] The relation of the temporal and eternal, the finite and the infinite, renders the negotiation of the ontological difference the defining activity of human existence. Kierkegaard's architecture of the self introduces a third dimension into a previously flat binary. Rather than potentially unbalance the dialectic by identifying the divine with one pole, he rather understands that *both* poles are only rightly related to by humanity under the aegis of a divine that transcends both. Thus, "spirit" is, at once, the relation of the person's corporeal and incorporeal aspects, its own reflexive self-relation, and its constituting relation to the divine. "Spirit," furthermore, mediates between and balances the conflicting metaphysical claims on the individual, such as those of time and eternity, or freedom and necessity. Like Evagrius, Kierkegaard understands the necessity of *integrating* these claims, rather than pursuing only one pole.

Key to this proper integration, indeed, the very site of the "third term" itself rests, for both thinkers, in the imagination: the faculty by which one relates, not only to the world, but also to oneself. For Evagrius, the human mind rather passively receives information through its senses. These pieces of information Evagrius terms *noemata*, "impressions," which literally "make an impression" upon the mind, like, for example, a seal in wax. Though the mind of the monk is, in some sense, at the mercy of his senses

---

4. Kierkegaard, *Sickness*, 43.
5. Ibid.
6. Ibid., 44.

in the reception of *noemata*, these "impressions" do not "shape" the mind in any meaningful way, but, rather, become the spur for a subsequent chain of thought that is, as we have seen, morally decisive. The Greek term used by Evagrius to designate these thoughts is suggestive, too: *logismoi*. Its root in *logos* (word), implies, not merely a dumb impulse, but a complex, and often conscious psychological construction by which inspiration and temptation are received and processed. Evagrius makes strikingly clear the decisive moral freight of active, conscious ruminations: he admonishes his reader that to let the mind wander in insidious resentment at the time of prayer to the image of a brother with whom he is in conflict, for example, blasphemously defies him, "for certainly what the mind sees while praying is worthy of being acknowledged as god."[7]

Evagrius' use of the term "sees" is significant: *noemata* are *sensory* impressions of materiality and inextricably bound up with embodiment. Indeed, for Evagrius, thought regarding material things can be described as chains of images or fantasies. Despite the near-instantaneous succession of one picture upon another,[8] this idea of mental "movement"[9] has similar overtones of spatio-temporal progress to the metaphor of the journey though the desert to the city, noted above, further emphasizing the dynamic nature of Evagrius' worldview and the impossibility of stasis therein. However, in order to process, manipulate, and move amongst these images and impressions of the physical world and the passions associated with it, in which thought consists, the mind requires an imaginative figure of the body with which to "think" the physical world. This self-concept, as the distinctive mark of its own subjectivity, lacks a face, "for it is incapable of creating a form of this within itself since it has never seen itself." Nevertheless, "with this figure then our mind does everything interiorly—it sits and walks, gives and receives in its intellect."[10] With regard to the material realm, then, the human mind is not reflexively imageless. Indeed, the body is the instrument, both physically and mentally, of our thought-in-the world. The mechanics of the imagination demonstrate and enact the necessity of the body to the mind.

Nevertheless, this relation is dynamic and changeable. An over-emphasis on one aspect of the self at the expense of another results in sin and a degradation of being. In Evagrius, the roots of the "Eight Deadly Thoughts," the direct progenitors of our more familiar Seven Deadly Sins, are rooted in,

---

7. Evagrius, *Logismoi*, 37.
8. Ibid., 25.
9. Ibid.
10. Ibid.

or express their frustration through, not only negative cognitions, but negative emotions, such as sorrow and anger. The passions, as we noted above, are ambivalent. Indeed, if anger is a longing for revenge, then, "sadness is a dejection of soul and is constituted from thoughts of anger, for . . . the frustration of revenge produces sadness."[11] The frustration of avarice produces sadness, too,[12] as will the frustration of vainglory.[13]

Like anger, sadness "takes away the perceptions of the soul."[14] This kind of unhappiness, therefore, consists in a misdirection of the imagination regarding its desires and its response to their disappointment. It is therefore suggestive that for the sin of sadness, Evagrius uses the Greek *lupes*, which indicates pain. Indeed, situated at the centre of Evagrius' schema of the sins, sadness follows behind each, like a sting in the tail. Evagrius' metaphors become nightmarishly maternal-parasitic: sadness is "a worm in the heart that consumes the mother that gives it birth . . . when sadness is begotten, it provokes much toil, and since it stays even after the birth pains, it causes not a little suffering."[15] It destroys that on which it feeds. To be "bound by sadness" is to have been "vanquished by the passions" for "sadness is constituted by the frustration of an appetite, and an appetite is joined to every passion."[16] It is implied that, not only is sadness the common consequence of abandonment to the passions, it might even be said to be inevitable. Moreover, from this inevitability, there can be no return: only "one who has overcome the passions will not be *dominated* by sadness."[17] Sadness is the obverse side of the pleasures of the world.

Indeed, sadness is a peculiar sin, for while the others tempt the sinner with satisfaction and pleasure, sadness actively destroys pleasure, even spiritual pleasure.[18] Moreover, "A monk afflicted by sadness cannot move the mind towards contemplation or offer up pure prayer, for sadness poses an obstacle to all that is good."[19] Here, sadness interrupts that metaphor of progress through the desert by which Evagrius describes the monastic life. As well as obstructing his path, it also weighs down the traveller, linked

---

11. Evagrius, *Thoughts*, 5.1.
12. Ibid., 5.17.
13. Ibid., 5.18.
14. Ibid., 5.25.
15. Ibid., 3.4.
16. Evagrius, *Praktikos*, 5.10.
17. Evagrius, *Thoughts*, 5.11, italics mine.
18. Ibid., 5.5.
19. Ibid., 5.6.

with "fetters on the feet"[20] and being "bound in irons."[21] This, then, is the greatest danger of sadness: while other passions exacerbate the beastliness in humanity, sadness dampens the divine.

In contrast, the "deadly thought" of *acedia* involves an imagination both overactive and petty, preoccupied with escapist fantasies and speculations that feed an adulterous dissatisfaction with one's vocation. Though no direct translation of the Greek term exists, *acedia* was perhaps rendered most evocatively by John Cassian. The Latin monastic theologian renders the term "weariness or dejection of heart,"[22] recalling Evagrius' slightly less sympathetic descriptor "a relaxation of soul which is not in accord with nature [and] does not resist temptation nobly."[23] He regards it as the monk's loss of "perseverance"[24] in his vocation that, rather, "considers his own satisfaction to be a precept."[25]

Yet it seems that *acedia* cannot be adequately defined—it can only be narrated. In the *Praktikos*, he links it with the "noonday demon" of Psalm 90. He describes how it distorts the experience of time, lengthening the hours until the monk seeks any imaginative distraction from his present state. He envisions himself elsewhere, performing other work, or remembers his family and former friends; he imagines the long life of asceticism facing him and its burdens.[26] What is particularly dangerous about this thought pattern is its very appearance of reasonableness: the acediac monk is able, with its help, to construct impressive and sensible structures to circumvent his duties and undermine his vocation while seemingly exercising the best part of his humanity, his reason. Rather than regarding his dissatisfaction as the symptom of a deeper spiritual malaise, either that of sadness or of *acedia*, he regards it as the problem in itself. Thus, while sadness destroys the appreciation of spiritual pleasures, *acedia* is the disease of what part of the human remains. This demonstrates the potentially dangerous pliability of the imagination that constructs the reality of beings made at once corporeal and incorporeal.

The mutability of one's experience of time, founded in mankind's dynamically moral character, is further explicated by Kierkegaard, who, once again, sharpens the point. His understanding of the time in which humans

---

20. Ibid., 5.7.
21. Ibid., 5.8.
22. Cassian, *Twelve*, 10.1.
23. Evagrius, *Thoughts*, 6.1.
24. Ibid., 6.5.
25. Ibid., 8.7.
26. Evagrius, *Praktikos*, 12.

live is one that receives its necessary validation from the "eternal" that makes up an equally necessary part of human existence. Indeed, the distinction between past, present, and future "appears only through the relation of time to eternity and the reflection of eternity in time. . . . [T]he infinite succession of time is an infinitely contentless present (this is the parody of eternity) . . . ,"[27] while the *moment* is a fullness rather than an empty passage, where "time and eternity touch each other."[28] He further notes the colloquial interchangeability of terms relating to the future and to eternity as preserving the latter's association with time and thus writes that, together, the future and the moment posit the past.[29] It is this future, too, corresponding both to time and to freedom as the *possible*, and its relation to the past, which "corresponds to anxiety in the individual life."[30] Kierkegaard locates anxiety in temporality and grounds the psychological experience in the metaphysics of anthropology.

Thus, it is eternity that provides time with a present capable of experience, rather than an empty passage of featureless, indifferently extended existence. Moreover, it provides time with the "continuity" that enables it to pass in linear fashion. "Only with the moment does history begin."[31] To Kierkegaard, as humans are a synthesis of the temporal and eternal, "eternity is the essential continuity, and demands this continuity of man, that he be conscious of himself as spirit and have faith."[32]

Indeed, an important corollary to, and illustration of, both Evagrius' and Kierkegaard's understanding of this dynamically moral anthropology is their common interest in comparing human attitudes to demonic ones. Demons form the lowest stratum of Evagrius' vertical cosmology. Characterized as "heavy," the most attached to material pleasures and selfishness, it is they who inspire, manipulate, and capitalize upon those thoughts in humans that inspire the irascible and concupiscible passions. In line with other aspects of the literature of the desert, Evagrius understands the individual monk's struggle with his own conscience and weaknesses as equally a grappling with infernal forces. That he is faced with inhuman powers, however, does not excuse the monk from moral agency. Indeed, it rather enjoins on him a responsibility to resist the promptings and persuasions of his enemies. Neither does it displace the locus of sin entirely outside the human subject.

27. Kierkegaard, *Concept*, 85–86.
28. Ibid., 87.
29. Ibid., 89.
30. Ibid., 91.
31. Ibid., 89.
32. Kierkegaard, *Sickness*, 138.

While, even to modern eyes, the detailed and consistent characterization of demons as specific actors in the desert drama is too prominent and lively to be explained away as metaphor or disdained as myth, the interaction of these forces with humanity are subtle and occur as much on a subjective level as they do on an objective one. The demons make use of the human individual's foibles, histories, and habits, not just to destroy an enemy, but to make their adversary *like them*: characterized by selfishness, wrath, and greed, with a thick and heavy being, fallen far from heaven.

To do so, the demons employ a number of tactics. At the extreme, these can include sensory hallucination of flames in the cell, and the attack of terrifying monsters.[33] Evagrius develops this tradition further, beyond the attempt to confound and horrify with unearthly powers usually attributed to demonic hallucinations. A conscientious psychologist in his theology and practice, he ties the experience of hallucinations and "fantasies" to the sin of pride: as the proud man's attachment to his own self and status distances him from God, he succumbs to cowardice and paranoia and begins to imagine danger to his person lurking everywhere. Indeed, in this state, the monk can be said to be "abandoned" by God to be "the plaything of the demons."[34]

The hallucinations and fantasies conjured by the demons not only prey on the monk's conscious mind, but in his dreams, too. Indeed, this is a tactic commonly and troublingly employed to destabilise the monk and draw him into sin. For Evagrius, whose spiritual program advocates a great deal of self-cultivation and control, that one should be taken by surprise in the vulnerability of sleep is particularly worrying. Their assault is holistic and, though it is keyed to our humanity, is not of a human character. Thus, in addition to these sly diagnostic promptings, evil spirits use dreams to destabilize the concupiscible and irascible parts of the soul, rendering them less controllable and, the following day, more prone to fall to temptation. Conversely, "those inclined to anger and irascibility are apt to fall victim to frightening visions."[35] More subtly, the experience of shameful or terrifying dreams can humiliate and dishearten the monk during his waking hours, or, indeed, compound the distress of one already troubled.[36] Like the seductive ruminations of the restless acediac monk, demonic forces attempt to manipulate and degrade human moral character by inhabiting and perverting the imagination in which that character finds the crucible of its integration.

33. Evagrius, *Thoughts*, 27.
34. Ibid.
35. Ibid.
36. Ibid.

However, though the temptations offered by the evil spirits can uncover the sinful desires that remain within the monk despite his efforts, those unclean forces are dependent on their own observation of externally observable behaviors to determine the character of their adversary. "The Lord alone is a knower of hearts."[37] They thus become the mirror-image of the monk is his own conscientious self-observation and imaginative self-construction. "The demons arm themselves with evil actions; once armed they treat harshly those who armed them."[38] The agency of these beings is intimately bound up with the behavior and spiritual state of individual humans, while not being reduced to such. Once again, the positing of spiritual adversaries in no way displaces the moral locus outside of the subject. Even more so, it is this claustrophobic entanglement that characterizes the nature of the demonic threat, which is a paradoxical enemy that, though it comes from without, stimulates self-harm from within. For, as noted above, humanity's own subjectivity is faceless: only the Lord can know one's own heart.

Kierkegaard's stance with regard to the demonic is more ambiguous. He uses the term in order to illuminate the ontological and substantive character of human moral states. Although, unlike Evagrius, he does not dwell on the possibilities of demonic interaction, it is in this very existential, totalizing aspect of the "demonic" human experience that demonstrates the seriousness with which Kierkegaard, too, takes the far end of the moral "sliding scale." To become devilish is to become inhuman, and to become so in not just a philosophical, but in a theological sense. Indeed, in a moral cosmos under the Christian God, to decline from one's proper state, and, as we shall see, to sequester oneself from the spiritual ground of being, can be understood in no other sense. The aim of the demonic, in Kierkegaard, might be said to be convincing the human that it does not exist.

For Kirkegaard, the demonic is to be in a state of sin such that one is not anxious about the possibility of being entrapped in (more) evil, but rather anxious about the possibility of the good itself—and the relation that this entails with others, but most especially with the all-good Creator Himself. As he notes, "The demonic manifests itself clearly only when it is in contact with the good, which comes to its boundary from the outside. For this reason, it is noteworthy that the demonic in the New Testament first appears when it is approached by Christ."[39] The anxiety of the demonic, thus, is to shut itself up, alone, in an "inclosing reserve." In an intriguing

37. Evagrius, *Logismoi*, 37.
38. Ibid., Appendix 3.
39. Kierkegaard, *Concept*, 119.

counterpoint to Evagrius, whose demons are forced to "read" the character of their victims through observation of their behavior, in Kierkegaard, the demonic, when it comes into contact with the good "blurts" out the truth of its own nature in an "unfree disclosure" as the nature of God forces it to read the truth of its own heart: just as, for Evagrius, only God is the one who has access to the deep truths of human nature.

This kind of communication-in-relation, however, can only occur within the continuity of time. The inclosing reserve of the demonic therefore attempts to reject time, living in what Kierkegaard characterizes as "the sudden," a persistent false present over-freighted with possibility that would collapse under its own weight if it were not, paradoxically, utterly insubstantial. The empty abstractions of inclosing reserve are contentless, even as they are innumerable—like the murmuring "as ifs" of *acedia*. It is an attempt to pervert imagination into a single dimension, the imagination subsuming relation within itself. Instead of the simplicity of unity-in-diversity that ought to characterize the tripartite human, the demonic imagination attempts to usurp the unity of simplicity though a multiplicity of near-nothingness that affectively stretches insubstantiality beyond the bounds of time.

It is for this reason that the demonic is "the boring."[40] "The continuity that corresponds to the sudden is what might be called extinction. Boredom, extinction, is precisely a continuity in nothingness[;] . . . the prodigious span of time evokes the notion of the dreadful emptiness and contentlessness of evil."[41] The "sudden" "does not belong among natural phenomena, but is a psychical phenomenon"[42] seeming to be the mind without the body. However, "the ambiguity of the phenomenon . . . indicates that it belongs in all spheres: the somatic, the psychic, and the pneumatic. This suggests that the demonic covers a much larger area than is commonly assumed, which can be explained by the fact that a man is a synthesis of psyche and body sustained by spirit, and therefore a disorganization in one shows itself in the others."[43] Most fundamentally, however, the demonic belongs to the synthesizing relation that is the spirit, as seen in its characteristic residence in the imagination, discussed above. Ironically, moreover, though "the sudden" acts as a rejection of the particularity of action in favor of dreaming phantoms, it is, in fact, a rejection of humanity's *eternal* aspect: its relation to, and groundedness in, the divine. Like Evagrius' demons of *acedia*, the

---

40. Ibid., 132.
41. Ibid., 133.
42. Ibid., 130.
43. Ibid., 122.

demonic in Kierkegaard distracts and swaddles its victim,[44] as "men are not willing to think eternally earnestly but are anxious about it, and anxiety can contrive a hundred evasions. And this is precisely the demonic."[45]

It may be seen, thus, how, for both Evagrius of Pontus and Søren Kierkegaard, an imbalance in the "third term" that relates the corporeal and incorporeal aspects of humanity comes to expression in an infection of the imagination with a melancholia that is obsessive, phantasmal, and empty and whose selfishness, paradoxically, acts to dissolve the self that hosts it. However, it may also be seen that the experience of melancholy is, in fact, situated at the crux of the moral cosmos described by both, and that the reaction to it is decisive in forging the character, and, thus, the very nature of the individual.

For the ancient monk Evagrius, sadness could be as deadly as any other "evil thought." Indeed, it, too, could prey upon the imagination, haunting the monk with visions of past indiscretions such that he could be blinded to present efforts towards the good. However, Evagrius writes that there is also a certain "godly sadness." It can spur the soul to reflection upon, and grief over, its sins. Like the venom of a viper, "administered in a manner beneficial to humans, destroys the venoms of other animals." Sadness must be used, but it must be *mastered* as much as any other passion.[46] If the "warfare" of sadness is moderate, it "renders the anchorite tried and tested, for he teaches him to approach none of the things of this world."[47] Thus this passion, bound into the inevitable frustration of all the others in this finite world, can reveal the limited nature of all the others, if it is observed with the conscientious self-reflection that is part of Evagrius' abstinence: "when this spirit afflicts people, it can be for them an opportunity for a good repentance."[48] In such a repentance, the imagination, impelled by suffering, energetically modifies its own self-concept, using it to pursue and grasp at different thoughts and behaviors. Sadness, thus, is the only "evil" thought

---

44. In fact, he describes the demonic as like "a game in which two persons are concealed under one cloak as if there were only one person, and one speaks and the other gesticulates arbitrarily without any *relation* to what is said. Similarly, the beast has taken on human form and now constantly jeers *at him* by gesticulation and farce" (italics mine). Note how even in Kierkegaard's more psychological approach to the issue, the demonic is still conceived of as a relation, the theological-metaphysical implications of moral degradation making the individual alien to his very (God-given and therefore fundamentally good) self. Ibid., 119.

45. Ibid., 154.
46. Evagrius, *Logismoi*, 12.
47. Ibid.
48. Ibid.

that can be used for good, and the only demon who falls victim to his own wiles.

For Kierkegaard, developing this psychological-spiritual observation quite profoundly, to face despair is to be forced to develop "spirit," or else to perish. Kierkegaard endured the suffocation of melancholia, first his father's and then his own, throughout his life.[49] He draws on his experiences in his literature and his philosophy; he committed his struggles to his voluminous journals. As described above, melancholy and anxiety are, for him, quite explicitly the result of an improper relation in the dialectical metaphysic that constitutes human ontology. Their devastating effect is evidence of the extremity of the paradoxical nature of our existence. Once the Christian understands the theological implications of his sorrow or anxiety, these states "become serving spirit[s] that against [their] will lead him where he wants to go."

Indeed, for Kierkegaard, melancholic states such as despair and anxiety, inhabiting this revelatory space, are, in fact, quite *necessary* to one's progress as a Christian: to him, "the possibility of this sickness [unto death] is man's advantage over the beast; to be aware of this sickness is the Christian's advantage over natural man."[50] We have seen how demonic anxiety attempts to reject the divine "axis" of human existence as well as its created particularity. For Kierkegaard, despair, too, is *in itself* an "imbalance in a relation of synthesis" that makes up a man as "a relation that relates to itself."[51] The imaginative atemporality described above is experienced, "because despair . . . has to do with the eternal in a person,"[52] and "eternity is something humanity cannot be rid of."[53] Yet, equally, it cannot be rid of its finite nature. A self without finitization is dissolved in the phantoms of unchecked possibility, that, "succeed one another with such speed that it seems as though everything were possible, and that is the very moment the individual himself has finally become nothing but an atmospheric illusion."[54] His understanding of despair is that the ability to understand it is a Christian privilege that contextualizes the experience within humanity's metaphysical location. Equally,

---

49. "[T]he father thought the son's melancholy was his fault, and the son thought the father's was his fault, and so they never spoke of it to each other." Kierkegaard, *Diary*, 33.

50. Kierkegaard, *Sickness*, 45.

51. Ibid.

52. Ibid., 47.

53. Ibid.

54. Ibid., 66.

> I will say that this is an adventure every human being must go through—to learn to be anxious in order that he may not perish either by never having been in anxiety or by succumbing in anxiety. Whoever has learned to be anxious in the right way has learned the ultimate.[55]

For the Christian, therefore, despair and anxiety are "absolutely educative"[56] once understood, they can become both the motor and the map towards a proper relation of the spirit to the body and the soul, and of the entire person to God. "Whoever is educated by his anxiety . . . is educated according to infinity."[57] They must be experienced in their full, devastating force in order to bring one to the incomprehensible paradox of absolute possibility that necessitates the "leap" into the incomprehensible absurdity of faith, but also "what Hegel, in his way, correctly calls the inner certainty that anticipates infinity."[58] For the Christian, who has put himself in the right relation to his anxiety in order to be able to learn profundity from it, "anxiety becomes a serving spirit that against its will leads him where he wants to go."[59]

Nevertheless, despair claims this status not in itself, but as the possibility of its own annihilation in faith. Thus, "to be cured of this sickness is the Christian's blessedness."[60] However, though it may be necessary for one to pass through this stern pedagogy, to do so, and then to leave it behind, is the Christian's duty. As Kierkegaard notes, nevertheless, despite the Christian's advantage contained in the possibility of despair, for example, "it is the greatest misfortune and misery to actually be in despair; no, it is ruin."[61] The cure for despair must be the achievement of the synthesis whose simultaneous possibility and imbalance it signals. "Not being in despair must mean the annihilated possibility of the ability to be in it."[62] Once one is properly "educated" by despair, rather than subverting the dialectic of one's being by

---

55. Kierkegaard, *Concept*, 155.
56. Ibid.
57. Ibid., 156.
58. Ibid., 157; in this way, Paul Ricoeur demonstrates the dichotomous understanding of Kierkegaard's thought as a "dialectic without mediation" when he writes, "Despair is the negative version of Abraham's faith," which does not acknowledge the important part despair can play on the road to faith. Ricoeur, "Kierkegaard and Evil" in Bloom, ed., *Kierkegaard*, 49–58.
59. Kierkegaard, *Concept*, 159.
60. Kierkegaard, *Sickness*, 45.
61. Ibid.
62. Ibid..

tending towards one pole in favor of another, one rather grounds their relation, that is, "spirit" in the transcendent paradox of the creator.

This is powerfully narrated in his meditation on Abraham's ascent of Mount Moriah to sacrifice his firstborn and only son, Isaac, *Fear and Trembling*. This work posits that the demands of philosophical morality can offer no account of Abraham's terrible piety and concludes that this kind of heroic faith is born in the frightful abandonment of the principles and obligations that guard worldly living in favor of an "absurd" faith that, utterly without evidence, reason, or justification, somehow believes in the generosity of God. Thus, faith, born out of the devastation of one's expectations concerning mundane life, pushes the imagination utterly beyond itself into a pillar of cloud where it blindly waits to see God's face.

In the thought of Evagrius, too, the goal of Christian life is to overcome the temptations and trials associated with sin and, by thus bringing the *psyche* and *nous* into a correct balance with *soma*, perfect human nature by pressing beyond it. As noted, for the ancient monk, humans "process" the experience of existence through an imaginative self-construction that operates upon sensory "impressions" on the mind. However, the most perfect thoughts, those in which there is no danger of sin, are non-sensual—what Evagrius terms, "imageless," such as the concept of "The Word" in the Gospel of John.[63] On a trajectory of consummation similar to that of Kierkegaard, human nature is perfected by an integration of the self that is then, transforming the body *and* the mind through the soul, capable of reaching beyond itself, and in faith coming to imagine beyond its own imagination.

Thus, the emotional impact of melancholy is such that it not only presents a danger to one's own health and the health of one's faith if badly handled; but also uncovers that humanity's finite nature can only be satisfied by the infinity of the divine. This, however, does not demand the destruction or transcendence of finitude itself, for example, through the denial or destruction of the body. Instead, it demands that the whole of the person be integrated and harmoniously self-relating. The site of this relating, dynamic, changeable, and expressing itself in the imagination, is the soul. However, this self-relation is only made possible in relation to the Creator; and the establishment of the human being in the divine demands that the integration of tripartite personhood is completed by a "leap" of the self into the seamless and satisfying imagination of God.

---

63. Corrigan, *Soul*, 79.

# Bibliography

Cassian, John. *The Twelve Books of John Cassian on the Institutes of the Coenobia and the Remedies for the Eight Principal Faults*. Translated by E. C. S. Gibson in *A Select Library of Nicene and Post-Nicene Fathers of the Christian Church*, Second Series, Volume 11. New York, 1894. Accessed 11/06/2014, http://www.osb.org/lectio/cassian/inst/index.html.

Corrigan, Kevin. *Evagrius and Gregory: Views of the Soul in Late Antiquity*. Ashgate Studies in Philosophy and Theology in Antiquity. Burlington, VT: Ashgate, 2009.

Evagrius. *Kephalia Gnostica*, http://www.ldysinger.com/Evagrius/02_Gno-Keph/00a_start.htm, Accessed 13/6/2014.

———. *On the Eight Thoughts* in *Evagrius of Pontus: The Greek Ascetic Corpus*. Translated and introduced by Robert E. Sinkewicz, 73–90. Oxford: Oxford University Press, 2006.

———. *Peri Logismon* in *Evagrius of Pontus: The Greek Ascetic Corpus*. Translated and introduced by Robert E. Sinkewicz, 153–82. Oxford: Oxford University Press, 2006.

———. *Praktikos* in *Evagrius of Pontus: The Greek Ascetic Corpus*. Translated by and introduced by Robert E. Sinkewicz, 93–114. Oxford: Oxford University Press, 2006.

Kierkegaard, Søren. *The Concept of Anxiety*. Translated and edited by Reider Thomte and Albert B. Anderson. Princeton, NJ: Princeton University Press, 1981.

———. *The Diary of Søren Kierkegaard*. Edited by Peter Rhode. New York: Citadel, 1987.

———. *The Sickness Unto Death*. Translated by Alistair Hannay. London: Penguin, 2004.

Ricoeur, Paul. "Kierkegaard and Evil." In *Modern Critical Views: Søren Kierkegaard*, edited by Harold Bloom, 49–58. London: Chelsea House, 1989.

# SECTION IV
## The Soul's Regard

# 13

## Strategies of the Gift

### Body and Soul in John Paul II and Levinas

NIGEL ZIMMERMANN

THE PROBLEM OF THE body-soul relationship is treated by Emmanuel Levinas and St. John Paul II as one of describing the manifestation of the other person in terms of the gift. The soul, assuming such an objective reality exists, is taken to bear itself in the world only in so far as it is manifested in the body. However, in describing the significance of the body in Levinas and John Paul II, two differing trajectories of the gift emerge, which meet in convergence and departure. Both thinkers draw upon a phenomenologically informed set of intellectual commitments, and both incorporate language that relies on some cognizance of religious grammar for its interpretation. In this chapter, two fundamental strategies employed by Levinas and John Paul II will be studied, and it will be shown that they yield differing results for the place of the human person in relation to a trajectory of the gift. In Levinas, that strategy is a "hesitation" before embodied presence, and in John Paul II, the strategy is a "pause." Such differing strategies carry consequences for the manner in which the soul is understood.

Whereas Levinas' account of the body benefits only the event of alterity in the face of the Other, John Paul II's account is explicitly theological, relying on an analogical paradigm that displays the significance of the divine Other within the human experience of inter-subjectivity. Indeed, Levinas' account of the body too easily merges otherness into inter-subjectivity, reducing that which is strange and alien to a ghost-like category—seemingly less than human—because it is all too absolute. For example, the absolute Other can never meet the self in an intimacy of friendship on its own terms, for its essential substance is that of ethical demand and responsibility. Such a demand is posited in the sheer eventfulness of the ethical consequences of the manifestation of the other in the world. Levinas describes it as follows:

> The body of course has always been taken to be more than a chunk of matter. It was taken to house a soul, which it had the power of expressing. The body might be more or less expressive, and had parts which were more or less expressive. The face and the eyes, those mirrors of the soul, were especially the organs of expression. But the spirituality of the body does not lie in this power to express what is inward. By its position it realises the condition necessary for any inwardness. It does not express an event; it is itself this event.[1]

In other words, Levinas avoids the language of manifestation as such; he prefers to view the body as the condition for an inner reality (assumedly which could be named the soul). The soul, for Levinas, is not realized in the world through the body, but instead the soul is made manifest inwardly through the presence of a body. That is to say, the body makes possible an interior experience which may be investigated according to the category of the soul.

On the other hand, John Paul II's reluctance to reduce the otherness evident in the face of the other in such a way moves his trajectory in an otherwise direction. For John Paul II, the other person is irreducibly singular without falling into a disregard for the categories of community or communion. John Paul II views the other person in the logic of the gift, which bears some likeness to Levinas' notion of the sheer givenness of the Other, but the concreteness of the human body is interpreted in such varying ways that the trajectories of their gift-language differ substantially. For John Paul II, the theological origin of any appropriate reflection on embodied human life is found in Scripture, in which a vision of human flourishing is orientated by its foundation within a divinely-ordered plan.[2] Such an orientation protects philosophical enquiry from subjugating the human person to its embodied existence, or in turn, keeping the soul from subjugating the body. In his work *The Acting Person* (published originally before his election as Pope, and so under his baptismal name Karol Wojtyła), John Paul II argues, "we cannot discuss the human body apart from the whole that is man, that is,

---

1. Levinas, *Existence and Existents*, 72.
2. John Paul II, *Man and Woman He Created Them: A Theology of the Body*, 19:6.

without recognizing that he is a person."³ John Paul II, like Levinas, takes seriously the event of alterity in the face of the other person, but does so with attentiveness to the intrinsic irreducibility of the human person.

To complicate the relationship between Levinas and John Paul II further, it is significant that they became friends through shared philosophical interests, and carried on a dialogue respected and attended to by one another for many years. For example, John Paul II writes of Levinas in his book-length interview, *Crossing the Threshold of Hope*. In referring to Levinas' account of the face and its relationship to the divine command not to kill, John Paul II proclaims that they are "ingeniously joined in Levinas, and thus become a testimony for our age."⁴ For John Paul II, the provocative thought of Levinas provides a challenging philosophy of the suffering person that ought to be taken up and treated with seriousness. In turn, Levinas writes of John Paul II in the French language edition of *Communio* as the "phenomenological Cardinal," and one who retains a "particularly sensitive and unfailing solidarity with the entire structure of ethics; which determines a phenomenology of that which is human within that of transcendence."⁵ Much more can be said of the dialogue between the Polish Cardinal Archbishop who became Pope, and the Lithuanian-French Jewish philosopher, but for now let it suffice to say that such a dialogue suggests a fruitfulness in pursuing a dialogue between their differing approaches to the other person, precisely on the significance of the body in relation to the soul.⁶

The place of the body in Emmanuel Levinas is a shifting locality of significance in his wider philosophical work. At times it seems the body of the other signifies alterity in its incarnate presence, transporting that which is transcendent into the immanent context of subjectivity. This is detected in sections of Levinas' *Totaite et Infini*, in which the explicit conjoining of authentic ethics with the face relies on the function of sense and touch to communicate subjective presence. For example, Levinas turns to the notion of "enjoyment," in which the human subject experiences an order that renders sensibility possible.⁷ Enjoyment, for Levinas, is the intentionality

---

3. John Paul II, *The Acting Person*, 203. It is important to note that Tymieniecka's translation of the original Polish text into English is not universally accepted as an authentic rendering of Karol Wojtyła's original argument. Having said that, this particular reference is not controversial, and it aligns with the French translation, which is altogether more reliable. See John Paul II, *Personne et acte*.

4. John Paul II, *Crossing the Threshold of Hope*, 210–11.

5. Levinas, "Notes sur la pensée philosophique du Cardinal Wojtyła," 87.

6. For further study of theological themes in Levinas, see my work, *Levinas and Theology*.

7. Levinas, *Totality and Infinity: An Essay on Exteriority*. See especially B. Enjoyment

that secures self-representation in the world. It is a reaching out within the world that takes nourishment from the material existence of the "substantial plenitude of being," and thus embraces not only the things of the world, but a relation with those things.[8] Enjoyment is an intentional self-representation, and one might add that for Levinas it is described with the flavor of hopeful optimism. It is a positive picture of enjoyment, and it is contrasted by Levinas against *the same*, which is that movement of Being that short-circuits the overwhelming uniqueness of the other, resulting in a depleted, vandalized, and incomplete picture of the mystery of the human person. In this account, the body plays a crucial role because it is the site of possibility for such enjoyment. That is to say, the experience of corporeality places the person in a relationship to the world that enacts the drama of all that one is and all that one hopes for, within one's experience of both the self and the world. Levinas takes up the language of "sinking one's teeth" into the substance of the world; of an incarnate existence that owes its whole animation to the fact of its corporeality.[9] It is worth quoting Levinas at length:

> To posit oneself corporeally is to touch an earth, but to do so in such a way that the touching finds itself already conditioned by the position, the foot settles into a real which this very action outlines or constitutes—, as though a painter would notice that he is descending from the picture he is painting.[10]

In other words, one is not simply grounded in the world, but one's body places the self in the materiality of the world. In this way, the soul experiences the world in a contingent manner by way of its reliance on the body. The foot "settles into a real" and expresses a desire for self-realization in such a context, which might be viewed as an optimistic description of corporeality and of the significance of the body. The notion of the foot settling into an authentic expression of the "real" places Levinas within a perspective that recognizes the body's self-expression, as well as the earthy shaping of the body by forces outwith the power of the human person. The body is both a presence that shapes experience, as well as a presence shaped by the world. It can be seen elsewhere that such an account sits in tension with Levinas' understanding of the way in which the body sits within the order of the gift. This is because Levinas' chief concern is not the relationship of the person with the world as such, but with the ethical content of the

and Representation, 1–5.
  8. Ibid., 133.
  9. Ibid., 117.
  10. Ibid., 128.

relation of the self to the other. In considering the other party in the context of sociality, Levinas maintains that a certain inequality always pervades the exchange between the two, such that the other person is primarily configured as *the Other*. Indeed, Levinas argues strictly against any presupposition of universal truths into which "subjectivity could be absorbed," and the possibility that a relationship of "communion" might be contemplated.[11] For Levinas, the other remains always *the* Other, and therefore a transcendent category as far as one's own experience of otherness can be described. Such an account carries a risk that the body of the other itself is, as it were, disenfranchised. If alterity is the constitutive factor in the event of the other person, then the body also must be construed as merely a natural operation of particularizing difference in the world. The body is not to be enjoyed, shared, or attended to as a gift in its own terms, but reduced to the material stamp of a ghostly intrigue. Because of this, the soul is not construed by Levinas as carrying any ontological value per se, nor of conveying a meaning or language indicative of anything other than an interior subjectivity.

The tension between Levinas' account of "enjoyment" in the world and his negation of the body as a corporeal presence of significance within itself can be seen further in *Autrement qu'être*. The following words characterize the development of Levinas' negative assessment of the body:

> Hospitality, the-one-for-the-other in the ego, delivers it more passively than any passivity from links in a causal chain. Being torn from oneself for another in giving to the other the bread from one's mouth is being able to give up one's soul for another. The animation of a body by a soul only articulates the-one-for-the-other in subjectivity.[12]

First, Levinas indicates that the self is gifted to oneself in authenticity, precisely in the giving of the I for the other. It is a sacrifice of the self's own good for the other that describes the authentic expression of the self. Such a sacrifice entails the sense of being torn, separated and, in its phenomenality, deconstructed within the world. Second, Levinas describes the self-gift for the other, particularly pronounced in the tearing of sustenance from one's lips for the other, as an event that is markedly corporeal. It relies upon the sensations of the body for its expression. This echoes Levinas' earlier more positive account of enjoyment in the world. It is an offering configured in the substance of the flesh and an ethical activity of care for the other in and through the body.

11. Ibid., 251.
12. Levinas, *Otherwise than Being: or Beyond Essence*, 79.

As such, Levinas' giving of bread for the other is both a spiritual and an en-fleshed exercise in which the action of giftedness to and for the sake of another person grants proper form to the self's relationship with another. It is not simply the concrete presence of one's body that returns the self self-ward; it is rather the sacrificing of one's body for the other that reveals the true self. For Levinas, ethical care for the other returns the self to self-authenticity. This account of ethics offers self-revelation as a kind of excess.[13] Because it is an excess, it opens up the space in which the "conditions" of giving are made possible.[14] By this, it can be seen how the gift of bread to the other entails more than simply offering an object of worth, but describes the character of self-donation, or self-giving, in what can be called a logic of the gift. Even as it lurks in the mire of unethical in-authenticity, the human person is called out by responsibility to give for the suffering other. In giving for the other absolutely, Levinas' accent on alterity intensifies the difficulty in securing a relationship between the body of the other person, and the other as a philosophical category. Levinas' account privileges ethical responsibility, but a responsibility for who, or what, exactly? This question will be explored further below.

In a similar vein, John Paul II calls for a "pause" before the mystery of human subjectivity.[15] In an act of humility, he wishes to avoid a rush into describing the human person in its subjectivity, and instead calls for careful meditation upon the existential depths that lay hidden within the structures of human personhood. Such a pause can be detected in a circumspective way in Levinas.[16] The pause cannot be characterized as a ponderous reflection, but is rather an intellectual manoeuvre that interrupts the philosophical anthropological tradition, which is as theoretically important as the chronological interruption of sociality before the face of the other. John Paul II attempts to hold together the integral aspects of the human person in its psychical and bodily dimensions, avoiding modern dualism through a defense of human subjectivity. As he argues, "[s]ubjectivity is, then, a kind

---

13. Webb, "The Rhetoric of Ethics as Excess: A Christian Theological Response to Emmanuel Levinas." Webb identifies a natural link between the categories of ethics and excess, rooted in the Jewish (and Christian) concern for the widow, the stranger, and the poor. He views the scriptural demandingness of the ethical as a constant "extravagance" over the demands of the everyday and normally expected. To be ethical is not to meet an expectation, but to go beyond it.

14. Mansfield, *The God Who Deconstructs Himself: Sovereignty and Subjectivity between Freud, Bataille, and Derrida*, 112.

15. John Paul II, *Person and Community*, 213.

16. For example, Michael Purcell describes something not dissimilar to the "pause" in his phenomenological description of "hesitation" before the Other. See Michael Purcell, "On Hesitation before the Other."

of synonym for the irreducible in the human being."[17] In facing the other person, John Paul II resists swift descriptions and prejudicial objectifications by honoring the irreducibility of the person; philosophy stands with head bowed. In this way, John Paul II's account does not view philosophy as shuffling hesitantly before the embodied human being, but exercises an intentional humility before the tremendous mystery of humanity. Indeed, John Paul II remarks that to resist such a pause is itself to risk putting aside exactly that in the *humanum* that makes a person human.[18] This is not to say that the human person is a static object—something like a statue or a painting—but rather that he or she is a singular work of irreducible theatre offered in the dynamism of a thinking subject. John Paul II identifies in the human subject a moral conflict between good and evil that is itself irreducible to the natural world, despite the positive objectivity accorded to its description in the Aristotelian tradition. The pause before the mystery— a contemplative moment—does not mean the evasion of description, but rather a newness of the descriptive approach. This approach is given by way of phenomenology, in which objective values and their penetration in the conscience is witnessed with new perception, an observation Levinas makes of John Paul II.[19] Furthermore, John Paul II's Thomist realism is enhanced by phenomenology's aptitude for the intuitive movement of objective realities, especially that of the human person.[20] It is important to view John Paul II's contribution for its ingenuity here, but also for its profound continuity within the Western tradition.

In the "pause," it is seen that what is in fact appearing to the observer of human subjectivity is transcendent to the simple operation of cognitive understanding. It is a fullness of meaning that incorporates descriptive language even as it exceeds the possibility of language. Despite this transcendence, it remains immersed in the event of human experience. John Paul II argues:

> The irreducible signifies that which is essentially incapable of reduction, that which cannot be reduced but can only be disclosed or revealed. Lived experience essentially defies reduction. This does not mean, however, that it eludes our knowledge; it only means that we must arrive at the knowledge of it differently,

---

17. See "Subjectivity and the Irreducible in the Human Being," in John Paul II, *Person and Community*, 211.

18. Ibid., 215.

19. Buttiglione, *Karol Wojtyla: The Thought of the Man Who Became Pope John Paul II*, 276.

20. Lawler, *The Christian Personalism of Pope John Paul II*, 46.

namely, by a method or means of analysis that merely reveals and discloses its essence. The method of phenomenological analysis allows us to pause at lived experience as the irreducible.[21]

It is an irreducibility that, according to its own inner structure, is *given* to us, "disclosed" or "revealed."[22] Two points are of importance in these words.

The first is that the irreducible in the human person is given as a quality of resistance, a dignity that cannot be compromised.[23] It refuses comprehensive explanation and cannot be bracketed out from its embodied context. Its only interpretation is through an appreciation of its intuitive content; intentionality itself is not sufficient. This implies a certain quality of resistance, almost of dogged recalcitrance, in the inner life of the embodied person, that which we call the soul. In this language of irreducibility, we discover that the soul, rather than being a passive presence in the human person, is a dynamically resistant presence that is deeply invested in the way in which the person manifests itself in the world.

The second point is that the disclosure of the irreducible is not given in formal categories, but according to its own order, which, according to John Paul II, is chiefly phenomenological. Only the method of phenomenological analysis allows such a disclosure. Even then, such a disclosure does not give itself entirely to the receiver, but allows the receiver to pause in an active reception to the disclosure. In this way, the irreducible reflects John Paul II's personalism, which always avoids falling into subjectivism.[24]

The reference of John Paul II to that which can be "disclosed" or "revealed" places the power of discovery over other human persons primarily in their own hands.[25] That is to say, what may be discovered is only that which can be disclosed or revealed by an other. The dramatic ethics of irreducibility that occurs in John Paul II's phenomenological reading of the *humanum* holds together the integrated whole of the human person as well as describing its soulful resistance to thematizations and ideological reductions.

For John Paul II, this action allows a permeation of the "whole essence" of the experience of human subjectivity to be made manifest.[26] That is not to say that it allows a fully comprehensible description of the hu-

21. John Paul II, *Person and Community*, 215.
22. Ibid.
23. Lawler, *The Christian Personalism of Pope John Paul II*, 69.
24. Ibid., 22.
25. John Paul II, *Person and Community*, 215.
26. Ibid., 216.

man person, but rather the fullness of subjectivity is disclosed, leading to a phenomenological contribution of a "trans-phenomenal understanding... of the richness proper to human existence...."[27] While the strategic step of taking a pause is of great help in recognizing the limits of sensory description regarding the human person, our own subjective experience in relation to others seems to enjoy a more numerous array of the modes of human knowing. The pause cannot be purely cognitive, because it is not limited to the methodology of the philosopher in any formal sense. The pause is contemplative, and so belongs to all human experience. A convergence on this line of thinking can be found in Levinas when he insists that responsibility for the other is "awakened" by the call of the other's face, which is a pre-cognitive, non-formal moment.[28] The consequences of this awakening are not dissimilar to John Paul II's pause, which yet reveals a divergence between John Paul II and Levinas, that of the relationship of the pause or contemplative posture before the other, and the embodied other.

The body of the other person—the human body—en-fleshes the irreducibility of the human subject. Such an irreducibility is not contained by the body, but situated by it, and therefore coincides with language that might otherwise be used for the soul. In both Levinas and John Paul II, it converges as a mystery to be accepted as gift, both to the one whose body makes the other present in the world, and to the one who contemplates the mystery of the other person in the intentional gaze. And yet it is at this point of convergence that the place of the body highlights two differing trajectories in the logic of the gift at work in Levinas and John Paul II. These trajectories appear close to one another in their insistence that the other person is to be received ethically as a gift, but they depart most significantly through the role they attribute to reciprocity in human inter-subjectivity. It must be kept in mind that for John Paul II, his approach to the *humanum* seeks to hold the insights of the Aristotelian-Boethian anthropological heritage in close approximation to the contemporary personalistic impulse (the pause). He sees in such a relationship between the traditions a space in which essential and burning questions concerning the human person ought to be pursued and, by consequence, in which the most fruitful of anthropological-ethical challenges might be faced.[29] As such, John Paul II locates a philosophical

---

27. Ibid.

28. "The Awakening of the I," in Levinas, *Is it Righteous to Be?: Interviews with Emmanuel Levinas*, 182.

29. In this way, Wojtyła's early essays in *Person and Community* and his dramatic productions such as *The Jeweler's Shop* interpret and illustrate each other. They cannot be read apart from one another. See John Paul II, *The Jeweler's Shop: A Meditation on the Sacrament of Matrimony, Passing on Occasion into a Drama*.

basis for what eventually became his highly reciprocal structure of the nuptial mystery as his chief paradigm of alterity.[30] In John Paul II, the gift of the other is pondered in a contemplative posture; an interior silence receives the gift of the body and complements it with one's own gifted body. In this way, the human soul reaches out through materiality for the sense and touch of communion with another.

Reciprocity—denied profoundly by Levinas—appears as a substratal feature of John Paul II's anthropology.[31] The divine statement in Gen 2:18, "[i]t is not good that the man should be alone," affirms the impossibility that the human person should "realize his essence or find his 'norm' without communion with others."[32] The Creator makes possible the response of joy when, after the creation of woman, the man exclaims, "she is flesh from my flesh and bone from my bones" (Gen 2:23). According to John Paul II's philosophical-theology, reciprocity follows God's acknowledgement that the human person cannot fulfill its destiny without the other. It is not only an embodied other who appears in the text, but one whose own body has the capacity for reciprocal and mutual union. Sexuality and personhood are intimately related here, for one cannot be thought of apart from the other. The gift is not given so that the self might find pleasure, happiness, or even the good, but so that the primary gift of the divine-self might be revealed in the reciprocity of male and female.[33] In this way, the category of revelation serves a similar purpose in John Paul II as that of ethics in Levinas. The revelation of the divine image constitutes, for John Paul II, the basis of prayer and self-realization, thus showing forth the path of ethical responsibility.

For Levinas, an opposing principle is at work, that of ethics as the revelatory substance of subjective existentiality. John Paul II's turn to the nuptial paradigm allows then both contemplation and action in an embodied communion of persons. Indeed, the fullness of the two reveals also the absence borne in the presence of only one. Angelo Scola, an interpreter of John Paul II, puts it this way:

> Sexuality (man and woman, sexual difference) thus demonstrates its coessentiality with human nature, through that polarity which indicates reciprocity. I, who exist as a man of the male

---

30. This approach came to be known, largely through his weekly audiences presented as Pope John Paul II, as the "theology of the body," as collected in John Paul II, *Man and Woman He Created Them*.

31. This was in reference to Martin Buber's insistence on reciprocity as the means by which the "thou" could be protected from reduction to an "it." See Martin Buber, *I and Thou*.

32. John Paul II, *Man and Woman He Created Them*, 14:2.

33. Ibid., 14:5.

gender, do not exhaust the whole of being man. I always have before me, almost as a counterimage, the other way of being man, which is inaccessible to me.[34]

The inaccessibility of the other person's interiority is therefore related—via the somatic whole of the body—to the sexual nature of personal subjectivity. This discovery is a source of freedom for the human person, who is not reduced to bodily passions and therefore not constrained by the body.[35] This is a multi-layered account of the gift. The body is a gift to the self that makes possible the personal gift of the self to the other; the result of which is the communion of the soul with another. In this way, the body is the condition of the gift of the soul. The gift is a conscious movement of the body, which allows for the spousal meaning of the body to enact its drama within creation.[36] Love makes its appearance at this point in John Paul II's anthropology, in which the reciprocity of male and female, consciously imagined, is the "power to express love" to the other.[37] Carl Anderson has interpreted the structure of the gift in terms of a cognitive, pre-active recognition of givenness that ends in blessing.[38] Recognizing the gift in terms of personhood is to receive the gift, before any other action.

There is a beatifying directionality in the spousal meaning of the body, achieved in the complementary relationship of reciprocity.[39] John Paul II quotes *Gaudium et Spes* 24, which articulates that man is uniquely created for his own sake and may only find himself through the "gift of self."[40] While Levinas' self-donation is an exhaustive insomnia that places the self always at the disposal of the other, John Paul II's account renders possible the fostering of the good in the context of *communion*. The embodied orientation towards the good is in part based on the mutual recognition of the *imago Dei* in the other, but is also based on the strange motivation of the divine in creating man to begin with.

Original innocence is the state that makes possible a mutual recognition of the gift in the spousal meaning of the body. In Gen 2:25, the man and the woman look upon each other and experience no shame. For John Paul II, this is an overlooked text, in which "welcoming" and "accepting" the

---

34. Scola, *The Nuptial Mystery*, 119.
35. John Paul II, *Man and Woman He Created Them*, 14:6.
36. Ibid., 15:1.
37. Ibid.
38. Anderson and Granados, *Called to Love: Approaching John Paul II's Theology of the Body*, 67.
39. John Paul II, *Man and Woman He Created Them*, 15:5.
40. Ibid.

embodied beauty of the other in the nuptial relationship constitutes a recognition of what is inherently a gracious gift.[41] John Paul II seeks to counter a lingering Manichaeism in his own Catholic tradition, but which can also be witnessed in the purview of contemporary culture.[42] In this and more generally, John Paul is at pains to rebuke the Manichaen heresy, which derived from texts in the third century that taught a radical dualism between spirituality (the light) and materiality (the world). The body and sexuality were negated sorely, and such a position results in a refusal of the goodness and beauty of material and spiritual goods. The refusal of the other is considered not just the rejection of the gift, but its loss.[43] Moreover, the refusal of the other person is a flattening out of what is intended to be a mutual self-donation for the greatness of the other. This reciprocity is described in terms of a co-habitual serving of the wellbeing of the nuptial other.

Levinas also envisages an asymmetry in the ethical relationship, but his approach disallows the inclusion of reciprocity.[44] Certainly, a reciprocity of dignity is manifest in the inter-subjectivity of the two. Yet, in an ethical sense, the relationship is a thoroughgoing asymmetry of self-donation. One discovers the truth of one's own dignity through an ethos of sacrifice for the other.[45] In turn, one finds that a new gift arises from the exchange: the gradual awareness of a new "gift of self" in correlation to the consciousness of the original gift of the other.[46] While this reflection is centered on the original states of human existentiality, John Paul II is concerned to ensure they orbit within the range of grace, such that by the same, contemporary persons might re-imagine the body in their own historical situation. The "theological prehistory," as it were, constitutes the basis for a new theological aspect of the "*ethos of the body.*"[47] Reciprocity then has both a theological and an ethical dimension. Theologically, it is a strict term, denoting a rigorous reciprocal possibility in the mutual recognition and exchange of the *imago Dei* in terms of a lived experience of the body. Ethically, reciprocity is experienced in a radical asymmetry, in which the self finds itself through giving itself away for the other. John Paul II argues that "[o]riginal innocence manifests and at the same time constitutes the perfect

---

41. Ibid., 17:3.

42. See ibid., 35:3, 41:4, 44:5–6, 45:1–5, 46:1, 4, 49:6, 55:3, 62:5, 77:6, 78:1, 82:6, 83:3, 85:5, 117B:2.

43. The "antithesis" of the gift. Ibid., 17:3.

44. Scola, *The Nuptial Mystery*, 120.

45. John Paul II, *Man and Woman He Created Them*, 17:4–6.

46. Ibid., 17:5.

47. Ibid., 18:3.

ethos of the gift."[48] This innocence, which is being "pure of heart," allows the imaging forth of the other stripped of garments and of the world itself. In consciousness of the gift, the other may be received as a free gift, but elicits a free response of ethical hospitality. And as this original *ethos* takes form, John Paul II locates in marriage the "primordial sacrament," which is constituted upon the concrete presence of male and female in an embodied relationship of care and mutual regard.[49] What is, in effect, the sacrament of asymmetrical reciprocity, opens up the logic of the gift to others, not as a hidden or discrete exchange, but as one known consciously and enacted in a festal mood. Truth and love issue forth an extended exchange of the gift that, despite the horizon of death and sin, remains intact through the *imago Dei* in the integrated whole that is the human body.[50]

Moreover, for John Paul II's anthropology, the other, if he or she is to be received in the full value to which the ensouled body is a witness, must be understood always to be a sexual person. To think otherwise is to destabilize the human body. According to Angelo Scola, "[r]elation to the other is never constituted independently of their sexuality."[51] In the paradigm of alterity, the nuptial mystery constitutes one flesh but two bodies, which axiomatically relies on the mutual gift of the entire body, male and female. In this reading, the nuptial mystery acts as the guarantor of bodily otherness and of the integrity of the body in its reciprocity. The knowledge of this mystery allows for other aspects of the Paschal mystery to unfold more clearly. For example, the Eucharistic celebration of the Christian tradition, in which the Bride and Bridegroom relationship is dramatized in God's divine presence in the sacrament, relies on a typological significance of the almost mundane, domesticated, and recognizable experiences of marriage. That is, the significance of the liturgical drama of marriage is confirmed by a social realization of those countless married moments that appear in the natural world; travelling together, the rearing of children, domestic disputes, and the realization of different priorities in a community of the two. Marc Ouellet calls this the historical guarantee of the mutual "knowledge" and "recognition" of the divine Bridegroom and earthly Bride.[52] This helps to maintain an integrated role for sexuality in an account of the body, in which the whole of life's drama is seen in a liturgical and theological perspective. In spousal perspective, it is the recognition of an irreducible subjectivity that

48. Ibid., 18:5.
49. Ibid., 19:3–6.
50. Ibid., 19:6.
51. Scola, *The Nuptial Mystery*, 126.
52. Ouellet, *Divine Likeness: Toward a Trinitarian Anthropology of the Family*, 165.

is intimately related to its own embodiment. John Paul II's hermeneutics of the gift radicalizes the human person in the movement of gift exchange, in which it acts as a constant reference point that makes the gift possible. Furthermore, his use of the nuptial mystery necessitates a new coincidence of *eros* and *ethos*:

> It is necessary continually to rediscover the spousal meaning of the body and the true dignity of the gift in what is "erotic." This is the task of the human spirit, and it is by its nature an ethical task. If one does not assume this task, the very attraction of the senses and the passion of the body can stop at mere concupiscence, deprived of all ethical value, and man, male and female, does not experience that fullness of "eros," which implies the upward impulse of the human spirit toward what is true, good, and beautiful. It is, therefore, indispensable that ethos becomes the constitutive form of eros.[53]

John Paul II is explaining here the ethical task of rediscovering an aspect of theological anthropology he views as being overlooked among many in the church. He locates in the spousal meaning of the body a language of gift that is phenomenologically received in the presence of the body itself. *Eros* is invoked as the formal means in which *ethos* might be re-approached. Desire is re-interpreted positively, allowing the possibility of gifting by way of the body. By this, John Paul II indicates a regulative role of the nuptial mystery in a new development of the theology of the body. It is a dense, but crucial passage. He calls for a phenomenological reading of the spousal meaning of the body, recognizing the spousal intuition of the human body. Further, he is seeking out the gift of the erotic (which is not bound to the language of sexuality). This "spiritual" task in itself is not limited to theology, but is a common "ethical" task, relying on a transcendent hope beyond the immediate sensations and passions of the body.[54] John Paul II addresses this wider application directly:

> Does it not embrace every human being and, in some sense, everything created, as the Pauline text on the "redemption of the body" in Romans indicates (see Rom 8:23)? In this sense, the *sacramentum magnum* is indeed a *new* sacrament of man in Christ and in the Church: *the sacrament "of man and of the world*," just as the creation of man, male and female, in the image of God was the original sacrament of man and of the world.[55]

53. John Paul II, *Man and Woman He Created Them*, 48:1.
54. Ibid.
55. Ibid., 102:7.

This notion of the nuptial sacrament as a mystery of man and the world is then applicable to each human person. It is woven through concrete experiences of the body in alterity as well as in its theological application.

Levinas and John Paul II accent differing aspects of alterity in its embodied perspective. In Levinas, the form of ethics is illustrated as a deferential posture of self-kenosis before the epiphany of the face.[56] The other carries an infinity of meaning and possibility, transcendent in its capacity for otherness and its directionality, a centering upon the human "before all system."[57] Indeed, by this, "God comes to mind."[58] The kind of sociality that follows Levinas' logic requires a radical asymmetry in inter-subjectivity. What matters is that the gift of the other is not besmirched in any way by one's own body. The "pure gift" of the other is always a gift beyond, towards a "not yet" of responsibility which is foreshadowed in the ethical.[59] For him, the soul is never reached and never heard, nor is it manifest in the world. Despite their otherwise agreement on the asymmetry of the relation with the embodied other, John Paul II maintains the possibility of human reciprocity because of what animates the body. In this sense, John Paul maintains that the human person rests within the certainty of an ultimate symmetry defined by reciprocity, but one grounded in the lively human experience of difference. He does so by an appeal to the inherent good affirmed by the biblical logic of the body in its nascent human narrative. For John Paul II, a crucial integrity is maintained by affirming the relationship between sexuality, erotic desire, and ethics in the human body, through which one can also perceive the possibilities once more of family and community.

Accounting for the place of the embodied human person in John Paul II and Levinas is to reflect on differing trajectories of the gift. In the former, a theological paradigm of reciprocal nuptial *communio* places the body in an integrated order of love in which human souls intermingle in the complexities of the world. In the latter, the body becomes subject to an alterity that seeks no such common humanity according to the soul, community or relationship. Because John Paul II's account is philosophical and theological, it allows for both the demands placed upon the body in its material suffering as well as a measure of anticipated glory. It centers upon the inclusion of incarnation as a category that re-interprets human experiences

56. Levinas, *Totality and Infinity: An Essay on Exteriority [Totalité et infini: essai sur l'extériorité]*, 199.

57. "Discussion Following 'Transcendence and Intelligibility,'" in Levinas, *Is it Righteous to Be?: Interviews with Emmanuel Levinas*, 270.

58. "Discussion Following 'Transcendence and Intelligibility,'" in ibid.

59. Kearney, "Desire of God," in Caputo and Scanlon, *God, the Gift, and Postmodernism*, 118.

of the body in light of narratives concerned with divine-human mingling, the shadow of death, and resurrection. It does not limit itself to a positive rendering of incarnate experience, but is informed by the content of a particularized experience of divine-human intimacy within the person of the divine *Logos*. In this way, John Paul II's approach takes up a rich discourse that serves the humility of the other within the context of *communio*. It is the gift that gives itself most perfectly in the coincidence of *eros* with *ethos*, which, perhaps ironically, Levinas cannot avoid: "In *Desire* are conjoined the movements unto the Height and unto the Humility of the Other."[60] For Levinas, otherness is the epiphany also of human responsibility before an experiential glory or "height." Between Levinas and John Paul II, it can be seen that the approach to reciprocity results in particular ways of viewing how such a height is received and responded to. John Paul II affirms a theological insight that Levinas cannot commit to philosophically: that the gift of the other is profoundly shown forth in the arrival of the third, whose interruption of the same is the very epiphany of *corporeal* existence. Whereas Levinas' account of the third is a new instance of alterity that marks the self as responsible, John Paul insists that the body is a site of alterity's invitation to serve out the good. In other words, Levinas disregards the significance of the body, and John Paul views it as essential.

Levinas is confronted by John Paul II in an approach that both converges, and departs, when it reflects upon the place of the human person. The categories of the body and the soul cannot avoid a turn towards themes of incarnation, materiality, and the corporeality of the human subject in its encounter with others. What Levinas denies in corporeality, John Paul II affirms in his phenomenological observation: "the *other*, after all, is also an *I* for whom I can be an *other*."[61] In his vision of the human person, the soul is irreducible to the concepts and totalities of the world, precisely because of its intimacy with the body. The interweaving of nuptial themes with ethical responsibility indeed has the capacity to receive and to love the other, and to allow one's intentional gaze to turn towards the nascent person, whose own body is radically contingent on others. Levinas hesitates before the significance of the gift of ensouled and embodied existence, whereas John Paul II pauses. As it has been shown, the space between a "pause" and a "hesitation" is profound.

---

60. Levinas, *Totality and Infinity*, 200.

61. "Participation or Alienation?," in John Paul II, *Person and Community: Selected Essays*, 201.

# Bibliography

Anderson, Carl A., and José Granados. *Called to Love: Approaching John Paul II's Theology of the Body*. New York: Doubleday, 2009.
Buber, Martin. *I and Thou*. Translated by Ronald Gregor Smith. 1937. Reprint. London: Continuum, 2004.
Buttiglione, Rocco. *Karol Wojtyła: The Thought of the Man Who Became Pope John Paul II*. Grand Rapids: Eerdmans, 1997.
Caputo, John D., and Michael J. Scanlon, eds. *God, the Gift, and Postmodernism*. Bloomington, IN: Indiana University Press, 1999.
John Paul II. *The Acting Person*. Translated by Anna-Teresa Tymieniecka. Analecta Husserliana. Dordrecht: Reidel, 1979.
———. *Crossing the Threshold of Hope*. Translated by Vittorio Messori. London: Cape, 1994.
———. *The Jeweler's Shop: A Meditation on the Sacrament of Matrimony, Passing on Occasion into a Drama*. Translated by Boleslaw Taborski. San Francisco: Ignatius, 1992.
———. *Man and Woman He Created Them: A Theology of the Body*. Translated by Michael Waldstein. Boston: Pauline, 2006.
———. *Person and Community: Selected Essays*. Translated by Theresa Sandok. New York: Lang, 1993.
———. *Personne et Acte*. Translated by Gwendoline Jarczyk. Saint-Maur (Val-de-Marne): Parole et silence, 2011.
Lawler, Ronald David. *The Christian Personalism of Pope John Paul II*. Chicago: Franciscan Herald, 1982.
Levinas, Emmanuel. *Existence and Existents [De L'existence À L'existant]*. Translated by Alphonso Lingis. The Hague: Nijhoff, 1978.
———. *Is It Righteous to Be?: Interviews with Emmanuel Levinas*. Translated by Jill Robbins. Stanford: Stanford University Press, 2001.
———. "Notes Sur La Pensée Philosophique Du Cardinal Wojtyla." *Communio* 4 (juillet-aout 1980) 87–90.
———. *Otherwise Than Being: Or Beyond Essence [Autrement Qu'être Ou Au-Delà De L'essence]* [Translation of: Autrement qu'être. 2nd ed.]. Translated by Alphonso Lingis. Pittsburgh: Duquesne University Press, 1998.
———. *Totality and Infinity: An Essay on Exteriority [Totalité Et Infini: Essai Sur L'extériorité]* [Translation of: Totalité et infini.]. Translated by Alphonso Lingis. Pittsburgh: Duquesne University Press, 2004.
Mansfield, Nick. *The God Who Deconstructs Himself: Sovereignty and Subjectivity between Freud, Bataille, and Derrida*. New York: Fordham University Press, 2010.
Ouellet, Marc. *Divine Likeness: Toward a Trinitarian Anthropology of the Family*. Grand Rapids: Eerdmans, 2006.
Purcell, Michael. "On Hesitation before the Other." *International Journal of Philosophy & Religion* 60 (2006) 9–19.
Scola, Angelo. *The Nuptial Mystery*. Translated by Michelle K. Borras. Grand Rapids: Eerdmans, 2005.
Webb, Stephen H. "The Rhetoric of Ethics as Excess: A Christian Theological Response to Emmanuel Levinas." *Modern Theology* 15.1 (1999) 1–16.
Zimmermann, Nigel. *Levinas and Theology*. London: T. & T. Clark Bloomsbury, 2013.

# 14

# Redeeming Duality

## Anthropological Split-ness and Embodied Soteriology

LEXI EIKELBOOM

## Introduction

THERE HAVE BEEN MANY recent theological attempts to argue for a more holistic anthropology than that which substance-dualism has traditionally provided.[1] The proponents of holistic anthropology have several motives—an increased recognition of the importance of the body,[2] a respect for scientific research that points towards physicalism,[3] and a desire to reflect biblical anthropology,[4] for example. However, the desire for

---

1. Examples include Warren S. Brown's and Nancey Murphy's non-reductive physicalism in Murphy and Brown, *Did My Neurons Make Me Do It?* and N. T. Wright's biblical argument for integrated persons in "Mind, Spirit, Soul and Body: All for One and One for All, Reflections on Paul's Anthropology in his Complex Contexts."

2. Green, *Body, Soul, and Human Life*, 131: "We do what we are—that is, one's deepest commitments are unavoidably exhibited in one's practices, so that attention focuses on 'embodied life,' disallowing the possibility that the 'real' person might be relegated to one's interior life."

3. Shults, *Reforming Theological Anthropology*, 179: "One of the factors in the decline of substance dualism is discoveries in Neurobiology."

4. Murphy, *Bodies and Souls, or Spirited Bodies?* 37: "most of the dualism that has appeared to be biblical teaching has been a result of poor translations."

a more holistic anthropology, whether of the materialist or non-reductive physicalist variety, is also motivated by a theological suspicion of split-ness itself. If Christians affirm the existence of the soul in some sense, they must also accept that the human includes differentiation. This is not necessarily to say that every affirmation of the soul implies two distinct, ontological or substantial objects that could exist apart from their unification. However, even if one argues for a soul conceptualized in non-substantialist terms,[5] this implies non-coincidence. Any sort of conjunction or integration, no matter how total, implies a previous non-identity between these parts or dimensions. Moreover, this is a difference that is more significant than merely the difference between parts of the body, for example, which can all be addressed or even reduced to biological enquiry, while any concept of the soul cannot be investigated or described in these same terms. The human transects various planes of reality. I call this significant difference "split-ness" and I argue that this idea in itself is uncomfortable because if humans are essentially split, that is, non-identical with ourselves, then our ideas about what soteriological holism and healing mean are challenged. We see in ourselves the divisions that are caused by and lead to sin and fallenness, and this makes us uncomfortable with split-ness in general. In contrast to our division, God's perfection involves simplicity. Thus, we associate goodness with simplicity and duality with sin. We assume our own eschatological perfection will involve simplicity, just as God is perfect in his simplicity.

If a theological discomfort with the idea of a split anthropology is one of the motives for the rejection of dualist conceptions of the soul, it is important that we investigate this idea's theological merit. This paper is a consideration of what it would mean theologically if there were a disjunction at the heart of our identity that was not the result of sin, that would not be erased in the eschaton. It is not intended as an attempt to argue for one specific sort of anthropology, but rather to investigate the concept of anthropological split-ness itself in a fashion that reaffirms its value for anthropologies of whatever kind. The first section will consider the ways in which a desire to affirm wholeness and reject duality is a part of arguments for a holistic anthropology. This desire is tied to the larger eschatological and ethical concern to affirm the resurrection of the body and responsible living in the world. The second and third sections are a theological critique of this desire to overcome anthropological disjunction, which appeals to an alternative understanding of the resurrection of the body. This demonstration relies

---

5. Such as, for example, Klein's narrative account of the soul in Klein, *The Nature of the Soul: The Soul as Narrative*.

heavily on the thought of Giorgio Agamben. While Agamben is not himself a confessional theologian, he nevertheless opens imaginative possibilities for thinking about anthropological difference theologically. I use him here as a prompt for theological reflection.

This paper is therefore an argument for the importance of retaining the language of duality as a recognition of difference within our nature. It is an argument that can be used as part of a larger argument for a Christian, holistic substance-dualism that does not devalue the material,[6] but could also be used to support alternative accounts of theological anthropology that consider difference to be an important part of human nature, but do not want to conceive of it in substantialist terms.[7] I here attempt to consider carefully the difference between the sort of dualism that leads to devaluations of the material, and is complicit with sin and brokenness, and a duality that is amenable to human salvation. I use the term "division" to indicate the former, problematic dualism, and various terms such as split-ness, duality, and difference, to designate the latter.

## The Desire for Holism

Recent theological arguments for a more holistic anthropology have largely been based upon a reassessment of the biblical understanding of the person, in which, it is claimed, no explicit distinction is made between body and soul. Specifically, theologians and biblical scholars such as H. Wheeler Robinson, Karl Barth, Rudolf Bultmann, and more recently Joel B. Green and N. T. Wright, have largely come to replace the dualist account of the person with a more holistic and physicalist account, based on the argument that Hebrew anthropology is holistic and that this holistic anthropology is consistent across the Old and New Testaments. Joel B. Green claims, for example, that Hebrew words such as *nephesh*, *basar*, and *ruach*, which designate the person in the Old Testament, are not contrasting parts of the person. Rather, they all are used in ways that are both soul-like and body-like. *Nephesh* denotes the human person, but is also used of animals, *basar* refers to both fleshly and spiritual dimensions of the person, and *ruah* is the life of the person.[8] He thus asserts that anything resembling the soul is never spoken of as independent of or outside the body. In the New Testament, likewise,

---

6. This is the sort of dualism supported by John W. Cooper, for example. See Cooper, *Body, Soul, and Life Everlasting*.

7. N. T. Wright might be an example of this, although he prefers to conceive of anthropological difference as multiple, rather than binary.

8. Green, "Bodies—That Is, Human Lives," 157–58.

*psyche* and *pneuma*, words that are often translated as "soul" and "spirit," are much closer to the Old Testament concept of *nephesh* and *ruah*—the life of a person—than they are to the platonic idea of an immortal soul, since the New Testament nowhere talks about a soul that is independently immortal. On the basis of these sorts of textual interpretations, Green, Wright, and others argue that while early Christian dualism is considered to be a result of Greek anthropology, there is no evidence that this Greek anthropology was adopted by Paul and the other writers of the New Testament, despite its influence on other Jewish thinkers, such as Philo and Josephus.[9]

However, biblical scholars acknowledge that inferring the sort of anthropology that this language *does* support is more challenging, and must be based on more than just the vocabulary itself. All of the theologians and biblical scholars mentioned above argue that the biblical narrative supports an anthropology that is more holistic than a dualism in which it is possible for the soul to be separated from the body.[10] Karl Barth, for example, argues that Jesus is one whole man, rather than a union of two substances that can be separated. He says that "Jesus is true man in the sense that He is a whole man, a meaningfully ordered unity of soul and body . . . so much so that one might miss the reality of their difference."[11] As a result, the cure of souls is always bound up with the cure of bodies and the person who follows Christ is "on the way to the same whole manhood which is His own mystery."[12] This Christological wholeness has the ontological implication for Barth that

---

9. N. T. Wright, "Mind, Spirit, Soul and Body"; Green, "Bodies—That Is, Human Lives," 162–63; Bultmann, *Theology of the New Testament* 1:191–211. While this interpretation has recently become influential, it is not the only possible interpretation of the biblical evidence. George H. Kooten, for example, argues that the anthropologies of Paul and Philo are more similar than they are different in that they stress the similarity between God and man as pneumatic. The fall is not the division of the human, but its reduction from *psyche* and *pneuma*, to only a psychic being. The *pneuma* is that by which God and human are joined (Kooten, *Paul's Anthropology in Context*, 271–311). James Barr, in *The Garden of Eden and the Hope of Immortality* argues that the holistic interpretation of persons in Scripture became the dominant reading because society lost interest in the immortal soul such that "much in the turn against immortality of the soul was not a return to the fountainhead of biblical evidence but a climbing on the bandwagon of modern progress" (99).

10. Wright is a partial exception in that he does allow for the possibility of an intermediate state in which the soul is temporarily separated from the body, although this is something negative as it is the result of death. It is not based on an inherent capacity of the soul for immortality, but is dependent upon God's grace and power. Wright, *Surprised by Hope*, 183–87.

11. Barth, *CD* 3/2: 340.

12. Barth, *CD* 3/2:, 327–28.

the term "soul" simply designates the life of the body.[13] Similarly, Green argues that the Hebrew person is an integrated whole based on the fact that humanity's being made in the image of God is based on its being embedded in covenant relationship, such that humans are inseparable from their embodied, communal existence. "Soul" simply designates those embodied capacities that make such relationships possible.[14] Moreover, he argues that Jesus affirms this holistic anthropology in his healing ministry, in which his concern for those he encounters is always simultaneously a concern for their bodies and their spiritual and social situations, such that he does not allow the body to be distinguished from other dimensions of life. Green concludes that "The New Testament writers insist on the concept of soteriological wholism . . . ."[15] Thus, Green makes an unsubstantiated leap from the fact that Jesus is concerned with bodies, implying that soteriology is holistic in the sense that it concerns the whole person, to the conclusion that the soul is simply a term that can be reduced to the bodily capacity for relationship.

One of the theological concerns behind this leap is precisely the desire to affirm such "soteriological wholism." Warren S. Brown and Brad D. Strawn, for example, argue that substance-dualism leads persons to live split lives, to turn their spiritual attention inward, towards the state of an internal soul, rather than outward, towards their relationship with God and the world. They argue that if we consider ourselves to be "wholly integrated physical beings," then there is no interior part to distract us from our concern for our relationship to God, others, and our physical environment.[16] Holistic anthropology is therefore, in part, a response to feminist and ecological critiques of a Christianity that has often, historically, tied up the separation of body and soul with patriarchal denigration of bodily experience and lack of creation care.[17] According to this model, salvation is not a matter of individualistic redemption, but of the restoration of relationship. This concern for a holistic soteriology is also bound up with a renewed emphasis on the resurrection of the body, which has been strongly championed by N. T. Wright. Soteriology is holistic because the salvation for which Christians hope is the resurrection of the body at the time of Christ's second coming, when the New Earth will be established. Wright argues from the New Testament that "the eschatological reality will be a fully integrated and

---

13. Ibid., 350.
14. Green, "Bodies—That Is, Human Lives," 157–58.
15. Ibid., 173.
16. Brown and Strawn, *The Physical Nature of Christian Life*, 7, 14.
17. See, for example McCulloch, *The Deconstruction of Dualism in Theology*. McCulloch does not herself believe that all dualisms necessarily lead to patriarchy.

renewed humanity . . . ."[18] He says that Paul's view of salvation is human integration, that God will be all in all, and all will be brought into the one body of Jesus Christ in the church.[19] We do not escape this world for another, but God comes to rule earth as he does heaven. Human wholeness is therefore rooted in the larger restoration to wholeness of creation in general through heaven coming down to earth as the body of Christ, the church—new Jerusalem.[20]

While I affirm the impulse towards a greater theological concern for the body and the earth, and the notions of harmony and restoration that are here appealed to as part of the Christian understanding of salvation, I do not think that the kind of anthropological holism put forward here is the only way to account for these dimensions of what we hope for. A soteriology that is rooted in the bodily resurrection and involves the entirety of our existence, rather than a single ephemeral part, does not necessarily preclude split-ness within the person. Not every understanding of holism necessarily implies this assumption. If holism simply refers to the salvation of the whole of a person, then there is no objection. However, the assumption that if the whole of the person is saved there can then be no distinction within the person is unjustified. Thus far, the bodily nature of our resurrection has not been demonstrated to preclude there being a split or differentiation that is a part of our nature. It simply means that the whole of our nature will be saved, though not necessarily all in the same way.

Not all of the above theologians suggest this. Wright, for example affirms the radical difference between heaven and earth, while affirming their union in the new creation,[21] just as he describes the person as a "differentiated unity." Despite this affirmation, however, very little is said about the nature of this differentiation. The descriptions that are provided suggest that differences are merely a matter of different perspectives, rather than ontological in any way, as is indicated by describing things like body, soul, and mind as "multi-faceted descriptions of the whole" and "all aspects of the one."[22] For Ray S. Anderson also, difference is merely conceptual. The soul is merely the self-identity of the body, grounded in "the existence of the whole person as a unity."[23] Similarly, Brown and Strawn have no recognition of

18. Wright, "Mind, Spirit, Soul and Body."
19. Ibid.
20. Wright, *Surprised by Hope*, 25, 116. Biblical references include Rom 8; Rom 12, and 1 Thess 5:13.
21. Ibid., 116.
22. Wright, "Mind, Spirit, Soul and Body."
23. Anderson, "On Being Human," 189, 193.

anthropological difference at all, referring to persons as "wholly integrated physical beings."[24]

## The Fear of Duality

The argument for holism is partly the result of a desire to emphasize the embodied and contextual nature of salvation against a recent emphasis on individualism and escapism in many churches. While this impulse is admirable, there is nothing in these doctrines that precludes a conception of differentiation or split-ness within the human that is more than a mere conceptual difference. John W. Cooper acknowledges that substance-dualism has often led to bifurcations of other sorts, such as between spiritual conversion and social justice, but argues nonetheless that there are "no necessary connections between the body-soul distinction and this catalogue of false dichotomies."[25] This association of duality with other, harmful divisions demonstrates that the adoption of a holistic anthropology is partially motivated by a fear of such harmful dualisms.

A particularly poignant example of this is found in the Christian philosopher Lynne Rudder Baker's argument for "constitutionalism," and against mind-body dualism. She argues that in light of the fact that there are not strong enough arguments that would make mind-body dualism logically or biblically necessary, we ought to reject it based on the belief that one ought not to introduce bifurcations into reality where they are unnecessary, since we make better sense of the world when we do not bifurcate it.[26] She argues that since a non-split description of the person accounts for all of the things that we care about in defining the person, such as the existence and continuation of personal identity, in the interest of parsimony we should not introduce a split where it is not necessary.[27] Baker's rationale for the rejection of a split within the human is in this case based on a privileging of logical parsimony and epistemological ease of understanding. Moreover, Baker suggests that "constitutionalism," the more holistic anthropology that she puts forward, provides an obvious, logical reason for the embodied nature of life after death in that our personhood is dependent upon our bodies.[28] The implication is that mind-body dualism makes the resurrection of the body an unnecessary add-on to the faith. However, this overlooks

---

24. Brown and Strawn, *Physical Nature*, 14.
25. Cooper, *Body, Soul & Life Everlasting*, 181.
26. Baker, "Christians Should Reject Mind-Body Dualism," 334.
27. Ibid., 335.
28. Ibid., 337.

the fact that in Christian theology, the embodied nature of our resurrection is primarily the result of our participation in Christ's bodily resurrection, rather than the result of our own, independent anthropology. To forget this is to make the theological mistake of making immortality independent of God, which is precisely one of the fears regarding dualism, namely that the soul's immortality is located in its own nature, rather than in relationship to God.[29] Likewise, in this case, it is the resurrection that is made to be dependent on our own anthropology, rather than on Christ. This demonstrates that anthropological holism does not necessarily guard against the mistakes associated with dualism. In this example, the division between body and immortal soul is simply recast as a division between anthropological resurrection that can be understood independently of theology, and Christ's resurrection. Harmful, soteriological bifurcations may persist despite a holistic anthropology.

This points to a second problem with Baker's approach. Namely, she assumes that once we have demonstrated that a bifurcation is not necessary for explanatory reasons, removing it is a simple matter. I argue instead that split-ness is not something that we can so easily escape, and our responsibility, as the above example demonstrates, is instead to differentiate between theologically problematic divisions and theologically faithful differentiations. The fear of harmful dualisms cannot be allowed to become a fear of duality itself as the result may be a holistic anthropology that nevertheless allows other, harmful divisions to persist out of sight. The contemporary philosopher Giorgio Agamben considers our inability to escape duality. Agamben suggests that "life" itself is a concept that cannot be defined, but only divided. He says of life that

> this thing that remains indeterminate gets articulated and divided time and again through a series of caesurae and oppositions that invest it with a decisive strategic function in domains as apparently distant as philosophy, theology, politics, and—only later—medicine and biology. That is to say, everything happens as if, in our culture, life were what cannot be defined, yet, precisely for this reason, must be ceaselessly articulated and divided.[30]

Thus we divide vegetable life from animal life, and divide up the animal kingdom into various tiers and categories. Most notably we divide ourselves

29. I am not here suggesting that Christians who accept dualism believe that the soul can exist independently of God, but Platonic and Cartesian dualisms suggest that immortality is not fundamentally dependent on the bodily resurrection of Christ, but is an inherent characteristic of the soul, and Christian dualism is sometimes, rightly or wrongly, associated with Platonic or Cartesian dualism and rejected on that basis.

30. Agamben, *The Open*, 13.

from the rest of the animal kingdom. The Genesis account of the man's recognition of his difference from the animals that he names over against his unity with the woman created of his own body is consistent with Agamben's assessment.

Much of Agamben's work is an engagement with and exposure of the various splits in our cultures and societies that we have attempted (unsuccessfully) to conceal. The central theme of his anthropology is that there is a split at the very heart of what it means to be human. Indeed, Alex Murray has suggested that all of Agamben's work emerges "out of this sense that there is something irresolvably split at the heart of the human . . . and that we construct our world by simultaneously attempting to cover up the split (giving meaning to words, the human), yet also relying on that split to construct narratives and stories that can explain our own existence."[31] Agamben's book *The Open: Man and Animal* considers how our humanity is constructed and negotiated as an interaction with this split. Our divisions of life are not arbitrary, but are in the service of the anthropological machine—the apparatus according to which we generate our identity. The distinguishing characteristic of the human is its ability to recognize itself as human, such that in order truly to be human it must recognize itself as such. The human must raise itself above its own animality.[32] Its identity is based upon self-recognition and therefore requires that a division be introduced between human and non-human, as in Genesis. But in making this division, the human also acquires a split in its nature, between its animal component (*homo*)—the human as object, and the higher component that recognizes itself as human (*sapien*)—the human as subject.[33] The result is that "The animal-man and the man-animal are the two sides of a single fracture, which cannot be mended from either side."[34] "*Homo sapien*, then,

---

31. Murray, *Giorgio Agamben*, 20–21.

32. Agamben, *The Open*, 26.

33. While we often think about this split between the animal component and the human component as the division between body and soul, Agamben also describes it in terms of language. The human is distinguished from the animal as that which has language. However, the human does not have a distinct voice in the way that other animals do, such that the human's possession of language is based upon a lack or an absence. He asks "Is there a human voice that is the voice of man as the chirp is the voice of the cricket or the bray is the voice of the donkey? And if it exists, is this voice language? What is the relationship between voice and language, between *phonē* and *logos*? And if such a thing as the human voice does not exist, in what sense can man still be defined as the living being which has language?" Agamben, *Infancy and History*, 3–4. These various splits in the human such as body/soul, human/animal, and voice/language are not different splits, but various perspectives on the split nature of the human.

34. Agamben, *The Open*, 36.

is neither a clearly defined species nor a substance; it is, rather, a machine or device for producing the recognition of the human."[35]

This machine operates through the externalization of this opposition between human and inhuman. A determinate identity known as "human" is always presupposed and then mapped onto an opposition between human and inhuman, such that certain beings are included in the category and others are excluded. The notion of the human as an identifiable unity is presupposed, and something else which is identified as not-human, is then excluded. This not-human other is usually the animal, but the machine is an example of another possible not-human other. The difficulty with this logic of inclusion and exclusion is that it generates a zone of indeterminacy in which certain humans are animalized because they do not correspond to the pre-identified category of "human." This logic plays a part in political atrocities, such as genocide, the concentration camp, and colonialism.[36] So, because the caesura between body and soul is exteriorized into a division between the human species and non-human species, humanity becomes violently defined according the exclusion of that which is arbitrarily deemed not-human.

The more we try to understand ourselves as a unity, over and against other unities, pushing the split within ourselves to the periphery of our existence in order to make it do the work of generating our identity, the more we generate violence as well. Attempts to cover over our splitness are therefore merely new examples of the anthropological machine at work. For example, Agamben is suspicious of recent physicalist attempts to "biologize" humanity. He suggests that one cannot construct a personal identity based on biological data alone, although this is in fact what is now being attempted through biometric technology.[37] Such an identity is one that is stripped of will and community, and is reduced to biological markers. And yet, at the same time, this biological identity is promised the ability to assume multiple social personae at will, through phenomena like the internet,[38] although these identities do not belong to the person in any physical, biological way. This is another example of an attempt to cover-over the split in humanity between something like body and soul, by reducing the meaning and identity of the person to its body. However, we are blinded to the fact that this split continues out of sight as a distinction between physical identity, and willed social identity independent of the body. The more we attempt to

35. Ibid., 26.
36. Ibid., 37, 22.
37. Agamben, *Nudities*, 51.
38. Ibid., 53.

reduce the identity of the human person to his or her body, the more social identity and relationship become bifurcated from it. We do not overcome the split, we simply replace it with a different split, often one that is more exaggerated than that between body and soul.

By attending to Agamben's thought in this way, I do not mean to suggest that recent theological attempts to imagine a holistic anthropology introduce the *same* split between the biological and the social (indeed, this is precisely what thinkers such as Brown are attempting to fight against in locating our identity in bodily community), but rather to draw attention to the hitherto unperceived risks implicit in attempting to establish such a unity at all. Agamben's arguments for the indispensability of anthropological division draw attention to the peril of superficially "covering over" difference such that it re-emerges in dangerous and hidden forms. Even Wright notes that there are biblical examples of integrations and unities of death and sin. In Ephesians 4, for example, mind, body, understanding, and heart have all been integrated through being given over to sin and death.[39] Romans 1 also connects the darkening of heart, knowledge, and imagination with various sorts of bodily sin. Not all unity and holism is good. Given that it is more difficult than we might think to remove bifurcation from human nature, the ethical and theological implications of a split nature and the ways in which such a split could be compatible with Christian soteriology and eschatology must be considered seriously.

## Redeeming Split-ness

Agamben is clearly not sympathetic towards the anthropogenic machine and the split that powers it. His approach to split-ness, however, is to avoid covering it over hastily through premature unifying and universalizing tendencies. A more appropriate way to think about our identity is to be more attentive to this split itself, to confront the paradox:

> In our culture, man has always been thought of as the articulation and conjunction of a body and a soul, of a living thing and a *logos*, of a natural (or animal) element and a supernatural or social or divine element. We must learn instead to think of man as what results from the incongruity of these two elements, and investigate not the metaphysical mystery of conjunction, but rather the practical and political mystery of separation.[40]

---

39. Wright, "Mind, Spirit, Soul and Body."
40. Agamben, *The Open*, 16.

We are so accustomed to thinking of ourselves as a conjunction of two things that we gloss over the obvious point that in order for there to be a conjunction, there must first be some sort of separation, no matter how slight. Thus, even if we, as Christians, want to affirm that the person participating in the realities of salvation and the eschaton is an integrated whole, we must nevertheless come to terms with the fact that certain dimensions or components of the person which are different from one another have been integrated, and this internal differentiation must play some part in our anthropology.

I will here continue to follow Agamben's indications for how it is that we might think about such split-ness or differentiation in the context of salvation and eschatology. While Agamben is not a theologian, he nevertheless frequently engages with theological themes, thinkers, and ideas. Examples include his work on Paul's letter to the Romans, messianism, sacrifice, judgment day, and redemption. Dickinson, in *Agamben and Theology*, draws several further theological parallels that Agamben does not explicate, but that are nevertheless convincing.[41] Moreover, Agamben does not think about his interest in these theological concepts as a simple looting of the tradition, but as an attempt to re-affirm what he believes to be the real, more originary, messianism that has been bent out of shape through its complicity with the anthropological machine. For example, he opens his commentary on the Letter to the Romans by saying

> First and foremost, this seminar proposes to restore Paul's letters to the status of the fundamental messianic text for the Western tradition. This would seem a banal task, for no one would seriously deny the messianic character of the Letters. And yet, this is not self-evident, since two thousand years of translation and commentary coinciding with the history of the Christian church have literally cancelled out the messianic, and the word Messiah itself, from Paul's text.[42]

This is not to say that Agamben is a Christian thinker, but his objections to Christianity are against certain dimensions of the institution of Christianity and not against Christ himself or the church understood in a particular way. Christian theology has the choice of whether to ignore this move on Agamben's part, or openly to consider whether it has something to learn from Agamben's use of its own concepts. The following explication proceeds

---

41. For example, "Parabasis," the notion that a transcendent actor is transposed into the spectating audience in order to transform it into participants, is a possible way to think about the incarnation of Christ. See Dickinson, *Agamben and Theology*, 33.

42. Agamben, *The Time That Remains*, 1.

according to the latter conviction. It is not intended as dogma, but as an imaginative prompt for how Christians can think about what it might look like for a split nature to be redeemed.

The way in which Agamben addresses splits is by deactivating them, so that while they are still present, they are no longer operative; they do not power an anthropological machine. This does not involve denying or covering the split, but dividing it further. One specifically theological example of this is Agamben's description of the social dimensions of salvation in his commentary on Paul's epistle to the Romans, mentioned above. The principle of the Jewish law is division. It divides the Jews from the Gentiles. However, messianic salvation does not obliterate the division between Jews and Gentiles, thereby producing a sameness or equality between them that allows all to be saved. Gentiles do not become Jews or vice versa. Rather, the division between Jews and Gentiles is itself divided. Paul sets the division *sarx/pneuma* to work against the division of the law. This is not a division that is identical to the law, but it is not external to it either.[43] It is "a separation to the second power, a separation which, in its very separateness, divides and traverses the divisions of Pharisaic laws,"[44] such that the category "Jew" is further divided into Jew according to the flesh, and Jew according to the spirit, and the same occurs with the category "Gentile." Some Jews are now not Jews and some non-Jews are not non-Jews. Thus, in dividing the division, a remnant or remainder is opened up that cannot be associated with either Jew or non-Jew, making it impossible for a category perfectly to coincide with itself.[45] Agamben defines this remnant as "neither the all, nor a part of the all, but the impossibility for the part and the all to coincide with themselves or with each other."[46] The result is that the legal operations of the Jew-Gentile division are rendered inoperative; not abolished, but suspended. Agamben believes this point to be important because it demonstrates that salvation for Paul is not a universalizing "production of the Same."[47] Salvation is not a matter of holistic integration.

The anthropological machine operates in the same way as the law, in that it is based on the logic of inclusion and exclusion. Rendering this machine inoperative according to the same messianic logic would therefore involve dividing the division between soul and body, such that neither can one side of the split coincide precisely with itself leading to the logic of

43. Ibid., 49.
44. Ibid., 46.
45. Ibid., 50–51.
46. Ibid., 55.
47. Ibid., 52.

inclusion and exclusion, nor can they coincide with one another and be synthesized into a third, universal identity. The division between body and soul, or animal element and human element, is also divided by the *sarx/pneuma* division, such that the category "body" is divided into "body according to the flesh" and "body according to the spirit," and the category "soul" becomes "soul according to the flesh" and "soul according to the spirit." We do not here have a simple substance-dualism, but nor is the soteriological movement one of holistic integration. Rather, the person becomes "the sieve in which creatural life and spirit, creation and redemption, nature and history are continually discerned and separated, yet nevertheless continue to conspire toward their own salvation."[48] Agamben says that salvation, with respect to the human and animal, means precisely that "neither must man master nature nor nature man. Nor must both be surpassed in a third term that would represent their dialectical synthesis[;] . . . what is decisive here is only the 'between,' the interval or, we might say, the play between the two terms, their immediate constellation in a non-coincidence."[49] This approach to salvation as the multiplication of difference in a constellation is attractive because it causes us to question what it is that we mean when we think about salvation as harmony or unity. Rather than assuming that it implies an undifferentiated whole, which is not significantly different from a monad, Agamben reminds us of the relational dimension of salvation and allows this dimension to permeate the person.[50] In the same way that salvation does not imply that we become equal to God or subsumed by God, but that our difference from God is retained even in eschatological intimacy, redeemed anthropology is one in which the relationship of the person to itself is of the kind that is made possible in its difference from itself.

Agamben finds a resource for imagining what this might look like in patristic and medieval discussions surrounding the nature of the resurrected body. One of the frequent questions with respect to the resurrected body in these discussions was "If one's body is going to be raised materially at the *parousia*, how much of it must be raised if it is to be materially the same as one's pre-resurrection body?" The answers to this question understandably became quite convoluted, such that the idea of an "integral material

48. Agamben, *The Open*, 82.

49. Ibid., 83.

50. Significantly, this emphasis on relationality is a large part of the turn to holism, since this anthropology recognizes the person as determined in relationship to God, world, others, and even self. Despite this fact, however, and the assertion that the rejection of dualism needn't lead to monism, this relationality is not permitted to enter into the self's relation to itself, or if it is, we are never told how this is possible or what it looks like. Shults, *Reforming Theological Anthropology*, 181–83.

identity" eventually became replaced with a conception of the resurrected body in which the body's image, or likeness to itself, remains immutable, but its material composition is in a state of ebb and flow.[51] An example of this is Aquinas' metaphor for the resurrected body as a city which retains its identity as this or that city, even as the residents continually change. He says that "In like manner, while certain parts are on the ebb and others are being restored to the same shape and position, all the parts flow back and forth as to their matter, but remain as to their species; and nevertheless the selfsame man remains."[52]

This opens up the possibility of a certain movement appropriate to the post-resurrection body, both as a whole as well as with respect to its internal processes. This glorified-movement is distinct from the movement of our present bodies in that it is not goal-directed. The glorified bodies move like dancers, without aim or necessity, only in order to exhibit their agility.[53] Likewise, with respect to bodily functions such as digestion, there is operation without teleology. So, "[t]he organ or instrument that was separated from its operation and remains, so to speak, in a state of suspension, acquires, precisely for this reason, an ostensive function; it exhibits the virtue corresponding to the suspended operation."[54] The organs cannot be used, they can only be displayed through a movement of "inoperativity," or Sabbath rest—a sort of empty repetition in which the functions of the body are not directed towards a goal, but exhibit themselves in a movement for the glorification of God.[55]

---

51. Agamben, *Nudities*, 93.

52. Aquinas, *Summa Theologiae*, suppl., q. 80, a. 4.

53. Agamben, *Nudities*, 95–96. Aquinas quotes Augustine saying that the resurrected body will possess movement without fatigue and the ability to eat without hunger. *Summa Theologiae* I, q. 97, a. 4.

54. Agamben, *Nudities*, 98.

55. Agamben does not put this extrapolation forward as an interpretation of Aquinas or Augustine, but as his own description. Retaining the form of something while emptying it of its traditional content is a common move for Agamben. For example, in *The Coming Community*, Agamben retains the concept of community but empties it of the categories according to which belonging to a community usually take place (race, interests, biology, etc.) and makes the criteria for community the concept of belonging itself, emptied of any other category of belonging. I interpret Agamben as doing something similar in this case, such that the movements of the body are emptied of any of the reasons for which such movement usually takes place and are simply exhibited in themselves. Arguably, these movements are the opposite of empty since they are here fulfilled in their purpose. However, Agamben's point is that we cannot think what this would look like independently of the processes in which they are here involved, such that this movement appears empty and without purpose from our perspective.

According to this account, the resurrected person, in a sense, continues to be split, but the split of soul/body becomes a split between the likeness of the body and the movement of the body. The body's image or likeness to itself, on the one hand, is the site of the immutability and eternity of the resurrected body, but there exists on the other hand a certain kind of movement, or rhythm of ebb and flow, that is also appropriate to the resurrected body. A glorified anthropology is one in which man is traversed by two different sorts of redemption appropriate to both sides of the split. On the one hand, there is a raising of the soul to immutability, but this would be artificial without the saving of the body for its own distinct salvation precisely as creaturely and transient. However, this is not to say that these two things—immutable likeness and material movement—map perfectly onto soul and body. The soteriological remnant means that the glorified body is that in which the immutable likeness (soul) includes some of that which is not immutable—the movement of the material. The body's likeness to itself is a moving likeness because the material is in motion. Likewise, glorified material movement always contains its immutable likeness and is freed from transience and teleology. Yet these things are not identical to one another. Their difference is what allows for their interaction. The division between soul and body is itself divided such that the strict division between immutable soul and mutable body is problematized to create new eschatological categories of moving soul and immutable body. These do not replace immutable soul and mutable body, but they enter into the relationship of the person to itself thereby preventing the duality from being a simple opposition between one part and another. The parts here cannot coincide with themselves, but are always related to themselves at the same time as they are related to their other. This is what Agamben means when he says that soul and body remain distinct, but they conspire together towards their salvation. On this account, salvation is not a matter of attempting to master and overcome the body-soul relationship, but of learning to rest within its non-identicality. Unification comes about, not through fusion, but through further differentiation. The implication of Agamben's emphasis on the split within the human is that the unifying movement that is the relationship between the two sides of the split is made possible by their non-coincidence. The split-ness is itself the location of salvation, and not a barrier to be overcome.

In this depiction, salvation is an anthropological self-relationship which is freed from the goal-directedness of the anthropological machine, and the tendency towards the domination of one side of the split over the other. Instead, the split is exhibited to the glory of God. According to this understanding, the split is so fundamental to human nature that it will, in some glorified way, persist in the eschaton. Disjunction and salvation, caesura and glorification, are not mutually exclusive. Duality itself is not a result of sin that must be overcome in salvation. It is only the violent uses to which this split-ness is put that are overcome.

## Conclusion

I have put forward Agamben's anthropology as an alternative to anthropological holism as a possible way of thinking about the redeemed person as someone for whom relationship penetrates the core of their being. Holism gives us a picture of atomistic anthropology in which persons are externally in relationship, but are internally monads, albeit multi-faceted monads. Recall Anderson's statement above that the soul is the self-identity of the body. The implication of this picture is that the person can be delineated and circumscribed in opposition to other identities. The self is known through a kind of conceptual mapping. As Agamben points out, however, this way of thinking can have violent consequences. If, in contrast, we think about redeemed anthropology as a redeemed duality, then salvation is not only a restored relationship-in-difference between the person and the world, and the person and God, but also between the person and itself. This self is not known through simple identification, but through participating in and undergoing the movements of this self-relation in and through the process of salvation.

Agamben's account is helpful because while he recognizes the problematic dimensions of dualism, he does not therefore hastily reject all duality, but seriously considers how these problematic elements could be redeemed. According to this account, the human is the site of two modes of salvation that intersect one another. It is an account of creaturely perfection that does not exclude non-coincidence. Agamben's doubling of the duality neither overcomes it into a monad of sameness, nor allows it to remain a simple opposition between two identities, but retains the relationality and difference within the person, while also allowing these differences to work together to make a redeemed person, rather than pulling apart from one another as in Platonic or Cartesian dualism, for example. In this way, Agamben's description is an important exploration of how anthropological difference can correspond to our doctrines of soteriology and bodily resurrection in the eschaton. This is an attempt to imagine a salvation that is appropriate to our nature, rather than one that covers over our nature, by considering that if human salvation involves integration, it also presupposes separation and therefore requires a unity and integration that respects this differentiation.

This is not say that Agamben's suggestions are sufficient for a theological account of the redemption of a split. We noted above that ultimately the persistence of the person in Christian theology must be made possible through his or her participation in the resurrection of Christ, regardless of whether we conceptualize this in terms of the resurrection of the body only, or include the concept of the immortality of the soul. There is very little about this in Agamben, and it is an important concept that would need to be introduced into Agamben's description from elsewhere. Nevertheless, it is not difficult to conceptualize a self-relation that is simultaneously redemptively interrupted and thereby held together in Christ, for example.[56]

Finally, describing soteriological anthropology as participation in the movements of self-relation implies that these points are important not only for our doctrine of soteriology, but also for how it is that we experience these movements of salvation now. Christians believe that eschatological redemption is already breaking into the now, as is demonstrated in the resurrection of Christ, and enacted on the Sabbath. Agamben says that on the Sabbath "what is done ... becomes undone, rendered inoperative, liberated and suspended from its 'economy,' from the reasons and aims that define it during the weekdays...."[57] If much of our work with respect to anthropology is directed towards defining ourselves over-against that which is other, the Sabbath represents those eschatological moments when we suspend the concepts of soul and body from the economy of the anthropological machine and participate in their redemption by learning to live in the unified tension of their non-coincidence.

## Bibliography

Agamben, Giorgio. *Infancy and History On the Destruction of Experience*. Translated by Liz Heron. London: Verso, 1993.
———. *Nudities*. Translated by David Kishik and Stefan Pedatella. Stanford, CA: Stanford University Press.
———. *The Coming Community*. Translated by Michael Hardt. Minneapolis, MN: University of Minnesota Press, 1993.
———. *The Open: Man and Animal*. Translated by Kevin Attell. Stanford, CA: Stanford University Press.
———. *The Time That Remains: A Commentary on the Letter to the Romans*. Translated by Patricia Dailey. Stanford, CA: Stanford University Press, 2005.
Anderson, Ray S. "On Being Human: The Spiritual Saga of a Creaturely Soul." In *Whatever Happened to the Soul? Scientific and Theological Portraits of Human*

---

56. One example of someone who might be able to provide this is Søren Kierkegaard in *The Sickness unto Death*.
57. Agamben, *Nudities*, 111.

*Nature*, edited by Warren Brown, Nancey Murphy, and H. Newton Malony, 175–194. Minneapolis, MN: Fortress, 1999.
Baker, Lynne Rudder. "Christians Should Reject Mind-Body Dualism." In *Contemporary Debates in Philosophy of Religion*, edited by Michael L. Peterson and Raymond J. Van Arragon, 327–38. Oxford: Blackwell, 2004.
Barr, James. *The Garden of Eden and The Hope of Immortality*. London: SCM, 1992.
Barth, Karl. *Church Dogmatics* III.2: The Doctrine of Creation. Translated and edited by G. W. Bromily, T. F. Torrance. London: T. & T. Clark, 2004.
Brown, Warren S., and Brad D. Strawn. *The Physical Nature of Christian Life: Neuroscience, Psychology & the Church*. Cambridge: Cambridge University Press, 2012.
Brown, Warren S., et al., eds. *Whatever Happened to the Soul? Scientific and Theological Portraits of Human Nature*. Minneapolis, MN: Fortress, 1999.
Bultmann, Rudolf. *Theology of the New Testament*. Vol 1. New York: Scribner's Sons, 1951.
Cooper, John W. *Body, Soul & Life Everlasting: Biblical Anthropology and the Monism-Dualism Debate*. Grand Rapids: Eerdmans, 1989.
Dickinson, Colby. *Agamben and Theology*. London: T. & T. Clark, 2011.
Green, Joel B. "'Bodies—That Is, Human Lives': A Re-Examination of Human Nature in the Bible." In *Whatever Happened to the Soul? Scientific and Theological Portraits of Human Nature*, edited by Warren Brown, Nancey Murphy, and H. Newton Malony, 149–74. Minneapolis, MN: Fortress, 1999.
———. *Body, Soul, and Human Life: The Nature of Humanity in the Bible*. Grand Rapids: Baker Academic, 2008.
Kierkegaard, Søren. *The Sickness Unto Death*. Edited and translated by Howard V. Hong and Edna H. Hong. Princeton, NJ: Princeton University Press, 1983.
Klein, Terrance W. *The Nature of the Soul: The Soul as Narrative*. Farnham, UK: Ashgate, 2012.
Kooten, Guert Henrik van. *Paul's Anthropology in Context: The Image of God, Assimilation to God, and Tripartite Man in Ancient Judaism, Ancient Philosophy, and Early Christianity*. Tübingen: Mohr Siebeck, 2008.
McCulloch, Gillian. *The Deconstruction of Dualism in Theology: With Special Reference to Ecofeminist Theology and New Age Spirituality*. Carlisle, UK: Paternoster, 2002.
Murphy, Nancey. *Bodies and Souls, or Spirited Bodies? Human Nature at the Intersection*. Cambridge: Cambridge University Press, 2006.
Murphy, Nancey, and Warren S. Brown. *Did My Neurons Make Me Do It?*. Oxford: Clarendon, 2007.
Murray, Alex. *Giorgio Agamben: An Introduction*. London: Routledge, 2010.
Shults, F. LeRon. *Reforming Theological Anthropology: After the Philosophical Turn to Relationality*. Grand Rapids: Eerdmans, 2003.
Wright, N. T. "Mind, Spirit, Soul and Body: All for One and One for All, Reflections on Paul's Anthropology in his Complex Contexts." Paper presented at the Society of Christian Philosophers, Regional Meeting, Fordham University, 2011. Online: http://ntwrightpage.com/Wright_SCP_MindSpiritSoulBody.htm. Accessed November 15th, 2013.
———. *Surprised by Hope*. London: SPCK, 2007.

# 15

## Music and Liminal Ethics

### Facilitating a "Soulful Reality"

FÉRDIA J. STONE-DAVIS

Very simply, "soul" is the medium in which we dwell as human beings. There is no other space in which we could humanly live. As the possessors of souls, we are able to move our bodies, whose parts are coherently held together in a pattern that can itself be described as soul. A soulful reality is a shape deemed "living" by virtue of its capacity to reposition and reshape itself within its environment.[1]

"Futility music" and "gender coercion" can force human beings like Muhammed al-Qatani to cause themselves psychic rather than physical pain. Deriving directly from who they are or have chosen to be as enculturated human beings, that is, as persons, not only as sensate biological organisms—this psychic pain attacks its target and causes self-betrayal in the intrasubjective space that many religious traditions call the soul.[2]

---

1. Milbank, "The Politics of the Soul," 1; available at http://theologyphilosophycentre.co.uk/papers/Milbank_PoliticsOfTheSoul.pdf.
2. Cusick, "'You are in a place that is out of the world . . .': Music in the Detention Camps of the 'Global War on Terror,'" 17. Cusick states: "[t]he purpose of such "futility" techniques as "loud music" and "gender coercion" is to persuade a detainee that resistance to interrogation is futile." Ibid., 1 (abstract).

THIS ARTICLE TAKES AS its starting-point the conception of the soul as "the medium in which we dwell as human beings." It also acknowledges that this dwelling occurs relationally, since it is only in response to and in dialogue with an environment that a "soulful reality" can emerge. It is on this basis that a consideration of music is undertaken. Music operates by means of thresholds, encouraging a certain porosity that mediates notions of "inner" and "outer" in a unique way, and facilitating the development of the subject as both "interior" and "exterior," both "active" and "passive," as both "giver" and "recipient." On this basis, music practices have the capacity to enable and constrain the subject, and processes of world-making. The chapter will proceed in three steps: first, the idea of world-making will be elaborated; second, music's mode of being as threshold will be set forth, as will the impact of its constitutive thresholds upon the more fundamental one between subject and other; third, noting the resistance and vulnerability of the encounters that occur between subject and other in the music event, steps towards a liminal ethics will be made. It will be suggested that the thresholds in operation within a music event can be evaluated, as can their capacity to facilitate the development of a "soulful reality," with wonder standing as a marker of the tension between intimacy and resistance, proximity and distance.

## World-Making

By world-making I refer to attempts to make sense of the human person, the environment in which she is situated, and the relationship between the two.[3] Such attempts necessarily rely on and arise from an interaction between the subject and her environment, which includes the physical world, but also other subjects. Within this interaction a sense of feeling "at-home" in the world is enabled. Such attempts do not arise simply from intellectual effort, but emerge more fundamentally through physical interaction: "life goes on in an environment, not merely *in* it but because of it, through interaction with it. No creature lives merely under its skin, its subcutaneous organs are means of connection with what lies beyond its bodily frame."[4] Thus, "by the time we think about things, or explicitly perceive them as what they are, we have already been immersed in their pragmatic meaning."[5]

---

3. Limiting world-making to the human person acknowledges the imaginative character of the response to the environment that distinguishes human action from other forms of animal action.

4. Dewey, *Art as Experience*, 12.

5. Gallagher, "Philosophical Antecedents of Situated Cognition," 39. This resonates

It is by virtue of the dynamic between the subject and her environment that certain objects in the world afford different interpretations and uses in particular situations and to certain individuals or groups: "perceptual specification is a reciprocal relationship between the invariants of the environment and the particular capacities of the perceiver."[6] For this reason, a stick will afford throwing or burning depending upon the mode of engagement that a subject has with the object, which is influenced in turn by the circumstances informing the engagement. Thus, time and space are not neutral frames since they are related in the first instance to the kinds of activity in which the subject is engaged; it is on this basis that ideas of "quick" and "slow," "far" and "close," are determined.[7]

## Music, World-Making and Threshold

The interaction between the subject and her environment, the process of world-making (which occurs both physically and imaginatively), happens within music as well. It does so by virtue of music's mode of existence, which involves thresholds. A threshold (*limen*) is a point at which transition occurs. However, that which is most significant about thresholds is not the *moment of crossing* but the *relation* that is brought about at the *instant before that crossing*, since it is here that binaries such as "inside" and "outside," "subject" and "object," are transcended, brought into relation, and held in tension. In relation to the music event,[8] then, different but interrelating thresholds are at work—"sensory," "processual," and "relational." The thresholds operate *in* time but also *across* time and impact upon a more fundamental threshold between the subject and that which is "other" than the subject, creating an

---

with Ingold's understanding of the "taskscape" which encompasses the myriad activities that comprise "dwelling." Ingold, "The Temporality of the Landscape."

6. Clarke, *Ways of Listening*, 44.

7. Gallagher, "Philosophical Antecedents of Situated Cognition," 41. This of course stands against conceiving time and space as absolutes, which is typically thought to occur primarily in the course of modernity. Edward Casey explains: "Beginning with Philoponus in the sixth century A.D. and reaching an apogee in fourteenth-century theology and above all in seventeenth-century physics, place has been assimilated to space. The latter, regarded as infinite extension, has become a cosmic and extra-cosmic Moloch that consumes every corpuscle of place to be found within its greedy reach. . . . [I]n the course of the eighteenth and nineteenth centuries place was also made subject to time, regarded as chronometric and universal, indeed as 'the formal *a priori* condition of all appearances whatsoever,' in Kant's commanding phrase" (Casey, *The Fate of Place: A Philosophical History*, x).

8. To think of "music as event" is to keep in mind that music is a temporally-performed practice, occurring in action, within particular contexts.

attunement that relies upon porosity.[9] Although it is difficult, as well as unwise, to unpick the thresholds from one another (since they are mutually reliant) one might distinguish between them within a music event in order to bring certain features to light, relating them to the creation of a "soulful reality."

## *"Sensory" thresholds*

In broad terms, music is sound organized in and through physical activity. It is thus dependent upon "sensory" thresholds. Unlike the relationship between other media and the human senses the effect is immediate and to a degree unstoppable. The aural threshold is easily trespassed, so to speak, commingling the interior and the exterior. It is not only the aural threshold that is easily crossed, however, but the entire body, which internalizes external sounds: "the human experience of sound involves, in addition to the sympathetic vibration of the ear-drums, the sympathetic vibration of the resonators of the body. Sound, shaped and resonating with the properties of the internal and external configurations, textures and movements of the objects of the external world, can thus be felt in addition to being heard."[10] This immediacy of sound to the ear and the body extends further, underpinning the performance of music, as types of sounds are shaped in their production, which occurs through varying forms of physical engagement. Thus, composer Trevor Wishart notes:

> the morphology of intellectual-physiological gestures (an aspect of human behaviour) may be translated directly into the morphology of sound-objects by the action of the larynx, or the musculature and an instrumental transducer. The translation of performance-gesture into the gestural-structure of the sound-object is most complete and convincing where the technology of instrument construction does not present a barrier. Thus, vocal music where there is no socially-constructed mechanical intermediary—and particularly where performance practice has not become dominated by a notation-based system of theory—is the most sensitive carrier of gestural information.[11]

---

9. Elsewhere, I have unpacked thresholds in implicit terms through the moments of "impact," "absorption," and "ekstasis" which are identifiable within the music event. Stone-Davis, *Musical Beauty*, 161 ff.

10. Shepherd and Wicke, *Music and Cultural Theory*, 127.

11. Wishart, *On Sonic Art*, 17–18.

"Sensory" thresholds underpin the physical impact music has on subject(s) and object(s), and it is this that facilitates world-making in "real" time and space. Sound is heard and orients the subject within her physical surroundings: "[r]eflexively turning to look for the source of sound or ducking when you hear something coming from behind would make little sense unless you were aware of sound sources."[12] However, it is not a simple conception of a sound-source that results, for sound imparts information about the environment and the interaction that gives rise to it:

> Because the pattern of frequency components that comprise the vibration of an object and the way that pattern changes over time is determined by the nature of the object and the events that caused it to vibrate, that pattern and the way it changes provide a great deal of information about the object and the interaction that produced the vibration.[13]

Within music practices, "sensory" thresholds provide another means of orientation and world-making: the shaping of sounds allows co-ordination between those making music and extends outwards, making communication with others possible. In short, the "sensory" thresholds of music show knowledge to be grounded in processes informed by the subject "going beyond" herself. Here, subjects, objects, and the environment are gathered together.

## "Processual" thresholds

As physically produced, arising in and through a succession of events that are in some way contiguous with and reliant upon one another rather than standing discretely, music is bound up with "processual" thresholds, since it is only ever in transition. This can be seen in the aspects that constitute the musical experience, including physical processes, such as the dissipation of sound and its organization as it moves through time and space, as well as

---

12. O'Callaghan and Nudds, "Introduction: The Philosophy of Sounds and Auditory Perception," 1–25 (12).

13. Matthew Nudds, "Sounds and Space," 69–96 (71). Thus: "[w]e can perceive the size of an object dropped into water, that something is rolling, the material composition of an object from the sound of an impact, and the force of an impact. We can distinguish objects with different shapes, and we can tell the length of a rod dropped onto the floor. When something is dropped, we can hear whether it bounced or broke. We are good at recognising natural sounds, such as footsteps, hands clapping, paper tearing, and so on. We can tell that a cup is being filled and when it is full" (ibid., 70).

the imaginative processes that accompany these.[14] Here, sound is shaped and transformed into an imaginative realm of intention with its own "field of force."[15] The production of sounds, organized and transmitted, opens up "a phenomenal space of tones" in which the subject is situated and to which she responds.[16] Thus, the "processual" thresholds of music rely upon the resistances built into the physical production of sound and the negotiation of a tone's development that imbues imaginative time and space with shape and feel, giving a sense of height, depth, and extension. As Roger Scruton notes, the timbre of tones allows perception of them as more or less thick, as having a weight and mass, and clusters of tones can appear as "open," "hollow," "filled," and "stretched."[17] Moreover, music consists of many structural levels, spanning from "outlines" supplied by extended configurations of tones, through "inlines" that are more fractional, including those emerging from gesture and articulation such as the "sigh" that accompanies a slurred intervallic movement downwards, and the shape of tones (whether they are short or long, light or heavy). It is in this way that tones are given musically expressive contours that feed into longer configurations. Thus, in both real and imaginative time and space the subject is "taken beyond" its seemingly discrete existence, and is set in relation.

## *"Relational" thresholds*

The music event is also grounded in "relational" thresholds, which can be conceived in terms of a set of concentric circles.[18] These reflect the dynamism of musical activity as it extends itself, bringing together discrete existences at every level of the social, including objects, people, ideas, events, activities, and modes of communication. However, significantly, even the central point upon which the circles converge is not singular, but is relational. Musical activity involves the relation of the subject to that which is "other," including the relationship between the subject and the material object that issues forth the sound upon being struck, plucked, bowed, blown, or programmed, and the relationship of the subject to a set of similar other

---

14. A discussion of music and time can be found in Stone-Davis, *Musical Beauty*, 167–78. For an exploration of "Music, space, and subjectivity," see Clarke, in *Music, Sound and Space*, 90–110.

15. Scruton, *The Aesthetics of Music*, 17.

16. Ibid., 75.

17. Ibid., 78.

18. The types of relations invoked by music here have some similarities to the "assemblages" remarked upon by Georgina Born in her article "Listening, Mediation and Event: Anthropological and Sociological Perspectives," 79–89, see especially 87–88.

material objects, the space within which the sound is produced, and the sets of interpersonal relationships that are forged. Moreover, the music event brings the subject and these various sets of relations into contact with a myriad of other relations since it draws together past, present, and future. Thus, music allows the interaction between the subject and her environment to be honed and/or restructured by modifying the subject's way of being in the world as she goes about her everyday activities. The imaginative time and space of the musical place can entrain and support the subject so that she can achieve more within a particular context, for example, the use of music to order the bodies of subjects doing aerobics.[19] It can also reshape and personalize the soundscape within which the subject is immersed, for example, through the use of mobile audio devices, so that "manageable sites of habitation"[20] or, in my terms, a "world-within-a-world," can be created.[21]

In other terms, then, music's capacity to world-make through the "sensory," "processual," and "relational" thresholds upon which it depends implicates it in the development and sustenance of the soul, for it undercuts divisions of "inner" and "outer," "nature" and "culture" and allows the human person to "reposition and reshape itself within its environment." It is on this basis that a "liminal ethics" becomes important.

## Wonder, the Co-Existence of Proximity and Distance, and Liminal Ethics

To summarize: understanding music by means of threshold brings to light the porosity of the subject within the music event, where she stands at the threshold of the dichotomies of "subject" and "object" (and thereby "interior" and "exterior," "active" and "passive," "giver" and "recipient"). Herein, the subject becomes sensitized to the other, to the otherness of the other, and simultaneously, to the other's proximity. It is fruitful to consider this

---

19. Tia DeNora identifies core components of this process, where music organizes bodily activity: "warm up," "pre-core," "core," "cool-down," and "floor exercises." *Music in Everyday Life*, 90–91.

20. Bull, *Sounding Out the City*, 2.

21. World-making also happens at a meta-level by means of intellectual reflection, which sets certain frameworks in place which not only throw into relief certain aspects of human beings and the world but in doing so influence and shape understandings and practices of music. For an example of the ways in which understandings of music are underpinned by surrounding philosophies, see Stone-Davis, *Musical Beauty*; Bowie, *Music Philosophy and Modernity*. For an example of how philosophies impact on music practices specifically see Goehr, *The Imaginary Museum of Musical Works*.

process through the notion of "wonder," for wonder points to the intimate nature of the contact that the music event yields.[22]

By wonder I do not simply mean that which can accompany epistemological and material curiosity. Such wonder is grounded in a drive for knowledge that in some sense seeks to possess and is always looking to assimilate, looking for the next thing to be known or grasped. This wonder is associated with appropriation, since it is allied with a desire to bring experience under reason and is to a degree instrumental in focus: the object is analyzed and made intelligible by the subject.[23] A more fitting understanding of wonder resonates with something like the phenomenological reduction that was advocated by Merleau-Ponty. Here, the conscious conceptual mode of engagement with the world is suspended and the intentional threads that bind the subject to the world are slackened. In this way, the world is revealed as "strange and paradoxical."[24] This slackening is expressed elsewhere: "To return to the things in themselves is to return to that world which precedes knowledge, of which knowledge always *speaks*, and in relation to which scientific schematization is an abstract and derivative sign-language, as is geography in relation to the countryside in which we have learnt beforehand what a forest, a prairie, or a river is."[25]

It is this type of wonder that we can see at work in the music event. Music impacts physically, announcing its presence, eliciting the attention of the subject, and inviting the subject's engagement. Within such experiences, the usual approach to the world is deferred for we do not experience in order to acquire a particular knowledge. Rather, the drive to rationalize and instrumentalize is postponed and one becomes exposed to that which is unforeseen and potentially disruptive, since that which is presented lies beyond our conscious conceptual frameworks and resists reduction. As a result, such experiences do not stand instrumentally, but are ends in themselves. Moreover, the other gives itself, but never completely.

Thus understood, wonder turns our attention to a fundamental element of the music event and forms the basis of what we might call a "liminal ethics," since it is a marker of both intimacy and resistance, a co-existence, as it were, of proximity and distance. A liminal ethics, then, arises from the recognition that the music event relies upon and operates by means of thresholds. It allows one to approach a music event and detect which

22. Stone-Davis, *Musical Beauty*, 185–90.

23. For a detailed consideration of different understandings of wonder see Ronald W. Hepburn, "The Inaugural Address: Wonder," 1–23.

24. Merleau-Ponty, *Phenomenology of Perception*, xv.

25. Ibid., x–xi.

thresholds are at work, and how. More importantly, it acknowledges that these thresholds are underpinned by another, the one between subject and other, and that a certain irreducibility of one to the other must remain intact. It is on the basis of this more fundamental threshold that the "sensory," "processual," and "relational" can be evaluated, for the fact that certain thresholds *are* at play does not mean that they *ought* to be so. It is only in this way that a "soulful reality" can be enabled, that is, the capacity of a subject to "reposition and reshape" herself within an environment.

In relation to this, it is important to state that it is not only human subjects who are to be cast as "other" in the music event, but rather the music too, since the subject-like character of music is fundamental to the proximities that are inaugurated. For music not only arises from creative intentionalities and agencies, but transcends these, such that it exhibits its own intentionality and agency. To explain: the human person exists simultaneously as both object and subject.[26] Roger Scruton elaborates: "We are animals swimming in the currents of causality, who relate to each other in space and time. But, in the I-to-you encounter we do not see each other in that way. Each human object is also a subject, addressing us in looks, gestures and words, from the transcendental horizon of the 'I.'"[27] Within the inter-subjective encounter, then, an "over-reaching intentionality" takes place as "I," the subject, discern the presence of the "I" of "you," the object. This over-reaching attends other encounters as well, including musical ones. Scruton says: "It [music] moves as *we* move, with reasons for what it does and a sense of purpose (which might at any moment evaporate, like the purposes of people). It has the outward appearance of the inner life, so to speak, and although it is heard and not seen, it is heard as the voice is heard, and understood like the face—as a revelation of free subjectivity."[28] In short: the relationship between subject and musical object takes on something of the quality of a subject-subject relation.[29] Importantly, we do not simply respond to the music with our ears but are sensitized to it by means of its physical affect on our bodies.

---

26. Roger Scruton views this as a cognitive (rather than an ontological) dualism. *The Soul of the World*, 34ff.

27. Ibid., 62.

28. Ibid., 121. See also Pattison, *Seeing Things*. Pattison argues for the cultivation of person-like relationships in relation to visual artifacts since they exhibit intentionality and agency. In part, according to Pattison, this is due to the fact that such objects "have been created by human persons who have filled them with intention, emotion, agency and communication" (ibid., 204).

29. See Pattison discussing theologian Sally McFague in ibid., 210.

So what is the nature of the proximity that is encountered, or rather, what is the quality of what emerges by means of wonder? In broad terms, the relationship between subject and other is one characterized by vulnerability. For the other presented in and through the music event is always *given* to the subject. Although the other never gives itself completely, for that which is given is only ever *partial* and resists complete reduction, acquisition, and mastery, the process of giving involves a measure of vulnerability, since reception is never entirely controlled or controllable. Vulnerability does not obtain simply for that which is other, however, but pertains to the subject as well. In issuing forth, the other makes a demand upon the subject, since utterances (musical and otherwise) are performed and act upon us, offering an interpellation. That is, they address us, in some sense call us into being and constitute us in doing so. Thus, meaning and value do not derive simply from the subject but, rather, are something received as they are responded to. They are in process, are not instrumental, and entail a posture of vulnerability, for being acted upon involves exposure. Thus, Jean-Louis Chrétien says in *The Call and the Response*: "To listen is to be opened to the other and transformed by the other at our most intimate core. Intimacy, in these ways of thinking, is neither escape nor shelter, but rather the place of broader exposure."[30]

## Levinas, the other, and liminal ethics

The notion of wonder indicates something of the resistance and vulnerability of the encounters that occur at threshold points, where proximity and distance co-exist. It is this that must remain intact in order for the human subject to achieve a "soulful reality." To unpack this further, an engagement with the thought of Emmanuel Levinas will be beneficial.

One of Levinas' primary concerns is embodied in the title of *Totality and Infinity*. Levinas is opposed to forms of totalization, since they do not take account of the particularity of that to which they attend, but, rather, force particularity into preconceived systematizations. Levinas states: "The meaning of individuals (invisible outside of this totality) is derived from the totality. The unicity of each present is incessantly sacrificed to a future appealed to to bring forth its objective meaning. For the ultimate meaning alone counts."[31] Infinity stands in contrast to totality for, Levinas says, "Consciousness then does not consist in equaling being with representation, in

---

30. Chrétien, *The Call and the Response*, 63.
31. Levinas, *Totality and Infinity*, 21–22. My italics.

tending to the full light in which this adequation is to be sought, but rather in overflowing this play of lights."[32]

In opposition to totality, and drawing out what is meant by infinity, Levinas focuses on the particularity of the other, specifically its unrepresentability. It is upon the basis of this that Levinas establishes an ethics. In *Totality and Infinity* the "face" of the other manifests its unrepresentability: "The way in which the other presents himself, exceeding *the idea of the other in me*, we here name face."[33] He continues: "The face of the Other at each moment destroys and overflows the plastic image it leaves me, the idea existing to my own measure."[34] In a later work, a paper entitled "Language and Proximity," it is "touch" that provides the model.[35] Levinas says:

> The ethical does not designate an inoffensive attenuation of passionate particularisms, which would introduce the human subject into a universal order and unite all rational beings, like ideas, in a kingdom of ends. It indicates a reversal of the subjectivity which is open upon beings and always in some measure represents them to itself . . . into a subjectivity that enters into contact with a singularity, excluding identification in the ideal, excluding thematization and representation—an absolute singularity, as such unrepresentable.[36]

It is on this basis that touch is, for Levinas, "an event of proximity and not of knowledge."[37] For even in becoming proximate with another, the other always remains elusive: "To approach the other is to still pursue what is already present, to still seek what one has found, to not be able to be quits with the neighbor. It is like caressing: the caress is the unity of approach and proximity. In it proximity is always also an absence."[38] Allying the music

---

32. Ibid., 26. In the "Conclusions" to the book, Levinas states: "The Heideggerian thesis that every human attitude consists in 'bringing to light' . . . rests on the primacy of the panoramic" (ibid., 294). For Levinas, the panoramic is another form of totalization, "[f]or vision is essentially an adequation of exteriority and interiority: in it exteriority is reabsorbed in the contemplative soul and, as an *adequate idea*, revealed to be a priori . . . ." (ibid., 295).

33. Ibid., 50.

34. Ibid., 50–51.

35. In *Totality and Infinity* touch is not understood positively, as in the later text. It is likened to vision, both offering a means of totalization: "By the hand the object is in the end comprehended, touched, taken, borne and *referred* to other objects, clothed with signification, *by reference to* other objects" (ibid., 189).

36. Levinas, "Language and Proximity," 116.

37. Ibid.

38. Ibid., 120.

event with touch and proximity is in line with its mode of being and the thresholds that comprise it: sound is not simply aural, but is *bodily*, affecting us *physically*. Moreover, proximity is resonant with wonder as I have outlined it, since it indicates a relation that resists reduction and completion. In doing so, it also accords with the implicit movement of desire that wonder invokes: reason's desire to bring that which is experienced under its control remains unfulfilled. Thus, the subject is attracted by that which is other, but does not, and cannot, assimilate it. In Levinas' terms:

> In the neighbor's presence there then rises an absence by virtue of which proximity is not a simple coexistence and rest, but non-repose itself, restlessness. Not an intentional movement tending to fulfilment, and which is in this sense always *less* than the plenitude of this fulfilment. Here it is a hunger, glorious in its insatiable desire, a contact by love and responsibility.[39]

It is within the dynamic interaction between subject and that which is other than it that the potential of a liminal ethics starts to open up. For Levinas, there is a clear asymmetry at work in the relation between subject and other, since the other always initiates by virtue of the fact that the presence of the face of the other issues a call. In this way, before the subject is able to speak about the face, "[t]he face speaks."[40] The face precedes and is in excess of any description and conceptualization. Likewise, for Levinas, a caress "takes form in the contact without this signification turning into an experience of a caress. In this caress proximity remains proximity and does not become an intention of something, although the caress could become an expressive gesture, a bearer of messages."[41]

It is here that we reach a key moment in Levinas' treatment of the aporetic quality of the face and, indeed, touch. For its resistance to conceptualization does not command silence but, rather, issues a call to the subject and thereby sets discourse in motion. Indeed, Levinas says: "[t]he face speaks. The manifestation of the face is already discourse."[42] The subject responds to the call by taking up a dialogical position. In this way, the distance between subject and other is maintained, as is the particularity of the other such

---

39. Ibid., 122. In "Phenomenology of Eros" in *Totality and Infinity*, Levinas elaborates: "The caress consists in seizing upon nothing, in soliciting what ceaselessly escapes its form toward a future never future enough, in soliciting what slips away as though it *were not yet*. It *searches*, it forages. It is not an intentionality of disclosure but of search: a movement unto the invisible" (ibid., 257–58).

40. Ibid., 66.

41. Levinas, "Language and Proximity," 118.

42. Levinas, *Totality and Infinity*, 66.

that a stance of vulnerability is taken up. Levinas says: "Conversation, from the very fact that it maintains the distance between me and the Other . . . consists in recognizing in the Other a *right* over this egoism."[43] Upholding distance even in the proximity of the other sets a resistance in place, since every meaning becomes contestable: "In discourse the divergence that inevitably opens up between the Other as my theme and the Other as my interlocutor, emancipated from the theme that seemed a moment to hold him, forthwith contests the meaning I ascribe to my interlocutor."[44]

The resonances of this discussion with the music event and with a liminal ethics are striking. As we have seen, music operates by means of thresholds, bringing the subject and the many-layered otherness of that which is other than the subject into intimate proximity. In this way, the music event provides a means by which a "soulful reality" can be manifested, since the subject thereby responds to, explores, and dwells in the world, yet in a way that is always resistant, since it is infinitely other and is never fully comprehended.

## Liminal Ethics in Practice: Restlessness, Resistance, and "Balanced Asymmetry"

Approaching music practices with a liminal ethics in mind, that is, with a view to the thresholds at play in the music event, brings to light the restlessness that is ideally entailed. At the same time, it advances an awareness of the responsibility that accompanies involvement in the music event. The main emphasis of Levinas' discussion is on maintaining the integrity of the other in relation to the subject. Indeed, Levinas is very clear that the relationship between the subject and the other is asymmetrical. This is undoubtedly the case at some level, since the subject is already open onto that which is encountered. It is always in some way already in response. However, in accord with the thresholds at work in the music event, and thus within a liminal ethics, I would suggest that a "balanced asymmetry" is at work: just as the other is so by virtue of its relation to the subject, so the reverse is true, that is, the subject is "other" to the other and therefore issues a call and elicits response.[45] This is not to posit "alterity" as a category that assimilates both

43. Ibid., 40.
44. Ibid., 195.
45. Indeed, Jacques Derrida notes the necessity of this type of move to the coherence of Levinas's thought: "The movement of transcendence toward the other, as invoked by Levinas, would have no meaning if it did not bear within it, as one of its essential meanings, that in my ipseity I know myself to be other for the other." "Violence

subject and other with a totalizing force, but is to insist upon the non-appropriation of subjectivity, whether it is mine, yours, or that of music. Thus, in thinking through a liminal ethics, not only must the otherness of the other be upheld as irreducible, but so must the irreducibility of the subject(s).

The three thresholds identified in relation to music at the outset of the chapter, "sensory," "processual," and "relational," are helpful to structuring thoughts about and ensuring the respective irreducibilities of subject and other. Through them one can become aware of which thresholds are at work and in doing so one can question whether they ought to be sustained. This might entail an attention to the physical and imaginative execution of music and its relation to the processes upon which it relies, and attention to and reflection upon the relations that are set in place. In doing so, the "sensory" thresholds invoked might be addressed. In what follows, the music practices examined stand as limit cases. Indeed, there are many others that are more nuanced in their capacity to enable and constrain the creation and sustenance of a "soulful reality." However, it serves as a clear illustration of how a liminal ethics might work in practice.

## *Music Immersion Program*

The "Music Immersion Program" was initiated by Judge Paul Sacco in Fort Lupton, Colorado, in 1998, responding to occurrences of "noise violation." It was formulated such that it would subject offenders to an equivalent "noise." To this end, the program places offenders under controlled conditions for up to an hour,[46] playing them music thought to be antithetical to their tastes. The aims of the program are apparently twofold: retribution and education.[47] The success of the program is not of concern here, although establishing this would be problematic in any case.[48] Rather, it is the motiva-

---

and Metaphysics: An Essay on the Thought of Emmanuel Levinas," 157. He continues further on: "That I am also essentially the other's other, and that I know I am, is the evidence of a *strange symmetry* whose trace appears nowhere in Levinas's descriptions" (ibid., 160, my italics).

46. Offenders had to listen "without talking, chewing gum, sleeping, or breaks." Hirsch, "'Do You Really Want to Hurt Me?' Music as Punishment in the United States Legal System," 35–53 (39).

47. Ibid., 43.

48. "The judge claims the outcome of the "Music Immersion Program" is a drop in repeat offences—a recidivism rate of less than 5%. . . . The police chief in Fort Lupton, however, observes that offenders, upon completing the program, resume their normal activities, but are simply more cautious" (ibid., 43). The offenders are asked to complete evaluation forms. However, as Hirsch notes, the usefulness of these is limited since the forms are "completed on site and are not anonymous" (ibid., 44).

tion behind the program that is important. It is so, since it bears directly on music's capacity to world-make and thus enable a "soulful reality." Within the program, it is the "sensory" and the "relational" thresholds that are of most significance, although "processual" thresholds are implicitly involved, since the "antithetical" musics are selected and arranged into a playing order onto CDs for the violators' listening sessions.

The "sensory" threshold is paramount in considering the "Music Immersion Program": as mentioned at the outset, the aural threshold is easily trespassed and both the designation of an incident as a "noise violation" and the nature of the consequent punishment are based upon this fact. Although the central notion at stake here, "noise," might broadly be defined as "unwanted sound," and although the offenders have exceeded the accepted volume range when playing car stereos, it is clear that decibel level is not the only issue at stake. Indeed, the "relational" thresholds at work are manifold: the notion of "unwanted sound" is highly dependent, since sound and music inaugurate different "relational" thresholds, including interpersonal and spatial, and these are shaped by other relations invoked in and through music, including those that are aesthetic and ideological.[49]

Hirsch notes the complexity of the history of noise legislation and regulation and, in doing so, reflects to some degree on the "relational" thresholds at stake.[50] In doing so, she recounts a case that arose in 1921 in New York City, where, as a result of a tenant hosting late-night musical gatherings in her flat, a complaint was filed. At the trial, one neighbor reported that he had been kept awake by "an absolute riot," declaring how, as a result, he had imagined building "a pounding machine" over the offending tenant's

---

49. R. Murray Schafer notes that the term noise has a variety of meanings, but identifies four primary ones: unwanted sound; unmusical sound; any loud sound; disturbance in a signalling system (*The Soundscape: the Tuning of the World*, 182). The contingency of the designation "noise" is well-attested and, although Hirsch primarily identifies the noise under scrutiny as unwanted sound it is clear that other definitions are at work. It is in terms of the last definition, the disturbance of a signalling system that focuses Marie Thompson's attempt to detach noise from any moral and aesthetic considerations. She conceives noise as affect: "Noise . . . is to be thought of as a verb rather than a noun; instead of referring to a human judgement of sound, noise is recognised [as] a process of interruption that induces a change" (p. 13). Thus, "[t]he 'goodness' or 'badness' of noise, its wantedness or unwantedness, its intentionality or unintentionality, can be thought of as secondary, or contingent, to a (dis)continuous complex that connects noise's affective impact on the aesthetic to its affective impact on the flows of social networks, its affective impact on communicative and informational channels, and its artistic manifestations" ("Productive Parasites: Thinking of Noise as Affect," 31–32).

50. Hirsh, "Do you really want to hurt me?", 36–38.

bedroom ceiling.[51] Both the fact that a complaint was filed, and that such an effect was brought about in the neighbor such that he imagined retaliation, makes clear the sensory impact of sound, the vulnerability involved in the encounter, and the "relational" thresholds that can be invoked, here between two neighbors. However, the matter is further complicated by the fact that other witnesses for the defendant testified that the music performed was not "noise" since it had great "artistic character." Interestingly, the judge agreed and the case was dismissed.[52]

Here the contested nature of "noise" becomes clear, since whether or not music is classed as such depends in part upon the relations it invokes, including whether or not it is considered to be aesthetically "good." Clearly, this judgment itself is dependent upon other factors, including whether a music is one to which *I* relate or not. Music can accrue a dichotomous character by virtue of the relations that it invokes. It is this dichotomous character that is central to, and is potentially exacerbated by, the "Music Immersion Program": those prosecuted are subjected to hearing what they are thought likely to consider as "noise," just as they have subjected others to the same. That is, the offenders are made to listen to "music they don't like."[53]

Clearly, the use of music as a means of punishment is problematic, since it rests on assumptions about identities and associated musical likes and dislikes. Indeed, it has been criticized on this basis. Stuart Laven notes: "While there is no 'smoking gun' upon which one could conclude that any particular car stereo ordinance was adopted as a way to deal with the culture of rap music and those who enjoy it, there is enough circumstantial evidence to at least negate the argument that the emergence of rap music and car stereo noise ordinances is simply coincidental."[54] In addition, the use of the program to serve as a means of education in musical appreciation is a troubled enterprise. Apart from the fact that, given the intimate connection between music and identity, it may serve to elicit or perpetuate negative associations with certain forms of music[55] (especially when enforced by sources of authority), it also presumes that education occurs because the forms of music to which offenders are subjected are preferable to the ones currently enjoyed.[56] The "relational" thresholds set in place seek to reduce

51. Ibid., 37.
52. Ibid.
53. Ibid., 39.
54. Laven, "Turn Down the Volume." Quoted in Hirsh, "Do you really want to hurt me?" 47.
55. Ibid., 48.
56. Debatably, support for the twofold aim of the program as punishment and education can be found in the fact that, following the assessment of evaluation forms,

that which is conceived as "other" to the same. In so doing, the aim is to *force* subjects' repositioning, rather than enabling the subject to do so herself.

Interestingly, Hirsch concludes her article by saying: "Given the various reactions to and concerns regarding music as punishment, it is difficult to render an ultimate verdict on the program."[57] This statement is made having both noted the inconclusive nature of any results as well as suggesting that the use of music as punishment stands on some kind of continuum with the use of music as torture, due to the "comparable loss of control" entailed.[58] Surely something is missing here, for even if a success rate were apparent, the question remains of whether the program is ethical. How might a liminal ethics help?

If liminal ethics leads us to identify the thresholds at work in particular music practices, it also causes us to enquire into their sustainability. In the case of the "Music Immersion Program," the balanced asymmetry proposed by a liminal ethics, that is, the irreducibility of both subject and other, is put at risk. The program seeks to shape a certain type of relationship between offenders and society, and this affects the dialogical relationships that result. On the one hand, the otherness of music is compromised through its reduction to certain associations, which are entrenched as they are deployed. On the other hand, the call that is issued arises from a motivation to reduce the otherness of the subject to the same, absorbing difference within a totalizing vision. Despite this attempt to assimilate, it is important to notice that some form of dialogue and restlessness is still enabled, for it is this fact that renders fallacious the equation of music as punishment and music as torture. Indeed, it is unclear how they involve a "comparable loss of control" in the context of the music event: in the case of the "Music Immersion Program," enrolled perpetrators know the length of their experience (one hour). Moreover, even though they are not allowed distractions during this time, they are still able to exert some power over whether and how they engage with the music (thus some of the offenders "laughed as certain musical selections, such as Cartman's abrasive *Come Sail Away*, began").[59] In short, those exposed to music are still capable of some form of self-governed response.

It is this that distinguishes this instance of music punishment from music as torture, where the network of otherness held in tension within

---

which were completed after immersion, songs that received too much positive feedback were removed from subsequent listening session CDs. Ibid., 40.

57. Ibid., 48.
58. Ibid.
59. Ibid., 49.

the music event is not just compromised but potentially obliterated. At one level the otherness of the music is effaced entirely as its intentionality and agency (its subjecthood) is undone. Suzanne G. Cusick reports the experience of one Guantanamo detainee, Ruhal Ahmed: "after a while you don't hear the lyrics, all you hear is heavy, heavy banging, that's all you hear. Um, you can't concentrate on the drums, or what the person's saying, all you hear is just loud shouting, loud banging, like metal clashing against metal. That's all it sounds like. *It doesn't sound like music at all.*"[60] In this instance, the music is appropriated in such a way that it ceases to be music; it is assimilated and projected as its "acoustical energy"[61] is used as an assertion of power. At another level, the otherness of the subject is compromised since a non-dialogical relationship is invoked and the subject is unable to "reposition and reshape itself within its environment": although detainees fight to maintain some sense of subjectivity by developing or adopting defensive techniques,[62] many detainees are unable to respond in this way and are assimilated to and become the call. The subject literally becomes the other. In an account of "acoustical harassment" at Camp Cropper, Cusick explains:

> The destruction of prisoner's subjectivities partly depends on the acoustically and philosophically salient fact that manipulations of the acoustical environment always produce the somatic effect of sympathetic vibration. Always compelled by the physical properties of sound to vibrate in their very bones with those sounds, the prisoners subjected to the music programme have no choice but to become, themselves, the characteristic sounds of their captors. This is, I argue, an ultimate violence that batters prisoners' bodies, shatters (however temporarily) the capacity to control the acoustical relationality that is the foundation of subjectivity and blasts away all sense of privacy, leaving in its place a feeling of paradoxically unprivate isolation.[63]

---

60. Cusick, "Musicology, Torture, Repair," paragraph 6. (Italics added by Cusick.) Of course, here a question of intelligibility and meaningfulness is at stake, and attention is implicitly returned to the issue of how noise is to be understood.

61. Ibid., paragraph 3.

62. "All day, every day, for as long as the music played, often with his fingers in his ears so that he could hear himself, Z would tell himself stories, tell himself jokes . . . anything to keep control of his acoustical agency, his speech, his thoughts" (Cusick, "Acoustemology of Detention in the 'Global War on Terror,'" 281).

63. Ibid., 276. Exploring the use of a detainee's attempt to cope with loud music at Camp Cropper, Cusick notes that the music's power was located in its disruption of "the call-and-response relationship with the world that characterises well-formed subjectivity" (ibid., 282).

In sum: understanding music as an event dependent upon "sensory," "processual," and "relational" thresholds draws attention to the porosity of the human subject, which is fundamentally relational. In doing so, we become aware of the simultaneous proximity and distance of that which is encountered within music practices and the accompanying need for a "balanced asymmetry." Here both the irreducibility of the other (which is in fact a network of othernesses) and the otherness of the subject are maintained. Wonder can be seen as a marker of this irreducibility and resistance as well as a measure of its realization, signaling the absence of assimilation and the existence of a dialogical restlessness. It is this, also, that stands as a marker of human and "soulful reality" and ought to be discernible if a music practice is a viable one.

## Bibliography

Born, Georgina. "Listening, Mediation and Event: Anthropological and Sociological Perspectives." *Journal of The Royal Musical Association* 135 (S1) (2010) 79–89.

Bowie, Andrew. *Music Philosophy and Modernity*. Cambridge: Cambridge University Press, 2007.

Bull, Michael. *Sounding Out the City: Personal Stereos and the Management of Everyday Life*. Oxford: Berg, 2000.

Casey, Edward S. *The Fate of Place: A Philosophical History*. Berkeley, CA: University of California Press, 2008.

O'Callaghan, Casey, and Matthew Nudds. "Introduction: The Philosophy of Sounds and Auditory Perception." In *Sounds & Perception: New Philosophical Essays*, edited by Casey O'Callaghan and Matthew Nudds, 1–25. Oxford: Oxford University Press, 2009.

Chrétien, Jean-Louis. *The Call and the Response*. Translated by Anne A. Davenport. New York: Fordham University Press, 2004.

Clarke, Eric F. "Music, Space, and Subjectivity." In *Music, Sound and Space: Transformations of Public and Private Experience*, edited by Georgina Born, 90–110. Cambridge: Cambridge University Press, 2013.

———. *Ways of Listening: An Ecological Approach to the Perception of Musical Meaning*. Oxford: Oxford University Press, 2005.

Cusick, Suzanne G. "Acoustemology of Detention in the 'Global War on Terror.'" In *Music, Sound and Space: Transformations of Public and Private Experience*, edited by Georgina Born, 275–91. Cambridge: Cambridge University Press, 2013.

———. "Musicology, Torture, Repair." *Radical Musicology* 3.24 (2008) 24 pars. Online: http://www.radical-musicology.org.uk (12 August 2013).

———. "'You are in a place that is out of the world...': Music in the Detention Camps of the 'Global War on Terror.'" *Journal of the Society for American Music* 2.1 (2008) 1–26.

DeNora, Tia. *Music in Everyday Life*. Cambridge: Cambridge University Press, 2000.

Derrida, Jacques. "Violence and Metaphysics: An Essay on the Thought of Emmanuel Levinas," In *Writing and Difference*, translated by Alan Bass, 97–192. 2nd ed. London: Routledge, 1978.
Dewey, John. *Art as Experience*. New York: Perigee, 1934.
Gallagher, Shaun. "Philosophical Antecedents of Situated Cognition." In *The Cambridge Handbook of Situated Cognition*, edited by Philip Robbins and Murat Aydede, 35–51. Cambridge: Cambridge University Press, 2008.
Goehr, Lydia. *The Imaginary Museum of Musical Works: An Essay in the Philosophy of Music*. Oxford: Clarendon, 1997.
Hepburn, Ronald W. "The Inaugural Address: Wonder." *Proceedings of the Aristotelian Society*, Supplementary Volumes, 54 (1980) 1–23.
Hirsch, Lily. "'Do you really want to hurt me?' Music as Punishment in the United States Legal System." *Popular Music and Society* 34.1 (2011) 35–53.
Ingold, Tim. "The Temporality of the Landscape." *World Archaeology* 25.2 (1993) 152–74.
Levinas, Emmanuel. "Language and Proximity" in *Collected Philosophical Papers*. Translated by Alphonso Lingis, 109–26. Dordrecht: Nijhoff, 1987.
———. *Totality and Infinity: An Essay on Exteriority*. Translated by Alphonso Lingis. Pittsburgh, PA: Duquesne University Press 1969.
Merleau-Ponty, Maurice. *Phenomenology of Perception*. Translated by Colin Smith. London: Routledge, 1962.
Milbank, John. "The Politics of the Soul." Online: http://theologyphilosophycentre.co.uk/papers/Milbank_PoliticsOfTheSoul.pdf, accessed: 20 January 2014.
Nudds, Matthew. "Sounds and Space." In *Sounds & Perception: New Philosophical Essays*, edited by O'Callaghan and Matthew Nudds, 69–96. Oxford: Oxford University Press, 2009.
Pattison, Stephen. *Seeing Things: Deepening Relations with Visual Artefacts*. London: SCM Press, 2007.
Schafer, R. Murray. *The Soundscape: The Tuning of the World*. Vermont: Destiny, 1977.
Scruton, Roger. *The Aesthetics of Music*. Oxford: Clarendon, 1998.
———. *The Soul of the World*. Princeton, NJ: Princeton University Press, 2014.
Shepherd, John, and Peter Wicke. *Music and Cultural Theory*. Cambridge: Polity, 1997.
Stone-Davis, Férdia J. *Musical Beauty: Negotiating the Boundary between Subject and Object*. Eugene, OR: Cascade, 2011.
Thompson, Marie. "Productive Parasites: Thinking of Noise as Affect." *Cultural Studies Review* 18.3 (2012) 13–35.
Wishart, Trevor. *On Sonic Art*. Amsterdam: Harwood Academic Publishers, 1996.

# SECTION V
Vivacity

# 16

# The Soul and "All Things"
## Contribution to a Postmodern Account of the Soul

### W. Chris Hackett

*Anima quodammodo omnia est.*

To modern ears, "soul" sounds more poetic than scientific, or at least vaguely religious.[1]

## Introduction: The Concept of the Soul and Its Three-fold Necessity

THE SOUL IS A necessary concept for Christian theology, for an account of Christian religious experience and for the philosophy that cannot help finding itself thinking from within this domain—and perhaps, further, for any thinking that wants to do full justice to our human experience of ourselves and others as bearing permanent identities and inestimable value. This necessity is doubled when we recognize that the *soul*, like its perennial corollary concepts *God* and the *world*, is a concept that bears within itself a critique of the fundamental *mythos* of conceptual rationality: it asserts the primacy of personality and freedom over abstraction in the metaphysical

---

1. Koterski, *An Introduction to Medieval Philosophy*, 173.

domain (i.e., the domain of basic intelligibility) and it therefore bears within itself an appropriate, permanent element of deconstruction for every systematization, every conceptualization, every account of reality that considers ultimate reality coincident with that which one can think, with instrumental reasoning.

In a fundamental and paradoxical way, the *concept* of the soul (again, like "God" and the "world") conceptually *exceeds* its conceptuality, thereby performing the essential *critical* (we could even say, before and beyond Kant, "meta-critical") function basic to religious rationality—i.e., a thinking that is *more rational* precisely because it is "religious," because, that is, it senses that ultimate reality fundamentally exceeds its own grasp and it arrives to itself in its own activity as *devoted to* reality.

This fundamental and permanent critical value of the concept is furthermore (and here do we find its necessity tripled) tied to the fact that, like its corollary concepts that pertain to the ultimately and irreducibly real, the concept of the soul is unavoidably *given* to be thought (as its privileged place in the classic modern three-fold division of metaphysics, *metaphysica specialis*, surely indicated). For believers who reflect rationally, for meta-critical thinkers especially, the "immortality of the soul" attains to the level of "dogma": *unconditionally* given to be thought.[2] Dogma gives rise to thought, and furthermore, a specific kind of thought, thinking that thinks beyond the boundaries of its own conditions, since dogma fundamentally exceeds these conditions that reason would attempt to give itself. Dogma can therefore become, and in fact must become, the condition for the most properly "critical" approach of a thinking truly come of age.

The soul is therefore a permanent feature of religious or "theological" thinking.[3] The validity of this thinking can be challenged, but the necessity of the concept for this thinking is not in doubt. This three-fold necessity, as I have sketched it above, is today only a promise, however, as if the necessity itself has become wholly un-compelling, and in fact wholly invisible to our thinking. How do we understand, and in fact revive this necessity today, after the era, if we can speak this way—and I am compelled to—of the *death*

---

2. The dogmatic assertion of the thoughtlessness of dogma ought to be laid to rest. Dogma is meta-critical, the crystallization for reason of that which exceeds reason and never ceases to demand of it *greater* activity. See Sergius Bulgakov's sane motto for intellectual work from 1917 that "we set a conscious (and in this sense 'critical') and principled dogmatism against a pusillanimous and barely conscious adogmatism that in its own way is also dogmatic" (*Unfading Light*, 77).

3. The thinking—as far as I am concerned—that aspires to think under, within, and for the sake of the universal reign of Christ (as opposed to the reign of nothing). For the conception of "theological thinking," in fidelity to which I attempt to place these reflections, see Lacoste, *From Theology to Theological Thinking*.

*of the soul*, strictly concomitant with the "death of God"?[4] The following reflections attempt to gather together some crucial dimensions of the soul's history in Christian thinking in order then to give the first indications of a proposal regarding the resurrection of the soul for contemporary thought, after its death in modernity. The remarkably wealthy and fruitful "background," culminating in Thomas Aquinas' conception of the "immortality of the soul" as necessary condition for the activity of theology itself, is not only a perennial source for the renewal of the concept, but would also serve as a sort of measure of richness by which any renewal of the concept must be ultimately judged.

I will first elucidate some critical dimensions of the concept of the soul (§§ 1–2) before "foregrounding" the most suggestive moments of its erasure in modernity (§ 3), in order, finally, to propose a first sketch for a renewal of the intelligibility of the concept by means of a synthesis of phenomenology and the spiritual senses (§ 4).

## § 1 Background: Some Aspects of the Soul in Scripture and Tradition

Not only is the immortality of the soul a dogma (with a relatively clear biblical proof text in the Wisdom of Solomon 3:1–4), but the term itself (*psuchē*) is used throughout the Old and New Testaments: for example, in the second creation account itself, where Adam receives the breath of life in his nostrils in order to become "a living soul" (Gen 2:7),[5] and much later, in the reflections on the living beings of the "new creation," the baptized and especially the martyred dead are considered essentially as "souls" (see Heb 6:19; 1 Pet 1–2; Rev 6:9, 20:4). The creation account reveals that to be human is to be alive and to be a living human is to be a "soul": the essence of the humanity of man, its defining feature, is to be alive, which means, unique among the creatures of the earth, to be intrinsically and even *a priori* (the word is not misplaced here) open to the divine presence, to breathe with the breath of life, imparted by the creative spirit of God in a way unlike every other "living creature" (*nefesh*): the formation of the *adam* from the *adamah* by the "Lord God" through the intimate impartation of the "breath of life" as

---

4. Foucault's line that concluded *Les mots et les choses*, 1966, about the face sketched in the sand washed away by the tide, is commonly cited here, and I refer to it simply for the record. See Foucault, *The Order of Things*, 387: "As the archaeology of our thought easily shows, man is an invention of a recent date. And one perhaps nearing its end. . . . If those arrangements were to disappear as they appeared . . . then one can certainly wager that man would be erased, like a face drawn in sand at the edge of the sea."

5. *Et factus est homo in* animam viventem.

a sort of co-breathing in the second creation account (2:7) may be taken as a correlate synonymous parallelism with the first creation account's introduction of the "image and likeness" (1:26–27). This re-expression of the general idea in intimate terms matches the parallelism of the names of God used in both accounts (Elohim and then YHWH-Elohim). To be a soul as the New Testament materially demonstrates, is to be identified as *destined* in one's humanity for God, to be from God, with God, and for God, which is the essence of life, in the creaturely and most acutely human sense.[6] To express the essential, the soul, for this biblical tradition, is one's permanent "interiority," the permanent "+" or "more than" that marks humanity, and by which *our humanity* is for us both gift and task. This spiritual "openness" or essential divine interiority is of course fundamentally personal and therefore relational; the soul *is* one's essential existence inasmuch as it *is* being-before-God; the soul is, in other words, the total human person seen from the vantage of God, grasped by God, held in existence by God, a grasp that in no way *depends* on the body, drawn from the earth and "animated" by the divine breath (though still perhaps not normatively grasped *without* the body, since, for this tradition, as I will elaborate below, the human person *is* soul and body, together). To be a soul is to be a creature, to be given oneself by God, bearing the *gift* of an integrity and self-possession (and hence freedom) that at the same time signifies one's *task*, grounded in, ratifying and bringing to completion one's absolute ontological dependence on the Creator through its absolute redundance in *freedom*—the return of the gift that redoubles the original giving.[7] The concept of soul captures the point of intersection of this polarity of freedom between gift and task that marks the human creature and makes of our being such a fruitful and elusive antinomy.[8]

The Christian soul lives on after death, as in Plato (and Aristotle; at least the active intellect for the latter, which is not hylemorphic and is divine . . .),[9] but, even more, it lives on in its individual, creaturely identity, as

---

6. This is especially clear in the data of the Gospels (see Mark 8:36–37; 12:30 and parallels), but is essential to the diverse material referenced above.

7. In both testaments, the word soul, *néfesh* and *psyche* (LXX and NT), is found most often in the specific formula, "love the Lord your God with all your heart, mind, soul and strength," and its variations. See especially Deuteronomy 6:5; 10:12; 11:13; 13:3; 26:16; 30:2, etc, and Matt 22:37 and parallels.

8. I am wholly indebted to Sergius Bulgakov for the language used in the last sentences of this paragraph. Gift and task is the way he articulates the relation of image and likeness in the human being, and the "synergy" of divine and human activities in Christ paradigmatically. See *Unfading Light*, Section 3, 285–435, and *The Lamb of God*, Sections 2.4 (140–55) and 4.2 (247–60).

9. This is a hotly debated question. See *De anima* III, 5, 430a22–24, for a text that

the identifiable and stable form that *informs* a body, even when separated from the body. It is the doctrine of the creation-out-of-nothing-toward-God, grounded in the inexhaustibly intelligible will of the Creator, which demands this fundamental transformation of the Platonic-Socratic doctrine of the immortality of the soul: the created soul as such possesses an intrinsic and permanent purpose in God.[10] So Thomas Aquinas says, "the human soul retains the being of the composite after the destruction of the body, since the being of the form is the same as that of its matter, that is, to be composite" (*ST* 4, 5, repl obj 2): separated from the body, the soul possesses perfect being, nothing is lacking for its operation, though at the same time it does not possess perfect specific nature, which requires the body. The soul is in fact the form of the body, but it is also the form—I do not know how else to put it—of the *whole* human person, of the soul *and* body. This necessary redundance of the soul as "form of the form" leads us to a further, classical distinction between the soul and what the Christian tradition calls the "heart," which is material and spiritual at once, naming the person in his intellect and will and affections, the seat of his actions and origin of his self-revealing acts in the world. The "heart," therefore, articulates the "interlacing" (as it were) of soul and body that defines our human being: on the one hand, the irreducible spiritual dimension of the material body (the body is body only as informed, spiritually) and, reciprocally, the material dimension of the spiritual side of human nature (the soul as composite being, that is, as form *of the body*, which it remains even apart from the body in death).

For Christianity it is an essential dimension of the meaning of human being that the soul, the humanity of man grasped in God and destined by God, can and does live on in its integrity, apart from the body, whether in the state of beatitude or damnation, union or separation, or somewhere in between. In fact, the possibility of an "intermediate state"—for those in Christ who die before the final consummation of all things—is itself the goad, historically speaking, that first calls for the unique Christian proposal of the immortality of the soul. The soul lives on in its personal and individual integrity even when the material dimension of the total human person, the body, dies. Far from being alien to Christian revelation, the so-called "Greek" conception of the "immortality of the soul" is therefore demanded all the more acutely by the new metaphysical event brought about by Christ: his resurrection and ascension, that is, his conquest of death, and the

---

seems to suggest the immortality of the soul for Aristotle.

10. Creation out of nothing means nothing if it is not creation towards God, which is the purpose, and hence, intelligible principle of creation. The world, and the soul most uniquely, partakes of the divine intelligibility itself.

"metamorphosis" of finitude it entails.[11] Here the humanity of man, beyond what Greek thought could have anticipated (but that is a banal observation) opens up towards a radically new, radically unforeseen sense of the "weight" of its own significance in the gratuity of divine love that opens a share of its own eternity to the finite creature.

What follows Christ's conquest of death in the resurrection of his body after three-day death is the so-called "delay" of his return to bring to a completion for all of us what is accomplished already in him. The New Testament therefore records for us a problem for faith that surely seems alien to us today: this delay of the return of Christ lasts long enough in fact that people in Christ are dying. The problem arose with remarkable force for the earliest Christian communities of the apostolic era: what happens to those who have died "in Christ" before the final resurrection, who have already, through baptism passed through death and into the life of the world to come? St. Paul answered this deeply existential question of faith in his typical aphoristic style: "to be home in the body is to be apart from the Lord," "to be apart from the body is to be at home with the Lord" (see 2 Cor 5:1–10). That is to say, as the broader Letter to the Corinthians makes clear: death is the dissolution of the body and the separation of those who have died from us; and although not permanent, since it only lasts until the resurrection of the body, death is nevertheless a real separation, a gulf that *only God can cross*. The conviction of faith regarding the immediate presence of the resurrected Christ to the Christian who has separated from the body through death leads to the further conviction that this presence of the Resurrected One overcomes the power of death and eclipses even its power to separate the soul from the body and the beloved from the community. The ultimate eclipse of course—St. Paul is at pains to say—occurs with the resurrection of the body, its reunion with the soul and translation into glory in a new and undying unity as a "spiritual body," but it already occurs for the dead in the present by means of the soul's union with God that death does not destroy because of the soul's essential communion with Christ. "What can separate us from the love of God in Christ?" Paul therefore feverishly exclaims in a famous passage from Romans 8. Not even death. This conquest of death is, indeed, the soul of the Christian faith. "Whether in the body or out of the body," the Christian is compelled to believe that we are all "alive in Christ" (see 1 Thess 5: 10). This overcoming of death is so complete for Paul that the intermediate state for the beloved soul between death and resurrection now even has a fundamental advantage over that of the living

---

11. I use the title of Emmanuel Falque's book, *The Metamorphosis of Finitude*, though at a critical distance from some of his most problematic assumptions, as will be described below.

here below: through death one is now *fully present* to Christ, in communion with the one who overcame death and ascended to the Father's embrace; the soul, though separated from the body and from the community here below, is simply now there where he is.[12]

As a coda to this section we can recall that by the fourteenth century, as is well known, the debate regarding the beatitude of such a soul, apart from the body, but "with Christ in God," is dogmatically crystallized: Benedict XII's *Benedictus Deus* promulgated in 1336 affirmed that those who have died in Christ, the *beati*, the saints, enjoy, paradoxically, the fullness of the beatific vision, even while lacking their fully human character; that is, while separated from the body. This division within the heart of their humanity is nevertheless no obstacle, by the power of God which raised Jesus from the dead, to their full participation in God's blessedness. The text states in unequivocal directness: "Even before their reunification with their bodies and the general judgment [the souls of the blessed] . . . see the divine nature in an immediate vision, face to face, without the mediation of any creature."[13]

## § 2 The High Point: The "Immortality of the Soul" as Condition for Theology in St. Thomas Aquinas

Beyond all that could be said in our context regarding the fascinating and much commented-upon papal teaching just mentioned, for the direct task at hand I will only retain a single observation regarding its profound significance for the practice of Christian faith, particularly in relation to the "communion of saints."

The conviction of the perfect beatitude of, as it were, "imperfect" creatures, allows believers *in via*, in the state of pilgrimage, to invoke the saints with perfect confidence in their intimate "proximity" to God. This is, as it were, the pastoral significance of the teaching of the separated soul's present beatitude. Related to this, there is also a deeply implicit theological significance of the teaching as well: I would propose that it justifies Thomas Aquinas' account of *sacra doctrina*, that is, theology as an activity for believers in the state of pilgrimage here below. In short, it makes *sacra doctrina* possible. And it does so in the following way: If the divine science is, most basically, God's knowledge of himself, then our access to it depends on

---

12. For the above remarks especially, see Joseph Ratzinger's classic discussion of the biblical and Christological background of the doctrine of the immortality of the soul in, *Eschatology: Death and Eternal Life*.

13. Denzinger, *Enchiridon Symbolorum*, 1000 [*The Sources of Catholic Dogma*, 30th ed.].

revelation;[14] now revelation is, at least from the perspective of the question of the nature of theology, the fundamentally soteriological activity whereby God shares his own self-knowledge with human beings.[15] Revelation is, in the first place, historical events—the Creator's "words and deeds" (to invoke the refrain of Vatican II's *Dei Verbum*)—but it is specifically the *elevation* of historical events to the level of what, on ancient philosophical accounts, could only be held by abstract principles; that is, to the level of eternal truths.

This relation of historical event wed to eternal truth in revelation can be understood by analogy to the incarnation itself by which material reality, in the flesh of a whole human being, is elevated to the heights of divine reality. In order to recall this Christian enlargement of Greek categories, I invoke here Jean Daniélou's discussion of the Scriptural concept of the "once and for all" (*ephapax*), which (as developed by Augustine in *City of God*) inserts a new category into the Greek context.[16] The latter context simply turned on a basic distinction between the eternal (that which has no beginning and no end) and the temporal (that which has a beginning and an end). Christianity introduced a new category, which we can call the *event*: that which has a beginning and no end. The creation, and then all the moments of sacred history culminating in the new creation, are events in this sense. This third concept allows patristic Christianity to conceive of *the soul*, which has a beginning, but an eternal destiny.[17] For Christianity the finite no longer lies in tragic contrast to the infinite (either swallowed up by its reality or set over-against it in utter alienation), but rather elevates the finite into new proximity to the divine realms, an elevation that is paradoxically expressive of its *now strange finitude*—how to express it?—an ever-greater finitude in being ever-greater than finitude.[18]

Now this revelation is for us here below, from the days of the apostles to the present, mediated by the church, most centrally in its liturgical and sacramental practice, since this practice is an extension through time and space of God's very incarnate activity in Christ, if the central image of the church as body of Christ, her head, is to be taken as seriously as Scripture takes it; that is, as a real description of ecclesial experience. The Scriptures themselves, the church's authoritative record of the founding events of God's

---

14. See *Summa Theologica* (*ST*) I, q. 1, a. 7.

15. See *ST* I, q. 1, a. 1.

16. See Heb 10:10, 12. See Augustine, *City of God* XII.

17. See especially Gregory of Nyssa's self-conscious but implicit rebuke of a (merely) Platonic doctrine (for which "resurrection" means merely the eternal abiding of the soul in God) in his dialogue *On the Soul and the Resurrection*.

18 See Daniélou, "Conception of History in the Christian Tradition"; and the discussion of Marc Nicholas in his *Jean Daniélou's Doxological Humanism*, 26–29.

revelatory action, stand at the center of her tradition that lives and moves *within* this liturgical-sacramental context: sacred doctrine is (normatively) taught "not by mere learning," says Thomas quoting Dionysius, "but by experience of divine things."[19]

The church, moreover, spans heaven and earth; it pierces eternity and fills up time from end to end. It is a trans-historical reality (it is not a coincidence that the image of the relation of the soul and body is a common patristic and medieval trope for understanding the cosmic nature of the church).[20] Now if there are those in heaven who enjoy the beatific vision—that is, the knowledge of God as God knows himself, albeit according to a creaturely mode, however paradoxical that mode is in the case of "deiform" humanity, *totus Deus sed non totaliter*—and, if, together with them, we are in "mystical" and "real" communion with Christ as *our* head, then *by this very means*, the divine science as an activity is justifiable for us here below in our theological explication of sacred doctrine. We here below share in their activity of knowing God as those souls, who are "with Christ in God," share, through union with Christ, in God's activity of knowing himself. This sharing is grounded in the fact that the truth that God reveals to them is one with the truth that he reveals in history—*himself*. The difference between the *beati* and ourselves is that they see the essence of God, and we do not (since the highest knowledge attainable in this life is to know that we do not know the essence of God);[21] yet the articles of faith, the truths disclosed by revelation, stand for us in the place of what they see, and therefore as the principles of our sacred doctrine. What we know in principle and therefore implicitly, as the condition for all our knowledge, they know explicitly, having by grace attained the principle (as opposed to our merely presupposing

---

19. *ST* I, q. 1, a. 6, repl. obj. 3 (quoting *Divine Names*, 2). In this way the sacramental dimension is the unification of the speculative and practical dimensions that compose necessarily the mixed character of *sacra doctrina* as a science (and here we touch upon, of course, the unity of the three parts of the *Summa* itself, the *prima pars* being speculative, on God in himself and his act of creation; the *secunda pars* being practical, on the centerpiece of God's creation, man, endowed with freedom, who seeks to return to God; and the *tertia pars*, being sacramental, on the speculative-practical path or way that God gives in Christ for us to enact our passage to beatitude, which is, finally, an *incarnate* activity).

20. This is the theme, for example, of the fourth chapter of Maximus the Confessor's *Mystagogia*.

21. See his *Commentary on Boethius' On the Trinity*, I, 2, ad 1. This remains, even though, as Samuel Kimbriel rightly pointed out to me, that later in the *Commentary* Thomas says that knowledge of God's existence necessarily implies some confused knowledge of what God is. This is because, presumably, God is the identity of being and essence. We share in that knowledge by being ourselves, although at a remove from its immediacy like circles that can never close.

it as necessary but directly inaccessible);[22] what they know immediately, as *scientia divina*, we know through the medium of faith, and as *sacra doctrina*.[23] What is revealed in an historical mode, as far as theology is concerned, is the knowledge of God, "the science of God and of the blessed" in heaven, which serves as principles for sacred doctrine.[24] This is why theology is famously "subaltern," its principles being derived from a higher science. But, more acutely, the fact that humans, in this case the *beati* (and us, with Christ as our common head), participate in this science, therefore makes *theo-logy*, the knowledge of God, a *human* science. The upshot is therefore that theology is a fundamentally ecclesial activity (a sense in need of recovery), and as such it depends on the communion of saints, inasmuch as Christ and the *beati*, on the one hand, and ourselves, on the other hand, are as inseparable as a head and body are for a living person.

It is this integral unity of head and body (along with the corollary image of soul and body), the extension of this union in and through us here below, that makes theology as *sacra doctrina* possible.[25] Because there are now human beings, souls, who enjoy the fullness of divine science, we know that it is possible that we, human beings who do not see, may share in their vision, their perfect human sharing in the divine *scientia*, and which we already share to the degree that we share their life, the life of God, through our ecclesial-sacramental existence. Our real, living communion with them in Christ with God makes our participation in the divine science through revelation here below not only possible but even actual.

The entire argument can be expressed this way:

1. Man's salvation depends on the knowledge that God reveals, viz., our ultimate end and how we get there, since "the end must be first known by men who are to direct their thoughts and actions to it" (*ST* I, q. 1, resp.).

2. These truths exceed human reason and depend on revelation.

3. Theology is the work of this salvation inasmuch as it is involved with this knowledge that is revealed for our salvation (*ST* I, q. 1, resp.).

---

22. See *ST* I, q. 12, a. 1, resp.
23. See *ST* I, q. 1, a. 7, resp.
24. See *ST* I, q. 1, a. 2, resp.

25. The fundamental paradox remains that the *beati* enjoy the Vision while being incomplete in their humanity. Though implicit in Thomas, we must say that Christ's resurrected body stands in, as it were (as it does for us, though in a different way, through the sacraments), for the entirety of the *beati* as they await their bodies at the end of time.

4. Now it "pertains to the glory of the *beati*" to be "co-operators with God," that is, to "assist the needy for their salvation" (*ST* Suppl, q. 72, a. 1 resp).

5. Therefore, since our salvation depends on theological knowledge, the *beati* can and do aid us in this theological labor inasmuch as it pertains to our salvation.

6. They do this all the more insofar as "it is not on account of any defect in God's power that he works by means of second causes, but it is for . . . the more manifold outpouring of his goodness on things," which comes about "through his bestowing on them not only the goodness that is proper to them, but also the faculty of causing goodness in others" (*ST* Suppl q. 72, a. 2, repl obj 1).

We could also make the practical observation regarding the importance of the personal cultivation of the cult of the saints for the practice of theology, that is, for the theologian—whose task we can define, using the words of *Gaudium et spes*, as the research that possesses the task to "deepen the knowledge of revealed truth."[26] This is because theology depends on and is in fact wholly composed of what Aquinas, taking up a central theme of the fathers, called "friendship" with God, rooted in intimate knowledge with the living Christ, and which is only enriched, and thereby made more adequate, by "friendship" with the saints, *the* friends of God.[27] This is the manner we would have to fill out, from the vantage of this explication of Aquinas, the ancient maxim of Evagrius, so dear to the Christian tradition, that the theologian is "one who prays in truth"—but the immediate point I want to make here, and in this way sum up the preceding discussion, is that the concept of the soul, understood in this Christological-ecclesial sense, is not only necessary *in* theology, but it asserts itself as necessary *for* theology.[28]

With Thomas Aquinas the Christian account of the soul is not only realist and capacious but is also the condition for a right understanding of the theological enterprise itself. If for Aristotle metaphysics is an enterprise that

---

26. GS § 62.

27. See *ST* II–II, 23, 1, resp: "charity is the friendship of man for God." See also Marie T. Farrell, "Thomas Aquinas and Friendship with God," and especially Samuel Kimbriel, *Friendship as Sacred Knowing*.

28. I am indebted to Rudi te Velde for the perspective presented here. See the first chapter of his *Aquinas on God*, 9–30. He summarizes this view I have tried to flesh out here: "An insurmountable gap between the superior science and the subordinated science of the human intellect does not exist, since the superior science is not only the science of God but also of the *beati*. The science of the *beati* represents the necessary mediation between the divine intellect knowing the principles and the human intellect believing the principles."

can only be justified at its completion, the same can be said for theology: only the eschatological realization of sacred doctrine in the divine science of the blessed enjoying the status of *comprehensor* establishes the practice of theology in our present state of *viator*.

## § 3 The Modern Fall of the Soul

Despite all of the evident power and fruitfulness that to me so clearly appears in the concept of the soul, about which I have tried to give some selective indication above, the history of modern theology and philosophy, from the late Middle Ages,[29] is a story of decline and fall. This decline and fall, or erasure of the soul from the horizon of conceivability, is a matter of the nihilism intrinsic to instrumentalized reason that conceives only what it can control, and posits as real only what it can conceive: if the real can only be an "object" posited over-against and *for* a "subject," and this defines the real as such, the "subject" can never be real, since it can never satisfactorily become an object.[30] The soul (in a way similar to God and the world) transcends all our reflection on it, since, in its case, the thought that thinks always escapes the grasp of itself; the mind cannot become a clear and distinct object of itself.

The medievals fundamentally recognized this intrinsic transcendence proper to the phenomenon of the soul; their commitment to the properly apophatic character of the soul, despite the preparation for his viewpoint in a genealogy that is well-known, finds a point of transformation in Descartes.[31] Descartes, following Suárez's pseudo-Augustinian turn to the avowedly *notior*, "better-known," the being of the soul, for the sake of knowing the lesser-known, being as such, only clearly establishes the dualism of the interior world of subjectivity set over against the external world of objects, mediated in knowledge by representation.[32] He conceives of the

29. See, on the concept of soul in medieval thought, Joseph W. Koterski, SJ, *An Introduction to Medieval Philosophy: Basic Concepts*, 173–200.

30. See, for example, Martin Heidegger, *Basic Problems of Phenomenology*, § 13, 122–39 and "The Age of the World Picture," *The Question Concerning Technology and Other Essays*, 115–54.

31. For this genealogy let us look no further than Hans Urs von Balthasar's *The Glory of the Lord*, vols. 4–5, *The Realm of Metaphysics*, in Antiquity and the Modern Age, respectively.

32. For Suárez a mental concept, the *conceptus formalis entis*, is the means for establishing the *conceptus obiectivus entis*, the concept of being as unified sense of reality and the condition for objective philosophical knowledge. For Descartes, see Descartes' Second *Meditation*, and secondarily, the Sixth. More generally see Olivier Boulnois, *Être et représentation*, especially chapters 8 and 9, 405–503, not concerned directly with

soul as "thinking substance" and reduces the body to mere extension that can be completely bracketed without altering the human essence, identified with the former. Reality is thereby divided into two fundamental categories: *res cogitans* and *res extensa*. Descartes can only think the soul, on the one hand, and body, on the other, in a separated fashion: their intelligibility is predicated on their distinction. In his *Treatise of Man*, for example, he starts with the body and moves to the soul. As he states in the text's first line: "These men will be composed, as we are, of a soul and a body. First, I must describe the body on its own, then the soul, and finally I must show how these two natures would have to be joined and united in order to constitute men who resemble us."[33] In his later treatise, *Passions of the Soul*, he starts, by contrast, with an analysis of the basic features of the soul and moves to the body. In both cases, he divides in order to unite, but the union is only a matter, famously, of a tenuous, hypothetical point of contact, which can only problematize their respective realities as he conceives them.[34]

In no way eclipsing Descartes' fundamental division, Kant only expresses its implications. He conceives the soul as inconceivable, wholly out of bounds for reason, a "metaphysical" and therefore strictly impossible, "pseudo-rational" concept. It is "necessary" (like "God" and the "world") insofar as reason inevitably tends towards the unconditioned. And in the case of the soul specifically, a concept is needed that would represent "the subjective conditions of representation."[35] But the problem perceived by Kant is that no analysis of the activity of thinking can ever lead to knowledge of that which thinks (as happens in Descartes), since no object appears, only the phenomena of thought. He replaces the soul of Descartes with an empty "I think" that is posited only as a necessary condition for thought. The bare, logical identity of I=I of the transcendental unity of apperception that is necessarily presupposed by thought is not a "metaphysical object," but rather a mere transcendental condition necessarily posited by the analysis of thinking.[36]

---

Descartes, but the fulfillment of the Suárezian tradition in Kant.

33. Descartes, *Treatise of Man*, 1.

34. Both texts seem to portray Descartes as a dualist full stop. But see Jean-Luc Marion's recent radically revisionary attempt to destroy this "myth" in his *Sur la pensée passive de Descartes*. According to Marion, the sixth *Meditation* discovers a *cogitatio* in a passive modality and which becomes a third element along with body and (active) mind. This third mode anticipates the phenomenological concept of the flesh and conceives of a level of the human person as a unity prior to the abstract differentiation between soul and body, as non-extended and extended thing (as Michel Henry fundamentally pointed out earlier in his work on Descartes).

35. Kant, *Critique of Pure Reason*, A406/B4333, 304.

36. Ibid., A400, 364.

Heirs of this tradition (about which much more could be said), contemporary religious thinkers (there are exceptions[37]) almost seem incapable of conceiving of the soul as anything but a "dead metaphor." I will only refer to an exemplary case that demonstrates this.

Emmanuel Falque, in his *Métamorphose de la finitude* (2004), concerned with articulating the Christian and theological conception of finitude, runs with courage through the gauntlet laid down by Nietzsche and Heidegger—viz., that finitude as such, conceived without contrast with some gratuitous divine infinity that saves its intelligibility, is the only manner of adequately conceiving our essential humanity—and argues for a radicalization of the "philosophical" account of finitude *by means of* the very "theological" data given by Scripture and tradition. For this author, this means releasing ourselves from the language of the "soul," replacing it with the phenomenological concept of "flesh" (or "lived body"), and replacing the, as it were, "otherworldly" attitude that concerns itself with a ("literal") resurrection of the body, with an interpretation of resurrection as life lived in the present:[38]

> What was true for the Middle Ages is certainly true also for our present age . . . : metamorphosis of finitude as the *resurrection of the body*. But our language today has changed, because culture has modified its expression as much as it has modified what is basic and given. Philosophers after Nietzsche . . . rarely speak in terms of the body (*corpus*) and the soul (*anima*) when it is a question of bodily subsistence (*Körper*) and the lived experience of the body (*Leib*). A division between the spiritual and the bodily (as if a soul without a body could be conceived) is no longer acceptable, even in the supposed separation of body and soul at the moment of death.[39]

37. See John Milbank, "The Soul of Reciprocity, Part One: Reciprocity Refused" and "The Soul of Reciprocity, Part Two: Reciprocity Granted." In these articles Milbank reproposes the concept of the soul as an alternative to modern subjectivity and postmodern rejection of that very subjectivity. The soul, for Milbank, taking up the challenge picked up and put down by Augustine in *De Trinitate* V–VII, is defined by an ontology of relation conceived as "reciprocity," gift exchange. The present proposal would ultimately attempt to develop its theses in collaboration with what Milbank proposes here.

38. My remarks above regarding the biblical and traditional data are enough to conclude that this approach clearly does not do justice to the Christian faith, even if part of the biblical data indeed conceives of resurrection as life lived in the present, on this side of death. For the New Testament only draws this conclusion insofar as the promise of resurrected body and impending divine judgment is embraced as the all-determining reality that invades the present order from wholly beyond it.

39. Falque, *The Metamorphosis of Finitude*, 151. See also, earlier: "A veritable

But the author, whose daring and often perceptive analyses have much to commend them on many points, gives away the game to those whom he feels he has to answer, which he does only by accepting the whole tenor of their critique *as they propose it*, rather than in discerning the inadequacy of their critique precisely there, where it is most penetrating. For the "ontotheological tradition of metaphysics," however determinative of modern thinking, whether theological or philosophical, does not at all determine theological thinking itself, which, penetrated by revelation, is already undertaking the work of "overcoming" the instrumental, nihilistic tendencies of reason.[40] The author's inability to transcend the critique of Christianity as nihilism that motivates both Nietzsche and Heidegger, only lands him more firmly, if in a negative fashion, within the ontotheological itself, it would seem to me.[41]

In the light of this example, one would have to be pardoned for reading the stepping stones of Descartes and Kant as a pathway that abruptly ends in the middle of a river, and overrun by a swelling attempt to kill the soul as a theological and philosophical concept and even as having any religious and human significance whatsoever.

Taking a step back, one is compelled to say that the upshot of modern thought, however quickly sketched here, is to make the soul *unintelligible*—and to make God *impossible* and the world only intelligible through the equation of truth with that which the mind can possibly grasp, and hence reducing *life*—that to which "soul" classically refers[42]—to the instrumentally measurable. God, the soul, and the world, as I have stressed from the outset of these reflections, are three fundamental organizing concepts for reason that can only be separated, then, at the direst cost to our understanding of each.

---

'phenomenal' body to body confrontation takes place between St. Paul and Nietzsche, not so much to extract the soul from the body and thus make it abstract (immortality) as to consecrate a certain Christian type of resurrected bodilness—according to the spirit (*pneuma*) or in a way of openness to God—and thus to make that resurrected bodiliness incarnate here" (55). The tenor of Falque's entire argument is to overcome a sort of two-worlds dualism in response to Nietzsche's avowed definitive critique of Christianity by means of a rejection and replacement of the concept of soul with the phenomenological concept of flesh (vs. body), which is achieved by a sort of reification of the data of phenomenology, in my view.

40. See n. 3, above.

41. The "metamorphosis of finitude" by Christianity, the radicalization and overcoming of nihilism by religious thought, here seems to remain finally only at the level of a metamorphosis of Christianity by still-modern accounts of finitude.

42. Aristotle, *On the Soul* I, 1, 402 a7: "the soul is in some sense the principle of animate life" (*The Complete Works of Aristotle*, vol. 1, 641).

This erasure of the soul is achieved, to express things directly in the form of a clarified thesis, by the undoing of the fundamental primacy, for metaphysical reflection, of absolute personality and freedom coincident with the highest intelligibility that is articulated by Christianity in the concept of the Logos (as the locus of divine intelligibility in God the Son, who is the ever-present source of the intelligibility of the world). This is replaced ultimately with the harsh limitations of the capacity for abstraction of merely human rationality detached from freedom, now made opaque and irrational. Here the intelligibility of the world itself is reduced to mere mechanism; "spirit" is evacuated from the world. Yet it is the living personality alone that, as the coincidence of freedom and intelligibility, can hold together the basic metaphysical antinomy of absolute singularity and absolute universality that does justice to the profundity, the reciprocal complexity and simplicity, in which human experience finds itself immersed.[43] For the medievals, by contrast to this dim picture, the "rational soul" enjoyed by human beings, enabling them to enter into the inexhaustible intelligibility of the world, is precisely the principle of freedom *and* reason: to separate these elements (as happened in the late Middle Ages, crystallized in Descartes) is to lose the intelligibility of the concept of the *soul*, with dire consequences for our understanding of *God* (since, as the premise on which Augustine's entire thought rests shows, the soul's relation to the world is a vague and essential indication to us of God's own excess over the world, an excess which can only be conceived of apophatically) and the *world* (since the soul's excess over the world is only a matter of still ever remaining a part of it, indeed, the part of the world that conceives the world as such in its totality as world).

## § 4 Contribution to a Postmodern Account of the Soul

As a result of this history of the erasure that reaches its classic expression in Kant, articulated here with the most minimal conceptuality, the theology and religious philosophy from last century even to the present, which to our eyes today can only appear as so timid and embattled in this respect, hardly touches the concept of the soul, except, it seems, to be done with it. Where do we turn from here? Here I will summarize the themes before commenting upon them, but in any case these are only the barest remarks that will have to be taken up much more fully on another occasion.

---

43. The history of modern thought would likewise show that if the concept of God as "+", grasped through apophasis as ever-greater intelligibility in his very freedom as the Absolute, is undone, so also does the soul as "+", as antinomical unity of finitude and infinity in the human, become impossible.

The budding revival of the tradition of the "spiritual senses" is already, to my mind, leading to a renewed approach, since it shows us, as we will see below, that monism (or immanentism) and dualism are two poles that reason must impossibly hold together, which it does by reminding us that human being is problematically ordered towards two "worlds" that correspond to two fundamental horizons of the soul, heaven and earth, and that one's work in this life, as led by the liturgy, is to reorder oneself towards the harmony of these worlds, which in reality, as eschatologically disclosed, is a harmony that they most truly *are*.[44]

Besides the revival of the spiritual senses originating out of brief moments in the *oeuvres* of Rahner and Balthasar,[45] there are others who have rightly sensed the permanence of the concept of soul and have sought to rethink it. Michel Henry, for example, in 1966, wrote an underappreciated essay asking the honest question: "Does the Concept 'Soul' Mean Anything?"[46] His answer is yes, but only if the soul (obviously, as we have seen) is rescued from modern dualisms and rearticulated (not so obviously) from the starting point of his "enstatic" phenomenology, emerging from the "phenomenology of the body." The latter is derived first from Maine de Biran's conception of the self-affirmation intrinsic to the feeling of effort that is even more fundamental than the abstract and vacuous thought of myself of the Cartesian cogito (abstracted, that is, from the domain of its native intelligibility, experience, and conceived as set over-against the body, which is then conceived as a mere mechanism animated from outside).[47] Like the tradition of the spiritual senses, Henry sees the soul as articulating the interior dimension of the total human person, its presence to God that is paradoxically direct, limitless, and endlessly rich in many folds and unfoldings (but from which it is somehow alienated, and in being so, is alienated from itself).

This phenomenology begins with the absolute coincidence of affective experience with itself, and, as Henry will later articulate forcefully, is rooted

---

44. See for example Chrétien, *Symbolique du corps*; Pickstock, "Liturgy and the Senses," and "The Ritual Birth of Sense"; Gavrilyuk and Coakley, *The Spiritual Senses*.

45. Two articles by Karl Rahner, originally published in French, in 1932 and 1933, respectively ("The Doctrine of the 'Spiritual Senses' in Origen," *Theological Investigations* 16: 81–103; "The Doctrine of the 'Spiritual Senses' in the Middle Ages," *Theological Investigations* 16:104–34) and a long section in the first volume of Balthasar's "theological aesthetics": *The Glory of the Lord vol. 1: Seeing the Form*, 365–425. One can consult also Balthasar's study of Bonaventure in the subsequent volume of *The Glory of the Lord*, vol. 2: *Clerical Styles*, 260–362, which relies heavily on Rahner's second essay.

46. "Le concept d'âme a-t-il un sens?" *Revue philosophique Louvain* 64 (1966), 5–33, translated as "Does the concept 'soul' mean anything?"

47. *Philosophy and Phenomenology of the Body*.

in its awareness of itself as pure *pathos*, as living, but living as received from another and in another, the First Living, the Son in God.[48] No longer can we simply or most fundamentally say, says Henry (like Merleau-Ponty), that I *have* a body (and therefore "am" a soul in *this* way), but rather I, as human, *am* my body, the "lived" body. The former statement, that I "have" a body, may be relatively true, but it misses the essential regarding human nature: what I am, I am *as incarnate*. This being a body of the "I," of the soul, is what already transcends the objective bodily dimension, that can only be, from this vantage, an *abstraction* away from the I that is "flesh," enjoying the feeling of life in immediate experience of itself, which is the essential dimension of myself as human. This abstraction can move in either direction, either towards the "immaterial" substance of a detached subjective soul, or towards the "material" substance of the objective body, but as an abstraction, it would lead us away from the *thing itself*. The fundamental distinction becomes for Henry to be sure that between "flesh" and "body," following Husserl's fecund distinction between *Leib* (the body as lived through by a subject) and *Körper* (body as object, out there, as a thing other than the real me that perceives it).[49] According to Henry, then, the soul—the essential aspect of who I am, my permanent and essential interiority—can no longer be identified with an abstract intellective activity, detached from the material dimension as inert and mute object set over-against it, but rather must be a living "flesh" that precedes and grounds this dichotomy ruled by representation and alienation. For Henry, this flesh is eternal, indestructible, and partakes of the divine life itself.[50] It is in this way that Henry can be taken to re-enliven the principle aspects of classical Christian and indeed Aquinas' anthropology apart from its perversion into the so-called "substantialist" metaphysics of now-dead modern philosophy to which the soul has been until now banished, and which seems to fall so short of the integrity of human experience of itself as alive and as lived.[51]

---

48. This absolute passivity of life, lived as received in the life of God, is the basic premise investigated in his *I Am the Truth*.

49. For a clear statement of the distinction in Husserl himself see *Ideas II* (Hua IV, 145), 152.

50. It is precisely here that we would have to separate him from Emmanuel Falque's use of the flesh over-against soul, for Henry identifies flesh and soul. One could read him as presenting only a new phenomenological commentary on the Christian tradition in this way, one that would presumably be able to preserve its essential theses. But this is controversial and would have to be demonstrated in the face of the readings of Henry that tie him more to the gnostic aberrations than to Christian orthodoxy.

51. For this see Jean-Yves Lacoste discussion in his contribution, "Orientations contemporaines" to the article "Âme-cœur-corps" in his *Dictionnaire critique*, 39–41.

One does not have to subscribe to the philosophy of Michel Henry in every respect in order to grasp, and to be grasped by, the demand it poses to any thinking that would rehabilitate the soul as a living concept. At such a remove from his doctrine (assisted by the doctrine of the spiritual senses), we can tentatively intuit something of its permanent significance. With this observation I will close these remarks.

One can grasp the pattern of rehabilitation I would propose through the startling words with which Henry ends the aforementioned essay: "And the concept of 'soul' has a meaning, if it refers, not merely to a reality, but to the fundamental structure of all possible reality."[52] Besides an essay published twenty years later in a special issue of the French edition of *Communio* dedicated to the soul,[53] Henry never brings up the concept in any sustained way subsequent to this very early article. What do we grasp through this quotation? In the letter of Henry's thought, the reference seems plain: the interiority of subjectivity is alone real, grounded in itself as ground, as transparent feeling of life, albeit a ground that is a pure receptivity to the higher life of God, which is its origin. The world of "representation," of transcendence, is only at best a shadow world, a fallen world, an illusory veil evacuated of any significance, though it proposes itself as the only real "world" and thereby hides its origin in immanence. But, if I can express myself thus, in the "spirit" of Henry's thought, the "two" worlds of immanence and transcendence are really, finally, truly one world. This is because transcendence is founded on immanence and, *when rightly perceived*, a work of transforming perception, which is the whole task of Henry's philosophy, can only be inexhaustibly expressive of it.[54] Henry makes this explicit in little book on Kandinsky, whose paintings, on his reading, make visible the invisible, and are thereby, in our terms, an exercise precisely of the spiritual senses. There he poses the question: "Does this one and the same external reality [the irreality of the 'world'] become real, however, only insofar as it is experienced

---

52. "Does the concept 'soul' mean anything?," 114. My present reflection may be taken as a sort of extended gloss on this suggestive statement, understood, not dogmatically—i.e., not in fidelity to Henry's doctrine, but aphoristically, as a suggestive goad to reflection.

53. "Représentation et auto-affection," 77–96. This article essentially repeats what Henry offers in 1966, which is a refiguring of the soul through the phenomenon of life: the experience of life, "autoaffection," is, as it were, the inexhaustible manifestation of that to which the soul classically refers.

54. On this account, Henry's thought is best understood as a critique of modernity and its ways of seeing, including its ways of seeing the history of philosophy. For a (relatively) clear justification of this view, see *Seeing the Invisible*, especially the final chapter "Art and the Cosmos," 133–42.

inwardly in the pathos of its invisible subjectivity and is Life?"[55] Reality does not merely manifest *my own* subjective interiority as in Romantic Idealism, but rather manifests *its own* proper interiority, a depth of life in which I, as a living soul, uniquely participate—the Life of God.

One can properly illumine Henry's "aphorism" by setting beside it a sentence from Andrew Louth, found in his entry on "les sens spirituels" in Lacoste's celebrated *Dictionnaire critique de théologie*. This quotation can draw together, as I have now suggested, the tradition of the spiritual senses and Michel Henry's thought:

> This interior world [to which are calibrated the spiritual senses] sometimes seems to be imagined according to the model of the Platonic realm of Forms, where the truth is essentially immaterial. But sometimes, and more profoundly, [this world of the spiritual senses] is the totality of the created world, seen in its properly creaturely value, a transfigured world, seen by means of senses that are spiritually transfigured.[56]

We can observe at least two essential theses suggested here. First, the permanent "interiority" of the human being is not an interiority necessarily or even essentially opposed to the "external" world; instead, true understanding of this interiority, of the soul (the "organ of communion with God"),[57] is found, indeed recovered, within a converted existence through which the world of creation is experienced, perhaps in this life hardly more than in various degrees of anticipation in its intended unity, as transparent to God—which the liturgical order itself symbolically brings about. It is our very material senses that are themselves transfigured, as Balthasar first fundamentally argued in the first volume of *The Glory of the Lord*.[58] Second, the problematically unified order of things in God, a *problematization* that is the whole essential pathos of religious consciousness,[59] is ordered not according to a static dualism ("Platonic" in the profane sense), but *eschatologically* and

---

55. Henry, *Seeing the Invisible*, 134.

56. Section II.4 of the entry "Spirituelle (théologie)," *Dictionnaire critique de théologie*, 1344–47. Quote is found on p. 1346, of the third edition, first column.

57. For this phrase see Brague, "L'âme du salut."

58. See fn. 45 above. I quote the essence of his proposal here: "Spiritual senses, in the sense of Christian mysticism, presuppose devout bodily senses which are capable of undergoing Christian transformation by coming to resemble the sensibility of Christ and Mary" (378).

59. See Bulgakov, *Unfading Light*: "Religion flows out of a sense of the rupture between the immanent and transcendent, and at the same time an intense attraction to it" (72–73).

dynamically, that is, as "being-towards" its own transfiguration, a defining pursuit in which the believer partakes as a creature of this world.

As was seen above at the conclusion of section 3, the medieval concept of the soul as simultaneously and co-extensively intellect and will was concomitant with an "integrated" conception of God as co-extensively the same, whose freedom and intelligibility are one in his divinity. We will have to join to that a further conclusion here that to recover the soul, therefore, as a compelling concept we must at the same time rediscover reality as self-evident to human experience—the reality of which I speak is *the reality of God, rightly perceived*, and therefore the mystery of ourselves as souls, as the opening of the world to him, an opening that comes from God, and completes itself by opening to him in freedom. The world, and ourselves, alienated from God, and hence blind to his glory manifest in and through the world, the spirituality of our senses dulled, are nevertheless destined for this glory, as revealed by the incarnation of God in Jesus Christ. And it is the liturgy, which is only the extension of the incarnation through time in the church, that therefore reveals the soul because the liturgy performs a symbolic "redistribution of the field of experience,"[60] or in other words enacts a transfiguration of the world in its totality, that, by human activity joined with God's, en-souls the world, makes this field into a theophanic presence, of which it is the essential dignity of human being, of the *embodied soul*, to bring about, by performing its "service."

The soul is the precise point of intersection of two worlds, heaven and earth, and through the senses it peers out in both directions; its gift and task is its very enacting of the free liturgical "harmonization" of these two worlds, since through this "work," this liturgy, like a passage, the divine presence flows into the created order and saves it. To "perceive" God in the world is *to be* a soul. What else can the believer, who has already inchoately received this gift of vision, say? *Esse est percipere*.

The soul is, *in a sense*, all things because it is, *in the senses*, divine.

## Bibliography

Aquinas, St. Thomas. *Summa Theologica*, 5 vols. Translated by the Fathers of the English Dominican Province. New York: Benzinger Brothers, 1948.
Aristotole. *On the Soul. The Complete Works of Aristotle*, vol. 1. Edited by Jonathan Barnes. Princeton, NJ: Princeton University Press, 1984.
Balthasar, Hans Urs von. *The Glory of the Lord vol. 1: Seeing the Form*. Translated by Erasmo Leiva-Merikakis. San Francisco: Ignatius, 1982.
Boulnois, Olivier. *Être et représentation*. Paris: Presses universitaires de France, 1999.

60. See Lacoste, *Experience and the Absolute*, for this rather Rancière-like phrase.

Brague, Rémi. "L'âme du salut." *Communio* 12.3 (1987).
Bulgakov, Sergei. *The Lamb of God*. Translated by Boris Jakim. Grand Rapids: Eerdmans, 2008.
———. *Unfading Light*. Translated by Thomas Alan Smith. Grand Rapids: Eerdmans, 2012.
Chrétien, Jean-Louis. *Symbolique du corps: La tradition chrétienne du Cantiques des Cantiques*. Paris: Presses universitaires de France, 2005.
Daniélou, Jean. "Conception of History in the Christian Tradition." *The Journal of Religion* 30 (1950) 171–79.
Denzinger, Heinrich. *The Sources of Catholic Dogma*. 30th ed. Translated by Roy J. Deferrari. Fitzwilliam, NH: Loreto, 1955.
Descartes, Rene. *Treatise of Man*. Translated by Thomas Steele. Hall. New York: Prometheus, 2003.
Falque, Emmanuel. *The Metamorphosis of Finitude*. Translated by George Hughes. New York: Fordham, 2012.
Farrell, Marie, T. "Thomas Aquinas and Friendship with God." *Irish Theological Quarterly* 61 (1995) 212–18.
Foucault, Michel. *The Order of Things*. New York: Random House, 1970.
Gavrilyuk, Paul, and Sarah Coakley. *The Spiritual Senses: Perceiving God in Western Christianity*. Cambridge: Cambridge University Press, 2011.
Heidegger, Martin. "The Age of the World Picture." In *The Question Concerning Technology and Other Essays*, translated by William Lovitt, 115–54. New York: Harper, 1982.
———. *Basic Problems of Phenomenology*. Translated by Albert Hofstadter. Indianapolis: Indiana University Press, 1988.
Henry, Michel. "Does the Concept 'Soul' Mean Anything?" *Philosophy Today* 13.2 (1969) 94–114.
———. *I Am the Truth: Toward a Philosophy of Christianity*. Translated by Susan Emanuel. Stanford, CA: Stanford University Press, 2002.
———. "Le concept d'âme a-t-il un sens?" *Revue philosophique Louvain* 64 (1966) 5–33.
———. *Philosophy and Phenomenology of the Body*. Translated by Gerard Etzkorn. The Hague: Nijhoff, 1975.
———. "Représentation et auto-affection." *Communio* 13.3 (1987) 77–96.
———. *Seeing the Invisible*. Translated by Scott Davidson. New York: Continuum, 2005.
Husserl, Edmund. *Ideas II*. Translated by Richard Rojcewicz and Andre Shcuwer. Dordrecht: Kluwer Academic, 1989.
Kant, Immanuel. *Critique of Pure Reason*. Translated by Norman Kemp Smith. New York: McMillan, 1965.
Kimbriel, Samuel. *Friendship as Sacred Knowing: Overcoming Isolation*. Oxford: Oxford University Press, 2014.
Koterski, Joseph W., SJ. *An Introduction to Medieval Philosophy: Basic Concepts*. Oxford: Wiley-Blackwell, 2009.
Lacoste, Jean-Yves. "Âme-cœur-corps." In *Dictionnaire critique de théologie*, 3rd ed., 39–41. Paris: Presses universitaires de France, 2007.
———. *From Theology to Theological Thinking*. Translated by W. Chris Hackett. Charlottesville, VA: University of Virginia Press, 2014.
Marion, Jean-Luc. *Sur la pensée passive de Descartes*. Paris: Presses universitaires de France, 2013.

Maximus the Confessor. *Mystagogia. Corpus Christianorum. Series Graeca*, vol. 69. Edited by C. Boudignon. Tournhout, Belgium: Brepols, 2011.

Milbank, John. "The Soul of Reciprocity, Part One: Reciprocity Refused." *Modern Theology* 17.3 (2001) 334–91.

———. "The Soul of Reciprocity, Part Two: Reciprocity Granted." *Modern Theology* 17.4 (2001) 485–507.

Nicholas, Marc. *Jean Daniélou's Doxological Humanism*. Eugene, OR: Pickwick, 2013.

Pickstock, Catherine. "Liturgy and the Senses." *South Atlantic Quarterly* 109.4 (2010) 719–41.

———. "The Ritual Birth of Sense." *Telos* 162 (2013) 29–55.

Rahner, Karl. "The Doctrine of the 'Spiritual Senses' in Origen." In *Theological Investigations* 16, 81–103. London: DLT, 1979.

———. "The Doctrine of the 'Spiritual Senses' in the Middle Ages," *Theological Investigations* 16, 104–34. London: DLT, 1979

Ratzinger, Joseph. *Eschatology: Death and Eternal Life*. Translated by Michael Waldstein. Washington, DC: Catholic University of America Press, 1988.

# 17

# The Soul at Work

## A Reading in Catholic Romanticism

### SIMONE KOTVA

DRESDEN, THE WINTER OF 1828–29. In the final months of a life not wanting in notoriety, Friedrich Schlegel (born 1772) delivers a set of curious lectures "concerning in particular the philosophy of language and words."[1] They are the third part of a trilogy, collectively christened the Philosophy of Life (*Philosophie des Lebens*),[2] which argues that the Divine telos of the soul, "the full and living centre of consciousness,"[3] lies in the restoration of the imago Dei. Despite this stolid appeal to doctrine, Schlegel's late *Philosophy of Life* has caused continual embarrassment for scholars of Romanticism, focusing the eye on its apparent heterodoxy with regard to a professed Catholicism, coupled with its enthrallment to a "Christian-vitalist occultism."[4] This has contributed to the unfortunate neglect of a significant chapter in the philosophical theology of "high" German Romanticism

---

1. Schlegel, *Philosophy of Language*, 349–555.

2. The two antecedent parts being the *Philosophy of Life* (1827) and *Philosophy of History* (1828). To avoid undue confusion "Philosophy of Life" will refer to Schlegel's project as a whole and *Philosophy of Life* to the lecture series of the same name.

3. Schlegel, *Philosophy of Language*, 448.

4. Anstett, "Mystisches und Okkultistisches," 132–50. In this paper, "vitalism" corresponds to Schlegel's use of *lebendig* and *Lebendigkeit* ("lively, living," "vitality") to articulate his belief in organic, "living" forces and his refutation of a mechanistic order of inert matter. For the relevant theories, see Richards, *Romantic Conception of Life*, 207–324, 511–54.

(c. 1815–48), to which the present paper addresses itself. I will argue that an attention to Schlegel's little-known theory of the soul reveals less heresy than orthodoxy, as its author defends classical theism and the doctrine of creation *ex nihilo* from the "dark spirit of negation" he believed G. W. F. Hegel to have unleashed upon the homeland.[5] This challenge to (rather than outright critique of) Idealism does indeed transpire as a species of Romantic vitalism, but one whose idiosyncrasies were characteristic of Schlegel's intellectual context—the short-lived Catholic Renaissance that thrived in the first few decades of the nineteenth century—rather than of a willful eclecticism.[6] It was the aim of this loose-knit fraternity (which included figures such as F. W. J. Schelling and Franz von Baader) to temper, creatively, *Naturphilosophie* and its ideas of organic "forces" (*Kräfte*) by suggesting that the intrinsic animation of matter and human artifice is dependent on (rather than equal to) the vitality and efficacy of God. In what follows, we will see how, for Schlegel, the artifice of language in particular is given a vitalist interpretation in order to support his Catholic construal of vitalism as the devotional activity of the soul. In place of a descriptive ontology, vitalism traces the love of God intimated by Socrates (as *philosophia*) and worked out by the tradition of Christian mysticism.[7] This, as he calls it, "positive" (rather than dialectically indifferent) Doctrine of Faith (*Glaubenslehre*) is a riposte to secular vitalism, one whose strengths as well as weaknesses offer a sobering example for the contemporary dialogue between theology and immanentist philosophies of life.

## Schlegel's Vitalism: Beyond Poetic Pantheism

> In the Philosophy of Life, even the method must be a living one.[8]

It was the events of Schlegel's conversion to Catholicism in 1808, coupled with his subsequent emigration to Austria, that served permanently to divide his audience and obscure his contributions to theology. On the one hand, he is the "early" co-editor of the radical journal *Athenaeum* (1798–1800), founding father of the Romantic movement; on the other, the "late" conservative in the employ of Austria's infamous Prince Clemens von Metternich, writer

---

5. Schlegel, *Philosophy of Language*, 543.

6. For the Anglophone history of the movement, see O'Meara, *Romantic Idealism*.

7. *KFSA* 8, 529–45. Unless otherwise stated, all translations from the *KFSA* are my own.

8. *KFSA* 10, 9.

for the Catholic *Ölzweige*.⁹ With a few notable exceptions, studies of Romantic literature, philosophy, and even theology have consistently favored the early Schlegel as their subject-matter, partly for geo-political reasons (the German liberal versus the Viennese Catholic), but more fundamentally for the volte-face that does appears in Schlegel's work as it begins to move in a theological direction.¹⁰ It manifested itself as a public rejection of Spinozism and pantheism (in 1808), followed by an ongoing polemic directed both at the thought of pantheism and Idealism, putting his later work at odds with earlier endorsements of Spinoza as "the general basis and support for every individual kind of mysticism."¹¹ At this point, a few remarks on Schlegel's changing attitude toward Spinozism and pantheism will clarify the far from obvious presuppositions of his swan song in the *Philosophy of Language*. Of particular importance is the distinction Schlegel makes between theological vitalism and an "absolutist" pantheism, distinctions that will shed light on the "occultist" components of Schlegel's psychology.

Schlegel's rejection of pantheism was a reflection of the permanent confusion in terminology caused by the Pantheism Controversy (1783 to 1786) which had been incited by the polemics of Friedrich Heinrich Jacobi. In nuce, the latter had argued (following Gotthold Ephraim Lessing's supposed confession to Spinozism) that Spinoza's belief in a deterministic universe controlled by an immanent Godhead was the necessary outcome of the *Aufklärung* appeal to reason as a way to faith: "rational theology" meant theology deterministically reduced to reason.¹² To overcome the implied

---

9. Goethe expressed his exasperation "that in the highest light of reason and understanding, of world-comprehension, an extraordinary and highly educated talent is mislead to bury itself." Quoted in O'Meara, *Romantic Idealism*, 122. Goethe's critical standpoint was perpetuated by Heine, *History of Religion*, 152 and is still discernible in contemporary treatments of Schlegel's thought. See for instance Hellerich, *Religionizing, Romanizing Romantics*, for a particularly scathing interpretation of Schlegel's theology; and Beiser, introduction to *Early Political Writings*, xviii–xxii, for a more sensitive but still confused reading of Schlegelian religiosity. Schlegel's volte-face was recently made the subject-matter of an academic conference, Figuren der Konversion: Tagung der Friedrich Schlegel-Gesellschaft, held at the Johannes Gutenberg-Universität, Mainz, April 8–10, 2010.

10. The literature on early Schlegel is too voluminous to cite; for a good survey, see Millán-Zaibert, *Friedrich Schlegel*. For the literature that touches on Schlegel's Catholicism, see Körner, "Friedrich Schlegels katolische Glaubensbekenntnis?" 349–56; Anstett, *La Pensées religièuse* and "Mystisches und Okkultistisches," 132–50; Dempf, "Der frühe und der späte Friedrich Schlegel," 79ff; Behler, introduction to *KFSA* 8, 9 and 10; O'Meara, *Romantic Idealism*, 120–26; Vincelette, *Recent Catholic Philosophy*, 22–31 and Keiner, *Hieroglyphenromantik*, 138–97. Only the work by Anstett, which is sadly out of date with the *KFSA*, offers a full-length study of Schlegel's theology.

11. Schlegel, *Dialogue on Poetry*, 87.

12. Beiser, *The Fate of Reason*, 44–108.

radical divide between faith and reason, Jacobi suggested a paradoxical "fatal leap," a *salto mortale*, from reason into faith. In 1787 Johann Gottfried Herder responded to this (as he perceived it) abuse of Spinoza's metaphysics with a book that defended the substance-monism of the *Ethics* by redefining it in terms of a force-monism, replacing substance with the language of "forces" derived from G. W. Leibniz: "everywhere organic forces (*Kräfte*) alone can be active, and every one of them makes attributes of an infinite God known to us."[13] Herder's Spinoza was not the rationalist of geometric method, but the mystic of vital energies and material evolution, bringing the seventeenth-century thinker in line with the latest speculative ventures in the biological sciences. It was this Spinoza (rather than the philosopher himself) whom Schlegel applauded as the prophet of the pre-established cult of the *anima mundi*, which the early Romantics perpetuated as children of the *Goethezeit*.

Thus Schlegel adopts the idea of immanent forces; though, as we shall see, he would eventually construe these in terms of a force-dualism, distinguishing between Divine and created vitality. But even at this early stage, he is not entirely at ease with its denomination of "pantheism" and "Spinozism." In 1806, whilst residing in Paris and frequenting Catholic salons, he finds himself qualifying the terms in the following manner:

> Pantheism is the entrance to truth for our age—if it is taken scientifically (*Wissenschaftlich*) and mechanically it leads to Nature-Philosophy (*Naturphilosophie*) and astrology. If it taken poetically (as in the ideas of Novalis and myself) it leads 1) to the religion of all religions, without exceptions 2) through further research to the distinctions between true and simple religions and thus finally to true Catholicism.[14]

The distinction Schlegel is forced to make between a "bad" and a "good" pantheism, the latter of which is the remit of religious practice whilst the former represents scientific observation deprived of a theological dimension, is conditioned by Herder's and Jacobi's conflicting uses, from which Schlegel still wants positively to distance himself. For Jacobi, "pantheism" designates a methodology—that of rational reduction—by which one is able to view the world only after one has established the way it is known (epistemology). Schlegel will later refer to this method as "absolutization," where, as it were, the "pan" of "pantheism" has come to stand for reduction, rather than vitalist animation: for his elevation of the "I," Fichte is

13. Herder, *God: Some Conversations*, 104.
14. *KFSA* 19, 250, §374.

likewise a pantheist (an "absolutizer") of a single principle.¹⁵ For Herder, by contrast, pantheism really does describe the world (it is alive with forces); it is an ontology, not a methodology.

What Schlegel might have in mind by a "poetic" pantheism beyond both methodology and the vitalism of *Naturphilosophie* is clarified two years later, in his first (and only) monograph, *The Language and Wisdom of the Indians*, a historical survey of Sanskrit literature, theology, and philosophy. In its second book, Schlegel gives a developmental narrative of the six schools of Brahmanical philosophy, to be taken as paradigms or quasi-archetypes for the evolution of religion in general. Retrospectively summarizing the thesis of the *Language and Wisdom*, in the *Philosophy of Language* Schlegel explains that history begins with the Divine revelation of the "real vitality inherent in all existence," a generally held "creed of nature, enforced by the universal feeling of mankind, and originally held by all the nations of the earth."¹⁶ In the *Language and Wisdom* this vitalism constitutes an ur-monotheism (*Urmonotheismus*) or "primeval Christianity,"¹⁷ an original revelation that then passes through historical stages of successive deterioration and confusion, culminating in the modern "error" of a pantheism of "pure reason," a variation on the "scientific" pantheism of 1806, which is here denounced roundly as the scourge of contemporary philosophy (F. W. J. Schelling's recent appropriation of pantheism being the implicit target).¹⁸ Intermediate to this reigning heresy, however, is the intriguing "mythological" pantheism, a misguided hypostatization (absolutization) of "real vitality" into personifications, deities, and other supernatural powers. Though removed from original revelation, unlike its "rational" kindred, "mythological" pantheism preserves something of the ur-monotheism. Though both pantheisms are denounced, the latter is able to safeguard a kernel of that earlier, Romantic rhetoric of a "poetic pantheism."

Already in this work of his middle period, it is evident that "further researches" compelled Schlegel to refrain from throwing out the baby with the bath water. Whilst "pantheism" is found wanting as a suitable term to describe the vitalist revelation, the revelation itself is fortified (as demonstrated by its iteration in the *Philosophy of Language*). This observation gives us reason to question the attractive narrative of Nicholas Riasanovsky, who argues that the premature death of early Romanticism was caused by the intrinsic

    15. The polemic against an over-confidence in the Absolute is scattered throughout the *Philosophy of Language*, but particularly concentrated in Lecture IX, 528–51.
    16. Schlegel, *Philosophy of Language*, 526.
    17. Stroc-Oppenberg, introduction to *KFSA* 8, cxliv–cli.
    18. *KFSA* 8, 191–255 and 243. For the Schlegel-Schelling polemics, see Behler, "Friedrich Schlegel und Hegel," 224–26 and O'Meara, *Romantic Idealism*, 121–26.

deficiencies of neo-Spinozist pantheism; Schlegel's evidence suggests in its stead a less dramatic though certainly more confusing transformation of neo-Spinozism into a theologically determined vitalism.[19] The *Philosophy of Language* illustrates this in a rare display of self-criticism, where Schlegel is regretful of his youthful resort to Spinozism, explaining that the popularity of the term has led to a situation where his original *poetisch* ("poetic") has been demoted to the "innumerable . . . figures of *dichterisch* ('poetical') pantheism" since "so many poets and other popular writers are a kind of half or whole, conscious or unconscious, Spinozists—to use this name in a wide and general sense."[20] As Schelling would likewise point out, this poetical generation uses pantheism simply to express an immediate enthusiasm by God, rather than indicating any awareness of the underlying Pantheism Controversy.[21] For Schlegel, this eventuated a concomitant inability to separate Spinoza's twofold sin of subscribing both to an ontological (mythological) pantheism (*Deus sive natura*) and to a methodological pantheism (of "pure reason"), in that Schlegel believed his *Ethics* to represent the definite account of truth, an instance of intellectual hubris (absolutism).[22]

To combat these two species of pantheism, Schlegel insists that the original revelation of vitalism must predicate not only our conception of matter, but likewise our philosophical procedures: "In the Philosophy of Life, even the method must be a living one."[23] A vitalist method will see ideas themselves participating in an "eddying stream," ever-changing and growing with the epochs of human consciousness.[24] This is the tenor of both the *Philosophy of Life* and the *Philosophy of Language* where Schlegel argues for philosophy as the engagement with "living" ideas over "dead" abstractions.[25] This is so, he explains, because philosophy, as a Neoplatonic *philosophia*, is a continual striving for wisdom, an "infinite yearning" (*unendliche Sehnsucht*) that is justified by the fact that what the philosopher is yearning for is itself infinite: namely, God. "Yearning for the Infinite" (*Sehnsucht nach dem Unendlichen*) is philosophy's true, theological calling, distinct both from a pursuit of absolute knowledge (whether secular or sacred), as well as the study and exposition of doctrine (the theology of

19. Riasanovsky, *The Emergence of Romanticism*.
20. Schlegel, *Philosophy of Language*, 499.
21. Schelling, *On the History of Modern Philosophy*, 178.
22. Schlegel, *Philosophy of Language*, 495–96.
23. *KFSA* 10, 9.
24. *KFSA* 10, 355.
25. Behler has helpfully collated Schlegel's vitriolic rhetoric against "dead" philosophy in his "Schlegel und Hegel," 217, 243, 249.

the schools).[26] This creaturely yearning for the Creator (a theistic distinction Schlegel is at great pains to retain) is mirrored in its accompanying vitalist imagery. Critically distancing itself from Herder's use of "forces" to describe God's nature, Schlegel sees the fact of vitality as an earthly analogy to the transcendent vitality of the Divine. In contrast to Schelling, for whom organicism entails a primordial matrix for undifferentiated forces of good and evil, for Schlegel, vitality is created wholly good as slumbering potentials dependent on the rousing word of God, which stirs them into life and enables their first turning toward Him. It is to this Divine con-version that the soul is instrumental.

## The Soul: Figuration and Restoration

Over the course of ten lectures, the *Philosophy of Language* offers a theoretical account of the soul, aspects of which are anticipated in scattered notebook entries and the articles Schlegel published in the *Ölzweige*, the Viennese journal of Catholic thought which ran from 1819 to 1823. The *Philosophy of Language*, however, knits together these earlier ideas into a more pronouncedly vitalist framework, attempting to demonstrate a "living method" at work. In the following outline of the theory, these earlier pieces will nonetheless come in useful, as Schlegel's untimely death occurred before he had begun to edit and expound the more suggestive passages of his final lectures.[27]

The premise of Schlegel's theory of the soul, which is shared across the *Philosophy of Life* trilogy, is that humanity is made in the image of God. First, she is made, or created, standing in a particular relationship to God, who, though he creates the world *ex nihilo*, does so "for something."[28] Schlegel shares this assertion of the doctrine of creation with Baader, the Catholic intellectual who exercised an immense influence on the early Romantics, and with whom Schlegel carried on a life-long correspondence. For both these thinkers *creatio ex nihilo* challenged the immanent Spirit of Hegelian philosophy, "the nought of the dark world of shadows, which has now become real and consequently evil."[29] In Schlegel's view, evil is never part of the Divine plan, but is ever the result of a creature exercising its creative

---

26. Schlegel, *Philosophy of Language*, 429.

27. As it is, we have only Schlegel's preliminary indications in the margins of the text beside those paragraphs he wished to return to when preparing the manuscript for publication.

28. Schlegel, *Philosophy of Language*, 543

29. Ibid.

faculty (*Fantasie*) in opposition to God.³⁰ To deny the event of creation is to aid evil in its proliferation, an evil one is then able to detect in the tendencies of poetical pantheism.³¹

Second, humanity is imaged. She is essentially representational, or "figurative" (*Bildlich*), because, as he explains in his notebooks, "the human being itself, in its entire and innermost essence (*Wesen*) is an image (*Bild*), a likeness (*Ebenbild*) and a representation (*Abbild*) of God—as indeed creation itself, in which He reveals his innermost being, is thought of as a reflection, a mirror and image of His concealed glory."³² Schlegel's contributions to the *Ölzweige* develop this theme, arguing that because of their figured natures, human beings encounter the world imaginatively through a "childlike sense" of *Bildlichkeit*, the "figurative faculty," not to be confused with the treacherous *Fantasie*.³³ *Bild*, "image," the common word also for "picture" and "painting," is a nominal formation from the verb *bilden*, "to shape, form." The abstract noun *Bildung* came to mean "education" in the sense of "formation," used in the eighteenth-century *Bildungsroman* as a humanist alternative to the life of formative *imitatio Christi*.³⁴ By opting for *Bildlichkeit* over *Bildung*, Schlegel, for whom the latter had become "an entirely corrupt concept,"³⁵ is showing his theological colors: *Bild* and *Ebenbild* are the Mosaic "image and likeness" of Genesis 1:26.³⁶ Employing *Bild* synonymously with symbol in the *Philosophy of Language*, Schlegel explains that "it is only figuratively (*bildlich*) that . . . [the idea of God] can be at all indicated. It is by symbols alone that such can be conceived or comprehended."³⁷ This aesthetic category of *Bildlichkeit* does not, for Schlegel, depict the Divine nature exactly (or reduce it entirely), rather, images express the nature of

---

30. *KFSA* 19, [X] § 199. The trope of Satan as "fantasist" is a common one. See Baader, *Vorlesungen und Erläuterungen*, 72–73: "The Devil was the first poet . . . ."

31. For Schlegel's rejection of radical evil, see his remarks on Jacob Böhme in *KFSA* 19, [X], §7: "(. . . God's whole nature (*Wesen*) is nothing but love, mercy is wholly one with his being).—the farther we move from the midpoint of God, the more difficult is the return."

32. *KFSA* 8, 565.

33. "Anfangspunkte des Christlischen Nachdenkens. Nach dem Sprüchen des Angelus," in *KFSA* 8, 563, the companion piece to "Von der wahren Liebe Gottes und dem falschen Mystizismus. Ein Nachtrag der Heiligen Bernhardus," *KFSA* 8, 546–84; both originally published between 1819 and 1820.

34. For the theological versus secular developments of this term see Stahl, *Die religiöse und die humanitätsphilosophische Bildungsidee*.

35. *KFSA* 19, 172, §153.

36. Unlike the church fathers, but like the German Protestant tradition, Schlegel does not discriminate between *Bild* and *Ebenbild*.

37. Schlegel, *Philosophy of Language*, 457.

creaturely existence, imperfectly mirroring the Creator, as Platonic Ideas relate to their mimetic copies. This mirroring function is crucial, as without it we would not be able to realign our *imago Dei* with its Divine prototype. Again, pace Hegel, the aim of the historical unfolding is not an upward spiral toward absolute knowledge, but "the restoration in man of the lost image of God."[38]

This embodied perspective afforded by the *imago Dei* means that human life is defined in terms of its "inner" life, viz., the life perceived and felt by consciousness (*Bewusstsein*). Unlike later psychology and phenomenology, however, the core of these experiences are not human but Divine, being divinely created.[39] "Consciousness" is here the umbrella term by which Schlegel indicates the inner life in order to situate its parts: the "general" soul (the body's animating principle), the spirit, and the manifold faculties, all of which are subservient to their guiding principle, the "thinking" and "loving" soul, the center of both body and mind. The thinking soul, in itself pure and incorruptible, retains the image of God, participating in Him as the "primary source [and] recollection of eternal love."[40] Through a Christian version of Platonic *anamnesis* (recollection), Schlegel explains how it is consciousness (reacting to day-to-day impressions) that initiates this process of restoration which can then clear the path for the illumination of the soul's imago, the relationship between consciousness and soul being roughly that of expression and essence, where the former is the active manifestation or diagnosis of the inner, true state. Schlegel explains that this emphasis on the inner life is not a capitulation to the force of a Fichtean "I"; on the contrary, life becomes inner only in relation to God to whom it strives in our two formulae: "the yearning for the infinite," interchangeable with "an infinite yearning." The movement is fittingly given its own symbolic figuration in an etching (after a drawing by the author's niece Auguste von Buttlar) which illustrates the first edition, printed so as to complete the last, unfinished, sentence of the *Philosophy of Language*. The nymph-like cherub is in fact the soul, Psyche being distinguished from angels by her butterfly wings. She is ascending from earth to heaven, brandishing the broken shackles of, we may conjecture, Hegel's "dark spirit of negation."[41]

38. *KFSA* 9, 3.
39. Schlegel, *Philosophy of Language*, 392. Emphasis mine.
40. Ibid., 411.
41. Vienna, 1830, 313.

Figure 1: The Soul of "Infinite Yearning"

## The Soul's Hieroglyph

The soul as living figure—as literal *imago Dei*—is reinforced by the pictorial representation of the soul as a hieroglyphic alphabet, the idea of a primitive "sacred writing" Schlegel derives from the interest occasioned by Jean-François Champollion's deciphering of the Rosetta Stone in 1822.

We begin with observing that consciousness is fourfold, consisting of reason, will, understanding, and fancy (*Fantasie*, not *Bildlichkeit*, since this latter is the provenance of the "loving" soul), to which belong the four intermediary faculties of memory, judgment, desiring (or volition), and conscience. This doubled fourfold is then juxtaposed to human nature proper, which is, on the classical model, triple or triune, consisting of body, (animating) soul, and spirit (or the "idea of God"). At the centre of both is the loving soul, a unified circle or "midpoint." Together consciousness, human nature, and soul make up a twelve-letter "alphabet of consciousness."[42]

It is an "alphabet" because the role of consciousness is to put into relation, with the help of reason and fancy, the building-blocks of speech impressed in the soul at the time of the original revelation. Language, Schlegel believes, is the singular characteristic of human nature, being "a true copy (*treuer Abdruck*), a shifting *diorama*, as it were, of man's inward self."[43] Here Schlegel is entering upon favorite territory: the debate surrounding the origin of language, which he had first theorized in *Language and Wisdom*. As in the earlier monograph, Schlegel takes Johann Georg Hamann's side against Herder, critiquing the latter's Enlightenment "naturalist" position, which argued that language had developed over the course of time, arising through the imitation of bird-calls and the articulation of emotive outcries. Adam, in this view, had no intelligible language; what was given him by God was the capacity for speech, rather than speech itself. Against this popular thesis, Schlegel stubbornly insisted on the old Adamic thesis that language was given by God to humankind in such a way that it arose not "piecemeal," but through the gift of revelation: "at once and in its totality out of the full inner and living consciousness of man," albeit not in a uniform package, but in dialects appropriate to the dispositions of each stage in the development of consciousness.[44]

"Alphabet," though selected in part as a fitting metaphor, rapidly comes to exceed a merely suggestive role. At first we see this in the rehearsal of the outmoded theories that so irritated (not to say bewildered) his audience.[45] Thus Schlegel elaborates how the different parts of speech correspond to different aspects of human nature: aspirates (being ethereal) are a mark of spirit, and so of antiquity; a language rich in them (Greek being the obvious example) belongs to an archaic civilization with great intellectual traditions,

---

42. Schlegel, *Philosophy of Language*, 456–57. Cf. *KFSA* 8, 551, "if only we have once found the correct midpoint—namely God— . . . then life moves in ever wider circles and spreads itself out in waxing power (*Kraft*) and plenitude."

43. Ibid., 402.

44. Ibid., 402–3. Schlegel's philosophy of language has, unlike his *Philosophy of Life*, received repeated attention, though without sufficient attention to its theological implications. See Fiesel, *Die Sprachphilosophie der deutschen Romantik*; Nüsse, *Die Sprachtheorie Friedrich Schlegels*, and most recently, Keiner, *Hieroglyphenromantik*. In Anglophone scholarship, Schlegel's work is accorded an unusual (though brief) mention in Riley, "Some German Theories of the Origin of Language," 626–29.

45. As evidenced in a letter lamenting the demise of Schlegel's genius written by Ludwig Tieck to August Wilhelm, Schlegel's elder brother, shortly after Schlegel's death. See Lüdeke and Lohner (eds), *Ludwig Tieck und die Brüder Schlegel*, 191. The opinion of Tieck is repeated in Eichner, *Friedrich Schlegel*, 140–44.

and so on. The (animating) soul corresponds to vowels, and, as we might expect, consonants represent somatic gravity.[46] The theory gains momentum once Schlegel concludes his exegesis of the phonemes which the letters signify, and turns to their visible figuration. For Schlegel, the most primitive and also fundamental form of the individual letter was the hieroglyph, the word or syllable depicted not through the composition of mediatory signs corresponding to specific sounds (as in the hieroglyphically devolved Hebrew, Greek, and Roman alphabets), but immediately, by a single image (the wavy line signifying "water").[47] It is in this specific (rather than "poetically pantheistic") sense that Schlegel can claim that visual art, or the symbolic figure,

> in its inmost essence . . . is a language of nature of a higher and spiritual kind . . . an inward hieroglyphical writing and original speech of the soul, which is immediately intelligible to all susceptible natures. . . . For the eternal and fundamental feelings of the soul are awakened, or rather re-awakened, in these inner soul-words of true art.[48]

Before we sang, shouted, or discoursed, we wrote, or were ourselves inscribed with images. This "original speech" is the direct outcome of our imaged creation, since "humankind . . . is nothing other than the created word, the faint echo and very imperfect copy of the uncreated and eternal." The *imago Dei* reverses a "naturalist" theory that would place writing at the endpoint of human development. Instead, humankind as literal word entails, long before Jacques Derrida's critique of orality, the primacy of writing as a form of original speech. It is a thesis drawn from a Neoplatonically-informed Christian Kabbalah, transmitted to Schlegel via Hamann and Baader, who were intrigued by the Kabbalist anti-naturalist idea that letters and phonemes possessed inherent vitality.[49] Rather than pursue these ideas to their occult conclusion in alphabet-mysticism, Schlegel chooses to give them a doctrinal grounding: the created word is not stowed away in a Hermetic grimoire, but revealed in the "child-like" faculty of figuration, which is the gift of the Creator to His creation.

46. Schlegel, *Philosophy of Language*, 461–65.

47. Middle Egyptian writing recorded by a complex writing system which combined basic pictorial representation with a highly abstract syllabic alphabet, but Schlegel is interested only in the primitive stage, still discernible in the archaic form of the characters.

48. Schlegel, *Philosophy of Language*, 436. Emphasis mine.

49. For the influence of Christian Kabbalah on Catholic Renaissance thinkers, see Benz, *The Mystical Sources of German Romantic Philosophy*, 47, and Koslowski, *Philosophien der Offenbarung*, 186–87.

Similarly, Schlegel's alphabet is outlined in terms that subtly subvert a Hermetic interpretation. If we recall, the alphabet is a composite of three basic geometrical shapes: circle ("loving" soul/"midpoint"), quadrangle (fourfold consciousness) and triangle (triune human nature).

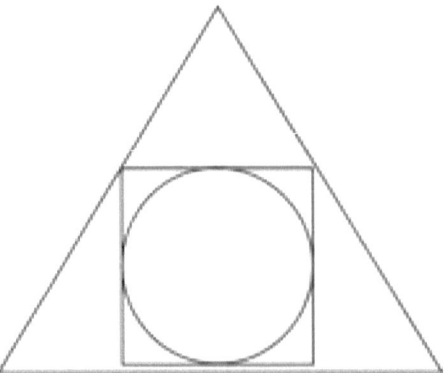

Figure 2. Pictorial representation of the Alphabet of Consciousness

In assembling these shapes according to the *Philosophy of Language*, we see how Schlegel draws on Hermetic number symbolism, ideas most likely conveyed to him, as Michael Elsässer suggests, by Baader, and a paper by the latter, "On the Pythagorean Quadrangle in Nature or the Four Parts of the World (*plagae mundi*)."[50] In Pythagorean number mysticism the quadrangle was interpreted as the original form of the circle, a paradox that the ancient world articulated as the task of "squaring the circle." It was a mathematical conundrum that received mystical analogies, translated into the quintessence of a spiritual quest. In Michael Maier's 1617 collection of "emblems" illustrating alchemical secrets, the *Atalanta Fugiens*, we find the quest as the first step required in order to create the Philosopher's Stone: "make of the man and woman a Circle, of that a Quadrangle [i.e., square the circle], of this a Triangle, of the same a Circle and you will have the Stone of the Philosophers."[51]

---

50. Schlegel, *Philosophy of Language*, 475–77. Elsässer, *Kritik am Ding*, 118–21, 155–59. Baader, "Ueber das pythagoräische Quadrat," 247–68.

51. Maier, *Atalanta Fugiens*, Emblem XXI.

Figure 3. Maier's alchemical emblem of
The Philosopher's Stone (left), with schematic (right)

The geometric sigil of the Philosopher's Stone (right) resembles Schlegel's alphabet, with a decisive caveat: Meier depicts spiritual completion with a monistic circle (union with the Divine One), whilst Schlegel opts for a Trinitarian threefold (union of the Christian Godhead). Again, this is reminiscent of Baader, who, like Schlegel, allows the triangle to complete his squared circle. The quadrangle, representing the immanent world of spatial "corners" (the *plagae mundi*) and the circle, representing the transcendent unity of the Divine, are both visually and theologically fulfilled in the triangle (the Trinity), in which the Creator completes and redeems the world ("squares the circle") through the incarnation. In a footnote to his article, Baader depicts this Trinitarian squaring elegantly with the "familiar symbol" of a triangle pierced by a circle.[52]

Figure 4. Baader's threefold "squaring" the circle.

---

52. Baader, "Das pythagoräische Quadrat," 267.

Thus, while Schlegel's Dresden audience were busy expressing their disappointment at the ease with which this once enlightened thinker now mingled outmoded ideas of language theory with curious theosophy, Catholic doctrine, and modern vitalism, they unwittingly lost sight of the radical and daring project of their lecturer, namely, to uncover a theological genealogy of vitalism from within its largely heretical articulations.[53] His theory of the soul exemplifies this aim, composed as it is of occult components that are deliberately misread so as to situate them in relation to the original revelation of a "real vitality." Schlegel defends the primacy of the soul's inner life only insofar as this life is seen to be but one part of a reciprocal exchange, the dynamic "yearning" for the infinite which sets in motion the restoration of the lost image of God. In the hands of Schlegel, vitalism is turned from speculative organicism (*Naturphilosophie*) to a pioneering outpost of Catholic doctrine, seeking a new way of articulating the fundamental movement of creation as it tends toward and is directed by God. While the *Philosophy of Language* answers the question of why the soul is vital (namely, because it is a "created word" striving to be iterated), it now remains to be seen how the soul puts its capacities to use in the "living method"—the "further researches" of "poetic pantheism"—indicated above.

## The Soul at Work: Liturgy and Prayer

For Schlegel, the living soul is the soul at work, consciously turning itself toward God through liturgical devotion and prayer which exercise the "child-like sense": this, I argue, is what Schlegel means by a "living method." Being of a more experientially contingent nature than a general theory of the soul, this conclusion is only hinted at in the *Philosophy of Language*; for its articulation we must look to Schlegel's notes and private correspondence. Intimations, however, are found in the penultimate lecture of the *Philosophy of Language*, where Schlegel explains that true knowledge is not the result of raising ourselves to a Divine level, but of allowing ourselves to let this level "take hold of our minds" as we "feel and draw out the latent presence of God in objects (*Gegenständen*)." He hastens to qualify this apparent pantheism of a "real vitality" by adding that these objects be viewed not immanently, but in relation to the transcendent God, as they have "proceeded from the Deity[,] stand before His omniscient eye and are seen by Him."[54]

A possession by the Divine (reminiscent of the mania that grips the enthusiast in Plato's *Phaedrus* 244a) enables the soul to communicate with

---

53. See above, n. 45.
54. Schlegel, *Philosophy of Language*, 547.

the "effectual potency of the life-enlightened spirit in which every thought is at once an act, and every word a power."[55] In thus taking the first steps toward restoration, the soul is mirroring the very essence or nature (*Wesen*) of God, which, as Schlegel noted down, "is at the same time His action."[56] The difference between the Divinely created soul of the human being, and the soul of the Divine, is that there is in the latter no discrepancy (no "infinite striving") between life-force and expression, between act and figuration. It comes as no surprise that Schlegel, the Catholic convert, sees the superlative instance of this possession, where the Divine vitality communes with that of creation, taking place in the liturgy of the Eucharist:

> The concept of transubstantiation receives an entirely different appearance if one imagines it as a restoration or a retrieval of transfigured nature, whose inmost core is the real life-matter .... [T]he transfigured body [of the host] is itself not only the image of God, but also the force (*Kraft*) of God.[57]

The Eucharist is here what Astrid Keiner calls a Schlegelian *Realsymbol*, or "true symbol," a hieroglyph which is immediate and non-representational, because it embodies what it (re)presents, as earthly images can never do satisfactorily.[58] This is why, again, Schlegel is emphatic regarding the importance of the aesthetically visual as part (rather than predicate) of the theological. In the *Philosophy of Life* he writes that an "altar-less" Christianity, "divested of every symbol and mystery, would be merely a philosophical view and opinion ... but not a religion," not because the pictorial trumps the devotional, but because symbols are the necessary manifestation of that inner *Bildlichkeit* of the "original" (psychic) "speech": iconoclasm is a violence against the human soul.[59]

If the Eucharist is where the soul is able to receive the vitalized symbol of the Divine passionately, as it were, prayer is the means by which the soul is invited to work actively toward the vitalization of its own re-figuring. In his notebooks Schlegel reflects that "we only reach the knowledge of God through life and through personal experience, primarily ... through prayer," the latter defined simply as "faith, hope, and love in actu."[60] Prayer, particu-

---

55. Schlegel, *Philosophy of Language*, 449. Emphasis mine.

56. *KFSA* 19, 382, §206. The note is a riposte to Schleiermacher's distinction between a "hidden" and "revealed" God, a bifurcation Schlegel believes is antithetical to the "true [Catholic] doctrine of revelation."

57. *KFSA* 19, 342, §274.

58. Keiner, *Hieroglyphenromantik*, 129.

59. *KFSA* 10, 241.

60. *KFSA* 19, [X] §283, §229.

larly mystical prayer, became an all-consuming occupation during the last decade of Schlegel's life, a practice begun during the theologically formative years 1817–23. Among other spiritual literature, both he and Dorothea, his wife and fellow convert, steeped themselves in Baroque mysticism, reading Ignatius of Loyola's *Spiritual Exercises* and Theresa of Avila's autobiography with particular fervor, the latter which Schlegel refers to as a great aid in his own prayer-life.[61] Schlegel's mention of Avila is a testimony to what is perhaps the most remarkable—and remarkably misunderstood—dedication by a nineteenth-century philosopher to practicing "love in actu," the animated correspondence with his "soul-sister in Christ" Christine von Stransky. In the epistolary exchange, begun after a chance meeting in 1821, Schlegel and Christine attempt a course of remote healing, petitioning for the cure of physical and spiritual afflictions through fervent intercession. Woven into the pious rhetoric of Schlegel's surviving letters is the conviction that an understanding of vitalism supplies prayer with a practical manual, since it, like all else in the created order, participates in life. Prayer is not merely a hopeful desire, but a very real force, subject to being directed—and misdirected—by the human person. Notoriously, Schlegel also interpreted the new "sciences" of animal magnetism and mesmerism as forces related to prayer, suggesting that the exercise of them could help ensure the Divine teleology of prayer before it departed the sphere of earthly vitality. Dorothea observes that at this time Schlegel was becoming increasingly preoccupied with the occult sciences,[62] apparently developing his statement jotted down years previously, that "prayer is nothing but magnetism,"[63] a statement that has unfortunately led later detractors to draw his theological praxis in too mystical a light.[64] In truth, the importance of animal magnetism and the occult sciences for Schlegel is less eccentric than his commentators have allowed. His starting point is that of a theological vitalist who must take seriously any theory purporting to explain the forces at work in nature, hence the interest in speculative therapies. However, Schlegel converts these pseudoscientific therapies into a *labora:* animal magnetism is re-interpreted as the

---

61. *KFSA* 30, 285, 404, and 432. On the Schlegels' reading list we also find Bernard of Clairvaux's *The Love of God*, Thomas à Kempis' *The Imitation of Christ*, and Angelus Silesius' *Cherubic Wanderer*.

62. *KFSA* 30, 387.

63. Elsässer, *Kritik am Ding*, 104. This method of "Christianized" magnetic healing had been pioneered by Schlegel in an earlier correspondence with the Countess Lešniowska, *KFSA* 35, 1–206.

64. See Elsässer, *Kritik am Ding*, 92–93, who expresses doubts as to the sincerity of Schlegel's Catholicism, and Eichner, *Friedrich Schlegel*, 140–44, for a wholly disparaging account of Schlegel's interests in animal magnetism.

conversion "through the Christian faith and through prayer" of the "natural magnetism of pagan antiquity,"[65] in other words, of the restoration of the original revelation of a "real vitality" from its mythological interpretation to its true meaning in Christ (as Divine love). Schlegel's surviving letters to Christine overflow with reflections on the efficacy of the "treatment," which purportedly led to an astonishing episode of stigmata in his confidante.[66]

Albeit idiosyncratic, this prayer-life was for Schlegel the exterior symbol of psychic restoration, a divinely directed activity which operated on the principle of reciprocity, reminiscent of what in his earlier work he had termed a *Wechselerweis* or *Wechselbegriff* ("oscillation-concept"), between the vitality of the world and the vitality of God.[67] Its aesthetic is that of an excess of figuration, a cataphatic, "positive philosophy," which leads, in the classical way of the *via negativa*, toward an essential apophaticism: "one cannot see God in himself, in this essentiality (*Wesenheit*); but one can indeed see all things in God."[68] In the deceptive lull between two periods of upheaval and revolution, this vitalism of sacrament and prayer seemed to herald a rejuvenation of the Catholic Church: "We live in a wonderful age," exclaims Dorothea in 1822, while Schlegel writes to Christine that he believes "the most important part of my life is yet to come."[69]

## Conclusion: The Fate of Catholic Romanticism

Schlegel's theory of the soul affords a glimpse of Catholic Romantic thought at its zenith. Only a few years after his death, its unique milieu, open to harnessing heady speculation to doctrinal ends, came under fire from Rome, and was discouraged by a resurgence of neo-Thomism in the 1830s, and further disrupted by the revolutions of 1848.[70] Schlegel's choice to deliver the *Philosophy of Language* in Dresden (and not in Vienna like its two companions), tells of the optimism Schlegel still harbored for both the project and its method, aside from being undertaken for personal reasons (Dresden was the home of his sister's family). For Schlegel it was important to face this

---

65. *KFSA* 19, [X] §287.
66. *KFSA* 30, 638.
67. Frank, "'Wechselgrundsatz,'" 26–50.
68. *KFSA* 19, [X] §44. Schlegel's sense of "positive philosophy," similarly employed by Schelling as a piece of anti-Hegelian rhetoric, is most likely informed by the traditional distinction between a "scholastic" and a "positive" (i.e., practically oriented) philosophy, for which see Ignatius, *Spiritual Exercises of Saint Ignatius*, §363.
69. *KFSA* 30, 380–81, 337.
70. O'Meara, *Romantic Idealism*, 121.

skeptical audience in order to dispatch his Catholic *Philosophy of Life* with evangelizing urge straight into the country from whence had sprung the philosophy of Hegel, whose universalizing (pantheistic) Spirit epitomized for Schlegel the theological hazard played by German philosophy.[71] Ernst Behler, collaborator on the critical edition of Schlegel's complete works, charitably suggests that we read this zenith of Catholic Romanticism as a proto-*Lebensphilosophie*, a herald of those philosophies of the later nineteenth century that developed vitalism in a specifically psychological direction, leading to the beginnings of phenomenology and existentialism.[72] This was a ferment out of which arose a host of distinct but related thinkers: Franz Brentano, Wilhelm Dilthey, Ludwig Klages, Edmund Husserl, and Martin Heidegger; as well as, in Schlegel's Paris, Main de Biran, Félix Ravaisson, Henri Bergson, and the "French Spiritualists." Tempting though it is to fashion Schlegel into the progenitor of not only Romanticism but the entire tradition of "Continental" Philosophy, it does not move beyond a superficial comparison of rhetorical form (the references to "life") to the examination of argumentative content. Behler's comparison moderates Schlegel into a benign "spiritual realist" in place of the controversial Catholic thinker of the *Philosophy of Language*.[73] The theological concerns of the *Philosophy of Life*, exemplified in Schlegel's theory of the soul and its subversion of both secular and occult philosophy, will hopefully have done something to complicate this ascription. Rather than revealing a continuity with later life-philosophies, Schlegel's vitalism, grounded in theism, *creatio ex nihilo*, and devotional praxis, is notably discontinuous with its successors: by and large, these have abandoned their Catholic beginnings for a more "poetical" Spinozism. More convincing, for this reason, is the argument of Peter Koslowski, who suggests that the Catholic Renaissance is Modernity's path less trodden, an alternative to Hegelianism and Marxist conceptions of mind and history.[74] While Koslowski is writing about Schelling and Baader, the argument is equally applicable to Schlegel, and makes the lessons of the *Philosophy of Life* all the more prescient, as the Catholic theologian Aloïs Dempf, a lone advocate of Schlegel's "positive philosophy," asserted over half a century ago.[75] Prescient in that today, as it was during the 1820s, the philosophical landscape facing theology is dominated by ontologies that are variations of absolutizing ("pantheistic," in the Schlegelian sense) ontologies

---

71. *KFSA* 10, 520.
72. Behler, "Schlegel und Hegel," 226–29.
73. Behler, introduction to *KFSA* 10, xxxi–xliii.
74. Koslowski, *Philosophien der Offenbarung*.
75. Dempf, "Der frühe und der späte Friedrich Schlegel," passim.

and methods: we need think only of the neo-Spinozist and neo-vitalist philosophies sparked by the work of Gilles Deleuze in the recent movement of Speculative Realism and Object Oriented Ontology to note the parallels.[76] If it is the desire of theology to respond constructively to these philosophies with its own account of "vitality," the example of Schlegel shows that it might do so by first revisiting its early Catholic developments, before deferring to latter-day representatives.[77] The resulting analysis is as unassuming as it is grandiose: though at present our souls are covered over with scrambled hieroglyphs, the analogical connection between human and Divine vitality means that, if we engage in both passive possession by and active yearning for God, we may yet become sacramentally transfigured images. Human beings will then be true figures of coincident Kraft and image, in order to reflect, as Schlegel explains, the basic equivalence of thought—language—and Being—life.[78]

## Bibliography

### Works by Schlegel

Schlegel, Friedrich. *Kritische Friedrich-Schlegel-Ausgabe (KFSA)*. Edited by Ernst Behler with Jean-Jacques Anstett and Hans Eichner. Paderborn/München/Wien: Ferdinand Schöningh, 1958–.

### Particular volumes referred to

KFSA 8. *Studien zur Philosophie und Theologie*. Edited by Ernst Behler and Ursula Struc-Oppenberg. 1975.
KFSA 9. *Philosophie der Geschichte. In achtzehn Vorlesungen gehalten zu Wien im Jahre 1828*. Edited by Jean-Jacques Anstett. 1971.
KFSA 10. *Philosophie des Lebens. In fünfzehn Vorlesungen gehalten zu Wien im Jahre 1827 und Philosophische Vorlesungen inbesondere über Philosophie der Sprache und des Wortes. Geschrieben und vorgetragen zu Dresden im Deczember 1828 und in den ersten Tagen des Januar 1829*. Edited by Ernst Behler. 1969.
KFSA 19. *Philosophische Lehrjahre 1796–1806 nebst philosophischen Manuskripten aus den Jahren 1796–1828*. Zweiter Teil. Edited by Ernst Behler. 1971.
KFSA 30. *Die Epoche der Zeitschrift Concordia (6 November 1818–Mai 1823)*. Edited by Eugène Susini 1981.

76. See the self-presentation given by Bryant, Srnicek and Harman, "Towards a Speculative Philosophy," 1–19.
77. As is the case with Michel Henry, in many ways Deleuze's "theological" respondent, who develops his arguments from the standpoint of a phenomenological method.
78. Schlegel, *Philosophy of Language*, 526.

KFSA 35. *Tagebuch über die magnetische Behandlung der Gräfin Lesniowska 1820–1826.* Edited by Ursula Behler. 1979.

## Translations

Schlegel, Friedrich. *Dialogue on Poetry and Literary Aphorisms.* Translated by Ernst Behler and Roman Struc. Philadelphia: Pennsylvania State University Press, 1968.
Schlegel, Friedrich. *Philosophy of Language.* In *Schlegel's Philosophy of Life and Philosophy of Language*, translated by A. J. W. Morrison, 349–555. London: Bohn, 1847.

## Works by other authors

Anstett, Jean-Jacques. *La Pensées religièuse de F. Schlegel.* Paris: Société d'Édition des Belles Lettres, 1941.
———. "Mystisches und Okkultistisches in Friedrich Schlegels Spätern Denken und Glauben." *Zeitschrift für Deutsche Philologie* 88 (1969) 132–50.
von Baader, Franz. Vorlesungen und Erläuterungen zu Jacob Böhme's Lehre. Leipzig: Herrmann Bethmann, 1855.
———. "Ueber das pythagoräische Quadrat in der Natur oder die vier Weltgegenden [1798]." In *Gesammelte Schriften* Vol. 3, 247–68. Leipzig: Bethmann, 1852.
Behler, Ernst. "Friedrich Schlegel und Hegel." *Hegel-Studien* 2 (1963) 224–26.
Beiser, Frederick. *The Fate of Reason.* Cambridge: Harvard University Press. 1987.
———. "Introduction." In *The Early Political Writings of the German Romantics*, xviii–xxii. Cambridge: Cambridge University Press, 1996.
Benz, Ernst. *The Mystical Sources of German Romantic Philosophy.* Translated by Blair R. Reynolds and Eunice M. Paul. Alison Park, PA: Pickwick, 1983.
Bryant, Levi, et al. "Towards a Speculative Philosophy." In *The Speculative Turn: Continental Materialism and Realism*, 1–19. Melbourne: re.press, 2011.
Dempf, Aloïs. "Der frühe und der späte Friedrich Schlegel." In *Weltordnung und Heilsgeschichte*, 79ff. Einsiedeln: Johannes, 1958.
Eichner, Hans. *Friedrich Schlegel.* New York: Twayne, 1970.
Elsässer, Michael. *Friedrich Schlegels Kritik am Ding.* Hamburg: Meiner, 1994.
Fiesel, Eva. *Die Sprachphilosophie der deutschen Romantik.* Tübingen: Mohr, 1927.
Frank, Manfred. "'Wechselgrundsatz': Friedrich Schlegels philosophische Ausgangspunkt'. *Zeitschrift für philosophische Forschung* 50.1–2 (1996) 26–50.
Heine, Henrich. *On the History of Religion and Philosophy in Germany and Other Writings.* Translated by Howard Pollack-Milgate. Cambridge: Cambridge University Press, 2007.
Hellerich, Siegmar. *Religionizing, Romanizing Romantics: The Catholico-Christian Camouflage of the Early German Romantics: Wackenroder, Tieck, Novalis Friedrich & August Wilhelm Schlegel.* Frankfurt am Main: Lang, 1995.
Herder, Johann Gottfried. *God: Some Conversations.* Translated by Frederick Henry Burkhardt. Berkeley, CA: Veritas, 1940.

Keiner, Astrid. *Hieroglyphenromantik: zur Genese und Destruktion eines Bilderschriftmodells und zu seiner Überforderung in Friedrich Schlegels Spätphilosophie.* Würzburg : Königshausen & Neumann, 2003.
Koslowski, Peter. *Philosophien der Offenbarung. Antiker Gnostizismus, Franz von Baader, Schelling.* Paderborn: Ferdinand Schöningh, 2001.
Körner, Joseph. "Friedrich Schlegels katolische Glaubensbekenntnis?" *Hochland* 15 (1917) 349–56.
Lüdeke, Henry, and Edgar Lohner, eds. *Ludwig Tieck und die Brüder Schlegel.* München: Winkler Verlag, 1972.
Maier, Michael. *Atalanta Fugiens.* Oppenheim: Johann Theodori de Bry, 1617.
Millán-Zaibert, Elizabeth. *Friedrich Schelgel and the Emergence of Romantic Philosophy.* Albany, NY: State University of New York Press, 2007.
Nüsse, Heinrich. *Die Sprachtheorie Friedrich Schlegels.* Heidelberg: Winter, 1962.
O'Meara, Thomas. *Romantic Idealism and Roman Catholicism: Schelling and the Theologians.* Notre Dame, IN: University of Notre Dame Press, 1982.
Riasanovsky, Nicholas. *The Emergence of Romanticism.* Oxford: Oxford University Press, 1992.
Richards, Robert J. *The Romantic Conception of Life.* Chicago: Chicago University Press, 2002.
Riley, Helene M. Kastinger. "Some German Theories of the Origin of Language from Herder to Wagner." *The Modern Languages Review* 74 (1979) 626–29.
Schelling, F. W. J. *On the History of Modern Philosophy.* Translated by Andrew Bowie. Cambridge: Cambridge University Press, 1994.
Stahl, E. L. *Die religiöse und die humanitätsphilosophische Bildungsidee, und die Entstehung des deutschen Bildungsroman im 18. Jahrhundert.* Bern: Haupt, 1934.
Vincelette, Alan. *Recent Catholic Philosophy: The Nineteenth Century.* Milwaukee, MN: Marquette University Press, 2009.

# 18

## Soul Music and Soul-less Selving

WILLIAM DESMOND

### I: Why Soul Music and Not Self Music?

WHILE THERE IS SUCH a thing as "soul music," there is no such thing as "self music." Why is this? What is the difference between the two? And is not the language of "self" all pervasive in our cultures, while the language of soul seems to have gone into eclipse, especially among the more modernly educated persons? Why is this? What might be at issue in the music of the soul in soul music, and the music-less self without soul. "Oh self, self, self. At every turn nothing but self"—so expostulates Charles Dickens's Martin Chuzzlewit.[1] And yet for all this all-pervasiveness, why no self music and why soul music, music of the soul? It is true that Walt

---

1. Dickens, *The Life and Adventures of Martin Chuzzlewit*, 95: Chuzzlewit has just burned a new will in exasperation after an exchange with Picksniff—everyone wants his money. Is Chuzzlewit immune from self, self, self? For he goes on to say: "Heaven help us, we have much to answer for! Oh self, self, self! Every man for himself and no one for me!" Then the narrator offers the thought: "Universal self. Was there nothing of it in these reflections, and in the history of Martin Chuzzlewit, on his own showing?" Of course, Dickens had a genius for names, for the signature of souls, so to say, even when to all appearance, there is nothing but self, self, self. In his feel for the music of demotic English, he also had great "negative capability." He referred to himself as the "great imitator," and would mimic his characters in a mirror, then rush back to his desk and put them down in words; as if he had no self, and yet was the fertile place where selves with soul come to expression—even his soul-less selves have souls.

Whitman's celebrated poem is called "Song of Myself."[2] But the song of myself, when it is truly singing, is soul music—it is not just self, self, self. And so the question again: Why soul music and no self music? Why even when there is a song of self without the music of the soul, there might be no singing selving at all?

A first remark: soul music is associated with certain styles of black singing. Ray Charles has said: "Some people tell me I'd invented the sounds they called soul—but I can't take any credit. Soul is just the way black folk sing when they leave themselves alone."[3] Leave themselves alone: get out of the way and let soul pass through . . . .

One huge thing worth noting is the history of suffering of such a people—a suffering endured, yet turned into song, and indeed transformed by singing. One need only think of Gospel music, and how out of Gospel music so many other forms of passionate, pathos-filled, and vigorous singing emerge to branch off into the wide world.[4] Blues: the color of a soul; not the experience of a self.[5]

Speaking of color, I cannot help but draw attention to the category of "blue-eyed soul." The eyes are the windows of the soul, it is said, but what is blued-eyed soul? A soul that is blue, a soul colored blue? One might suggest that the term "blue-eyed soul" refers us to an *entirely non-dualistic* way of speaking, since crucial features of the body, the focal features of the face, the eyes are in the soul, *are* the soul as embodying itself, singing out itself to us. Blue-eyed soul is the name for black music not sung by a black but by a white singer who sings black. The voice of the singer rings forth as black, though the singer is white; rings forth from a world that in one way is inimitable, but that in another way can be shared, and more, can be intimately lived together outwardly from this deeper voice within. The source of the voice is more than the white surface of the skin. It is soul. I admit many now might cringe in political correctness at this use of words like "white" and "black," charged are they can be with social and political agendas.[6] But

---

2. Opening lines: "I celebrate myself, and sing myself, / And what I assume you shall assume, / For every atom belonging to me as good belongs to you." Quoted from edition edited by Sandburg, 24.

3. See Cousineau, *Soul: An Archaeology*, 1.

4. Of course, the ways of the world are also exploitative, and Martha Bayles in *Hole in our Soul* shows us how soul can be for sale, indeed the many ways soul-music was often sold out. Her fine book is a celebration of the soul of the music and a lamentation for its abuse.

5. See James Baldwin's celebrated story, *Sonny's Blues*.

6. Think of the blue-eyed rhetoric of the white music of the Aryan nation. Think of such black-face minstrels as Al Jolson, now not to be respectably heard.

blue-eyed soul is not an agenda, but a singing from a space of being, prior to and beyond such agendas.

My favorite blue-eyed soul singer from a youth not entirely misspent: Dusty Springfield. With such a singer how could one lose one's soul or squander its longing? Growing up in England of Irish Catholic stock, her real name was Mary Isobel Catherine Bernadette O'Brien.[7] What a singer! When one looks at some of her performances on YouTube a thrill along the spine still comes with some of her singing . . . there is an entirely singular signature, and in that sense she is self, herself and nothing but herself—but it is not the self of the singer that communicates the spread of the thrill—it is soul . . . blue-eyed soul. There is loss, loneliness, lament, appeal, longing, amazement. The voice raises the banal to the exalted, making more of the less, transforming, ensouling . . . all things simple and deep, intimate, heartbroken and sultry. "I close my eyes and count to ten, and when I open them you're still here; I close my eyes and count again, I can't believe that you're still here . . . ." This is a song of the primal astonishment of being in love, astonishment before the being of the beloved. The ordinary perception of seeing and not seeing is disturbed and disarrayed—and yet the seeing is more fully completed in being again and again surprised by the loved one, simply as there before one. The song sings the incredible miracle of love surprised.

Enough singing the praises of Dusty, and back again to the question: Why then is there soul music and not self music? Or are we entirely to give free range to self language in a tuneless modality—hearing nothing of beauty, singing nothing of soul? Can we relate soul and self in a manner that also restores to selving something of its soul, something too of its music? Is there a music of soul that spreads itself abroad even more universally and soulfully than soul music and in which soul music participates?

## II: Soul-lessness

Soul, under many names, has echoes of a primal word in many cultures: *atman, psuche, anima, Geist, nephesh, prana, duk,* breath, the principle of life. It is difficult to define, and yet resists reduction. Even in an age of science and technology, these ways of speaking persist. People will not forfeit their souls easily.

Nevertheless, if the soul has lost its meaning for many (Cavell speaks of "soul-blindness"), there are diverse factors involved in this.[8] I think that

---

7. See Bartlett, *Dusty: An Intimate Portrait of a Musical Legend.*
8. See Barrett, *Death of the Soul: From Descartes to the Computer.*

certainly attention must be paid to the ambition to *univocally determine all being* that has expanded in modernity into a project claiming to be on a par with the whole. I want to suggest that there is more to soul than can be made the object of such univocal determination. Being more, it is also not indeterminate; there is something overdeterminate to it, in excess of determination and self-determination. There is a mystery to it, in the end. Moreover, the project of determination passes seamlessly with a project of self-determination, and hence the huge presence of the language of self coexists with a view where there is nothing so absent as self. Soul suffers in the projects of determination and self-determination. We need other ways to think of selving to allow soul to communicate out of its overdeterminate mysteriousness.[9]

Relative to the project of determination and determinability: I am thinking of the objectification of being, wherein all that is is determined to be an object of scientific investigation and possible technological exploitation. The qualitative textures of things do not count in this project of universal quantification, this *mathesis universalis*. Of course, if things are massively objectified, this goes with the huge subjectification of the human being, the self as it will come to be known. Which comes first: the subjectification or the objectification? Since objectification is a project of the subject, there is a sense in which the subjectification is prior, even though this may not appear so at the outset. We make things objective, but changes in ourselves then set in motion other changes, not only to things other to us, but also in how we relate to ourselves, how we understand ourselves. One of these changes has to do with the de-souling of nature as other to us (following the objectification), and with this the creeping soul-lessness of the ensuing self (following the subjectification).

We find this twinning of objectification and subjectification in the Cartesian language of the *res extensa* and the *res cogitans*. The extended thing is determined by the thinking thing, and then the thinking thing is subjectified. As subjectified the thinking thing does not tap into its root in nature: it is over against nature, it is above nature, determining it. It is feathering its own nest of self-determination, and perhaps not feathering it, but fouling it. And then we find self, self, self: self circulating around self. We might say that the univocalizing on the two sides, the subject and object,

---

9. What I say here has some relevance to the recently debated question: what comes after subjectivity? I have spoken of this in Desmond, "Agapeic Selving and the Passion of Being: Subjectivity in the Light of Solidarity." There I also reflect on the language of throwing, *jacere* as in pro-ject, ob-ject, sub-ject, intersub-ject; this is not the language of soul, but a version of the *conatus essendi* that covers over the porosity of being as the matrix of souling—and truer selving.

hides a flight from the equivocity of soul music, and indeed any possibility of an ensouled world (*anima mundi*). In addition, there is the taking over of what the ancients took as the key mark of soul, namely as principle of motion, as self-moving. This now is driven in the direction of autonomy (self-motion) and self-determination. I would venture that the reason why an entire configuration of human being as autonomous did not earlier emerge had nothing to do with the absence of freedom but with the fact that it was not evident that to be free was to be autonomous, and autonomous in connection with determinability and univocalization. *In actu* there was too much of porosity to othernesses that did not enter the self-circling of autonomy. Modern autonomy is a construction of freedom erected on the basis of soul-less selving and the soul without music.

The soul is sent underground in this, or sent beyond "nature," beyond the body. It is not there as participating in the body of being—on the surface of things. For on the surface there is an aesthetic communication of depth and surface. The body is a singing word—it is there where the first languages find utterance. Here we find a certain separation of body and soul that makes the body into a neutral thereness, and the soul into the ghost in the machine. There is then no soul music of the body; no musical bodying of the soul; no wording the body. We become deaf to what Vico heard: song as the first language.

I want to stress at the outset that the loss of the soul in the vocabularies of science and philosophy does not obviate the persistence of expressions of the soul in our existential lives. What other kind of life is there finally, if not existential? We do not live in theories. We should take this persistence (of the expressions of soul) very seriously as thinkers. The theorist is not himself or herself a theory. I have argued in connection with life that the surface is a threshold of communication with the deepest; the threshold is a saturated surface, for there sur-faces what communicates itself. This is like the face of another: absolutely there, and yet there as a mystery beyond subjectification and objectification. One can be intimately in communication with this person, this before-one-present mystery in the sur-face that faces one. There is no need of a dualism of surface and depth, outer and inner—the outer is the uttering of the inner, the inner is the intimacy of the outer communicated. The sur-face is the threshold of communication where the mystery of singularly embodied being is offered. I will not repeat the arguments I offered in favor of a way that is neither objectivizing nor subjectivizing with respect to life, but *mutatis mutandi* these considerations also have relevance to the enigmatic persistence of soul.[10]

---

10. Desmond, "On the Surface of Things: Transient Life and Beauty in Passing."

There is no need to have a negative view of scientific findings, but philosophically one cannot take these as the acme of truth. They are truths formulated in a well-determined framework, which itself is configured according to inclusions and exclusions, that is to say, in abstraction from the full overdeterminacy of given being as such.[11] The framework is set forth with as much univocal precision as possible, but as the word "precision" suggests, there is a *cut* (scisio: scissors) in the fullness of the given, a cut that as abstraction is manipulable and determinable in a way that the full overdeterminacy is not—for all determinations ultimately derive from it as the original matrix of being and intelligibility. Manipulation is itself a cut—cut out from, perhaps cut off from the fullness of the overdeterminacy. (The phenomenologist makes the point sometimes in terms of the *Lebenswelt*.) What I have called the saturated surface of things hints at a less abstracted figuring forth of the fullness of the overdeterminacy. The view is that what flowers forth in human existence, apart from any prior permission from a scientific scheme, can be immensely revealing about the truth of the matter. So even if scientific discourse has dispensed with the soul, the issuing forth in life of such a happening as soul music can be of great importance in communicating something true(r) about soul.

There are different pathways to different truths, and the pathway of science may not at all be the right one when it comes to soul. (The same point applies to rational psychology, as I will indicate below.) The pathways through music, art, religion, the ordinary ways of talking, may be the truer ways. In that regard, what perhaps we need to do is not offer a scientific theory; it is to search out traces, signs, reminders of something, once named soul, exceeding determination and self-determination. No scientific certainty can be offered in such a probing exploration. More often than not, metaphorical, imagistic ways of speaking have to be invoked, not because of an evasion of thought, but because the appropriate thought of soul must necessarily clothe itself in metaphorical and analogical likenesses. The

---

11. I begin to suffer from glaucoma, and sometimes what I see is a blob, more or less distinct, but more indistinct than earlier. I might take these blobs for what is there, but I know there is more sharp determinacy there, since I have seen it. Yet the other conclusion is not warranted: namely, that what I see is an indeterminacy that I make determinate. To the contrary, the sharp determinacy is saturated—it is surplus to what I could ever determine—it is overdeterminate, not indeterminate; and if I were to see by a more powerful light, and if my eyes were up to it, I might see more of the overdeterminacy—but I would not see all that is there. The blob seems indeterminate, but I have seen more, and know it is not such a blob at all. Think of the refreshing of a landscape after a heavy rain, and the same determinacies shine with a new freshness, as if a new light fell on them. One might be graced by sight, by access of the light and see the same things, but see them in this other light; but what is there is no less an overdeterminacy for us, not an indeterminacy in itself.

saturated surfaces of things are signs communicating living realities like soul. Hence the notably metaphorical character of quite a bit of, say, the *Phaedo*.[12]

## III: Souling: From Animation to Reification

I will return to selving below, but I want to illustrate the loss of the soul in modernity by looking briefly at Aristotle's vision, contrasting it with the reification of soul that occurs after Descartes. It might seem more appropriate to contrast Plato and Descartes as offering two forms of dualism. There is a tendency in this direction in Plato, though there is more at play there, and if there is dualism it is not of the same sort as in Descartes. But that is a tale for another time, though I will return below to the musical Socrates on the vigil of death.

With Aristotle, as with many of the ancients, it is the living being and its unity, as well as its power of moving itself, that is centrally at stake. The soul is not some dematerialized stuff haunting the grosser stuff of the body. Soul is in the deepest intimacy of the living being and on the outermost surface of its bodily communication. It is hard to describe the intimacy of this unity without risking, in modern-wise, some kind of reduction to unfinessed materialism. Much of our modern materialism takes form according to the heritage of the objectifying-subjectifying dualism already suggested, but Aristotle's unity of soul and *soma* is in a different metaphysical space, reflecting a different ontological ethos and dwelling in the world than the more typical modern one. The ensouled being is a living integrity, even though it can be marked by a plurality of powers. Soul shows itself in the pluripotent integrity of the living being that is and becomes itself. The powers are revealed in how it is, how it does itself, how it goes and utters itself. The soul is the original of the powers, and in some beings the original pluralization of powers is richer than in others. Hence Aristotle's fruitful scheme of the vegetative, animal, and rational souls. In all cases, our attention is drawn to a dynamic integrity of being, which displays a pluralization of powers, up to the instance of beings manifesting themselves in rational powers.

The soul is the living self-pluralizing integrity. Soul is in the body and enfolds body in its manifest materiality, and so too the body is in the

---

12. Though there is our need for dialectical argumentation, there is also our need for myth; see *Phaedo* 114d. Also *Phaedrus* 246a: to speak of the Idea of soul would be an entirely divine and blessed discourse, nevertheless it is within human power to describe the soul in a figure (or likeness: *eikōn*).

soul: there is a rich immanence that cannot be either dualized absolutely or materialistically reduced. The ensouled integrity is also ecstatic as well as self-relating—it is out beyond itself in communication with what is other; and yet in being out beyond, it is a holding of itself together in that dynamic integrity of being it is.[13] See the plant out beyond itself in the flower turning to the sun, later folding into itself at dark; and yet in turning out and turning in relative to what is other, it is always itself. Consider the animal's mobility: witness to an increased range of power, marking the spread of its self-transcendence, as not rooted in one place, like the plant; and yet in this spread, the animal *is itself* in its sensitive and sensible self-transcendence. And most of all with the rational being, the being of logos, we find the being out beyond itself and yet entirely intimate to its own integrity of being. There are the famous enigmatic sayings in *De Anima*: somehow the soul is everything (431b, 21–22); *nous* is the power to be and become all things (430a14–17). I find these famous sayings (echoed by Aquinas: intellect as *potens omnia facere et fieri*) to be very important for our music of the soul. For music, in its fluid resonance, is like the water of Thales. In one way, water is everything in being able to take on all forms, and yet in another way it is nothing in that it is never there if we try to fix it as one frozen form. I would not say it is a nothing and an everything (in *posse*), just as an indeterminacy awaiting determination, and self-determining. I would say it an overdeterminacy—more than everything determinate and self-determining, and nothing as enabling the determinate and the self-determining.[14] A potency that is a plenipotency is not a mere potential but already a kind of fullness (*plenum*) and hence not just an indeterminacy. Because it is a plenipotency it can be a pluripotency. I will connect this below with the porosity of being.

Aristotle's is a marvelous thinking of the soul. I notice that he situates his reflections on the soul as part of *physics*. Of course, the sense of the physical (*ta phusika*) here is not the mechanical order of earlier modernity when the soul comes to be put in question. *Phusis* as *natura* is as much *natura naturans* as *natura naturata*, nature in its overdeterminate power of becoming, nature as determinately natured (which need not mean mechanically determined). The soul in relation to *phusis* cannot be thought of as a dematerialized spook. What nature means here is not the objectified concatenation of centers of effective power that we find in the modern version. It is emergent, it is growing, it is blossoming, so well described

---

13. Joe Sachs gets at something of this in his translation of *entelecheia* as "being-at-work-staying-itself," in *Aristotle's On the Soul and on Memory and Recollection*, 189–90.

14. See Emily Dickinson's poem, "The Brain—is wider than the Sky—." Should we perhaps not say, with a bow to Aristotle: "The Soul—is wider than the Sky—."

by the twentieth-century Aristotelian, Heidegger.[15] It is the matrix of the self-becoming of beings, beings that are more than ontological centers of *becoming*, since to be at all they have to have *come to be*—given to be before they can begin to become themselves, or give themselves to themselves. Determination and self-determination always derive from sources more primordial and not to be described as just determinate or self-determining.

But let us now look, again briefly, at what becomes of the soul in modernity, and Descartes is the familiar and obvious paradigm. The movement is from *animation to reification*, and the reification marks both the objectification and subjectification of being. In Descartes there is the now familiar dualism of the *res extensa* and *res cogitans*. This might seem to fall within a Platonic paradigm, but what we find is the project of mathematical and technological objectification, for the certainty of which philosophical reflection is to provide the epistemological warrant or certification. The famous *cogito* argument is not to be eschewed, though it has been relentlessly assaulted in more recent times. It is a peculiar argument—there is indeed something incontrovertible in the denial of self (if this is the right word). What is being denied is doing the denying and hence is affirmed even in the denial itself. The issue now, granting a certain incontrovertibility, is what is it that is doing the denial and affirming itself in the denial.[16] Here the answer: the *ego cogitans*—and this *res cogitans* is then identified with *spiritual substance*, set off by an ontological gulf from the *res extensa*, the neutral wax-like stuff of the world around us. The term "*res*" carries the objectification: "thing," but with the implication of a determinability that fixes itself and nothing but itself. I mean this not only as an objectification and determination but also

15. See W. James' "Concerning Fechner" in *A Pluralistic Universe*, Lecture IV. On Fechner himself, see *Religion of a Scientist: Selections from Gustav Theodor Fechner*. There is music of the soul in Fechner—see the lovely description of plant life that James cites: it is reminiscent of a lyrical Aristotelianism. James is enthusiastic and diffident at once. Enthusiastic: in being enchanted by the vision of Fechner—a thick version of idealism/panpsychism, not the thin version of American transcendentalism, as he suspected that to be. Diffident: in that his own skeptical side, coming from science, keeps him from going overboard in terms of voicing the vision as *his own conviction*; he delights in playing the music of another, and it is as beautiful as James can sing, but it is of another, and so he cannot be accused of being the singer simply—he would sing, one feels, but he could not quite—so song becomes reporting another, even a little singing of another (a "cover" as the musicians say), but it is not quite the pouring forth of the song from one's own being, as one's own being. In that sense it is not quite soul music.

16. It is only too well known that something of this incontrovertibility is affirmed by Augustine before Descartes, but Augustine has no "project" to found a new science of nature. The incontrovertibility counters the soul's evasions of its own truthful porosity to truth—truth as intimate and other to the soul's claim to be the truth. The soul music of Augustine is prayerful and not geometrical, and sung from a space of sacred intimacy more hyperbolically interior even to the soul's own intimacy with itself.

as a certain univocalization. It is as a consequence of univocal determinability that we find ourselves fixed in dualism; for to be the one thing it is, the *res* must incontrovertibly be not the other things, and between the one and the other there opens a gulf of difference, in the end not intermediated or open to intermediation.

The *res extensa* seems to open up the vista of objectified neutralized thereness; and it seems also to define by necessary complement the *res cogitans*, the subjectivity for whom or for which this neutralized other is there at all. But this subjectivity itself undergoes a reification in being determined as thinking *thing*. It is in this determination, identified with the soul, that the soul begins to be lost. For the soul is not a thing. This is not at all intended as a depreciation or making inferior of things. I would defend things as ontologically thick,[17] in fact, and see no point in an absolute dualizing of things and persons, say. But qua *res*, the univocal fixity of the soul begins to live a life that is continuous with the modern project of determinate objectification, even though carried out through a process of subjectification. My point is this: soul music ceases, because it is the determinability, the fixability that is now at stake. Music witnesses to *flowing form*; but flowing form requires more than univocal stasis for its determination—for it is more determining than determined—and hence exceeds complete determination. Fluid form is a *forming in passage*; and if we see a unity in the flow of passage, it is a strange unity that is itself by exceeding itself, and that yet is in intimate self-relation in this being beyond itself, in this being of itself in the moving of itself.[18]

17. See my *Being and the Between*, chapter 8, "Things."

18. Aristotle connects soul and *nous* with form (the form of forms: *ho nous eidos eidōn, De Anima*, 432a3). I would say that there is more to form than form—there is forming and its dynamic power has to be taken into account. Form as articulated points beyond itself to forming as articulating. There is life that is passing in the form, and hence the form is not just form. This is why the fluid form of music is so appropriate to the soul as souling, and indeed perhaps also to the self as selving. The source of the fluid form is not just another form and hence there is an element of beyond determinability and self-determination about its power(s). This also is consistent with the overlap of mathematics and music, in respect of form, but if the form is forming then in a sense the music is more primal than the mathematic, for it is attuned to, it is the attuning of the source powering the forming qua forming, and not just crystallized in (determinate) form. A more general point might be made relative to all beauty in so far as we think of this in terms of *splendor formae*: form has no splendor if it is only form considered as a determinate structure; for form shines, but shining with splendor is more than fixed form; thus we say a picture shimmers, that is to say, radiates, and exceeds fixation in determinate form, even though it is in the determinate form itself that the radiation of the splendor is singularized. The same point holds for the communication of music, and hence Kant's metaphor below of the perfumed handkerchief is not at all inapposite: it is the diffusion that is at stake, the diffusion beyond the determinate and

Of course, music is not mathematics, though both are intimately connected, as the Pythagoreans long ago realized. Mathematics tends to form, while music tends to forming. The music begins to fade with the project of the modern mathematicization of nature. Think of the difference of Kepler and Galileo. Nature for both may be the book written in the language of mathematics, but the former still heard the music in the mathematics, while in the latter the mathematics had taken over in a form that recessed the music.[19] My question: does not the same happen to music when the self comes to the fore, when the self is intent on being the source of determination and on being itself the realization of self-determination? We find it hard to hear soul music; we find it perplexing even to know what it means to listen for it. That is why *all the arts*, and music not least, are *guardian angels of this easily lost listening*. An ear for music is asked of all the powers of the senses. We have to listen when we look, listen when we touch and shape, listen when the body dances, listen when the tongue tastes and words.[20]

What of the long-standing argument which connects soul with *simplicity*? Is not this consonant with the desire for univocal determinability? Is not this too the meaning of simplicity? But this is too simple by far. Simplicity is the most unsimple of things. God's simplicity—what is this? Surely this simplicity is infinitely rich, just in its being uncompounded. On first appearance, it would seem we have to think an origin that in its uncompounded character seems to leave no juts of complexity by which we might hang our determinations by the skin of articulated differences. Otherwise, this would be "the night in which all cows are black," in Hegel's sarcastic jibe at Schelling's absolute as the *Indifferenzpunkt*.[21] And yet this divine simplicity is the absolutely full, the absolutely overfull. Here we begin to border on paradox, indeed touch on mystery: the infinitely overfull is so absolutely simple that when we try to determine it, it comes before us as nothing—nothing in particular. This paradoxical doubleness is deeply important for the soul: the soul as surplus seems beyond finite determinability and yet

---

determinable boundary of fixed form; the diffusion of the music is carried by the moving form, the fluid forming as it is in passing. One might note also the musical reference of soul in respect of the image of the lyre in the *Phaedo* (86c), an image that occasions criticism of soul considered as a harmony; though the source of the music as forming beyond form is not the same as the musical instrument on which the music is played. See *De Anima*, 407b30–408a10 for criticism of soul as a harmony.

19. See Desmond, *Being and the Between*, 95–97.

20. Augustine (*De Trinitate*, XV, X, 18) refers to the words of the heart (*locutiones cordis*) and how in the soul the outer distinction of seeing and hearing is abrogated: seeing is hearing, hearing is seeing (*non est aliud atque aliud videre et audire*). On this see Chrétien, *The Call and the Response*, 49.

21. Hegel, *Phänomenologie des Geistes*, 19; *Phenomenology of Spirit*, §16.

seems like a nothing, but it is a nothing that is the power to be or become everything (again with a bow to Aristotle).[22]

The language of self begins to take over with the *res cogitans*, with this self of reification in a double sense—reification of what is other to itself as objective, reification of itself as spiritual subject. Thus one can make sense of the paradoxical development in this modern univocalization: it can go in the direction of a more brutal reification and reduction, or likewise veer in the direction of an unleashing of subjectivity unmoored from any anchor in being. So we find: the materialisms of modernity on the one hand, the idealisms on the other, and their de-sublations.

True, the Cartesian view of the soul seems a fit made for the question of *immortality*, and this with respect to its simplicity.[23] But with the reification, there is the recessed being at work of the soul and this too unanchored from nature; and as a non-natural thing, it is a question as to how we are then to determine it, how then to pin it down. This is not at all easy, and can come to appear scandalous when the project of univocal determinability has matured to the point of demanding an analogous univocalization of the soul. But there is no mathematicization of the soul, no technology of its music. We are tempted with a material science, whether phrenology in earlier centuries, or neurophysiology in our own time. The de-naturing of soul contributes to a desire for soul's determinate objectification, which, in turn, leads to the disappearance of soul and its replacement with a variety of other seemingly plausible forms of determinability. But there is no such soul.

In the quest of the substantial soul, the issue deteriorates also on the side of the empiricists. I think of Locke's description of substance as an

---

22. One reason soul as simple is not determinable simply or simply determinate is because it is the determining source of singular determinations and in excess of complete determination; and it is also not "self" as formation of self-determination. Not that there is not self-determining going on, but the soul as source of determining is more before determination and more beyond. "Selving" comes to be on the surface of this mysterious source, is the sur-facing of soul. More on this below.

23. Descartes talks about the soul as being the most easily known of all. I think this has to do with intimacy. In one sense, what he says is true; there is this (elusive) intimacy of being; but what is the nature of the knowing of it? If it is an intimate knowing, how determinate or determinable is it? Most close to itself, most far from itself; most known to itself and most unknown to itself? Since the knower is the knowing and the known, there is no "distance" of objectification (by and through which the subject can determinately grasp itself). For we are not only participants; one is it—and yet there is more to it than one can univocally determine. It is a mystery rather than a problem, in Gabriel Marcel's sense. Even at that, it is not easy to say *what it is*, since the saying of what it is intimately participates in it. Compare Descartes on the soul as the most easily known with Heraclitus (fragment 45) on the impossibility of finding the limits of the soul, "so unfathomable is its *logos*."

"I know not what" that yet has to be invoked to sustain the properties of the thing taken in as impressions by the acts of sensation. How sustain the claims made about an "I know not what"? Of course, if determinability is required big time we are in a pickle. One thinks of the arguments about Lockean substance by the divine Stillingfleet to the effect that it cannot be an "I know not what" if we can say about it that it is an "I know not what." And then there is the relentless assault by Berkeley following on this as to the redundancy of this concept of substance, certainly material substances as such. There remain only spirits, as Berkeley calls them, all perhaps rather too cliptly. Of course, the overdeterminacy of the issue of soul tends not to be honestly enough acknowledged in all of this, and the kind of sanity of the Aristotelian fidelity to nature is not given its proper due. Berkeley claims to demolish material substance, Hume tries to demolish spiritual substance, and the self, considered as a fixed substance, is held to dissolve in a flux of impressions. Of course, Hume had to be himself to look for his self, and had to continue to be himself when he himself (who is he?) found there was no self to be found. The aesthetic determinability of soul proves a failure with the empiricists, as the dianoetic determinability does with the rationalists.

## IV: Soul, Self(-Activity), and Kantian Equivocation

I take Kant here as a witness to the mess. I refer to his discussion of rational psychology, a scholastic discipline dealing with the soul, but soul considered as this simple substance. We find this in his treatment of the paralogisms of pure reason in the *Critique of Pure Reason* (Second Division, Book II, chapter I). What seems to be at work here is Kant's strategy of showing a contradiction, indeed an illusion reason cannot avoid, a deep-seated equivocity in reason itself concerning the notion of the soul as simple substance, and as treated in a speculative theory. Rational psychology equivocates between the dianoetics and aesthetics of the matter, between claims made by reason and claims which seem to offer an empirical affirmation. That is, in treating of the soul as simple substance, we claim to make assertions about the soul purely on the basis of reason, and its consideration of the "I think"; in the process we move from rational considerations, but end up with seemingly empirical claims. For Kant, however, nothing of cognitive worth is to be ascribed to these claims. One might say, apropos of the twinning of subjectification and objectification, that we move from the side of rational subjectivity, but only it seems to end up on the side of an empirical reality. This move cannot be justified. Rational psychology is vitiated by contradiction and equivocation.

At face value, there seems to be here a certain working out of the doublet of the *res cogitans* and *res extensa*, considered as amenable to univocal determination.[24] This discussion of the paralogisms was seen by many as dealing a death blow to rational psychology. Or is it the death of the soul? A death warrant perhaps, but not direct death. It is the death warrant of a certain way of conceiving the soul, but this cannot be taken to exhaust the issue, or to deliver us over to a truer approach. In fact, Kant does bring the soul back, *via* his practical philosophy, where the autonomy of the moral self is sovereign, and *via* the postulate of immortality. Practical reason can still address the great themes of special metaphysics, God, freedom, the soul. But where is the music in Kant's moral philosophy? Is there any soul music in this postulate of its immortality? I cannot hear it. I hear nothing.

It bears remarking that this turn to practical philosophy is configured by Kant in terms of *moral self-determination*, which does what univocal rational determination cannot do in a theoretical sense. There is nothing of the living overdeterminacy of souling in all of this. And, of course, the recessed presuppositions of the dualistic contraposition of the *res cogitans* and *res extensa* are still very much at play. If we find these presuppositions problematic in terms of understanding soul—as we must—then another approach is required. Perhaps the problem is the recessing of the intimacy of soul in the dualistic language—the self either as a determinable thing or as source of self-activity. We have difficulty seeing the determinate and self-determining self as the outcome of a process of selving, itself reaching more deeply into intimate sources of souling and being ensouled. These intimate sources are idiotic from the standpoint of surfaced determinations and projects of self-determinations of the selving. As intimate they return us more into the *passio essendi* and deeper still into the porosity of being, which is neither active nor passive.[25]

Another important upshot here with Kant is the turn away from soul *towards self-activity*, and so towards the being of selving as *conatus essendi*, and following this the emphasis on practical willing as most essential to the being of selving. Soul is pathological, as intimate with the *passio essendi*;

---

24. One could say that Kant's critique of the paralogisms is continuous with his critique of the *ontological argument*. There is no justified transition or inference from rational concept (possibility) to reality or existence. There is a gulf between the two that cannot be bridged by rational thought alone.

25. Nor is it *protē hulē* either, though there is a likeness to the Platonic *khōra* (this interests me more than what deconstruction has made of the *khōra*). The matrix of ongoingness is neither simple being nor becoming. How speak of that mother? Paul Weiss speaks of the *dunamis* and I have written on this in "Creativity and the *Dunamis*," in *The Philosophy of Paul Weiss: Library of Living Philosophers*, 543–57.

and there is also the matter of the primordial givenness to itself.[26] This is a complication taken over by the great idealists, where the quest to give an articulation of pure activity is to be found (consult the whole problem of spontaneity and receptivity here). Moreover, the matter is there developed in a manner that again wants to embed self in nature. Hegel and Schelling do this somewhat differently. I will say something below about this in relation to Hegel who, while recuperating something of the ontological embeddedness (evident in his great respect for Aristotle and his *De Anima*), has a view of spirit and nature that, in the end, comes to remind one more of the modern conception, rather than Greek *phusis*.

One might wonder here how in Kant the farewell to rational psychology, and the promotion of moral postulates, leave us with regard to music and the soul. Undoubtedly music does not fare very well. Kant has a very diffident attitude, perhaps even an easily irritated attitude. So I infer from the things he says in the *Critique of Judgment* where he compares music to the dandy and his perfumed handkerchief. The perfume works on everyone involuntarily. It does not ask of us our permission, but with no by-your-leave it works on us before we can insulate ourselves in the circle of self-determination. It is as if we would be better off, if only we could be *Stoics without noses*. Music, like perfume, touches us, "gets up our nose," caresses us or hits us, in any event, it moves us at a level of being below or beyond the defenses of our autonomy, self-circulated in its rational security. It moves us before we know we have been moved. Perhaps just as bad, it seems, is the unsavory aspect of its relative indeterminability. Music is not above board, Kant avers. In this it is unlike poetry, which shows its hand, as he puts it. Like perfume, music can be everywhere and nowhere, passing through the pores of our bodies, indeed our souls, proving so moving that the body (self-moving like a soul) might move itself to its beat and tap its feet, clap its hands, and more outrageously, even make it desire to dance. Music ensouls, animates the body. Indeed the moving power of music passes beyond fixed determination and self-determination, gets through to the porosity, reopening it, and resonating with the soul.

We can see here how selving configured as autonomous self-determination is diffident about the intimate communication of music, which touches us at depths of soul before rational self-consciousness. This is all pathological for Kant. There is no soul music here. I find that the interesting thing about music is that it would give the lie to the notion of soul substance as a spiritual thing. In that sense, it would confirm perhaps one side of Kant's

---

26. I have articulated the meaning terms like the *passio essendi* elsewhere, for instance, *The Intimate Strangeness of Being: Metaphysics after Dialectic*. Something of their meaning will become more evident as we proceed.

discussion in the paralogism, but what this would open up for consideration does not find its place in Kant's way of negatively, critical thinking.

A last remark on soul in Kant, concerning his move to the level of pure practical reason where the antinomy of moral autonomy opens beyond itself towards the immortality of the soul.[27] The argument is that we must postulate the immortality of the soul as part of the resolution (*Aufhebung*) of the antinomy of pure practical reason. This is the antinomy between virtue and happiness, resolved in the *summum bonum* which, through God, ensures that merited happiness is enjoyed by the virtuous in exact proportion to their moral worthiness to be happy. What is this deathless soul that is implicated in overcoming the antinomy of pure practical reason and completing the moral doctrine in the *summum bonum*? Where is the music of the soul in the other world? Just as Kant seemed somewhat irritated with the singing of spiritual hymns here in this life, one suspects that Kant did not anticipate much singing there in the next world either. What an eternal irritation it would be to him, given that it was such a terrestrial agitation that he had to take his revenge in a footnote.[28]

Be that as it may, it seems the moral toil goes on, as each soul tries to earn its right to be happy—its rightful worthiness to merit happiness. There is no free music for this soul. Kant seems to moralize the glory of eternal life, now somewhat faded in true glory, since he does not allow the soul to enjoy itself there until it has paid its moral dues. Otherwise heaven would be like *spiritual South Sea Islands* whose natives seem to him disgustingly happy in eating, lounging around, and, *mon Dieu*, reproducing (*Fortpflanzung*).[29] For Kant there seems no great banquet in the divine eschatology, with wine, woman, and song (if you like, resurrected in the dimension of hyperbolic transfiguration). God forbid, again. God is not the mystery of overabundant gifts to whom we sing, but the paymaster general of moral merit. There is no hymn of soul music in eternity. The pagan Nietzsche is far closer to soul music when his Zarathustra sings: all joy wills eternity, wills deep, deep eternity!

---

27. Death, of course, means *facing the music* and we must not forget the ethical and religious dimensions of this question of deathlessness, evident in Plato's *Phaedo*, and in the Christian thinkers like Augustine and Aquinas. These ethical and religious concerns are bound up with *eschatological justice*. The rational psychology of modern thought is not richly attuned to the issue of eschatological justice—though there is a pale echo of it in Kant's postulates of immortality and God.

28. Kant, *Critique of the Power of Judgment*, §53; see my *Art, Origins, Otherness*, 78 (hereafter *AOO*).

29. Kant, *Groundwork of the Metaphysics of Morals: A German-English Edition*, 74–75.

## V: Substance, Soul, Subject: Hegel's (Self-Determining) Spirit

I want to pay some attention to Hegel since he is amphibolous in a revealing way: he tries to recuperate something of the Aristotelian way in a post-Kantian space, but in the end he tilts towards a superposition of a logic of self-determination on the living overdeterminacy of soul. The result resounds in his philosophy of music whose notes are quite close to the music of the soul, but not concordant. There is something out of tune.

Hegel speaks about soul in connection with his philosophy of subjective spirit. Technically the discussion appears first under the heading of anthropology, which he connects with the soul in nature, passing thence through phenomenology, where we encounter the soul coming to appearance out of nature, coming finally to psychology proper, wherein Hegel's philosophy surpasses soul as such in the direction of a more adequate expression of spirit.[30] Overall Hegel is dealing with the emergence of spirit from nature, and its development out of this toward its own liberation from nature as such. This liberation from nature is into spirit's being for itself and into its more and more consummate self-determination. While the details of his account are often richly suggestive, and while he praises Aristotle's *De Anima* as in a class of its own (*Encyclopedia,* §378), the unfolding of his account as a whole is oriented to the emergence and consummation of subjective spirit, and its *Aufhebung* and supersession by objective spirit. The whole process is governed by the teleology of spirit as journeying towards the (self) constitution of its own proper self-determination, finally consummated at the level of absolute spirit.

The soul is explicated as the first appearance of spirit out of nature and its externality. The true root for Hegel is not nature, but freedom. I would say Hegel takes over the critique of soul as simple substance and he needs to do so if he is to move to the self-activity of spirit. Noticeable in his discussion is his reaction to any dualism of matter and spirit, body and soul; such dualism leads to his critique not only of materialism, but also to his critique of questions so dualistically posed about the relation of body and spirit as two substances. Hegel makes references to Descartes, Malebranche, and Leibniz as seeking through God differently to bring the two substances into unity or community. He criticizes this way of thinking. In a sense,

---

30. Hegel treats extensively of the soul throughout the section on subjective *Geist* in Hegel, *Enzyklopädie der Philosophischen Wissenschaften im Grundrisse*; *Hegel's Philosophy of Mind: Being Part Three of the Encyclopedia of the Philosophical Sciences*; see also *Lectures on the Philosophy of Spirit (1827–1828)*.

materialism is to be dematerialized, while spirit is to be concretized in its determinate appearance.

Hegel is one of the idealists who developed the notion of pure activity (an idea in Fichte). One can map something of this in terms of a certain reaction to the spiritual substance of rational psychology and Kant's critique of it. This critique is accepted at one level, and at another level, there is an extraordinary expansion coming from the critique that might be summarized in Hegel's words: from substance to subject.[31] This is a central catchword for the *Phenomenology of Spirit*, and it adds significantly to the theme. Substance is selfless, lacking in true subjectivity, as Hegel suggests in connection with Spinoza's substance. Moving from substance to subject is the phenomenology of spirit, *Geist*, the *logos* of appearing spirit. What of soul in this? We must give up simple substance to make the move and transformation of substance to subject, but soul can find some place in this process. It provides something of the needed threshold and transition between nature and spirit.

I note that Hegel is Aristotelian, but not entirely so. Where he discusses the soul in his anthropology, it is just on this threshold between nature and spirit, where the transition from the former to the latter is effected. The embeddedness in nature is Aristotelian, and the emergence from nature mimics Aristotle in one sense, in that with the rational powers we come upon the fullest form of soul. But Hegel's account is not Aristotelian in another sense, in that the threshold, once crossed, tends to the subordination of nature in the very act of spiritually sublating it. Hegel's is an intrinsically interesting discussion, but it is very modern with regard to nature and spirit. Nature is something that spirit will overcome—nature is spirit in its self-externality, not spirit in its full and hence proper self-relation. There the idea is outside of itself and in a sense it is scattered abroad. The soul initiates the bringing of the scattering back to self-relation. It does so as in the body and as emergent in the body. For obviously the body and our being embodied are important for Hegel. More, as the expression of spirit, the human form is the only true vehicle of spirit in nature, as he puts it in his *Aesthetics*.[32] Yet in the end *Geist* is self-surpassing, not only of nature, but of itself also, and is not to be reduced to bodily form only. I might put it: the selving of *Geist* is more than the aesthetics of souling. The soul as witnessing to spirit emergent in nature has about it an immediacy, but immediacy is connected with a beginning and thus with a sense of indeterminate possibility. Hence, if there is

---

31. Hegel, *Phänomenologie des Geistes*, 19; *Phenomenology of Spirit*, §17.

32. *Hegel's Aesthetics: Lectures on Fine Art*, vol.1, 78; (abbreviated, *HA*); *Vorlesungen über die Ästhetik*, in Hegel, *Werke in zwanzig Banden*, I, 110 (abbreviated *VA*).

an opening of soul here the immediacy must be mediated. Finally, with mediation we traverse a movement from the indeterminacy of the immediate, through various forms of determination, towards the end of more and more fulfilled self-determination.

Note that while we might find here hints of the porosity of being and the *passio essendi*, they tend to fall under the governance of a teleology of endeavor (the *Trieb* of the Idea?) where the *conatus essendi* is in search of fuller and fuller rational self-determination. The soul does seem to be intimately idiotic in one sense, but it is more idiotic in a deficient rather than a saturated sense, an indeterminate rather than overdeterminate sense. And the threshold once crossed, nature does not show itself to have quite the blooming surplus character it might be said to have in the Greek notion of *phusis*. Where then is the soul music in Hegel? It is not denied, but there is a selving more ultimate than soul, and to invest in soul too much is to hinder the self-completing process of this selving.

Pure activity determines itself in a plurality of forms—but practically speaking it is oriented to "the free will which wills the free will," as Hegel puts it in the *Philosophy of Right*.[33] There is more, of course, than a bare free will that wills the free will. Hegel is a complex modern thinker in offering a teleology of selving oriented to *social self-determination*, not an archeology which finds soul called up from surplus naturing, and which finds uttering from the idiotic sources of the intimate affirmation of the "to be," with its porosity and *passio*, with its suffering and endeavor. In the move from substance to subject *via* soul, there is more stress on the end through human endeavor and activity than on the sacredness of suffering and receiving. Suffering and receiving may be beginnings but they are not the end and the end is what determines the point of the whole. This concern with the end, the *telos*, is very Aristotelian, of course, but once again Hegel is not fully an Aristotelian, even when he crowns his *Encyclopedia* (§577) with a speculative hymn covering Aristotle's thought thinking thought (*noēsis noēsis noeseōs*). One suspects Plato was the greater at offering an archeology of the good and not only a teleology; moreover, an archeology which points back to the intimate soul in its own cavernous darknesses, its prenatal intimacies with true being, its outreach to the good above itself, above us all, the good that gives us to be here and now, that allows us to stand on the surface of the earth and in the light that gives us being and intelligibility and growing. Hegel talks about the impotence of nature. It does not seem to be the mother, matrix of all fertile possibility. *Geist* is the true progenitor. Hegel is not a dualist,

---

33. Hegel, *Outline of the Philosophy of Right*, §27.

to be sure, but he is more concerned to complete the modern turn towards self-determination than return to or retrieve forgotten archaic resources.[34]

And what of the music of soul? Interestingly, Hegel importantly sees the connection between music and the soul. In line with his teleological tilt to self-determination, and his location of soul at the beginning, which is only indeterminate, we find him identifying *music* with the romantic art *par excellence* (HA, vol. 1, 88, 528; vol. 2, 889; VA, I, 122; II, 141; III, 133). Romantic art is the art of interiority. Hear Hegel:

> For expression in music is the object-free inner life, abstract subjectivity as such. This is our entirely empty self, the self without any further content. Consequently the chief task of music consists in making resound, not the objective world itself, but, to the contrary, the manner in which the inmost self is moved to the depths of its personality and conscious soul (*Seele*). The same is true of the effect of music. What it claims as its own is the depths of a person's inner life as such; it is the art of the soul and is directly addressed to the soul (*Gemüt*). (HA, vol. 2, 891; VA, III,135)

There is much that is suggestive about this and that bears thought,[35] but something about the indeterminate immediacy of soul does not bear enough thought for Hegel. Thus we find him remarking on the thoughtless virtuosity we sometimes find in music:

> musical production may easily become something utterly devoid of thought and feeling, something needing for its apprehension

---

34. In his later *Lectures on the History of Philosophy*, Hegel gives more evidence of a sympathetic appreciation of the ancients—though again perhaps as too much prefiguring his own ultra-modern, totally up-to-date system.

35. One thinks of Hegel's understanding of the human voice "as the freest, and in its sound the most perfect instrument[;] . . . the human voice can apprehend itself as the sounding of the soul itself, as the sound the inner life has in its own nature for the expression of itself, an expression which it regulates directly. . . . [I]n song the soul rings out from its own body. . . . So, for example, the Italians are a people of song, *ein Volk des Gesanges*"(HA, vol. 2, 922; VA, III, 175). "[The] free sounding of the soul in the field of music—this is alone melody" (HA, vol. 2, 930; VA, III, 185). Hegel makes a positive reference to Pythagoras (HA, vol. 2, 924; VA, III, 177–78). Music is connected to tone and tonality: "music takes the soul of tone, working itself free from spatial matter, in the qualitative differences of sound and in the movement of the ever-rolling stream of time" (HA, vol. 2, 894; VA, III, 139). Here he mentions mathematics, and also compares music and architecture. In an inward sensuousness heard in the inner ear, the development and unfolding of tones is by way of interplays of repetition and variability, sameness and dissonance; and while the unfolding is fluid in its variability, there is a return to itself. Something of this is connected to the feeling soul. Still, this is the "I" in its barest of immediate indeterminacy; the soul or "I" here is all but nothing.

no previous profound cultivation of mind or heart. On account of this lack of material not only do we see the gift for composition developed at the most tender age but very talented composers frequently remain throughout their life the most ignorant and empty-headed of men. (*HA*, vol. 2, 954; *VA*, III, 217)

We hear, once again, that it is the indeterminacy of beginnings that is stressed by Hegel, and with this also a certain deficiency of determinacy, not to say immaturity of rational self-determination. It is not the too-muchness of the musical soul that he hears, but the not-enoughness of the indefinite, of the immaturity of the too indeterminate, of a dearth and poverty of thought and spiritual culture. The overdeterminacy of fullness that pours forth in soul music is not heard, for its too-muchness cannot be heard amongst the emptiness of indeterminacy, just like the voice in the wilderness. Hegel thus:

> Music, for example, which is concerned only with the completely indeterminate movement of the inner spirit and with sounds as if they were feeling without thought, needs to have little or no spiritual material present in consciousness. Therefore, musical talent announces itself in most cases very early in youth, when the head is empty and the heart little moved, and it may sometimes attain a very considerable height before the spirit and life have experience of themselves. Often enough, after all, we have seen very great virtuosity in musical composition and performance accompanied by a remarkable barrenness of spirit and character.
>
> In poetry, on the other hand, it is quite different. (*HA*, vol. 1, 28; *VA*, I, 47)

You might interpret some of these statements of Hegel as touching on the porous idiocy of the soul, but their significance as idiotic for Hegel is precisely to be superseded in the direction of a more rational self-determination. On the threshold of this idiocy, Hegel can only drive forward to more and more rational self-determination. The "object-free inwardness" (*HA*, vol. 2, 892; *VA*, III, 136) that music expresses is too indeterminate for him. There is a logic of self-determination always at work. The soul is an immediacy in the sense of indeterminacy, not in the sense of a secret overdeterminacy of living. There follows the drive from soul to selving and then selving is in essence a matter of self-determination. The self-determination takes over the souling, and wins over its porosity—wins it over not by the wooing of the music, but in terms of the will that wills itself. The *Trieb* of the *conatus* defines the move from the indeterminate to the determinate to the self-determining. The selving then proves not porous enough, risks losing its intimacy with the *passio*. In its music the soul does not sing itself as received into being. The soul does not know itself as wooed and wooing. In its music it does not receive the given note from the secret source; it works on its own notes.

I find a redeeming feature to Hegel's way of thinking in his appreciation of dialectic as enabling a dealing with *transitions* and *thresholds*.[36] This shows something of the capacity for "two thinks at a time," as James Joyce put it. A threshold opens up on more than one side, and hence we can move back and forth, we can move up and down, we can move out and in. The fluidity of moving on the threshold is important, and this is very relevant to the fluid forming that we can be said to experience in music. The question of how we move on the threshold is all important, and whether we are so driven to the end that the antecedents are either left behind, or perhaps used as stepping stones to attaining the end. In Hegel's case, the antecedents are not simply left behind and also are not simply stepping stones. The antecedents are taken up into the unfolding process and hence contribute to the living substance of that unfolding, now taking new and sometimes surprising forms in the unfolding itself. Nor are the stages of unfolding stepping stones simply, since stages might take on the fuller form of an entirely developed world that is fully for itself, if not the absolute fullness itself. It is not a means to an end merely, even if in the end, it does serve the becoming of a fuller end beyond itself.

These complexities in Hegel's understanding are not to be underestimated or undervalued, but the tilt of the unfolding in the process is still in the direction of the end, with the beginning understood as an indetermination to be further determined, in view of the self-determination to be attained rather than attuned in achieved teleology. The threshold serves this teleological process of self-determination, as does the indetermination of the beginnings, as well as the plural forms of determination we find along the way and its stages. But music as threshold, as soul music, intimates a different sense of origin, and hence also a different sense of determinacy and self-determination. This I have called the overdeterminacy, though again without hiding the need of paradoxical language of fullness and emptying. The surplus character is intimate even in the minimalism of the least unfolding; you might say, the affirmative is in the negative, but in a way that does not fit Hegelian negativity.[37]

---

36. See also Férdia Stone-Davis' essay in this volume, which also touches on the subject of music and thresholds.

37. See Hegel, *Science of Logic*, 56 where he talks about "the inner negativity of the determinations as their self-moving soul, the principle of all natural and spiritual life."

As with Kant, it is not surprising that in Hegel there is a final preference for poetry as preeminent, and one can see in this a predilection for determination and determinability. In a way too it is also a preference for the promise of the diurnal life of the spirit, a preference for surpassing the nocturnal intimacy of the musical. The spiritual is understood as more essentially diurnal than nocturnal.[38] Is there a dark night of the soul in Hegel's way of thinking? I cannot conceive Hegel as writing a hymn to the night (as Novalis did). I cannot see him like Zarathustra singing a *Nachtlied*; nor for that matter that most tender song that came to Nietzsche on hearing at evening the voice of the unseen gondolier from the bridge in Venice. It is hard to think of Hegel as a musically Orphic thinker, and for all his talk of staring the negative in the face and converting it into the positive, as one with the power of music to descend into hell and even move the powers of Acheron. In fact, Hegel sardonically suggests that the notes of Orpheus "sufficed for wild beasts which lay around him tame, but not for men who demanded the contents of a higher doctrine" (*HA*, vol. 2, 908; *VA*, III, 157).[39] One wonders, of course, who could be such a singing thinker. Perhaps only a god or God could be the singer of such soul music that all horror is forgiven, all broken promises of the good reinstated, indeed festively fulfilled. Were one allowed to mix Greek and Jew, such an Orphic singer would be Christ.

## VI: Selving with Soul

The Hegelian "self" determines itself "upwards," so to say, through the rational self-sublation of its own soul. But hell knows no peace. And what if the dialectical negativity that moves up thus might also move down, and now not preserving but negating the rational self? Might it not lead to a de-sublation of *self without soul*? In truth, after Hegel, one does see signs of this de-sublation and it does not bring us back to the soul, rather more to the ab-ject "subject" than the rational subject. The thrown down self, the abject, goes back into the dark, but it is not the dark night of the soul. Indeed, in this going down, the "self" is a kind of dark night where every dawning is a false dawn, masking, surfacing over, what lies down deep beneath. This going down is to be found in Schopenhauer and Nietzsche and others later.

---

38. It is worth asking if there would ever be soul music without the black churches and their Gospel music. And if there would be that black music without Africa? Go figure Hegel! Riddle me Africa. But Africa for Hegel does not figure in his scheme of world history. Is it an indeterminacy whose night does not get the honor of offering even a small fillip of progress in dialectical determination. Ironically, black Africa is blank.

39. See Marchenkov, *The Orpheus Myth and the Powers of Music*.

But where is the soul in entry to its own night? And does it not also seem as if what makes the living being to be living at all (formerly, soul) lies "behind" or "below" it as the "thing"—obscene and a horror and not good: not the soul, but the evil "thing." If so, self-sublating subjectivity is de-sublated and subjected to the "thing." We might call this *the horror version of reification*—the subject not merely objectified but subtended by the "thing." When the "subject" knows it as thus subtended, it sees itself as the abject subjected by the "thing."

This is a motive to come back directly to the theme of soul music and soul-less selving. Even if there is a stress on self, self, self, that is not good for the soul, the point cannot be to do away entirely with self.[40] Not at all. I spoke above of soul and *selving* when considering objectification and subjectification. I adopt "selving" as a term from G. M. Hopkins and adapt it now in tune with the present theme. I quote Hopkins:

> As kingfishers catch fire, dragonflies dráw fláme;
> As tumbled over rim in roundy wells
> Stones ring; like each tucked string tells, each hung bell's
> Bow swung finds tongue to fling out broad its name;
> Each mortal thing does one thing and the same:
> Deals out that being indoors each one dwells;
> Selves—goes itself; myself it speaks and spells,
> Crying Whát I do is me: for that I came.[41]

In this marvelous poem, we are arrested by the eye catching flare of fire, but also by the resonance of music in the splash of water that has entered deep in the well, or in the tolling bell that tongues perhaps its angelus, the message broadcast being that mortal things word themselves. Their wording is their selving.

---

40. Think of Charles Taylor's suggestion of the "buffered self" in *A Secular Age*, 27. This for him is a modern construction. But where he sees the premodern self as "porous," I see the porosity of being as elementally constitutive in an ontological sense, not just an historical cultural mark of "earlier" peoples. To be is to be porous. Buffered selves lose their souls.

The porosity of being is related to what Keats speaks of as "negative capability," earlier mentioned in connection with Dickens. Keats also spoke, of course, of the "vale of soul making." In one sense, the soul is not made, it is created, and endowed with powers, and with these powers it participates in making a self: the world is a vale of self-making in that sense. But prior to making is what is not made but what enables making; and what enables making is in itself not self-enabled. It is enabled not as self-made but as endowed, that is, as received into being from a source other than itself: God (speaking theologically).

41. Hopkins quotes taken from *Poems*, edited by Robert Bridges.

How now relate selving and soul? A suggestion: the uttering of the soul is its outering, and this uttering is where selving takes form. Selving is the outering of souling; this also entails the wording of being ensouled. Souling is not to be reified in the ensouling of things. This is why it, the wording, is more like a singing. The souling comes to the embodiment of a selving, coming to be from a secret origin, given to be as itself, an intimate and finite origin(al). For it is received into being as creature—as singing creature, both created and creative. Being created and being finitely creative are mirrored in the doubleness of the *passio essendi* and the *conatus essendi*. Soul, then, is witness to an intimacy of being more original than selving, but in the intimacy of souling there is something more than soul that endows its being. Soul comes to itself as enabling selving from a source beyond both selving and souling.[42]

How relate this to what has gone before? To recall the narrative I offered: as soul has been objectified and self subjectified, being a self has tended to become enmeshed with determinability and self-determination. Self is a relatively surface event, if that is the right way to put it. We are often tempted to speak of layers or depths of self and this is not wrong, but the implication is this: we standardly take for self what has been firmed in terms of a more available determination. This is the selving that has come to be the more constant character, and our fix on this is not always with patient attention to the more recessed selving out of which the self is expressed. We do not attend enough to the saturated surplus of the surface, and hence miss the soul. To attend to soul asks of us to be attuned to the recessed reserves of being. But again, this is not entirely accurate, if we think only of a vanishing depth, since the soul is as much out as in; it outwards itself and is the inner in the outer, which is never just outer, just as the inner is never just inner. My suggestion is that the soul-less selving of modernity comes to be in the collusion of objectification and subjectification, and does so not only in terms of more fixed determinability but in terms of what is stirring secretly in the soul—the urge to be free, the urge to be released. But here this urge now takes the form of a quest for self-determination. This is a quest for an autonomy that risks forgetting as much the inward otherness of itself, as of the outward otherness with which it is always in communication, always co-implicated.

There is a variety of ways of being free, ways that are not necessarily just autonomous, for instance, not just self-circling self-determination, but our

---

42. Emerson is wonderfully suggestive in relation to the Over-soul: "Man is a stream whose source is hidden. Our being is descending into us from we know not where" (Essay IX, "The Over-soul," in *Collected Works of Ralph Waldo Emerson, Volume II: Essays: First Series*, 159).

being released; or our being sung into being from beyond ourselves; or our singing selving of ourselves beyond our self. In being self, in being itself, this soul-less selving sets itself over against otherness outside, also made soul-less, and sets itself over its own inward otherness—both of which then are thought to be heteronomies to be subordinated to autonomy. The *conatus essendi* takes shape as the will to self-determination, but in doing so forgets its own more original *passio essendi* which is itself as more intimately and vulnerably porous. It forgets the porosity of soul that makes it participant in an open space of communication, indeed communion. It covers over the porosity of soul as an empty abyss, a threatening nothing within innerness, as well as reconfiguring outer otherness as a soul-less heterogeneity separate from itself. The selving on the surface of self-determination thus tries to snip the umbilical cord that ties it to its own soul—and no nourishment from the womb of the porosity comes up to it, even though in this, all its endeavor is still an affair of being "birthed with" (*con-natus*). It thinks it gives birth to itself, and forgets its being received into being, its being initiated—always through an other or others—an other or others who are with it, before it is with itself. Soul music opens access to the *passio essendi* and the porosity, and when the opening is allowed, we ourselves are allowed, free(d), released differently—into the song of life that is never our own, even when it is most intimately our own.

Thus I would use the language of selving, and in a manner that carries the resonance of souling. I cannot go into the fuller dimensionalities of selving, beyond recalling that out of the idiot self comes the aesthetic selving, bound up more articulately with our full aesthetic being in rapport with the aesthetic happening of being as intimately other to us; recalling then the erotics of selving where the thrust of self-transcending in search of another comes to itself in being with the other; recalling further the agapeics of selving which witnesses to a surplus generosity of being at work in the selving which is not simply for selving itself and alone but for giving beyond self. This last is selving in service of goodness that is willing to be there and to give of itself fully there for the good of the other as other. For it does not find just itself in the other, but finds the other as other, and finds that just finding itself is not what finding or being found is all about.[43]

Soul(ing) reminds us that there a radical intimacy to the living being which empowers communication but which is more than this or that communication. This is why its powers are not more ordinary determinate powers, since these powers invoke the *porosity* and the *passio essendi*, relative to which we have to grant the priority of being given to be to giving

---

43. On selving, see again *Being and the Between*, chapter 9.

beyond ourselves, as well as give up insisting on self-giving that gives only self or gives only for itself. Souling reminds us of the secret endowment of which we are in primal receipt before any acting or endeavoring on our part.

Soul is particularly connected with the intimacy of the idiotic self as naming the threshold of night and day, the night of our being and the day; the threshold of dawning and awakening; the threshold allowing intimacy with the nocturnal powers slumbering in our being; the threshold releasing passage into the diurnal powers we more normally associate with the self, with the processes of selving. The soul is night, the selving is day. In the passages from the idiotic through agapeic selving, there is a dawning of day, even as there is also return to night. This means there is no selving without suffering, though this is double, since return to night with us can mean both the horror of the nightmare and the healing of the prophetic dream.

When I say the soul is something idiotic, idiocy here has the meaning of the intimate, to be sure. It also has the meaning of the idiosyncratic, in the sense of the singular. This is connected with the sense of simplicity associated with the soul. But this intimate singularity is not autistic in the sense of being turned back into self as a closed or enclosed monadism. Rather it is a singular opening of an intimate field of communication. Here is the connection with the porosity of our being. This is itself not initiated by us, but rather it is a between-space where we begin to wake to ourselves and other things, where things dawn on us, where we dawn on ourselves, where the others dawn on us. This prior field of communicability is indicated by the word "idiot," as when we speak of an idiom—a singularly inflected way of communication. There is no need here to set self-relation and other-relation in opposition. Our participating singularity in the open porosity of communication births us in the promising field of the intimate universal. This intimate field of communication is related, one might suggest, to our nature as *beings in prayer*. Is this field of communication perhaps why the thought of a kind of panpsychism or *anima mundi* cannot be quite suppressed, when our participation in the field of communication, in the porosity of being, indicates no final or absolute impermeability between ourselves and what is other to us? It is not that the "more" is like us, or that we are like it, but that we are together in a metaxological community that cannot be defined by *partes extra partes*. It is a kind of metaxological "all in all." Sometimes it seems even like a kind of mystical promiscuity in which, nevertheless, a mysterious and absolute chastity marks the being together of all things, when they are themselves in their most intimate truth. Interestingly, there are forms of music in which we have that double experience of pure chastity and nuptial *sun-ousia*. We are being penetrated and penetrating; receiving joy and offering back rejoicing.

There is here a connection with my above remarks on Kant and Hegel on music, a connection which brings to mind the renegade Kantian and Hegel-hater: Schopenhauer. If I am not mistaken, Schopenhauer has a feeling for something prior to the determinate and self-determining self. He speaks of this in terms of what he calls *the will*, but he should have talked about the *passio essendi* and the *porosity*. There is too much of the *conatus essendi*, the striving of the will (*Streben nach dem Unendlichen*) in his description of the ultimate metaphysical origin. He realizes the problem with the Kantian dualism. Kant does not pursue the way "self" puts its ontological roots intimately into a certain darkness of being (even though he does refer to an unknowable X). This is why Schopenhauer is close to the heart of the matter when he talks about music as the direct copy of the will—except it is not a copy of the will. Music comes out of the intimacy, the porosity rather than the will. It comes out of the soul, in the sense I am here trying to suggest, not the modern spiritual substance.

Recall again Kant's attitude to music and the porosity of being, his irritation that his autonomy might be overcome, as it were, with perfumes. Think of his phobic reaction to the threat of a sweat coming on: he would stop his afternoon walk, rest under the shade of a tree, until the danger of the sweats passed and the porosity sweating brings; safe again, the pores of his being closed up, he would resume his walk. (Might one see this as a protection against the infernal condition of which G. M. Hopkins, seer of spirit, spoke with witness: "Selfyeast of spirit a dull dough sours. I see/ The lost are like this, and their scourge to be/As I am mine, their sweating selves, but worse"?[44]) Now consider Schopenhauer. He thinks there is a release from the relentless striving of the *conatus essendi* which we find in the artistic genius and more radically the saint. The artist as genius, as excessive contemplative intellect, somehow escapes the fate of being in the bondage of the will. The artistic genius is free(d), if only for some few privileged moments, while the ascetic saint is graced with or sustains this freedom more fully. Lifted above the incessant becoming of will, its ever renewed lack and restlessness, the artist attains the Platonic Idea in a contemplative composure replete with metaphysical significance about the most ultimate nature of being, which is named by Schopenhauer as Will. The individual arts offer will-less knowledge of Ideas, an indirect knowing of Will itself, but music alone is not knowledge of Idea, but directly of will itself. This is its privileged position. "Unlike the other arts, then, music is in no way the image of ideas; but rather the *image of the will itself (Abbild des Willens selbst)*, whose objective form the ideas are also: it is for this very reason that the

---

44. This is from Hopkins' poem: "I wake and feel the fell of dark, not day."

effect of music is so much more powerful and penetrating than that of the other arts: since the latter only speak of the shadow (*Schatten*), while music speaks of the substance (*Wesen*)."[45]

There is more in the primal root of the soul, retreating into darkness.[46] Schopenhauer shows himself attuned to the power of music to open up the porosity of being. Music speaks to what is profoundly *intimate* to the human being. Melody: the "secret history of the intellectually enlightened will"[47]— not quite the right way to put it, but moving in the space of a right attunement. My question: whence comes that festive joy we often have in music; whence the peace even in and through dissonance, if the Will as origin is as Schopenhauer describes it? Surely it cannot be an *eros turannos*; there must be more of the agapeic in it?[48] More often than not, Schopenhauer's sense of the will corresponds dominantly to the *conatus essendi* rather than the *passio essendi*. Sometimes perhaps he mingles these two together, but I would say it is to the *passio essendi* that music first addresses itself. The language of the will is not the most apt way of talking here. There is something before the will that wills itself. The *passio essendi* has to do with our being given to be, prior to our giving ourselves to be, determining ourselves this way or that. Thus there is something on the *other side* of will, something *not voluntary*, about the intimate appeal of music. The appeal has to do with gift. It has to do with what is secret to the idiotic selving. The power of music to open up again the porosity of being is remarkable. It communicates its intimate appeal beyond the fixation of this or that determinate formation of our selving. If music has this significance for the intimacy of being, and its porosity, its ultimate origin cannot be as Schopenhauer describes the will. Schopenhauer's self-insistent will cannot account for the opening up of the porosity of being in which the powers of communicability and communi-

---

45. Schopenhauer, *The World as Will and Representation*, vol. 1, 257.

46. Platonic erotics does not deny that darkness, nevertheless the soul's eros is brought to its consummation in relation to beauty, and one might say that there is a *musical logos of philosophical reason* that gives harmonious voice to that eros. The soul's eros is not lost in the night. Schopenhauer's recommendation of music and its metaphysical consolation comes out of a desire for escape from the tyrannical eros, the dark origin named Will. Schopenhauer less redoubles Platonic themes as *doubles* them in a way that is not Platonic, given his view of the ultimate origin as a tyrannical erotic will. See *AOO*, 152–53; also 240n32 on Heidegger and song.

47. Schopenhauer, *The World as Will and Representation*, vol. 1, 259.

48. One should not forget that the original Will, the *Wesen* is itself even darker than all the shadows! An ultimate darkness that casts shadows (of itself)—how is this possible at all? Any shadow needs light, but an original darkness is devoid of light, so how then can it cast a shadow of itself? With light, or a light other than the darkness? But what could that light then be, given the ultimate (pre-)supposition that everything is the outcome of Will, the dark origin?

cation come to form, and within which the expressions of music, and all art, show themselves intimate with the *passio essendi* prior to our *conatus essendi*. The original giving of the porosity is agapeic.[49]

It is difficult to avoid paradoxical language in regard to this prior porosity: neither passive nor active, but both passive and active; neither beyond nor immanent, but both beyond and immanent; neither strange nor intimate, yet both intimate and strange; not mine, not thine, but both mine and not mine at all, and both thine and not thine too; not unknown nor known, but both unknown and yet as if known already; neither one nor many, but both one and many; not simply given nor giving, but both given to itself and self-giving. This paradoxical language is beyond the dialectical language of the coincidence of opposites. It is more resonant of the metaxological poise between opposites, in the fluent passage between them.[50]

---

49. What words to call on to express what is prior to determination and beyond self-determination? My suggestion overall is that our stress on "self" has been so foregrounded that we become less attuned to what is recessed, just in that foregrounding. Will, will to power: these are not good ways of describing the recessed. They offer languages more at home in the foreground, rather than the recessed intimacy of being. The ethos of self-determining will becomes more self-affirming, but the patience in the selving does not get the right acknowledgment or mindfulness. But it is out of what is thus recessed that music springs. This indicates something about the nature of the recessed that is not entirely one with describing the expressed in the language of will (to power). Thus Schopenhauer is a participant in soul music, as it were, but he cannot quite make sense of the meaning of this participation, how it touches the intimacy of being, as it does. We are released from will into a Sabbath of peace, but his language of will does not quite jell with the festive celebration that is part of the meaning of Sabbatical festivity. The mutation of autonomy into tyrannical eros does not help soul music, for this music breaks forth to console even the tortured self in its subjection to the inexorability of will. The abject self lurks already there in this inexorability—even though later, whether defiant or abject, it will be even less willing to confess its confused, even corrupt condition.

50. The soul is self-moving in both Plato (*Phaedrus*, 245c–246a) and Aristotle (*De Anima*, III, 9). Soul names an originality of moving, an initiation of moving, of life, of being. But if the soul is self-moving, is one "side" of it mover and the other "side" of it moved? Hence one side passive, one side active? How make sense of this? Or is there a middle, neither passive nor active. There is an intriguing connection here between soul and the middle voice (see Davis, *The Soul of the Greeks*, ch. 12, "The Grammar of Soul," 207). One might connect the active with the endeavoring *conatus*, the passive with the *passio*, and the middle with the prior porosity. The modern selving tilts in the direction of the endeavor as self-determining; selving as *conatus* over-takes the *passio* and the porosity, and hence loses the middle and its meaning.

## VII: Soul Music and More: More Than Self Alone with Itself

To round off these reflections, though not quite in any finale, I want to broaden the question and ask: more than soul music as a genre of music, should we perhaps understand soul music in something like the broader Greek sense concerning *ta musika*, the musical things? The musical things have everything to do with what a later age will deem humanistic studies, or indeed liberal arts (*artes liberales*). A self without soul music is devoid of these liberal and humanizing arts. These call for finesse and not just geometrical technique. There is a Platonic sense of soul music in this regard, and its care is for the pedagogy of the *psuche*. Without that care soul-less selving produces results in which the music of life, the poetry of being, evaporates—and we have *technē* without art, art in the more deeply wooed sense called for by music.

Selving springs out from, and must always remain in contact with, soul in this musical sense, and hence must be marked by ontological fidelity to what is *before* its own determinacy and self-determination, and what also is *more*, in pointing beyond self to what is above it. One should remember that music refers us to the muses, and these recall the gift of receiving from sources of inspiration we can call on, but cannot command. We can call on and can recall, and we must listen to those sources, if our own being is to be animated by soul-music—if our existence is to become a singing life.[51] The muses are the daughters of Mnemosyne—and memory in the deep metaphysical sense is connected to music. The more deeply wooed sense of art comes only with true courtesy for these daughters.

I mention three indicators here. A first indicator has to do with *origin*. I find myself thinking of Nietzsche and his first-born book: *The Birth of Tragedy from the Spirit of Music*.[52] One must stress this last part: origin in the spirit of music. One can see here a kind of regress to, if not recuperation of, sources of animation prior to the determinations of reason, out of which human outering and uttering come richly. We have to drop back down into the darkness of this prior animation for creativity to come. But again it cannot be commanded. The Greeks were right: it has to be wooed and we have to accept our recipient status. We are beneficiaries of its gift, honored by it, not masters of its energy. To a huge degree this source is identified with the Dionysian by Nietzsche and there are questions to be asked about this.

---

51. There would be then a song of self not the same as the song of myself of Walt Whitman—though in truth his song is more than of himself, it sings of that more . . . .

52. Nietzsche, *The Birth of Tragedy*.

As far as I can see the matter in Nietzsche, there is no trace of the agapeic promise of the gift. There is too much of *eros turranos* and its equivocity, not least inherited from Schopenhauer and turned in a different direction, putatively "yes-saying." In truth, there is a sign of the porosity here, though it is then taken over by a *conatus essendi* as defined by will to power affirming itself, sometimes ferociously. Nietzsche never worked out the equivocities of receiving and self-affirming. Nevertheless, the redeeming power of music comes. If there is a kind of "aesthetic theodicy," as Nietzsche does suggest, what does this say about the saving power? If there is a Sabbath of the will, as Schopenhauer says, what does this say about the redemptive power of the releasing source? The source does not have to be taken in their willful sense, their godless sense. One might see them both as trying to restore the soul music to the self, but with the sometimes forced strains of the soul-less self.

A second indicator has to do with *end*: I am thinking of Socrates at his end. Nietzsche touches on the point of the "musical Socrates" and this is very germane to the matter. The matter now is the eve of death and the perplexity about the deathlessness of the soul, broached by Socrates and his companions in the prison. The setting of their conversation is the anticipated end of a singular life, the beginning of perhaps another life. Eschatological perplexity hovers over the dialogue—perhaps the most dualistic in one sense, but one has to consider the occasion: this is not the beginning of a Dionysian orgy but a fare-well into death, the greatest mortal mystery perhaps, not less than the mystery of life itself. The setting in prison is dictated by the religious duty to avoid polluting Athens by putting someone to death during the sacred time of the yearly festival during which a state ship is sent to Delos to thank the god Apollo for delivery of the youth from the sacrificial death exacted by the Minotaur. It recalls Theseus in the labyrinth, finally gaining release from the appeasing sacrifice of fourteen youths to the Minotaur. In the case of Socrates, there has been a long interim between judgment and execution, the interim prolonged by the delay in the ship's return. The ship is now close by. This stay of execution creates a time in between life and death which is entirely enfolded in sacred festival. In that between time, neither immersed in life nor yet passing over into death, the worry of Socrates is about the dream that has come to him in the past, and that now again has visited him, namely, with the admonition about making music: "make music and work at it" (*Phaedo*, 60e). He does try his hand at music, and since he is not a maker of myths, he takes some of the fables of Aesop as the substance of his songs, though a hymn to Apollo is also mentioned (60d).[53] He comes to wonder rather if he should continue what

---

53. Some have mocked this, Nietzsche included, but there is something elemental

he has always been doing since he thought that perhaps philosophy was the true music and that his dream was like the cheers that encourage runners of a race. Nevertheless, Socrates thought homage must be paid to music, and the musical soul, and there is something sacred about it. That is clear.

Clear also is that there is a musical moment even when the arguments for the deathlessness of the soul do not always completely convince, in the sense of putting all perplexity to rest. Yet even if the *logoi* give no apodictic certainty, there is to be no misology. At certain limits argument becomes appeal and exhortation. Further, Socrates is quite honest that in face even of the crestfallen deflation of argumentative certainty, we still might resort to charms and songs (*Phaedo*, 77e) to keep the soul primed and not lacking in confidence or hope. There is edifying music on the boundary between life and the beyond of this life.

All this is by way of qualification also of the stark dualistic picture most frequently associated with Plato and the *Phaedo*. Further, the immortality of the soul is not just a matter of offering a univocal theoretical argument about a simple substance. It is not that we must eschew metaphysical arguments, but metaphysics here must acknowledge the issue of eschatological vision. An eschatological vision is not the same as a teleology of self-determination (pace Hegel and Kant above). There is something beyond the logics of determination and self-determination. The question is tied to the matter of the last things (*ta eschata*), of ultimate justice and ethical judgment on the singular soul. This is metaphysical in a metaxological sense as dealing with a threshold where a perplexity about ultimate justice cannot be entirely resolved within immanence itself but in immanent time points to the beyond of immanence. The eschatology of the *metaxu* crossed the boundary between metaphysics/ethics and religion. Thus, the issue is also trans-ethical (if we think of ethics in the Kantian sense). It is beyond immanent autonomy, since the divine measure that will judge cannot be also folded back into any morality of autonomy and (social) self-determination. The soul music resounds from beginning to end . . . even unto eschatological judgment where there may be glorious song, but perhaps also not music but weeping and gnashing of teeth.[54] The question of eschatological vision is

---

about Aesop—there is nothing aesthetic in the foppish, "cultured" sense about such fables; they come up from below, from the often inarticulate ground of the demos and its folk-memory. Folk wisdom comes from nowhere, and yet it has a ground and hold in the elemental constancies of the human condition which, again and again, keep getting resurrected.

54. On the need for myth, see *Phaedo* 114 d. See Pieper, *The Platonic Myths*. The *Republic* is centrally concerned with justice, but in the myth of Er, Socrates is concerned with justice in an *eschatological perspective*, as he is with the vision of the other world in the *Phaedo*. One notes also how all these visions seem to have an essentially

bound up with what I speak of in terms of *posthumous mindfulness*: mindfulness beyond the normal division of life and death, and on the lookout for the worthy to be affirmed in life, and in death . . . the good of the "to be."[55]

There is a sense in which Nietzsche is not so un-Platonic after all, not so different to Socrates at the end. One thinks of his own anticipation of arriving in Hades into the company of great figures and of him having converse with four pairs of thinkers: Epicurus and Montaigne, Goethe and Spinoza, Plato and Rousseau, Pascal and Schopenhauer. Over against their greatness, he would be tested, he will be perhaps purged, he will judge and be judged.[56] This is uncannily like Socrates' anticipation of meeting the heroes on arrival in the next world, and putting them to the kinds of questions that have consumed his soul in this life (*Apology*, 40e–41c). Again we have to cease to think in simplistic dualisms—of which I would not accuse Plato. In the *Pheadrus*, it is said that to give an account of the idea of the soul would be divine and that a likeness is more fitting for us humans. We are not totally bereft of articulations. Hence again our need for the image and the myth (the chariot, the horses and charioteer, the singing cicadas). The sacred story is more resonant of the music of the soul than is the bare

---

underground dimension, and their concern is emerging from under ground to the surface of a beautiful world. One thinks of the images in Plato comparing us to the fish that lift their heads above the water, and get a glimpse of another world (*Phaedo*, 109b–110b); or of the chariot rising and falling in the empyrean *Phaedrus*, a vision of our earth, if not seen from above, touched by what is above, and touching it; and then there is the prophesy of the other world to come, where we will not have images of the gods but the gods themselves actually will dwell in the sacred groves and temples (*Phaedo*, 111b–c).

55. When one witnesses the astonishing singularity of an infant once born, one is perplexed by Plato's perplexity about the prenatal intimacy of the soul with being; and one wonders about pre-existence, beyond determinate life and death, and our being delivered into life, being delivered over to life and death.

56. One notes at the close of the *Birth of Tragedy*, the reference to sacrifice: the voice of an "old Athenian . . . with the eyes of Aeschylus," and the invitation to "follow me to a tragedy, and sacrifice with me in the temple of both deities" (*Basic Writings*, 144). In "Mixed Opinions and Maxims," §408 (*Human all too Human*): "*The Journey to Hades*: I too have been in the underworld, like Odysseus, and I shall yet return there often; and not only sheep have I sacrificed to be able to talk with a few of the dead, but I have not spared my own blood. Four pairs did not deny themselves to me as I sacrificed: Epicurus and Montaigne, Goethe and Spinoza, Plato and Rousseau, Pascal and Schopenhauer. With these I must come to terms when I have long wandered by myself; they shall tell me whether I am right or wrong; to them I want to listen when, in the process, they tell each other whether they are right or wrong . . ." [*The Portable Nietzsche*, 67]. The allusion is to Odysseus in Hades (*Odyssey*, book 11) in response to Circe's instructions (book 10). Odysseus encounters many in Hades: his erstwhile companion Elpenor, his mother Antikleia, Ariadne, Tiresias, Agamemnon, Achilles, Ajax, to name some.

concept. The image and myth tend to be concretizing and sometimes even singularizing in ways that the concept does not and cannot be.

Soul may have lost its meaning for many, but if we follow the path I have indicated we are brought to the threshold of mystery, where soul is not a bad name for something that has evaporated in the self-determination of selving in our time. It is a matter of acknowledgement of an overdeterminacy rather than knowledge of a determinate matter that we can pin down with univocal fixity. There may be no positive knowledge of the soul in the sense of an absolutely determinate concept, but this does not mean we do not know the soul. Beyond absolutely determinate and univocal knowledge, there can be a kind of *metaxological nescience on the threshold*, especially on the boundary of the ultimate between—between life and death, between death and the life that is beyond death. Heraclitus (fragment 45): "You could not search out the furthest limits of the soul, even if you traversed all of the ways; so unfathomable is its logos."[57] All the ways Heraclitus mentions are the songlines along which the aboriginal ancestors went on walkabout. Without soul, the selving goes on pointless walkabout, for it cannot hear the songlines. It sees only wasteland around it, not secret sources of support.

My third indicator comes back to the *middle*: I must be content to conclude by returning to the poem of G. M. Hopkins which helped me hear the music of the word "selve." I have already cited the first part of the poem, and it brings out the sense of everything as selving, and indeed of the musical sounding of selving. But there is more than selving, even in selving, and to see this one needs to recite the second part. Body and soul are together in a vision of the incarnate God. The incarnate God is more than the Nietzschean body, more than the Platonic soul. The music of the soul is called to hear the song of the divine, in the saturated surface of all things, in the elemental self-affirmation of all being, and then in the selving that the soul makes for itself in being pleasing in the sight of God. Here is the second part:

> Í say móre: the just man justices;
> Kéeps gráce: thát keeps all his goings graces;
> Acts in God's eye what in God's eye he is—
> Chríst—for Christ plays in ten thousand places,
> Lovely in limbs, and lovely in eyes not his

---

57. Deserving of more attention is W. B. Yeats' poem "A Dialogue of Self and Soul" where soul "fix(es) every wandering thought upon/ That quarter where all thought is done:/Who can distinguish darkness from the soul?" Yeats, *The Poems*, 284–86. I have said something about that poem in connection with forgiveness in "It is Nothing: Wording the Release of Forgiveness," 1–23, especially 13–15.

To the Father through the features of men's faces.

I perform a variation on a theme of Hopkins. I say more—but is it more of the same? More of the self? Yes, and no. We have come to the selving of all things, and there was music in things before this express affirmation. But there is more: The just man justices. If justicing keeps grace, there is more to the just self than its own moral justice. *Keeps*—but what keeps and what is keeping? I venture this keeping is not a matter of possession, but of safeguarding, a sacred duty of holding in trust, as we do when we are confided a gift or an endowment. (An older usage: one has a job to do and one gets one's keep—the shelter and essential nourishments that sustain one's life.) To keep grace is to guard grace, to husband it, to shepherd it. To be the shepherd of this gracing is to be a graced self. In graced selving, the sacred source of soul brims up from the bottomless well and, so to say, christens the selving. With such soul music, we taste ourselves, but the taste is not bitter, not sour. (I hear the echoing air of a darker poem of Hopkins.) We are not gall to ourselves, we are not heartburn. Selfyeast of soul no longer a dull dough sours. Our lot is not to be as are the lost, our own sweating selving. (If we sweat, it is the porosity coming to be unclogged again, the selving no longer clotting on itself.) The soul is leavened and as song rises in it, it rises into song. This might even be a song of myself, but if so, this is the music of no longer soul-less selving.

## Bibliography

Baldwin, James. *Sonny's Blues*. London: Penguin, 1995.
Barrett, William. *Death of the Soul: From Descartes to the Computer*. Oxford: Oxford University Press, 1987.
Bartlett, Karen. *Dusty: An Intimate Portrait of a Musical Legend*. London: Robson, 2014.
Bayles, Martha. *Hole in our Soul: The Loss of Beauty and Meaning in American Popular Music*. Chicago: University of Chicago Press, 1995.
Chrétien, Jean-Louis. *The Call and the Response*. Translated by Anne Davenport. New York: Fordham University Press, 2004.
Cousineau, Phil. *Soul: An Archaeology*. New York: HarperCollins, 1995.
Davis, Michael. *The Soul of the Greeks*. Chicago: The University of Chicago Press, 2011.
Desmond, William. "Agapeic Selving and the Passion of Being: Subjectivity in the Light of Solidarity." In *Post-Subjectivity*, edited by Christoph Schmidt, Merav Mack, and Andy R. German, 81–106. Cambridge: Cambridge Scholars Press, 2014.
———. *Art, Origins, Otherness*. Albany, NY: SUNY, 2003.
———. *Being and the Between*. Albany, NY: SUNY, 1995.
———. "Creativity and the Dunamis." In *The Philosophy of Paul Weiss: Library of Living Philosophers*, edited by L. Hahn, 543–57. Chicago: Open Court, 1995.
———. *The Intimate Strangeness of Being: Metaphysics after Dialectic*. Washington, DC: Catholic University of America Press, 2012.

———. "It is Nothing: Wording the Release of Forgiveness." Presidential Address, ACPA, *Proceedings of the American Catholic Philosophical Association* 82 (2008) 1–23.

———. "On the Surface of Things: Transient Life and Beauty in Passing." In *Radical Orthodoxy: Annual Review 1*, edited by Neil Turnbull, 19–50. Eugene, OR: Cascade, 2012.

Dickens, Charles. *The Life and Adventures of Martin Chuzzlewit*. Harmondsworth, UK: Penguin, 1968.

Emerson, Ralph Waldo. *Collected Works of Ralph Waldo Emerson*, Volume II: Essays: First Series. Cambridge: Belknap, 1980.

Fechner, Gustav Theodor. *Religion of a Scientist: Selections from Gustav Theodor Fechner*. Edited and translated by Walter Lowrie. 1946. Reprint. Whitefish, MT: Kessinger, 2007.

Hegel, G. W. F. *Hegel's Aesthetics: Lectures on Fine Art*. Vol 1. Translated by T. M. Knox. Oxford: Clarendon, 1975.

———. *Enzyklopädie der Philosophischen Wissenschaften im Grundrisse* (1830). Edited by Friedhelm Nicolin and Otto Pöggeler. Hamburg: Meiner, 1991.

———. *Hegel's Philosophy of Mind: Being Part Three of the Encyclopedia of the Philosophical Sciences*. Translated by W. Wallace. Oxford: Oxford University Press, 1971.

———. *Hegel's Lectures on the History of Philosophy*. Translated by E. S. Haldane and F. H. Simson. London: Routledge and Kegan Paul, 1892–96.

———. *Lectures on the Philosophy of Spirit (1827–1828)*. Translated by with an introduction by Robert R. Williams. Oxford: Oxford University Press, 2007.

———. *Outline of the Philosophy of Right*. Translated by T. M. Knox, revised and introduction by Stephen Houlgate. Oxford: Oxford University Press, 2008.

———. *Phänomenologie des Geistes*. Hamburg: Meiner, 1952; *Phenomenology of Spirit*. Translated by A. V. Miller. Oxford: Clarendon, 1977.

———. *Science of Logic*. Translated by A. V. Miller. New York: Humanities, 1969.

———. *Werke in zwanzig Banden*, Bande 13–15. Edited by E. Moldenhauer and K. M. Michel. Frankfurt: Suhrkamp, 1970.

Hopkins, Gerard Manley. *Poems of Gerard Manley Hopkins*. Edited by Robert Bridges. London: Humphrey Milford, 1918.

James, William. "Concerning Fechner." In *A Pluralistic Universe*, 68–87. Lincoln, NE: University of Nebraska Press, 1996.

Kant, Immanuel. *Critique of the Power of Judgment*. Edited by Paul Guyer, translated by Eric Matthews. Cambridge: Cambridge University Press, 2000.

———. *Groundwork of the Metaphysics of Morals: A German-English Edition*. Edited and translated by Mary Gregor and Jens Timmerman. Cambridge: Cambridge University Press, 2011.

Marchenkov, Vladimir. *The Orpheus Myth and the Powers of Music*. Hillsdale, NY: Pendragon, 2009.

Nietzsche, Friedrich. *Basic Writings of Nietzsche*. Translated by Walter Kaufmann. New York: Modern Library, 1992.

———. *The Portable Nietzsche*. Edited and translated by Walter Kaufmann. New York: Penguin, 1977.

Pieper, Josef. *The Platonic Myths*. Introduction by James V. Schall, translated by Dan Farrelly. South Bend, IN: St. Augustine's Press, 2011.

Sachs, Joe. *Aristotle's On the Soul and on Memory and Recollection*. Santa Fe, NM: Green Lion, 2001.
Schopenhauer, Arthur. *The World as Will and Representation*. Vol 1. Translated by E. F. J. Payne. New York: Dover, 1966.
Taylor, Charles. *A Secular Age*. Cambridge: Harvard University Press, 2007.
Whitman, Walt. *Poems of Walt Whitman*. Edited by Carl Sandburg. New York: Modern Library, 1921.
Yeats, W. B. *The Poems*. Edited by Daniel Albright. London: J. M. Dent, 1990.

# Name and Subject Index

acedia, 236, 238, 240–41
aestheology, 42, 49, 55–57
aesthetic(s), 40–42, 45, 49, 51–52,
    57, 216, 337, 345, 347
  anthropology, 42
  of conversion, 219–22
  experience, 52, 55–57
  of justice, 228
  of liturgy, 53–54, 56
  of music, 299
  of noise, 300
  of selving, 377
  of the soul, 215, 356, 364, 369
  theodicy, 383
  theological, 228–29, 232n45
Agamben, Giorgio, 85, 268, 273–83
agency, 3–4, 118–20, 132, 203, 239,
    293, 302
  moral, 237
Ahmed, Ruhal, 302
Al-Farabi, 100
Al-Kindi, 100
Al-Qatani, Muhammed, 285
alterity, 81, 249, 251, 253–54, 258,
    261, 263–64, 297
amateur, the, 51–57
*anamnesis*, 338
anatomy, 93–109
  of being, 99, 99n32, 101
  etymology of, 94
  as knowledge (of the soul), 93,
    104–8
  as theology, 106–7, 109
Anderson, Carl, 259
Anderson, Ray S., 271, 282
Andrewes, Lancelot, 214

angels, 150, 152–53, 157, 163,
    168–69, 338
Anthony the Great, 232
Anthropic principle, 192
anthropology, 4–5, 10–13, 114–21,
    124, 132, 135, 139, 145–47,
    149–70, 207, 231, 233, 237,
    257–61, 269, 273–77, 281–
    82, 324, 368–69
  aesthetic, 42
  Aristotelian, 116
  atomistic, 282
  Augustinian, 115–16
  dualistic, 115, 118, 269, 277
  Eucharistic, 61, 66–76
  Greek, 269
  Hebrew, 268
  holistic, 146, 152, 164, 266–73,
    276, 282
  moral, 237
  Pauline, 269n9
  philosophical, 135, 146, 254
  physicalist, 132
  redeemed, 279, 282
  spiritualistic, 33
  split, 266–83
  techno-, 42
  theological, 4, 60, 66, 118, 120,
    126, 146, 150, 169, 262, 268
apophaticism, 9, 139, 157, 162, 318,
    322, 347
Aquinas, Thomas, 10n27, 13n32,
    14n35, 74n62, 87–88,
    115–16, 120, 126, 155, 280,
    280n55, 309, 311, 313–17,
    324, 359, 367n27

Arasse, Daniel, 54
Aristotle, 4, 14, 19, 41, 43–44, 49–52, 80–83, 87–88, 93–94, 98–102, 100n37, 105–6, 116–17, 156, 193, 202, 255, 257, 310, 311n9, 317, 358–59, 360n15, 361n18, 363–64, 366, 368–70, 381n50
art, 4, 41–42, 47–48, 55–58, 206, 341, 357, 381–82
   cult of, 42, 49, 55
   as liturgy, 53–55
   as successor of Christianity, 55–58
atheology, 40–41, 43–46, 55, 57
Atkins, Peter, 189–90
Auden, W. H., 220, 222n26
Augustine, Bishop of Hippo, 14, 16, 25–26, 28, 34–39, 48, 57, 87, 115–16, 150–59, 162, 168–69, 280n55, 314, 320n37, 360n16, 362n20, 367n27
auto-affection, 81–82, 325n53
Avicenna, see Ibn Sina
Avramova, Sofia, 160

Baader, Franz von, 331, 336, 341–43, 348
Bacon, Francis, 80, 109, 201–2
Baker, Lynne Rudder, 115, 119–21, 123–24, 132, 272–73
Balthasar, Hans Urs von, 323, 326
baptism, 73, 214, 312
Barfield, Owen, 100n37
Barlaam of Seminara, 154–55, 157, 159, 161–62, 166
Barth, John, 205
Barth, Karl, 268–69
Basil the Great, 152, 166
Bataille, Georges, 40
Bayles, Martha, 353n4
beatific vision, 158, 313, 315
behaviorism, 176, 181
Behler, Ernst, 348
Benedetti, Alessandro, 103n54
Bergson, Henri, 27n7, 84, 348
Bernard of Clairvaux, 165, 346n61
Bertolacci, Amos, 100–1

Beuys, Joseph, 52
Bichat, Xavier, 82
biology, 27n7, 122n28, 190, 273
   evolutionary, 4, 27
Bloom, Harold, 215, 220
Böhme, Jacob, 337n31
Bradshaw, David, 157
Brentano, Franz, 27, 103n48, 348
Brown, Warren S., 266n1, 270–71, 276
Buber, Martin, 258n31
Bulgakov, Sergius, 308n2, 310n8
Bultmann, Rudolf, 268
Buttlar, Auguste von, 338

Calvinism, 44
capitalism, 44–45, 58, 202, 204, 206
Carlino, Andrea, 108n72, 108n72
Carpi, Berengario da, 103n54
Cary, Phillip, 158
Casey, Edward, 287n7
Catholicism, 32, 53–54, 57–58, 214, 260, 330–33, 336, 341n49, 344–49
causality, 9, 84, 118, 187, 293
   efficient, 89, 116, 123
Cavell, Stanley, 354
Chalmers, David, 190
Champollion, Jean-François, 339
Charles, Ray, 353
Chesterton, G. K., 19
Chrétien, Jean-Louis, 20, 20n48, 294
Christ, Jesus, 18, 31, 60, 62–67, 69, 72–73, 75, 126, 128–31, 153, 158, 163, 167, 226, 229, 239, 262, 269, 271, 273, 277, 308n3, 310n8, 311–14, 315n19, 316–17, 326n58, 347, 374, 386
   as the archetype of the human person, 67
   ascension of, 311
   communion with, 76, 312–13, 315–16
   hypostatic union of, 139, 139n16, 141

incarnation of, 38, 57, 115, 120, 126, 128, 152, 167, 169, 263–64, 277n41, 314, 327, 343
passion of, 62–63, 129
resurrection of, 46, 62, 64–65, 73, 120, 130–33, 273n29, 283, 311–12
return of, 312
as *telos*, 60, 62, 66
Christology, 61, 135, 139, 152, 159, 169–70, 313n12, 317
Chalcedonian, 157
church, 19, 44, 47–48, 53, 56, 66, 131, 214, 222–23, 226, 229, 262, 271–72, 277, 314–15, 327, 347, 374n38
Churchland, Patricia, 5n17, 9, 9n27, 123
Churchland, Paul, 5n17
Clarke, W. Norris, 17
Climacus, John, 161
cloud of witnesses, 131, 133
Coleridge, Samuel Taylor, 216
communion,
  with God/Christ, 65, 65n18, 69–74, 76, 169, 259, 312–13, 315–16, 326
  with others, 15, 32, 71, 74, 138, 145–46, 250, 253, 258–59, 316, 377
  of saints, 313, 316
conscience, 25, 28, 204, 237, 255, 339
  religious, 29
consciousness, 3–4, 9n27, 10, 17, 25, 27n5, 81, 87–88, 115, 118–19, 121–23, 128, 132, 139n12, 178–82, 186–87, 189–91, 200, 206, 260–61, 294, 330, 335, 338, 340, 366, 372
  of death, 30–31
  problem of, 176–77, 181
  fourfold, 339, 342
  religious, 326
conversion, 16–17, 213–29, 272, 331, 347
  aesthetic, 220, 222

difficult, 219–20, 226–29
of the soul, 216, 219, 224, 229
secularized, 215
Cooper, John W., 268n6, 272
Copernicus, Nicolaus, 192
correlationism, 88–89
cosmos, 87–88, 130–31, 239
  as divinely ordered, 88
  moral, 241
  political, 85–86
  of soul, 15
*creatio ex nihilo*, 87, 311n10, 331, 336
Creed, Apostles, 69
Crick, Francis, 2–3, 9n27
Cullmann, Oscar, 75n64
cult, 41n4, 46, 53–54, 214, 333
  of art, 41–42, 49, 55
  democratic, 47–48
  secular, 55
Cusick, Suzanne G., 285n2, 302, 302n63

Daniélou, Jean, 314n18
Dante Alighieri, 209
Davies, Sir John, 1n1, 10n27
Dawkins, Richard, 122n28
death, 10n27, 19, 25, 46, 58, 60, 67, 69–71, 73–74, 129–31, 133, 136, 142–43, 180, 207, 222, 224–26, 228, 261, 264, 269n10, 272, 276, 309–13, 367n27, 383, 385, 385n55, 386
  as the denial of God, 69
  destruction of, 33, 72
  experience of, 25–39, 76
  of God, 41, 44, 55, 309
  and identity, 74
  knowledge of, 30
  as liberation from the body, 73
  as non-prosopic/non-relation, 138, 145
  as separation, 63, 312, 320
  of the soul, 308–9, 365
  time as, 61–62, 64
  victory over, 31, 62–63, 67, 69, 311–12

## Name and Subject Index

Defoe, Daniel, 199–205, 207, 209
deification, 143–44, 150–51, 153, 159, 167–68, 218
Deleuze, Gilles, 84, 349, 349n77
Delphic Oracle, 6, 10, 12–13, 94, 96, 105
Demetrakopoulous, George, 156
democracy, 41n4, 47–48
Democritus, 95n8, 190
demonic, the, 16, 85–86, 166, 219, 223, 226, 232, 237–41, 241n44, 242
Dempf, Aloïs, 348
Dennett, Daniel, 14, 115, 119, 119n11, 121, 121n21, 122, 122n28, 123, 123n35, 124, 124n38, 126, 132
Derrida, Jacques, 55, 297n45, 341
Descartes, René, 14, 19, 26, 84–85, 87, 102, 108, 116–17, 175, 177, 179–85, 191–92, 195, 201–2, 318–19, 321–22, 358, 360, 360n16, 363n23, 368
despair, 229, 242–43, 243n58
Dickens, Charles, 352, 352n1, 375n40
Dickinson, Colby, 277
Didymus the Blind, 155
Dilthey, Wilhelm, 348
Dionysius the Areopagite, 161, 315
disability, 2
divine science, 100, 313, 315–16, 318
Donne, John, 10n27
Dreyfus, Hubert L., 83n15, 89
Driesch, Hans, 27n7
dualism, 33, 74–75, 114–15, 137, 146, 178–80, 189, 254, 260, 269, 270n17, 273, 279n50, 282, 293n26, 321n39, 323, 355–56, 368, 385
  of body and mind, 123, 194, 272
  of body and soul, 14, 17, 30, 37, 39, 72, 74–75, 79, 120
  Cartesian, 116–117, 126, 132, 181, 185, 193, 199, 273n29, 282, 318, 326, 358, 360–61
  force-, 333

of functionality, 74
Kantian, 379
substance, 9, 101, 266–268, 270, 272, 279
Duns Scotus, John, 116, 116n5, 117, 117n6, 155

Eckhart, Meister, 35
Edelstein, David, 2
embodiment, 68, 127, 234, 262, 376
Emerson, Ralph Waldo, 376n42
empiricism, 30, 95n14, 204, 363–64
encounter, 2–3, 14, 81–82, 137, 213, 229, 264, 286, 294, 300, 337, 368
energies (divine), 149–50, 153, 155, 159, 166
Enlightenment, 47, 117, 175, 180, 205
Epicurus, 385, 385n56
epistemology, 125–26, 158, 272, 333, 360
eschatology, 31, 38–39, 64–65, 88, 164, 220, 267, 270–71, 276–77, 279, 281, 283, 318, 323, 326, 367, 367n27, 383–84, 384n54
  of the body, 130, 132
Eshelman, Raoul, 206
ethics, 3, 95–98, 121, 250–54, 254n13, 256–58, 260–64, 267, 276, 367n27, 384
  liminal, 286, 291–92, 294, 296–98, 301
Eucharist, 60–61, 64–67, 73, 75–76, 150, 261, 345
Evagrius Ponticus, 149, 160, 165–66, 231–41, 244, 317
evolution, 4, 10, 26–27, 30–31, 79, 121n21, 122, 122n28, 191–92, 333
experience, 3, 11, 14, 16–17, 25–28, 49–50, 52, 81–82, 84, 177, 190, 213, 237–39, 241–44, 249, 252–53, 255–56, 260, 263–64, 270, 296, 320, 322–25, 325n53, 326–27, 345, 353, 372, 378

Name and Subject Index   395

aesthetic, 52, 55–56
  of death, 26, 29–39
  of the divine, 315, 338
  ecclesial, 314
  musical, 288–89, 373
  mystical, 35, 39, 150, 157–58
  noetic, 52
  religious, 56, 307
  subjective, 177, 181–82, 250–51, 257
  of time, 38, 60–61, 65, 75, 236
existentialism, 200, 200n2, 348

face, the, 249–51, 254, 263, 293, 295–96, 353, 356
Fagerberg, David, 74n63
Fall, the, 36, 232, 269n9
Falque, Emmanuel, 312n11, 320, 321n39, 324n50
Fechner, Theodor, 360
feminism, 270
Fichte, Johann Gottlieb, 333, 338, 369
first-person perspective, 115–16, 119–20, 123–24, 128–29, 132–33, 199
Flogaus, Reinhard, 155–57, 159
form, 1, 74n62, 80, 96, 102–3, 116–17, 117n5–6, 130, 201–2, 311, 337, 359, 361, 361n18
Foucault, Michel, 309n4
François de Sales, 166
Franklin, Benjamin, 44
Franzen, Jonathan, 200, 200n2
freedom, 48, 70, 143, 145, 147, 233, 237, 259, 307, 310, 315n19, 322, 327, 356, 365, 368, 379
Freud, Sigmund, 49, 55
friendship, 2, 18, 35, 250, 317, 317n27
functionalism, 121, 121n21

Gaddis, William, 205
Gaia, 193–94
Galen of Pergamon, 93–95, 95n14, 96, 97, 97n26, 98–104, 106, 109
Galilei, Galileo, 362

Gellner, Ernest, 100n37
Gibson, William, 1n2
gift, 8, 17, 19, 54, 63n8, 73, 76, 85, 124n37, 125–26, 128–29, 131, 169, 229, 249–50, 252–54, 257–64, 310, 310n8, 320n37, 327, 341, 367, 372, 380, 382–83, 387
Gilson, Étienne, 125
Goethe, Johann Wolfgang von, 205, 332n9, 385, 385n56
Golitzin, Alexander, 157, 165
good, 7, 84, 239–41, 258, 262–63, 370, 374
  common, 96, 98–99, 232, 259, 264
grace, 31, 88, 131–32, 145, 150–52, 154, 157–58, 162, 164, 214, 221, 228, 260, 269n10, 315, 379, 386–87
  prevenient, 83
Green, Joel B., 268–70
Greene, Graham, 215
Gregory of Nazianzus, 155
Gregory of Nyssa, 125, 155, 161, 314n17
Gregory of Sinai, 149–50, 153, 155, 167

habit/*habitus*, 10, 81–84, 86, 89, 127–28, 131, 162, 238
Hadot, Pierre, 96
Hall, Robert, 101
Hamann, Johann Georg, 341
Hausherr, Irénée, 152, 165–66
heart, 16, 34n27, 54, 97, 150, 152, 158, 160, 163–68, 212–14, 217, 222, 226, 235–36, 239–40, 261, 276, 310n7, 311, 362n20, 372; see also *kardia*
Hegel, Georg Wilhelm Friedrich, 50, 88, 243, 331, 336, 338, 347n68, 348, 362, 366, 368–71, 371n35, 372–74, 374n38, 379, 384
Heidegger, Martin, 26, 61, 88, 320–21, 348, 360
Heisenberg, Werner, 190
hell, 143–47, 192, 374

## Name and Subject Index

Heller-Roazen, Daniel, 87
Henry, Michel, 81–82, 84, 319n34, 323–24, 324n50, 325, 325n53, 349n77
Heraclitus, 363n23, 386
Herder, Johann Gottfried von, 333–34, 340
Hermeticism, 341–42
hesychasm, 149–52, 154–57, 160–63, 166
Hippocrates of Kos, 95, 95n8, 96n19, 97–98
Hirsch, Lily, 298n48, 299, 299n49, 301
Hobbes, Thomas, 184
hope, 14, 34, 34n27, 39, 46, 49, 132, 138, 151, 158, 262, 270, 345, 384
    eschatological, 38
    ontological, 32, 35, 38–39
    Paschal, 69
    soteriological, 48
Hopkins, Gerard Manley, 375, 379, 386–87
humanism, 89, 103, 337, 382
    Byzantine, 159
    secular, 58
Hume, David, 83–84, 89, 364
Husserl, Edmund, 27, 324, 348
Hussey, Edmund, 155
hypostasis, 137–42, 146–47, 151, 169
    human, 16, 137, 140, 142
hypostatic union, 126, 139, 139n16, 140–41, 146

Ibn Sina, 81, 94, 99, 99n30, 100–1, 101n40, 102–3, 109
Ică, jr., Ioan I., 159
idiocy, 365, 370, 372, 377–78, 380
Ignatius of Loyola, 166, 346
imagination, 49, 51, 132, 231–36, 238, 240–41, 244, 276
*imago Dei*, 150, 163, 169, 259–62, 270, 330, 336, 338–39, 341, 344–45
incarnation,
    individual, 70, 70n41
    of Jesus Christ; *see* Christ, Jesus, incarnation of
individuation/individualization, 26, 29–31, 42–43, 46, 52
    psychic, 49, 52
Industrial Revolution, 193
Ingold, Tim, 287n5
intellect,
    contemplative, 379
    discursive, 160, 162–63
    divine, 157–58, 317n28
    human, 98, 103, 109, 116, 126n43, 150–53, 158, 160–66, 168, 170, 192, 234, 310–11, 317n28, 327, 359, 380
    intuitive, 151–52, 160, 162
    pure, 185, 192
intentionality, 4, 81–82, 119, 251, 256, 293, 293n28, 296n39, 299n49, 302
irony, 205, 211, 224
Isaac the Syrian, 167–68
Ivanka, Endre von, 155

Jacobi, Friedrich Heinrich, 89, 332–33
James, William, 118, 360n15
Jefferson, Thomas, 117
John of Damascus, 155
John Paul II (Pope), 249–51, 254–64
Jonson, Ben, 211–14, 214n11, 221, 226
Josephus, Titus Flavius, 269
Joyce, James, 205, 373
Jugie, Martin, 154, 169

Kabbalah, Christian, 341
Kandinsky, Wassily, 325
Kant, Immanuel, 19, 79, 84, 88–89, 287n7, 308, 319, 319n32, 321–22, 361n18, 364–65, 365n24, 366–67, 367n27, 368–69, 374, 379, 384
*kardia*, 151–52, 160, 164–65
Keats, John, 375n40
Keiner, Astrid, 345

## Name and Subject Index 397

Kepler, Johannes, 362
Kessler, Eckhard, 105
Kierkegaard, Søren, 16, 231, 233, 236–37, 239–41, 241n44, 242–43, 243n58, 244, 283n56
Kim, Jaegwon, 4n14
Kimbriel, Samuel, 211n1, 315n21, 317n27
Klages, Ludwig, 348
Knight, G. Wilson, 228n31
knowledge, 13, 19, 36, 39, 47, 56, 94–95, 100–1, 125, 158, 163, 169, 178, 185, 255, 261, 276, 289, 292, 295, 315, 319, 344, 386
  absolute, 335, 338
  anatomical, 94–96, 104–7
  of one's death, 26, 30, 32
  of the divine/God, 106–7, 154, 162–63, 168, 313, 315n21, 316–17, 345
  of divine union, 153
  of God as God knows himself, 313, 315
  as habituated, 127
  immanent, 151, 155, 169
  mechanical, 202
  noetic, 50
  philosophical, 318n32
  as representation, 103, 103n51, 108n75, 318
  scientific, 11, 124
  self-, 5, 7–8, 11–12, 94, 96, 99, 108, 314
  of soul, 7, 14, 93–94, 95n8, 96, 96n17, 102, 107–8, 108n70, 131, 386; *see* soul, knowledge of; *see* "know thyself"
  spatialized, 109
  triune nature of, 169–70
  univocal, 386
"know thyself", 4, 6–8, 93–96, 96n17, 97–104, 104n57, 105–8, 108n73, 109; *see* Delphic Oracle
Konstantinou, Lee, 206

Kooten, George H., 269n9
Koslowski, Peter, 348
Kukkonen, Taneli, 101
Kyd, Thomas, 216, 218–19
Kydones, Prochoros, 156

Landsberg, Paul Ludwig, 25–39
Last Supper, 65–66
Laven, Stuart, 300
Lazarus Saturday, 62, 66, 69
Leibniz, Gottfried Wilhelm, 333, 368
leisure, 19, 41n4, 42, 45, 48
  as the new *otium* of the people, 46–58
Leroi-Gourhan, André, 51
Lessing, Gotthold Ephraim, 332
Levinas, Emmanuel, 249–55, 257–60, 263–64, 294–95, 295n32, 296, 296n39, 297, 297n45, 298
Lewis, C. S., 5n15, 72–73
Lison, Jacques, 156
liturgy, 19, 41, 46, 49, 53–58, 62, 64–65, 67, 68, 73, 131, 162, 261, 314–15, 326–27, 344–45
  anatomical, 106n65
  art as, 53–55
Locke, John, 79–80, 117, 120, 132, 178, 182–84, 363–64
Lössl, Josef, 156–57, 159
love, 5, 18–19, 28, 31–32, 46, 47n24, 49, 56–57, 63–65, 70–71, 72n54, 76, 76n66, 143–44, 151, 162–63, 169–70, 229, 259, 261, 263, 312, 338, 345–47, 354
  in the Trinity as relation between Father and Son, 154–55, 169
Lovelock, James, 193–94
Luizzi, Mondino de, 103
Luther, Martin, 45

Macarius (Pseudo), 149, 165–66
Macrina the Younger, 125–26
Maier, Michael, 342–43

## Name and Subject Index

Maine de Biran, François-Pierre-Gonthier, 80–81, 83, 89, 323, 348
Malebranche, Nicolas, 368
Marcel, Gabriel, 32, 363n23
Marion, Jean-Luc, 319n34
Marx, Karl, 84, 202, 348
Mary, mother of God, 128, 150, 326n58
materialism, 14, 33, 79, 89, 101, 118–19, 123, 132, 181, 190–91, 267, 358–59, 363, 368–69
Maxime the Huts Burner, 150
Maximus the Confessor, 135–147, 315n20
McCabe, Herbert, 121–22, 127, 131
McDowell, John, 89
McGinn, Colin, 177, 181, 186, 195
mediation, 53, 86, 131, 139, 231, 233, 286, 313–14, 317n28, 318, 370
melancholy/melancholia, 231, 241–42, 242n49, 244
Melanchthon, Philip, 93–94, 105, 105n62, 106, 106n66, 107, 107n68, 108n70, 109
memes, 121–22, 122n28, 123–24, 125n38, 128, 133
memory, 35, 38, 46, 83, 98, 150, 178, 182–83, 184, 339, 382
mentalism, 83
Merleau-Ponty, Maurice, 10–11, 81–82, 83n15, 84, 89, 292, 324
metaphysic(s), 51, 78, 83, 85–86, 88–89, 99–101, 105, 114, 119, 123, 125, 176, 188, 213, 233, 276, 307–8, 317, 319, 321–22, 358, 365, 379, 382, 384
   of anthropology, 237
   of Aristotle, 99–100, 317
   Augustinian, 157
   Cartesian, 126
   dialectical, 242
   event of, 311
   hypothesis of, 29, 39
   modern, 108, 115, 132, 324
   Plato's, 184
   of science fiction, 179–82
   of Spinoza, 106
metaxology, 378, 381, 384, 386
Metternich, Prince Clemens von, 331
Meyendorff, John, 154–56, 161, 165
Milbank, John, 15, 285, 320n37
mind, 9–10, 14–15, 57, 68n33, 78–80, 83–89, 97, 101, 103, 116, 120, 126–27, 132n, 151–55, 158, 160–70, 175–82, 186, 188–90, 192, 194, 201, 203, 231–35, 238, 240, 244, 271–72, 276, 310n7, 318, 319n34, 321, 338, 348, 372
   divine, 87, 106–7, 163, 167–68
   philosophy of, 4, 118, 121
   as a power of the soul, 87–88
mind-body problem, 175–76, 188–89, 194, 272
mnemotechnology, 42, 47–48
modes of existence, 137, 147
money, 44–45
monism, 14, 33, 161, 181, 208, 279n50, 323, 333, 343
Monothelite controversy, 135
Montaigne, Michel de, 212–13, 224–25, 385, 385n56
Montero, Barbara, 83n15
Moore, Steven, 200
Mount Tabor, 67, 73, 150
Murphy, Nancy, 14, 68, 68n34, 115, 118–19, 119n11, 120–21, 126, 266n1
Murray, Alex, 274
Music Immersion Program, 298, 298n48, 299–301

Nagel, Thomas, 88
Nash, Ronald, 158
nature, 78–80, 82, 84–89, 95, 107, 109, 114n1, 137, 138, 138n10, 139, 139n12, 140–42, 144, 167, 188–89, 233, 236, 241, 244, 268, 271, 274, 279, 282, 291, 311, 341, 346,

355–56, 359, 362–64, 366,
  368–70, 378–79
 divine, 139, 139n16, 313, 336–
  37, 337n31, 345
 domination of, 201–2
 human, 1, 4, 10n27, 12, 66, 85,
  102, 139, 139n16, 140–41,
  146, 231, 240, 244, 258, 268,
  276, 281, 311, 324, 339, 340,
  342
 manipulation of, 11, 86, 202
 mathematicization of, 362
 split, 274n33, 276, 278
Neoplatonism, 26, 136, 149, 157
neuroscience, 2, 4, 97, 115, 118
Newton, Isaac, 185
Nicephorus the Monk, 153, 166
Nietzsche, Friedrich, 49, 320–21,
  321n39, 367, 374, 382–83,
  383n53, 385–86
nominalism, 154
nous/ νοῦς, 50, 86, 136n2, 150–54,
  157, 160–65, 167, 169, 232,
  244, 359, 361
Novalis (Georg Philipp Friedrich
  Freiherr von Hardenberg),
  333, 374
novel (literary), 17, 199–200, 200n2,
  201, 203–8
nuptial mystery, 258, 260–64, 378

Object Oriented Ontology, 349
Ockham, William of, 103
Ontological argument, 86,
ontological difference, 233, 365n24
ontology, 13n32, 31–39, 68, 81–86,
  100–101, 115, 119–22,
  124–26, 132, 136, 142–43,
  146–47, 170, 188, 191, 213,
  233, 239, 242, 253, 269, 271,
  310, 320n37, 331, 334–35,
  348, 358, 360–61, 366, 379,
  382
 logicized, 100–101
 as politicized, 85
 relational, 67, 75–76
 speculative, 82
Origen, 136, 155, 161, 232

Ouellet, Marc, 261

Palamas, Gregory, 149–70
pantheism, 79, 332–35, 344, 348
 controversy, 332, 335
 poetic, 331, 334–35, 337, 341,
  344
panpsychism, 360n15, 378
Park, Katherine, 105
participation,
 in communities, 127–28
 democratic, 47–51
 metaphysical, 15, 18, 52, 56–57,
  64–67, 69, 73, 76, 87–88,
  125, 131, 137, 143–45, 150,
  152, 160–62, 273, 277,
  282–83, 313, 316, 326, 338,
  346, 354, 356, 363n23, 378,
  381n49
Pascal, Blaise, 56, 208, 385, 385n56
Pattison, Stephen, 293n28
Paul, Saint, 107, 120n19, 161–62,
  221, 262, 269, 269n9, 271,
  277–78, 312, 321n39
Percy, Walker, 202
performance/performativity, 17, 83,
  200–201, 207, 212, 288
person(s)/personhood, 2–4, 7, 14,
  32, 34, 61–64, 71–73, 85, 96,
  115, 118–20, 126
 as becoming, 137–39, 226
 biological identity, 275, 285
 capacity for change, 226
 communion of, 17–18, 258, 270
 composite nature of, 139–41
 constitution view of, 119–20,
  132
 despair of, 242
 dignity of, 27
 as dynamic, 67, 255
 Eucharistic, 60, 66–67, 75–76
 and experience of death, 25–39,
  130, 138
 faculties of, 135–36
 freedom of, 142–47, 259
 fullness of, 224
 ghostly quality of, 120

person(s)/personhood (*continued*)
  as gift, 249–50, 257, 259–60, 262–63
  as identified with the hypostasis, 142
  identity of, 61, 74–76, 82, 178–79, 182–84, 272, 275–79
  inner life of, 176, 179, 256, 293, 338, 344, 371, 371n35
  irreducibility of, 27, 121, 126, 142, 250–51, 255–57, 264
  narrative, 123–33
  in relation to nature, 138–39
  ontological status of, 32, 119
  as microcosm, 105
  mystery of, 252, 256–57, 263, 356
  name of, 167
  as priest, 75–76
  as "punctual self", 117, 132
  rejection of salvation, 145, 147
  relationality of, 138, 139n12, 147, 204, 229, 231–33, 250–55, 257–60, 263–64, 279, 279n50, 281–82, 286, 291, 293, 293n28, 299, 310
  responsibility of, 254
  resurrected, 281
  as connected to the soul, 142
  as created in the image of the Trinity, 138
  tripartite, 244; *see also* soul, as tripartite
  uniqueness of, 31
  unity of, 28, 39, 115–16, 137, 141, 145–46, 271, 310, 319n34, 323
  wholeness of, 137, 140–42, 145–47, 152, 164, 175, 177, 229, 243–44, 256, 268, 270–72, 311, 323
phenomenology, 10, 12, 16, 25, 82, 88–89, 249, 251, 254n16, 255–57, 262, 264, 292, 309, 323, 324n50, 338, 348, 349n77, 357, 368–69
  of death, 26–30, 38
  of flesh, 319n34, 320, 321n39
  of givenness, 81
  of intention, 81–82
  of time, 38
Philo of Alexandria, 85, 269, 269n9
Philoponus, John, 287n7
Philosopher's Stone, 342–43
philosophy,
  analytic, 100n37, 101n40, 177–78
  ancient, 85, 100, 152, 160, 314
  of contemplation, 7–8
  Continental, 348
  medieval, 26, 85
  of mind, 4, 118, 121
  modern, 78
  moral, 108, 365
  natural, 94, 104, 104n57, 105, 117
  *Naturphilosophie*, 331, 333–34, 344
  practical, 365
  Scholastic, 102
  Scientific, 118
  as a way of life, 96
physicalism, 9, 14, 68,70, 98–99, 115, 118, 132, 266, 268, 275
  non-reductive, 68, 115, 118, 118n10, 132, 266n1, 267
  reductive, 119n11, 123, 132
physics, 95, 175, 178, 189–91, 287n7, 359
  envy of, 189–90
Pickstock, Catherine, 58, 87, 108n75, 125
pilgrimage, 8n25, 16, 67, 313
Planudis, Maxim, 154
Plato, 5, 7n20, 8n25, 26–27, 69, 74n63, 75, 75n63, 86–87, 94, 97–98, 155, 158, 160–61, 183–84, 190, 193, 269, 273n29, 282, 310–11, 314n17, 326, 338, 344, 358, 360, 365n25, 367n27, 370, 379, 380n46, 381n50, 382, 384–85, 385n54–56, 386
Plested, Marcus, 165
politics, 6, 15, 40–42, 46–47, 49–52, 56, 68, 84–87, 98, 176, 178,

184, 204, 214–15, 220, 224, 273, 275–76, 332, 353
Porter, Roy, 192
postmodernism, 295, 205–8, 320n37, 322–27
prayer, 41n4, 49, 65, 149–53, 161–62, 164–68, 203, 208, 219, 223, 225, 234–35, 258, 317, 344–47, 360n16, 378
  demonic, 219
  of Jesus Christ, 164, 167
Priestley, Joseph, 117
Protestantism, 44, 55, 93, 108n70, 203–4, 337n36
Purcell, Michael, 254n16
purgatory, 32
psychology, 4, 10, 27, 27n5–6, 86, 93, 101–3, 105, 118, 163, 167, 176, 181, 184, 216, 234, 237–38, 241n44, 242, 332, 338, 348, 368
  rational, 357, 364–66, 367n27, 369
Proclus, 6
Proust, Marcel, 53, 55
Pythagoras of Samos, 99, 193, 371n35

Quayle, Anthony, 225

Rahner, Karl, 323, 323n45
Ravaisson, Félix, 80, 82–84, 348
Rawls, John, 58
reason, 27, 30, 68n34, 86–87, 116, 150, 158, 160, 162–63, 170, 175, 178, 183–85, 202, 236, 244, 292, 296, 308, 308n2, 316, 319, 321–23, 332, 332n9, 333, 339–40, 364, 382
  instrumental, 308, 318
  medical, 95n14
  moral, 118n10
  practical, 365, 367
  pure, 334–35, 364
  scientific, 97, 191

reciprocity, 257–58, 258n31, 259–61, 263–64, 287, 320n37, 322, 344, 347
Reformation, 31, 214
  Counter-, 166
relationality, 17–18, 60–61, 64, 66–76, 138, 139n12, 144, 147, 204, 229, 231–33, 250–60, 263–64, 279, 279n50, 281–82, 286, 290–91, 293, 293n28, 299, 302–3, 310
relativity, theory of, 190
Renaissance, 31, 93–94, 103, 105, 107, 109
  Catholic, 331, 341n49, 348
repetition, 46, 54–57, 73, 131, 280, 371n35
representationalism, 103, 103n51, 108n75, 318
*res cogitans/res extensa*, 116, 120, 199, 201, 319, 355, 360–61, 363, 365
Riasanovsky, Nicholas, 334
Richardson, Samuel, 200, 200n2, 204
Ricoeur, Paul, 243n58
Robinson, H. Wheeler, 268
Romanides, John, 155, 162
Romanticism, 330, 334
  Catholic, 347–49
  German, 330
Rousseau, Jean-Jacques, 385, 385n56

Sacco, Paul, 298
Sachs, Joe, 4n14, 359n13
*sacra doctrina*, 313, 315n19, 316
sacrament(s), 67, 73, 79, 262, 314–15, 315n19, 316, 316n25, 347, 349
  of marriage, 261–63
sacrifice, 15, 46, 244, 253–54, 260, 277, 294, 383, 385n56
sadness, 34, 235–36, 241; *see also* melancholy/melancholia
Saturday, Holy, 228
Sawday, Jonathan, 103n52, 105n63
Scheler, Max, 25–27, 27n7, 28–30, 32–33, 35, 35n32, 37–38

Schelling, Friedrich Wilhelm Joseph, 331, 334–36, 347n68, 348, 362, 366
Schlegel, Friedrich, 330–49
Schleiermacher, Friedrich, 345n56
Schmemann, Alexander, 60–76
Schopenhauer, Arthur, 34, 374, 379–80, 380n46, 381n49, 383, 385, 385n56
Schupbach, William, 105
Scola, Angelo, 258, 261
Schafer, R. Murray, 299n49
science fiction, 178–82
Scruton, Roger, 290, 293, 293n26
secularism, 44, 46–48, 53, 55, 58, 68, 115, 192, 215, 220, 229, 331, 348
self; *see* person/personhood
Selkirk, Alexander, 200
sexuality, 184, 258–63
Shakespeare, William, 211–29
Shell, Alison, 215, 215n13, 220n22, 225n27
Sherwood, Polycarp, 140
Silesius, Angelus, 346n61
sin, 16, 31, 36, 38, 73, 130n64, 144, 221, 224, 234–35, 237–39, 244, 261, 267–68, 276, 282, 335
   original, 36
Sinkewicz, Robert E., 155–56
Smith, James K. A., 128
Socrates, 5–13, 15, 16n39, 17–19, 94, 99, 182, 311, 331, 358, 383–84, 384n54, 385
soteriology, 48–49, 142, 157, 267, 270–71, 273, 276, 279, 281–83, 314
soul, 1–20,
   as "all things", 14, 86, 327, 359, 386–87
   as anatomically understood, 93–109
   as animating, 116–17, 117n5, 338–39, 341, 366
   apophatic character of, 9, 12, 318, 322n43
   beatitude of, 313, 316; *see also* beatific vision
   belief that it is imaginary, 3, 3n10, 8–9, 118
   body, and it's relation to, 27, 70, 72, 74–76, 135–47, 249–52, 268–69, 269n10, 270, 272, 274–76, 278–79, 281, 285, 310, 312, 315, 319–20, 356, 358, 366, 368, 386; *see also*, dualism, of body and soul
   as communion with God/others, 70–71, 76, 258–59, 263–64, 312
   concept of, 307–9, 322
   conversion of, 216, 219, 224, 226–29, 336
   as cosmos, 15, 79
   cultivation of, 6, 9, 11–12, 238, 372
   dark night of, 374
   after death, 58, 70, 74, 142, 180, 310
   deathlessness of, 367n27, 383–84
   and the decline of usage/belief in, 4n14, 8, 114–15, 118, 175–95, 318–22, 352, 354–55, 357–58, 360–67, 386
   despairing, 229
   dignity of, 8
   as disembodied/incorporeal, 27–28, 74, 116–17, 142, 179–80, 320
   as dissected to obtain knowledge, 96–97, 100n37, 109
   as divine, 8, 327
   as sharply distinct from body, 199
   dualism with body; *see* dualism, of body and soul
   as embodied/corporeal, 117, 167, 180, 256, 261, 327, 358
   as a mode of encounter, 213, 229, 264; *see also* encounter
   erasure of, 318, 322

soul (*continued*)
   existence of, 27, 88, 96, 146, 213, 249, 267
   eyes as windows of the, 353
   face, as a mirror of, 250; *see also* face, the
   as form of the body, 74n62, 96, 102, 116, 250, 311
   as "form of the form", 311, 361n18
   as ghost in the machine, 356, 358–59
   hypothesis of, 3, 5, 5n17, 8, 10, 12, 15
   idiocy of, 370, 372, 378
   as *imago Dei*, 339
   immaterial, 28, 101–2
   immortality of, 26, 29, 68–69, 73, 78, 96–97, 102, 104n57, 135, 141–42, 144, 145n34, 146–47, 180, 269, 269n9–10, 273, 308–9, 311, 311n9, 363, 367
   immutable, 281
   as imprisoned, 27, 70, 75n63, 116, 167
   inhabiting the, 12, 19
   inner life of, 176, 179, 182, 256, 293, 338, 344, 371
   as an integrating form, 80, 231
   as the intersection between humanity and God, 327, 340–41, 386
   intimacy of, 363n23, 365, 370, 378–79, 385n55
   irreducibility of, 264; *see also* person(s)/personhood, irreducibility of
   knowledge of, 5, 7–8, 11–12, 14, 93–94, 95n8, 131; *see also* "know thyself"
   -less selving, 352n1, 356, 375–77, 382, 387
   as a living concept, 325–26
   as a microcosm, 85–86, 88, 169–70
   music of the; *see* soul music
   noetic, 49–52
   ontological dimension of, 38
   organic, 105
   overdeterminacy of, 355, 357, 359, 364–65, 368, 386
   persistence of, 114, 323, 356
   and personal identity, 69–70, 73–74; *see also* person(s)/personhood, identity of
   pilgrimage of, 8n25, 16, 67, 226, 313
   porosity of, 377
   pre-existence of, 136
   as principle of animate life, 322n42
   rational, 98, 105, 116, 116n5, 117, 117n6, 127, 150, 165, 322, 358
   Scriptural background, 309–10
   as secluded, 191
   secular, 215
   sensitive, 49–50, 116
   as simple substance, 136, 141, 279, 364, 368–69, 384
   as connected to simplicity, 362, 363n22, 364
   as "steered", 211–16, 220–21, 226, 229
   as a indispensable feature of theology, 308, 317
   as "thinking substance", 319, 338
   time of the, 37
   Trinitarian nature of, 151, 157, 169
   as tripartite, 7, 35, 41, 43–44, 49–51, 97, 161–62, 183, 231, 240, 244
   unintelligibility of, 319, 321
   unity with body, 15, 93, 139n16, 146, 167, 209, 232, 269, 316, 319n34, 358
   univocalization of, 355–56, 361, 363, 386
   vegetative, 43, 49–50, 105, 116, 358
   at work, 344
soul music, 1, 19, 352–53, 353n4, 354, 356–57, 360n15–16, 361–62, 365–67, 370,

soul music (*continued*)
    372–74, 374n38, 375, 377,
    381n49, 382–84, 387
    resounding of, 384
soulful reality, 285–86, 288, 293–94,
    297–99, 303
Speculative Realism, 349
Spinoza, Baruch, 332–33, 335, 369,
    385, 385n56
Spinozism, 332–33, 335, 349
spiritual body, 71–72, 133, 312
Springfield, Dusty, 354
*Star Trek*, 179
Sterne, Laurence, 204
Stiegler, Bernard, 40–58
Stillingfleet, Edward, 364
Stoicism, 68, 97, 149, 161, 165, 366
Stransky, Christine von, 346
Strawn, Brad D., 270–71
Suárez, Francisco, 318, 318n32
sublimation, 49, 55–57
substance, 2, 27, 116, 118, 136–38,
    138n10, 139, 139n12,
    140–42, 143n28, 146–47,
    178, 180, 190, 269, 275, 333,
    363–64, 368–70, 373, 380
    dualism; *see* dualism, substance
    immaterial, 324
    -less inexistence, 144–46
    material, 324
    simple, 136, 141, 279, 364,
    368–69, 384
    soul, 366
    spiritual, 319, 360, 364, 369, 379
Symeon the New Theologian, 149,
    153, 157, 165–66
synaesthesia, 87

Taylor, A. E., 8n25
Taylor, Charles, 58, 89, 117, 214,
    379n40
technics, 41, 47, 52, 55
teleology/*telos*, 29, 70, 86, 88, 104,
    201–2, 280–81, 370–71, 373
    Christ, as, 60, 62
    of the heavenly city, 47
    of nature, 95
    of prayer, 346
    of self-determination, 371, 373
    of selving, 370
    of the soul, 88, 330
    of spirit, 368
    of time, 66
    of truth, 131
temporality, 15, 25, 28–31, 34–39,
    44–45, 53, 60, 70, 125,
    129, 190, 221, 223, 231,
    233–34, 236–37, 240, 287n8,
    289–91, 293, 314, 383–84
    as death, 61–63
    phenomenology of, 38
    redeemed, 62–66, 75
    as relational, 66–67, 75–76
Teresa of Avila, 34–35, 346
Tertullian, 100n37, 117
theophany, 155, 157–58, 327
Theophilus of Antioch, 155
Theoleptos of Philadelphia, 150,
    152, 155, 162–63
theology of the body, 258n30, 262
*theoria*, 11
Thomas à Kempis, 346n61
Thompson, Francis, 18
Thompson, Marie, 299n49
thresholds, 18, 286–88, 292–93,
    296–97, 301, 356, 369–70,
    372–73, 378, 384, 386
    processual, 289–90, 294, 298–99,
    303
    relational, 290–91, 293, 298–
    300, 303
    sensory, 288–89, 293, 298–99,
    303
Thucydides, 85
Thunberg, Lars, 136n2, 139n16, 140
time; *see* temporality
Tollefsen, Torstein, 136
Tolstoy, Leo, 205
transcendental unity of
    apperception, 319
transubstantiation, 345
Trinity, Holy, 126, 153, 157, 165–70,
    343
    analogies of, 150–51, 153, 164,
    169
Tsirpanlis, Constantine, 155

unity, 13, 153, 155, 279
   of being, 28
   with body; *see* soul, unity with body
   of body and mind, 180
   of a composite, 117n5
   between creatures and God, 36–37
   of the Divine, 343
   of divine and human nature, 139n16
   of necessity and universality, 31
   of the person, 16, 30, 32–33, 39, 115, 183, 240, 271–72, 275–76, 282, 312, 322n43, 358

Vesalius, Andreas, 104–5, 104n57, 107–9
Vidal, Fernando, 93–94
Vico, Giambattista, 356
Vinci, Leonardo da, 213
vitalism, 78, 84, 89, 330–36, 344, 346–49
   Romantic, 331
vitality, 4, 9, 12, 14, 18, 29, 38, 336, 344, 347
   Divine, 345, 347, 349
   Kabbalist, 341
voluntarism, 79, 116

Wallace, David Foster, 199–200, 205–9
Ware, Kallistos, 72n54, 76n66, 167
Watt, Ian, 201, 203

Weber, Max, 44
Weiss, Paul, 365n25
Whitehead, Alfred North, 80
Whitman, Walt, 353, 382n51
Wilkins, Eliza Gregory, 96n17
will, 98–99, 115–17, 122–24, 214, 222, 242–43, 275, 311, 327, 339, 372, 379–80, 380n46, 380n48, 381n49
   divine, 116–17, 311
   free, 68n34, 135, 142–43, 145n34, 146, 370
   to live, 34
   to power, 381n49, 383
   to self-determination, 377, 381n49
Wishart, Trevor, 288
Wittgenstein, Ludwig, 88
Wojtyła, Karol; *see* John Paul II (Pope)
wonder, 107, 286, 291–92, 294, 296, 303
Wordsworth, William, 109
world-making, 286–87, 289–91, 299
Wright, N. T., 268–71, 276
Wundt, Wilhelm, 27

Yannaras, Christos, 143–44, 145n34
Yeats, W. B., 386n57

Zappa, Frank, 212
Zizioulas, Metropolitan John of Pergamon, 138n10

www.ingramcontent.com/pod-product-compliance
Lightning Source LLC
Chambersburg PA
CBHW021929290426
44108CB00012B/769